URBAN LABOR ECONOMICS

The aim of this book is to study the links between urban economics and labor economics. Different models of urban labor economic theory are examined in the initial two parts of this book: first urban search-matching models (Part 1) and then urban efficiency wages (Part 2). In Part 3, we apply these models to analyze urban ghettos and their consequences for ethnic minorities in the labor market. Professor Zenou first provides different mechanisms for the so-called spatial mismatch hypothesis, which postulates that housing discrimination introduces a key frictional factor that prevents minorities from improving access to job opportunities by relocating their residences closer to jobs. He then explores social networks, which tend to be affected by spatial factors, as workers who are physically close to jobs can be socially far away from them. Based on these models, the author offers different policies aiming at fighting high unemployment rates experienced by ethnic minorities residing in segregated areas.

Yves Zenou is Professor of Economics at Stockholm University and a Senior Research Fellow at the Research Institute of Industrial Economics (IFN). He is also affiliated with the Groupe d'Analyse des Itinéraires et Niveaux Salariaux (GAINS, Le Mans, France), the Centre for Economic Policy Research (CEPR, London), and the Institute for the Study of Labor (IZA, Bonn). He was previously Professor of Economics at the University of Southampton, UK, and a Research Fellow at the Center for Operations Research and Econometrics (CORE, Belgium). He is editor of *Regional Science and Urban Economics* and associate editor of the *Journal of Urban Economics*. His publications have appeared in leading journals such as *Econometrica, Review of Economic Studies, Journal of Economic Theory, International Economic Review, Journal of Labor Economics,* and the *Journal of Public Economics.*

Urban Labor Economics

YVES ZENOU
Stockholm University

CAMBRIDGE UNIVERSITY PRESS

Cambridge, New York, Melbourne, Madrid, Cape Town, Singapore, São Paulo, Delhi

Cambridge University Press
32 Avenue of the Americas, New York, NY 10013-2473, USA

www.cambridge.org
Information on this title: www.cambridge.org/9780521698221

First published 2009

Printed in the United States of America

A catalog record for this publication is available from the British Library

Library of Congress Cataloging in Publication data

Zenou, Yves.
Urban labor economics / Yves Zenou.
p.   cm.
Includes bibliographical references and index.
ISBN 978-0-521-87538-7 (hardback : alk. paper) –
ISBN 978-0-521-69822-1 (paperback : alk. paper)
1. Labor economics.   2. Urban policy.   I. Title.
HD4901.Z46   2009
331.2'1091732–dc22   2009006838

ISBN 978-0-521-87538-7 hardback
ISBN 978-0-521-69822-1 paperback

Till Tina, Julie, Emma och Oliver
Tack för er kärlek

Contents

Preface and Acknowledgments

The intended reader of this text is typically a last-year undergraduate, a graduate student in economics, or a researcher. People in connected fields (sociology, geography, urban planning, regional science, transportation, etc.) as well as policy makers with some background in economics should also be interested, especially in the last part of the book. Indeed, the techniques used in this book are not complicated and are now quite standard, and the main requirement is to be interested in the issues and have a good ability to use simple models and algebraic manipulations. I have homogenized the different models and the different chapters of this book by using the same notations and the same type of approach throughout. So the reading should be quite smooth. I have also included various appendices, which should help the reader understand the different chapters.

This book is the outcome of my research, which started twenty years ago. It has thus been a long time in the making. In August 1987, when I finished my master's degree in economics and econometrics at Université de Paris 10 (Nanterre), I was looking for a possible dissertation topic for a PhD. I had the chance to meet Gerard Ballot, professor at Université Pantheon-Assas (Paris 2), who suggested that the analysis of spatial labor markets could be an interesting and challenging topic. I decided to embark on this journey, having for sole reference the seminal paper of Harris and Todaro published in *American Economic Review* in 1970. In my dissertation, I studied the spatial aspects of labor markets, from both a theoretical and empirical perspective. I then met Jacques Thisse, professor at CORE in Belgium, who really taught me how to do research. My intellectual debt to him is immense. We wrote several articles together on the theory of local labor markets, some of which are included in this book. Jacques introduced me to Masahisa Fujita and

Tony E. Smith, the leaders of the regional science group at the University of Pennsylvania. As a junior researcher, working in 1995 with Masa and Jacques, two well-established urban economists, was a very challenging experience for me. I learned a great deal from this collaboration. My meeting with Tony E. Smith was also decisive. He taught me about the rigor of mathematics and how to prove theorems. Simplicity, kindness, and complexity are certainly good ways of describing Tony. At that time, I also worked with Marcus Berliant, who taught me mathematical tools I had never heard of before, such as differential topology. Diving into the world of general equilibrium, with its infinite dimensions and manifolds, was a very important experience. It helped me understand how a general equilibrium is calculated and how one proves its existence and uniqueness. I then collaborated with Jan K. Brueckner, who helped me fathom how to write simple models in order to capture complex economic situations. After having had these different mentors, I was able to work on my own and collaborate with younger researchers.

One of these researchers was particularly important to me: Antoni Calvó-Armengol. I met him in 1998, when we were both researchers at Centre d'Enseignement et de Recherche en Analyse Socio-Economique (CERAS) in Paris. Even though Toni was very young (nine years younger than me), I was extremely impressed by his energy, curiosity, creativity, and way of solving complicated mathematical problems. He taught me how to use the "right" model for the "right" question. He also introduced me to graph and social network theory, which is an important part of my research today. We published eight papers together, and we still have papers in progress. I was very close to him. Unfortunately, he tragically died at the age of 37 on November 3, 2007. I will miss him immensely. Two younger researchers have also influenced me: Etienne Wasmer and Eleonora Patacchini. Etienne has basically introduced me to search-matching theory. Thanks to Eleonora I am now writing a lot of empirical papers. Our endless discussions on how to write a model that can be tested have helped me think differently about theory.

I have also gained enormously from research collaborations with (in alphabetic order): Olof Åslund, Coralio Ballester, Gérard Ballot, Philippe Batifoulier, Harminder Battu, Marcus Berliant, Alberto Bisin, Nicolas Boccard, Jan K. Brueckner, Antonio Cabrales, Antoni Calvó-Armengol, Joan de Martí, Chengri Ding, Louis Eeckhoudt, Masahisa Fujita, Frédéric Gannon, Pieter Gautier, Laurent Gobillon, Florence Gofette-Nagot, Jonathan Hamilton, Mohamed Jellal, Maurice Kugler, John Östh, Eleonora Patacchini, Stephen Ross, Maria Saez-Marti, Paul Seaman, Harris Selod, Anna Sjögren, Tony

E. Smith, Yan Song, Sebastien Steinmetz, Jacques Thisse, Isabelle Thomas, Thierry Verdier, Jackline Wahba, Etienne Wasmer, and Xavier Wauthy. I have taught urban economics for a number a years. I am therefore grateful for all constructive comments received over the years from students at Southampton University, UK; Université du Maine, France; Uppsala University, Sweden; and Beijing University, China. I also thank Marcus Berliant, Antoni Calvó-Armengol, and Joan de Martí for extensive comments on earlier drafts.

I have been extremely privileged in the support, funding, and hospitality I received from the Research Institute of Industrial Economics (IFN), where most of this book has been written. I am also indebted to the Department of Economics at Stockholm University for the stimulating environment provided when the last part of this book was written.

Scott Parris at Cambridge University Press has been a supporter of this book since the very beginning. I thank him for his constant encouragement. I am also very grateful to the four anonymous readers who made extensive and very helpful comments on an early draft of the book.

This book has been a long journey, and I am not sure it would have ended without the support and love of my family. My wife, Tina, was always by my side. Her critical mind helped me phrase my research questions in a simpler way. My children, Julie, Emma, and Oliver, helped me focus on other things than research. This is the best motivation for writing a book.

Introduction

It is commonly observed in OECD (Organisation for Economic Co-operation and Development) countries that unemployment is unevenly distributed among cities. The incidence of unemployment varies between the regions of a country (Isserman, Taylor, Gerking, and Schubert, 1986; Gordon, 1987; Blanchflower and Oswald, 1994), cities of different sizes and functions (Marston, 1985), inner and outer areas of cities, and between urban and rural areas. There are also stark spatial differences in incomes. For example, in the United States, the median income of central city residents is 40 percent lower than that of suburban residents. This has renewed interest in the spatial dimension of unemployment and, more generally, of the labor market.

According to the U.S. Bureau of the Census, in large U.S. cities, the unemployment rate is much higher in the city center than in the suburbs. This is, in particular, due to the fact that U.S. city centers are generally characterized by ghettos and poverty. Even if the European situation is more complex and less uniform, the general tendency is similar – but opposite. Indeed, poor and unemployed workers tend to reside on the outskirts of the city while rich workers tend to live close to the city center. The spatial concentration of unemployment and poverty makes the workings of urban labor markets a vital concern for urban residents.

The labor market is therefore *not* a global market in which the labor force is homogeneous. Quite the opposite. There is an increasing heterogeneity of the labor force as well as a thinner segmentation of this market into submarkets characterized by a fairly weak mobility between segments. For example, the existence of regional/urban labor markets is a well-established fact. Workers and firms only interact in local labor markets whose size is much smaller than that of the national market, and few people move from one market to another (Armstrong and Taylor, 1993; Bartik, 1996; Hughes

1

and McCormick, 1994; Topel, 1986). Yet, in the standard neoclassical model, economic agents do not choose with whom they exchange goods or labor. They are supposed to operate in an impersonal market where nobody needs to know the identity of the other party in the transaction. Therefore, explaining the existence of local labor markets is beyond the reach of the standard paradigm. A new approach is thus required that explicitly accounts for the possibility of local markets pulling subgroups of agents together. Such an extension should also allow for the determination of the size of these markets, since it is precisely their geographical extension that limits the reality of the global market.

Very few theoretical attempts have, in fact, been made to better understand the workings of urban labor markets. Indeed, traditionally, labor economists do not directly incorporate space into their studies (see, e.g., Layard, Nickell, and Jackman, 1991; Pissarides, 2000; Cahuc and Zylberberg, 2004), even though there are some well-known empirical studies of local labor markets (see, e.g., Holzer, 1989; Eberts and Stone, 1992). Similarly, despite numerous empirical studies, the theory of urban labor economics has been relatively neglected in urban economics. In most advanced urban textbooks (see, in particular, Fujita, 1989; Fujita, Krugman, and Venables, 1999; Fujita and Thisse, 2002), it is mainly assumed that there is perfect competition in the labor market and the issue of urban unemployment is not even discussed. One of the aims of this book is to bring labor economics to urban economists and urban economics to labor economists.

I believe that we need to fathom the way labor markets work in cities, in particular the way wages and unemployment are locally determined. This will eventually help us better understand urban ghettos and design adequate policies aiming at fighting against these urban problems.

This book is mainly based on my own research over the last twenty years, even though I discuss other related urban labor models. It must be clear that this book is focusing on *urban* labor economic theory, that is, papers that explicitly model both the land/housing market (where both the location of workers and the price of land/housing are endogenous) and the labor market (where both wages and unemployment are endogenous) and analyze their interactions. There are also regional models (for instance, in the migration and economic geography literatures) that deal with regional labor markets, where a city/region is a point in space. That is not what this book is about.

This book is about urban labor market theory and, as such, it deals with two different markets. This is a difficult task because it brings together two different branches of economics, labor economics and urban economics.

This is why it is crucial for the reader to master the modeling of these two markets. This takes a large part of the book, namely the first two parts. Indeed, in Parts 1 and 2, we focus on search-matching and efficiency wage models, respectively, which are the main theories in labor economics, because they have the strongest empirical support. Each part has the same structure. We start with the standard urban framework of monocentric cities and see how the labor market affects (and is affected by) this urban structure. Both Chapters 1 and 4 describe the standard models of urban labor economics, focusing on search-matching (Chapter 1) or efficiency wages (Chapter 4). Then, in Chapters 2 and 5, we expose the different possible extensions of these benchmark models, keeping the same spatial monocentric city structure. Finally, in the last chapter of each part (Chapters 3 and 6), we deal with non-monocentric (or polycentric) cities. In particular, we show how this polycentric structure, which is increasingly common in modern cities (e.g., Los Angeles), affects the labor market outcomes of workers, which, in turn, affects the spatial structure of the city. In these chapters, we also deal with agglomeration economics and, in particular, with the endogenous formation of a monocentric city with endogenous wages and unemployment.

After these first two parts, the reader should be able to master the main tools and have a clear understanding of the way urban labor economic models work. It is only then that we deal with applied and policy-relevant issues. Indeed, as already noted, (big) cities are characterized by uneven distributions of unemployment and poverty. In particular, some areas (inner cities in the United States) accumulate poverty, low-skilled workers, few jobs, and a high proportion of ethnic workers. This is particularly true in most American cities, which exhibit a high level of racial segregation and stark socioeconomic disparities between neighborhoods. In general, white city dwellers experience much better labor-market outcomes than inner-city black workers. An important debate has focused on the existence of a possible link between residential segregation and the adverse labor market outcomes of racial minorities. Empirical studies have shown that such a link exists (see, for instance, Cutler and Glaeser, 1997). However, it remains unclear which economic mechanisms account for the link. It is thus crucial for policy makers to understand the causes and consequences of these poverty pockets and how they can be dealt with appropriately. For this purpose, we need a proper theoretical approach that incorporates both land and labor markets. Indeed, it is because they are located in specific areas that these groups of workers (minorities) experience adverse labor market outcomes. Moreover, it is because they experience high unemployment rates (and earn low wages when employed) that they are "forced" to live in these rundown areas. So any policy that would like to address these issues should be based on urban labor economic models. Therefore, we will use the tools and models exposed in the first two parts of this book to address the issues of poverty and adverse labor market outcomes of ethnic minority workers in ghettos.

Indeed, as expressed by Eberts (1994): "Urban labor markets are characterized by the spatial proximity of households and businesses, which offers firms and workers advantages that lead to more efficient markets, enhanced productivity, and greater economic success." But, by offering the greatest opportunity for economic success, cities attract both the most talented and successful individuals and the most disadvantaged (Glaeser, Kahn, and Rappaport, 2008). This is the paradox of cities since they stand as a stark dichotomy between those who have succeeded and those who have not. This is particularly true for ethnic minorities, like blacks and Hispanics in the United States, Indians, Pakistanis, and Bangladeshis in the UK; North Africans in France, etc., whose earning gap to whites is quite large (for example, in the United States, in 1991, black household median income was 60 percent of white household income). One popular explanation is that, for minorities and low-skill workers, access to the urban labor market is impeded by physical barriers of spatial isolation. This is what we investigate in the first two chapters of Part 3 (Chapters 7 and 8) by analyzing the so-called spatial mismatch hypothesis, initiated by Kain (1968). It stipulates that residing in urban segregated areas distant from (and poorly connected to) major centers of employment growth, minority workers face strong geographical barriers to finding and keeping well-paid jobs. In the U.S. context, where jobs have been decentralized and blacks have remained in the central part of cities, the main conclusion of the spatial mismatch hypothesis is putting forward distance to jobs as the main reason for the high unemployment rates and low earnings among blacks. Since the study of Kain, hundreds of studies have been carried out trying to test the spatial mismatch hypothesis (see, in particular, the literature surveys by Holzer, 1991; Kain, 1992; Ihlanfeldt and Sjoquist, 1998). The weight of the evidence suggests that bad job access indeed deteriorates labor market outcomes, especially for ethnic minorities, thus confirming the spatial mismatch hypothesis.

In Chapter 7, we use the search framework developed in Part 1 to give some microeconomic foundation for the spatial mismatch theory. In particular, we show that workers' job search efficiency may decrease with the distance to jobs and, in particular, workers residing far away from jobs may have few incentives to search intensively. In that case, distance to jobs can

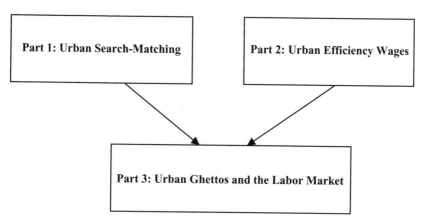

Figure I.1. Outline of the book.

be harmful because it implies low search intensities. In Chapter 8, using the efficiency wage approach exposed in Part 2, we show that workers may refuse jobs that involve commutes that are too long because commuting to that job would be too costly in view of the proposed wage. We also show that if workers' productivity negatively depends on distance to jobs, employers may discriminate against residentially segregated workers because of the stigma or prejudice associated with their residential location.

Clearly, distance to jobs is crucial for understanding why ethnic minorities experience adverse labor market outcomes. But this is not the whole story. There are other elements at stake since even when black workers live close to jobs (like in New York City), they still have problems finding a job. Social networks are obviously an important part of the story and are not always related to the distance to jobs. There is indeed strong empirical evidence showing that social networks play an important role in the job search and job finding processes. Individuals seeking jobs read newspapers, go to employment agencies, browse on the Web, and mobilize their local networks of friends and relatives. In Chapter 9, we focus on the relationship between non-market interactions (or peer effects and social networks) and urban economics through the labor market. In particular, we study how residential location determines social interactions, which, in turn, affect labor market outcomes.

In a nutshell, the way this book has been written can be described by Figure I.1.

In Parts 1 (urban search-matching models) and 2 (urban efficiency wage models), I give the main theoretical ingredients for understanding the way urban economic theory works. Once the reader has mastered these theoretical tools, we show in Part 3 how these tools can be used to address the issue of urban ghettos. In Chapters 7 and 8, using both the efficiency wage and the search-matching approaches, I give some theoretical foundations for a well-established empirical fact: spatial mismatch between ethnic minorities' residence and job locations. Finally, in the last chapter of the book, I highlight the role of labor market networks in cities.

PART 1

URBAN SEARCH-MATCHING

Introduction of Part 1

There is a vast amount of literature on search and matching theory that emphasizes the importance of flows in the labor markets (Mortensen and Pissarides, 1999; Pissarides, 2000). These models, now widely used in labor economics and macroeconomics, have greatly enriched research on unemployment as an equilibrium phenomenon, labor market dynamics, and cyclical adjustment. The starting point of the analysis is to recognize that labor markets are characterized by search frictions. This means that it takes time for workers to find a job and for firms to fill up a vacancy so that unemployed workers and vacant jobs can coexist in equilibrium, a feature not possible in a standard Walrasian world (i.e., a frictionless world where workers and firms can move costlessly and instantaneously between working and not working). Because of these search frictions, the contacts between workers and firms depend on the market variables and the arrival rate of contacts for workers increases with the number of unemployed searchers, while the arrival rate of contacts for firms increases with the number of vacant firms. A constant-return to scale function is a convenient way of capturing these properties, which is referred to as the "matching function" (Pissarides, 1979). Indeed, the matching function relates job creation to the number of unemployed, the number of job vacancies, and the intensities with which workers search and firms recruit. It successfully captures the key implications of frictions that prevent an instantaneous encounter of trading partners.[1,2]

However, the spatial dimension is absent in all these models, even if it has been recognized for a long time that distance interacts with the diffusion of information. For example, in his seminal contribution to search, Stigler (1961) puts geographical dispersion as one of the four immediate determinants of price ignorance. The reason is simply that distance affects various costs associated with search. In most search models, say for example Diamond (1982), distance between agents or units implies a fixed cost of making another draw in the distribution. In other words, a spatial dispersion of agents creates more frictions and thus, more unemployment. This is a weakness of the analysis since empirical evidence supports the idea of a clear _spatial dimension of labor markets_ (see, for example, the survey by Crampton, 1999).

The interaction between space and labor markets is complex, however. The aim of this part is to capture some of the phenomena at work and, in particular, account for the spatial dimension of search.

The first search paper that (implicitly) introduces space is the famous island model of Lucas and Prescott (1974). This model formalizes the idea of search frictions through space by introducing a large number of separated labor markets (islands) where one firm is located in each island subject to productivity shocks. The authors refer to the locations as "islands" populated at any moment by firms that cannot move among islands while workers can. The wage is competitively determined on each island. Consequently, the distribution of wage offers represents productivity differentials across different islands (or locations) at a given point in time. As productivity on each island is subject to idiosyncratic shocks, workers need to spend some effort in locating better matching opportunities and eventually relocating across islands in their pursuit of wage gains. This is because communication among islands is imperfect in the sense that each worker only knows the current wage on his or her own island, that these differences exist, and their extent as described by the wage offer distribution function. This knowledge motivates investment in search as a means of finding an island where labor is more highly rewarded than on the island currently occupied. The main

---

[1] For theoretical surveys of search-matching models, see Mortensen (1986, 1988), Mortensen and Pissarides (1999a,b); Pissarides (2000); Rogerson, Shimer, and Wright (2005); and Postel-Vinay and Robin (2007).

[2] Empirical evidence of search and matching models is well-documented. See, in particular, the surveys by Devine and Kieffer (1991); Davis, Haltiwanger, and Schuh (1996); Petrongolo and Pissarides (2001); Eckstein and Van den Berg (2007); and Yashiv (2007).

result is to characterize an economy with unemployed workers (i.e., those who are currently on islands where labor productivity happens to be below the opportunity cost of working) and employed workers with different wages, both results due to spatial frictions.

Even if this model is interesting, the spatial analysis is quite shallow in the sense that there is no land/housing market. The island story is just a metaphor for characterizing search frictions.

In this first part of the book, we explicitly deal with the urban aspects of search-matching models by modeling both labor and land markets. In Chapter 1, we will first present some simple models of urban search-matching. In the benchmark model, search effort is exogenous, but still affects the matching function. We relax this assumption because distance to jobs is a crucial channel through which space affects the labor market. Indeed, workers who live further away from jobs may have poorer labor market information and be less productive than those living closer to jobs (Seater, 1979). This is particularly true for younger and/or less-skilled workers who rely heavily on informal search methods to obtain employment (Holzer, 1987).[3] The reliance on these informal methods of job search suggests that information on available job opportunities may decay rapidly with distance from home (Ihlanfeldt and Sjoquist, 1990). Thus, we develop a model where distance to jobs affects workers' search efficiency, and study its impact on land and labor market outcomes.

In Chapter 2, we further extend the basic urban search-matching models. We consider the following interesting extensions of the benchmark model: workers' heterogeneity in training costs, endogenous job destruction, positive workers' relocation costs, and wage posting instead of wage bargaining.

Finally, in Chapter 3, we study the case of non-monocentric cities. We study rural-urban migration by extending the standard Harris-Todaro model to incorporate search frictions and an explicit land market. Following the seminal contribution of Salop (1979), we also analyze an urban framework when there is a finite number of job centers and a continuum of workers. In that case, workers will have different productivities while firms will have different job requirements. Some jobs will be matched to workers, even though the productivity of the match is quite low. We will consider both wage bargaining and wage posting models.

---

[3] We will investigate the issue of social networks in more detail in the last chapter of this book.

CHAPTER ONE

Simple Models of Urban Search-Matching

1. Introduction

The search-matching model is by now the standard workhorse of labor economists (Pissarides, 2000). In this chapter, we first develop a canonical model of *urban* search-matching, i.e., we introduce a land market[1] into a standard search-matching model. The link between the land and the labor market is realized through the average search intensity of unemployed workers. Indeed, the latter depends on the location of all unemployed workers in the city, which is endogenously determined in the land-use equilibrium. The location of workers, in turn, depends on the outcomes of the labor market. To understand the way the two markets operate, we first develop a simple model in which search intensity is exogenous (Section 2). Due to this assumption, only one urban pattern emerges in equilibrium: employed workers reside close to jobs while unemployed workers live on the periphery of the city. In Section 3, we extend this benchmark model by assuming that workers' search intensity depends negatively on their residential distance to jobs. This leads to two urban-land-use equilibrium configurations in which unemployed workers either reside close to or far away from jobs. In Section 4, unemployed workers endogenously choose their search intensity and we are able to show that they search less, the further away they reside from jobs. Besides the two previous urban configurations, there is a third urban equilibrium (the *core-periphery* equilibrium) where unemployed workers reside both close to (short-run unemployed workers) and far away (long-run unemployed workers) from jobs while employed workers live in between them. In each model, we explore the labor market

---

[1] Throughout this book, individuals consume land directly and thus we use the terms "land" and "housing" interchangeably.

10

consequences (job creation, unemployment and wages) of the urban-and-use pattern. In particular, we find that the land rent depends negatively on unemployment benefits, but positively on workers' productivity. The size of the city increases with the unemployment benefits, but decreases with the firms' entry cost or the job-destruction rate, and commuting costs increase unemployment, but decrease firms' job creation. Finally, in Section 5, we discuss some robustness results.

It is well-documented that both the labor and the housing market are subject to frictions. This first chapter assumes that the labor frictions are more important and consider the extreme case where all workers have zero relocation costs. Chapter 2 will explore the situation where housing frictions are more important so that mobility costs within the city will be very high (see sections 4 and 5 in Chapter 2).

2. The Benchmark Model

There is a continuum of ex-ante identical workers whose mass is N and a continuum of M identical firms. Among the N workers, L of them are employed and U are unemployed, with $N = L + U$. The workers are uniformly distributed along a *linear, closed,* and *monocentric* city. Their density in each location is taken to be 1. All land is owned by *absentee landlords* and all firms are exogenously located in the Central Business District (CBD) and consume no space. Workers are assumed to be infinitely lived, risk neutral, and decide their optimal place of residence between the CBD and the city fringe. There are *no relocation costs,* either in terms of time or money. This assumption will be relaxed in Chapter 2.

Each individual is identified with one unit of labor. Each employed worker goes to the CBD to work and incurs a fixed monetary commuting cost τ per unit of distance. When living at a distance x from the CBD, he/she also pays a land rent $R(x)$, consumes $h_L = 1$ unit of land and z_L unities of the non-spatial composite good (which is taken as the numeraire so that its price is normalized to 1) and earns a wage w_L (which will be determined at the labor market equilibrium).[2] The budget constraint of an employed worker is thus given by:

$$R(x) + \tau x + z_L = w_L. \tag{1.1}$$

Because of risk neutrality, we assume that preferences of all workers are given by $\Omega(z_L) = z_L$ so that the *instantaneous* (indirect) utility of an employed

---

[2] Subscript L refers to the employed whereas subscript U refers to the unemployed.

worker located at a distance x from the CBD is equal to:

$$W_L(x) = w_L - \tau x - R(x). \tag{1.2}$$

Concerning the unemployed workers, they commute less often to the CBD since they mainly go there to search for jobs. So, we assume that they incur a commuting cost $s\tau$ per unit of distance, where $0 < s \leq 1$ is a measure of search intensity or search efficiency; s is assumed to be exogenous. For example, $s = 1$ would mean that unemployed workers go every day to the CBD (as often as employed workers) to search for jobs. Observe that, here, we assume that unemployed workers need to go to the CBD to obtain information about jobs. This is why they need to commute there. If, for example, $s = 0$, which is excluded here, they would never find a job. We will discuss alternative ways of gathering information about jobs through search below.

The *instantaneous* (indirect) utility of an unemployed worker residing at a distance x from the CBD is equal to:

$$W_U(x) = w_U - s\tau x - R(x), \tag{1.3}$$

where w_U is the unemployment benefit. We assume w_U to be exogenously financed by taxpayers who reside elsewhere (for example absentee landlords).[3] Let us describe the labor market. A firm is a unit of production that can either be filled by a worker whose production is y units of output or unfilled and thus unproductive. To find a worker, a firm posts a vacancy. A vacancy can be filled according to a random Poisson process.[4] Similarly, workers searching for a job will find one according to a random Poisson process. In aggregate, these processes imply that there is a number of contacts per unit of time between the two sides of the market that are determined by the following matching function:[5]

$$d = d(\bar{s}U, V), \tag{1.4}$$

where $\bar{s}$ is the average search efficiency of the unemployed workers, U and V the total number of unemployed workers and vacancies, respectively. Observe that $U = uN$ and $V = vM$, where u is the unemployment rate and v the vacancy rate. Contrary to Pissarides (2000), where both U and V are defined with respect to the total labor force N, V is here the number of vacant jobs defined as a fraction of the total mass of firms. As all workers are

---

[3] In search-matching models, w_U is often interpreted as the utility of leisure.
[4] The random Poisson process is formally defined in Appendix B at the end of this book.
[5] This matching function is written under the assumption that the city is monocentric, i.e., all firms are located in one fixed location.

atomistic and (ex-ante) homogenous, they choose the same search intensity s so that $s = \bar{s}$. Observe that $\bar{s}U$ is the level of unemployment measured in efficiency units.

As in the standard search-matching model (Mortensen and Pissarides, 1999; and Pissarides, 2000), we assume d to be increasing in both its arguments, concave and homogeneous of degree 1 (or equivalently having constant returns to scale).[6] The *matching function d* summarizes all details of the meeting process in a manner analogous to the way a *production function* summarizes a production process. Indeed, it describes a relationship between the inputs ($\bar{s}U$ and V) and the output of the meeting process.

Given the matching function (1.4), we can determine the rate at which vacancies are filled. It is equal to: $d(\bar{s}u\,N, v\,M)/(v\,M)$. By constant return to scale, it can be written as

$$d(1/\theta, 1) \equiv q(\theta)$$

where

$$\theta = \frac{v\,M}{\bar{s}u\,N} \tag{1.5}$$

is a measure of *labor market tightness* in efficiency units and $q(\theta)$ is a Poisson intensity. Using the properties of d, it is easily verified that $q'(\theta) \leq 0$: the higher the labor market tightness, the lower the rate at which firms fill their vacancy. Similarly, the rate at which an unemployed worker with search intensity s leaves unemployment is

$$a = \frac{s}{\bar{s}} \frac{d(\bar{s}u\,N, v\,M)}{u\,N} \equiv s\theta q(\theta).$$

Once more, by using the properties of $d(.)$, it is easily verified that $[\theta q(\theta)]' \geq 0$: the higher the labor market tightness, the higher the rate at which workers leave unemployment since there are relatively more jobs than unemployed workers. Also, the higher the search intensity s (unemployed search more actively for jobs), the higher is this rate $s\theta q(\theta)$. We can now write the matching function as follows:

$$q(\theta)V = d(\bar{s}U, V) = \theta q(\theta)\bar{s}U.$$

This implies that the two meeting rate functions, $q(\theta)V$ and $\theta q(\theta)\bar{s}U$, represent the average rates at which unemployed workers and vacancies

---

[6] In most empirical studies, the assumption of constant returns to scale of the matching function is verified (see, e.g., Blanchard and Diamond, 1989, 1990; Petrongolo and Pissarides, 2001).

meet potential partners. Finally, the rate at which jobs are destroyed is exogenous and denoted by δ.

The matching function captures the frictions that search behaviors of both firms and workers imply. If there are no frictions in this model, then unemployment or vacancies disappear, and jobs are found or filled instantaneously. Indeed,

$$\lim_{\theta \to 0} [\theta q (\theta)] = \lim_{\theta \to +\infty} q (\theta) = 0 \qquad (1.6)$$

and

$$\lim_{\theta \to +\infty} [\theta q (\theta)] = \lim_{\theta \to 0} q (\theta) = +\infty. \qquad (1.7)$$

That is, if $\theta \to 0$, then the number of unemployed is infinite and thus, firms fill their jobs instantaneously (no frictions on the firm's side), whereas if $\theta \to +\infty$, the number of vacancies is infinite and thus, workers find a job instantaneously (no frictions on the worker's side).

At the micro level, a matching function (1.4) can be derived from specific specifications of the meeting process.[7] What is crucial is that even with ex-ante identical agents (i.e., workers and firms) and no wage distribution, there can exist search frictions captured by the matching function.[8] The traditional micro-foundation behind the aggregate matching function is the so-called urn-ball model and *coordination failures* inherent to this model can explain the emergence of search frictions. Let us give the intuition (borrowed from Petrongolo and Pissarides, 2001) of this result. Consider firms as urns and workers as balls. If all workers and firms are ex-ante identical and if only one worker can occupy each job, an uncoordinated application process by workers will lead to overcrowding in some jobs and no applications in others. The search frictions that lead to the existence of unemployment and vacancies in equilibrium are here the lack of information about other workers' actions (i.e., to which firm workers send their job application). To be more precise, consider U workers who know exactly the location of V job vacancies and send one application each. If a vacancy receives one or more applications, it selects an applicant at random and forms a match. The other applicants are returned to the pool of unemployed workers to apply again. The matching function is derived by writing down an expression for the number of vacancies that do not receive any applications. It is easily

---

[7] For simplicity, when exposing the microfoundations of the matching function, we assume $s = \bar{s} = 1$.

[8] It is assumed that there is a constraint on the number of job applications.

shown that, as V becomes large, the matching function is equal to:

$$d(U, V) = d\left(1 - e^{U/V}\right).$$

(1.8)

This matching function is a particular case of our general matching function and exhibits the same properties. Naturally, other specific meeting processes can give rise to a similar matching function (see Mortensen and Pissarides, 1999; Petrongolo and Pissarides, 2001). A common story is that workers know where vacancies are, but do not know which particular vacancies other workers will visit, allowing for the possibility that some workers are unable to fill vacancies because they were "second in line". This structure once more reduces the aggregate meeting process to an "urn-ball" process in which the labor market is visualized as V "urns" (i.e., vacancies) and U "balls" (i.e., workers), each ball having a probability $1/V$ of being directed to any given urn. An exponential matching function similar to (1.8) is once more obtained. Hall (1977, 1979); Butters (1979); Pissarides (1979); Montgomery (1991a); Peters (1991); Blanchard and Diamond (1994); Cao and Shi (2000); Julien, Kennes, and King (2000); Burdett, Shi, and Wright (2001); Smith and Zenou (2003c) and Albrecht, Gautier, Tan, and Vroman (2004)[9] all derive the number of contacts that will occur in some interval, as a function of the number of vacancies and searching workers that is immediately implied by this structure. Lagos (2000) proposed an alternative micro approach by deriving an aggregate matching function without assuming ex-ante meeting frictions, but by deriving these as a distinctive feature of the possible equilibria. Agents choose between heterogeneous locations. In equilibrium, some fail to match since too many of them choose locations where matching payoffs are high. The matching function obtained takes the form of a min function, i.e., $d(U, V) = \min\{U, V\}$. Since the empirical studies of the aggregate matching function have pointed to a Cobb-Douglas functional form (Petrongolo and Pissarides, 2001), Stevens (2007) has recently proposed a new model for the matching process, based on a "telephone line" Poisson queuing process. Her model gives a microfoundation for a Constant Elasticity of Substitution (CES) matching function, and is approximately Cobb-Douglas when search costs are approximately linear.

---

[9] In Montgomery (1991); Cao and Shi (2000); Julien, Kennes, and King (2000) and Burdett, Shi, and Wright (2001), the microfoundation for search frictions comes from a mixed-strategy equilibrium of an underlying coordination game. Thus, search frictions arise because when all other agents look for jobs haphazardly, those workers that remain have similar incentives to search haphazardly. In all these papers, the symmetric mixed-strategy equilibrium generates an exponential matching function at the limit.

Let us now focus on the equilibrium of the benchmark model. A steady-state equilibrium requires that an urban-land-use equilibrium and a labor market equilibrium are solved *simultaneously*. It is convenient to first present the former and then the latter.

2.1. Urban-Land-Use Equilibrium

Let us define the land market equilibrium.[10] The land market is assumed to be *competitive* so that all workers (employed and unemployed) take land rents in the city as given. Since all workers within a group are assumed to be identical, it must be that, in equilibrium, they all reach the same maximum utility level independent of location. If this were not true, some individual might increase his/her utility level by imitating the residential choice of an identical individual with a higher utility. Thus, an incentive to make a new decision would exist and such a situation could not be an equilibrium. We call the common maximum utility achieved by workers of employment status $es = U, L$ in equilibrium the equilibrium utility and we denote it by W_{es}. The relationship between W_{es} and $W_{es}(x)$ (given by (1.2) and (1.3)) is:

$$W_{es} = \max_x W_{es}(x) \qquad es = U, L$$

that is, the equilibrium utility W_{es} is the maximum utility attainable in the city under the market rent curve $R(x)$. We are now able to define the bid-rent, a concept widely used in urban economics (see, e.g., Fujita, 1989). The bid-rent indicates the maximum land rent that a worker of type i located at a distance x from the CBD is ready to pay in order to achieve equilibrium utility W_{es}. Formally, the bid-rent $\Psi_{es}(x, W_{es})$ of an individual of employment status es residing at a distance x from the CBD is the inverse of the utility function $W_{es}(x)$ and it is equal to:

$$\Psi_L(x, W_L) = w_L - \tau x - W_L \qquad (1.9)$$

$$\Psi_U(x, W_U) = w_U - s\tau x - W_U. \qquad (1.10)$$

These bid-rents are both linear and decreasing in x and it is easy to verify that $\Psi_L(x, W_L)$ is steeper than $\Psi_U(x, W_U)$ because $0 < s < 1$.

We assume that land not occupied for residential use is utilized for agriculture and there is no vacant land in the city. Let us denote by R_A

---

[10] In Appendix A at the end of this book, we provide an overview of urban economics. It is quite useful for the reader who is not familiar with this literature.

the agricultural land rent, by $n_{es}(x)$ the distribution of workers of type $es = U, L$ at distance x, that is, the mass of workers of type es between distance x and $x + dx$ is $n_{es}(x)dx$, and by $\mathcal{L}(x)$ the land distribution in the city, that is, the amount of land available for housing between distance x and $x + dx$ is $\mathcal{L}(x)dx$ (for a circular city, $\mathcal{L}(x) = 2\pi x$ while for a linear city, as in this case, $\mathcal{L}(x) = 1$). We have the following definition (Fujita, 1989):

Definition 1.1. *An equilibrium land use with employed and unemployed workers consists of a pair of utility levels W_{es}, $es = U, L$, and a land rent curve $R(x)$ such that, at each $x \in [0, +\infty)$:*

(i) $R(x) = \max \left\{ \max_{es} \Psi_{es}(x, W_{es}), R_A \right\}$,

(ii) $R(x) = \Psi_{es}(x, W_{es})$ *if* $n_i(x) > 0$,

(iii) $n_U(x) + n_L(x) = \mathcal{L}(x)$ *if* $R(x) > R_A$.

Condition (i) means that the market rent curve $R(x)$ is the upper envelope of the equilibrium bid-rent curves $\Psi_{es}(x, W_{es})$ of all worker types ($es = U, L$) and the agricultural rent line R_A. This ensures that no type es individual can achieve a utility level higher than W_{es}, $es = U, L$, and no farmers can make a positive profit. Condition (ii) ensures that if some workers of type es reside at distance x, they actually obtain the equilibrium utility W_{es}. Condition (iii) states that if the land rent at x exceeds the agricultural land rent, all land must be used for housing. Conditions (i), (ii) and (iii) together imply that whenever the equilibrium land rent exceeds the agricultural land rent, the land is used by the workers with the highest equilibrium bid-rent. In other words, these conditions guarantee that each location is occupied by a highest-bidding activity.

The following remarks are in order. First, since we assume that all workers (whatever their type) consume one unit of land and that the size of each population of workers is equal to U and L, for unemployed and employed workers, then the city fringe is always equal to $N = U + L$. Second, we did not write the market clearing condition for land since it is always satisfied by assumption. Indeed, since we assume that there is one unit of land available in each location, and since each worker consumes one unit of land, then at each $x \in [0, N]$, total demand for land is always equal to the existing amount of land. Third, the population constraints that ensure that every worker resides somewhere in the city are also always satisfied since housing consumption has been normalized to 1. Fourth, since the city is linear and the size of each population is equal to U and L, $n_B(x)$, $n_W(x)$ and $L(x)$

have constant values (i.e., are independent of x). Finally, because bid-rents are well-behaved, (essentially $\Psi_{es}(x, W_{es})$ is continuous and decreasing in both x and W_{es}; see Fujita, 1989), in equilibrium, the market rent curve $R(x)$ is continuously decreasing up to the city fringe N.

Definition 1.1 is quite general and we here focus on an equilibrium where the land rent paid by the unemployed workers is equal at the boundary to the agricultural land rent and the land rent paid by the two groups is the same at distance L from the CBD. Together with condition (*iii*) and the fact that employed workers have steeper bid-rents than unemployed workers, this allows us to restate Definition 1.1 as followed (for simplicity, assuming that $R_A = 0$):

Definition 1.2. *An urban-land-use equilibrium with no relocation costs, fixed-housing consumption and fixed search intensity is a triple* (W_L^*, W_U^*, $R^*(x)$) *such that:*

$$\Psi_L(L, W_L^*) = \Psi_U(L, W_U^*) \tag{1.11}$$

$$\Psi_U(N, W_U^*) = R_A = 0 \tag{1.12}$$

$$R^*(x) = \max\left\{\Psi_L(x, W_L^*), \Psi_U(x, W_U^*), 0\right\} \quad \textit{at each } x \in (0, N]. \tag{1.13}$$

Equations (1.11) and (1.12) reflect equilibrium conditions in the land market. Equation (1.11) says that in the land market, at frontier L, the bid-rent offered by the employed is equal to the bid rent offered by the unemployed. Equation (1.12), in turn, states that the bid rent of the unemployed must be equal to the agricultural land at the city fringe. Equation (1.13) defines the equilibrium land rent as the upper envelope of the equilibrium bid-rent curves of all worker types and the agricultural rent line. As a result, the employed reside between 0 and L, whereas the unemployed reside between L and N. Furthermore, for this equilibrium to exist (see, e.g., Fujita, 1989), the equilibrium land rent must be everywhere continuous in the city. This equilibrium is illustrated in Figure 1.1.

By solving (1.11) and (1.12), we easily obtain the equilibrium values of the instantaneous utilities of the employed and the unemployed, which are given by:

$$W_L^* = w_L - \tau x_b^* - s\tau\left(x_f^* - x_b^*\right) \tag{1.14}$$

$$= w_L - \tau L - s\tau (N - L)$$

$$W_U^* = w_U - s\tau x_f^* = w_U - s\tau N. \tag{1.15}$$

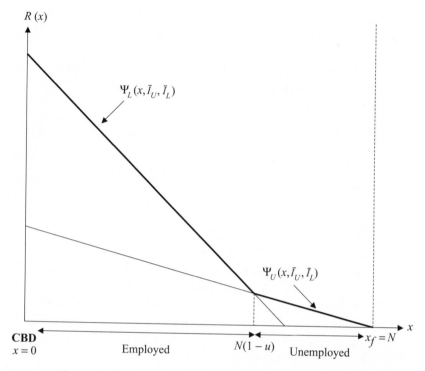

Figure 1.1. The urban-land-use equilibrium (The segregated city).

The employment zone (i.e., the residential zone for employed workers) is thus $(0, L]$ and the unemployment zone (i.e., the residential zone for unemployed workers) is thus $[L, N]$. By plugging (1.14) and (1.15) into (1.9) and (1.10), we easily obtain the land rent equilibrium $R^*(x)$. This is given by:

$$R^*(x) = \begin{cases} \tau\,(L - x) + s\tau\,(N - L) & \text{for} \quad 0 \le x \le L \\ s\tau\,(N - x) & \text{for} \quad L < x \le N \;. \\ 0 & \text{for} \quad x > N \end{cases} \qquad (1.16)$$

2.2. Steady-State Equilibrium

We are now able to solve for the labor market equilibrium and thus, the steady-state equilibrium. The unemployment rate is defined by $u = U/N$. We have:

Definition 1.3. *A (steady-state) labor market equilibrium (w_L^*, θ^*, u^*) is such that, given the matching technology d, all agents (workers and firms) maximize* *their respective objective function, i.e., this triple is determined by a steady-state condition, a free-entry condition for firms and a wage-setting mechanism.*

Agents discount the future at rate r and have rational expectations. In steady-state, the Bellman equations for the employed and unemployed are given by, respectively:[11]

$$r I_L = w_L - \tau L - st \, (N - L) - \delta \, (I_L - I_U) \tag{1.17}$$

$$r I_U = w_U - s \tau N + s\theta q(\theta) \, (I_L - I_U), \tag{1.18}$$

where I_L and I_U denote the discounted expected lifetime utility of an employed worker and a job seeker, respectively. The first equation that determines I_L states that an employed worker today obtains $W_L^* = w_L - \tau L - st \, (N - L)$, but can lose his/her job at rate δ and then obtains a negative surplus equal to $I_U - I_L$. Observe that the flow into unemployment results from job-specific (or idiosyncratic) shocks to job matches that reach the exogenous rate δ. These shocks may be explained by shifts in demand or productivity shocks. Here, the arrival of a shock leads to a closing down of the job, i.e. the dissolution of the match, because the shock moves the value of the match output from a high to a low level, at which it is not profitable for the firm to operate. In Chapter 2, we will endogenize δ by considering a more general framework where the firm can either continue production or close the job down after the occurrence of a shock. For the job seeker, I_U states that he/she obtains $W_U^* = w_U - s \tau N$ today, but may find a job at the rate $s\theta q(\theta)$, and then have a surplus equal to $I_L - I_U$. Because there are no relocation costs, in equilibrium all workers must reach the same utility level independently of their location in the city, i.e., $I_L = \overline{I}_L$ and $I_U = \overline{I}_U$. Combining (1.17) and (1.18), we obtain:

$$\overline{I}_L - \overline{I}_U = \frac{w_L - w_U - (1 - s) \tau L}{r + \delta + s\theta q(\theta)}. \tag{1.19}$$

By plugging (1.19) into (1.17) and (1.18), we finally get:

$$r \overline{I}_L = \frac{\delta w_U + [r + s\theta q(\theta)] \, w_L - \tau \, \{\delta s \, N + (r + s\theta q(\theta)) \, [s N + (1 - s) \, L]\}}{r + \delta + s\theta q(\theta)} \tag{1.20}$$

$$r \overline{I}_U = \frac{(r + \delta) \, w_U + s\theta q(\theta) w_L - s \tau \, \{N (r + \delta) + \theta q(\theta) \, [s N + (1 - s) \, L]\}}{r + \delta + s\theta q(\theta)}. \tag{1.21}$$

---

[11] For the derivations of the Bellman equations, see Appendix B at the end of this book.

Indeed, the discounted lifetime utility of an employed and an unemployed worker is a convex combination of the unemployment benefit w_U and the wage w_L, net of spatial costs. The weights are determined by the exit rates, which are different for employed and unemployed workers. It is easily verified that:

$$\lim_{r \to 0} r \overline{I}_L = r \overline{I}_U = \frac{\delta w_U + s\theta q(\theta) w_L - s\tau \left\{\delta N + \theta q(\theta) \left[s N + (1-s) L\right]\right\}}{\delta + s\theta q(\theta)}.$$

When there is a zero interest rate, i.e., $r \to 0$, workers have no intrinsic preference for the present so that they only care about the fraction of time they spend employed and unemployed. Therefore, the lifetime expected utilities are not state dependent. Indeed, over their lifetime, workers are totally indifferent between being employed today for T periods and then becoming unemployed for T' periods, and being unemployed today for T periods and then becoming employed for T' periods (which is not true if $r > 0$ since the present and the future are discounted differently). In other words, the only aspect that is of importance for them is the fraction of their lifetime they spend employed and unemployed, and not when they are in a specific employment state. In Chapter 2, we will study such a model for which $r \to 0$ in more detail.

Let us now focus on the case $r > 0$ and denote the intertemporal profit of a filled job and a vacancy by I_F and I_V, respectively. If c is the search cost for the firm per unit of time and y is the product of a match, then, in steady-state, I_F and I_V can be written as:

$$r I_F = y - w_L - \delta(I_F - I_V) \tag{1.22}$$

$$r I_V = -c + q(\theta)(I_F - I_V), \tag{1.23}$$

which implies that:

$$I_F - I_V = \frac{y - w_L + c}{r + \delta + q(\theta)}.$$

We assume that firms post vacancies up to a point where:

$$I_V = 0. \tag{1.24}$$

This is a free-entry condition. From (1.24) and using (1.23), the value of a job is now equal to:

$$I_F = \frac{c}{q(\theta)}. \tag{1.25}$$

Finally, plugging (1.25) into (1.22) and using (1.24), we obtain the following decreasing relationship between labor market tightness and wages in equilibrium:

$$\frac{c}{q(\theta)} = \frac{y - w_L}{r + \delta}. \tag{1.26}$$

In words, the value of a job $(y - w_L)/(r + \delta)$ is equal to the expected search cost $c/q(\theta)$, i.e., the cost per unit of time multiplied by the average duration of search for the firm. As a result, firms' job creation is endogenous and determined by (1.26). Observe that the free-entry condition $I_V = 0$ was written under the assumption that the total mass of firms, or equivalently, the total number of jobs, is equal to M. We thus have:[12]

$$M = \underbrace{(1 - u)\ N}_{\text{Total filled jobs}} + \underbrace{v\ M}_{\text{Total vacant jobs}} \tag{1.27}$$

which is equivalent to:

$$\frac{M}{N} = \frac{1 - u}{1 - v}. \tag{1.28}$$

Moreover, using (1.5) and the fact that $s = \bar{s}$, (1.27) can be written as:

$$\frac{M}{N} = 1 - u(1 - \theta s). \tag{1.29}$$

In this context, since the unemployment rate u is determined by a flow condition that is given below (see (1.36)) and θ by (1.26), M will adjust for (1.28) or (1.29) to hold. If we instead assume that $M = 1$, i.e., the number of firms is fixed to 1, then a free-entry condition cannot be written such as (1.26), and θ will be directly determined by $v = 1 - (1 - u)\,N$. Indeed, in that case, as soon as u is calculated from the flow equation, then v is deduced from this equation and $\theta = vM/su\,N$ is exogenous and determined by (1.5).[13]

Let us now determine the wage. In each period, the total intertemporal surplus is shared through a generalized Nash-bargaining process between the firm and the worker. The total surplus is the sum of the surplus of the

---

[12] Naturally,

$$(1 - u)\ N = (1 - v)\ M.$$

[13] In section 2 in Chapter 9, we assume that the number of jobs is fixed so that there will not be a free-entry condition.

workers, $\overline{I}_L - \overline{I}_U$, and the surplus of the firms $I_F - I_V$. In each period, the wage is determined by:

$$w_L = \arg\max_{w_L}(\overline{I}_L - \overline{I}_U)^\beta (I_F - I_V)^{1-\beta}, \qquad (1.30)$$

where $0 \leq \beta \leq 1$ represents the bargaining power of workers,[14] $\overline{I}_U$ the value of continued search and I_V equals the employer's value of holding the job vacant, i.e., $\overline{I}_U$ and I_V are the values of the agent's outside options. Observe that $\overline{I}_U$ does not depend on the current location of the worker who will relocate if there is a transition in his/her employment status. The maximization (1.30) implies that the worker's share of the match surplus is the constant β, formally

$$\overline{I}_L - \overline{I}_U = \beta \left(\overline{I}_L - \overline{I}_U + I_F - I_V \right),$$

which is equivalent to:

$$(1 - \beta) \left(\overline{I}_L - \overline{I}_U \right) = \beta \left(I_F - I_V \right). \qquad (1.31)$$

Solving (1.30) or (1.31) leads to the same result. The first-order condition of (1.30) yields:

$$\frac{\beta}{1 - \beta} \left(\frac{\partial \overline{I}_L}{\partial w_L} - \frac{\partial \overline{I}_U}{\partial w_L} \right) I_F + \left(\overline{I}_L - \overline{I}_U \right) \frac{\partial I_F}{\partial w_L} = 0. \qquad (1.32)$$

Since the wage is negotiated in each period, $\overline{I}_U$ does not depend on the current wage, w_L and so $\frac{\partial \overline{I}_U}{\partial w_L} = 0$. Since by (1.17), $\frac{\partial \overline{I}_L}{\partial w_L} = 1/(r + \delta)$, by (1.25), $I_F = c/q(\theta)$ and by (1.22), $\frac{\partial I_F}{\partial w_L} = -1/(r + \delta)$, equation (1.32) can be written as:

$$\overline{I}_L - \overline{I}_U = \frac{\beta}{1 - \beta} \frac{c}{q(\theta)}. \qquad (1.33)$$

Then, using (1.19) and (1.26), we finally obtain:

$$w_L = (1 - \beta) [w_U + (1 - s) \tau L] + \beta (y + cs\theta). \qquad (1.34)$$

In search-matching models, the wage-setting (WS) curve (a relation between wages and the state of the labor market, here θ) replaces the traditional labor-supply curve and is here given by (1.34). The wage can be seen as a weighted average of unemployment income $[w_U + (1 - s) \tau L]$ and current and future matching productivity $(y + cs\theta)$, the weights being β and

---

[14] For the interpretation of this parameter β, see Binmore, Rubinstein, and Wolinsky (1986).

$1 - \beta$, respectively. Let us now interpret this wage in more detail. The first part $(1 - \beta) [w_U + (1 - s) \tau L]$ is what firms must pay to induce workers to accept the job offer: Apart from the unemployment benefit, firms must exactly compensate the transportation cost difference (between the employed and the unemployed) of the employed worker who is the furthest away from the CBD, i.e., located at $x = x_b = L$. This is referred to as the *compensation effect*. The second part $\beta (y + cs\theta)$ gives the worker a fraction β (the bargaining power) of the surplus. This is referred to as the *outside option effect*. The first effect is a pure spatial cost since $(1 - s) \tau L$ represents the space cost differential between employed and unemployed workers paying the same bid-rent whereas the second effect is a mix of labor and spatial costs. Observe that θ has a positive impact on w_L, implying, in particular, that unemployment has a negative effect on wages. It is also interesting to note that search intensity s has an ambiguous effect on wages. On the one hand, when s increases, unemployed workers more often go to the CBD, so that the difference in commuting costs between employed and unemployed workers becomes lower. As a result, firms need to compensate employed workers less and thus, there is a decrease in wages. On the other hand, when s increases, unemployed workers find jobs at a higher rate and therefore, their outside option is better, which leads to an increase in the wage.

An interesting and new result is the fact that the wage (1.34) increases with commuting costs, τ. Indeed, when τ increases, firms need to compensate more the employed workers for their additional commuting costs compared to the unemployed workers. In the real world, firms often offer transport-related fringe benefits (Barber, 1998), which include monetary and non-monetary transport benefits (company cars, travel benefits, subsidized travel, etc.). For example, using information on firms' recruitment strategy in the United Kingdom, Van Ommeren, Van der Vlist, and Nijkamp (2006) show that workers' journey-to-work time induces firms to offer transport benefits to job applicants. Other evidence of the fact that firms reimburse workers' commuting costs is documented by Rouwendal and Van Ommeren (2007) for the case of the Netherlands.

Let us close the model. Since each job is destroyed according to a Poisson process with arrival rate δ, the number of workers who enter unemployment at time t is $\delta(1 - u_t)$, and the number who leave unemployment is $\theta_t q(\theta_t) s \, u_t$. The evolution of the unemployment rate is thus given by the difference between these two flows

$$\dot{u} = \delta(1 - u_t) - \theta_t q(\theta_t) s \, u_t, \qquad (1.35)$$

where $\overset{\bullet}{u} = du/dt$ is the variation in unemployment with respect to time t. In steady-state, the rate of unemployment as well as the market tightness are constant, $u_t = u, \theta_t = \theta$ and therefore, these two flows are equal (flows out of unemployment equal flows into unemployment). We thus have:[15]

$$u^* = \frac{\delta}{\delta + s\theta q(\theta)}. \tag{1.36}$$

It is easily verified that $\frac{\partial u^*}{\partial \theta} < 0$. Indeed, workers leave unemployment at a faster rate with a tighter labor market and thus, unemployment must decrease for (1.36) to hold. Furthermore, by using (1.6) and (1.7), we easily obtain that:

$$\lim_{\theta \to 0} u^* = 1 \text{ and } \lim_{\theta \to +\infty} u^* = 0.$$

When there are no search frictions on the workers' side, then the unemployment rate is equal to zero since job seekers instantaneously find a job ($u^* = 0$). If, on the contrary, firms do not experience any search frictions, then all workers must be unemployed ($u^* = 1$) for firms to instantaneously find a worker.

There is another more intuitive way of representing equation (1.36). Indeed, (1.36) can be written as:

$$\delta N(1 - u) - v\frac{M}{N}q\left(\frac{vM}{suN}\right) = 0,$$

and we obtain the so-called *Beveridge curve*. This is a downward sloping curve in the $u - v$ space, which once more expresses the search frictions since lower unemployment can only be achieved by creating more vacancies.

Now, by combining (1.26) and (1.34) and observing that $L^* = N(1 - u^*)$, the market solution that defines the equilibrium θ^* is given by:

$$y - w_U = \frac{c}{q(\theta^*)}\left[\frac{r + \delta + \beta s\theta^* q(\theta^*)}{1 - \beta}\right] + (1 - s)\tau N(1 - u). \tag{1.37}$$

Let us study its properties in (θ, u). We have:

$$\frac{\partial u}{\partial \theta} = -\frac{c}{q(\theta)^2}\frac{r + \delta}{1 - \beta}q'(\theta) + \frac{c\beta s}{1 - \beta} > 0.$$

---

[15] Using (1.35), it is easily shown that:

$$\lim_{t \to +\infty} u_t = u^*.$$

Thus, the steady-state u^* is a stable equilibrium.

Indeed, when unemployment increases, it is easier for firms to find a worker and thus, they create more jobs, which increases θ. Now by combining (1.36) and (1.37), we obtain:

$$\frac{c}{q(\theta^*)}\left[\frac{r+\delta+\beta s\theta^*q(\theta^*)}{1-\beta}\right] - (1-s)\tau N\frac{\delta}{\delta+s\theta^*q(\theta^*)}$$

$$+ (1-s)\tau N - (y-w_U) = 0. \tag{1.38}$$

Denote the left-hand side of this equation by $\Lambda(\theta)$. Then, it is easily verified that:

$$\Lambda'(\theta) > 0, \lim_{\theta\to 0}\Lambda(\theta) = -\infty \text{ and } \lim_{\theta\to+\infty}\Lambda(\theta) = +\infty.$$

This implies that there exists a unique θ^* that solves (1.38). Plugging this value into (1.34) and (1.36) gives a unique wage w^* and a unique unemployment rate u^*.

2.3. Interaction Between Land and Labor Markets

To study the interaction between the land and the labor market, let us write the four equilibrium equations that determine the four key endogenous variables, $R^*(x)$, W_L^*, W_U^* and θ^*. Using the values of w_L and u^*, given by (1.34) and (1.36), and by observing that $L^* = N(1-u^*)$, we obtain:

$$R^*(x) = \begin{cases} \tau(N-x) - (1-s)\tau N\frac{\delta}{\delta+s\theta^*q(\theta^*)} & \text{for } 0 \le x \le N\frac{s\theta^*q(\theta^*)}{\delta+s\theta^*q(\theta^*)} \\ s\tau(N-x) & \text{for } N\frac{s\theta^*q(\theta^*)}{\delta+s\theta^*q(\theta^*)} < x \le N \\ 0 & \text{for } x > N \end{cases}$$

$$W_L^* = (1-\beta)w_U + \beta\left(y+cs\theta^*\right) + (1-s)\beta\tau N\frac{\delta}{\delta+s\theta^*q(\theta^*)}$$

$$- [1-(1-s)(1-\beta)]\tau N$$

$$W_U^* = w_U - s\tau N$$

$$y - w_U = \frac{c}{q(\theta^*)}\left[\frac{r+\delta+\beta s\theta^*q(\theta^*)}{1-\beta}\right] + (1-s)\tau N\frac{s\theta^*q(\theta^*)}{\delta+s\theta^*q(\theta^*)}.$$

The key variable is θ^*, which appears everywhere except in the utility function of unemployed workers. Compared to the standard job-matching model with no space (Pissarides, 2000, Ch. 1), apart from the land market, the main difference resides in equation (1.37) and thus, in the determination of the equilibrium job creation rate θ^*. Indeed, there is an additional term, $(1 - s) \tau N (1 - u^*)$, which comes from the wage equation (1.34) which corresponds to the spatial wage compensation component. Interestingly, it depends on an endogenous variable u^*, which is here a measure of distance to jobs since the worker who resides the farthest away from jobs is located at $L^* = N (1 - u^*)$. This is why the two equations (1.36) and (1.37) are now linked together (which is not the case in Pissarides, 2000) and the comparative statics of θ^* are more complicated. By totally differentiating equation (1.38), we easily obtain:

$$\theta^* = \theta \left(\underset{+}{y}, \underset{-}{w_U}, \underset{-}{c}, \underset{-}{r}, \underset{?}{\delta}, \underset{-}{\beta}, \underset{?}{s}, \underset{-}{\tau}, \underset{-}{N} \right), \tag{1.39}$$

where a question mark means that the sign is ambiguous. The effects of y, w_U, c, and r are standard and can be found in Pissarides (2000). Indeed, an increase in productivity y or a decrease in the unemployment benefit w_U, or in the firms' search cost c, or in the discount rate r, or in the workers' bargaining power β, leads to more job creation because more firms enter the labor market, anticipating a higher expected profit. The new effects concern the parameters that enter in the term $(1 - s) \tau N (1 - u^*)$. Take, for example, the job destruction rate δ. There are two opposite effects, so the net effect on θ^* is ambiguous. Indeed, when δ increases, the unemployment rate increases, which leads to a higher job creation rate since firms need to compensate workers less in terms of wages ($(1 - s) \tau N (1 - u)$ decreases); the worker who is the furthest away is now closer to jobs. However, when δ increases, jobs are destroyed at a faster rate, which implies that less firms enter the labor market and thus, less jobs are created. Since the term $(1 - s) \tau N (1 - u)$ was absent in Pissarides (2000), only the last effect prevailed and therefore, an increase in δ was always reducing job creation θ^*.

Now take the spatial variables s and τ. For the commuting cost τ, it is quite easy to understand the intuition since it only enters in $(1 - s) \tau N (1 - u)$. So, when τ increases, spatial compensation in terms of wages increases and thus, less jobs are created. For search intensity, s, it is more subtle because s affects both spatial compensation and the efficiency of the labor market. An increase in search intensity reduces the unemployment rate. This has two effects. On the one hand, it decreases the spatial compensation of the wage, but on the other, it gives a better outside option for employed workers who demand higher wages. The net effect on wages and thus, on job creation θ^*, is therefore ambiguous. Once again, in Pissarides (2000, Ch. 5), only the second effect is present so that higher search intensity s always implies higher wages and lower θ^*.

The interaction between land and labor markets is here captured by the comparative statics exercise of θ^*, since the distance to jobs of the last employed worker affects wages and thus, job creation θ^*. To further study the interaction between these two markets, it must be observed that θ^* also affects both employment and unemployment zones and, as a result, land rent $R^*(x)$ in the employment zone. Indeed, when θ^* increases, less people are unemployed and thus, the employment zone augments while the unemployment zone shrinks. As a result, bid-rents and thus, the equilibrium land rent for employed workers increases at each $x \in [0, L]$. To be more precise, we have:

$$R^* = R \left(\underset{+}{y}, \underset{-}{w_U}, \underset{-}{c}, \underset{-}{r}, \underset{?}{\delta}, \underset{-}{\beta}, \underset{?}{s}, \underset{?}{\tau}, \underset{?}{N} \right).$$

The effects of each parameter on $R^*(x)$ can be derived from the effect of θ^* (see (1.39)). For example, when the productivity of a match y increases, θ^* increases, which reduces the unemployment rate. This extends the employment zone and workers are able to propose higher bids. Competition in the land market becomes fiercer in the employment zone and the land rent increases everywhere in that zone. Observe, however, that the spatial variables s, τ, N now have an ambiguous impact on R^*, because they have both a direct and an indirect effect on bid rents (through θ^*).

2.4. Welfare and Efficiency

Let us study the welfare of this economy. The equilibrium is clearly not efficient because of search externalities. Indeed, we have seen that the job-acquisition rate is positively related to V and negatively related to U, whereas the job-filling rate has exactly the opposite relationships. So, for example, negative search externalities arise because of the congestion that firms and workers impose on each other during the search process. Therefore, two types of externalities must be considered: negative intra-group externalities (more job seekers reduce the job-acquisition rate) and positive inter-group externalities (more searching firms increase the job-acquisition rate). As a result, the question of efficiency boils down to whether these two externalities cancel each other or whether one of them dominates the other. Since there is also the land market, we must see if there are additional externalities due to spatial frictions.

Let us determine the social welfare function. It is given by the sum of utilities of the employed and unemployed workers, the production of the firms net of search costs, and the land rents received by the (absentee) landlords. Being pure transfers, the wage w_L as well as the land rent $R(x)$ are thus excluded from the social welfare function. Using the fact that $v = \theta s u$, the latter can therefore be written as:

$$W = \int_0^{+\infty} e^{-rt} \left\{ \int_0^L (y - \tau x)dx + \int_L^N (w_U - s \tau x)dx - c \theta s u \right\} dt. \tag{1.40}$$

The social planner chooses θ and u which maximize (1.40) under the constraint (1.35). Indeed, we want to characterize the efficient solution when a social planner is affected by exactly the same externalities as the market economy and see whether it can do better than the decentralized equilibrium. These (search) externalities are captured by the constraint (1.35), which is the Beveridge curve.

In this problem, the control variable is θ and the state variable is u. Let ϑ be the co-state variable. The Hamiltonian is thus given by:

$$\mathcal{H} = e^{-rt} \{(1 - u)(y - \tau L) + u(w_U - s \tau L) - c s \theta u\}$$
$$+ \vartheta \left[\delta(1 - u) - \theta q(\theta)s u \right].$$

The Euler conditions are $\frac{\partial \mathcal{H}}{\partial \theta} = 0$ and $\frac{\partial \mathcal{H}}{\partial u} = -\dot{\vartheta}$. They are thus given by:

$$c e^{-rt} + \vartheta q(\theta) [1 - \eta(\theta)] = 0 \tag{1.41}$$

$$[y - w_U - (1 - u) \tau N(2 - s) - \tau N u s + c s \theta] e^{-rt}$$
$$+ \vartheta [\delta + s \theta q(\theta)] = \dot{\vartheta}_k, \tag{1.42}$$

where $\eta(\theta) = -q'(\theta)\theta/q(\theta)$ is the elasticity of the matching function with respect to unemployment. Let us focus on the steady-state equilibrium where $\dot{\theta} = 0$. By differentiating (1.41), we easily obtain that $\dot{\vartheta} = -r\vartheta$.[16] By plugging this value and the value of ϑ from (1.41) into (1.42), we obtain:

$$y - w_U = \frac{c}{q(\theta)} \left[\frac{r + \delta + s\theta q(\theta)\eta(\theta)}{1 - \eta(\theta)} \right] + (1 - s) \tau N(1 - u). \tag{1.43}$$

To see if the private and social solutions coincide, we compare (1.37) and (1.43). We have the following result.

---

[16] The transversality condition is given by:

$$\lim_{t \to +\infty} \vartheta \, u_t = 0$$

and is obviously verified.

Proposition 1.1. *In a spatial search-matching model with fixed search intensity, where the employed reside close to jobs and the unemployed far away from jobs, the market equilibrium is efficient if and only if:*

$$\beta = \eta(\theta). \tag{1.44}$$

Condition (1.44) is referred to as the Hosios-Pissarides condition and is exactly the same as in the standard matching model without space (Pissarides, 2000, Ch. 8). The land market is thus efficient (Fujita, 1989). Concerning the labor market, for a class of related search-matching models, Hosios (1990) and Pissarides (2000) have established that the negative intra-group externalities and the positive inter-group externalities just offset one another in the sense that a search equilibrium is socially efficient if and only if the matching function is homogenous of degree one and the worker's share of surplus β is equal to $\eta(\theta)$, i.e., the elasticity of the matching function with respect to unemployment. Naturally, there is no reason for β to be equal to $\eta(\theta)$ since these two variables are not related at all and, therefore, the search-matching equilibrium is, in general, inefficient.[17] When β is larger than $\eta(\theta)$, there is too much unemployment, creating congestion in the matching process for the unemployed. When β is lower than $\eta(\theta)$, there is too little unemployment, creating congestion for firms. In our present model, we have exactly the same externalities (intra- and inter-group externalities). The spatial dimension does not entail any inefficiency, so this is why the Hosios-Pissarides condition still holds, i.e., $\beta = \eta(\theta)$. Observe that since the equilibrium is efficient when $\beta = \eta(\theta)$, the social planner also likes unemployment since it has a social role by facilitating trade at low transaction costs. Indeed, the higher unemployment is, the less costly it is to fill vacancies. This is why workers' bargaining power β must be related to the elasticity of the matching function $\eta(\theta)$. The greater this elasticity is, the more important it is to have plenty of unemployed workers around to facilitate job matching. This means a high shadow value of unemployed workers, which corresponds to a high β in equilibrium.

3. Search Effort as a Function of Distance to Jobs

So far, workers' search intensity was exogenous and independent of residential location. There is strong evidence showing that distance to jobs does

---

[17] If search is directed (and not purely random like here), then it can be shown that the search equilibrium is efficient (Moen, 1997).

have an impact on search behavior.[18] In this section, following Wasmer and Zenou (2002, 2006), we would like to endogeneize s by assuming that

$$s(x) = s_0 - s_a x, \qquad (1.45)$$

where $s_0 > 0$ and $s_a > 0$. For the search intensity to always be positive, we impose that $s_0 > s_a N$. In this formulation, s_0 is the information about jobs that is available and not distance-related while s_a is the loss of information per unit of distance. Since the job acquisition rate is defined as $(s_0 - s_a x)\theta q(\theta)$, $s_a \theta q(\theta)$ is the marginal decrease in the job acquisition rate for an unemployed worker. When $s_a = 0$, we have returned to the previous model. The linearity assumption will be very useful in the urban-land-use analysis. So, with this formulation, when workers are further away from jobs, they search less intensively. Moreover, $\bar{s}$, the aggregate search efficiency in a city, will now depend on the average location of the unemployed since it is given by

$$\bar{s} = s_0 - s_a \bar{x}. \qquad (1.46)$$

Thus, we are integrating the land and the labor market even more because from now on, both markets need to be solved simultaneously to determine the steady-state equilibrium.

Since the model becomes quite complicated, we will slightly change the way s was viewed in the previous section. Indeed, in Section 2, search intensity s was affecting both the number of trips unemployed workers make to the CBD to gather information and the job acquisition rate. This was mainly because the only way workers were gathering information about jobs was by going to the CBD. Here, we make the other extreme assumption that unemployed workers do not need to go to the CBD at all to obtain information about jobs. They obtain information either locally through newspapers, local employment agencies, etc. or through firms' ads, and it is not costly. So, basically, when someone is searching more intensively, he/she reads more newspapers or more often checks the ads. In this context, (1.45) states that distance to jobs has a negative effect on workers' search intensity because, by living further away, it becomes more difficult to obtain information about jobs which has a discouraging effect on search intensity. In Section 4 below, we will consider a more general model where s is endogenous and affects both the number of trips to the CBD and the job acquisition rate. Observe that in the present model, unemployed workers

---

[18] We will discuss this issue in more detail in Chapter 7.

still need to go to the CBD to shop and meet friends (as in the previous section).

3.1. Urban-Land-Use Equilibrium

In contrast to Section 2, we cannot use the instantaneous utilities to solve the urban-land-use equilibrium. Indeed, now, when workers decide how much to bid for land, they have to take into account the future prospects in the labor market since this will partly be determined by their location. The job-acquisition rate of a worker residing at a distance x from the CBD is, as above, given by:

$$a(x) = s(x)\theta q(\theta) = (s_0 - s_a x)\theta q(\theta), \qquad (1.47)$$

but now depends on a worker's residential location and on the average location of the unemployed since θ depends on $\bar{s}$ (see 1.5). Hence, let us write the Bellman equations for employed and unemployed workers. By denoting the commuting cost of employed and unemployed workers, respectively, by τ_L and τ_U,[19] these equations are given by:

$$r I_L = w_L - \tau_L x - R(x) - \delta (I_L - I_U)$$

$$r I_U = w_U - \tau_U x - R(x) + a(x)(I_L - I_U),$$

where $\tau_U < \tau_L$ because unemployed workers only go to the CBD to shop while employed workers go there to shop and work. As stated above, search intensity only affects the job acquisition rate $a(x)$ and not the commuting cost of the unemployed. The main difference is that the value of $\bar{s}$ will depend on the average location of the unemployed $\bar{x}_U$ and thus, on the prevailing urban equilibrium. Since there are no relocation costs, the urban equilibrium is such that each group of workers enjoys the same level of utility whatever their residential location, i.e., $I_L = \bar{I}_L$ and $I_U = \bar{I}_U$. Bid rents can be written as:

$$\Psi_L(x, \bar{I}_U, \bar{I}_L) = w_L - \tau_L x + \delta \bar{I}_U - (r + \delta)\bar{I}_L \qquad (1.48)$$

$$\Psi_U(x, \bar{I}_U, \bar{I}_L) = w_U - \tau_U x + a(x)\bar{I}_L - [r + a(x)]\bar{I}_U. \qquad (1.49)$$

These bid-rents are linear (because $s(x)$ is linear in x) and decreasing in x. However, in contrast to Section 2, no clear urban pattern emerges because

---

[19] In the previous section, we had: $\tau_L = \tau$ and $\tau_U = s\tau$.

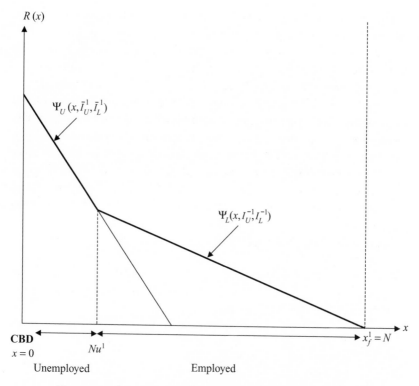

Figure 1.2. The urban-land-use equilibrium (The integrated city).

workers are trading off commuting costs and access to jobs. We have the following result:[20]

Proposition 1.2.

(*i*) *If*

$$\tau_L - \tau_U < w_U \theta^1 q(\theta^1)(\overline{I}_L^1 - \overline{I}_U^1) \qquad (1.50)$$

we have Equilibrium 1 (Figure 1.2) in which the unemployed live close to jobs.

(*ii*) *If*

$$\tau_L - \tau_U > w_U \theta^2 q(\theta^2)(\overline{I}_L^2 - \overline{I}_U^2) \qquad (1.51)$$

Equilibrium 2 (Figure 1.1) prevails and the employed live close to jobs.

---

[20] Superscript $k = 1, 2$ refers to Equilibrium k.

The unemployed workers would like to live close to jobs, both because they save on commuting costs and reduce their unemployment duration (which is the inverse of $a(x)$). For employed workers, it is only commuting costs that drive their choice. Equation (1.50) states that if the differential in commuting costs per unit of distance between employed and unemployed workers is lower than the marginal expected return of search for unemployed workers, then the latter bid away the employed workers and occupy the city center. If, on the contrary, (1.51) holds, then employed workers live close to jobs while unemployed workers reside on the outskirts of the city. Observe that these conditions depend on the endogenous variable θ that will be determined in the labor market equilibrium. So, at this stage, we do not know if both of them can hold simultaneously so that multiple equilibria prevail.

Given conditions (1.50) and (1.51), we have the following definitions:

Definition 1.4. *The urban-land-use Equilibrium 1 with no relocation costs, fixed-housing consumption and endogenous search intensity is a 5-tuple* $(I_L^{1*}, I_U^{1*}, x_b^{1*}, x_f^{1*}, R^{1*}(x))$ *such that:*

$$x_b^{1*} = N u^1 \tag{1.52}$$

$$x_f^{1*} = N \tag{1.53}$$

$$\Psi_U(x_b^{1*}, \overline{I}_U^{1*}, \overline{I}_L^{1*}) = \Psi_L(x_b^{1*}, \overline{I}_U^{1*}, \overline{I}_L^{1*}) \tag{1.54}$$

$$\Psi_L(x_f^{1*}, \overline{I}_U^{1*}, \overline{I}_L^{1*}) = 0 \tag{1.55}$$

$$R^{1*}(x) = \max\left\{\Psi_L(x, \overline{I}_U^{1*}, \overline{I}_L^{1*}), \Psi_U(x, \overline{I}_U^{1*}, \overline{I}_L^{1*}), 0\right\} \text{ at each } x \in \left(0, x_f^{1*}\right]. \tag{1.56}$$

Definition 1.5. *The urban-land-use Equilibrium 2 with no relocation costs, fixed-housing consumption and endogenous search intensity is a 5-tuple* $(I_L^{2*}, I_U^{2*}, x_b^{2*}, x_f^{2*}, R^{2*}(x))$ *such that:*

$$x_b^{2*} = N\left(1 - u^2\right) \tag{1.57}$$

$$x_f^{2*} = N \tag{1.58}$$

$$\Psi_U(x_b^{2*}, \overline{I}_U^{2*}, \overline{I}_L^{2*}) = \Psi_L(x_b^{2*}, \overline{I}_U^{2*}, \overline{I}_L^{2*}) \tag{1.59}$$

$$\Psi_U(x_f^{2*}, \overline{I}_U^{2*}, \overline{I}_L^{2*}) = 0 \tag{1.60}$$

$$R^{2*}(x) = \max\left\{\Psi_L(x, \overline{I}_U^{2*}, \overline{I}_L^{2*}), \Psi_U(x, \overline{I}_U^{2*}, \overline{I}_L^{2*}), 0\right\} \text{ at each } x \in \left(0, x_f^{2*}\right]. \tag{1.61}$$

Equilibrium 2 (the segregated city) is displayed in Figure 1.1 while Equilibrium 1 (the integrated city) is illustrated in Figure 1.2. Using (1.48), (1.49), (1.52) (or (1.57)), and replacing them in (1.54) (or (1.59)) and (1.55) (or (1.60)), we obtain:

$$I_L^k - I_U^k = \frac{w_L^k - w_U - (\tau_L - \tau_U)x_b^k}{r + \delta + (s_0 - s_a x)\theta^k q(\theta^k)} \qquad k = 1, 2, \qquad (1.62)$$

where w_L^k, u^k, θ^k will be determined at the labor market equilibrium k. The average search intensity in equilibrium k is equal to:

$$\bar{s}^k = s_0 - s_a \bar{x}^k \qquad k = 1, 2, \qquad (1.63)$$

where $\bar{x}^k$ is the average location of the unemployed in equilibrium k. It is easily verified that $\bar{x}^1 = N u^1/2$ and $\bar{x}^2 = N\left(1 - u^2/2\right)$. Since $\bar{x}_1^1 < \bar{x}^2$ (this is always true because $u^1 + u^2 < 2$), the average search efficiency in Urban Equilibrium 1 is higher than in Urban Equilibrium 2, i.e., $\bar{s}^1 > \bar{s}^2$. This result is not surprising. Indeed, in the integrated city (Equilibrium 1), the unemployed reside closer to the CBD than in the segregated city (Equilibrium 2) and thus, the rate at which they leave unemployment is on average higher.

3.2. Steady-State Equilibrium

We can now close the model as before. For each equilibrium $k = 1, 2$, we have a free-entry condition that gives the following labor demand curves:

$$\frac{c}{q(\theta^k)} = \frac{y - w_L^k}{r + \delta}. \qquad (1.64)$$

We can also determine a bargained wage for each equilibrium $k = 1, 2$. These are given by:

$$w_L^k = (1 - \beta)\left[w_U + (\tau_L - \tau_U)x_b^k\right] + \beta\left[y + \left(s_0 - s_a x_b^k\right)\theta^k c\right]. \qquad (1.65)$$

Equations (1.65) give the two wage-setting curves (WS_1 and WS_2) and are both positively sloped in (θ_k, w_k). It can be shown that the curve WS_1 is steeper than WS_2, but the intercept of WS_1 is lower. The reason why WS_1 is steeper than WS_2 is the following. The slope of these curves represents the ability of workers to exert wage pressures when the labor market is tighter. Thus, for a given labor market tightness, a more efficient labor market, i.e., $\bar{s}^1 > \bar{s}^2$, leads to a higher wage pressure per unit of θ and thus, a steeper WS_1 curve. The intercept is higher in Equilibrium 2, however, since when $\theta = 0$, the outside option effect vanishes and only the compensation effect remains. Since the same marginal worker is further away in Equilibrium 2, he/she must have a higher compensation for his/her transportation costs.

We can finally determine the steady-state conditions on flows:

$$u^k = \frac{\delta}{\delta + \bar{s}^k \theta^k q(\theta^k)}. \qquad (1.66)$$

As stated in the previous section, the above equation defines a downward sloping curve referred to as the Beveridge curve in the (u^k, V^k) space. The interesting feature of these Beveridge curves is that they are indexed by $\bar{s}^k$, which depends on the spatial dispersion of unemployed workers in equilibrium $k = 1, 2$. It can be shown that, in the plane (θ, w), the Beveridge curve in Urban Equilibrium 2 is always above the Beveridge curve in Urban Equilibrium 1. Indeed, a lower $\bar{s}^k$ is associated with an outward shift of the Beveridge curve in the $u^k - V^k$ space because more vacancies are needed to maintain the steady-state level of unemployment. If s_a increases or s_0 decreases, the Beveridge curve is shifted away from the origin meaning that the labor market is less efficient. The same would arise if the city size were to increase: unemployed workers would be further away from jobs.

By combining (1.64) and (1.65), we obtain the following market equilibrium equation:

$$y - w_U = \frac{c}{q(\theta^k)} \left[\frac{\delta + r + \theta^k q(\theta^k) \left(s_0 - s_a x_b^k \right) \beta}{1 - \beta} \right] + x_b^k \left(\tau_L - \tau_U \right). \qquad (1.67)$$

If we define

$$\widehat{\theta} = \frac{1 - \beta}{\beta} \frac{(\tau_L - \tau_U)}{s_a c}$$

we have the following result:

Proposition 1.3. *There exists a unique and stable steady-state equilibrium* $(I_L^{k*}, I_U^{k*}, x_b^{k*}, x_f^{k*}, R^{k*}(x), w_L^{k*}, \theta^{k*}, u^{k*})$, $k = 1, 2$, *and only the two following cases are possible:*

  (*i*) *If* $\widehat{\theta} < \theta^{1*} < \theta^{2*}$, *Urban Equilibrium 1 prevails;*
  (*ii*) *If* $\theta^{2*} < \theta^{1*} < \widehat{\theta}$, *Urban Equilibrium 2 prevails.*

These two possible cases are plotted in Figures 1.3 and 1.4, respectively. Inequalities in (*i*) and (*ii*) replace (1.50) and (1.51). Observe that multiple urban equilibria can never arise (i.e., having both a segregated and an integrated city) because, according to Proposition 1.3, the condition for

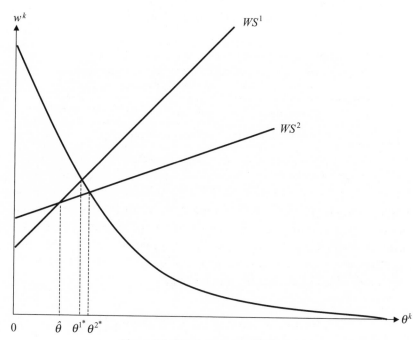

Figure 1.3. Steady-state equilibrium 1.

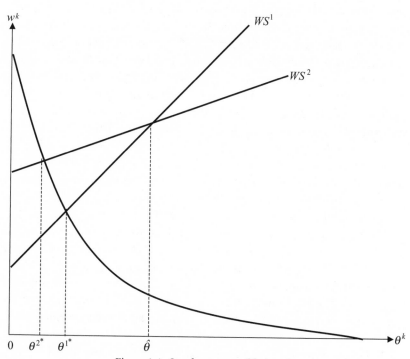

Figure 1.4. Steady-state equilibrium 2.

Table 1.1. *Interaction between land the labor markets*

	Exogenous wages	Endogenous wages
$s_a = 0$	No Interaction	Partial Interaction ($LME \rightarrow LE$)
$s_a > 0$	Complete Interaction	Complete Interaction

($LME \rightarrow LE$ means that the interaction is from the land market equilibrium to the labor equilibrium)

multiple equilibria is $\theta^{2*} < \widehat{\theta} < \theta^{1*}$ and it can never be verified since the intersection of the labor demand curve with the wage-setting curve never satisfies this condition. This is because $\widehat{\theta}$, initially defined as the intersection point between the two wage-setting curves, is also the critical value that determines which urban equilibrium prevails.

3.3. The Role of Space in Search-Matching Models

3.3.1. Interaction Between Land and Labor Markets.
The interaction between land and labour markets is partly due to the dependence of search efficiency on distance. To show this, we proceed a contrario: we first assume that wages are exogenous and $s_a = 0$. In this case, both markets are independent. When we relax exogenous wages and keep $s_a = 0$, then we have returned to Section 2 and there is a one-way interaction between markets: the labor market does not depend on the land market, but the land market equilibrium depends on the labor market equilibrium through labor market tightness as workers locate in one configuration or the other, notably depending on θ^*.

Finally, as soon as $s_a > 0$, there is a general equilibrium interaction between the two markets. Indeed, one of the key assumptions of our model is that the search efficiency, s, of each worker depends on the distance between residence and the job center, i.e., $s = s(x)$ with $s'(x) < 0$. This implies that the land and labor markets are interdependent. Indeed, on the one hand, the labor market strongly depends on the land market since the equilibrium values of u^{k*}, V^{k*} and θ^{k*} are affected by the value of $\bar{s}^k$. On the other hand, the land market strongly depends on the labor market since the inequality (1.50) or (1.51) determining the land market equilibrium configuration depends on the value of θ^{k*}. Table 1.1. summarizes our discussion.

3.3.2. Decomposition of Unemployment.
We pursue our analysis by determining the part of unemployment that is only due to spatial frictions. For

simplicity, we focus on Equilibrium 2 where the unemployed live far away from jobs. The analysis for the other equilibrium is straightforward since it is nearly identical. We also normalize the total population so that $N = 1$. Let us start with exogenous wages. In this case, θ^2 is constant and determined by (1.64). By using (1.66), the unemployment rate is given by:

$$u^2 = \frac{\delta}{\delta + \theta^2 q(\theta^2) \left[s_0 - s_a(1 - u^2/2) \right]}. \tag{1.68}$$

Let us further define:

$$u_0^2 = \frac{\delta}{\delta + \theta^2 q(\theta^2) s_0}, \tag{1.69}$$

the part of *unemployment that is independent of spatial frictions*, i.e., when $s_a = 0$. By a Taylor first-order expansion for small s_a/s_0, we easily obtain:

$$u^{2*} = u_0^2 \left[1 + \frac{s_a}{s_0} \left(1 - u_0^2 \right) \left(1 - u_0^2/2 \right) \right] = u_0^2 + u_\sigma^2, \tag{1.70}$$

where $u_\sigma^2 \equiv u_0^2[s_a(1 - u_0^2)(1 - u_0^2/2)/s_0]$ is the *unemployment rate that is only due to spatial frictions* and u_0^2 is defined by (1.69). Observe that u_σ^2 is increasing in s_a/s_0, the parameter representing the loss of information through distance to jobs and null when $s_a = 0$. Observe also that pure frictional unemployment u_0^2 affects u_σ^2 in the following way:

$$\text{If} \quad u_0^2 < 1 - \frac{\sqrt{3}}{3} \approx 0.42\,, \quad \text{then} \quad \frac{\partial u_\sigma^2}{\partial u_0^2} > 0.$$

In general, $u_0^2 < 0.42$ so that u_0^2 has a positive effect on u_σ^2, showing the full interaction between land and labor markets. This is quite natural: higher "spaceless" unemployment u_0^2 has a positive effect on search frictions due to spatial heterogeneity (this is a side effect of the dispersion of space on the unemployed themselves, which increases the average distance to jobs).

Overall, compared to the non-spatial case, unemployment increases because of the loss of information due to spatial dispersion of agents and also due to the wage compensation of commuting costs. However, it also tends to decrease because of the outside option effect that reduces wages.

3.4. Welfare

Let us now proceed to the welfare analysis. The first issue we address is the respective efficiency of the two types of land market configurations. Since there are no multiple equilibria in the land market, we cannot Pareto-rank

Table 1.2. *Parameter values*

$y = 1$ General Productivity	$r = 0.05$ Pure discount rate
$\delta = 0.1$ Job-destruction rate	$\beta = 0.5$ Workers' share of surplus
$s_0 = 1$ Search intensity that is independent of distance to jobs	$\eta(\theta) = 0.5$ Search elasticity of matching
$N = 1$ Total population	$\tau_L = 0.4$ Employed commuting cost
$w_U = 0.3$ Unemployment benefit	$\tau_U = 0.1$ Unemployed commuting cost
$c = 0.3$ Cost of vacant job	

the equilibria and it is difficult to compare them. Nevertheless, we are able to investigate what happens to the welfare difference in the range of parameters around the frontier separating the two types of land market equilibria.

3.4.1. *Welfare Comparison Between the Two Cities.* We first investigate the welfare of the city and study how it varies in each urban configuration. For each city, we use the welfare function $\mathcal{W}$ defined by (1.40). To see how this quantity varies and if it can be compared across cities, let us proceed to a simple numerical resolution of the model. We normalize the total population to 1, i.e., $N = 1$ and use the following Cobb-Douglas function for the matching function: $d(\overline{s}^k u^k, V^k) = \sqrt{\overline{s}^k u^k V^k}$. This implies that $q(\theta^k) = 1/\sqrt{\theta^k}$, $\theta^k q(\theta^k) = \sqrt{\theta^k}$ and, whatever the prevailing urban equilibrium, the elasticity of the matching rate (defined as $\eta(\theta^k) = -q'(\theta^k)\theta^k/q(\theta^k)$) is equal to 0.5. The values of the parameters (in yearly terms) are displayed in Table 1.2.

Table 1.3. gives the results. In this table, we have chosen to vary a key parameter, s_a, the loss of information per unit of distance (remember that workers' search intensity is defined by $s(x) = s_0 - s_a x$). This parameter s_a varies from a very large value 1 (where City 1 is the prevailing equilibrium) to a very small value 0.1 (where City 2 is the prevailing equilibrium). The cut-off point is equal to $s_a = 0.522$. The sign '$-$' indicates the 'limit to the left', whereas the sign '$+$' indicates the 'limit to the right'.

The first interesting result of this table is that when we switch from an integrated city (Equilibrium 1) to a segregated city (Equilibrium 2), for values very close to the cut-off point $s_a = 0.522$, the unemployment rate u^{k*} nearly doubles (from 6.85% to 12.4%). However, it is clear that this result is due to the spatial part of unemployment u_σ^k since the non-spatial part u_0^k is not at all affected by this increase. Indeed, when we switch from

Table 1.3. *Comparison between cities*

s_a	City	$u^{k*}(\%)$	$u_0^{k*}(\%)$	$u_\sigma^{k*}(\%)$	u_σ^{k*}/u^{k*}	θ^{k*}	x_b^{k*}	$\bar{s}^{k*}$	Welfare
1	1	6.86	6.64	0.22	0.03	1.98	0.069	0.966	0.715
0.75	1	6.85	6.69	0.16	0.02	1.95	0.069	0.974	0.714
0.6	1	6.85	6.72	0.13	0.02	1.93	0.069	0.979	0.714
0.55	1	6.85	6.73	0.12	0.02	1.92	0.069	0.981	0.714
0.525	1	6.85	6.73	0.15	0.02	1.92	0.069	0.982	0.714
0.522+	1	6.85	6.73	0.12	0.02	1.92	0.069	0.982	0.714
0.522−	2	12.4	6.73	5.65	0.46	1.92	0.876	0.511	0.712
0.52	2	12.4	6.74	5.63	0.45	1.91	0.876	0.512	0.712
0.5	2	12.1	6.82	5.31	0.44	1.86	0.879	0.530	0.713
0.25	2	10.0	7.81	2.20	0.22	1.39	0.900	0.763	0.727
0.1	2	9.15	8.35	0.80	0.09	1.20	0.909	0.905	0.732

Equilibrium 1, where the unemployed are close to jobs and are very efficient in their job search ($\bar{s}^1 = 0.982$), to Equilibrium 2, where the unemployed reside far away from jobs and are, on average, not very active in their search activity ($\bar{s}^2 = 0.511$), the spatial part of unemployment changes values from 0.12 to 5.65. Another way of seeing this is to consider column 6 (u_σ^k/u^{k*}): the part of unemployment which is due to space varies from 2% to 46%. So the main effect of switching from one equilibrium to another is that search frictions are amplified by space and consequently, there is a sharp increase in unemployment rates. Here, spatial access to jobs is thus crucial for understanding the formation of unemployment.

The last column of the table shows the value of welfare $\mathcal{W}^k$ when s_a varies. The result is very striking: even though unemployment rates are higher in Equilibrium 1 than in Equilibrium 2, this does not imply that the general welfare of the economy is higher in the first equilibrium. Indeed, even though the unemployed workers are better off in Equilibrium 1 (lower unemployment spells and lower commuting costs), employed workers can, in fact, be worse off because of much higher commuting costs in Equilibrium 1. In the above table, it is interesting to see that in the vicinity of $s_a = 0.522$, switching from Equilibrium 1 to Equilibrium 2 does not involve any considerable change in the welfare level (from 0.714 to 0.712). Naturally, this is just a numerical example and we do not have any general results. However, we are confident that it can be generalized since the same qualitative results have been obtained in the numerous simulations performed by us.

3.4.2. Welfare Within Each City. The shape of the city thus has little impact on welfare, since in the segregated city, what is lost from lower search efficiency is gained through lower commuting costs. We now investigate the issue of the optimality of the decentralized equilibrium *within each land market equilibrium.*

In our present model, we have exactly the same externalities (intra- and inter-group externalities) as in the previous section. The spatial dimension does not entail any inefficiency so that it is easily verified that for each equilibrium $k = 1, 2$, Proposition 1.1 and thus condition (1.44) still hold.

4. Endogenous Search Intensity and Housing Consumption

So far, we have assumed that search intensity was either exogenous or depending on distance to jobs. In the present section, following Smith and Zenou (2003a), we would like to endogenously derive the search behavior of workers and show under which condition their search intensity negatively depends on distance to jobs.

In this section, workers' search intensity s affects both the number of trips to the CBD and the job acquisition rate. Hence, when an unemployed worker wants to obtain information about jobs, he/she needs to go to the CBD. Moreover, here, the workers' search intensity s can be interpreted as the fraction of commutes to the CBD and thus, s is between $\underline{s_0} > 0$, its minimum value and 1. If $s = 1$, the unemployed workers go to the CBD as often as the employed workers, i.e., every day.

4.1. The Model

We assume that all workers have identical preferences among consumptions bundles (h_{es}, z_{es}) of land (*housing*), h_{es}, and *composite good, z_{es}*, which can be represented by a log-linear utility for $es = U, L$:[21]

$$\Gamma(h_{es}, z_{es}) = h_{es}^{\alpha} \, z_{es}^{\omega} \tag{1.71}$$

with $\alpha, \omega > 0$, and $\alpha + \omega < 1$. Each *employed* worker living in location x has the standard budget constraint

$$h_L R(x) + \tau x + z_L = w_L, \tag{1.72}$$

---

[21] We take a Cobb-Douglas utility function to obtain closed-form solutions.

where z_{es} is taken as the numeraire good with unit price. For an *unemployed* worker at x, we have the following budget constraint:

$$h_U R(x) + s\tau x + z_U = w_U. \tag{1.73}$$

Maximizing utility (1.71) subject to (1.72) yields the following *land demand for employed workers* at x:

$$h_L(x) = \frac{\alpha}{\alpha + \omega} \cdot \frac{w_L - \tau x}{R(x)}. \tag{1.74}$$

Similarly, maximizing (1.71) subject to (1.73) yields the following *land demand for unemployed workers* at x:

$$h_U(x) = \frac{\alpha}{\alpha + \omega} \cdot \frac{w_U - s\tau x}{R(x)}. \tag{1.75}$$

We can now derive the following indirect utility

$$\Omega_L(x) = \chi (w_L - \tau x)^{\alpha + \omega} R(x)^{-\alpha} \tag{1.76}$$

for each *employed* worker at x, where $\chi = [\alpha/(\alpha + \omega)]^\alpha [\omega/(\alpha + \omega)]^\omega$ and the following indirect utility

$$\Omega_U(s, x) = \chi (w_U - s\tau x)^{\alpha + \omega} R(x)^{-\alpha} \tag{1.77}$$

for each *unemployed* worker at x, where in this case s is now included as a relevant choice variable. The discounted expected lifetime utilities for employed and unemployed workers (Bellman equations) are now given by:

$$r I_L = \Omega_L(x) - \delta [I_L - I_U(s, x)] \tag{1.78}$$

$$r I_U(s, x) = \Omega_U(s, x) + s\theta q(\theta) [I_L - I_U(s, x)], \tag{1.79}$$

where $\theta = V/(\bar{s}U)$ and $\Omega_L(x)$ and $\Omega_U(s, x)$ are given by (1.76) and (1.77), respectively. Using (1.78) and (1.79), we obtain:

$$I_L - I_U(s, x) = \frac{\Omega_L(x) - \Omega_U(s, x)}{r + \delta + s\theta q(\theta)} > 0. \tag{1.80}$$

Since there are no relocation costs, at any urban equilibrium it must be that $r I_L = r \bar{I}_L$ and $r I_U(s, x) = r \bar{I}_U$. Unemployed workers optimally choose s^* by maximizing (1.79). We obtain:

$$r \frac{\partial I_U(s, x)}{\partial s} = -\chi \tau x (\alpha + \omega)(w_U - s\tau x)^{\alpha + \omega - 1} R(x)^{-\alpha}$$

$$+ \theta q(\theta) (\bar{I}_L - \bar{I}_U) = 0. \tag{1.81}$$

There is a fundamental trade-off between short-run and long-run benefits for an unemployed worker. On the one hand, increasing search effort s

is costly in the short run (more commuting costs) but, on the other, it increases the long-run prospects of employment. Using (1.76), the first-order condition (1.81) can be written as:

$$\Omega_U(s, x) \frac{(\alpha + \omega) \tau x}{w_U - s\tau x} = \theta q(\theta) \left(\overline{I}_L - \overline{I}_U \right). \qquad (1.82)$$

Now, observe that by plugging (1.80) into (1.78), we obtain:

$$\Omega_U(s, x) = r\overline{I}_U - s\theta q(\theta) \left(\overline{I}_L - \overline{I}_U \right). \qquad (1.83)$$

As a result, by plugging the value of $\Omega_U(s, x)$ from (1.83) into (1.82), we finally get:

$$s^*(x) = \frac{(\alpha + \omega)}{[1 - (\alpha + \omega)]} \left[\frac{w_U}{(\alpha + \omega) \tau x} - \frac{r\overline{I}_U}{\theta q(\theta) \left(\overline{I}_L - \overline{I}_U \right)} \right]. \qquad (1.84)$$

We have the following result:

Proposition 1.4.

(i) *In each location x, there is a unique search intensity s that maximizes (1.79).*

(ii) *For any prevailing job acquisition rate, $\theta q(\theta)$, and constant lifetime values, $\overline{I}_L$, $\overline{I}_U$, the optimal search intensity function, $s(x)$, for unemployed workers is given for each location, x, by*

$$s(x) = \begin{cases} 1 & \text{for } x \leq x(1) \\ \frac{(\alpha+\omega)}{[1-(\alpha+\omega)]} \left[\frac{w_U}{(\alpha+\omega)\tau x} - \frac{r\overline{I}_U}{\theta q(\theta)(\overline{I}_L-\overline{I}_U)} \right] & \text{for } x(1) < x < x(\underline{s_0}) \\ s_0 & \text{for } x \geq x(\underline{s_0}) \end{cases}$$

$$(1.85)$$

where

$$x(s) = \frac{w_U}{\tau} \cdot \frac{\theta q(\theta) \left(\overline{I}_L - \overline{I}_U \right)}{s \left[1 - (\alpha + \omega) \right] \theta q(\theta) \left(\overline{I}_L - \overline{I}_U \right) + (\alpha + \omega) r\overline{I}_U}$$

$$(1.86)$$

which is the unique inverse function of (1.85).

The proof of Proposition 1.4 is given in Appendix A.4.1 at the end of this chapter and shows why it is optimal for workers to have constant search intensities close to and far away from the CBD. Figure 1.5 describes $s(x)$. There is a *non-linear decreasing* relationship between the residential

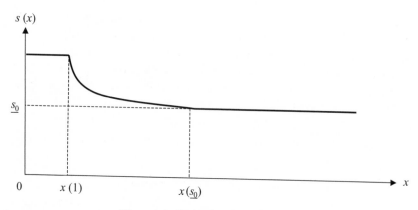

Figure 1.5. Optimal search intensities.

distance to jobs of unemployed workers and their search intensity, s. In fact, individuals living sufficiently close to jobs search every day, $s = 1$, whereas those residing far away provide a minimum search intensity, $s = \underline{s_0}$. Workers living in-between these two areas experience a decrease in their search intensity from $s = 1$ to $s = \underline{s_0}$. The intuition runs as follows. As stated above, there is a fundamental trade-off between short-run and long-run benefits of various location choices for unemployed workers. Indeed, locations near jobs are costly in the short-run (both in terms of high rents and low housing consumption), but allow higher search intensities which, in turn, increase the long-run prospects of reemployment. Conversely, locations far from jobs are more desirable in the short-run (low rents and high housing consumption), but only allow infrequent trips to the CBD jobs and hence, reduce the long-run prospects of reemployment. Therefore, for workers residing further away from the CBD, it is optimal to spend a minimal search effort whereas workers residing close to jobs provide a high search effort. Compared to the previous section, we have endogenized the relationship between s and x and have provided a mechanism that explains why search intensity is a decreasing function of distance to jobs.

For interior $s^*(x)$, that is search intensity for workers living between $x(1)$ and $x(\underline{s_0})$, we can perform a comparative statics analysis. An interesting and non-standard result is that when the unemployment benefit w_U increases, workers' search intensity s^* also increases. Indeed, since

$$\frac{\partial \Omega_U(s, x)}{\partial s} = -\chi \tau x (\alpha + \omega)(w_U - s\tau x)^{\alpha+\omega-1} R(x)^{-\alpha} < 0,$$

then $\partial^2 \Omega_U(s, x)/\partial s \partial w_U \geq 0$ since $\alpha + \omega < 1$, which means that an increase in w_U reduces the marginal cost of searching and thus, workers

put more effort into their search activities. For the same reason, we have
the reverse result for the commuting cost per unit of distance τ since
$\partial^2 \Omega_U(s, x)/\partial s \partial \tau \leq 0$. So, when transportation becomes cheaper (for example because of transportation subsidies or better public transportation),
then unemployed workers search more intensively. Another interesting result concerns land rent. For a given x, an increase in land rent $R(x)$ increases
the search intensity since $\partial^2 \Omega_U(s, x)/\partial s \partial R \geq 0$. Finally, not surprisingly,
an increase in labor market tightness increases search intensity.[22]

4.2. The Different Urban-Land-Use Equilibria

We have determined the optimal search intensity of the unemployed workers in each location in the city (Proposition 1.4). Given this function $s(x)$,
one may ask where do unemployed and employed workers locate in the
city? The basic trade-off for employed workers is between commuting costs
and housing consumption whereas for the unemployed, it is between com-
muting/search costs, housing consumption and search intensity (and thus
duration of unemployment). As usual, in order to determine the urban-
land-use equilibrium, we must define the bid rent function for each group
of workers.

Given the utilities and lifetime values above, we now define the equilibrium bid-rents. It follows from (1.78) that the bid-rent function of the
employed workers in each location, x, is equal to:

$$\Psi_L(x, \overline{I}_U, \overline{I}_L) = \left[\frac{\chi(w_L - \tau x)^{\alpha+\omega}}{r\overline{I}_L + \delta\left(\overline{I}_L - \overline{I}_U\right)} \right]^{1/\alpha} . \qquad (1.87)$$

As usual, this bid-rent is decreasing in x but is no longer linear, which
implies that more than two urban configurations can emerge. The bid-rent
function for unemployed workers is considerably more complex, in that it
depends on the optimal search intensity level in each location. Using (1.79),
we obtain the following bid-rent function for unemployed workers in each
location x:

$$\Psi_U(x, \overline{I}_U, \overline{I}_L) = \left[\frac{\chi\left[w_U - s(x)\tau x\right]^{\alpha+\omega}}{r\overline{I}_U - s(x)\theta q(\theta)\left(\overline{I}_L - \overline{I}_U\right)} \right]^{1/\alpha} , \qquad (1.88)$$

---

[22] Using a panel of English sub-regional data, Patacchini and Zenou (2005; 2006a) show
that optimal search intensity is higher in areas characterized by higher costs of living (i.e.,
higher land rent) R and/or higher labor market tightness θ.

where $s(x)$ is given by (1.85). It should be clear that the bid-rents are calculated such that the lifetime utilities of both employed and unemployed workers, $\bar{I}_U$ and $\bar{I}_L$, are spatially invariant. Compare, for example, an unemployed worker residing close to jobs and another unemployed worker living far away from jobs. The former has a lower search (commuting) cost and a higher chance of finding a job but consumes less land, whereas the latter has a higher search (commuting) cost and a lower chance of finding a job but consumes more land. The bid-rent defined by (1.88) exactly compensates these differences by ensuring that these two workers obtain the same lifetime utility, $\bar{I}_U$. This is not true for the current utility of the unemployed $\Omega_U(s, x)$ because, as can be seen in (1.83), the land rent does not compensate for $s(x)$. In fact, the unemployed residing close to jobs have a lower current utility than those living far away from jobs because they provide more search intensity (indeed, using (1.83), it is easily seen that $\Omega_U'(x) > 0$). However, because they search more intensively, they have a higher chance of finding a job and, hence, in the long-run they compensate for the short-run disadvantage so that all unemployed workers obtain the same $\bar{I}_U$ in equilibrium.

Definition 1.6. *An urban-land-use equilibrium is such that:*

$$R(x) = \max\{\Psi_L(x, \bar{I}_U, \bar{I}_L), \Psi_U(x, \bar{I}_U, \bar{I}_L), R_A\} \tag{1.89}$$

$$\rho_{es}(x) > 0 \Rightarrow R_{es}(x) = R(x), \quad es = U, L \tag{1.90}$$

$$h_U(x)\rho_U(x) + h_L(x)\rho_L(x) \le \mathcal{L}(x) \tag{1.91}$$

$$R(x) > R_A \Rightarrow h_U(x)\rho_U(x) + h_L(x)\rho_L(x) = \mathcal{L}(x) \tag{1.92}$$

where R_A is agricultural land rent, $\rho_L(x)$ and $\rho_U(x)$ denote, respectively, the population densities of employed and unemployed workers at x, and $\mathcal{L}(x)$ is the land distribution in the city.

This is a quite general definition similar to Definition 1.1 since we do not know what the urban equilibrium looks like. Equations (1.89) and (1.90) state that land at each x is assigned to the highest bidder and there is no vacant land in the city. Equation (1.91) is the *land capacity condition* that no more land be consumed than what is available and equation (1.92) is the *land filling condition* that all land with rents higher than agricultural rent must be occupied by workers. Observe that, as defined in Section 2, $\mathcal{L}(x)dx$ is the amount of land available for housing between distance x and $x + dx$. Observe also that, by definition, $\rho_{es}(x) = \mathcal{L}(x)/h_{es}(x)$.

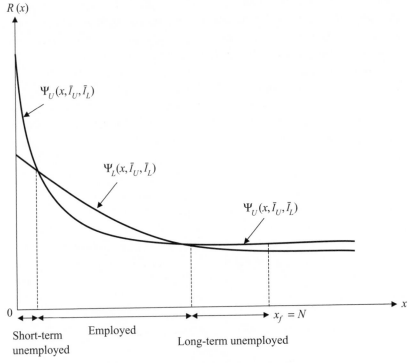

Figure 1.6. The core-periphery equilibrium.

4.3. Classification of Equilibrium Land-Use Patterns

Different urban configurations can emerge with the non-linear bid-rents defined by (1.87) and (1.88). Indeed, the land market being perfectly competitive, all workers propose different bid-rents at different locations and (absentee) landlords allocate land to the highest bids. So, depending on the different steepness of the bid-rents (as captured by their slopes), in each location, employed workers can outbid or be outbidden by unemployed workers. An example of the equilibrium rent function defined by (1.89) is shown in Figure 1.6. In particular, this figure illustrates a case where unemployed workers occupy both a central core of locations and a peripheral ring of locations around the CBD, separated by an intermediate ring of employed workers. Other urban configurations may also emerge. For example, the unemployed can occupy the core of the city and the employed the suburbs. The reverse pattern may also prevail.

Since we want to focus on interesting urban configurations in which unemployed workers can outbid employed workers for peripheral land in equilibrium, we shall assume

$$w_L < \frac{w_U}{\underline{s_0}}. \tag{1.93}$$

Proposition 1.5. *In equilibrium, there are exactly three possible locational patterns:*

(i) *A central core of employed surrounded by a peripheral ring of unemployed.*

(ii) *A central core of unemployed surrounded by a peripheral ring of employed.*

(iii) *Both a central core and a peripheral ring of unemployed separated by an intermediate ring of employed.*

This proposition shows that in a framework where workers' search intensity is location dependent, different urban equilibrium configurations can emerge.[23] In the first one (i), referred to as the *segregated equilibrium*, the employed occupy the core of the city and bid away the unemployed in the suburbs. In the second one (ii), referred to as the *integrated equilibrium*, the unemployed reside close to the CBD, have high search intensities and experience short unemployment spells. In this case, the former tend to remain unemployed for a longer period of time since their search intensity is quite low. Finally, the third case (iii), referred to as the *core-periphery equilibrium*, is when there are two categories of unemployed: the short-term ones who reside close to jobs and the long-term ones who live in the periphery of the city. To be consistent with Section 3, the segregated equilibrium is referred to as Equilibrium 1 (Figure 1.1), the integrated equilibrium as Equilibrium 2 (Figure 1.2), and the core-periphery equilibrium as Equilibrium 3 (Figure 1.6).

4.4. The Steady-State Labor Equilibrium

For each equilibrium $k = 1, 2, 3$, we can calculate the steady-state labor equilibrium, which is still defined by Definition 1.3. Indeed, (θ^k, w_L^k, u^k) is

---

[23] The proof of Proposition 1.5 can be found in Smith and Zenou (2003b).

a steady-state labor equilibrium k if the following equations hold:

$$\frac{c}{q(\theta^k)} = \frac{y - w_L^k}{r + \delta} \tag{1.94}$$

$$w_L^k = \arg\max_{w_L^k} (\bar{I}_L^k - \bar{I}_U^k)^\beta (I_F^k - I_V^k)^{1-\beta} \tag{1.95}$$

$$u^k = \frac{\delta}{\delta + \bar{s}^k \theta^k q(\theta^k)}. \tag{1.96}$$

The key variable that differs between equilibria is clearly $\bar{s}^k$ since its value depends on the average location of the unemployed. However, we have seen (Proposition 1.4 and Figure 1.5) that two *constant* search intensity levels for unemployed workers can emerge: all unemployed workers in the central core search with *full intensity*, $s = 1$, and all in the peripheral ring search with *minimum intensity*, $s = s_0$. These constant-search-intensity patterns are particularly easy to analyze. Moreover, Proposition 1.5 shows that essentially all equilibrium properties of the system can be studied in terms of these simple cases. For the other two possible locational patterns it is clear that, as long as the equilibrium bid-rent curves, Ψ_U and Ψ_L, do not cross in the region $[x(1), x(s_0)]$, only maximum and minimum search intensities will be involved. In fact, the region $[x(1), x(s_0)]$ can be shown to be relatively small. This assertion is supported by the following result, which shows that if utility is "almost linearly homogeneous" in the sense that $\alpha + \omega$ is close to one, the interval $[x(1), x(s_0)]$ is necessarily very small:

Proposition 1.6. *If $\alpha + \omega \approx 1$, then in equilibrium $|x(1) - x(s_0)| \approx 0$.*

Proof: It is sufficient to observe from (1.86) that for any given lifetime values and hiring probability $(\bar{I}_L^k, \bar{I}_U^k, \theta^k q(\theta^k))$, locations $x(1)$ and $x(s_0)$ have a common limiting value, $\frac{w_U}{\tau} \frac{\theta^k q(\theta^k)(\bar{I}_L^k - \bar{I}_U^k)}{r \bar{I}_U^k}$, as $\alpha + \omega \to 1$. ∎

Hence, if a diminishing marginal utility (along rays) is sufficiently small, then equilibrium can be safely assumed to involve only maximum and/or minimum search intensities for unemployed workers. With these observations, we now restrict the attention to the constant-search-intensity case. To complete the analysis, we must calculate $\bar{s}^k$ for each equilibrium k. Observing that, in contrast to the two previous sections and since workers consume different amounts of land, $\bar{s}^k$ is no longer the search intensity of an unemployed worker residing in the average location.

For any given *lifetime values*, $\bar{I}_L^k$, $\bar{I}_U^k$, with $\bar{I}_L^k > \bar{I}_U^k$, and *hiring probability*, $\theta^k q(\theta^k) \in (0, +\infty)$, we define the following set of functions. First, let function s be defined by (1.85) with ranges $x(1)$ and $x(s_0)$, given by (1.86). In terms of s and $(\bar{I}_L^k, \bar{I}_U^k, \theta^k q(\theta^k))$, we may then define the additional functions, Ω_U^k, Ψ_L^k, Ψ_U^k, and R^k, by (1.83), (1.87), (1.88) and (1.89), respectively. Using Ψ_L^k, Ψ_U^k, and R^k, we next define the *indicator functions*, φ_{es}^k, $es = U, L$, specifying the relevant regions occupied by unemployed and employed workers, respectively:

$$\varphi_{es}^k(x) = \begin{cases} 1, & \Psi_{es}^k(x, \bar{I}_U^k, \bar{I}_L^k) = R^k(x) \\ 0, & \text{otherwise} \end{cases}, \quad es = U, L. \tag{1.97}$$

It can be shown (Smith and Zenou, 2003b) that these indicator functions are only ambiguous on a set of measure zero [i.e., the equality $\Psi_L^k(x) = \Psi_U^k(x)$ holds only on a set of measure zero in the interval of relevant distances, x]. Hence, the general set of locational equilibrium conditions [(1.90),(1.91),(1.92)] above can now be sharpened by noting in the present case that at almost every distance, x, at most one of the population densities, $\rho_L^k(x)$ and $\rho_U^k(x)$, can be positive. Hence, by substituting (1.74) and (1.75) into (1.92), and observing that, by definition, $\Psi_{es}^k(x) = R^k(x)$ iff $\varphi_{es}^k(x) = 1$, it follows that the appropriate *population densities* must have the form (in a linear city where $\mathcal{L}(x) = 1$):

$$\rho_L^k(x) = \frac{\mathcal{L}(x)}{h_L^k(x)} = \left(\frac{\alpha + \omega}{\alpha}\right) \frac{\Psi_L(x, \bar{I}_U^k, \bar{I}_L^k)}{w_L^k - \tau x} \tag{1.98}$$

$$\rho_U^k(x) = \frac{\mathcal{L}(x)}{h_U^k(x)} = \left(\frac{\alpha + \omega}{\alpha}\right) \frac{\Psi_U(x, \bar{I}_U^k, \bar{I}_L^k)}{w_U - s^k(x)\tau x}, \tag{1.99}$$

where $s^k(x)$ can only take constant values 1 or s_0. Since $N = U^k + L^k$, with these functions, we can now give a formal general definition of $\bar{s}^k$, U^k, L^k as follows:

$$\bar{s}^k = \frac{1}{U^k} \int_0^N s^k(x)\varphi_U^k(x)\rho_U^k(x)dx \tag{1.100}$$

$$U^k = \int_0^N \varphi_U^k(x)\rho_U^k(x)dx \tag{1.101}$$

$$L^k = \int_0^N \varphi_L^k(x)\rho_L^k(x)dx. \tag{1.102}$$

Equation (1.100) defines $\bar{s}^k$ in terms of the search intensities, $s^k(x)$, and population densities, $\rho_U^k(x)$, in each location x occupied by unemployed workers [i.e., with $\varphi_U(x) = 1$]. Equation (1.101) defines the population totals for employed and unemployed workers, together with the accounting condition ($N = U^k + L^k$) that all workers are either employed or unemployed.

Since Equilibria 1 and 2 are particular cases of Equilibrium 3, let us now characterize the latter.

4.5. The Core-Periphery Steady-State Equilibrium

In this equilibrium, the unemployed workers who reside close to jobs are short-run unemployed[24] since their search intensity is $s = 1$ while those who live far away from jobs are long-run unemployed.[25] Denote by x_{b_1} the border between short-run unemployed and employed workers, and by x_{b_2} the border between long-run unemployed and employed workers. We have the following general definition.[26]

Definition 1.7. *Assume $x_{b_1}^{3*} \leq x(1)$ and $x_{b_2}^* \geq x(s_0)$, where $x(.)$ is defined by (1.86). Then, a core-periphery steady-state equilibrium (Equilibrium 3) with endogenous search intensity is a 11-tuple $(\overline{I}_U^{3*}, \overline{I}_L^{3*}, x_{b_1}^{3*}, x_{b_2}^{3*}, x_f^{3*}, U^{sr*}, U^{lr*}, \overline{s}^{3*}, \theta^{3*}, w_L^{3*}, R^*(x))$ such that:*

$$\Psi_L^3(x_{b_1}^{3*}, \overline{I}_U^{3*}, \overline{I}_L^{3*}) = \Psi_U^3(x_{b_1}^{3*}, \overline{I}_U^{3*}, \overline{I}_L^{3*}) \tag{1.103}$$

$$\Psi_L^3(x_{b_2}^{3*}, \overline{I}_U^3, \overline{I}_L^3) = \Psi_U^3(x_{b_2}^*, \overline{I}_U^3, \overline{I}_L^3) \tag{1.104}$$

$$\Psi_U^3(N, \overline{I}_U^3, \overline{I}_L^3) = R_A = 1 \tag{1.105}$$

$$\int_0^{x_{b_1}^{3*}} \rho_U^k(x) dx = U^{sr*} \tag{1.106}$$

$$\int_{x_{b_1}^{3*}}^{x_{b_2}^{3*}} \rho_L^k(x) = N - U^{sr*} - U^{lr*} \tag{1.107}$$

$$\int_{x_{b_1}^{3*}}^{x_f^{3*}} \rho_U^k(x) = U^{lr*} \tag{1.108}$$

$$R^*(x) = \max\left\{\Psi_L(x, \overline{I}_U^{3*}, \overline{I}_L^{3*}), \Psi_U(x, \overline{I}_U^{3*}, \overline{I}_L^{3*}), 0\right\} \quad \text{at each } x \in \left(0, x_f\right] \tag{1.109}$$

---

[24] When we refer to short-run unemployed workers, we use superscript sr and denote them by U^{sr}.

[25] When we refer to long-run unemployed workers, we use superscript lr and denote them by U^{lr}.

[26] For analytical simplicity and without loss of generality, agricultural land rent R_A is now normalized to 1 and not to zero.

$$\overline{s}^{3*} = \frac{U^{sr*} + \underline{s_0}U^{lr*}}{U^{sr*} + U^{lr*}} \tag{1.110}$$

$$u^{3*} = \frac{\delta}{\delta + \overline{s}^{3*}\theta^{3*}q(\theta^{3*})} = \frac{U^{sr*} + U^{lr*}}{N} \tag{1.111}$$

$$\frac{c}{q(\theta^{3*})} = \frac{y - w_L^{3*}}{r + \delta} \tag{1.112}$$

$$w_L^{3*} = \arg\max_{w_L^{3*}}(\overline{I}_L^{3*} - \overline{I}_U^{3*})^\beta(I_F^{3*} - I_V^{3*})^{1-\beta} \tag{1.113}$$

where $\rho_L^k(x)$ and $\rho_U^k(x)$ are given by (1.98) and (1.99), respectively.

This definition of equilibrium encompasses both urban and labor markets. First, by definition, full search intensity, $s = 1$, is optimal for core unemployed workers and thus, in equilibrium, from (1.85), it has to be true that the core boundary point, $x_{b_1}^{3*}$, must satisfy $x_{b_1}^{3*} \leq x(1)$. Similarly, minimum search intensity, $s = \underline{s_0}$, is assumed to be optimal for peripheral unemployed workers, so that the peripheral boundary point, $x_{b_2}^{3*}$, must satisfy $x_{b_2}^{3*} \geq x(\underline{s_0})$. Second, for core-periphery land-use to be an equilibrium, it must be that the bid rents cross twice (equations (1.103) and (1.104)), the bid-rent of the long-run unemployed equals R_A at the city fringe (equation (1.105)), the population constraints must be satisfied (equations (1.106)–(1.108)), and the equilibrium land rent must be the upper envelope of all bid-rents in the city (equation (1.109)). Finally, the equilibrium land market conditions are given by (1.110)–(1.113).

This is obviously quite messy, but it can be shown that there is a unique equilibrium where it is really $\overline{s}^{3*}$ that makes the link between the labor market and the land market. To give some intuition of the way the labor market operates, let us show how the wage is calculated. The Bellman equations for employed and short-run and long-run unemployed workers are, respectively, given by:

$$r\overline{I}_L^3 = \Omega_L(x) - \delta\left(\overline{I}_L^3 - \overline{I}_U^3\right) \tag{1.114}$$

$$r\overline{I}_U^{sr} = \Omega_U^{sr} + \theta^3 q(\theta^3)\left(\overline{I}_L^3 - \overline{I}_U^3\right) \tag{1.115}$$

$$r\overline{I}_U^{lr} = \Omega_U^{lr} + \underline{s_0}\theta^3 q(\theta^3)\left(\overline{I}_L^3 - \overline{I}_U^3\right). \tag{1.116}$$

Since, in equilibrium, it has to be that $r I_U^{lr} = r I_U^{sr} = r\overline{I}_U^3$, by combining (1.115) and (1.116), we have

$$\Omega_U^{lr} - \Omega_U^{sr} = \left(1 - \underline{s_0}\right)\theta q(\theta)\left(\overline{I}_L^3 - \overline{I}_U^3\right) > 0.$$

Once more, this underscores the essential difference between unemployed workers in the central core (short-run unemployed workers) and those in the periphery (long-run unemployed workers). Those in the central core give up short-run utility for long-run utility gains. Hence, if the lifetime value, $\overline{I}_U^3$, of all unemployed workers is the same, then the short-run utility for those in the periphery must be greater than for those in the central core.

As in the previous section, let us determine the wage through bargaining between the firm and the worker. First, observe that since workers are not attached to location (they freely relocate each time they change employment status), the wage will be the same for all employed workers. Then, by solving (1.103)–(1.105), and using (1.87) and (1.88), one obtains:

$$\overline{I}_L^{3*} - \overline{I}_U^{3*} = \frac{\chi \left(w_U - \underline{s_0}\tau x_f^{3*} \right)^{\alpha+\omega}}{r + \delta + \underline{s_0}\theta^{3*}q(\theta^{3*})} \left[\left(\frac{w_L^3 - \tau x_{b_2}^{3*}}{w_U - \underline{s_0}\tau x_{b_2}^{3*}} \right)^{\alpha+\omega} - 1 \right],$$

where $x_{b_2}^{3*}$ and x_f^{3*} are determined by (1.106)–(1.108). Since the first-order condition of the Nash-bargaining is given by:

$$\frac{\beta}{1-\beta} \left(\frac{\partial \overline{I}_L^{3*}}{\partial w_L^3} - \frac{\partial \overline{I}_U^{3*}}{\partial w_L^3} \right) I_F + \left(\overline{I}_L^{3*} - \overline{I}_U^{3*} \right) \frac{\partial I_F}{\partial w_L} = 0$$

and since $I_F = c/q(\theta^{3*})$ and $\frac{\partial I_F}{\partial w_L^3} = -1/(r+\delta)$, a non-linear relationship that defines the bargain wage w_L^3 can be obtained.

4.6. Interaction Between Land and Labor Markets

Compared to the previous model (of Section 3), the land and labor markets are even more integrated. First, it is even clearer here how city structure affects workers' labor market outcomes. We have three different city structures, described by Figures 1.1, 1.2, and 1.6, which imply very different labor market outcomes for ex-ante identical workers. Moreover, we also better understand why workers living far away from jobs search less intensively than those residing closer to jobs. It is simply because they have less incentives since their land price is low and their housing consumption is small. There is also a new implication generated by this model: the impact of the labor-market variables on the growth of the city. Indeed, since housing consumption is now endogenous, city size is no longer measured by N, the number of people living in the city, but also includes population density (which is the inverse of housing consumption).

To illustrate this issue, take Equilibrium 1 (Figure 1.1), where unemployed workers reside far away from jobs and, for simplicity, assume that $x_b^* \geq x(\underline{s_0})$, so that all unemployed workers provide a search intensity equal to $s(x) = \underline{s_0}$, $\forall x$. We have the following new definition where we normalize agricultural land to 1:

Definition 1.8. *An urban-land-use equilibrium where unemployed workers reside far away from jobs, with no relocation costs, endogenous housing consumption and endogenous search intensity is a 5-tuple* $(\overline{I}_L^{1*}, \overline{I}_U^{1*}, x_b^{1*}, x_f^{1*}, R^{1*}(x))$ *such that:*

$$\Psi_U(x_b^{1*}, \overline{I}_U^{1*}, \overline{I}_L^{1*}) = \Psi_L(x_b^{1*}, \overline{I}_U^{1*}, \overline{I}_L^{1*})$$

$$\Psi_U(x_f^{1*}, \overline{I}_U^{1*}, \overline{I}_L^{1*}) = 1$$

$$\int_0^{x_b^{1*}} \frac{1}{h_L(\overline{I}_L^{1*}, \overline{I}_U^{1*})} dx = \left(1 - u^{*1}\right) N$$

$$\int_{x_b^{1*}}^{x_f^{1*}} \frac{1}{h_U(\overline{I}_L^{1*}, \overline{I}_U^{2*})} dx = u^{*1} N$$

$$R^{1*}(x) = \max\left\{\Psi_L(x, \overline{I}_U^{1*}, \overline{I}_L^{1*}), \Psi_U(x, \overline{I}_U^{1*}, \overline{I}_L^{1*}), 0\right\} \text{ at each } x \in \left(0, x_f^{1*}\right].$$

In this definition, $\Psi_U(x_b^*, \overline{I}_U^{1*}, \overline{I}_L^{1*})$ and $\Psi_L(x_b^{1*}, \overline{I}_U^{1*}, \overline{I}_L^{1*})$ are defined by (1.87) and (1.88), $h_L(\overline{I}_L^1, \overline{I}_U^1)$ and $h_U(\overline{I}_L^1, \overline{I}_U^1)$ by (1.74) and (1.75) where $R(x)$ has been replaced by the bid-rents defined in (1.87) and (1.88), respectively. The model can be closed exactly as in the previous section. Therefore, the equilibrium labor market variables θ^{1*}, w_L^{1*}, and u^{1*} are still determined by equations (1.94), (1.95), and (1.96) with $s(x) = \underline{s_0}$, $\forall x$, and $\overline{s} = \underline{s_0}$.

Since the model becomes quite complicated, let us run some simple numerical simulations. We use the same assumptions as in Section **3.4.1** and the same numerical values as in Table 1.2, with some differences due to the specificity of the model. First, as stated above, search intensity is now independent of distance to jobs and we fix it to $\underline{s_0} = 0.1$. This means that unemployed workers have a very low search intensity (if employed workers search every day, then unemployed workers search every ten days) because they all reside far away from jobs. As a result, we still assume that commuting costs τ are equal to 0.4, which implies that $\tau_L = \tau = 0.4$ and $\tau_L = \underline{s_0}\tau = 0.04$. Second, there are some new parameters, which are set as follows: $\alpha = \omega = 1/4$. By running the simulations, we obtain the following equilibrium steady-state values:[27]

$$\theta^* = 10.46; \ u^* = 0.24; \ w_L^* = 0.85; \ x_b^* = 0.26; \ x_f^* = 0.30.$$

Not surprisingly, the unemployment rate is quite high (24%) because unemployed workers, who reside far away from jobs, do not search very intensively. The wage is relatively high (85% of the productivity) and the replacement ratio, w_U/w_L^*, relatively low (35%). The employed workers, who live between $x = 0$ and $x = x_b^*$, occupy 87% of the city. Indeed, even though 24% of the workers are unemployed, they occupy a smaller part of the city because their housing consumption is much smaller than that of employed workers. This is mainly because the wage w_L^* is very high compared to the unemployed benefit.

Let us now examine how the different variables affect the size of the city, i.e., x_f^*. Figures 1.7a and 1.7b report the simulation results. First, when there is an increase in the unemployment benefits w_U, the size of the city also increases, even if the effect on x_b^* is extremely small. This is due to the fact that the unemployment rate u^* increases since firms create less jobs (θ^* decreases) and the housing consumption of unemployed workers rises. As a result, even though the employment area is not affected (the wage and the housing consumption of employed workers increase but their number is lower), there is a sharp increase in the unemployment area which, in turn, raises the size of the city. In contrast, an increase in the firms' entry cost c or the job-destruction rate δ, reduces the size of the city as well as the employment area. Indeed, wages and job creation decrease while unemployment increases, which means that there is less competition in the land market and lower housing consumption for all workers. If we look at the effect of search intensity $s = s_0$, we have exactly the reverse results, i.e., both x_b^* and x_f^* increase because of lower unemployment and higher wages. However, this increase is not very important because job creation decreases since it becomes more expensive to hire workers. Finally, looking at the effect of commuting costs τ on equilibrium outcomes, we find that x_b^* and x_f^* decrease because of higher competition in the land market (access to the CBD is more valuable), unemployment is increased and job creation reduced despite the increase in wages (firms need to compensate more workers for their commuting costs).

---

[27] For simplicity, we omit superscript 1 characterizing equilibrium variables.

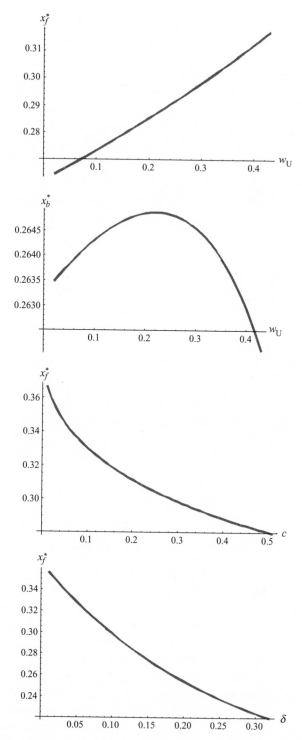

Figure 1.7a. Impact of labor market variables on the growth of cities.

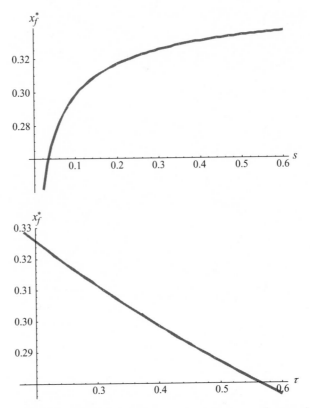

Figure 1.7b. Impact of search intensity and commuting costs on the growth of cities.

5. Discussion

5.1. Fixed-Housing Consumption

The previous model of endogenous housing consumption was admittedly quite complicated, even though we were able to completely characterize it. In fact, one of the complications came from the fact that housing consumption was endogenously determined. Imagine now a similar model, but with fixed housing consumption.

Each individual's search efficiency s now only depends on his/her job search effort denoted by e, with $s'(e) > 0$ and $s''(e) \leq 0$. As above, each interview is carried out in the employment center and thus involves transport costs. We denote by $e\tau x$ (i.e., $\tau_U = e\tau$) the search costs associated with a level of effort e for a worker living at a distance x from the employment center. Let us write the Bellman equation of the unemployed workers. It is given by:

$$r I_U = w_U - e \tau x - R(x) + \theta q(\theta) s(e) (I_L - I_U), \qquad (1.117)$$

while the value of employment is equal to:

$$r I_L = w_L - \tau_L x - R(x) - \delta (I_L - I_U).$$

The unemployed worker located at a distance x from the employment center chooses e^* which maximizes his/her intertemporal utility (1.117). The first-order condition on effort yields:

$$s'(e^*)\theta q(\theta)(I_L - I_U) = \tau x. \qquad (1.118)$$

Once more, when choosing the optimal search effort e^*, workers trade off short-run costs of commuting against long-run gains. By totally differentiating (1.118), we obtain:

$$\frac{\partial e^*}{\partial x} = \frac{\tau}{\theta q(\theta) s''(e^*)(I_L - I_U)} < 0 \qquad (1.119)$$

and thus

$$\frac{\partial s}{\partial x} = s'(e)\frac{\partial e}{\partial x} < 0. \qquad (1.120)$$

The bid-rent functions are given by (1.48) and (1.49) with $\tau_L = \tau, \tau_U = e^*(x)\tau x$, and $a(x) = s [e^*(x)] \theta q(\theta)$, where $e^*(x)$ is given by (1.118). The bid-rent of the employed workers is linear and such that

$$\frac{\partial \Psi_L(x, \overline{I}_U, \overline{I}_L)}{\partial x} = -\tau < 0,$$

while the bid-rent of unemployed workers is non-linear and its slope is given by:

$$\frac{\partial \Psi_U(x, \overline{I}_U, \overline{I}_L)}{\partial x} = -\tau \left[\frac{\partial e^*}{\partial x} x + e^*(x) \right] + s'(e^*)\frac{\partial e^*}{\partial x}\theta q(\theta) \left(\overline{I}_L - \overline{I}_U \right)$$

which, using (1.118), yields

$$\frac{\partial \Psi_U(x, \overline{I}_U, \overline{I}_L)}{\partial x} = \frac{\partial e^*}{\partial x} \left[s'(e^*)\theta q(\theta) \left(\overline{I}_L - \overline{I}_U \right) - \tau x \right] - \tau e^*(x)$$

$$= -\tau e^*(x) < 0.$$

It can also be verified that

$$\frac{\partial^2 \Psi_U(x, \overline{I}_U, \overline{I}_L)}{\partial x^2} = -\tau \frac{\partial e^*}{\partial x} = -\frac{\tau^2}{\theta q(\theta) s''(e^*)(I_L - I_U)} > 0.$$

As in Proposition 1.5, we here have three urban configurations. If the slope of $\Psi_U(x, \overline{I}_U, \overline{I}_L)$ is steep enough close to the CBD, i.e., $e^*(0) > 1$, then the integrated equilibrium (Equilibrium 2) emerges while if we have the reverse, i.e., $e^*(0) < 1$, then the segregated equilibrium (Equilibrium 1) prevails. Finally, if $e^*(N) < 1 < e^*(0)$, then a core-periphery equilibrium (Equilibrium 3) emerges. Naturally, the latter analysis will be easier since the population densities are now equal to 1 which implies, in particular, that $x_{b_1}^3 = U^{sr}, x_{b_2} = N - U^{lr}, x_f^3 = N$. However, search intensities are no longer constant close to or far away from the CBD, which makes the analysis slightly more complicated.

5.2. Gathering Information about Jobs

So far, the way workers gathered information about jobs was mainly by commuting to the CBD. Now, imagine the following. Each unemployed individual commutes to the center to gather information about jobs. This is not the only way of obtaining information since job information can also be obtained by buying newspapers or calling friends. However, each return trip from the residential location to the employment center allows the worker to have some additional information that is not accessible without going to the center (for example, looking at some ads that are locally posted in the city center or having interviews with employment agencies that are located in the city center).

If τ and ι denote, respectively, the *pecuniary* and *time* cost per unit of distance to commute to the employment center, then for unemployed workers the total cost per return trip of gathering information about jobs in the employment center is given by:

$$\tau x + \iota x. \tag{1.121}$$

We can now determine the *total* cost of gathering information about jobs at a distance x from the employment center. It is given by:

$$(\tau + \iota) e x, \tag{1.122}$$

where, as in the previous section, $0 \leq e \leq 1$ is the search-effort rate provided by each unemployed worker. For example, $e = 1$ would be searching every day while $e = 1/2$ would be searching every other day. Obviously the higher is e, the more often the unemployed worker must travel to the employment center to gather information about jobs. In this formulation, x is a measure of job access (how "well" the unemployed worker is connected to jobs) while

e is a measure of search intensity (how many hours per day the unemployed worker spends searching for a job).

The budget constraint of an unemployed worker living at a distance x from the employment center is equal to:

$$w_U = z + R(x) + C(e) + (\tau + \iota) e x, \qquad (1.123)$$

where $C(e)$ denotes all searching costs that are not distance-related. The latter encompass the costs of buying newspapers, making phone calls, etc. We assume that $C(0) = 0$, $C'(e) > 0$ and $C''(e) > 0$. In this formulation, the total cost of searching is thus $C(e) + (\tau + \iota) e x$, which encompasses both search costs that are not distance-related and costs that involve commuting to the employment center.

Let us now focus on employed workers. They have the following budget constraint:

$$w_L = z + R(x) + (\tau + \iota \, w_L) x. \qquad (1.124)$$

The time cost of commuting for an employed worker residing at a distance x from the CBD is $\iota \, w \, x$; in accordance with empirical observation, it increases with income. As usual, w_L is the opportunity cost of leisure (even though this is not explicitly modeled here). The Bellman equations for unemployed and employed workers can be written as:

$$r I_U = w_U - C(e) - (\tau + \iota) e x - R(x) + \theta q(\theta) s(e) (I_L - I_U) \quad (1.125)$$

$$r I_L = w_L (1 - \iota x) - \tau x - R(x) - \delta (I_L - I_U). \qquad (1.126)$$

The unemployed worker located at a distance x chooses e^* that maximizes his/her intertemporal utility (1.125). The first-order condition yields:

$$\theta q(\theta) s'(e^*) (I_L - I_U) = C'(e^*) + (\tau + \iota) x. \qquad (1.127)$$

By totally differentiating (1.127), we obtain:

$$\frac{\partial e^*}{\partial x} = \frac{\tau + \iota}{\theta q(\theta) s''(e^*)(I_L - I_U) - C'(e^*)} < 0,$$

and thus

$$\frac{\partial s}{\partial x} = s'(e^*) \frac{\partial e^*}{\partial x} < 0.$$

Our previous results are thus robust to different search costs. It is easy to check that the employed workers' bid-rent is linearly decreasing in x, while that of unemployed workers will be decreasing and convex in x. Once more, we will have the above three urban configurations and the labor-market analysis can be carried out.

6. Notes on the Literature

The idea of combining search and space is not new and goes back at least to Stigler (1961). Some informal models have been provided (see, for example, the book by Fisher and Nijkamp, 1987) but, as observed by Cheshire (1979), there has been a lack of theoretical framework for understanding the way spatial labor markets operate. Simpson (1992) has really been the first to propose a theoretical framework combining search and space.[28] In this book, Simpson (1992) summarizes his different contributions to this literature. However, even though the analysis of the land market is well-developed in Simpson (1992), the analysis of the labor market is not. Only workers search and neither job creation nor labor demand is included in the analysis. As a result, the entire matching process between workers and firms is not determined, which results in a very partial analysis of the urban land market. To the best of our knowledge, Wasmer and Zenou (1997, 2002) were the first to propose a complete analysis of the urban search model in which both a labor market with search frictions and a land market are explicitly modeled. Helsley and Strange (1990), Kim (1991), Sato (2001), and Coulson, Laing, and Wang (2001) have also proposed early urban search models, but the location of employed and unemployed workers is not explicitly determined.[29] The benchmark models of Sections 2 and 3 are based on Wasmer and Zenou (1997, 2002). The model developed in Section 4 is based on Smith and Zenou (2003a,b) and Zenou (2008a). Finally, Section 5 is based on Wasmer and Zenou (2002) and Patacchini and Zenou (2005).

APPENDIX A1. PROOF OF PROPOSITION 1.4

Let us first establish the uniqueness of solutions to (1.82). Thus, we partially differentiate (1.81) once more to obtain:

$$r\frac{\partial^2 I_U(s, x)}{\partial s^2} = -\chi\tau x (\alpha + \omega) \left[1 - (\alpha + \omega)\right](w_U - s\tau x)^{\alpha+\omega-2} R(x)^{-\alpha}$$

$$-\theta q(\theta)\frac{\partial I_U(s, x)}{\partial s}. \tag{A1.1}$$

[28] Jayet (1990a,b) and Van Ommeren, Rietveld, and Nijkamp (1999), propose interesting spatial search models, but the land market is not explicitly modeled.

[29] The model of Coulson, Laing, and Wang (2001) is exposed in detail in Section 3 of Chapter 7.

Observing that the first term in the numerator is negative, we may conclude that

$$\frac{\partial I_U(s, x)}{\partial s} \geq 0 \implies \frac{\partial^2 I_U(s, x)}{\partial s^2} < 0. \tag{A1.2}$$

In particular, this implies that stationary points of (1.79) can only be local maxima and thus, [by continuity of (1.81)] there is at most one stationary point. Thus, in each location x, there is at most one solution to (1.82).

Let us now prove the second part of the proposition.

First, note that in equilibrium, this optimal lifetime value must agree with the prevailing lifetime value, I_U, for unemployed workers, i.e., that $I_U(s, x) = I_U$ in (1.82). Note also that in equilibrium, we must have (1.83). Hence, by substituting these results into (1.82) and solving for s, we obtain

$$s(x) = \frac{(\alpha + \omega)}{[1 - (\alpha + \omega)]} \left[\frac{w_U}{(\alpha + \omega) \tau x} - \frac{r \overline{I}_U}{\theta q(\theta) (\overline{I}_L - \overline{I}_U)} \right] \tag{A1.3}$$

with a unique inverse function, $x(s)$, given by (1.86).

In terms of this inverse function (1.86), it at once follows from (1.81) that

$$\frac{\partial I_U(s, x)}{\partial s} \gtrless 0 \Leftrightarrow x \lessgtr x(s). \tag{A1.4}$$

Let us now prove parts (i), (ii), and (iii) of (1.85). They are established, respectively, as follows:

(i) $[x < x(1)]$: Observe from (A1.4) and (A1.2) that $x < x(1) \implies \partial I_U(1, x)/\partial s > 0 \implies \partial^2 I_U(1, x)/\partial s^2 < 0$, so that $I_U(\cdot, x)$ must be increasing near $s = 1$. Hence, if there is some $s_1 \in [s_0, 1)$ with $I_U(s_1, x) > I_U(1, x)$, it then follows from the continuity of (1.81) that $I_U(\cdot, x)$ must achieve a differentiable minimum at some point interior to $[s_1, 1]$. But since this contradicts (A1.2), it follows that no such s_1 can exist and hence, that $I_U(1, x)$ is maximal.

(ii) $[x > x(s_0)]$: Once more, by (A1.4), $x > x(s_0) \implies \partial I_U(s_0, x)/\partial s < 0$, so that $I_U(\cdot, x)$ must be decreasing near $s = s_0$. Hence, if there is some $s_1 \in (s_0, 1]$ with $I_U(s_1, x) > I_U(s_0, x)$, it once more follows from the continuity of (1.81) that $I_U(\cdot, x)$ must achieve a differentiable minimum interior to $[s_0, 1]$, which contradicts (A1.2). Thus, $I_U(s_0, x)$ must be maximal.

(*iii*) $[x(1) \leq x \leq x(s_0)]$: Finally, it also follows from (A1.4) that $x(1) \leq x \Rightarrow \partial I_U(1, x)/\partial s \geq 0$, and $x \leq x(s_0) \Rightarrow \partial I_U(s_0, x)/\partial s \leq 0$, so that, by continuity, there is some $s \in [s_0, 1]$ with $\partial I_U(s, x)/\partial s = 0$. Hence, $s = s(x)$ in (A1.3), and we may conclude from the uniqueness of the differentiable maxima observed above that $I_U[s(x), x]$ must be maximal. ∎

CHAPTER TWO

Extensions of Urban Search-Matching Models

1. Introduction

In this chapter, we extend the different models proposed in Chapter 1 by introducing workers' heterogeneity, high mobility costs and wage posting. In Section 2, workers are ex-ante heterogenous in terms of some idiosyncratic characteristics, which implies that, once they find a new job, they must bear a training cost that is match-specific and stochastically determined. Thus, there is a training decision rule because workers are not ready to accept a job if it implies extremely high training costs. In this model, the training cost is a sunk cost because it is of no use for the next job and it is thus forfeited. Moreover, after training, all workers are assumed to provide the same productivity and thus, are ex-post identical. Compared to the models in Chapter 1, the urban-land-use equilibrium is not affected while, in the labor market, there is a new equation: the training decision rule. This leads to a new source of inefficiency due to training costs. Indeed, in the market solution, workers tend to refuse socially beneficial jobs due to the fact that while workers bear all training costs, the revenues from production are divided between firms and workers through bargaining.

In Section 3, workers are ex-ante identical, but they are ex-post heterogenous in terms of match productivities. Contrary to Chapter 1, job destructions are now endogenous, which is consistent with the evidence of Davis, Haltiwanger, and Schuh (1996). More precisely, it is assumed that each job is characterized by a fixed irreversible technology, so that each time there is a technological shock, the quality of the match and the productivity deteriorate. New filled jobs start at the highest productivity value and a job is destroyed only if the idiosyncratic component of its productivity falls below some critical number. It is shown that workers with the highest wages (productivity) have the steepest bid-rent curves and are therefore located closest to the employment center. Unemployed workers have the lowest value of time and live at the edge of the city. These properties of the model are standard features of urban economic models with heterogeneity of workers that leads to differences in the steepness of bid-rent functions (see Chapter 1, Appendix A or Fujita, 1989). What is less standard is that such differences are not related to structural worker characteristics (such as education, age, or family composition), but to productivity levels that are only related to the job with which a worker is randomly matched. Each change in the productivity of the job with which a worker is matched immediately leads to a change in his/her wage, value of time, and thus, his/her residential location. This mechanism creates the relationship between productivity and location that is central to the analysis of the model. Compared to the "standard" urban search models of Chapter 1, new results are found. First, workers with high productivities and wages reside close to jobs, have low commuting costs and pay high land rents. Second, wages are a function of workers' productivity, the productivity gap between workers, and the reservation productivity below which jobs are destroyed. Third, higher commuting costs and higher unemployment benefits lead to more job destruction. Last, there is more interaction between the land and the labor market because workers' productivity now affects the land rent and the location of workers in the city.

Sections 4 and 5 introduce positive and high-mobility costs. In the former, workers can either be mobile (i.e., when their employment status changes, they decide to relocate to another part of the city) or immobile (i.e., when their employment status changes, they remain in the same location) while, in the latter, they can only be immobile because the cost of relocating is too high. The main result of Section 4 is to show that, compared to the benchmark model of Chapter 1 where all workers were assumed to be mobile, a new area in the middle of the city emerges in which employed and unemployed workers are immobile, pay the same land rent, and continuously overlap. The analysis is quite cumbersome, however. In contrast, the model proposed in Section 5 is much simpler since workers can only be immobile. In this section, we also assume perfect capital markets with a zero interest rate, so that workers only care about the fraction of time they spend employed and unemployed, respectively, during their lifetime. It is shown that wages increase with distance to jobs. It is also shown that the Hosios-Pissarides condition, which guarantees that the market equilibrium is efficient, no longer holds. A new and more general condition is needed because additional spatial frictions are created due to the fact that workers are stuck in their residential location. Finally, in the last section (Section 6), we consider a different wage-setting mechanism. While wages were determined by a bilateral bargaining between workers and firms in all previous models, in this section, maximizing-profit firms post wages by making a take-it-or-leave-it offer to workers. Moreover, we show that it is possible to obtain a wage distribution in equilibrium in the city. We also show how the interaction between the land market and the labor market is modified when wage posting instead of wage bargaining is considered.

2. Workers' Heterogeneity in Training Costs

In the benchmark model of Chapter 1 (Section 2), all workers were assumed to be ex-ante identical. We would now like to relax this assumption and introduce ex-ante heterogeneity, while keeping the model exactly as before. Following Sato (2004a), we assume workers to be ex-ante heterogenous in terms of some idiosyncratic characteristics. To be more precise, it is assumed that when an unemployed worker finds a job, he/she must bear a training cost, b, which is match-specific and stochastically determined, i.e., b is a random variable whose cumulative distribution function $G(b)$ is defined on the support $[0, \bar{b}]$. A worker does not know his/her b until he/she contacts a firm. When there is a contact, an endogenous job acceptance rule will determine whether the worker will accept a job. After the training, every worker-firm pair attains the same level of productivity, so that all employed workers receive the same wage. To summarize, there is heterogeneity ex-ante, but not ex-post.

2.1. Urban-Land-Use Equilibrium

The fact that workers are ex-post identical means, in particular, that the urban-land-use equilibrium can be analyzed as in the benchmark model in Chapter 1. The urban equilibrium can therefore still be described by Figure 1.1 in Chapter 1 and the instantaneous equilibrium utilities of employed and unemployed workers are therefore, respectively, given by:

$$W_L^* = w_L - \tau L - s\tau (N - L) \tag{2.1}$$

$$W_U^* = w_U - s\tau N, \tag{2.2}$$

while the land-rent equilibrium is still equal to:

$$R^*(x) = \begin{cases} \tau (L - x) + s\tau (N - L) & \text{for } 0 \le x \le L \\ s\tau (N - x) & \text{for } L < x \le N. \\ 0 & \text{for } x > N \end{cases} \tag{2.3}$$

2.2. Steady-State Labor Equilibrium

Let us now calculate the steady-state labor equilibrium. The discounted expected lifetime utilities of workers can now be written as:

$$r I_L = w_L - \tau L - s\tau (N - L) - \delta (I_L - I_U) \qquad (2.4)$$

$$r I_U = w_U - s\tau N + s\theta q(\theta) \left[E_b \left(\widehat{I_L} \right) - I_U \right], \qquad (2.5)$$

where $\widehat{I_L} = \max\{I_L - b, I_U\}$ and $E_b(\widehat{I_L})$ is the expectation of $\widehat{I_L}$ with respect to b. Hence, the only equation that changes is the one for unemployed workers, which is now given by (2.5). This is due to the match-specific training costs where $E_b(\widehat{I_L})$ represents the change in expected utility when an unemployed worker comes into contact with a vacant job. For firms, the Bellman equations are given by:

$$r I_F = y - w_L - \delta(I_F - I_V) \qquad (2.6)$$

$$r I_V = -c + q(\theta) \Pr(\text{accept})(I_F - I_V), \qquad (2.7)$$

where $\Pr(\text{accept})$ is the probability of the match being accepted by a worker when a firm contacts a worker. Because there are no relocation costs, it must be that, in equilibrium, all workers obtain the same utility level independently of their location in the city, i.e., $I_L = \overline{I}_L$ and $I_U = \overline{I}_U$. Let us denote the threshold value above which workers refuse to accept a job offer by $\widetilde{b}$, i.e., the reservation training level of a worker. Formally, $\widetilde{b}$ can be defined as:

$$\widetilde{b} = \overline{I}_L - \overline{I}_U. \qquad (2.8)$$

Indeed, when an unemployed worker is offered a job, he/she compares the expected value of this job, i.e., $\overline{I}_L - b$, and the expected value of remaining unemployed, i.e., $\overline{I}_U$. As a result, we have:

$$\Pr(\text{accept}) = G\left(\widetilde{b}\right)$$

and

$$E_b\left(\widehat{I_L}\right) = \int_0^{\widetilde{b}} \left(\overline{I}_L - b\right) g(b)db + \int_{\widetilde{b}}^{\overline{b}} \overline{I}_U g(b)db,$$

where $g(b)$ is the density function. Indeed, the expected utility of a job is calculated ex-ante, that is when the worker is unemployed and does know his/her b. So if he/she discovers that his/her b is between 0 and $\widetilde{b}$, then this worker will accept the job offer since $\overline{I}_L - b \geq \overline{I}_U$ while if the b is between $\widetilde{b}$ and $\overline{b}$, then $\overline{I}_L - b \leq \overline{I}_U$, and the worker prefers to remain unemployed.

Using (2.8), the fact that $G(\overline{b}) = 1$, and by integrating by parts, it is easily shown that:

$$E_b\left(\widehat{I}_L\right) = G(\overline{b})\overline{b} - \int_0^{\widetilde{b}} bg(b)db + \overline{I}_U \tag{2.9}$$

$$= \int_0^{\widetilde{b}} G(b)db + \overline{I}_U.$$

Furthermore, using (2.4), (2.5), and (2.9), we obtain:

$$\overline{I}_L - \overline{I}_U = \frac{w_L - w_U - (1-s)\tau L - s\theta q(\theta)\int_0^{\widetilde{b}}G(b)db}{r+\delta}, \tag{2.10}$$

which means that, using (2.8), we have:

$$\widetilde{b} = \frac{w_L - w_U - (1-s)\tau L - s\theta q(\theta)\int_0^{\widetilde{b}}G(b)db}{r+\delta}. \tag{2.11}$$

This is quite intuitive. The higher is the difference between wages and unemployment benefits, $w_L - w_U$, the higher is $\widetilde{b}$ since the value of a job increases and thus, workers are less picky. We have the reverse relationship between commuting costs $(1-s)\tau L$ and the threshold value $\widetilde{b}$ because higher commuting costs decrease the utility of working.

We can now close the model as in Chapter 1. First, using the free-entry condition $I_V = 0$, we calculate the value of a job as follows:

$$I_F = \frac{c}{q(\theta)G\left(\widetilde{b}\right)} \tag{2.12}$$

so that the firms' labor demand is given by:

$$\frac{y - w_L}{r+\delta} = \frac{c}{q(\theta)G\left(\widetilde{b}\right)}. \tag{2.13}$$

The value of a job (left-hand side of (2.13)) is equal to the expected search cost, i.e., the cost per unit of time multiplied by the average duration of search for the firm (right-hand side of (2.13)). Second, the wage is determined by the Nash-bargaining rule and is equal to:

$$w_L = \beta y + (1-\beta)\left[w_U + (1-s)\tau L + s\theta q(\theta)\int_0^{\widetilde{b}}G(b)db\right]. \tag{2.14}$$

Interestingly, the wage now compensates for *both* spatial costs $(1 - s)\tau L$ and training costs $\int_0^{\tilde{b}} G(b)\,db$ borne by workers. Finally, the unemployment rate is given by:

$$u^* = \frac{\delta}{\delta + s\theta q(\theta)G\left(\tilde{b}\right)}, \tag{2.15}$$

since a match is the product of a contact with a firm (which occurs at the rate $s\theta q(\theta)$) and an acceptance probability $G(\tilde{b})$. It is interesting to observe that there is a decreasing relationship between u^* and $\tilde{b}$ since when the threshold $\tilde{b}$ increases, workers are ready to accept more jobs (they are less picky) and, therefore, the unemployment rate decreases.

Let us solve the steady-state equilibrium. By observing that $L^* = N(1 - u^*)$, plugging the wage (2.14) and the unemployment rate (2.15) into (2.11) and into (2.13) gives, respectively:

$$\tilde{b}^* (r + \delta) = \beta \left[y - w_U - (1 - s)\tau N \frac{s\theta^* q(\theta^*)G\left(\tilde{b}^*\right)}{\delta + s\theta^* q(\theta^*)G\left(\tilde{b}^*\right)} \right. \\ \left. - s\theta^* q(\theta^*) \int_0^{\tilde{b}^*} G(b)\,db \right] \tag{2.16}$$

$$y - w_U = \frac{c}{q(\theta^*)G\left(\tilde{b}^*\right)} \left(\frac{r + \delta}{1 - \beta} \right) + (1 - s)\tau N \frac{s\theta^* q(\theta^*)G\left(\tilde{b}^*\right)}{\delta + s\theta^* q(\theta^*)G\left(\tilde{b}^*\right)} \\ + s\theta^* q(\theta^*) \int_0^{\tilde{b}^*} G(b)\,db. \tag{2.17}$$

These two equations determine the steady-state equilibrium $(\tilde{b}^*, \theta^*)$. It can be shown that (2.16) describes a *negative* relationship between $\tilde{b}$ and θ (labor supply curve), while (2.17) shows a *positive* relationship between $\tilde{b}$ and θ (labor demand curve). Indeed, when θ increases in (2.16), then workers become more picky since more jobs are available and thus, the threshold $\tilde{b}$ decreases. In contrast, when $\tilde{b}$ increases in (2.17), forward-looking firms anticipate that it will be easier to fill a vacancy and thus, more firms enter the labor market which creates more jobs and therefore increases θ. Sato (2004a) shows that if $\bar{b} \geq \beta(y - w_U)/(r + \delta)$, then there exists a unique steady-state equilibrium. This guarantees a possibility for sufficiently high training costs and excludes the case that, for some θ, workers accept any jobs. Figure 2.1 describes this equilibrium.

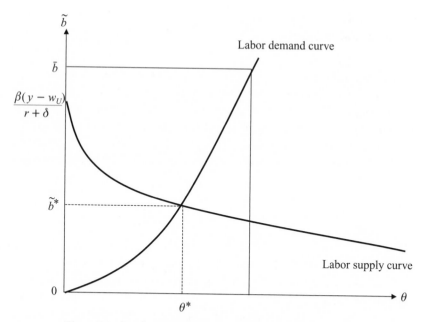

Figure 2.1. Steady-state equilibrium with hetrogenous workers.

2.3. Welfare

Let us study the welfare of this economy. As in the benchmark model in Chapter 1, the social welfare function is given by:

$$
\mathcal{W} = \int_0^{+\infty} e^{-rt} \left\{ \int_0^L (y - \tau x)dx + \int_L^N (w_U - s\,\tau\,x)dx - c\,\theta\,s\,u \right.
$$
$$
\left. - u\,s\theta q(\theta) \int_0^{\tilde{b}} bg(b)db \right\} dt. \tag{2.18}
$$

The only difference with the welfare function in the benchmark model is the term $u\,s\theta q(\theta) \int_0^{\tilde{b}} bg(b)db$, which is the total training costs borne by workers. The social planner maximizes (2.18) under the constraint

$$
\dot{u} = \delta(1 - u_t) - s\theta_t q(\theta_t) G\left(\tilde{b}\right), \tag{2.19}
$$

where $\dot{u}$ is the variation in unemployment with respect to time. Equation (2.19) describes the evolution of the unemployment rate. In this problem, the control variables are θ and $\tilde{b}$ and the state variable is u. Sato (2004a) proves the following result:[1]

Proposition 2.1. *In a spatial search-matching model with fixed search intensity and heterogenous workers where employed workers reside close to jobs and unemployed workers far away from jobs, the market equilibrium is not efficient. For a given θ, the labor supply condition (2.16) generates too little acceptance, i.e., $\tilde{b}^* < \tilde{b}^o$. Moreover, for a given $\tilde{b}$, the labor demand condition (2.17) generates an optimal level of job creation, i.e., $\theta^* = \theta^o$, if and only if:*

$$\beta = \cfrac{1}{1 + \left[1 - \cfrac{\int_0^{\tilde{b}} bg(b)db}{G(\tilde{b})\tilde{b}}\right] \cfrac{d(s\theta q(\theta))}{d\theta}}. \tag{2.20}$$

Here, in contrast to the benchmark model, there are two sources of inefficiencies. First, there is the job-creation inefficiency where, depending on the value of β, firms create too many or too few jobs as compared to the efficiency solution. This is due to the search externalities since firms do not take into account the impact of their entry on the labor market on workers' and other firms' outcomes. The condition (2.20) is a modified version of the Hosios-Pissarides condition (1.44), which guarantees that these search externalities are internalized by the planner. Second, and this is new, there is another source of inefficiency due to training costs. Indeed, at the market solution, workers tend to refuse socially beneficial jobs because, while workers bear all training costs, the revenues from production are divided through bargaining between firms and workers.

An interesting issue is whether we can find a subsidy rate, for example for the commuting costs, that guarantees that $\tilde{b}^* = \tilde{b}^o$. The answer is yes. Indeed, a subsidy reduces the commuting cost for both employed and unemployed workers, but the effect is stronger for employed workers since they more often go to the CBD. This raises the attractiveness of being employed which, in turn, increases the threshold value $\tilde{b}$. Thus, the planner can find the optimal value of this threshold which guarantees that $\tilde{b}^* = \tilde{b}^o$. It should be clear that the same kind of result can be obtained if the planner offers to subsidy the training cost instead of the commuting cost.

---

[1] Superscript o refers to the optimal solution.

2.4. Interaction Between Land and Labor Markets

There are three interesting results that link the urban market and the labor market. First, an increase in the commuting cost τ decreases both the reservation training level $\tilde{b}$ and labor market tightness θ, but increases the unemployment rate, u. This is because a rise in τ does not affect the labor demand curve (2.17), but does affect the labor supply curve (2.16). Therefore, higher commuting costs make workers more selective, which leads them to reduce their reservation training level. Firms then create less jobs and thus, there is an increase in unemployment. Second, an increase in city size N decreases both the reservation training level $\tilde{b}$ and labor market tightness θ, but increases the unemployment rate u. The intuition is similar to that with commuting costs since larger cities imply (on average) higher commuting costs for workers. Finally, an increase in search intensity s decreases $\tilde{b}$ only if the commuting cost τ is small. Indeed, as workers search more intensively, firms create more jobs, but the difference in the cost of living between employed and unemployed workers decreases. The net effect depends on the value of the commuting cost. Moreover, the relationship between s and θ is positive only if τ is high. The intuition is similar to that of s and $\tilde{b}$.

Let us now examine the impact of labor market variables on land rent. Thus, let us write the land rent defined in (2.3) using (2.15). We obtain:

$$R^*(x) = \begin{cases} \tau\,(N-x) - \dfrac{(1-s)\tau N\delta}{\delta+s\theta^* q(\theta^*)G(\tilde{b}^*)} & \text{for } 0 \le x \le L \\ s\tau\,(N-x) & \text{for } L < x \le N \ . \\ 0 & \text{for } x > N \end{cases} \qquad (2.21)$$

It can be seen that an increase in θ^*, the job creation rate, or $\tilde{b}^*$, the threshold value of the training cost, has a positive impact on equilibrium land rent. Indeed, if more jobs are created or if workers are less picky, then all individuals can propose higher bid-rents and thus, the housing price increases in all locations. In contrast to the benchmark model where all labor market variables had an impact on land rent only through θ^*, here it is both through θ^* and $\tilde{b}^*$. This means, for example, that a rise in search intensity, s, has a direct positive effect on $R^*(x)$ since it increases L^*, but only has two indirect effects on $R^*(x)$ through θ^* and $\tilde{b}^*$. As we have seen above, when commuting costs τ are high, then an increase in s increases θ^*, which, in turn, increases $R^*(x)$. However, when τ is small, an increase in s decreases $\tilde{b}^*$ which, in turn, reduces $R^*(x)$. The total net effect of s on $R^*(x)$ is thus ambiguous.

3. Endogenous Job Destruction

The previous model was interesting since it introduced an ex-ante workers' heterogeneity that we did not have in Chapter 1. However, since it was assumed that ex-post all workers were trained in such a way that they become identical in terms of productivities, the analysis, especially the land-use equilibrium, was relatively similar to what we did in Chapter 1. Sato (2001) has developed a similar framework with ex-ante productivity differences, but also allows ex-post heterogeneity in terms of matching productivities. However, this heterogeneity in the productivity space, which implies a distribution of wages, does not translate into a heterogeneity in the urban space since, in equilibrium, whatever their location in the city, all workers experience the same costs of living and thus, there is no direct correspondence between the heterogeneity in the productivity space and that in the urban space.

We now propose to extend these two approaches (Sato, 2001, 2004a) by introducing ex-post heterogeneity both in the productivity space and the urban space. Based on the fact that the labor market is characterized by large flows and job turnover (Davis, Haltiwanger, and Schuh, 1996), we also endogeneize the job destruction rate, which was until now assumed to be totally exogenous and characterized by the arrival rate, δ.

For this purpose, we follow Mortensen and Pissarides (1994) who propose to extend the basic non-spatial matching model to the case where the job destruction rate δ is endogenous. It is now assumed that each job is characterized by a *fixed irreversible technology*. To be more precise, the value of a match is no longer given by y, but by $y + \epsilon$ where y, as previously, denotes general productivity and ϵ is a parameter that is drawn from a distribution $G(\epsilon)$, which has a finite support $[\underline{\epsilon}, \overline{\epsilon}]$ and no mass point. It is assumed that a job is created with the highest productivity value, $y + \overline{\epsilon}$, capturing the idea that firms with new filled jobs use the best available technology. Then, a new value of productivity ϵ is drawn from $G(\epsilon)$ independently of the current value of ϵ when the productivity shock occurs at rate δ according to the Poisson process. Given that a new match is assumed to have the highest productivity, this implies that when the productivity shock occurs, the productivity of a new match always declines. A job is then destroyed only if the idiosyncratic component of its productivity falls below some critical number $\widetilde{\epsilon} < \overline{\epsilon}$. As a result, the rate at which jobs are destroyed is no longer given by δ, but by $\delta G(\widetilde{\epsilon})$. Since $\widetilde{\epsilon}$ is endogenous and will be determined by a reservation rule in equilibrium, job destruction is also endogenous. Since there will be a distribution of ex-post productivities $y + \epsilon$, there will also be a distribution of wages $w_L(\epsilon)$.

3.1. Urban-Land-Use Equilibrium

We extend the benchmark model of Chapter 1, Section 2, to the case of endogenous job destruction. For simplicity, it is assumed that $s = 1$ so that employed and unemployed workers commute as often to the CBD. We would like to slightly change the benchmark model to have a better link between wages and location. For this purpose, we consider a reduced form of a labor-leisure choice model, where working hours are adjusted until the marginal value of leisure time equals the wage rate. We assume that the *instantaneous* indirect utility of a type-ϵ worker at distance x, denoted by $W_L(\epsilon)$, is given by:[2]

$$W_L(\epsilon) = w_L(\epsilon)(1 - \iota x) - \tau x - R(x). \tag{2.22}$$

Here, the commuting time from distance x is equal to ιx, where $\iota > 0$ is the time spent per unit of distance. Observe that the time cost of commuting for a type-ϵ worker residing at a distance x from the CBD is $\iota w_L(\epsilon)x$; in accordance with empirical observations (Glaeser, Kahn, and Rappaport, 2008), it increases with income. As usual, $w_L(\epsilon)$ in (2.22) does not stand for the worker's actual income, but for the income that would accrue to an individual being employed all the time (the total amount of time is normalized to 1). Rearranging (2.22) yields:

$$\Psi_L(\epsilon, x, W_L(\epsilon)) = w_L(\epsilon)(1 - \iota x) - \tau x - W_L(\epsilon), \tag{2.23}$$

which is the bid-rent of a type-ϵ employed worker residing at a distance x from the CBD.

Inspection of (2.23) shows that, as usual, the bid-rent function is decreasing in x, with $\partial \Psi_L / \partial x < 0$. In the present model, this reflects the combined influence of the time cost of commuting and the monetary cost. Since $w_L'(\epsilon) \geq 0$ (see below), further inspection shows that, at a given x,

---

[2] Another way to justify (2.22) is that commuting is paid in units of time (with possibly an un-modelled transport sector). In that case, it would be natural to get rid of the term ιx in (2.22) so that:

$$W_L(\epsilon) = w_L(\epsilon) - \tau x - R(x).$$

However, here, the location patterns of all workers (both employed and unemployed) would be undetermined since all bid-rent functions would have the same slope τ.

an increase in ϵ makes the bid-rent slope more negative ($\partial^2 \Psi_L / \partial \epsilon \partial x < 0$). This means that high-$\epsilon$ workers have steeper bid-rent curves than low-ϵ workers. The intuitive reason is that *an extra mile of commuting reduces income more for a high-ϵ worker than for a low-ϵ worker*; a consequence of the higher net wage. Therefore, the high-ϵ worker requires a larger decline in land rent than a high-ϵ worker to maintain a given utility level. Comparing the residential locations of two groups, the group with the steeper bid-rent curve locates closer to the CBD. In the present model, this implies that *high-ϵ workers locate closer to the CBD than low-ϵ workers.*

As stated above, it is assumed that the unemployed commute as often to the CBD as the employed, i.e., $s = 1$. We also assume the unemployed's opportunity cost of time to be negligible since they do not work and, thus, time costs do not enter in their utility function.[3] As a result, the *instantaneous indirect utility* of an unemployed worker residing at distance x is:

$$W_U = w_U - \tau x - R(x) \tag{2.24}$$

and his/her bid-rent is equal to:

$$\Psi_U(x, W_U) = w_U - \tau x - W_U. \tag{2.25}$$

Since the wage is never equal to zero, any employed worker (whatever his/her ϵ-type) will have a steeper bid-rent than an unemployed worker (for that, compare (2.23) and (2.25)). To formalize this notion, we introduce the definition of residential equilibrium:

Definition 2.1. *A land-use-urban equilibrium consists of the following mapping $\epsilon(x)$ that assigns a worker of skill type ϵ to a location x, i.e.,*

$$\epsilon(x) = \bar{\epsilon} - \left(\frac{\bar{\epsilon} - \tilde{\epsilon}}{L} \right) x \quad \text{for} \quad 0 \le x \le L \tag{2.26}$$

a set of utility levels $W_L^*(\epsilon)$ and W_U^*, and a land-rent curve $R^*(x)$ such that:

(i) at each $x \in [0, L]$,

$$R^*(x) = \Psi_L(\epsilon(x), x, W_L^*(\epsilon))$$
$$= \max_{\epsilon} \Psi_L(\epsilon, x, W_L^*(\epsilon)) \tag{2.27}$$

---

[3] This is admittedly a simplifying assumption because the unemployed workers are also assumed to commute to the CBD. However, since their wage (i.e., unemployment benefit) is fixed, it does not vary with working hours and is lower than any wage earned by an employed worker; they have the lowest opportunity cost of time when commuting. Hence, assuming that time costs do not enter in their utility function is just a normalization assumption.

(*ii*)

$$\Psi_L(L, W_L(\widetilde{\epsilon})) = \Psi_U(L, W_U) \qquad (2.28)$$

(*iii*)

$$\Psi_U(N) = 0. \qquad (2.29)$$

Indeed, to define the urban equilibrium, we need to calculate the *assignment rule* between *location space* defined on $[0, L]$ and *productivity space* defined on $[\widetilde{\epsilon}, \overline{\epsilon}]$, since, in equilibrium, only workers with a productivity equal to or above $\widetilde{\epsilon}$ will work. Because we know that the relationship is negative and because of the linearity assumption of both the distribution x of workers in the city and the distribution ϵ of productivities, this relationship must be linear. Thus, we must find a linear and negative relationship between ϵ and x so that $\epsilon(0) = \overline{\epsilon}$ and $\epsilon(L) = \widetilde{\epsilon}$. The only equation that satisfies these requirements is given by (2.26). The mapping between the physical and productivity "distances" of workers involves a correlation between these distances. It should be noted that this result depends on the assumption of a fixed lot size and a uniform distribution of ϵ. As is well-known, variable land consumption can overturn the present inverse association between residential distance and the time cost of commuting (see, for example, Fujita, 1989, Ch. 2). With variable consumption, however, additional conditions could be imposed to guarantee that the two distances remain perfectly correlated. The same applies to a more general c.d.f. $G(\epsilon)$. All other equations have a similar interpretation as in the benchmark model. The only difference here is that we have a continuum of bid-rents and thus, we cannot, as in Chapter 1, define an equilibrium where bid-rents intersect for different workers. On the contrary, equation (2.27) means that in order to occupy a location x, each type-ϵ worker must propose the highest bid rent at this location x, that is:

$$\frac{d\Psi_L(\epsilon, x, W_L^*(\epsilon))}{d\epsilon}\Big|_{\epsilon=\epsilon(x)} = 0.$$

Since the wage $w_L(\epsilon)$ is endogenous, it must be determined before solving the urban-land-use equilibrium.

3.2. Steady-State Equilibrium

As usual, let us write the different discounted lifetime expected utilities of workers and firms. The steady-state Bellman equations for unemployed and employed workers are given by:

$$r I_U = w_U - \tau x - R(x) + \theta q(\theta) \left[I_L(\overline{\epsilon}) - I_U \right] \tag{2.30}$$

$$r I_L(\epsilon) = w_L(\epsilon)(1 - \iota x) - \tau x - R(x) + \delta \int_{\widetilde{\epsilon}}^{\overline{\epsilon}} I_L(\epsilon) dG(\epsilon)$$
$$+ \delta G(\widetilde{\epsilon}) I_U - \delta I_L(\epsilon) \tag{2.31}$$

while, for firms with a filled job and a vacancy, we have, respectively:

$$r I_F(\epsilon) = y + \epsilon - w_L(\epsilon) + \frac{\delta}{(\overline{\epsilon} - \widetilde{\epsilon})} \int_{\widetilde{\epsilon}}^{\overline{\epsilon}} I_F(\epsilon) d\epsilon + \delta G(\widetilde{\epsilon}) I_V - \delta I_F(\epsilon)$$
$$\tag{2.32}$$

$$r I_V = -c + q(\theta) \left[I_F(\overline{\epsilon}) - I_V \right]. \tag{2.33}$$

Equation (2.30) states that an unemployed worker who enjoys an instantaneous utility $w_U - \tau x - R(x)$ today can find a job at rate $\theta q(\theta)$ and, in that case, will start a job at the highest productivity level $y + \overline{\epsilon}$ and thus, will obtain an expected utility $I_L(\overline{\epsilon})$ with the highest wage level $w_L(\overline{\epsilon})$. Equation (2.31) states that an employed worker who is employed at a certain productivity level ϵ obtains an instantaneous utility given by: $w_L(\epsilon)(1 - \iota x) - \tau x - R(x)$, but can then be "hit" by a productivity shock at rate δ and will continue to work in that job only if the match is still productive, i.e., productivity is at least equal to $y + \widetilde{\epsilon}$. If not, that is, if the productivity of the match is less than $y + \widetilde{\epsilon}$, which happens with probability $G(\widetilde{\epsilon}) = \Pr \left[\epsilon \leq \widetilde{\epsilon} \right]$, the worker becomes unemployed and loses $I_L(\epsilon) - I_U$. The interpretation of equations (2.32) and (2.33) is similar to that of (2.30) and (2.31).

As in the benchmark model, firms post vacancies up to a point where $I_V = 0$. Using (2.33), the value of a *new* job is then equal to:

$$I_F(\overline{\epsilon}) = \frac{c}{q(\theta)}. \tag{2.34}$$

In each period, the total intertemporal surplus is shared through a generalized Nash bargaining process between the firm and the worker. The result of the bargaining gives the following sharing rule:

$$(1 - \beta) \left[I_L(\epsilon) - I_U \right] = \beta I_F(\epsilon) \tag{2.35}$$

and we obtain (see Zenou, 2007a):

Proposition 2.2. *Assume*

$$(1 - \beta)\iota L < \frac{\beta\,(\bar{\epsilon} - \tilde{\epsilon})}{(1 - \beta)\,w_U + \beta\,(y + c\theta + \bar{\epsilon})}. \qquad (2.36)$$

Then, the wage $w_L(\epsilon)$ is always strictly positive, given by

$$w_L(\epsilon) = \frac{(1 - \beta)\,w_U + \beta\,(y + \epsilon + c\theta)}{1 - (1 - \beta)\,\iota\,L\,(\bar{\epsilon} - \epsilon)\,/\,(\bar{\epsilon} - \tilde{\epsilon})} \qquad (2.37)$$

and increasing in ϵ.

Condition (2.36) guarantees that the wage is always strictly positive and increasing in ϵ. The wage (2.37) is a generalization of the non-spatial wage obtained by Mortensen and Pissarides (1994) (see equation (2.10) p. 42 in Pissarides, 2000, which is (2.37) when $\iota = 0$). As in the standard search-matching model, we have the same positive effects of w_U, y, c and θ on the wage, since they all increase the outside option for workers. The new element here is the spatial aspect of the negotiation where the employer must take into account the location x of workers. As in Chapter 1, firms must *compensate* workers for the transport cost difference between employed and unemployed workers for them to accept the job offer. However, the main difference as compared to the wage determined in Chapter 1 is that here, workers are ex-post heterogenous in terms of productivity ϵ and, because of the assignment rule (2.26), this translates into heterogeneity in terms of distance to jobs x. So the compensation is more complex which leads to a non-linear relationship between w and ϵ. Compared with the non-spatial model, what is interesting is that *here* the range of the distribution $\bar{\epsilon} - \tilde{\epsilon}$ does affect the wage. Indeed, in the non-spatial model of Mortensen and Pissarides (1994), wages depend on job productivity y, but not on the productivities of other jobs. Here, because of spatial compensation, the highest and the lowest productivity have an impact on the wage of every worker, whatever his/her productivity. Finally, because employed and unemployed workers have the same monetary commuting cost, only time cost (i.e., ι) affects the wage. Not surprisingly, the higher ι is, the higher the wage is since firms need to compensate more workers to induce them to accept the job offer. Observe that this comparative statics exercise (like those above) is performed for a given θ and a given L. In equilibrium, θ and $L = (1 - u)\,N$ will be affected by ι and thus, there will also be indirect effects of ι on w via θ and L.

As in the previous section, since workers are heterogenous, we need to determine a job-acceptance rule, which here will lead to a job destruction equation. We must solve the following equations:

$$I_F(\widetilde{\epsilon}) = 0$$

$$I_L(\widetilde{\epsilon}) - I_U = 0.$$

By the sharing rule (2.35), these two equations are equivalent and thus, it suffices to solve only one of them. Zenou (2007a) shows that, using (2.36) and solving one of these equations, the job-creation condition can be written as:

$$\frac{c}{q(\theta)} = \left(\frac{1-\beta}{r+\delta}\right) \frac{(\overline{\epsilon} - \widetilde{\epsilon})(1 - \iota L) + [(1-\beta)w_U + \beta(y + \overline{\epsilon} + c\theta)]\iota L}{[1 - (1-\beta)\iota L]}$$

(2.38)

while the job-destruction condition is given by:

$$(y + \widetilde{\epsilon})(1 - \iota L) - w_U - \frac{\beta c}{1-\beta}\theta + \frac{\delta(1-\iota L)}{2(r+\delta)}(\overline{\epsilon} - \widetilde{\epsilon}) = 0. \quad (2.39)$$

Equation (2.38) states that the firm's expected gain from a new job is equal to the expected hiring cost paid by the firm. In the non-spatial case, when $\iota = 0$, we obtain equation (2.14) p. 43 in Pissarides (2000). First, in the non-spatial case, the relationship between reservation productivity $\widetilde{\epsilon}$ and labor market tightness θ is *negative* because at higher $\widetilde{\epsilon}$, the expected lifetime of a job is shorter since, in any short interval of time dt, the job is destroyed with probability $\delta G(\widetilde{\epsilon})dt$. As a result, firms create fewer jobs, which leads to a fall in θ and thus, less job creation. This is no longer true in the spatial model since, as highlighted above, wages need to be spatially compensated. So, when $\widetilde{\epsilon}$ increases, the duration of jobs is shorter, but workers need to be compensated less, which increases θ. The net effect is thus ambiguous. If the spatial compensation effect is not too strong, i.e., if ι is not too high, then the relationship between θ and $\widetilde{\epsilon}$ is negative, as in the non-spatial model. Second, the impact of the discount rate r or the mismatch rate δ is similar to that of the non-spatial model since higher r or δ decreases job creation because the future returns from new jobs are discounted at higher rates. Third, contrary the non-spatial model, general productivity y, the cost of maintaining a vacancy c as well as the unemployment benefit w_U enter in the equation and thus affect the relationship between $\widetilde{\epsilon}$ and θ. Once more, this is due to the spatial aspect of wages, which implies that the firm's expected revenues and costs are no longer proportional to y. Finally, the spatial variable ι does affect the relationship between $\widetilde{\epsilon}$ and θ.

If ι increases, then firms will create less jobs because wages increase due to higher spatial compensation. Observe that all our comments were made at a given $L = (1 - u) N$. In the general equilibrium, there will be additional effects since u is also affected by θ and $\tilde{\epsilon}$ (see below).

Let us now comment on the job-destruction equation (2.39) and compare it to the non-spatial case when $\iota = 0$, which corresponds to equation (2.15, for the uniform distribution) in Pissarides (2000). In contrast to the job-creation equation, spatial and non-spatial equations are quite similar. This is mainly because job creation is directly affected by wages while job destruction is not. First, as in the non-spatial model, there is a positive relationship between θ and $\tilde{\epsilon}$ because at higher θ, the worker's outside opportunities are better, wages are thus higher, and so more marginal jobs are destroyed, which increases $\tilde{\epsilon}$. Second, all variables except ι enter in a similar way and have the same effects on the relationship between θ and $\tilde{\epsilon}$ as in the non-spatial model. Finally, the new element, ι is, the commuting cost per unit of distance. At given θ and L, it is easily verified that an increase in ι increases $\tilde{\epsilon}$, which implies that more marginal jobs are destroyed. Indeed, when ι is higher, net wages increase and thus the value of employment at each ϵ, i.e., $I_L(\epsilon)$, increases. As a result, since the value of unemployment I_U is not affected, $\tilde{\epsilon}$ must increase to satisfy condition $I_L(\tilde{\epsilon}) = I_U$.

To close the model, we must determine the steady-state unemployment rate. Since the number of workers who enter unemployment is $\delta G(\tilde{\epsilon})(1 - u) N$ and the number who leave unemployment is $\theta q(\theta) u N$, we have:

$$u^* = \frac{\delta G(\tilde{\epsilon})}{\delta G(\tilde{\epsilon}) + \theta q(\theta)}. \tag{2.40}$$

This equation is exactly the same as in the non-spatial model. All spatial variables will only indirectly affect the unemployment rate through both job creation θ (see (2.38)) and job destruction $\tilde{\epsilon}$ (see (2.39)).

We can now solve the urban equilibrium. As stated above, because there is a *continuum* of heterogenous workers, we *cannot* solve the urban equilibrium in a standard way by using the fact that the group with the steeper bid-rent curve locates closer to the job center (Fujita, 1989, Chapter 2). The latter is only possible if there is a *finite* of number of heterogenous workers. Brueckner, Thisse, and Zenou (2002) propose a solution to solve the location of workers when there is a continuum of them. Since we introduce Brueckner, Thisse, and Zenou (2002) in Chapter 3, we expose this method of determining the location of a continuum of workers in a monocentric city in Appendix A3 at the end of Chapter 3. Using this method, Zenou

(2007a) shows that the urban-land-use equilibrium is characterized by the following proposition:

Proposition 2.3. *Assume*

$$\frac{\iota L}{\bar{\epsilon} - \widetilde{\epsilon}} < \min\left\{\frac{\beta/(1-\beta)}{(1-\beta)\,w_U + \beta\,(y + c\,\theta + \bar{\epsilon})},\ \frac{1}{\bar{\epsilon} - \epsilon}\right\}. \qquad (2.41)$$

Then, there exists a unique residential equilibrium characterized by the assignment rule (2.26). The equilibrium instantaneous utilities of employed workers of type ϵ are given by:

$$W_L^*(\epsilon) = \frac{\beta^2\,(\bar{\epsilon} - \widetilde{\epsilon})}{(1-\beta)^2\,\iota L}\log\left[\frac{\bar{\epsilon} - \widetilde{\epsilon} - (1-\beta)\,\iota L\,(\bar{\epsilon} - \epsilon)}{\bar{\epsilon} - \widetilde{\epsilon} - (1-\beta)\,\iota L\,(\bar{\epsilon} - \widetilde{\epsilon})}\right] - \tau N$$

$$+ \frac{\beta\,(\epsilon - \widetilde{\epsilon})}{(1-\beta)} + \frac{[(1-\beta)\,w_U + \beta\,(y + \epsilon + c\,\theta)]\,(1 - \iota L)}{1 - (1-\beta)\,\iota L}, \qquad (2.42)$$

which are increasing and convex in ϵ, while the unemployed's utility is:

$$W_U^* = w_U - s\,\tau\,N. \qquad (2.43)$$

The land-rent equilibrium in the employment zone $R_L^*(x)$, i.e., for all $x \in [0, L]$, is equal to

$$R_L^*(x) = \frac{[(1-\beta)\,w_U + \beta\,(y + \bar{\epsilon}\,(1 - 1/L) + x\,\widetilde{\epsilon}/L + c\,\theta)]\,(1 - \iota x)}{1 - (1-\beta)\,\iota x}$$

$$- \frac{[(1-\beta)\,w_U + \beta\,(y + \widetilde{\epsilon} + c\,\theta)]\,(1 - \iota L)}{1 - (1-\beta)\,\iota L} + \tau\,(N - x) \qquad (2.44)$$

$$+ \frac{\beta\,(\bar{\epsilon} - \widetilde{\epsilon})}{(1-\beta)\,L}\left[\frac{\beta}{(1-\beta)\,\iota}\log\left[\frac{1 - (1-\beta)\,\iota x}{1 - (1-\beta)\,\iota L}\right] - 1 + x\right]$$

and is decreasing and convex in x. In the unemployment zone, i.e., for all $x \in [L, N]$, the land-rent equilibrium $R_U^*(x)$ is given by:

$$R_U^*(x) = \tau\,(N - x). \qquad (2.45)$$

This result establishes that there is a unique urban-land-use equilibrium and gives the exact values of all endogenous variables as a function of the exogenous parameters and the endogenous variables in the labor market, i.e., θ^*, $\widetilde{\epsilon}^*$, u^*. Observe that the way in which these labor variables affect the spatial variables $W_L^*(\epsilon)$, W_U^* and $R^*(x)$ is through wage setting. Indeed, as we have seen above, the wage (2.37) is affected by θ^*, $\widetilde{\epsilon}^*$, u^*, but the wage also affects the land market through the bid-rents. Indeed, workers with higher wages want to reduce their commuting time and thus, outbid workers with lower wages on the outskirts of the city. The steady-state equilibrium, which requires simultaneously solving the urban-land-use equilibrium and the labor market equilibrium, is a 7-tuple $(\theta^*, \tilde{\epsilon}^*, u^*, R_L^*(x), W_L^*(\epsilon), W_U^*, L^*)$ such that equations (2.38), (2.39), (2.40), (2.27), (2.28), (2.29), and

$$L^* = (1 - u^*)N \tag{2.46}$$

are satisfied. It can be shown that there is a unique steady-state equilibrium. What is interesting now is to analyze the interaction between the land and the labor market.

3.3. Interaction Between Land and Labor Markets

To study the interaction between the land market and the labor market, we run similar numerical simulations as in Section 4 in Chapter 1, by calibrating the model in order to obtain reasonable values of the unemployment rate and the job creation rate. In particular, we will focus our discussion on the differences between the spatial model and the nonspatial model. To obtain analytical solutions, we run some numerical simulations using specific parameter values and the following Cobb-Douglas function for the matching function:

$$d(u\,N, v\,N) = \sqrt{(u\,N)\,V},$$

where u is the unemployment rate and V the vacancy level. This implies that $q(\theta) = 1/\sqrt{\theta}, \theta q(\theta) = \sqrt{\theta}$ and the elasticity of the matching rate (defined as $\eta(\theta) = -q'(\theta)\theta/q(\theta)$) is equal to 0.5. The values of the parameters (in yearly terms) are the following:[4] output y is normalized to unity. The relative bargaining power of workers is equal to $\eta(\theta)$, i.e., $\beta = \eta(\theta) = 0.5$. Unemployment benefits have a value of 2 and the costs of maintaining a vacancy c are equal to 2 per unit of time, while general productivity is 4. The uniform distribution of ϵ is defined on the support $[0, 2]$, which implies that new jobs have a productivity equal to $y + \bar{\epsilon} = 6$ while, for the worse jobs, it is $y + \underline{\epsilon} = 4$. Pecuniary commuting costs τ are equal to 0.1, whereas time costs are equal to 0.07. The discount rate is $r = 0.05$, whereas the mismatch rate is $\delta = 0.15$ which means that, on average, there is a technological shock every six and years and a half. Finally, total population is normalized to 1. Table 2.1 summarizes these different values.

Let us calculate the steady-state equilibrium for the non-spatial model ($\iota = 0$) and the spatial model ($\iota > 0, \tau > 0$) using the parameter values

---

[4] We use slightly different values than those displayed in Table 1.2.

Table 2.1. *Parameter values*

$y = 4$ General productivity	$r = 0.01$ Pure discount rate
$\delta = 0.15$ Job-specific shock arrival rate	$\beta = 0.5$ Workers' share of surplus
$\underline{\epsilon} = 0, \overline{\epsilon} = 2$ Parameters of the distribution	$\eta(\theta) = 0.5$ Search elasticity of matching
$N = 1$ Total population	$\iota = 0.07$ Time commuting cost
$w_U = 2$ Unemployment benefit	$\tau = 0.1$ Pecuniary commuting cost
$c = 2$ Cost of vacant job	

given in Table 2.1. The numerical results of these two equilibria are displayed in Table 2.2.

The unemployment rate u^* and the reservation productivity $\widetilde{\epsilon}^*$ are lower and the job-creation rate θ^* is higher in the non-spatial model. Indeed, through commuting costs and land rent, urban space creates additional frictions in the labor market that lead to these differences. Let us examine these differences in more detail. In the non-spatial model, the wage, given by $4.69 + 0.5\,\epsilon$, varies between $w_L^*(\widetilde{\epsilon}^*) = 5.27$ and $w_L^*(\overline{\epsilon}) = 5.69$ while total productivity varies between $y + \widetilde{\epsilon}^* = 5.15$ and $y + \overline{\epsilon} = 6$. This means that firms keep some currently unprofitable jobs occupied. In fact, it is easily verified that all jobs with a productivity $\epsilon \leq 1.38$ are not currently profitable because $y + \epsilon \leq w_L^*(\epsilon)$ while jobs with a $\epsilon \in [1.38, 2]$ are profitable. As observed by Pissarides (2000), this means that some firms keep some currently

Table 2.2. *Steady-state equilibrium*

	Non-spatial model ($t = 0$)	Spatial model ($t > 0, \tau > 0$)
$u^*(\%)$	6.07	8.11
θ^*	1.77	1.69
$v^*(\%)$	10.77	13.71
$\tilde{\epsilon}^*$	1.15	1.53
$\epsilon^*(x)$		$2 - 0.51x$
$w_L^*(\epsilon)$	$4.69 + 0.5\,\epsilon$	$(4.69 + 0.5\,\epsilon)/(0.86 - 0.068\,\epsilon)$
$I_F(\epsilon)$	$-3.59 + 3.13\,\epsilon$	$-19.96 + 6.25\,\epsilon + 146.83/(12.60 + \epsilon)$
$W_L^*(\epsilon)$	$4.69 + 0.5\,\epsilon$	$2.95 + 1.48\,\epsilon + 7.30 \log[0.89 + 0.07\,\epsilon]$
W_U^*	2	1.95

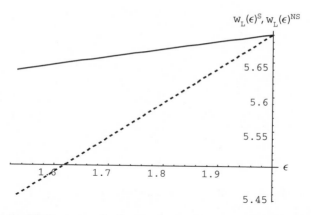

Figure 2.2. Equilibrium wage distribution for spatial and non-spatial models in the productivity space.

unprofitable jobs because of the possibility that a job productivity might change, which enables firms to start production at the new productivity immediately after arrival, without having to pay the recruitment cost (which is here quite high since $c = 2$) and forgo production during search. This is confirmed by looking at $I_F(\epsilon)$, the lifetime expected utility of a firm with a filled job, which is calculating using (2.32) and given by $-3.59 + 3.13\,\epsilon$. It is easily checked that it is always strictly positive for all $\epsilon \in [\tilde{\epsilon}^*, \bar{\epsilon}]$. So even if jobs with an $\epsilon \in [1.15, 1.38]$ are not currently profitable, firms keep them because their lifetime expected utility $I_F(\epsilon)$ is strictly positive in this interval. This is even more true in the spatial model. Indeed, because firms need to compensate for spatial costs, wages are always higher, but productivity is the same, and it is easily verified that, in our example, all jobs are currently unprofitable since $w_L^*(\epsilon) > y + \epsilon$, $\forall \epsilon \in [\tilde{\epsilon}^*, \bar{\epsilon}]$. However, in the same interval, it is also easy to check that the lifetime expected utility $I_F(\epsilon)$ is strictly positive. Figure 2.2 confirms what we said before. The spatial wage $w_L^{*S}(\epsilon)$ (solid curve) is always higher than the non-spatial one $w_L^{*NS}(\epsilon)$ (dotted curve) because of the need for firms to spatially compensate workers for commuting and land costs. In Figure 2.3, we compare the two expected lifetime utilities $I_F(\epsilon)$ (solid and dotted curves for spatial and non-spatial models, respectively) and show that they are always higher in the spatial model for $\epsilon \in [\tilde{\epsilon}^*, \bar{\epsilon}]$ because wages are much lower.

Let us now focus on the land market. Figure 2.4 compares the equilibrium instantaneous utilities in the spatial model (solid curve), given by $W_L^*(\epsilon)$, and the non-spatial model (dotted curve), given by $w_L^*(\epsilon)$. It is not clear which utility is higher because spatial wages are higher, but workers incur

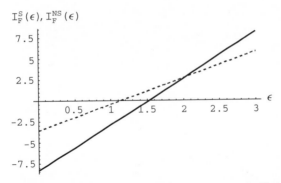

Figure 2.3. Comparison of lifetime expected utilities of firms with filled jobs between spatial and non-spatial models.

commuting and land costs. In Figure 2.4, it is seen that for low values of ϵ, the non-spatial utility is higher while we have the reverse for high productivity values. This is quite intuitive because when ϵ is low, wage differences are not too high, but spatial costs exist and thus, the non-spatial utility has a higher value. For high ϵ, we obtain the reverse result because the wage difference is sufficiently high to compensate for the spatial cost difference since the spatial wage (2.37) is non-linear in ϵ.

We would like to pursue our analysis of the interaction between land and labor markets by analyzing the impact of the key spatial variable, the time commuting cost ι, on the equilibrium labor market variables, u^*, $\widetilde{\epsilon}^*$ and θ^*. The effects are complex since ι directly affects the land market through land rent and the instantaneous utilities $W_L(\epsilon)$ and W_U, but also

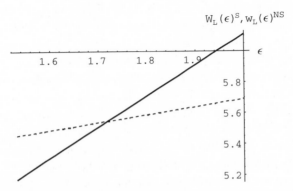

Figure 2.4. Comparison of equilibrium instantaneous utilities between spatial and non-spatial models.

Table 2.3. *Variation of the unemployment benefit*

	Non-spatial model ($\iota = 0$)				Spatial model ($\iota > 0, \tau > 0$)			
	$u^*(\%)$	θ^*	$v^*(\%)$	$\tilde{\epsilon}^*$	$u^*(\%)$	θ^*	$v^*(\%)$	$\tilde{\epsilon}^*$
$w_U = 0$	4.12	2.72	11.20	0.94	5.58	2.63	15.17	1.32
$w_U = 1$	4.95	2.25	11.12	1.04	6.76	2.16	14.61	1.42
$w_U = 2$	6.07	1.77	10.77	1.15	8.11	1.69	13.71	1.53
$w_U = 3$	7.69	1.31	10.04	1.27	10.07	1.22	12.33	1.65
$w_U = 4$	10.34	0.84	8.72	1.41	13.32	0.77	10.21	1.79

indirectly affects the labor market through wage. It can be shown that the relationships between u^* and ι and between $\tilde{\epsilon}^*$ and ι are increasing while that between θ^* and ι is decreasing. This should not be a surprise since higher commuting costs lead to an increase in wages (firms need to compensate workers for their spatial costs), which makes traveling to the job center even more costly. As a result, land rents increase and firms must compensate even more workers. Therefore, firms enter less in the labor market and create less jobs, which decreases θ^*. Moreover, since wages have increased, $I_L(\epsilon)$ the lifetime expected value of employment increases for each job ϵ, which implies that $\tilde{\epsilon}^*$, the reservation productivity below which jobs are destroyed, must increase for condition $I_L(\tilde{\epsilon}^*) = I_U$ to be satisfied. Since more marginal jobs are destroyed and less jobs are created, the equilibrium unemployment rate u^* is reduced following an increase in ι.

It can also be noticed that the equilibrium values are quite sensitive to a variation in the commuting cost, ι. Indeed, an increase in the commuting cost from $\iota = 0$ to $\iota = 0.15$ leads to an increase in the unemployment rate from 6.07% to 10.59%, an increase in the reservation productivity from 1.15 to 1.995, and a decrease in the job-creation rate from 1.77 to 1.6 (which corresponds to an increase in the vacancy rate from 10.77% to 16.91%). These are important effects due to the fact that the interaction between land and labor markets tends to amplify the effect of one variable on the other. To illustrate this point, let us consider an increase in the unemployment benefit w_U on u^*, $\tilde{\epsilon}^*$ and θ^*, both in the spatial and the non-spatial model. In both models, we obtain without any surprise that an increase in w_U leads to an increase in u^* and $\tilde{\epsilon}^*$ and a decrease in θ^*. What is interesting is the difference in the values of the endogenous variables. Table 2.3 reports these outcomes for $w_U = 0, 1, 2, 3$ and 4.

From Table 2.3, it is easily seen that the values of the endogenous variables are much higher in the spatial model than in the non-spatial one because of amplifying effects due to the interaction between land and labor markets. Indeed, when $w_U = 0$, the unemployment rate is 4.12% and the vacancy rate 11.20% in the non-spatial model while, in the spatial model, these figures are 5.58% and 15.17%, respectively. When $w_U = 4$, the differences are even larger with, for example, a 3% higher unemployment rate in the spatial model where each labor variable, like for example w_U, has an impact on both markets. Indeed, the unemployment benefit directly affects the wage since, at given θ and L, higher w_U implies higher wages which, in turn, affects the time cost of traveling. This increases competition in the land market since access to the job center becomes more valuable which, in turn, increases the wage since firms need to compensate more for spatial costs to induce workers to take a job. These amplifying effects lead to a higher unemployment rate and reservation productivity and lower labor market tightness in the spatial model.

4. Positive Mobility Costs

The models developed so far have no relocation costs. Although this assumption is quite frequent in urban economics, its relevance may depend on the nature of the labor market considered. Indeed, when unemployment and employment spells are short (i.e., a U.S. style labor market), it is not necessarily appealing. Indeed, even though residential mobility in the U.S. is quite high,[5] low-income households do not necessarily change their residential location as soon as they change their employment status. However, in a European context, long spells of employment and unemployment make it more likely that relocation and labor transitions coincide, in which case our benchmark assumption of absence of mobility costs is relevant. Indeed, in Europe, it is commonly observed that residential mobility is limited because of different costs. In particular, transaction costs, which include transaction taxes such as capital gains taxes and ad valorem taxes that are proportional to the housing value (e.g., stamp duties and sale taxes), are substantial barriers to mobility (see, e.g., Van Ommeren and Van Leuvensteijn, 2005). This is also confirmed by a recent study in the U.K. (Cho and Whitehead, 2005)

---

[5] Rosenthal (1988) shows that in the United States, the median renter moves roughly every one to two years, while the median homeowner moves every six to seven years. Even if why people move is not explained, this shows a high level of residential mobility in the United States, at least for renters.

which shows that people tend to change residential location for professional reasons, even though this mobility is lower in London (11.2% move) than in the Northern regions (between 17% and 22%). It has also been observed that homes tend to be less mobile than jobs. For example, Manning (2003) argues that approximately 20% of the workers have job tenure less than a year compared to 10% with a residential tenure of less than a year.

Consider the benchmark model developed in Chapter 1 (Section 2) where search intensity was exogenous and denoted by s. Following Wasmer and Zenou (2006), we will analyze how the assumption of positive relocation costs affects the urban land-use equilibrium described in Figure 1.1 and the resulting labor market outcomes. For simplicity, we assume the wage w_L to be exogenous.

4.1. Urban-Land-Use Equilibrium

Relocation costs are strictly positive and we denote by C the instantaneous amount of effort and money supported by individuals when they move (i.e., change residential location). *Four* groups of workers emerge in equilibrium: mobile employed and unemployed workers and immobile employed and unemployed workers. Employed workers are said to be mobile (respectively immobile) when, hit by a job-destruction shock, they decide to relocate to another part of the city (respectively stay in the same location). A similar definition of mobility is adopted for unemployed workers depending on the occurrence of a successful application to a job. By this definition, all workers were mobile in all models developed so far.

To keep the model tractable, we assume that these *four* groups always form spatially homogenous communities. In other words, we only focus on equilibria in which mobile employed workers are perfectly segregated, mobile unemployed workers are perfectly segregated, and finally immobile workers (both employed and unemployed) are integrated and randomly, but evenly, distributed in a part of the city. This latter part of the land market equilibrium is natural since, in the long run, immobile workers are distributed according to an ergodic distribution of the employment/unemployment process.

As stated above, we want to see how the urban configuration described in Figure 1.1 is modified when positive relocation costs are introduced. So we focus on an equilibrium where the employed are close to the city center and unemployed workers reside on the outskirts of the city. To be more precise, as the distance to the CBD increases from 0 to N, we will first have

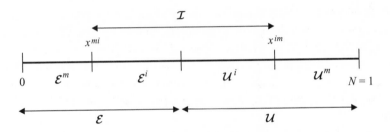

Figure 2.5. Areas of mobile and immobile workers.

mobile employed workers, then immobile employed/unemployed workers and, finally, mobile unemployed workers.

Let superscripts m and i indicate mobility and immobility. Denote by $\mathcal{E}$ and $\mathcal{U}$ the employment and unemployment areas, with $\mathcal{E} \cup \mathcal{U} = [0, N]$. Denote by $\mathcal{E}^m$ and $\mathcal{E}^i$ the subsets of $\mathcal{E}$ in which the employed are mobile and immobile, and by $\mathcal{U}^m$ and U^i the subsets of U in which the unemployed are mobile and immobile. Observe that E^i is the complement of subset E^m in E and U^i is the complement of subset U^m in U. Observe also, because of the assumption made above (groups always form spatially homogenous communities), that each subset, E^m, E^i, U^m and U^i, is connected and in the city, we have $E^m \cup E^i \cup U^i \cup U^m = [0, N]$. Among the immobile workers, the employment status is not relevant because when an employed worker who lives in E^i loses his/her job, he/she stays in E^i. The same applies for an unemployed worker in U^i who has found a job. As a result, we can define a subset $I = E^i \cup U^i = E^i = U^i$, which includes all immobile (employed and unemployed) workers. Finally, let us denote by x^{mi} and x^{im} the border between mobile and immobile employed workers, and immobile and mobile unemployed workers, respectively. The length of E^m and U^m is thus, respectively, given by x^{mi} and $N - x^{im}$, while the length of I is $x^{im} - x^{mi}$. Figure 2.5 illustrates these different sets.

As in the benchmark model, mobile employed workers leave their area after a shock to become unemployed in U^m and, likewise, mobile unemployed workers leave U^m only to relocate to E^m. As a result, in steady-state, the intertemporal utility of the immobile employed and unemployed workers must be constant over locations so that $I_U^m(x) = \overline{I}_U^m$ for all $x \in U^m$ and $I_L^m(x) = \overline{I}_L^m$ for all $x \in E^m$. Therefore, we can calculate the expected utility of the unemployed worker residing at $x = x^{im}$ so that $I_U^m(x^{im}) = \overline{I}_U^m$ and the expected utility of the employed worker at $x = x^{mi}$ so that $I_L^m(x^{mi}) = \overline{I}_L^m$. Thus, we obtain the following arbitrage equations in which moving costs are paid by mobile workers upon transition, i.e.:

$$r\overline{I}_L^m = w_L - \tau x - R(x) + \delta \left(\overline{I}_U^m - \overline{I}_L^m - C \right) \tag{2.47}$$

for $x \in \mathcal{E}^m = [0, x^{mi}]$ and

$$r\overline{I}_U^m = w_U - s \tau x - R(x) + s \theta q(\theta) \left(\overline{I}_L^m - \overline{I}_U^m - C \right) \tag{2.48}$$

for $x \in \mathcal{U}^m = \left[x^{im}, N \right]$. For immobile workers, we instead have:

$$r I_L^i(x) = w_L - \tau x - R(x) - \delta \left[I_L^i(x) - I_U^i(x) \right] \tag{2.49}$$

$$r I_U^i(x) = w_U - s \tau x - R(x) + s \theta q(\theta) \left[I_L^i(x) - I_U^i(x) \right] \tag{2.50}$$

for $x \in \mathcal{I} = \left[x^{mi}, x^{im} \right]$. Combining the last two equations, we obtain:

$$I_L^i(x) - I_U^i(x) = \frac{w_L - w_U - (1 - s) \tau x}{r + \delta + s \theta q(\theta)}. \tag{2.51}$$

We can now determine the bid-rent functions of all workers. We have:

$$\Psi_L^m(x, \overline{I}_U^m, \overline{I}_L^m) = w_L - \tau x - r \overline{I}_L^m - \delta \left(\overline{I}_L^m - \overline{I}_U^m + C \right)$$

$$\Psi_U^m(x, \overline{I}_U^m, \overline{I}_L^m) = w_U - s \tau x - r \overline{I}_U^m + s \theta q(\theta) \left(\overline{I}_L^m - \overline{I}_U^m - C \right)$$

$$\Psi_L^i(x, I_U^i(x), I_L^i(x)) = w_L - \tau x - r I_L^i(x) - \delta \left[I_L^i(x) - I_U^i(x) \right]$$

$$\Psi_U^i \left(x, I_U^i(x), I_L^i(x) \right) = w_U - s \tau x - r I_U^i(x) + s \theta q(\theta) \left[I_L^i(x) - I_U^i(x) \right].$$

We would like to focus on an urban equilibrium that is described by Figure 2.6 which is, in fact, an "extension" of that displayed in Figure 1.1 for positive relocation costs.

Let us now impose the conditions on the land market that guarantee that the equilibrium described in Figure 2.6 exists, i.e.,

$$R(x) = \begin{cases} \Psi_L^m(x, \overline{I}_U^m, \overline{I}_L^m) & \text{for all} \quad x < x^{mi} \\ \Psi_L^i(x, I_U^i(x), I_L^i(x)) & \\ = \Psi_U^i(x, I_U^i(x), I_L^i(x)) = \Psi^i(x) & \text{for all} \quad x^{mi} \leq x \leq x^{im} \\ \Psi_U^m(x, \overline{I}_U^m, \overline{I}_L^m) & \text{for all} \quad x^{im} < x < N \\ R_A = 0 & \text{for all} \quad x \geq N \end{cases}.$$

4.2. Steady-State Equilibrium

Denote by ϕ_U^i the fraction of immobile unemployed workers in the city. Then, we have:

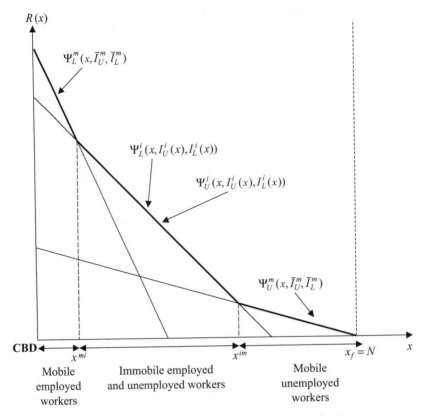

Figure 2.6. The urban-land-use equilibrium with positive relocation costs.

Definition 2.2. *A steady-state equilibrium with positive relocation costs, fixed housing consumption, fixed search intensity and exogenous wages, is a 10-tuple* $(\overline{I}_U^{m*}, \overline{I}_L^{m*}, I_U^{i*}(x), I_L^{i*}(x), x^{mi*}, x^{mi*}, u^*, \phi_u^{i*}, \theta^*, R^*(x))$ *such that:*

$$\overline{I}_L^m = I_L^i(x^{mi}) \tag{2.52}$$

$$\overline{I}_U^m = I_U^i(x^{im}) \tag{2.53}$$

$$I_L^i(x^{im}) = \overline{I}_L^m - C \tag{2.54}$$

$$I_U^i(x^{mi}) = \overline{I}_U^m - C \tag{2.55}$$

$$x^{mi}\delta = s\,\theta q(\theta)(N - x^{im}) \tag{2.56}$$

$$\Psi_L^m(x^{mi}, \overline{I}_U^m, \overline{I}_L^m) = \Psi_L^i(x^{mi}, I_U^i(x^{mi}), I_L^i(x^{mi})) \tag{2.57}$$

$$\Psi_U^m(x^{im}, \overline{I}_U^m, \overline{I}_L^m) = \Psi_U^i(x^{im}, I_U^i(x^{im}), I_L^i(x^{im})) \tag{2.58}$$

$$\Psi_U^m(N, \bar{I}_U^m, \bar{I}_L^m) = 0 \tag{2.59}$$

$$Nu = N\phi_u^i(x^{im} - x^{mi}) + N - x^{im} \tag{2.60}$$

$R^*(x)$

$$= \max\left\{\Psi_L^m(x, \bar{I}_U^m, \bar{I}_L^m), \Psi^i(x), \Psi_U^m(x, \bar{I}_U^m, \bar{I}_L^m), 0\right\} \quad at\ each\ x \in (0, N] \tag{2.61}$$

$$\delta N(1 - u) - s\theta q(\theta)Nu = 0 \tag{2.62}$$

$$\frac{c}{q(\theta)} = \frac{y - w_L}{r + \delta}. \tag{2.63}$$

Equations (2.52) and (2.53) guarantee the continuity of the intertemporal utility of workers with the same employment status (see Figure 2.7). Equations (2.54) and (2.55) impose that, upon a transition (from employment to unemployment or from unemployment to employment), immobile workers do not want to relocate. Indeed, it can be shown that the minimum of the employed workers' expected utilities in the "immobile workers" zone $\mathcal{I}$ is reached at x^{im} while, for unemployed workers, it is attained at x^{mi}. As a result, these two conditions guarantee that immobile workers will never relocate upon a shock. Figure 2.7 displays the different expected utilities in urban space $x \in [0, N]$.

Equation (2.56) is a steady-state condition on mobile workers which states that, upon a δ-shock (i.e., technological shock), mobile employed workers who reside in the mobile employment area $\mathcal{E}^m = [0, x^{mi}]$ relocate to the mobile unemployment area $\mathcal{U}^m = [x^{im}, N]$, while there is a corresponding flow of mobile unemployed workers accessing employment and relocating to the mobile employment area. Equations (2.57) and (2.58) guarantee that the bid-rent is continuous everywhere in the city and, as usual, (2.59) states that the bid-rent at the city fringe is equal to the agricultural land rent, which is normalized to zero. Equation (2.60) is the population constraint. Indeed, in the mobile unemployment zone $\mathcal{U}^m$, the length of which is $N - x^{im}$, all workers are unemployed whereas, among the immobile workers, there are only ϕ_u^i who are unemployed. Equation (2.61) guarantees that each location is occupied by the highest bidder. Finally, the last two equations close the model with the labor market analysis. As in the benchmark model, equation (2.62) states that the flows into and out of unemployment must be equal in steady-state while equation (2.62) corresponds to the free-entry condition of firms, $I_V = 0$. Since wages are exogenous when a firm enters the labor market, hiring an unemployed worker from the immobile area $\mathcal{I}$

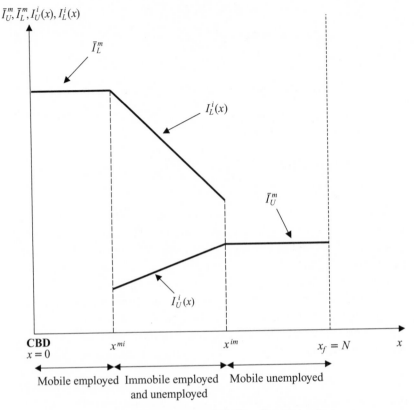

Figure 2.7. Expected utilities of all workers in the city.

or the mobile unemployed area $\mathcal{U}^m$ leads to the same expected profit and thus, the standard benchmark condition (2.62) applies here.[6]

We have the following result:

Proposition 2.4. *Assume*

$$\tau > s\tau + \frac{s\,\theta^* q(\theta^*)\,(1-s)\,\tau}{r+\delta+s\,\theta^* q(\theta^*)} + \frac{2r\,C^2\,[r+\delta+s\,\theta^* q(\theta^*)]}{(1-s)\,\tau} > s\tau.$$

$$(2.64)$$

---

[6] The analysis with endogenous wages is straightforward. Since mobile and immobile workers do not have the same outside option, there will be two wages in equilibrium and thus, the free-entry will be modified.

Then, the steady-state equilibrium is given by:

$$r\,\overline{I}_U^m = \left[\frac{(r+\delta)(w_U - s\tau N) + s\,\theta^*q(\theta^*)(w_L + \tau N)}{r + \delta + s\,\theta^*q(\theta^*)}\right]$$
$$- \frac{(r + 2\delta)\,s\,\theta^*q(\theta^*)}{r + \delta + s\,\theta^*q(\theta^*)}\,C \tag{2.65}$$

$$\overline{I}_L^m = \overline{I}_U^m + \frac{(w_L - w_U)}{r + \delta + s\,\theta^*q(\theta^*)} - \frac{(1-s)\tau\left[\delta\,x^{mi} + s\,\theta^*q(\theta^*)\,x^{im}\right]}{[r + \delta + s\,\theta^*q(\theta^*)]\,[\delta + s\,\theta^*q(\theta^*)]}$$
$$- \left[\frac{\delta - s\,\theta^*q(\theta^*)}{\delta + s\,\theta^*q(\theta^*)}\right]C \tag{2.66}$$

$$I_U(x) = \overline{I}_U^m + \frac{\left(x - x^{im}\right)}{\left(x^{im} - x^{mi}\right)}\,C \tag{2.67}$$

$$I_L(x) = \overline{I}_L^m + \frac{\left(x^{mi} - x\right)}{\left(x^{im} - x^{mi}\right)}\,C \tag{2.68}$$

$$x^{mi*} = \frac{s\,\theta^*q(\theta^*)N}{\delta\,[\delta + s\,\theta^*q(\theta^*)]} - \frac{2\,[r + \delta + s\,\theta^*q(\theta^*)]\,s\,\theta^*q(\theta^{**})}{(1-s)\,\tau\,[\delta + s\,\theta^*q(\theta^*)]}\,C \tag{2.69}$$

$$x^{im*} = \frac{s\,\theta^*q(\theta^*)N}{\delta\,[\delta + s\,\theta^*q(\theta^*)]} + \frac{2\delta\,[r + \delta + s\,\theta^*q(\theta^{**})]}{(1-s)\,\tau\,[\delta + s\,\theta^*q(\theta^*)]}\,C \tag{2.70}$$

$$u^* = \frac{\delta}{\delta + s\,\theta^*q(\theta^*)} \tag{2.71}$$

$$\phi_u^{i*} = \frac{x^{im} - N(1 - u^*)}{N(x^{im} - x^{mi})} \tag{2.72}$$

$$q(\theta^*) = \frac{c\,(r + \delta)}{y - w_L}. \tag{2.73}$$

The following comments are in order. First, condition (2.64) guarantees that the bid-rents of mobile employed workers are steeper than those of immobile workers (employed or unemployed) who, in turn, have a steeper bid-rent than mobile unemployed workers. As a result, the urban configuration looks like the one described in Figure 2.6. Second, the different expected utilities of workers are given by (2.65), (2.66), (2.67), and (2.68). It can be seen that mobile unemployed workers' expected utility $\overline{I}_U^m$ is decreasing in C, i.e., the cost of relocating in the city. This is not surprising since a mobile worker always relocates upon a shock. The effect of C on the other expected utilities is more complex because of the indirect effect on land rent. Indeed, when C increases, it is more costly for mobile workers to relocate and this translates into the land market since they bid more for land. Let us now focus on the size of the different areas $\mathcal{E}^m$, $\mathcal{U}^m$ and $\mathcal{I}$, which is given by (2.69) and (2.70). Subtracting (2.69) from (2.70), we obtain:

$$x^{im} - x^{mi} = \frac{2C \left[r + \delta + s \, \theta^* q(\theta^*) \right]}{(1 - s) \, \tau}. \qquad (2.74)$$

This is a key equation determining the size of the middle area (i.e., the immobile workers' area I) and thus, the cost imposed by the full-mobility assumption made in the benchmark model. The size of the immobile area $\mathcal{I}$ increases by C (indeed x^{mi} decreases by C while x^{im} increases by C; see (2.69) and (2.70)), and by all turnover rates (i.e., δ and $s \, \theta^* q(\theta^*)$), and decreases by $(1 - s) \, \tau$, i.e., the difference in commuting costs between employed and unemployed workers. Indeed, to remain immobile, fast transitions in the labor market (so that waiting for another employment transition to remain in the same location is the best strategy) or low gains from mobility in terms of commuting costs must be expected.

Finally, the last three equations (2.71), (2.72), and (2.73) are directly derived from (2.62), (2.60), and (2.63) using the values of x^{mi*} and x^{im*}.

To conclude this part, it can be observed that relocation costs indeed change the derivation of the equilibrium. This adds an area in the middle of the city in which employed and unemployed workers are immobile, pay the same rent, and continuously overlap. When relocation costs disappear (i.e., $C \to 0$), we have returned to the benchmark model. This section has thus generalized the frictionless land market.

5. Very High Mobility Costs

The previous model was a first step towards understanding the process of incorporating mobility costs in an urban search model. However, the model was quite cumbersome, especially the labor market analysis. We now propose a simpler spatial search-matching model in which mobility costs are so high that it is too costly for workers to relocate when a change in their employment status occurs.

5.1. The Model

We once more consider the benchmark model developed in Chapter 1 (Section 2) where search intensity was exogenous and denoted by s. The *instantaneous* (indirect) utilities of an employed and unemployed worker located at a distance x from the CBD are still given by:

$$W_L(x) = w_L - \tau x - R(x) \tag{2.75}$$

$$W_U(x) = w_U - s \tau x - R(x). \tag{2.76}$$

The steady-state unemployment rate is equal to:

$$u = \frac{\delta}{\delta + s \theta q(\theta)}, \tag{2.77}$$

where $\theta = v M/ (\bar{s} u N)$. As is well-known in a Poisson process, the steady-state unemployment rate $u = U/N$ and employment rate $1 - u$ correspond to the respective fractions of time a worker remains unemployed and employed over his/her infinite lifetime. Thus, we are able to calculate the expected utility of workers. For this purpose, we assume perfect capital markets with a zero interest rate,[7] i.e., $r \to 0$. With perfect capital markets, workers are able to smooth their disposable income over time so that at any moment in time, the disposable income of a worker is equal to his/her average net income over the job cycle. The expected utility of a worker residing in x is given by:

$$E\,W(x) = (1 - u)\,W_L(x) + u\,W_U(x)$$
$$= w_L - \tau x - R(x) - \frac{\delta\,[w_L - w_U - (1 - s)\,\tau x]}{\delta + s \theta q(\theta)}. \tag{2.78}$$

Observe that because workers are able to smooth their income over time, a worker's residential location remains fixed as he/she enters and leaves unemployment. In other words, the worker does not relocate after a change in his/her employment status.

5.2. Labor-Market Equilibrium

Let us first determine the expected utility of firms when $r \to 0$. The instantaneous profit function for a firm hiring a worker is $\Pi_F(x) = y - w_L(x)$ (we will show below that w is indeed a function of x) whereas for a firm with a vacant job, it is: $\Pi_V = -c$. As stated, there is a Poisson process on the firm's side in which $q(\theta)$ is the job-contact rate and δ is the exogenous

---

[7] When there is a zero interest rate, workers have no intrinsic preference for the present so they only care about the fraction of time they spend employed and unemployed. Therefore, the expected utilities are not state-dependent.

job-separation rate. In steady-state, flows into and out of vacancies are equal so that:

$$v \, M q(\theta) = \delta \, (1 - v) \, M. \qquad (2.79)$$

Observe that $\delta \, (1 - v) \, M = \delta \, (1 - u) \, N$ and thus, (2.79) can also be written as:

$$v \, M q(\theta) = \delta \, (1 - u) \, N. \qquad (2.80)$$

Therefore, solving (2.79) gives the value of the vacancy rate v as:[8]

$$v = \frac{\delta}{\delta + q(\theta)}. \qquad (2.81)$$

With zero interest rate, the expected profit of a firm $E \Pi$ is therefore equal to:

$$
\begin{aligned}
E \Pi(x) &= (1 - v) \, \Pi_F(x) + v \, \Pi_V \\
&= y - w_L(x) - \frac{\delta \, [y - w_L(x) + c]}{\delta + q(\theta)}. \qquad (2.82)
\end{aligned}
$$

Let us now determine the wage using the standard Nash bargaining rule. When a worker located at x accepts a job offer, he/she will get an expected utility of $E \, W(x)$ defined by (2.78) while if the negotiation fails, the worker obtains (2.76). Indeed, since all firms are identical, all job offers will be the same and thus, if a worker refuses a job offer today, he/she will refuse all job offers in the future. As a result, the worker will get the same utility of being unemployed all his/her life, which is equal to $W_U(x)$ since $r \to 0$. Thus, the surplus for workers located at x of accepting a job offer is equal to:

$$
\begin{aligned}
S_W &= E \, W(x) - W_U(x) = \left[\frac{s \, \theta q(\theta)}{\delta + s \, \theta q(\theta)} \right] [w_L - w_U - (1 - s) \, \tau \, x] \\
&= (1 - u) \, [W_L(x) - W_U(x)] \, .
\end{aligned}
$$

The value of the surplus is easy to understand since it means that, by accepting a job offer, the gain is the instantaneous surplus of being employed, i.e., $W_L(x) - W_U(x)$, during the fraction of time the worker is employed,

---

[8] Solving (2.80) would lead to

$$v = \frac{\delta}{q(\theta)} \frac{N}{M} (1 - u)$$

which using (2.77) gives:

$$\theta = \frac{v \, M}{s \, u \, N}.$$

i.e., $1 - u$. Similarly, for firms, if the negotiation fails, the firm will forever obtain Π_V and thus, the surplus is equal to:

$$S_F = E\Pi - \Pi_V = \left[\frac{q(\theta)}{\delta + q(\theta)}\right](y - w_L + c)$$
$$= (1 - v)\left[\Pi_F - \Pi_V\right].$$

For firms, the surplus of a match is the instantaneous profit difference of having a filled job during the fraction of time the job will be filled. The total surplus is thus $S = S_W + S_F$, and it is shared according to a bargaining between the worker and the firm. We obtain the following wage:

$$w_L^*(x) = (1 - \beta)\left[w_U + (1 - s)\tau x\right] + \beta(y + c). \tag{2.83}$$

This wage is very similar to the one calculated under zero relocation costs (see (1.34) in Chapter 1). There are two main differences, however. First, the labor market tightness θ, which had a positive impact on wages in (1.34), has no impact now. Indeed, when $r \to 0$ and workers are not mobile, the surplus of each agent is determined by the *instantaneous* utility difference and not the *intertemporal* one. So, when workers and firms bargain over the wage, they do not take into account the future propects such as the labor market tightness θ. Second, the spatial aspect of the wage is here captured by $(1 - s)\tau x$ and not by $(1 - s)\tau L$. Indeed, $(1 - s)\tau x$ is what firms must pay to induce workers to accept the job offer since they must exactly compensate the transportation cost difference between employed and unemployed workers in each location x. On the contrary, when workers are perfectly mobile, then it suffices to compensate the employed worker who is the furthest away from jobs.

That wages increase with distance to jobs is a well-established empirical fact. For example, using British data (the Labour Force Survey for 1993–2001 and the British Household Panel Survey for 1991–2000), Manning (2003) shows that an additional hour of commuting each day is, on average, associated with an increase in wages of 27 log-points. This applies even more for highly educated workers since those with more education and in higher-status occupations are more likely to have both high wages and a long commute.[9] These results are consistent with those found in the United States. For instance, Madden (1985) uses the Panel Study of Income Dynamics (PSID) to investigate how wages vary with distance to the CBD. She finds that for all workers who changed jobs, there is a positive relationship between wage change and change in commuting distance. Zax (1991), who

---

[9] For additional evidence, see also Van Ommeren and Rietveld (2007).

uses data from a single company and regresses wages on commutes, also finds a positive relationship.

As in the benchmark model, firms enter the labor market up to the point where their expected profit is equal to zero. When they enter the labor market, they do not know which wage they will pay, so ex-ante they expect to pay the average wage, $\overline{w}_L(x)$, since workers are uniformly distributed in the city. The free-entry condition is thus $E\,\Pi(N/2) = 0$, which leads to:

$$y - w_U = \left[\frac{\delta}{q(\theta^*)} + \beta\right] \frac{c}{(1 - \beta)} + (1 - s)\,\tau\,\frac{N}{2}. \qquad (2.84)$$

This is the equilibrium condition that determines job creation θ^*.

5.3. Urban-Land-Use Equilibrium

Let us now solve the urban-land-use equilibrium. For this purpose, we present the analysis of bid-rent with a land/housing market. Let us describe the timing of the model. Assume that there is an initial situation when workers pick locations without knowing their initial employment status. They will not change locations afterwards. Then, given zero discounting and income smoothing, people bid for rents given that they anticipate the time they will spend in each employment state. Thus, the whole structure of the analysis is: (*i*) initial period location determination; (*ii*) ensuing labor market shocks resulting in unemployment, wage, etc. In equilibrium, because of the competition in the land/housing market, all ex-ante identical workers will obtain the same expected utility, $E\,W$. It should be clear that the presence of high relocation costs means that there is no bidding after the initial location decisions. The bid-rent function of a worker residing at a distance x from the CBD can be written as:

$$\Psi(x, E\,W) = w_U + \beta\,(1 - u)\,[y - w_U + c - (1 - s)\,\tau x] - s\,\tau x - E\,W, \qquad (2.85)$$

which is decreasing and linear in x. This shows that the role of land rent is to compensate workers for commuting costs and for the wage, which depends on the time they spend in each state (employment versus unemployment). We have the following definition:

Definition 2.3. *An urban-land-use equilibrium with high relocation costs, fixed housing consumption and fixed search intensity is a 2-tuple $(E\,W^*, R^*(x))$ such that:*

$$\Psi(N, E\,W^*) = R_A = 0 \qquad (2.86)$$

$$R^*(x) = \max\left\{\Psi(x, E\, W^*), 0\right\} \quad \text{at each } x \in (0, N].$$ (2.87)

Solving these equations leads to:

$$E\, W^* = w_U + \beta \left[\frac{s\,\theta q(\theta)}{\delta + s\,\theta q(\theta)}\right] [y - w_U + c - (1 - s)\,\tau N] - s\,\tau N$$ (2.88)

$$R^*(x) = \begin{cases} \tau\,(N - x)\left[s + (1 - s)\,\beta\left(\frac{s\theta q(\theta)}{\delta + s\theta q(\theta)}\right)\right] & \text{for } x \le N \\ 0 & \text{for } x > N \end{cases}.$$ (2.89)

5.4. Interaction Between Land and Labor Markets

Let us study the general equilibrium effects on the impact of the different parameters on expected utility $E\, W^*$ and land rent $R^*(x)$. It is the labor market tightness θ that makes the link between land and labor markets. We obtain:

$$\frac{\partial E\, W^*}{\partial \delta} < 0 \quad \frac{\partial E\, W^*}{\partial y} > 0 \quad \frac{\partial E\, W^*}{\partial w_U} \gtrless 0 \quad \frac{\partial E\, W^*}{\partial c} \gtrless 0 \quad \frac{\partial E\, W^*}{\partial \beta} \gtrless 0$$

$$\frac{\partial E\, W^*}{\partial \tau} \gtrless 0 \quad \frac{\partial E\, W^*}{\partial N} \gtrless 0 \quad \frac{\partial E\, W^*}{\partial s} \gtrless 0.$$

Observe first that by looking at (2.88), it can be seen that the effect of δ on $E\, W^*$ is only indirect via θ and is negative since higher δ increases the fraction of time spent unemployed, which reduces the expected utility. For all other parameters, there are always two effects, a direct one and an indirect one via θ. Concerning productivity y, the effect on $E\, W^*$ is always positive because it directly increases the wage and thus, the expected utility, but it also increases job creation and the time spent employed. For w_U and c, the effects are ambiguous because they have a direct positive effect, but an indirect negative effect via θ since they increase wages and reduce job creation. Concerning the spatial variables τ and N, increasing them always reduces expected utility $E\, W^*$ because it both reduces job creation and increases competition in the land market. Finally, the ambiguity of β and s stems from the same types of direct and indirect effects via θ.

We also have the following results

$$\frac{\partial R^*(x)}{\partial y} > 0 \quad \frac{\partial R^*(x)}{\partial w_U} < 0 \quad \frac{\partial R^*(x)}{\partial c} < 0 \quad \frac{\partial R^*(x)}{\partial \delta} < 0 \quad \frac{\partial R^*(x)}{\partial \beta} \gtrless 0$$

$$\frac{\partial R^*(x)}{\partial \tau} \gtrless 0 \quad \frac{\partial R^*(x)}{\partial N} \gtrless 0 \quad \frac{\partial R^*(x)}{\partial s} \gtrless 0.$$

First, parameters y, δ, c, and w_U only indirectly affect equilibrium land rent $R^*(x)$ through θ^*. For example, when job matches are more productive, y increases and thus, firms create more jobs, which leads to an increase of θ. This implies that there is more competition in the land market and thus, land prices are augmented in all locations $x \in [0, N]$. The same reasoning applies for δ, c, and w_U, even though the effects are negative. It is particularly interesting to see that an increase in unemployment benefits, w_U, leads to lower land prices. This does not seem to be contradicted by what we observe when we compare countries like the U.K. which have low unemployment benefits, and other European countries (such as France, Germany, or Spain) where unemployment benefits are higher. It is indeed well-known that London is a much more expensive place to live in than Paris, Berlin, or Madrid. Second, the bargaining power of workers, β, acts both directly and indirectly on $R^*(x)$. Indeed, it is easily checked that

$$sign \frac{\partial R^*(x)}{\partial \beta} = sign \left[\underbrace{\frac{s\,\theta q(\theta)}{\delta + s\,\theta q(\theta)}}_{+} + \beta \underbrace{\frac{\partial (1-u)}{\partial \theta}}_{+} \underbrace{\frac{\partial \theta}{\partial \beta}}_{-} \right].$$

There is a direct positive effect since a higher β implies higher wages and thus, more capacity to pay for land. There is also an indirect negative effect since a higher β, which increases the wage, also reduces the job creation rate θ and thus, the time workers spend employed. This, in turn, reduces their bid-rent. The net effect is ambiguous. Finally, the effects of commuting costs τ and city size N on $R^*(x)$ are ambiguous. Indeed, when τ or N increases, there is a direct positive effect on land rents since access to jobs becomes more important, but there is also an indirect negative effect on land rents via θ^* since wages increase, firms create less jobs, and workers spend more time unemployed and bid less for land.

5.5. Welfare and Efficiency

As in the standard search-matching literature, market failures are caused by search externalities in the present model. We would now like to see whether the land market *with* high relocation costs creates additional market failures as compared to that *without* relocation costs (Chapter 1, Section 2). Thus, let us study the welfare of this economy. As in Chapter 1, the social welfare function for $r \to 0$ is given by:

$$\mathcal{W} = \int_0^N (1-u)(y - \tau x)\,dx + \int_0^N u(w_U - s\tau x)\,dx - v\,c$$

$$= (1-u)\left[yN - \tau \frac{N^2}{2} \right] + u\left[w_U N - s\tau \frac{N^2}{2} \right] - \theta\,s\,u\,N c.$$

Indeed, each worker located at $x \in [0, N]$, spends $1 - u$ fractions of his/her lifetime employed, where he/she produces y while spending τx on commuting costs, and u fraction of his/her lifetime unemployed, where he/she earns w_U and spends $s \tau x$ on commuting costs. Firms (whose total mass is 1) spend $v = \theta s u N$ fractions of their lifetime with vacant jobs, which costs them c. The planner solves $\max_{\theta, u} W$, subject to the constraint (2.77). We have:

Proposition 2.5. *If*

$$\beta = \frac{[\delta + s\theta q(\theta)] \, \eta(\theta)}{\delta + q(\theta) [1 - \eta(\theta) (1 - s\theta)]} \qquad (2.90)$$

holds, then the private and social outcomes coincide.

In Chapter 1, Section 2, we established that the spatial search equilibrium with zero relocation costs was socially efficient if and only if the matching function was homogenous of degree one (like here) and the worker's share of surplus β was equal to $\eta(\theta)$, i.e., the elasticity of the matching function with respect to unemployment (see (1.44)). This was referred to as the Hosios-Pissarides condition since the same condition holds in the non-spatial model. Here, this condition does not hold and, in fact, (2.90) can be considered as a *spatial* Hosios-Pissarides condition since high relocation costs imply new inefficiencies.[10] As a result, the standard Hosios-Pissarides condition does not hold here because of high relocation costs, which means that workers are stuck in their residential location, creating additional frictions and externalities.

Observe that when $s = 1$, i.e., unemployed workers commute to the CBD every day like employed workers, then the wage does not depend on any spatial element (see (2.83)) and it is equivalent to a static non-spatial wage. However, an inspection of (2.90) indicates that the non-spatial Hosios-Pissarides condition, $\beta = \eta(\theta)$, does not hold. This is because, wages being pure transfers, they do not affect the welfare function while the spatial frictions (due to workers' high mobility costs) still create inefficiencies.

5.6. Comparison with the Model with Zero Relocation Costs

From a technical point of view, the model with high relocation costs enormously simplifies the urban-land-use equilibrium because we end up with

---

[10] In Section 2 of this chapter, we also established a more general Hosios-Pissarides condition (see (2.20)). However, the inefficiencies were caused by training costs and not by space, like in the present model.

fewer categories of workers. For example, with zero relocation costs, any urban model aiming at explaining the labor market outcomes of black and white workers will have to deal with at least four types of workers; employed and unemployed black and white workers. This is very cumbersome to analyze. In Chapter 7, where we deal with black and white workers, we use the model with high relocation costs since only two types of workers are taken into account blacks and whites. If one wants to further study the labor market of black and white workers with two employment centers (the CBD and the SBD), we have eight types of workers in the zero relocation cost case while only four in that with high relocation costs. The calculation of the equilibrium values in the urban-land-use analysis is not analytically possible in the first category while in the second category, it will not pose any problems (see Chapter 8). This means that this model can really be used for further applications on any issues in an urban labor market with these heterogeneous agents: blacks and whites, men and women, high and low incomes, etc.

From an empirical perspective, there is plenty of empirical evidence showing that mobility and relocation costs are important for low-skill workers, especially in the United States. In particular, the spatial mismatch literature (Chapters 7 and 8) stipulates that, because low-skill black workers have high mobility costs, they experience high unemployment rates. In other words, they cannot (or do not) want to move to areas where there are jobs. There is a great deal of empirical evidence showing that black low-skill workers indeed have high relocation costs.

6. Wage Posting

So far, we have followed the standard search-matching literature (Pissarides, 2000) by assuming that the wage was determined by a bilateral bargaining between the firm and the worker. However, there is another strand of the literature (Mortensen, 2000, 2003) where firms post wages instead of bargaining with workers. This is a quite realistic feature in the real world. The aim of this section is to introduce a wage posting model in an urban land market. For this reason, we return to the assumption of zero relocation costs.

6.1. Ex-Ante Identical Workers

We consider exactly the same model as in the benchmark model of Chapter 1, Section 2. The only difference is that there is assumed to exist a wage cumulative distribution function $G(w_L)$ that is known by everybody, i.e., workers know $G(w_L)$, but do not know which firm offers which wage. The aim of this model is to endogenously determine this wage distribution.

6.1.1. Urban-Land-Use Equilibrium. As in the benchmark model, the definition of the urban land-use equilibrium is given by Definition 1.2 and the equilibrium utilities and land rents W_L^*, W_U^*, and $R^*(x)$ are determined by (1.14), (1.15) and (1.16), respectively.

6.1.2. Labor Market Equilibrium. Firms post wages. To focus on this aspect, we here follow the wage posting literature (Mortensen, 2000, 2003) by assuming that the total mass of firms is fixed to 1, so that there is no free-entry condition and thus, no endogenous job creation, and the contact rates for both firms and workers are exogenous and not determined using a matching function. Naturally, as shown by Mortensen (2003) and Gaumont, Schindler, and Wright (2006), including these two aspects in a wage posting model is straightforward and does not generally change the results.

The Bellman equation for employed workers is given by:

$$r I_L(w_L) = w_L - (1 - s)\,\tau\, N (1 - u) - s\tau\, N - \delta\,[I_L(w_L) - I_U].$$
(2.91)

We must determine the reservation wage rule, i.e., the wage below which workers refuse to accept to a job offer. It is given by:

$$I_L(w_L^r) - I_U = 0,$$

which, using (2.91), is given by:

$$w_L^r = r I_U + (1 - s)\,\tau\, N (1 - u) + s\tau\, N.$$
(2.92)

The Bellman equation for unemployed workers is given by:

$$r I_U = w_U - s\tau\, N + s\,a \int_{w_L^r}^{+\infty} [I_L(w_L) - I_U]\, dG(w_L),$$
(2.93)

where a is the *exogenous* job contact rate. Using (2.93), the wage reservation rule (2.92) can be written as:

$$w_L^r = w_U + (1 - s)\,\tau\, N (1 - u) + \frac{s\,a}{r + \delta} \int_{w_L^r}^{+\infty} \left(w_L - w_L^r\right) dG(w_L).$$
(2.94)

As in the benchmark model, we determine the dynamics of the unemployment level as follows:

$$\dot{u} = \delta(1 - u_t) - s\, a\, u_t \left[1 - G(w_L^r)\right].$$

The main difference as compared to the benchmark model is that a replaces
$\theta q(\theta)$ and there is an additional term $G(w_L^r)$. Indeed, at each time t, $1 - u_t$
employed workers lose their jobs at the rate δ while u_t unemployed workers
find a job at the rate $s\, a\, u_t[1 - G(w_L^r)]$, which is the product of the contact
rate $s\, a$ and the acceptation rate $1 - G(w_L^r)$ (workers only accept job offers
with wages at least equal to their reservation wage w_L^r). In steady-state,
$\dot{u} = 0$ and thus, the unemployment rate u^* is given by:

$$u^* = \frac{\delta}{\delta + s\, a\left[1 - G(w_L^r)\right]}. \tag{2.95}$$

Denote by $l(w_L)$ the employment level of a firm that offers a wage w_L to
its employees. We have:

$$l(w_L) = \frac{s\, a\, N}{\delta + s\, a_U\left[1 - G(w_L^r)\right]}. \tag{2.96}$$

Equation (2.96) specifies the steady-state number of workers available to a
firm offering any particular wage, conditional on the wages offered by other
firms, represented by the distribution $G(.)$, and the workers' reservation
wage, w_L^r.

Firms post wages. They are interested in maximizing steady-state profit
and will hire as many workers as are willing to accept. The profit of a firm
that sets a wage w_L is given by:

$$\Pi = \max_{w_L} (y - w_L)\, l(w_L), \tag{2.97}$$

where y is the productivity of a worker.

Proposition 2.6 (Diamond's Paradox). *At the Nash equilibrium, all firms set
the following wage:*

$$w_L^* = w_L^r$$

and thus, $G(w_L)$ is degenerated to one point $w_L^* = w_L^r$.

This result is due to the fact that $l(w_L)$ is independent of w_L. This is the
so-called Diamond's paradox (Diamond, 1971). The intuition is as follows.

In equilibrium, no firm will post anything but the workers' reservation wage, as a firm posting a higher wage $w_L > w_L^r$ could reduce w_L to w_L^r and make more profit per worker without changing the set of workers who accept.

In equilibrium, since all firms set $w_L^* = w_L^r$, and since $1 - G(w_L^r) = 1$, we have:

$$w_L^* = w_L^r = w_U + (1 - s)\,\tau\,N\left(\frac{s\,a}{\delta + s\,a}\right). \tag{2.98}$$

This is the equilibrium wage obtained by all workers. The unemployment benefit, w_U, is the only labor market part of the wage. It increases with w_L^* because $r\,I_U$ increases and thus, workers are more demanding and increase their reservation wage. This is what is obtained in the non-spatial search model. The spatial part of the wage, $(1 - s)\,\tau\,N\left(\frac{s\,a}{\delta + s\,a}\right)$, is what firms must give to workers to compensate for the spatial cost difference between employed and unemployed workers. This spatial compensation is calculated at $x = L = N\left(\frac{s\,a}{\delta + s\,a}\right)$, i.e., when the land rent of employed and unemployed workers is the same. In the benchmark model of chapter 1 with wage bargaining, we also obtained this spatial compensation $(1 - s)\,\tau\,L$ (see (1.34)).

Furthermore, if a increases or δ decreases, then wages increase because the spatial cost difference between employed and unemployed workers increases since employed workers are, on average, further away from jobs. Observe that

$$\frac{\partial w_L^*}{\partial s} \gtreqless 0 \Leftrightarrow s \lesseqgtr \frac{1}{2}.$$

Indeed, there are two opposite effects of an increase of s on the wage, w_L^*. On the one hand, increasing s reduces the spatial compensation since the spatial cost difference between employed and unemployed workers is smaller. On the other hand, it increases the chances of obtaining a job and thus, the employment rate, which then increases the distance to jobs for the employed worker located at $x = L$. This raises the spatial compensation and thus, the wage.

With this wage, we can determine the steady-state equilibrium. We obtain:

Proposition 2.7. *There is a unique steady-state equilibrium* $(w_L^{r*}, w_L^*, F^*(w_L), \Pi^*, u^*, W_U^*, W_L^*, R^*(x))$, *where* $w_L^{r*} = w_L^*$ *is defined by (2.98),*

$F^*(w_L)$ is degenerated to one point w_L^*,

$$\Pi^* = \frac{s\,a\,N}{\delta + s\,a}\left[y - w_U - (1-s)\,\tau\,N\left(\frac{s\,a}{\delta + s\,a}\right)\right] \qquad (2.99)$$

$$u^* = \frac{\delta}{\delta + s\,a} \qquad (2.100)$$

$$W_U^* = w_U - s\tau\,N = W_L^* \qquad (2.101)$$

and

$$R^*(x) = \begin{cases} \tau\,(s\,N - x) + (1-s)\,\tau\,N\left(\frac{s\,a}{\delta + s\,a}\right) & \text{for } 0 \le x \le L \\ s\tau\,(N - x) & \text{for } L < x \le N. \\ 0 & \text{for } x > N \end{cases} \qquad (2.102)$$

Observe that all workers participate in the labor market because all workers search for a job and all accept a job if getting an offer. Moreover, not surprisingly, $W_U^* = W_L^*$ and $I_L^* = I_U^*$.

6.1.3. Interaction between Land and Labor Markets. Let us derive some comparative statics results. First, by differentiating (2.99), we have:

$$\Pi^* = \Pi\left(\underset{+}{y}, \underset{-}{w_U}, \underset{+}{a}, \underset{-}{\delta}, \underset{?}{s}, \underset{-}{\tau}, \underset{-}{N}\right).$$

When y, the productivity of workers, increases, firms' profits increase. The effects of w_U, s, τ, and N only go through the wage w_L^* and thus, when they increase w_L^*, firms' profits are reduced. The ambiguity of s stems from the ambiguity of the effect of s on w_L^* mentioned above. On the other hand, a and δ affect both employment in the firm $l(w_L)$ and the wage w_L^*. As a result, when a_U increases or δ decreases, then there is an increase in both employment $l(w_L)$ and wage w_L^* and thus, the effect on profits is ambiguous. However, if productivity y is sufficiently high, then the first effect dominates the second and the net impact is positive. Second, by differentiating the equilibrium land rent (2.102), for employed workers, i.e., for $x \in [0, L]$, we obtain:

$$R_L^* = R\left(\underset{-}{x}, \underset{+}{a}, \underset{-}{\delta}, \underset{+}{s}, \underset{+}{\tau}, \underset{+}{N}\right).$$

These results are mainly due to effects on the competition on the land market. Indeed, when a increases or δ decreases, the employment level $N(1 - u^*)$ in the economy increases, which means that employed workers are, on average, further away from jobs. Access to the job center becomes more valuable, which increases competition in the land market since

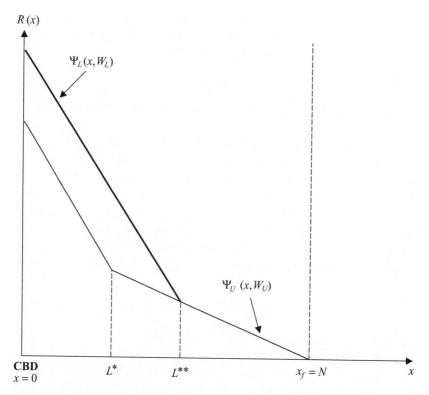

R(x)

$\Psi_L(x, W_L)$

$\Psi_U(x, W_U)$

CBD
x = 0   L*   L** $x_f = N$ x

Figure 2.8. Impact of an increase in a_U or a decrease in δ on land-rent equilibrium.

employed workers bear higher commuting costs than unemployed workers. As a result, housing prices increase everywhere in the city between $x = 0$ and $x = L$, but not in the unemployment area, i.e., when $x \in [L, N]$. This effect is illustrated in Figure 2.8. Before the shock (i.e., an increase in a or a decrease in δ), land rent is given by the normal line while after the shock, it is described by the thick line. The equilibrium values with one and two stars correspond to before and after the shock, respectively. Finally, an increase in τ, s, or N increases competition in the land market because it becomes more costly to travel to the job center and therefore, there is an increase in housing prices.

6.2. Ex-Ante Heterogenous Workers

We now assume there to be two types of individuals in the economy who differ according to the value imputed to leisure. This assumption ensures that at most two wages can be offered in equilibrium. Individuals are denoted by superscript $i = 0, 1$. Because the first individual is assumed to value leisure more than the second individual, we have:

$$s^1 > s^0, \qquad (2.103)$$

that is individuals of type 1 search more actively than those of type 0.

6.2.1. *Urban-Land-Use Equilibrium.* In equilibrium, there will be four types of workers: unemployed workers of types 0 and 1, with search intensities s^0 and s^1, and employed workers earning a wage w_L^1 and w_L^0, with $w_L^1 > w_L^0$ (this will be shown below). As we will also see below, in equilibrium, workers of both types 0 and 1 can earn the high wage, w_L^1, while only workers of type 0 can earn the low wage, w_L^0. As a result, for employed workers, types do not always correspond to wages. We now relax the assumption of housing consumption equal to 1 for all workers and assume that

$$h_L^1 > h_L^0 > h_U = 1, \qquad (2.104)$$

where h_L^i is the housing consumption of an employed worker earning a wage w_L^i and h_U is the housing consumption of an unemployed worker. Assumption (2.104) reflects the fact that richer workers consume more land, which is well-documented (see e.g. Glaeser, Kahn, and Rappaport, 2008). Observe that since the unemployed have the same revenue w_U, they consume the same amount of land, h_U. As above, we can write the bid-rent functions of an employed worker earning a wage w_L^i and a type-i unemployed worker located at a distance x from the BD as:

$$\Psi_L^i(x, W_L) = \frac{w_L^i - \tau x - W_L^i}{h_L^i}$$

$$\Psi_U^i(x, W_U) = w_U - s^i \tau x - W_U^i.$$

Observe that the type $i = 0, 1$ of a worker plays a role only when he/she is unemployed since it determines s^i. Type i is, however, irrelevant when a worker is employed since it is only the wage that is of any importance. As a result, in $W_U^i(x)$, superscript i indicates the type of workers while, in $W_L^i(x)$, it represents the type of wage a worker earns. As will be seen below, this is not true for the intertemporal utilities since someone employed must take into account that he/she may be unemployed in the future and thus, his/her type will be of importance even when employed. This is why there are four different instantaneous utilities, but five different intertemporal utilities. Depending on the assumptions we make, different types of urban equilibria can emerge. Because we want to be consistent with the previous section, we would like to focus on an equilibrium where employed workers reside closer to jobs than unemployed workers. Thus, we assume

$$h_L^1 < \frac{1}{s^1}, \tag{2.105}$$

which guarantees that, starting from the CBD, we first locate the type-0 employed, then the type-1 employed, then the type-1 unemployed and, finally, the type-0 unemployed.

Definition 2.4. *Assume (2.104) and (2.105). Then, an urban-land-use equilibrium with heterogenous workers is a 5-tuple* $(W_L^{0*},\ W_L^{1*},\ W_U^{0*},\ W_U^{1*},\ R^*(x))$ *such that:*

$$\Psi_U^0(N,\ W_U^{0*}) = R_A = 0$$

$$\Psi_U^0(N - U^0,\ W_U^{0*}) = \Psi_U^1(N - U^0,\ W_U^{1*})$$

$$\Psi_U^1(L,\ W_U^{1*}) = \Psi_L^1(L,\ W_L^{1*})$$

$$\Psi_L^1(L^0,\ W_L^{1*}) = \Psi_L^0(L^0,\ W_L^{0*})$$

$R^*(x)$
$$= \max\left\{\Psi_U^0(x,\ W_U^{0*}),\ \Psi_U^1(x,\ W_U^{1*}),\ \Psi_L(x,\ W_L^*), 0\right\}\ \text{at each } x \in (0, N].$$

Since $U^0 = u^0 N^0$, $L^0 = (1 - u^0) N^0$, and $L = N - u^0 N^0 - u^1 N^1$, solving these equations leads to:

$$W_U^{0*} = w_U - s^0 \tau N \tag{2.106}$$

$$W_U^{1*} = w_U - s^1 \tau N + (s^1 - s^0) \tau u^0 N^0 \tag{2.107}$$

$$W_L^{0*} = w_L^0 - \tau \left(N^0 + \frac{h_L^0}{h_L^1} N^1\right) + \tau u^0 N^0 (1 - s^0 h_L^0)$$
$$+ (1 - h_L^1 s^1) \frac{h_L^0}{h_L^1} \tau u^1 N^1 \tag{2.108}$$

$$W_L^{1*} = w_L^1 - \tau N + (1 - h_L^1 s^0) \tau u^0 N^0 + (1 - h_L^1 s^1) \tau u^1 N^1 \tag{2.109}$$

$$R^*(x) = \begin{cases} \tau\left(\frac{N^1}{h_L^1} + \frac{N^0 - x}{h_L^0}\right) - \tau\, u^0 N^0 \left(\frac{1}{h_L^0} - s^0\right) \\ \quad -\left(\frac{1}{h_L^1} - s^1\right)\tau\, u^1 N^1 & \text{for } 0 \le x \le L^0 \\[2mm] \tau\left(\frac{N-x}{h_L^1}\right) - \left(\frac{1}{h_L^0} - s^0\right)\tau\, u^0 N^0 \\ \quad -\left(\frac{1}{h_L^1} - s^1\right)\tau\, u^1 N^1 & \text{for } L^0 < x \le L \\[2mm] s^1\tau\,(N-x) - \left(s^1 - s^0\right)\tau\, u^0 N^0 & \text{for } L < x \le N - U^0 \\[1mm] s^0\tau\,(N-x) & \text{for } N - U^0 < x \le N \\[1mm] 0 & \text{for } x > N. \end{cases} \tag{2.110}$$

The effects are more complicated here than for the homogenous case, but the intuition remains the same. Indeed, the interaction between the land market and the labor market is performed through wages w_L^0 and w_L^1 and unemployment rates u^0 and u^1.

6.2.2. Labor Market Equilibrium. Firms post wages. Let $\varrho \in [0, 1]$ be the fraction of firms posting the high wage w_L^1 and thus, $1 - \varrho$ the fraction posting the low wage w_L^0. As in the previous section, given any distribution of posted wages $G(w_L)$, each worker of type i will have a reservation wage w_L^{ri}, such that he/she accepts a job if $w_L \ge w_L^{ri}$ and rejects it if $w_L < w_L^{ri}$, with $w_L^{r1} > w_L^{r0}$. It should also be clear that, in equilibrium, no firm will post anything other than the reservation wage of workers, as a firm posting $w_L \in \left(w_L^{r0}, w_L^{r1}\right)$ could reduce w_L down to w_L^{r0} and make a larger profit per worker without changing the set of workers who accept.

For unemployed workers, the reservation rule property implies that

$$I_L^{0,0} = I_U^0 \tag{2.111}$$

and

$$I_L^{1,1} = I_U^1. \tag{2.112}$$

where I_U^i is the value function of an unemployed worker of type $i = 0, 1$ while $I_L^{i,j}$ is the value function of an employed worker of type $i = 0, 1$ earning a wage $j = 0, 1$, where superscript j corresponds to a wage w_L^{rj}. Since we already know that the only two posted wages are w_L^{r1} and w_L^{r0}, the relevant steady-state Bellman equations for unemployed workers are given by:

$$r I_U^0 = W_U^{0*} + s^0 a_U \theta \left(I_L^{0,1} - I_U^0\right) \tag{2.113}$$

$$r I_U^1 = W_U^{1*}. \tag{2.114}$$

In this formulation, a value function $I_L^{1,0}$ cannot exist since a type-1 worker will always refuse a job offer with a wage w_L^{r0}. Indeed, type-1 workers accept the high wage w_L^{r1}, but not the low wage w_L^{r0}, while type-0 workers accept both wage offers.

Similarly, using the reservation rules (2.111) and (2.112), the relevant steady-state Bellman equations for employed workers are equal to:

$$r I_L^{0,0} = W_L^{0*} \tag{2.115}$$

$$r I_L^{0,1} = W_L^{1*} - \delta \left(I_L^{0,1} - I_U^0 \right) \tag{2.116}$$

$$r I_L^{1,1} = W_L^{1*}. \tag{2.117}$$

In steady-state, the unemployment rates $u^i = U^i / N^i$ are equal to:

$$u^0 = \frac{\delta}{\delta + s^0 a} \tag{2.118}$$

$$u^1 = \frac{\delta}{\delta + s^1 a \varrho}. \tag{2.119}$$

Indeed, workers of type 0 accept any job offer (w_L^{r0*} or w_L^{r1*}) while workers of type 1 only accept high-wage jobs, which arrive at rate $s^1 a \varrho$. As a result, the higher the fraction of firms posting the high wage, the lower the unemployment rate for type-1 workers. We can now easily calculate the equilibrium wages w_L^{r1*} and w_L^{r0*}. Indeed, the high wage w_L^{r1*} is determined by $W_L^{1*} = W_U^{1*}$, while the low wage w_L^{r0*} is determined by:

$$W_L^{0*} = \frac{(r + \delta) W_U^{0*} + s^0 a_U \varrho W_L^{1*}}{r + \delta + s^0 a_U \varrho},$$

where W_U^{0*}, W_U^{1*}, W_L^{0*}, W_L^{1*} are given by (2.106)-(2.108). Under some condition, it can be shown that $w_L^{r1*} > w_L^{r0*}$ (Zenou, 2007b). What is crucial here is the fact that competition in the land market (through commuting costs, for example) affects wage determination. Furthermore, we have:

$$\frac{\partial w_L^{r1*}}{\partial \varrho} = - \left(1 - h_L^1 s^1 \right) \tau N^1 \frac{\partial u^1}{\partial \varrho} > 0.$$

The high wage w_L^{r1*} depends on ϱ because an increase in ϱ has a negative effect on u^1, which affects the location of workers in the city (the employed are closer to jobs) and thus, competition in the land market and, ultimately, the wage. Furthermore, we have:

$$\frac{\partial w_L^{r0*}}{\partial \varrho} \gtrless 0.$$

A similar effect was present in the non-spatial model (see, e.g., Gaumont, Schindler, and Wright, 2006), but it was always positive. Here, the mechanism is quite different since it goes through u^1 and thus, while in the non-spatial model, competition in the land market went through the job contact rate, $s^0 a \varrho$.

Firms maximize steady-state profits. There are two types of firms $i = 0, 1$; those offering the high wage w_L^{r1*} (type-1 firms) and those offering the low wage w_L^{r0*} (type-0 firms). The profit of a firm of type i is given by:

$$\Pi^i = \frac{a_F^i \varsigma^i}{r + \delta} \left(y - w_L^{ri*} \right), \tag{2.120}$$

where ς^i is the probability of a random unemployed worker accepting a job offer at wage w_L^{ri*} and a_F is the rate at which a firm meets a worker. A job match is when these two events are realized, which occurs at the rate $a_F^i \varsigma$.

For a type-1 firm posting the high wage w_L^{r1*}, $\varsigma^1 = 1$ since a job offer is never turned down. On the contrary, for a type-0 firm posting the high wage w_L^{r0*},

$$\varsigma^0 = \frac{u^0 N^0}{u^0 N^0 + u^1 N^1},$$

since a job offer is only accepted by unemployed workers of type 0.

In order to avoid the Diamond's paradox, i.e., only the lowest wage is posted in equilibrium, a condition must be written that guarantees that both wages w_L^{r0*} and w_L^{r1*} coexist in equilibrium. For this reason, it must be that, in equilibrium, firms are indifferent between posting w_L^{r0*} and w_L^{r1*}; otherwise the two wages cannot coexist. This is an iso-profit condition $\Pi^1 = \Pi^0$, which is equivalent to:

$$\varrho^* = \left(\frac{\delta + s^0 a}{s^1 a} \right) \frac{N^1}{N^0} \left(\frac{y - w_L^{r1*}}{w_L^{r1*} - w_L^{r0*}} \right) - \frac{\delta}{s^1 a}. \tag{2.121}$$

Observe that ϱ enters in w_L^{r0*} and w_L^{r1*} through u^1. We have the following result:

Proposition 2.8. *The sufficient conditions for a non-degenerated labor market equilibrium (i.e., $0 < \varrho^* < 1$) to exist and be unique are $\underline{y} < y < \overline{y}$, where $\underline{y}$ and $\overline{y}$.*

Indeed, productivity y must be sufficiently high to reword all firms pay the lowest wage w_L^{r0*} and sufficiently low for firms not to pay the highest

Table 2.4. *Parameter values*

$y = 1.15$ Productivity	$r = 0.01$ Pure discount rate
$w_U = 0.32$ Unemployment benefit	$\delta = 0.01$ Job-destruction rate
$a_F = 1.5$ Firms' job contact rate	$a_U = 1.3$ Workers' job contact rate
$N = 10$ Total population	$N^0/N = 70\%$ Percentage of type-0 workers
$\tau = 0.1$ Pecuniary commuting cost	$N^1/N = 30\%$ Percentage of type-1 workers
$s^0 = 0.08$ Search effort of type-0 workers	$s^1 = 0.1$ Search effort of type-1 workers
$h_L^0 = 1.1$ Housing consumption of type-0 workers	$h_L^1 = 1.2$ Housing consumption of type-1 workers

wage w_L^{r1*}. In other words, to obtain wage dispersion, productivity y must have intermediate values between $\underline{y}$ and $\overline{y}$.

6.2.3. Interaction between Land and Labor Markets. We now run some numerical simulations in order to obtain reasonable values of the unemployment rates. The parameters values (in monthly terms) are the following: 70% of the workers have a high value of leisure. Output y is normalized to 1.15 while the unemployment benefit has a value of 0.32. Pecuniary commuting costs τ are equal to 0.1. The discount rate is $r = 0.01$, whereas the job-destruction rate is $\delta = 0.01$, which means that, on average, workers lose their job every eight years and four months. The contact rate of firms a_F is 1.5 while for workers it is $a_U = 1.3$, so that on average, they roughly have a contact every 20 days. Table 2.4 summarizes these different values and those for search efforts and housing consumption.

Let us calculate the steady-state equilibrium for these parameter values. The numerical results of the equilibrium are displayed in Table 2.5.

In equilibrium, 44.61% of the firms post the high wage w^{1r*}, which is slightly higher than w^{0r*}. Since the difference in search intensity between the two types is not very large, $\varrho^* = 0.4461$ implies that u^{0*}, the unemployment rate of workers of type 0, is much lower than u^{1*}, the unemployment rate of type-1 workers (8.77 versus 14.71%). Indeed, the arrival rates for type-0 and type-1 workers are given by $s^0 a = 0.104$ and $s^1 a \theta = 0.058$, respectively, which means that their average duration of unemployment is $9\frac{1}{2}$ and 17 months, respectively. Furthermore, ς^{0*}, the probability that a random unemployed worker accepts a job offer at wage, w_L^{r0*}, is equal to 58.19%. This means that firms that post the high wage will transform a contact into

Table 2.5. *Steady-state equilibrium*

	Base case
$\rho^*(\%)$	44.61
$u^{0*}(\%)$	8.77
$u^{1*}(\%)$	14.71
w^{0r*}	1.11
w^{1r*}	1.13
$\varsigma^{0*}(\%)$	58.19
$W_U^{0*}(I_U^{0*})$	0.24 (22.69)
$W_U^{1*}(I_U^{1*})$	0.2212 (22.12)
$W_L^{0*}(I_L^{0,0*};I_L^{0,1*})$	0.2269 (22.69; 22.41)
$W_L^{1*}(I_L^{1,1*})$	0.2212 (22.12)
$\Pi^* = \Pi^0 = \Pi^1$	1.73291

a match with probability 1, while this will be true only 58.19% of the time for firms posting the low wage since type-1 workers will always refuse such an offer. Since each firm has a contact with a worker every 20 days (i.e., $a_F = 1.5$), this also means that, on average, a match occurs every month for firms posting the low wage. Table 2.5 also gives the different utilities (both instantaneous and intertemporal) and it can be seen that, because of a fiercer competition in the land market for employed workers, their utilities are not always higher than those of unemployed workers. Finally, Figure 2.9 illustrates Proposition 2.9 by showing that for low values of productivity y (i.e., $\underline{y} \simeq 0.9$), $\varrho^* \leq 0$ while for high values of y (i.e., $\overline{y} \simeq 1.2$), $\varrho^* \geq 1$.

We would like to pursue our analysis by investigating the interaction between land and labor markets. For this purpose, we mainly study the impact of a key labor market variable, y, on equilibrium land price, $R^*(x)$. Figure 2.10 displays the result in the theoretical model (the variables with one and two stars are the equilibrium values before and after a change in y, respectively; the normal and thick lines correspond, respectively, to before and after the increase in y). Remember that L^i is the area in the city where the employed workers earning w^{ir*} reside while U^i is the area in the city where type-i unemployed workers reside. Looking at (2.110), an increase in y affects the bid-rents and thus, competition in the land market, only through u^1. In particular, y has a negative effect on u^1 since the latter is a

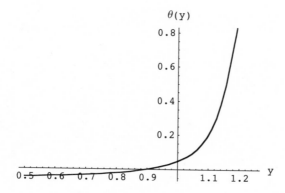

Figure 2.9. Impact of productivity y on θ.

negative function of ϱ, which is in itself a positive function of y. So when y increases, areas $L^0 = \left(1 - u^0\right) N^0$ and $U^0 = u^0 N^0$ are not affected while $L^1 = \left(1 - u^1\right) N^1$ expands and $U^1 = u^1 N^1$ shrinks (Figure 2.10). This is due to the fact that only the bid-rent of employed workers are affected by a change in y and this effect is positive. Indeed, by differentiating (2.110), at a given x, one obtains:

$$\frac{\partial R^*_{L^0}(x)}{\partial y} = \frac{\partial R^*_{L^1}(x)}{\partial y} = -\left(\frac{1}{h_L^1} - s^1\right) \tau N^1 \frac{\partial u^1}{\partial \varrho} \frac{\partial \varrho}{\partial y} > 0$$

and

$$\frac{\partial R^*_{U^0}(x)}{\partial y} = \frac{\partial R^*_{U^1}(x)}{\partial y} = 0,$$

where $R^*_{L^i}(x)$ and $R^*_{U^i}(x)$ are the equilibrium land rents at a distance x for employed workers earning w^{ir*} and type-i unemployed workers, respectively.

To better understand this result, Figures 2.11a, 2.11b, and 2.11c display the impact of y on land rent at $x = 0$, $x = L^0$, and $x = L$, respectively. In these figures, it can be seen that the relationship is positive for $R^*(0)$ and $R^*(L^0)$, but negative for $R^*(L)$. Indeed, as stated above, when y increases, the bid-rent of the employed increase because competition on the land market is fiercer due to the fact the unemployment rate u^1 decreases. So at $x = 0$ and $x = L^0$, land rents increase because the bid-rents of workers earning both w^{i0*} and w^{i1*} increase and these locations are not affected by a change in y (see Figure 2.10). Now, when y increases, $\Psi_L^1(x, W_L)$, the bid-rent of workers with high wages, increases while $\Psi_L^0(x, W_L)$, the bid-rent of type-0 unemployed workers, is not affected. As a result, the location

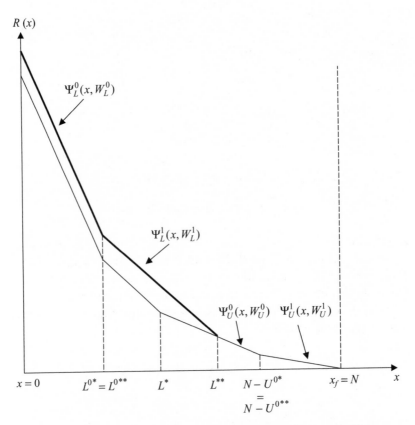

Figure 2.10. Impact of an increase in productivity y on land-rent equilibrium.

$x = L$ shifts rightwards (from L^* to L^{**}), which makes competition in the land market less fierce and thus, the land price decreases. This is an interesting effect of workers' productivity on housing prices. Similar results can be obtained with other labor market variables such as, for example, the job-destruction rate δ which only has an indirect effect on land-rent equilibrium through u^1.

7. Notes on the Literature

The model of Section 2 in which workers are ex-ante heterogenous in terms of some idiosyncratic characteristics, but ex-post identical was proposed by Sato (2004a). The models of Sections 3, 5, and 6 have been specifically written for this book and can be found as working papers in

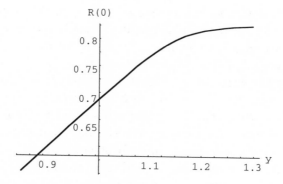

Figure 2.11a. Impact of productivity y on land rent at $x = 0$.

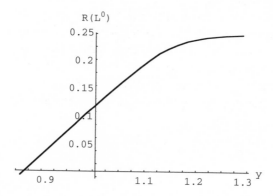

Figure 2.11b. Impact of productivity y on land rent at $x = L^0$.

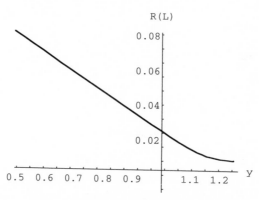

Figure 2.11c. Impact of the productivity y on the land rent at $x = L$.

Zenou (2007a, 2007b, 2008d). The job-destruction model was for the first time proposed by Mortensen and Pissarides (1994). In Section 3, we extend their model to incorporate the land market and the heterogeneity of workers in terms of location in the city. In Section 6, we propose a wage posting game instead of a bargaining wage. There is a strand of the search literature (Mortensen, 2000, 2003) where firms post wages instead of bargaining with workers. The starting point is the Diamond's paradox (Diamond, 1971) which says that when all workers are identical, then (even in the presence of search frictions) the only equilibrium is for all firms to post the reservation wage of workers. To obtain a wage dispersion and avoid Diamond's paradox, this model has been extended by introducing multiple job offers (Burdett and Judd, 1983), workers' heterogeneity (Albrecht and Axell, 1984), and on-the-job search (Burdett and Mortensen, 1998). In Section 6, we introduce a land market in a wage posting model. Section 5 extends the benchmark model of Chapter 1 to introduce high mobility costs. Even though some authors have discussed this issue in different search models (see, for example, Van Ommeren, Rietveld, and Nijkamp, 1998; 1999), this is the first model where both markets are totally integrated. Finally, the model of positive mobility costs (Section 4) was introduced by Wasmer and Zenou (2006).

CHAPTER THREE

Non-Monocentric Cities and Search-Matching

1. Introduction

Even if some large cities still have a monocentric structure (for example Paris, London, New York), plenty of others, especially in the United States, tend to be characterized by a more polycentric structure. Indeed, one of the most striking features of the American urban landscape has been the massive and continuous suburbanization of both people and jobs in the second half of the twentieth century. Whereas, on average, more than 57% of the Metropolitan Statistical Area (MSA) residents were located in a central city in 1950, the proportion of central city residents was already down to 40% in 1980 (Mieszkowski and Mills, 1993) and was still around 40% in the year 2000 (Anas, Arnott, and Small, 1998; Gobillon, Selod, and Zenou, 2003). In his famous book, Garreau (1991) coined the term "edge city" to describe this phenomenon of decentralization of jobs and families. This is related to the issue of urban sprawl (Brueckner, 2000; Nechyba and Walsh, 2004; Glaeser and Kahn, 2004). The emergence of edge cities and urban sprawl thus appears to be truly characteristic of U.S. cities and has major implications for the location of both jobs and people and their labor market outcomes. From a theoretical point of view, it is thus important to relax the assumption of monocentric cities and investigate to what extent multi-job centers affect the different results of Chapters 1 and 2.

In Section 2, we focus on ex-ante identical workers with two employment centers by examining rural-urban migration in a search-matching model. Workers trade off living in rural areas where full employment as well as low costs of living prevail with urban areas, which are characterized by search frictions, unemployment, high land rents, and commuting costs. We determine a steady-state equilibrium where workers are indifferent between living in the respective areas. We find that when there is an increase in the commuting cost in cities, land prices as well as wages increase while urban unemployment increases. There are amplifying effects because of the interaction between the land and labor markets and the fact that workers can choose between two different job centers.

In Section 3, we investigate the case of multiple job centers with ex-ante heterogenous workers and firms in terms of skills. In standard search-matching theory, ex-ante identical individuals choose reservation wages and search intensity by comparing the marginal benefits and costs of search and equating them at the margin (Pissarides, 2000; Ch. 1). Search costs include forgone earnings, time, and other resources devoted to search activities, while the benefits from search include a higher chance of leaving unemployment. In the present model, because workers and firms are ex-ante heterogenous and there are multiple job centers, workers have to decide how large an area to search (the extensive margin) and, holding the area constant, how much effort to put into searching (the intensive margin) since travel imposes costs. In particular, we show how commuting costs and the speed of the transportation system used affect wages, unemployment as well as the intensive and extensive margins.

Finally, Section 4 uses the same framework, but without search frictions and instead focuses on the equilibrium *assignment* between ex-ante heterogenous workers and firms in terms of skills. Two information structures are considered: either firms are not able to identify the skill type of workers prior to hiring or they can observe the cost of training borne by the worker prior to employment. The difference in the information structure turns out to have a dramatic impact on the workers' earnings since workers hired by a firm are not randomly drawn from the workforce as a whole. When a firm does not observe training costs, it offers the same wage to all potential employees, but makes them bear the training costs. Workers then select a firm which offers them higher net earnings than other firms. More precisely, workers whose skills are close to a firm's job requirement will be hired by this firm. As a consequence, self-selection leads to an endogenous segmentation of the labor market. The wage-setting game here is similar to the wage-posting game described in Section 6 in Chapter 2. On the other hand, when both firms and workers are able to observe the training cost prior to employment, each worker is engaged in a bargaining process with the nearest firm, using the potential offer of the second nearest firm as an alternative option. The wage-setting game is here similar to the wage-bargaining game proposed throughout Chapter 1. However, in that chapter, bargaining was bilateral whereas in the former, it is between the workers and his/her two "closest" firms.

We show that the corresponding distributions of earnings are very different in the two cases. In the imperfect information case, workers with the best match obtain the highest earnings. In the perfect information case, workers with the highest bargaining power (who are the poorest matches vis-a-vis the firm which employs them, but the best matches with an alternative firm) earn the highest net wages.

2. Rural-Urban Migration and Search

In this section, we analyze a model where rural workers can migrate to urban areas, so that two job centers (urban and rural) will prevail in equilibrium. We use a framework similar to that of the Harris-Todaro model (Todaro, 1969; Harris and Todaro, 1970).[1] In the standard Harris-Todaro model, a city differs from a rural area only because of the specificity of its labor market. Indeed, the main difference between rural and urban areas is that unemployment and high wages (that can be due to a minimum wage, efficiency wages, or search frictions) prevail in cities and not in rural areas. The main innovation of this section is to define a city in a more satisfactory way by explicitly modeling the land/housing market and the location of all workers in cities. Using the developments of Chapters 1 and 2, we will analyze a rural-urban migration model à la Harris-Todaro with a land market.

2.1. Model and Notations

There are two regions: an urban area (the city, denoted by superscript C) and a rural area (denoted by superscript R). As in the standard Harris-Todaro model, rural wages are assumed to be very flexible and thus, there is no unemployment in rural areas. Hence, the total population in rural areas is $L^R = N^R$, where L^R is the employment level and N^R the total population in rural areas. The total population in cities is equal to: $N^C = L^C + U^C$ (where L^C and U^C are the employment and unemployment levels in cities, respectively), with $N = N^C + N^R$ (where N denotes the total population in the economy). In this context, the unemployment level in cities is given by:

$$U^C = N - L^C - L^R. \tag{3.1}$$

---

[1] See Appendix C at the end of this book for a detailed presentation of the original Harris-Todaro model, especially for the search-matching case.

2.1.1. The City. There are assumed to be search frictions in the city and we use the standard search matching framework (Chapter 1) to model these frictions. As in Chapter 1, the starting point is the following matching function

$$d^C = d(\bar{s}U^C, V^C),\qquad (3.2)$$

where d^C is the total number of matches, V^C the total number of vacancies in the city, and $\bar{s} = s$ is the common workers' search effort. As usual, it is assumed that $M(.)$ is increasing in its arguments, concave and homogeneous of degree 1.

2.1.2. The Rural Area. The rural area is assumed to be frictionless, i.e., whoever decides to work in this sector finds a job instantaneously, so that there is no unemployment. If we believe that coordination failures give rise to search frictions,[2] one may ask why there is a significantly larger number of coordination failures in the city than in the rural area. It is, in fact, striking to observe that in rural areas, individuals work in agriculture and often within the family. Therefore, the search frictions should not be too large. Naturally, there are search frictions in rural areas, but they are much lower than in the city. Thus, for the sake of simplicity, we only assume search frictions in the city.

Thus, everybody can obtain a job in the rural area and it is assumed that the wage in the rural area is flexible enough to guarantee full employment; this wage is denoted by w_L^R. In the rural area, we have the following production function:

$$F(L^R)\quad \text{with } F'(L^R) > 0 \text{ and } F''(L^R) \leq 0,\qquad (3.3)$$

which means that rural productivity per worker is $y^R = F(L^R)/L^R$. The price of the good is taken as a numeraire and, without loss of generality, normalized to 1. As stated above, in the rural area, jobs are mainly menial and wages are flexible and equal to the marginal product, so that there is no unemployment. We thus have:

$$w_L^R = F'(L^R).\qquad (3.4)$$

In the city, each worker produces y^C and it is assumed that $\forall L^R > 0$, $y^C > y^R$.

---

[2] See Section 2 in Chapter 1 for a microfoundation of the matching function based on coordination failures.

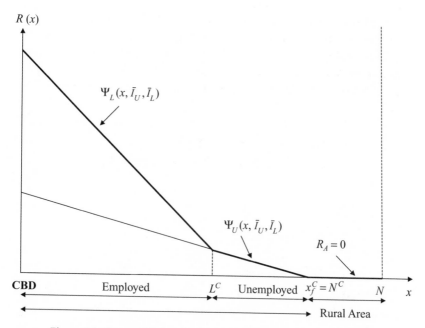

Figure 3.1. The equilibrium land rent in the city and in the rural area.

As in previous chapters, a steady-state equilibrium in cities requires *simultaneously* solving an urban-land-use equilibrium and a labor market equilibrium. For presentational convenience, we first present the former and then the latter.

2.2. The Urban-Land-Use Equilibrium

In region C, all workers are uniformly distributed along a *linear, closed,* and *monocentric* city. Even if there is migration, the city is still considered as closed because urban (employed as well as unemployed) workers will never consider a move to rural areas.[3] Their density in each location is taken to be 1. All land is owned by absentee landlords and all firms are exogenously located in the Central Business District (CBD) and consume no space. Workers decide on their optimal place of residence between the CBD and the city fringe. There are *no relocation costs*, neither in terms of time nor money.

The urban-land-use equilibrium is defined exactly as in Chapter 1, Section 2 (see Definition 1.2 and Figure 3.1), which means that, in cities,

[3] This will be formally shown below.

employed workers reside close to jobs while unemployed workers live on the outskirts of the city. Land rent in the rural area is exogenously given by R_A, the agricultural land rent, which is not normalized to zero.

As a result, the equilibrium instantaneous utilities of employed and unemployed workers and the equilibrium land rent in the city are, respectively, given by:

$$W_L^* = w_L^C - \tau \, L^C - s \, \tau \, \left(N^C - L^C \right) \tag{3.5}$$

$$= w_L^C - \tau \, L^C - s \, \tau \, \left(N - L^R - L^C \right)$$

$$W_U^* = w_U^C - s \, \tau \, N^C \tag{3.6}$$

$$= w_U^C - s \, \tau \, \left(N - L^R \right)$$

$$R^*(x) = \begin{cases} \tau \left(L^C - x \right) + s \tau \left(N - L^R - L^C \right) & \text{for } 0 \leq x \leq L^C \\ s \tau \left(N - L^R - x \right) & \text{for } L^C < x \leq N^C, \\ 0 & \text{for } x > N^C \end{cases}$$

$$\tag{3.7}$$

where w_L^C, w_U^C are the urban wage and the unemployment benefit, respectively, τ and s, the pecuniary commuting cost per unit of distance and the fraction of search trips to the CBD for the unemployed, respectively. The main difference to the benchmark model without migration (Chapter 1) is that the utilities of urban workers as well as the equilibrium land rent now depend on L^R, the level of employment in rural areas. This is due to the fact that rural-urban migration affects urban land prices. In particular, it can be seen that everywhere in the city, i.e., $\forall x \in [0, N^C]$,

$$\frac{\partial R^*(x)}{\partial L^R} < 0.$$

Indeed, since L^R will be determined by an equilibrium migration condition (see below), then when more workers are employed in the rural area, there is less migration to the city and thus, less competition in the urban land market so that there is a decrease in housing prices.

2.3. The Labor Equilibrium in Cities

The definition of the labor market equilibrium is exactly the same as in Definition 1.3 in Chapter 1 and we obtain the equilibrium values of labor-market tightness θ^{C*} and wage w_L^{C*} as follows:

$$\frac{c}{q(\theta^{C*})} = \frac{y^C - w_L^{C*}}{r + \delta} \tag{3.8}$$

$$w_L^{C*} = (1 - \beta)\left[w_U^C + (1 - s)\,\tau\,L^{C*}\right] + \beta\left(y^C + c\,s\,\theta^{C*}\right). \tag{3.9}$$

By combining (3.8) and (3.9), we obtain the equation defining θ^{C*}, which is given by:

$$y^C - w_U^C = \frac{c}{q(\theta^{C*})}\left[\frac{r + \delta + \beta\,s\,\theta^{C*}q(\theta^{C*})}{1 - \beta}\right] + (1 - s)\,\tau\,L^{C*}. \tag{3.10}$$

As usual, we must now close the model by writing a flow equation. Since there are interactions between rural and urban areas, this equation differs from (1.36) in Chapter 1. Each job is destroyed according to a Poisson process with arrival rate δ. Thus, the number of workers who enter unemployment in the city is δL^C and the number who leave unemployment in the city is $s\,\theta^C q(\theta)^C(N - L^C - L^R)$ since $U^C = N - L^C - L^R$ (see (3.1)). In steady-state, flows into and out of unemployment must be equal and we obtain the following steady-state relationship between urban and rural employment:

$$L^C = \frac{s\,\theta^C q(\theta^C)}{\delta + s\,\theta^C q(\theta^C)}\left(N - L^R\right). \tag{3.11}$$

2.4. The Rural-Urban Migration

Concerning rural-urban migration, we assume that a rural worker cannot search from home, but must first be unemployed in the city (to gather information about jobs) and then search for a job. As a result, as described in Figure 3.1, a rural worker who migrates to the city will first reside in the unemployment area anywhere between $x = L^C$ and $x = N^C = N - L^R$. He/she can then move into the employment area if he/she finds a job while living in the city. Hence, denoting the exogenous discount rate by r, the equilibrium migration condition can be written as:

$$I_U^C = \int_0^{+\infty} w_L^R e^{-rt}dt = \frac{w_L^R}{r}, \tag{3.12}$$

that is, rural workers will migrate to the city up to the point where their expected lifetime utility is equal to the expected utility they will obtain in cities.

Indeed, the left-hand side of this equation, I_U^C, is the intertemporal utility of moving to the city (remember that a migrant must first be unemployed) while the right-hand side, $\int_0^{+\infty} w_L^R e^{-rt} dt = w_L^R/r$, corresponds to the intertemporal utility of staying in rural areas.

Observe that we can now check that, in equilibrium, urban workers will never want to migrate to rural areas. Since the utility from staying in rural areas is equal to w_L^R/r and, in equilibrium, is given by I_U^C, it suffices to show that $I_L^C > I_U^C$. It is easily verified that:

$$
I_L^C - I_U^C = \frac{w_L^C - w_U^C - (1-s)\tau L^C}{r + \delta + s\theta q(\theta)}
$$
$$
= \beta \frac{\left[y^C - w_U^C + cs\,\theta^C - (1-s)\tau L^C \right]}{r + \delta + s\theta q(\theta)},
$$

which is strictly positive.

2.5. The Steady-State Equilibrium

We have the following definition.

Definition 3.1. *A Harris-Todaro equilibrium with search externalities and a land market is a 6-tuple $(\theta^{C*}, L^{C*}, L^{R*}, W_L^{C*}, W_U^{C*}, R^{C*}(x))$ such that (3.10), (3.11), (3.12), (3.5), (3.6), and (3.7) are satisfied.*

In fact, there are three unknowns θ^{C*}, L^{C*}, and L^{R*} and three equations (3.10), (3.11), and (3.12), to be determined (the other equations are independent). Equation (3.10) defines a relationship between θ^{C*} and L^{C*} that we can write $\theta^C = \theta(L^C)$. It is really the urban land market that introduces this relationship through the spatial compensation costs $(1-s)\tau L^{C*}$. In a standard non-spatial model, $\tau = 0$, and this equation defines a unique θ^{C*} as a function of parameters only. By differentiating (3.10), we obtain $\frac{\partial \theta^{C*}}{\partial L^{C*}} < 0$. Indeed, when L^{C*} increases, firms need to compensate more workers for their spatial costs and thus, there is an increase in wages (see (3.9)). As a result, less firms enter the labor market and thus, less jobs are created, so θ^{C*} decreases. Equation (3.11) defines a relationship between L^C and L^R and θ^C, i.e., $L^C = L^C(L^R, \theta^C)$. It can, for example, be seen that for a given θ^C, there is a decreasing relationship between L^C and L^R since more employment in the rural area implies that employment in the city must decrease for the steady-state condition on flows to be satisfied. Finally, the migration equilibrium condition (3.12) defines a relationship between L^R and L^C and θ^C, i.e., $L^R = L^R(L^C, \theta^C)$. For a given θ, there is a positive relationship between L^R and L^C since when L^C increases, employed workers are further away from jobs and thus, $I_L^C - I_U^C$ decreases. This, in turn, reduces the expected lifetime utility of an urban unemployed worker I_U^C and thus, less rural workers are attracted to the city (since they first obtain I_U^C). As a result, employment L^R increases in the rural area.

2.6. Interaction Between Land and Labor Markets

To study the interaction between land and labor markets, we run some numerical simulations in order to obtain reasonable values of the unemployment rate and the job creation rate in the city. As is usual, we use the following Cobb-Douglas function for the matching function:

$$d(sU^C, V) = \sqrt{sU^C V^C},$$

which implies that $q(\theta) = \theta^{-0.5}, \theta q(\theta) = \theta^{0.5}$. The production function in the rural area is also a Cobb-Douglas function and given by:

$$F(L^R) = \left(L^R\right)^{0.5},$$

The parameter values (in yearly terms) are the following. The total population is normalized to 100. The relative bargaining power of workers is equal to $\eta(\theta)$, i.e., $\beta = \eta(\theta) = 0.5$. unemployment benefits have a value of 4 and the costs of maintaining a vacancy c are equal to 1 per unit of time, while urban productivity is 10. Pecuniary commuting costs τ are equal to 0.1, whereas search effort is 0.5 (i.e., unemployed workers make half as many CBD trips as employed workers). The discount rate is $r = 0.05$, whereas the job-destruction rate is $\delta = 0.15$ which means that, on average, a job is destroyed every $6^1/_2$ years. Finally, total population is normalized to 100. Table 3.1 summarizes these different values.

Let us calculate the steady-state equilibrium using the parameter values given in Table 3.1. The numerical results of the steady-state equilibrium are displayed in Table 3.2.

If we take the economy as a whole, 62.23% of the workers are employed in the city while 28.90% work in the rural area. The rest of the workers are unemployed. So the unemployment rate in the economy is 8.87%, but that in the urban area, as measured by the number of unemployed workers over the urban active population (and not the entire population), is somewhat more than 12%. Roughly 20% of the urban jobs are vacant, and the number of vacant jobs per urban worker (employed and unemployed) is

Table 3.1. *Parameter values*

$y^C = 10$ General productivity	$r = 0.01$ Pure discount rate
$\delta = 0.15$ Job-specific shock arrival rate	$\beta = 0.5$ Workers' share of surplus
$N = 100$ Total population	$\eta(\theta) = 0.5$ Search elasticity of matching
$s = 0.5$ search intensity	$w_U = 4$ Unemployment benefit
$c = 1$ Cost of a vacant job	$\tau = 0.1$ Pecuniary commuting cost

somewhat more than 27%. There is an important productivity difference between rural and urban sectors, which results in stark wage differences. The housing costs in the city are quite high in the employment area, but very low in the unemployment area, thus capturing the idea that new migrants live in relatively distressed areas. For example, when a rural worker migrates to the city, he/she lives in the unemployment area where the highest land price is $x = L^C$, which is $R_L^{C*}(L^{C*}) = R_U^{C*}(L^{C*}) = 0.445$. Since

Table 3.2. *Steady-state equilibrium*

L^{C*}	62.23
L^{R*}	28.90
θ^{C*}	4.43
U^{C*}	8.87
u^{C*}	12.48
V^{C*}	19.65
v^{C*}	27.63
w^{R*}	0.093
y^{R*}	0.19
w^{C*}	9.66
W_L^{C*}	3.00
W_U^{C*}	0.45
$I_L^{C*} - I_U^{C*}$	2.11
$R_L^{C*}(x)$	$0.443 + 0.1(62.233 - x)$
$R_U^{C*}(x)$	$0.05(71.103 - x)$

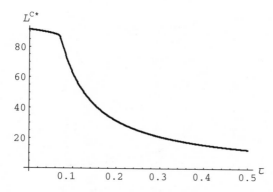

Figure 3.2a. Impact of commuting costs on urban employment.

the urban unemployment benefit is $w_U^C = 4$, this is 11% of the income. For an employed worker who lives in the more expensive location in the city, i.e., $x = 0$, the housing price is 6.66, which is nearly 69% of his/her income. However, since land rent compensates for spatial cost differences and the utility is the same within an employment group, employed workers are always better off both instantaneously ($W_L^{C*} - W_L^{C*} = 2.55$) and intertemporally ($I_L^{C*} - I_U^{C*} = 2.11$).

Let us now look at the interaction between the land and labor markets by analyzing the impact of a key spatial variable, the commuting cost τ, on the equilibrium variables, L^{C*}, L^{R*}, and θ^*. The effects are more complex since τ directly affects the land market through land rent and the instantaneous utility W_L^C and W_U^C, but also indirectly affects the labor market through wage. Figures 3.2a, 3.2b, and 3.2c display the comparative static effects of the impact of an increase in τ on L^{C*}, L^{R*}, and θ^*. When the commuting

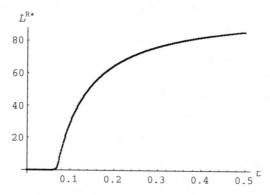

Figure 3.2b. Impact of commuting costs on rural employment.

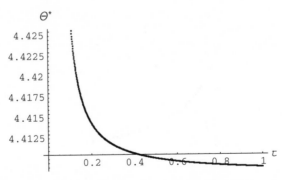

Figure 3.2c. Impact of commuting costs on urban job creation.

cost increases, land prices increase everywhere in the city (see (3.7)) and urban wages are also positively affected (see (3.9)) since firms need to compensate more workers for their spatial costs. As a result, firms create less jobs and thus, θ^{C*} decreases (Figure 3.2c). This leads to a decrease in urban employment L^{C*} (Figure 3.2a) and an increase in urban unemployment U^{C*}. Since urban wages and employment are lower, less people migrate and rural employment L^{R*} increases. There are once more amplifying effects because of the interaction between land and labor markets, but compared to the unemployment benefit policy, the effects are much more important because τ has a direct effect on land prices. For example, a small variation in τ (say from 0.1 to 0.15) leads to a huge variation in urban employment (from 62.23 to 41.58). In other words, a 33% increase in commuting cost τ (from 0.1 to 0.15) leads to a decrease in urban employment of nearly 50%. When $\tau = 0.1$, most people in the economy are employed in the city (62%) while when $\tau = 0.15$, most of them are employed in the rural sector ($L^{R*} = 53.48$ and $L^{C*} = 41.58$). This is because an increase in commuting costs both has a direct positive effect on land rents, which discourages migrants from moving to the city, and a direct positive effect on urban wages, which reduces job creation and thus, once more reduces migration. These two effects combined with search frictions lead to a stark impact of commuting costs on urban employment.

3. Job Matching and Search in Multicentric Cities

We would now like to pursue the analysis of non-monocentric cities by presenting a model with *multiple employment centers* and different transport modes.

3.1. Model and Notations

There is a continuum of workers and firms. The mass of workers is taken to be 1 and the mass of firms $M > 1$. Following Salop (1979), we model heterogeneity by means of a circle along which both workers' and firms' locations are uniformly distributed on the circumference $\mathbb{C}$ of a circle of length 1. This is the geographical space, and we denote by $0 \leq x_{ij} \leq 1/2$ the geographical distance between a worker located in i and a firm located in j.[4] As in Chapter 2, Section 5, mobility costs are so high that workers are unable to change their residential location. So basically firms' and workers' locations are exogenously fixed. However, contrary to the model of Chapter 2, Section 5, there are multiple job centers since firms and workers are uniformly distributed on the circumference of a circle.

In the present model, a match is the product of a (random) contact between a worker and a firm and an acceptation rule. To be more precise, job contacts arrive randomly to workers. Then, when workers have selected a job contact, they decide to apply or not to this job depending on the location of the firm. If we denote by $\hat{x}$, the maximum distance between a worker and a firm, beyond which a job is turned down, then workers will apply to all job announcements for which the commuting distance x is such $x \leq \hat{x}$. For firms, it is different. They advertize jobs and are ready to accept any worker who applies to the job since the workers' productivity is not affected by the geographical distance x between workers' and firms' location. However, all workers who reside at a distance $x > \hat{x}$ will turn down the job offer. It is easy to illustrate this process. Workers read newspapers and look at all job adds (this is the random contact rate). Then, once a job is located, they look at the address of the firm and decide to apply or not to the job offer depending on whether the distance x between the firm and the worker is lower or greater than $\hat{x}$.

At each moment in time, a worker can either be employed in a certain firm (or more exactly within a certain geographical distance from a firm) or unemployed. All unemployed workers search for a job and we assume there to be no on-the-job search. Similarly, at each moment in time, a firm can either have a filled position or an open vacancy (and in this case search for a worker). We denote by $u(i)$ the number of unemployed (or, equivalently, the unemployment rate) in location i and by $V(j)$, the number of vacancies in location j.

---

[4] Because it is a circle of length 1 where distance is measured on both sides, the maximum distance between a firm and a worker is $1/2$.

As in Marimon and Zilibotti (1999), we restrict the attention to the initial distribution such that the same proportion of workers is unemployed in all locations i, i.e., $u(i) = u$, $\forall i \in C$. It is easily shown (see Lemma 1 of Marimon and Zilibotti, 1999) that, in this case, a stationary equilibrium must have a uniform distribution of vacancies in all locations, i.e., $V(j) = V$, for all $j \in \mathbb{C}$.

There is a number of *contacts* per unit of time between the two sides of the market that are determined by the following standard matching function:

$$d \equiv d(\bar{s}\,u,\, V), \tag{3.13}$$

where s is the search intensity of each unemployed worker (i.e., how much effort he/she provides in the search process) and $\bar{s}$ represents the average intensity of search of all unemployed workers in the economy. This means that two aspects of the job search are taken into account in this model: *intensive* and *extensive* search. Indeed, workers decide on the intensity of search s, i.e., the number of hours per day devoted to search, but also the maximum area of search $\hat{x}$ (extensive search).

We can now model precisely the matching process between a worker and a firm. For a worker, a match will occur if and only if:

$$\text{Match} = \underbrace{d(\bar{s}u,\, V)/\bar{s}u}_{\text{Random contact}} \times \underbrace{2\hat{x}}_{\text{Probability to accept a job offer}}$$

Observe that the term $\hat{x}$ is multiplied by 2 because each worker considers the distance to jobs from both sides of his/her location. For a firm, a match will occur if and only if:

$$\text{Match} = \underbrace{d(\bar{s}u,\, V)/V}_{\text{Random contact}} \times \underbrace{2\hat{x}}_{\text{Probability to accept a job application}}$$

3.2. Firms Perfectly Observe Workers' Location

We assume that firms perfectly observe workers' location. Let us focus on individual decisions. For simplicity, we assume housing consumption to be fixed and normalized to 1 for all workers (employed and unemployed). The land rent R paid by workers (employed and unemployed) must be the same in each location since the number of unemployed and employed workers in each location is also the same. Furthermore, contrary to the standard result in urban economics where only one employment center prevails (as we have assumed in Chapters 1 and 2), here the land rent does not depend on distance to jobs because jobs are distributed around the circle and, over their lifetime, *workers change jobs, but not their residential location* so that the distance to jobs changes stochastically over time. As a result, in the steady state, average time and physical distance to jobs are the same for all workers and thus, land rent R does not depend on distance to jobs and has the same value in each location.

We are now able to write the *instantaneous* utility function of both unemployed and employed workers. Assuming risk neutrality for all workers, unemployed workers obtain the following instantaneous utility function:

$$w_U - R - C(s),$$

where w_U denotes the unemployment benefit, R the land rent in each location, and $C(s)$ the total cost of searching for jobs. The latter encompasses the costs of buying newspapers, contacting friends, phone calls, interviews, etc. We assume that $C(0) = 0$, $C'(s) > 0$ and $C''(s) > 0$. For an employed individual working at a geographical distance x, his/her *instantaneous* utility function is given by:[5]

$$w_L(x) - R - \mathbb{T} - \iota^1 w_L(x) \iota(x),$$

where $0 \le x \le 1/2$ denotes the distance between a residential location and a firm, $w_L(x)$ is the wage paid to workers at a distance x from the firm, $\mathbb{T}$ is the fixed cost of transportation[6] (for example, for a car, it will encompass the cost of maintaining a car, the insurance fees, etc. while, for public transportation, it is the daily or monthly ticket fees) and $\mathbb{T} + \iota^1 w_L(x) \iota(x)$ is the total cost of commuting as a function of the geographical distance to jobs.[7] Here, ι^1 is a positive coefficient, $\iota(x)$ the time it takes to commute to jobs when residing at a distance x and thus, $\iota^1 w_L(x)\iota(x)$ represents the total time cost for a person residing at a distance x from his/her job. Observe that unemployed workers have no fixed cost $\mathbb{T}$ of transportation because it is assumed that they find jobs without the need of commuting

---

[5] As will become clear below, the wage setting will be such that w_L is a function of x.

[6] This is a cost paid at each period.

[7] This is the common way of modeling transport cost in the transport mode choice literature; see, for example, LeRoy and Sonstelie (1983) and Sasaki (1990). For simplicity and without loss of generality, we have omitted the variable part of the commuting cost (i.e., the pecuniary commuting cost). Observe, however, that in a more general model, the link between commuting costs and the wage paid is obtained through a labor-leisure choice, which implies that a unit of commuting time is valued at the wage rate (see, for example, Fujita, 1989, Chapter 2). However, such a model is cumbersome to analyze and is not likely to yield any additional insights beyond those available from our simpler approach, which is consistent with the empirical literature showing that the time cost of commuting increases with the wage (see, e.g., Small, 1992, and Glaeser, Kahn, and Rappaport, 2008).

(for example, reading newspapers, contacting friends, etc.). As usual, the wage here represents the opportunity cost of time. We have:

$$\iota(x) = \frac{x}{\varpi}, \tag{3.14}$$

where ϖ denotes the (average) speed of journey to work. If, for example, an individual uses a car to go to work, then he/she has a higher fixed cost $\mathbb{T}$, but it takes less time to go to work (higher speed ϖ). As a result, distance to jobs can be measured in terms of physical distance x (i.e., number of miles) or time distance $\iota(x)$ (i.e., hours). In other words, two workers using different transport modes will not reach the same physical distance in the same period of time. Denoting the job destruction rate by δ, we have the following Bellman equations:

$$r I_L(x) = w_L(x) \left(1 - \iota^1 \frac{x}{\varpi}\right) - \mathbb{T} - R - \delta \left[I_L(x) - I_U(s)\right] \tag{3.15}$$

$$r I_U(s) = w_U - C(s) - R + s\,\theta q(\theta) \left[2 \int_0^{\widehat{x}} \left[I_L(x) - I_U(s)\right] dx\right], \tag{3.16}$$

where $r \in (0, 1)$ is the discount rate and $\widehat{x}$ is the maximum geographical distance for which the unemployed decide to take a job (beyond $\widehat{x}$, all jobs will be turned down by the unemployed).

Let us comment on these equations. Equation (3.15) has a standard interpretation. When a worker is employed today, he/she works at a distance x and he/she obtains an instantaneous (indirect) utility equal to $w_L(x)(1 - \iota^1 x/\varpi) - \mathbb{T} - R$. Then, this worker can lose his/her job with probability δ and, in this case, will experience a reduction in intertemporal utility equal to $I_L(x) - I_U(s)$. Let us now comment on equation (3.16). First, observe that $I_U(s)$ does not depend on x because firms cannot sort workers by location. When a worker is unemployed today, he/she provides a search effort s and his/her instantaneous utility is $w_U - C(s) - R$. Then, he/she may obtain a job and $s\,\theta q(\theta)$ represents the rate at which an unemployed worker has a contact with a randomly drawn firm. The match will then only be acceptable if the firm with which the worker has an interview turns out to be on a point along the arc of length $2\widehat{x}$, centered on the worker's location, otherwise it will be rejected. When this unemployed worker accepts a job offer at a distance x from his/her residential location, he/she obtains an increase in intertemporal utility equal to $I_L(x) - I_U(s)$. Finally, observe that the last term in (3.16) is not divided by $\widehat{x}$ since the unemployed worker searches in the whole circle (whose length and thus density are 1) and not only in the arc of length $2\widehat{x}$ centered on his/her location (whose density is $1/\hat{x}$. To make this last point clear, equation (3.16) can in fact be written as follows:

$$r I_U(s) = w_U - C(s) - R + s\,\theta q(\theta) \left[\int_0^1 \max\{[I_L(x) - I_U(s)], 0\}\,dx \right],$$

which shows that the worker searches everywhere in the circle and only accepts jobs that give him/her a higher expected utility than his/her current one. We can also write the Bellman equations for the firm. The expected discounted lifetime utility of a firm with a filled job and a firm with a vacancy, respectively, denoted by $I_F(x)$ and I_V, is given by:

$$r I_F(x) = y - w_L(x) - \delta\,[I_F(x) - I_V] \tag{3.17}$$

$$r I_V = -c + q(\theta) \left[2 \int_0^{\hat{x}} [I_F(x) - I_V]\,dx \right]. \tag{3.18}$$

The interpretation of (3.17) is similar to that of (3.15). Let us interpret (3.18). As stated above, workers' productivity y does not depend on their distance to jobs, x. As a result, all employed workers are identical from the firms' viewpoint. However, when a firm has a vacant job and pays c to search for workers, it has a probability $q(\theta)$ of having a contact with a worker anywhere in the circle, but knows that workers with a geographical distance greater than $\hat{x}$ from them will always turn down a job offer. As a result, even though firms are indifferent between hiring workers with different distances to jobs (since they all produce y), their area of research is limited to $\hat{x}$ because they anticipate that beyond this distance, workers will refuse to take a job.

3.2.1. Labor-Market Equilibrium. Firms enter the market up to the point where they make zero (expected) profits, i.e., $I_V = 0$. Using (3.17) and (3.18), we obtain:

$$\int_0^{\hat{x}} [y - w_L(x)]\,dx = \frac{c(r + \delta)}{2q(\theta)}. \tag{3.19}$$

For a given wage w_L, we can already examine the relationship between $\hat{x}$ and θ. Differentiating (3.19), we have $\partial\theta/\partial\hat{x} > 0$. This is quite intuitive. When the area of search increases so that workers are ready to accept jobs located further away, firms create more jobs (or equivalently more firms enter the labor market) because they have a greater chance of filling a vacancy (workers are less "picky" and I_V increases).

Let us now determine the wage setting. As stated above, we assume that firms perfectly observe the address and thus the location of each worker. We relax this assumption in Section 3.3 below. As usual, we assume that, in each period, the total intertemporal surplus is shared through a generalized Nash-bargaining process between the firm and the worker. Zenou (2007c) shows that the wage is given by:

$$w_L(x) = \frac{\beta\,(y + s\,c\,\theta) + (1 - \beta)\,[w_U - \mathbb{T} - C(s)]}{1 - (1 - \beta)\iota^1 x/\varpi}. \tag{3.20}$$

Observe that, for a given s, not surprisingly, the wage increases with labor market tightness θ since more vacancies or less unemployment increase the worker's outside option. Observe also that, for a given θ, an increase in workers' search effort s does not always lead to higher wages. There are, in fact, two opposite forces at work. Indeed, when s increases, workers have more of a chance of finding a job when unemployed and thus, their outside option rises. However, their cost of search $C(s)$ also increases which decreases their bargaining power. As a result, the net effect is ambiguous. Let us now comment on the properties of this wage for a given θ and a given s (since these are endogenous variables that will, in equilibrium, depend on all parameters). First, when the unemployment benefit w_U, workers' productivity y, or the workers' bargaining power β increases, firms increase the negotiated wage because the outside option for workers is higher. Second, let us see the impact of distance x and transport mode ϖ on wages. When x, the distance to jobs increases, workers spend more time commuting and thus, their opportunity cost of time rises. As a result, firms must increase wages to compensate workers for the increase in this cost. In contrast, when ϖ increases (workers use faster transport modes), wages are reduced because compensation is lower due to a lower opportunity cost of time.

We are now able to study the unemployed worker's decision s (search intensity). First, observe that when making this decision, the unemployed worker takes as given the unemployment rate u in the economy, the vacancy rate v in the economy, the average search intensity $\bar{s}$ (and thus $\theta = v/\bar{s}\,u$ the labor market tightness), land rent where he/she lives R, and the expected discounted lifetime utilities $I_U(s)$ and $I_L(x)$.

The expected discounted lifetime utility of an unemployed worker is defined by (3.16). Differentiating (3.16) with respect to s gives the following first-order condition:

$$-C'(s) + \theta q(\theta)\left[2\int_0^{\widehat{x}} [I_L(x) - I_U(s)]\,dx\right] = 0. \tag{3.21}$$

This is the behavioral equation for search intensity, s. The intuition of (3.21) is straightforward. For a given θ, when choosing s, the unemployed face a fundamental trade-off between short-run and long-run benefits. On the one hand, increasing search effort s is costly in the short run (more phone calls, more interviews, etc.) since it decreases instantaneous utility, but, on the other hand, it increases the long-run prospects of employment since workers then have a higher chance of obtaining a job. It can be shown that:

$$-C'(s) + \gamma\,\theta\,\frac{\beta}{1-\beta} = 0. \tag{3.22}$$

Observe that (3.22) is not a behavioral equation for search intensity, but a relation between intensity and labor market tightness that holds in equilibrium. We have: $s'(\theta) > 0$. This is quite natural since larger job opportunities (i.e., more vacancies or less job seekers) induce workers to search more. Since all individuals are identical, all unemployed workers choose the same search intensity s given by (3.22). As a result, the average search intensity, $\bar{s}$, is given by $\bar{s} = s$.

We can finally determine the value of $\hat{x}$, beyond which workers refuse to take jobs. It is given by

$$I_L(\hat{x}) - I_U(s) = 0$$

which is equivalent to:

$$\hat{x}(s, \theta) = \frac{y - w_U + C(s) + \mathbb{T} - s\,c\,\theta\,\beta/(1-\beta)}{y\,\iota^1/\varpi}, \tag{3.23}$$

which is assumed to be strictly positive.

One of the most interesting results here is the relationship between $\hat{x}$ and ϖ (for a given s and a given θ). It is easily seen that workers with a faster transportation mode (higher ϖ) are ready to accept jobs that are geographically further away than those who use a slower transportation mode. The intuition is as follows. When ϖ increases, the time cost of traveling becomes lower, which increases the instantaneous utility. As a result, workers can extend their area of search and thus, $\hat{x}$ increases. Now, if, for a given θ, we differentiate (3.23) with respect to s, we obtain:

$$\frac{\partial \hat{x}(s, \theta)}{\partial s} = \frac{C'(s) - c\,\theta\,\beta/(1-\beta)}{y\,\iota^1/\varpi}. \tag{3.24}$$

Indeed, when s increases, there are two effects on $\hat{x}$. On the one hand, it increases the present cost of searching so that workers are induced to extend their area of search, but on the other hand, it increases their chances of obtaining a job so that workers become more "picky" and thus, reduces $\widehat{x}$. The overall effect is thus ambiguous. However, if we evaluate this derivative at the optimal s, which is given by (3.22), we see that one effect thwarts the other so that the net effect is nil. Now, for a given s, we can differentiate (3.23) with respect to θ and we obtain: $\partial \widehat{x}(s, \theta)/\partial\theta < 0$. Indeed, for a given s, when θ increases, there are more opportunities in the labor market for workers since there are more vacancies and less unemployment. As a result, unemployed workers become more choosy and only accept jobs within a shorter distance from their residence.

3.2.2. *Steady-State Equilibrium and Comparative Statics.*

Since each job is destroyed according to a Poisson process with arrival rate δ, the number of workers who enter unemployment is $\delta(1 - u)$ and the number who leave unemployment is $2\widehat{x}s\theta\, q(\theta)\, u$, i.e., the probability that an unemployed worker finds an acceptable match $2\widehat{x}s\theta\, q(\theta)$ times the mass of unemployed u. In steady state, the rate of unemployment is constant and therefore, these two flows are equal (flows out of unemployment equal flows into unemployment). Thus, we have:

$$u = \frac{\delta}{\delta + 2\widehat{x}\,s\theta\, q(\theta)}. \tag{3.25}$$

We would like to focus on equilibria for which workers do not always accept job offers, i.e., $0 < \widehat{x}(s, \theta) < 1/2$. In equilibrium, we can now calculate average search intensity $\overline{s}^*$, average distance to work $\overline{x}^*$ and average commuting time $\overline{\iota}^*$. We have: $\overline{s}^* = s^*$, $\overline{x}^* = \widehat{x}^*/2$ and $\overline{\iota}^* = \overline{x}^*/\varpi = \widehat{x}^*/(2\varpi)$.

Proposition 3.1.

(*i*) When productivity y increases, $\theta^*, s^*, w_L^*, \widehat{x}^*, \overline{x}^*$, and $\overline{\iota}^*$ increase.

(*ii*) When the unemployment benefit w_U increases, θ^* and s^* decrease, but the effect on wages and search area is ambiguous. We indeed have:

$$\frac{\partial w_L^*}{\partial w_U} \gtrless 0 \Leftrightarrow \beta cs^* \frac{\partial \theta^*}{\partial w_U} + (1 - \beta) \gtrless 0$$

$$\frac{\partial \widehat{x}^*}{\partial w_U} \gtrless 0 \Leftrightarrow -c\frac{\beta}{1 - \beta} s^* \frac{\partial \theta^*}{\partial w_U} \gtrless 1.$$

(*iii*) When the destruction rate δ increases, u^* and $\widehat{x}^*$ (as well as $\overline{x}^*$ and $\overline{\iota}^*$) increase, but θ^*, w_U^*, and s^* decrease.

The first result (i) is very intuitive. Indeed, when the match between a firm and a worker becomes more productive, firms create more jobs, wages are higher, unemployed workers search more intensively because the rewards from obtaining a job are greater, and workers are ready to accept jobs located further away. As a result, on average, workers spend more time commuting to their jobs. An increase in unemployment benefits (result (ii)) has a negative impact on job creation and search intensity, but an ambiguous effect on wages and the maximum area of search. Indeed, an increase in w_U gives a better outside option for workers when negotiating their wage so that wages increase. However, because it becomes more costly to create a job, firms enter less in the labor market which, in turn, decreases the outside option for workers. These two opposite effects explain the ambiguous impact of w_U on $\hat{x}^*$. Finally, result (iii) shows that an increase in the job destruction rate reduces job creation, wages and search intensity, but increases workers' maximum area of search (workers are less picky since the risk of losing their jobs is higher) and, quite naturally, the equilibrium unemployment rate.

This model with multiple job centers is interesting since it shows that job matching between job seekers and firms depends on the distance between workers' residential location and firms' location. This feature was not present in all models with a single employment center, i.e., the monocentric city (Chapters 1 and 2). It must be acknowledged that, here, the land market is not fully analyzed since workers' location is exogenous. There is, however, a new spatial element since the mode of transportation (through the speed of a journey to work) influences how workers search at the extensive and intensive margins. Another new feature as compared to the models of Chapters 1 and 2 is that the average commuting time is endogenous, since workers chose the maximum area of search and thus their maximum commuting time. In Chapter 7, we will investigate the impact of transportation mode (through its speed) on workers' labor market outcomes, especially black and white workers.

3.3. Firms Do Not Observe Workers' Location

As above, the intertemporal surplus is shared through a generalized Nash-bargaining process between the firm and the worker. We assume that firms do not observe the location of workers or more precisely x the distance between the worker and firm. This is because either such information would be too costly to obtain or workers would have an incentive not to truthfully reveal where they live.

As a result, a worker and a firm will bargain only on the *observable* aspects of the negotiation.[8] However, even if firms do not know the exact location x of each worker, it is assumed that they know $\widehat{x}$. Thus, in the negotiation process, in order to calculate the surplus of workers, the values of employment is not given by (3.15), but by:

$$r I_L = w_L \left(1 - \iota^1 \frac{\widehat{x}/2}{\varpi}\right) - \mathbb{T} - R - \delta \left[I_L - I_U(s)\right], \qquad (3.26)$$

while the value of $I_U(s)$ is still determined by (3.16). The main difference between (3.15) and (3.26) is that the latter does not depend on x but on $\widehat{x}/2$. Indeed, firms do not know the location of each worker x, but infer that the expected distance each worker commutes is: $\mathbb{E}(x|x \leq \widehat{x}) = \widehat{x}/2$. Therefore, the wage w_L is determined by:

$$(1 - \beta)\left[I_L - I_U(s)\right] = \beta I_F, \qquad (3.27)$$

where now both I_L and I_F do not depend on x. By solving this equation, we obtain:

$$w_L = \frac{\beta y \left[r + \delta + 2s\,\theta\,q(\theta)\widehat{x}\right] + (r + \delta)(1 - \beta)\left[w_U - \mathbb{T} - C(s)\right]}{r + \delta + 2\beta s\,\theta\,q(\theta)\widehat{x} - (1 - \beta)(r + \delta)\iota^1 \frac{\widehat{x}}{2\varpi}}.$$
$$(3.28)$$

Now, since the wage does not depend on x, the free-entry condition is not anymore given by (3.19), but by:

$$2sq(\theta)\widehat{x}\left(\frac{y - w_L}{r + \delta}\right) = c. \qquad (3.29)$$

Using this equation, we can determine (implicitly) the wage (3.28) as follows:

$$w_L = \frac{\beta y \left[1 + c\,\theta/(y - w_L)\right] + (1 - \beta)\left[w_U - \mathbb{T} - C(s)\right]}{1 + \beta c\,\theta/(y - w_L)}. \qquad (3.30)$$

which is a second-degree equation in w_L. The model can then be closed as before. The equilibrium unemployment rate u^* is still given by (3.25), but the equilibrium values of $\widehat{x}^*$ and s^* are now different because the wage is now given by (3.27) and $I_L(x) - I_U(s)$ cannot be calculated from (3.27) since, in the wage bargaining, it is $I_L - I_U(s)$ and not $I_L(x) - I_U(s)$ that is taken into account. However, by taking these aspects into account and by solving the same programs, we can obtain the new equilibrium values of $\widehat{x}^*$ and s^*.

---

[8] Gautier (2002) uses a similar strategy to calculate the bargained wage between heterogenous workers and firms.

4. Job Matching and Assignment in a System of Cities

So far, we have only considered the matching problem between workers and firms caused by search frictions. Workers were either ex-ante homogenous (as in Chapter 1) or heterogenous (as in Chapter 2 and the previous section). Here we adopt another definition of job matching, not based on search frictions, but on the *assignment problem* between ex-ante heterogenous workers and firms.[9] The main issue is how to assign workers with different skills to jobs with different skill requirements. In contrast to the previous search models, we only consider *static* models. Because the assignment between firms and workers is not perfect in the *skill space*, firms will acquire *market power* over their potential workers. In the same vein, *geographical* separation gives firms market power over the workers residing in their vicinity, who attach themselves to the firm in order to reduce their commuting costs.

To be more precise, we study the assignment between a large number of workers and a small number of jobs (or firms), which is non-hierarchical since there is no ranking in any sense of the workers' types. Workers are assumed to be heterogenous in terms of both individual skill and urban location. In such a context, it becomes clear that the labor market and the land market are strongly connected, and that this connection is central for the understanding of the socio-economic forces at work in our modern cities. As a result, based on Brueckner, Thisse, and Zenou (2002), we here propose a new way of modeling urban labor markets and we will show how individual skills and urban locations play a fundamental role in the development of local labor markets. To reach this objective, as in Chapter 2, Section 3, we will consider a model linking two separate "spaces": *the skill space of workers* and *the physical space of cities*. We show how heterogeneity in the skill space is mirrored in the residential location choices of workers, drawing a connection between outcomes in the land and labor markets.

We will first focus on the case of *full employment*, i.e., all workers accept a job offer in equilibrium. In that case, since workers and firms are heterogeneous, it is clear that the information available to firms about workers is of importance in the wage formation process. Each firm has a specific technology such that workers can produce output only when they perfectly match the firm's skill needs. Since workers are heterogeneous, they have different matchings with the firm's job offer. In that case, workers need to be trained before starting to work so that even if ex-ante they have different

---

[9] Kim (1989, 1991) and Helsley and Strange (1990) were the first to propose assignment models in an urban framework.

skills, ex-post (i.e., after the training) they all provide the same productivity level. A crucial question that then arises is who will pay for the training costs. Since we consider two different information structures, two different ways of sharing the costs and returns of training may arise. In the first information structure (Section 4.1), it is assumed that *firms are not able to identify the skill type of workers prior to hiring, but they know the distribution of worker skills.* Workers know their own types and observe the firms' skill needs. Hence, workers are able to evaluate their training costs, but firms are not. In the second information structure (Section 4.2), *both the worker and the firm can observe the cost of training borne by the worker prior to employment.* Since the information structure is likely to vary with the specifics of the labor market, our framework thus shows that wage formation crucially depends on the industry as well as on the type of job. In particular, the difference in information structure allows us to determine how specific training costs are split between workers and firms.

In Section 4.3, we consider an economic environment in which not all workers take a job, which means that *unemployment* arises in equilibrium. In that case, each firm acts as a monopsony in the labor market and sets a wage that maximizes its profit. This is because firms no longer compete in the labor market and the training costs are borne by the workers.

4.1. Full Employment with Unobservable Skills

In this section, we assume that firms cannot observe the cost of training of a worker, but that the worker knows this cost. This seems to be a fairly natural assumption in the case of a *thick* market in which many people apply for a few jobs, thus making it very difficult for firms to observe workers' abilities. However, workers know their own types and observe the firms' skill needs. In order to induce the appropriate set of workers to take jobs with the most suitable firm, workers must pay at least some part of the cost of training. In addition, since the labor supply of a worker is inelastic, firms cannot offer a wage menu, so that the worker must pay all costs of training that are not observable to the firm (hence resolving the adverse selection problem). We focus on an equilibrium where all workers take a job (i.e., full employment).

4.1.1. *The Model.* Consider M firms producing a homogeneous good z,
which is sold on a competitive market (we take this good as the numeraire). There is a continuum of mass 1 of workers with heterogeneous skills. Workers are heterogeneous in the type of work for which they are best suited, but there is no ranking in any sense of these types of work. Each worker supplies

a fixed amount of labor provided that the resulting wage net of all costs is positive. Firms are heterogeneous both in terms of their skill/productivity needs and their urban locations. The model is *static,* there are *no search frictions* and there is *full employment.*

In the spirit of Sattinger (1993), a firm is identified with a job, while workers with heterogeneous skills only choose among a few jobs. As argued by Stevens (1994), in such a context, firms have different job requirements because they have incentives to differentiate their job offers in order to obtain market power in the labor market, thus allowing them to set lower wages. This implies that the labor market is an *oligopsony* where firms compete to attract workers. The type (or skill/productivity) of a worker i is given by his/her location y_i,[10] which is uniformly distributed along a circle $\mathbb{C}$ of unit length, called *skill space.* The skill requirement by firm j $(= 1, \ldots, M)$ is unique and given by $y_j \in \mathbb{C}$. Firms have different skill requirements because a firm's market power increases when it chooses a technology requiring a specific training which protects its location against infringements by rival employers (Stevens, 1994). We suppose that firms' skill requirements are evenly spaced along $\mathbb{C}$ so that the skill distance between two adjacent firms is $1/M$ (see Figure 3.3). As suggested by Economides (1989) and Kats (1995) in their analysis of the product market, this is likely to be an equilibrium of a game where firms strategically choose their technologies prior to their wages. The reason is that this configuration endows firms with the strongest market power in the labor market by relaxing wage competition.

If firm j hires a worker whose skill y_i differs from y_j, the cost of training the worker to meet the firm's skill requirement is a function of the distance $y_{ij} \equiv |y_i - y_j|$ and is given by $\nu|y_i - y_j|$, where $\nu > 0$ expresses the efficiency of the training process. More precisely, each firm j offers the same wage to all workers, conditional on the worker having been trained to the skill y_j. Each worker then compares the wage offers of firms and the required training costs, choosing to work for the firm offering the highest wage net of training costs. After training, all workers are identical from the firms' viewpoint since their *ex-post* productivity is observable and equal to $y > 0$. We assume y to be sufficiently large so that in equilibrium, all workers take a job (no unemployment in equilibrium). We will explicitly derive the condition that ensures equilibrium in the labor market. Each firm is then free to set its wage, and it hires all workers who want a job. Indeed, since workers pay the training cost, the firm correctly anticipates that workers choose the most suitable employer.

---

[10] This is an abuse of notation, since there is a continuum of workers. However, it is kept for ease of exposition.

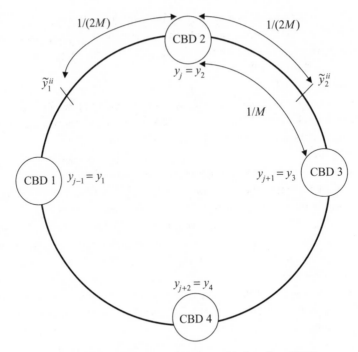

Figure 3.3. The skill space of workers with four firms/CBDs.

Each firm is described by its location in physical space (the city). As in Salop (1979), we assume that firm j is located at $y_j \in \mathbb{C}$, where the circle $\mathbb{C}$ is now interpreted as the physical substratum for urban activities. Note that we assume, without loss of generality, that firms' addresses in skill space are the same as their addresses in physical space. Although both spaces are identically described for notational simplicity, it should be clear that they are distinct and governed by different mechanisms. In such a context, it is natural to consider a firm as the CBD of the corresponding city where jobs are offered, recognizing that the firm represents the employment center in a city in which it is the only employer. Our physical space $\mathbb{C}$ thus contains M CBDs evenly spaced at a distance of $1/M$, implying that the M firms can be viewed as a *system of cities* competing to attract workers (Figure 3.3). Each worker chooses a location in $\mathbb{C}$ at a distance x from the firm in which he/she works. In this context, it is natural to define a local labor market as the set of workers hired by the same firm and commuting to the same CBD.

As in Fujita and Thisse (1986), the interaction between firms and workers is modeled as a two-stage process, reflecting the fact that firms have more market power than workers. In the first stage, firms simultaneously choose their wages at a Nash equilibrium; in the second, individuals decide where to live and how much of the consumption good z to consume at the residential equilibrium. Stated differently, we model the interaction between two markets, assuming that the labor market is *strategic* while the land market is *competitive*.

In this framework, a *market equilibrium* requires solving a two-stage game involving, first, a wage-setting problem whose solution is referred to as a *labor market equilibrium* and, then, a location and land rent problem whose solution is described by a *urban-land-use equilibrium*. In other words, a market equilibrium is a subgame perfect Nash equilibrium. As usual, the model is solved by backward induction.

4.1.2. Urban Equilibrium. The workers are uniformly distributed along each *monocentric* city. Their density in each location is taken to be 1. All land is owned by absentee landlords and each firm, which constitutes a CBD, consumes no space. As usual, workers are assumed to be risk neutral and decide their optimal place of residence between the CBD and the city fringe (this will be more precisely defined below). There are *no relocation costs*, either in terms of time or money.

Although a complete analysis of the labor market is given below, we find it useful to briefly summarize the results needed to describe the urban structure emerging in the second stage. Since workers must bear the training costs in order to take a job in the nearest firm along the circle $\mathbb{C}$, they earn different net wages. More precisely, the net wage is decreasing in skill distance: an employed worker situated at a distance y_{ij} from the nearest firm in skill space, called a *type-y_{ij} worker*, earns a wage equal to $w_L(y_{ij}) \equiv w_L - \nu\, y_{ij}$.

As said above, the circle showing firm and worker locations simultaneously represents both skill space and physical space. Since we assume that the circle has unit width and that workers each consume one unit of land, the entire unit mass of workers can be accommodated on the physical land area of the circle. Under symmetry, the workers within a distance of $1/(2M)$ on either side of a firm will commute to it. A key element of the residential equilibrium is a mapping that assigns the worker at a given location in physical space to a particular point in skill space. The question is the relationship between the commuting distances of these workers and their distance from the firm in skill space. Thus, we need to define an *assignment rule* similar to that defined in Chapter 2, Section 3. Next, we show that, in equilibrium, *these distances are the same*. In other words, a worker's physical distance from the firm coincides with his/her skill distance.

As in Chapter 2, Section 3, in order to generate a location pattern by skill type, we introduce a key assumption that links commuting costs to the wage paid. Indeed, we assume that the time cost of commuting for a type-y_{ij} worker (i.e., a worker of skill y_i working in a firm of skill y_j) residing at a distance x from the CBD is increasing with the wage w_L and is equal to: $w_L(y_{ij})\iota x$, where ι is, as before, the time cost of commuting per unit of distance x. As a result, the utility of a type-y_{ij} worker residing at a distance x from the CBD is given by:[11]

$$W_L^{ii}(y_{ij}) = w_L^{ii}(y_{ij})(1 - \iota x) - \tau x - R^{ii}(x). \qquad (3.31)$$

This utility is the equivalent of (2.22) using the notations of the present model. The bid-rent of a type-y_{ij} employed worker residing at a distance x from the CBD is therefore equal to:

$$\Psi_L^{ii}(y_{ij}, x, W_L^{ii}(y_{ij})) = w_L^{ii}(y_{ij})(1 - \iota x) - \tau x - W_L^{ii}(y_{ij}). \qquad (3.32)$$

As in Chapter 2, Section 3, the bid-rent function is decreasing in x, with $\partial \Psi_L / \partial x < 0$. Since $w_L'(y_{ij}) \leq 0$ (a higher skill mismatch implies lower wages; see below), further inspection of (3.32) shows that, at a given x, an increase in y_{ij} makes the bid-rent slope less negative ($\partial^2 \Psi_L / \partial y_{ij} \partial x > 0$). This means that low-$y_{ij}$ workers have steeper bid-rent curves than high-y_{ij} workers. The intuitive reason is that *an extra mile of commuting reduces income more for a low-y_{ij} worker than for a high-y_{ij} worker*, a consequence of the higher net wage. Therefore, the low-y_{ij} worker requires a larger decline in land rent than a high-y_{ij} worker to maintain a given utility level.

In comparing the residential locations of two groups, it is well known that the group with the steeper bid-rent curve locates closer to the CBD. In the present model, this implies that *low-y_{ij} workers locate closer to the CBD than high-y_{ij} workers*. We have the following definition of residential equilibrium:

Definition 3.2. *A residential equilibrium consists of a mapping $y_{ij}(\cdot)$ that assigns a worker of skill type $y_{ij}(x)$ to a location x, a set of utility levels $W_L^{ii}(y_{ij})$, and a land rent curve $R^{ii}(x)$ such that:*

(i) *at each $x \in [0, 1/(2M)]$:*

$$R^{ii*}(x) = \Psi_L^{ii}(y_{ij}(x), x, W_L^{ii*}(y_{ij}(x))) \qquad (3.33)$$
$$= \max_{y_{ij}} \Psi_L^{ii}\left(y_{ij}, x, W_L^{ii*}(y_{ij})\right)$$

---

[11] Superscript *ii* refers to the *imperfect information* case.

(*ii*)

$$\Psi^{ii}\left(\frac{1}{2M}\right) = 0. \tag{3.34}$$

Equation (3.33) states that the equilibrium land rent $R^{ii*}(x)$ in location x equals the maximum of the bid-rents across skill types, and that the skill type offering the highest bid at x is equal to $y_{ij}(x)$. Note that, as in other urban models with heterogeneous workers, the type of individual living at a given location is the highest bidder for land at that location. Because of our assumptions of a fixed lot size and no vacant land, the land rent at the edge of the city is undetermined. Since the value of this constant does not affect our results, we say in equation (3.34) that it equals the opportunity cost of land, which is assumed to be zero without loss of generality. The residential equilibrium is characterized as follows:

Proposition 3.2. *Assume that firms do not perfectly observe workers' skills. Then, when*

$$\iota < 2M \tag{3.35}$$

there exists a unique residential equilibrium characterized by:

$$y_{ij}(x) = x \quad \text{for} \quad 0 \le x \le 1/(2M) \tag{3.36}$$

$$W_L^{ii*}(y_{ij}) = w_L^{ii}\left(1 - \frac{\iota}{2M}\right) - \left(v\, y_{ij} + \frac{\tau}{2M}\right) + \frac{v\iota}{2}\left(\frac{1}{M^2} + y_{ij}^2\right) \quad \text{for}$$

$$0 \le y_{ij} \le 1/(2M) \tag{3.37}$$

which is decreasing and convex in y_{ij}, and

$$R^{ii*}(x) = (\iota\, w_L^{ii} + \tau)\left(\frac{1}{2M} - x\right) - \frac{v\iota}{2}\left(\frac{1}{4M^2} - x^2\right) \quad \text{for} \quad 0 \le x \le \frac{1}{2M} \tag{3.38}$$

which is decreasing and convex in x.

In Appendix A3 at the end of this chapter, we give the proof of this proposition. It is important because it provides a general solution for solving the location of all workers where there is a *continuum* of them. Equation (3.36) formalizes the above claim that low-y_{ij} workers locate closer to the CBD than high-y_{ij} workers.[12] Indeed, the mapping between the physical

---

[12] We use the type of argument and proof in Section 3 in Chapter 2.

and skill distances of workers involves perfect correlation between these distances; in other words, *the two distances are the same*. Condition (3.35) is a natural requirement because it says that commuting time from the edge of the city, which equals $\iota / (2M)$, is less than total time available (unity). This condition (3.35) also ensures that utility in (3.37) is a decreasing function of y_{ij}. The equilibrium utility levels themselves at different y_{ij} values are generated by the requirement that the highest bid for land at distance x is offered by a worker of type $y_{ij} = x$. Once these bids are derived, they can be used to generate the equilibrium land rent function in (3.38), which is the upper envelope of the bid-rents.

4.1.3. Labor Equilibrium. We now study the first stage of the model in which firms set wages, anticipating the resulting residential equilibrium. The labor market game is described as follows: (i) the players are the M firms; (ii) the strategies are the wages $(w_{L,1}^{ii}, \ldots, w_{L,M}^{ii})$ that are chosen simultaneously by firms and (iii) the payoffs are firms' profits. A labor market equilibrium w_L^{ii*} is a symmetric Nash equilibrium of the labor market game in which profits are strictly positive. Observe that the way the wages are determined here is exactly as in the wage-posting game (Chapter 2, Section 6) since firms post wages that maximize their profit.

The urban equilibrium determination assumed that all firms pay the same wage, which led to a symmetric system of cities. However, the equilibrium wage emerges from a process of strategic interaction among firms. In this process, a firm evaluates the gains from allowing its wage to deviate from those of nearby firms (cities). When a firm increases its wage, workers at the fringe of adjacent cities find it attractive to switch their employment location, enlarging the labor pool of the given firm. Equilibrium is achieved when such wage deviations are not profitable. To study this process, we assume that *all* workers earn a wage net of training cost that is sufficiently large for them to take a job in equilibrium.

Consider the marginal worker, whose physical and skill locations are denoted by $\widetilde{y}_1^{ii}$, and who is indifferent between taking a job in firms $j - 1$ and j. This worker is located at a distance $y_j - \widetilde{y}_1^{ii}$ from firm i and at a distance $\widetilde{y}_1^{ii} - y_{j-1}$ from firm $j - 1$. The value of $\widetilde{y}_1^{ii}$ that makes the worker indifferent between the two firms is the solution to the following equation: $W_L^{ii}(\widetilde{y}_{1j-1}^{ii}) = W_L^{ii}(\widetilde{y}_{1j}^{ii})$ which, using (3.31), is equivalent to:

$$
\left[w_{L,j-1}^{ii} - v\left(\widetilde{y}_1^{ii} - y_{j-1}\right) \right] \left[1 - \iota\left(\widetilde{y}_1^{ii} - y_{j-1}\right) \right] - \tau\left(\widetilde{y}_1^{ii} - y_{j-1}\right)
$$
$$
= \left[w_{L,j}^{ii} - v\left(y_j - \widetilde{y}_1^{ii}\right) \right] \left[1 - \iota\left(y_j - \widetilde{y}_1^{ii}\right) \right] - \tau\left(y_j - \widetilde{y}_1^{ii}\right).
$$

Two important aspects of this equation should be noted. First, the training costs are based on skill distances from the two firms that are equal to physical distances, reflecting Proposition 3.2. Second, firms know that the marginal worker must be located at the edges of the corresponding cities (here $j - 1$ and j), thus paying the same land rent at the residential equilibrium regardless of which CBD is chosen. Land rent equality is indeed a necessary feature of the land market equilibrium. As the wage of one city is varied, starting, say, at the symmetric equilibrium, an asymmetric equilibrium is obtained with rents once more equal at the boundary of cities $j - 1$ and j. Since boundary rents are always equal at all residential equilibria, they play no role in determining the location of the marginal worker, whose location depends entirely on wages net of commuting cost.

Solving for $\widetilde{y}_1^{ii}$ yields

$$\widetilde{y}_1^{ii} = \frac{w_{L,j-1}^{ii} - w_{L,j}^{ii} + [v + \tau + v\iota(y_{j-1} - y_j)](y_{j-1} + y_j) + \iota(w_{L,j-1}^{ii}\, y_{j-1} + w_{L,j}^{ii}\, y_j)}{2[v + \tau + v\iota(y_{j-1} - y_i)] + \iota(w_{L,j-1}^{ii} + w_{L,j}^{ii})}. \tag{3.39}$$

Similarly, it can be shown that the location of the individual $\widetilde{y}_2^{ii}$ who is indifferent between firms j and $j + 1$ is given by

$$\widetilde{y}_2^{ii} = \frac{w_{L,j}^{ii} - w_{L,j+1}^{ii} + [v + \tau + v\iota(y_j - y_{j+1})](y_j + y_{j+1}) + \iota(w_{L,j}^{ii}\, y_j + w_{L,j+1}^{ii}\, y_{j+1})}{2[v + \tau + v\iota(y_j - y_{j+1})] + \iota(w_{L,j}^{ii} + w_{L,j+1}^{ii})}. \tag{3.40}$$

The *labor pool* of firm j is given by the interval $(\widetilde{y}_1^{ii}, \widetilde{y}_2^{ii})$, whereas the corresponding mass of workers is equal to $\widetilde{y}_2 - \widetilde{y}_1$. Firm j's profit function is then written as follows:

$$\Pi_j^{ii} = (y - w_{L,j}^{ii})(\widetilde{y}_2^{ii} - \widetilde{y}_1^{ii}). \tag{3.41}$$

By comparing this profit function with the one given by (2.97) in Chapter 2, it can be seen that they are qualitatively the same since, in both cases, we solve a wage-posting game. The main difference lies in $l(w_L)$, the employment level in each firm, which is here a function of own wage w_j^{ii} and competitors' wages w_{j-1}^{ii} and w_{j+1}^{ii}. Thus, there is a trade-off between the cost of wages and competition with the other firms. Indeed, if one of the firms sets a very low wage, it has a low cost, but will lose workers to its competitors. Therefore, each firm chooses w_j^{ii} to maximize (3.41) subject to (3.39) and (3.40), taking w_{j-1}^{ii} and w_{j+1}^{ii} as given. Let us characterize the symmetric Nash equilibrium where all wages are identical. For this purpose, we need to define the utility of an unemployed worker. As in Chapter 2, Section 3, it is assumed that the unemployed workers commute as often to the CBD as the employed, i.e., $s = 1$. We also assume the unemployed's opportunity cost of time to be negligible, since they do not work and thus, time costs do not enter in their utility function. As a result, the *instantaneous* indirect utility of an unemployed worker residing at distance x is:

$$W_U^{ii}(x) = w_U - \tau x - R^{ii}(x). \tag{3.42}$$

We have the following result:

Proposition 3.3. *Assume that firms do not perfectly observe workers' skills. Then, when*

$$\iota < M \tag{3.43}$$

and

$$y > \frac{2M(2M+\iota)}{(2M-\iota)^2}w_U + \frac{3}{2M}v + \frac{2\tau}{2M-\iota} \tag{3.44}$$

there exists a unique symmetric market equilibrium in which the common wage is equal to:

$$w_L^{ii*} = y - \frac{2v(1-\iota/M)}{2M+\iota} - \frac{2(\iota y + \tau)}{2M+\iota} \tag{3.45}$$

and the utilities $W_L^{ii*}(y_{ij})$ and the land rent $R^{ii*}(x)$ are, respectively, given by (3.37) and (3.38) with (3.45) substituted in place of w_L^*. Finally, the equilibrium profit of each firm is given by:

$$\Pi^{ii*} = \frac{2}{M}\left[\frac{v(1-\iota/M)+(\iota y + \tau)}{2M+\iota}\right]. \tag{3.46}$$

First, the profit function is continuous in $(w_{L,j-1}, w_{L,j}, w_{L,j+1})$ and concave in $w_{L,j}$. Therefore, we can guarantee that there exists a Nash equilibrium in wages. This solution is unique since the first-order conditions are a system of linear equations in the wage of each firm. Observe that the condition (3.43), which is sufficient for concavity of the profit function, holds when transport costs are sufficiently low. Although more restrictive than (3.35), it is a weak requirement since it implies that the time cost must eat up less than half of the wage net of training cost, for the most distant worker. Second, condition (3.44) guarantees that all workers take a job and it is calculated such that the worker with the worst match, i.e., whose training cost is $v/(2M)$, agrees to work. Since the utility of an unemployed worker is given by (3.42), using (3.39) and the assignment rule (3.36), this condition can be written as:

$$W_L^{ii}\left(\frac{1}{2M}\right) = \left(w_L^{ii} - \frac{\nu}{2M}\right)\left(1 - \frac{\iota}{2M}\right) - \frac{\tau}{2M} - R^{ii}\left(\frac{1}{2M}\right)$$

$$> w_U - \frac{\tau}{2M} - R^{ii}\left(\frac{1}{2M}\right) = W_L^{ii}\left(\frac{1}{2M}\right).$$

Using (3.45), after some calculations, this inequality is equivalent to (3.44). This condition holds when y is sufficiently large and/or the unit costs ν, ι, and τ are sufficiently low.

Finally, the wage (3.45) equals the marginal productivity of labor ($w_L^{ii*} = y$) when all cost parameters ν, ι, and τ are zero, namely when there are no labor and urban heterogeneities. In addition, w_L^{ii*} monotonically increases when the number of firms rises because their market power weakens. As M approaches infinity, w_L^{ii*} converges to the competitive wage, which equals marginal productivity, y. The competitive model of the labor market is thus the limit of the spatial model of job assignment.

4.1.4. Interaction Between Land and Labor Markets. Using (3.43) and (3.44), by differentiating (3.45), it can be verified that:

$$\frac{\partial w_L^{ii*}}{\partial y} > 0, \quad \frac{\partial w_L^{ii*}}{\partial \tau} < 0, \quad \frac{\partial w_L^{ii*}}{\partial \iota} < 0, \quad \frac{\partial w_L^{ii*}}{\partial \nu} < 0, \quad \frac{\partial w_L^{ii*}}{\partial M} > 0.$$

$$(3.47)$$

Firms, which are *oligopsonists* in the labor market, thus find that their oligopsony power (as reflected in the magnitude of w_L^{ii*}) changes as parameters vary. Oligopsony power rises with ν, for example, causing the firm to reduce w_L^{ii*}. The reason is that aggregate labor supply to the firm, $\tilde{y}_2^{ii} - \tilde{y}_1^{ii}$, becomes *less elastic* as ν rises, as can easily be demonstrated. As is well known, the market power of an oligopsonist is greater the steeper (i.e., the less elastic) is the factor supply curve he/she faces. The same conclusion holds for ι and τ. As a result, by reducing the elasticity of aggregate labor supply, an increase in any of these parameters reduces the equilibrium wage paid by the firm.

Intuitively, each firm is able to use its proximity advantage in skill space in order to pay a lower wage to its workers, subtracting an amount equal to $2\nu(1 - \iota/M)/(2M + \iota)$ relative to the competitive wage, y. This, in turn, implies a decrease in the value of commuting time, which allows firms to further reduce the wage by an amount equal to $2(\iota y + \tau)/(2M + \iota)$ while still compensating workers for the cost of their journey to work. In other words, increasing ι or τ strengthens firms' market power, thus leading them to pay a wage that is further reduced below the competitive wage. All this implies that *firms exploit workers in both skill space and urban space*, with this exploitation leading to a wage lower than the competitive wage. The wage cut rises with the three cost parameters, but (as expected) falls with productivity, y.

Since the equilibrium profit is $\Pi^* = (y - w_L^{ii*})/M$, then the comparative statics results of τ, ι, and v are exactly the opposite to that of w_L^{ii*}. For y and M, we obtain:

$$\frac{\partial \Pi^{ii*}}{\partial y} > 0, \qquad \frac{\partial \Pi^{ii*}}{\partial M} \gtrless 0.$$

Indeed, higher productivity leads to higher profits. However, more firms imply more competition, and thus lower wages, but also a lower employment level $\tilde{y}_2^{ii} - \tilde{y}_1^{ii} = 1/M$. Thus, the effect of M on equilibrium profits is ambiguous.

Furthermore, after substituting (3.45) into (3.37), it is readily verified, using (3.47), that the equilibrium utility level of the type-y_{ij} worker is affected by the parameters in the same way as w_L^{ii*}, except that a change in v has an ambiguous impact on $W_L^{ii*}(y_{ij})$:

$$\frac{\partial W_L^{ii*}(y_{ij})}{\partial y} > 0, \qquad \frac{\partial W_L^{ii*}(y_{ij})}{\partial \tau} < 0, \qquad \frac{\partial W_L^{ii*}(y_{ij})}{\partial \iota} < 0,$$

$$\frac{\partial W_L^{ii*}(y_{ij})}{\partial v} \gtrless 0, \qquad \frac{\partial W_L^{ii*}(y_{ij})}{\partial M} > 0.$$

Finally, substituting (3.45) into (3.38), we obtain the equilibrium land rent $R^{ii*}(x)$ as a function of parameters only. By differentiating this equation, we have:

$$\frac{\partial R^{ii*}(x)}{\partial y} > 0, \qquad \frac{\partial R^{ii*}(x)}{\partial x} < 0, \qquad \frac{\partial R^{ii*}(x)}{\partial \tau} \gtrless 0, \qquad \frac{\partial R^{ii*}(x)}{\partial \iota} \gtrless 0,$$

$$\frac{\partial R^{ii*}(x)}{\partial v} < 0, \qquad \frac{\partial R^{ii*}(x)}{\partial M} \gtrless 0.$$

Indeed, an increase in productivity y increases the wage w_L^{ii*} which, in turn, increases the equilibrium land rent since all workers are richer and can bid more for land. Concerning the unit cost of training, v, there are two effects that go in the same direction. When v increases, there is a negative direct effect on utility, which decreases the bid-rent, and a negative indirect effect on wages (see (3.47)), which also reduces the bid-rent. For the three other variables, τ, ι, and M, there are two opposite effects. As can be seen from (3.38), an increase in τ, ι or M has a direct impact on land rent and an indirect impact via the wage w_L^{ii*}. The net effect is in general ambiguous. A condition that guarantees the direction of the effect can be found. For example, it is easily verified that

$$\frac{\partial R^{ii*}(x)}{\partial \tau} \gtreqless 0 \Leftrightarrow M \gtreqless \iota \left(\tau - \frac{1}{2} \right),$$

which means that if the number of firms is sufficiently large, the positive direct effect dominates the negative indirect effect (via wages) on equilibrium land rent.

4.1.5. Free-Entry. So far, the equilibrium has been calculated for a fixed number of firms. In particular, we have seen that for a fixed number of firms, the higher is the number of firms, the higher are the equilibrium wages because adjacent firms compete for workers who are better matches. Let us now analyze the case with free entry. Each firm that enters the market must pay a positive fixed cost, c, which corresponds to the cost of posting a vacancy in the search-matching model. In the long-run free-entry equilibrium, profits equal zero. Solving $\Pi^* - c = 0$, using (3.46), we have the following result:

Proposition 3.4. *Assume that firms do not observe workers' skills. Then, when all workers take a job, the equilibrium number of firms is implicitly defined by:*

$$2 \left(M^{ii*} \right)^3 c + \left(M^{ii*} \right)^2 c\iota - 2M^{ii*}(\nu + \iota y + \tau) + 2\nu\iota = 0. \quad (3.48)$$

Observe that to guarantee that all workers take a job in equilibrium, (3.44) is needed, which is here satisfied when M is replaced by M^{ii*}. It is easily checked that there is a unique real solution and two complex solutions to (3.48). Let us focus on the real solution. By running some numerical simulations (where $c = 0.1$, $y = 5$, $\tau = 1$), we obtain Figures 3.4 and 3.5. Not surprisingly, it can be seen that the number of firms M^{ii*} increases by ι and by ν (also by τ, which is not reported here). Indeed, when the cost of commuting or the cost of training increases, firms increase their monopsony power so that it becomes more difficult to poach workers outside the "natural" employment area of each firm. As a result, short-run wages decrease (see (3.47)) and more firms enter the labor market. Then, we can calculate the long-run equilibrium wage by plugging M^{ii*} into (3.45).

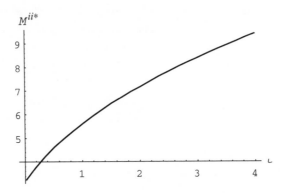

Figure 3.4. Impact of time costs on the equilibrium number of firms.

4.2. Full Employment with Observable Skills

We now turn to the model where firms are fully informed about the quality of individual job matches before hiring. Since each firm knows the skill type of each worker, firms can make different offers to workers of different skill types. The employer only cares about the sum of wage costs and its share of training costs, while the employee only cares about the wage net of any training costs he/she must bear. Thus, it is inessential who pays the training costs in that it is implicitly determined as part of the bargaining process. Furthermore, we will see that in this process each worker plays the second nearest firm against the nearest one in order to secure the highest offer.

Before determining the equilibrium wage, as in the previous section, the assignment rule between skill space and physical space must be calculated. In contrast to the previous case of imperfect information, here workers

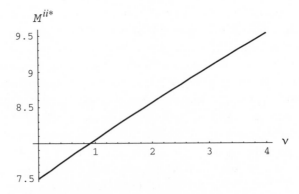

Figure 3.5. Impact of training costs on the equilibrium number of firms.

who are further away (i.e., located at a distance $y_{ij} = 1/(2M)$) will have the highest wage because they have the highest bargaining power since they are located at an equal distance $1/(2M)$ between the two adjacent firms. On the contrary, workers located the closest to firms (i.e., located at a distance $y_{ij} = 0$) will obtain the lowest wage, since they are also located at the longest distance from the adjacent firms, i.e., at a distance equal to $1/M$. Thus, the assignment rule must be given by:

$$y_{ij}(x) = \frac{1}{2M} - x \quad \text{for} \quad 0 \le x \le 1/(2M). \tag{3.49}$$

Let us now determine the wage. Denote by[13] $\tilde{y}_1^{pi}$ and $\tilde{y}_2^{pi}$ the outside boundaries of firm j's subsegments of the labor market. For workers with skill types in $[\tilde{y}_1^{pi}, y_j)$, only firm $j - 1$ can make the best alternative offer in order to counter firm j's offer, while for workers with skill types in $(y_j, \tilde{y}_2^{pi}]$, only firm $j + 1$ can make the best alternative offer to counter firm j's offer. As a result, there are only three agents in the bargaining process, that is the worker and the two firms j and $j - 1$ for workers in $[\tilde{y}_1^{pi}, y_j)$, and the worker and the two firms j and $j + 1$ for workers in $(y_j, \tilde{y}_2^{pi}]$. This implies that the Nash bargaining solution used throughout Chapter 1 cannot be applied here since the threat point is endogenous and determined by the alternative offer. The solution here in fact corresponds to Bertrand competition in wages: the employer offers just enough to bid the worker away from the rival firm (see also Chapter 2). Osborne and Rubinstein (1990, Section 9.2.2) show that this solution is an equilibrium of a game in which the buyers (here, the firms) have different reservation values, that is, productivity net of training and spatial costs. In the case of a wage tie, we assume that workers choose the nearest firm because this firm retains some leeway to raise its offer. In other words, this can be viewed as an ε-equilibrium in that the nearest firm can break the tie in wage offers by offering ε more than the competing rival.

Because competition for a worker type is independent of competition for any other worker type, the equilibrium net wages are easily derived. To be more precise, when a firm j bargains with a worker i located at a distance $y_{ij} \equiv |y_i - y_j|$, it offers the *highest net wage* that this worker can obtain by working in firm $j - 1$. This net wage is equal to ex-post productivity y minus the training costs in firm $j - 1$ and minus the spatial costs (i.e., commuting and housing costs) at his/her residential location where the correspondence between location in skill space and residential

---

[13] Superscript *pi* refers to the *perfect information* case.

location space is given by (3.49). Take a worker located at $y_i \in [\tilde{y}_1^{pi}, y_j)$, then his/her skill distance to firm $j - 1$ is equal to: $y_{ij} = y_i - y_{j-1}$. Thus, using (3.31), his/her net utility if working in firm $j - 1$ is given by:

$$
\left[y - v\left(y_i - y_{j-1}\right)\right](1 - \iota x) - \tau x - R^{pi}(x)
$$
$$
= y - v\left(y_i - y_{j-1}\right) - \left[\iota\left(y - v\left(y_i - y_{j-1}\right)\right) + \tau\right]x - R^{pi}(x),
$$

where the net wage is $y - v(y_i - y_{j-1})$. Using (3.49), we know that $x(y_{ij}) = 1/(2M) - y_{ij}$ and thus, $x(y_j - y_i) = 1/(2M) - (y_j - y_i)$. Observe that in the skill space, the distance $y_i - y_{j-1}$ is calculated between the location of worker y_i and the location of the *potential* firm y_{j-1}, where the worker has an outside option while, in the residential location space, the distance $x\left(y_j - y_i\right)$ is calculated between the location of worker y_i and the location of the *actual* firm y_{j-1} where the worker is employed. The two distances are thus different. As a result, the net utility is finally equal to:

$$
y - v\left(y_i - y_{j-1}\right) - \left\{\iota\left[y - v\left(y_i - y_{j-1}\right)\right] + \tau\right\}\left[\frac{1}{2M} - \left(y_j - y_i\right)\right]
$$
$$
- R\left[\frac{1}{2M} - \left(y_j - y_i\right)\right].
$$

Replicating the same reasoning for workers $y_i \in (y_j, \tilde{y}_2^{pi}]$, we obtain the following result:

Proposition 3.5. *Assume that firms perfectly observe workers' skills and (3.43). Then, when*

$$
y > \frac{4M^2}{(2M - \iota)^2}w_U + \frac{v}{M} + \frac{\tau}{2M - \iota} \tag{3.50}
$$

holds, in an equilibrium in which all workers are employed, workers with skill types $y_i \in [\tilde{y}_1^{pi}, y_i)$ receive net wages

$$
w_L^{pi}(y_{ij})
$$
$$
= y - v\left(y_i - y_{j-1}\right) - \left\{\iota\left[y - v\left(y_i - y_{j-1}\right)\right] + \tau\right\}\left[\frac{1}{2M} - \left(y_j - y_i\right)\right]
$$
$$
- R\left(\frac{1}{2M} - \left(y_j - y_i\right)\right) \tag{3.51}
$$

while workers with skill types $y_i \in (y_j, \widetilde{y}_2^{pi}]$ receive net wages

$$w_L^{pi}(y_{ij})$$

$$= y - v\left(y_{j+1} - y_i\right) - \left\{\iota\left[y - v\left(y_{j+1} - y_i\right)\right] + \tau\right\}\left[\frac{1}{2M} - \left(y_i - y_j\right)\right]$$

$$- R\left(\frac{1}{2M} - \left(y_i - y_j\right)\right). \tag{3.52}$$

Observe that the condition (3.50) is calculated such that the worker with the worst match, the one with skill $y_{ij} = 0$ (thus located at $x = 1/2M$), accepts a job offer. Using (3.31) and (3.42), and the assignment rule (3.49), this condition can be written as:

$$W_L^{pi}(0) = w_L^{pi}(0)\left(1 - \frac{\iota}{2M}\right) - \frac{\tau}{2M} - R^{pi}\left(\frac{1}{2M}\right)$$

$$> w_U - \frac{\tau}{2M} - R^{pi}\left(\frac{1}{2M}\right) = W_U^{pi}\left(\frac{1}{2M}\right).$$

Using (3.51) or (3.52), we obtain:

$$w_L^{pi}(0) = \left(y - \frac{v}{M}\right)\left(1 - \frac{\iota}{2M}\right) - \frac{\tau}{2M}, \tag{3.53}$$

since, for example for (3.51), $y_i = y_j$, $y_i - y_{j-1} = 1/M$, and $R^{pi}(\frac{1}{2M}) = 0$. It is now easily verified that the above inequality is equivalent to (3.50). When firms can make personalized offers based on skill types, workers who receive more training receive higher net wages. However, this is not because they are more productive than others, as in standard human capital models, but because their training costs in alternative firms are lower than those of others. Here, workers who are poorly matched with a firm have a better outside alternative than workers who are well matched with the same firm, thus increasing these workers' bargaining power. In particular, the worker with the worst match, that is, the worker in between two firms, succeeds in capturing his/her ex-post marginal productivity y net his/her training and spatial cost costs. At the other extreme, the worker with the best match, that is, the worker with skill $y_{ij} = 0$, has the lowest pay equal to $w_L^{pi}(0)$. As a result, *under asymmetric information, the distribution of earnings mirrors the match distribution, whereas when there is full information, this relationship is reversed.*

Let us now calculate the urban equilibrium. Its definition is still given by Definition 3.2, but with a different allocation of workers, since the assignment rule is now given by (3.49). Proceeding exactly as before, we can calculate the equilibrium land rent and the equilibrium utilities in each location.

4.3. The Case of Unemployment

Let us return to the case where firms could not perfectly observe workers' skills (Section 4.1). If condition (3.44) does not hold, then, as in Salop (1979), two market equilibrium configurations may emerge: either some workers do not take a job so that unemployment prevails in equilibrium or labor pools just touch and all workers are hired. Since the latter case is rather strange and not very interesting from an economic viewpoint, let us focus on the former.[14] Thus, we consider an economic environment where not all workers take a job, while the remainder of the setting is similar to that described in Section 4.1 of this chapter. In that case, each firm acts as a monopsony in the labor market and thus, in contrast to the previous case, is not affected by the wage policy of the other firms in the labor market. As previously, let us determine $\tilde{y}_1^u$ and $\tilde{y}_2^u$, i.e., the outer boundaries of the firm's labor pool (superscript u denotes the unemployment case). We need to determine the worker who is indifferent between working in firm j and not working. This worker is denoted by $\tilde{y}_1^u$ when he/she is to the left of firm j and by $\tilde{y}_2^u$ when he/she is to the right of firm j. Using (3.31), (3.42), and the assignment rule (3.36), we can thus define $\tilde{y}_1^u$ as follows:

$$\left[w_L^u - v\left(y_j - \tilde{y}_1^u\right)\right]\left[1 - \iota\left(y_j - \tilde{y}_1^u\right)\right] - \tau\left(y_j - \tilde{y}_1^u\right) - R^u\left(y_j - \tilde{y}_1^u\right)$$
$$= w_U - \tau\left(y_j - \tilde{y}_1^u\right) - R^u\left(y_j - \tilde{y}_1^u\right).$$

Solving this equation leads to the following two solutions that are both positive:

$$\tilde{y}_1^u = y_j - \frac{v + w_L^u \iota \pm \sqrt{\left(v + w_L^u \iota\right)^2 - 4v\iota\left(w_L^u - w_U\right)}}{2v\iota}. \tag{3.54}$$

In a similar way, we can define $\tilde{y}_2^u$ as

$$\tilde{y}_2^u = y_j + \frac{v + w_L^u \iota \pm \sqrt{\left(v + w_L^u \iota\right)^2 - 4v\iota\left(w_L^u - w_U\right)}}{2v\iota}. \tag{3.55}$$

---

[14] Thisse and Zenou (1998, 2000) and Jellal, Thisse, and Zenou (2005a,b) study this case, but without a land market.

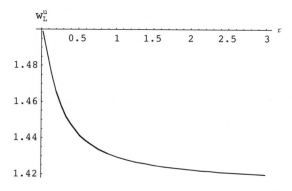

Figure 3.6. Impact of time costs on the monopsony wage.

The labor pool of firm j is then $[\widetilde{y}_1^u, \widetilde{y}_2^u]$ whereas the corresponding labor supply is equal to:[15]

$$\widetilde{y}_2^u - \widetilde{y}_1^u = \frac{v + w_L^u \iota \pm \sqrt{\left(v + w_L^u \iota\right)^2 - 4 v \iota \left(w_L^u - w_U\right)}}{v \iota}.$$

Each firm chooses w_L^u which maximizes the following profit: $\Pi^u = (y - w_L^u)(\widetilde{y}_2^u - \widetilde{y}_1^u)$. The wage obtained is implicitly defined in a cumbersome equation. To get some intuition, let us run some simple simulations by considering the smallest solutions in (3.54) and (3.55). Taking $w_U = 1$ and $y = 2$, we obtain Figures 3.6 and 3.7. It can be seen that both time costs ι and training costs v (or mismatch costs) have a negative impact on the monopsony wage. This result is not obvious since there are two opposite effects. On the one hand, as in the full-employment case, training and commuting costs increase the market power of firms so that they can reduce the wage. On the other hand, in the case of unemployment, since firms no longer compete in the labor market and since all these costs are borne by the workers, firms must compensate workers more when these costs increase in order to attract enough workers. In the case of the simulations, the net effect is negative.

---

[15] When $v = 0$, we have seen that the model with full employment remains meaningful. However, this is no longer true for the unemployment case because with workers being undifferentiated, the concept of isolated monopsonies no longer makes sense.

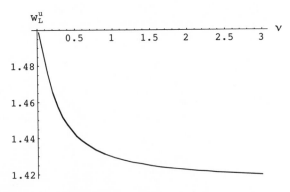

Figure 3.7. Impact of training costs on the monopsony wage.

We can close the model as before by solving the urban-land-use equilibrium. The latter is now defined as follows:

Definition 3.3. *A residential equilibrium with unemployment consists of mapping $y_{ij}(\cdot)$ given by (3.36) that assigns a worker of skill type $y_{ij}(x)$ to a location x, a set of utility levels $W_L^{u*}(y_{ij})$ for employed workers, a utility level for unemployed workers W_U^{u*}, and a land rent curve $R^{u*}(x)$ such that:*

(*i*) *at each $x \in [0, 1/(2M)]$:*

$$R^{u*}(x) = \Psi_L^u(y_{ij}(x), x, W_L^{u*}(y_{ij}(x)))$$
$$= \max_{y_{ij}} \Psi_L^u\left(y_{ij}, x, W_L^{u*}(y_{ij})\right) \tag{3.56}$$

(*ii*)

$$\Psi_L^u\left(\tilde{y}_1^u, W_L^{u*}(\tilde{y}_1^u)\right) = \Psi_U(\tilde{y}_1^u, W_U^{u*}) \tag{3.57}$$

(*iii*)

$$\Psi_U^u\left(\frac{1}{2M}\right) = 0. \tag{3.58}$$

The only difference in Definition 3.2 is that there is one more condition (i.e., (3.57)) since the bid-rent of the unemployed and the employed worker with the worst match must intersect at $x = \tilde{y}_1^u$, which is defined by (3.54). The model can be solved exactly as in the full-employment case to obtain the equilibrium values of all utilities and the equilibrium land rent.

5. Notes on the Literature

There is an important rural-urban migration literature. The first two seminal papers are Todaro (1969) and Harris and Todaro (1970),[16] even though there are important earlier papers (see, for example, Basu, 1997; Ray, 1998). These papers do not explicitly introduce search frictions in their models. There are, however, some papers that have search frictions in a rural-urban migration framework. The early models were using the old search approach where only one side of the market (the workers) was modeled (see, e.g., Fields, 1975, 1989; Banerjee, 1984; Mohtadi, 1989). There is also a more recent literature, which incorporates the search-matching approach à la Pissarides-Mortensen in a Harris-Todaro framework (Coulson, Laing, and Wang, 2001; Ortega, 2000; Sato, 2004b; Laing, Park, and Wang, 2005; Satchi and Temple, 2009; Albrecht, Navarro, and Vroman, 2009; Zenou, 2008b). However, none of these papers have an explicit land/housing market and the location of workers within areas is not modeled. To the best of our knowledge, Zenou (2008f) is the first to develop a model where both the land and the labor market are explicitly modeled in a rural-urban migration framework.[17] This is the model exposed in Section 2.

Sections 3 and 4 develop a research strategy that is becoming increasingly popular in labor economics. Following Salop (1979), this emerging body of literature models workers' and firms' skill heterogeneity by means of a circle along which both workers' skills and firms' needs are distributed[18] (Stokey, 1980; Kim, 1989, 1991; Helsey and Strange, 1990; Bhaskar and To, 1999; Marimon and Zilibotti, 1999; Fiorillo, Santacroce, and Staffolani, 2000; Hamilton, Thisse, and Zenou, 2000; Thisse and Zenou, 1998, 2000; Wauthy and Zenou, 2002; Abdel-Rahman and Wang, 2005; Tasnadi, 2005; Jellal, Thisse, and Zenou, 2005a,b; Zenou, 2007c). However, most of these papers "only" consider skill space and not urban space and thus, there is no analysis of land rent and workers' location. Kim (1991) was the first to introduce both land and labor markets with heterogenous workers using the circle as a device for modeling workers' and firms' heterogeneity. However, he does not explicitly consider the location of workers within the city and thus, does not have a complete correspondence between skill space and urban space. Brueckner, Thisse, and Zenou (2002) solve this problem by considering heterogeneity and therefore determining an assignment rule,

---

[16] See Appendix C at the end of this book for an exposition of these models.
[17] David (2008) proposes a model of open cities in an urban search framework.
[18] The problem of assigning workers to firms was first formulated by Roy (1951).

which gives the exact correspondence between skill space and urban space.[19] This is the model we present in Section 4. In fact, Brueckner, Thisse, and Zenou (2002) propose a model with full employment and a fixed number of firms. In Section 4, we extend their model to introduce free entry in the full-employment case and give a complete analysis of the unemployment case. Observe that because there is a *continuum* of heterogenous workers along the circle, we *cannot* solve the urban equilibrium in a standard way using the fact that the group with the steeper bid-rent curve locates closer to the job center (Fujita, 1989, Ch. 2). The latter is possible only if there is a *finite* of number of heterogenous workers (as, for example, in Hartwick, Schweizer, and Varaiya, 1976). Brueckner, Thisse, and Zenou (2002) propose a solution to solve the location of workers when there is a continuum of them. This method has been used by Selod and Zenou (2003) and Brueckner and Selod (2006). We expose this way of determining the location of a continuum of workers in Appendix A3 at the end of this chapter.

While there were no search frictions in the model of Section 4, the model of Section 3 proposes to introduce search frictions where workers and firms are ex-ante heterogenous *in* skill space. This model has been proposed by Zenou (2007c) for the perfect information case and by Gautier and Zenou (2008) for the imperfect information case.

APPENDIX A3. DETERMINING THE URBAN EQUILIBRIUM WHEN THERE IS A CONTINUUM OF WORKERS

Proof of Proposition 3.2

Existence: We establish existence by construction. For

$$R^{ii}\left(y_{ij}(x), x, W_L^{ii*}(y_{ij}(x))\right) = \max_{y_{ij}} R^{ii}\left(y_{ij}, x, W_L^{ii*}(y_{ij})\right),$$

it must be true that:

$$\frac{\mathrm{d}R^{ii}(y_{ij}, x, W_L^{ii*}(y_{ij}))}{\mathrm{d}y_{ij}}\Big|_{y_{ij}=y_{ij}(x)} = 0. \tag{3.59}$$

We use this equation to solve for the unknown function $W_L^{ii*}(y_{ij})$, which ensures that the bid-rent of a type $y_{ij}(x)$ worker is maximal in location x.

[19] There are other interesting models of search in cities that do not, however, incorporate the land/housing market. The aim of these papers is to explain agglomeration and the positive aspects of cities. See, in particular, Wheeler (2001); Berliant, Reed III, and Wang (2006); Teulings and Gautier (2009).

Using (3.32) to compute this derivative, (3.59) becomes:

$$-v - W_L^{ii\prime\prime}(y_{ij}(x)) + \iota v x = 0, \qquad (3.60)$$

where $W_L^{ii\prime\prime}(y_{ij}(x))$ is the derivative of W_L^{ii} with respect to y_{ij}. Since we want to solve for $W_L^{ii*}(y_{ij})$, this equation must be rewritten in terms of y_{ij}. Since our assumed mapping $y_{ij}(x) = x$ implies $x(y_{ij}) = y_{ij}$, we have:

$$-v - W_L^{ii*\prime}(y_{ij}) + \iota v y_{ij} = 0, \qquad (3.61)$$

and rearranging, we obtain:

$$W_L^{ii*\prime}(y_{ij}) = y_{ij} v \iota - v. \qquad (3.62)$$

Equation (3.62) constitutes a differential equation involving the unknown function $W_L^{ii*}(\cdot)$. Integrating, the solution is:

$$W_L^{ii*}(y_{ij}) = (v\iota/2)y_{ij}^2 - v y_{ij} + K, \qquad (3.63)$$

where K is a constant of integration.

To verify that this solution indeed maximizes $R^{ii}(\cdot)$, we need to check that the second-order condition holds for any solution to the first-order condition (3.60). This condition requires that $d^2 R^{ii}/dy_{ij}^2 < 0$, which from (3.60) implies that $W_L^{ii\prime\prime}(\cdot) > 0$. This inequality is verified using (3.63).

Substituting $y_{ij}(x) = x$ and $W_L^{ii*}(y_{ij}(x)) = W_L^{ii*}(x)$ from (3.63) into (3.33), we get the equilibrium land-rent at the given x, which equals:

$$\Psi_L^{ii}(x) = w_L^{ii} - K - (\iota w_L^{ii} + \tau)x + \frac{v\iota x^2}{2}. \qquad (3.64)$$

The constant K in (3.64) is determined by condition (3.34). Solving for K yields

$$K = w_L^{ii}\left(1 - \frac{\iota}{2M}\right) - \frac{\tau}{2M} + \frac{v\iota}{8M^2}.$$

Substituting K in (3.63) and (3.64), it is easily verified that the equilibrium utility is given by (3.37) and the city's equilibrium land-rent function by (3.38).

Since the land rent function is the upper envelope of downward sloping bid-rent curves, we know that it must be downward sloping and convex. Convexity of $\Psi_L^{ii}(\cdot)$ is clear from the inspection of (3.64), and the slope is negative when the derivative of (3.64) at the city edge is negative, i.e., $(2Mw_L^{ii} - v)\iota + 2M\tau > 0$. Since, by assumption, all workers take a job, it must be that $w_L^{ii} - vx > 0$ holds for any $x \leq 1/2M$. Therefore, $2Mw_L^{ii} - v > 0$ holds, ensuring that the first inequality above is satisfied and confirming that $\Psi_L^{ii\prime}(\cdot) < 0$.

Finally, since $x = y_{ij}$, the equilibrium utility of a type-y_{ij} worker is given by:

$$W_L^{ii*}(y_{ij}) = w_L^{ii} - v y_{ij} - \Psi_L^{ii}(y_{ij}) - [\iota(w_L^{ii} - v y_{ij}) + \tau] y_{ij}, \qquad (3.65)$$

which is equal to (3.37) after substituting for $\Psi_L^{ii}(y_{ij})$. While the net wage $w_L^{ii} - v y_{ij}$ is decreasing in skill type, we want to know whether utility from (3.63) is similarly decreasing in y_{ij}. Using (3.63), $W_L^{ii\prime}(y_{ij}) < 0$ requires

$$y_{ij} < \frac{1}{\iota}. \qquad (3.66)$$

Since $y_{ij} \leq 1/2M$, this inequality will hold if $\iota < 2M$ (equation (3.35)), a condition that must hold for commuting time from the edge of the city $(\iota/2M)$ to be less than total time available, which equals unity. Since $W_L^{ii\prime\prime}(\cdot) > 0$, the equilibrium utility level is a convex function of the skill type.

Uniqueness: To show uniqueness of the equilibrium, suppose that skill types y_{ij0} and $y_{ij1} < y_{ij0}$ reside at distances x_0 and x_1 where $x_1 > x_0$. This pattern differs from the mapping in (3.36). For workers of skill type y_{ij0} to reside at the close-in location x_0, they must outbid workers of type y_{ij1} for land at this location. But since the bid-rent curve of type y_{ij0} is flatter than that of type y_{ij1}, it follows that type y_{ij0} will also outbid type y_{ij1} for land at the more distant location x_1, where that type is assumed to live. This is a contradiction, and it rules out any location pattern in which skill type and location distance are not perfectly correlated. ∎

PART 2

URBAN EFFICIENCY WAGES

In the first part of this book, we have developed different models of urban search-matching. There is another dominant model in labor economics, which is the efficiency wage framework initially developed by Shapiro and Stiglitz (1984).[1] The initial idea was to explain unemployment by high and rigid wages[2] in order to give some microfoundations for the Keynesian framework. Indeed, because shirking is very costly and monitoring is imperfect, firms set a sufficiently high wage to induce workers to work hard.[3] In equilibrium, wages are too high as compared to the market-clearing wages and downward rigid. As a result, unemployment emerges in equilibrium. In the search-matching framework, search frictions were responsible for unemployment, while here, high wages are the main culprit. In this part,

---

[1] There are other versions of the efficiency wage models, but here we focus on the shirking version of Shapiro and Stiglitz (1984), since it is the most widely used.

[2] See the literature surveys by Akerlof and Yellen (1986) and Weiss (1991).

[3] In equilibrium, employed workers obtain "rents," which means that their (intertemporal) utility is strictly higher than that of the unemployed workers. Some researchers postulate that firms could design a contract that give not "rents" to workers (the so-called bonding critique, initially formulated by Carmichael, 1989). In that case, newly employed workers would post a "bond" that will be paid back to them later during their employment period. There are pros and cons on this debate and it is beyond the scope of this book to discuss the different possible contracts. The reader can consult the excellent book of Cahuc and Zylberberg (2004, Ch. 5) for an extensive discussion of this issue.

we will expose the different urban efficiency wage models, starting with the benchmark models and then extending them in different directions.

Whether search frictions and bargain wages or efficiency wages are the correct model for explaining unemployment and wage setting is a matter of empirical relevance. We have seen that there is a host of empirical papers showing the importance of frictions in the labor market. What about efficiency wages?

The standard way of testing the efficiency wage model is very *indirect*. Indeed, the traditional ways of testing the efficiency wage theory is to examine whether there are large wage differences between sectors for identical workers that are unexplained by observable worker characteristics. This literature (Dickens and Katz, 1987; Kruger and Summers, 1988; Murphy and Topel, 1990; Neal, 1993) mainly shows that these unexplained differences can be attributed to differences in supervision/monitoring rates.

However, it is not straightforward to *directly* test the efficiency wage model, which is more generally known as the "rational cheater model." Indeed, the latter stipulates that employees are rational cheaters who anticipate the consequences of their actions and shirk when the marginal benefit exceeds the costs, and firms respond to this decision calculus by implementing monitoring and incentive pay policies (i.e., efficiency wage) that make shirking unprofitable. Cappelli and Chauvin (1991) have proposed a direct test of this model by looking at the relationship between the rates of employee discipline and the relative wage premium across plants of the same large firm. Their result suggests that higher wage premiums are associated with lower levels of shirking, as measured by disciplinary dismissals. Centering the empirical investigation on the effect of safety supervision by host employers on the wage of contract maintenance workers, Rebitzer (1995) also finds that high levels of supervision are indeed associated with lower wage levels. Using data from the U.S. National Longitudinal Survey of Youth (NLSY) in 1992, Goldsmith, Veum, and Darity (2000) find that receiving an efficiency wage enhances an individual's effort and that individuals providing a greater effort earn higher wages.[4] However, as noted by Nagin, Rebitzer, Sanders, and Taylor (2002), there are two main problems in directly testing the shirking or rational cheater model. First, truly rational cheaters are more likely to engage in shirking behavior when such behavior is hard or expensive to detect. Second, should any association between monitoring and employee actions be found, it would be very difficult

---

[4]	See also Strobl and Walsh (2007) for a direct test of the efficiency wage between monitoring and effort.

to disentangle the effects of monitoring strategies from responses to other unobserved features of the firm's human resource system.

Resolving these problems requires a *natural experiment setting* in which monitoring levels are exogenously varied across similar sites and substantial resources are devoted to tracking the behavior of employees. Fehr, Kirchsteiger, and Riedl (1996) were the first to use experiments and show that higher wages indeed sharply reduce shirking. More recently, Nagin, Rebitzer, Sanders, and Taylor (2002) propose another experiment by collecting data from a large telephone solicitation company. The employees in this company work at 16 geographically dispersed sites. At each call center, telephone solicitors were paid according to the same incentive scheme, where the salary increased with the number of successful solicitations. This piece rate system, together with imperfect information about the outcomes of pledges, created incentives for employees to falsely claim that they had solicited a donation. To curb opportunistic behavior, the employer monitored for false donations by calling back a fraction of those who had responded positively to a solicitation. We are exactly in the framework of the shirking model of the efficiency wage. Nagin, Rebitzer, Sanders, and Taylor (2002) show that a significant fraction of employees behave according to the predictions of the shirking model. Specifically, they find that these employees respond to a reduction in the perceived cost of opportunistic behavior by increasing the rate at which they shirk.[5]

So far, we have seen that there is some empirical justification for the positive relationship between wages and effort, where the latter is not perfectly observable and thus, shirking is likely to arise. But another aspect of the Shapiro and Stiglitz (1984) model is that wage rigidity is the main explanation for (involuntary) unemployment. Indeed, in their model, firms refuse to reduce their wage even if some workers are ready to work for a lower wage because, in that case, the non-shirking constraint will not be met and thus, workers will shirk on the job. Different surveys of employers have shown that employers are indeed reluctant to reduce wages, even in the presence of high unemployment (Blinder and Choi, 1990; Agell and Lundborg, 1995; Campbell and Kamlani, 1997; Bewley, 1999). This is because employers believe that it would be unfair to employees to reduce their wages and that it would also have negative consequences in terms of work effort. Indeed, employers believe the main reason for avoiding pay cuts to be that they damage the morale and reduce productivity (Kaufman,

---

[5] There is a recent paper by Fehr and Goette (2007) which uses an experiment in a laboratory and shows that workers work more when wages are higher.

1982). In particular, firms are reluctant to hire workers who propose to work at a lower wage (Agell and Lundborg, 1995) because of the negative consequences it would have on workers' productivity. Fehr and Falk (1999) have studied the issue of downward wage rigidity in the framework of an experiment (in the laboratory) in which two groups, firms and workers, have the opportunity to agree on a wage contract through a mechanism of bilateral bidding. They show that under incomplete contracts, in which the effort level is not stipulated in advance, firms refuse to bid down the wage.

So, in the second part of this book, we are adopting this model to explain urban wages and unemployment.[6] This part, divided into three chapters, follows exactly the same structure as Part 1. In Chapter 4, we expose the simple models of the urban efficiency wage where the city is monocentric. We will first expose the benchmark urban efficiency wage model and then extend it to take into account more realistic situations such as endogenous housing consumption, open cities, resident landlords, long-run and free-entry of firms, different city structures, etc. In each model of Chapter 4, we show how the urban wage is set by firms and how urban unemployment is determined. We also calculate the equilibrium land rent in each location in the city. In Chapter 5, we provide different extensions of the benchmark model, for example, effort will vary with distance to the job center. As in Chapter 2, one important aspect that will be studied is when workers' relocation costs are no longer equal to zero, but are very high. In that case, each change in employment status will not necessarily imply a change in residential location. Once more, this will have a profound impact on labor and land market outcomes. In the last Chapter of Part 2 (Chapter 6), we relax the assumption of monocentric cities and investigate different urban structures with multiple job centers. We show how each structure affects the labor market outcomes of workers as well as the determination of land rent in the city. One interesting issue will be the study of rural-urban and urban-urban migration.

---

[6] To the best of our knowledge, the only test of the *urban efficiency wage* is due to Ross and Zenou (2008). Using the Public Use Microdata sample of the 2000 U.S. Decennial Census, their empirical results suggest that efficiency wages primarily operate for blue-collar workers, i.e., workers who tend to be in occupations that face higher levels of supervision. For this subset of workers, they find that longer commutes imply higher levels of unemployment and higher wages.

CHAPTER FOUR

Simple Models of Urban Efficiency Wages

1. Introduction

We now expose the simple models of urban efficiency wages. As in Chapter 1, we propose a model where housing prices and workers' location (land market), as well as wages and unemployment (labor market) are determined in equilibrium. This chapter constitutes the benchmark model of the urban efficiency wage theory we first developed in Section 2. In this simple model where workers' relocation is costless, the efficiency wage set by firms has two roles: to prevent shirking (incentive component) and ensure that workers are locationally indifferent (spatial compensation component). Indeed, as in the benchmark urban search model of Chapter 1, wages increase with commuting costs because firms need to compensate their employed workers for the additional commuting costs incurred when they leave unemployment. The land market and the labor market interact with each other since both wages and unemployment depend on commuting costs, and housing prices as well as location are, in turn, affected by workers' wages. In particular, we find that when the unemployment benefit increases, labor demand decreases and thus, the employment zone is reduced. This, in turn, increases the instantaneous utility of the employed workers and thus, the employed reduce their bid-rent, which decreases land prices in the city.

In Section 3, we introduce endogenous housing consumption and see how the results of the benchmark model are affected. We find that the urban efficiency wage is still positively affected by commuting costs because of the spatial compensation firms need to provide to their employed workers. The interesting aspect of this model is that city size is endogenous and depends on both the total number of workers and housing lot sizes.

In Section 4, we extend the benchmark model to the case of open cities and resident landlords. This complicates the model and introduces new interesting elements of the urban efficiency wage model.

Different city structures are investigated in Section 5. We examine whether living close to or far away from jobs affects the wages of employed workers and the urban unemployment that emerges in equilibrium. We find the effects of city structure on unemployment and welfare to be very small while those on wages are larger.

In the last two sections, we study the effects on firms' free-entry and long-run behavior (Section 6) and financed unemployment benefits (Section 7) on the urban and labor market equilibrium. The long-run equilibrium of the shirking model has nice properties. Indeed, because of the zero-profit condition, wages are solely determined by the parameters of the production function and the value of the free-entry cost. When unemployment benefits from employee taxes on local firms, then multiple equilibria are more likely to emerge; one with a high employment level and low efficiency wages and the other with the opposite.

2. The Benchmark Model

There is a continuum of ex-ante identical workers whose mass is N and a continuum of M identical firms. Among the N workers, there are L employed and U unemployed so that $N = L + U$. The workers are uniformly distributed along a *linear*, *closed*, and *monocentric* city. Their density in each location is taken to be 1. All land is owned by absentee landlords and all firms are exogenously located in the Central Business District (CBD) and consume no space. Workers are assumed to be infinitely lived, *risk neutral* and decide on their optimal place of residence between the CBD and the city fringe. There are *no relocation costs*, either in terms of time or money.

Each individual is identified with one unit of labor. As in the standard efficiency wage model without space (see Shapiro and Stiglitz, 1984), there are only two possible levels of effort: either the worker shirks, has zero effort, $e = 0$, and contributes to zero production or he/she does not shirk, provides full effort, $e > 0$, and contributes to e production levels. Each employed worker goes to the CBD to work and incurs a fixed monetary commuting cost τ per unit of distance. When living at a distance x from the CBD, he/she also pays a land rent $R(x)$, consumes $h_L = 1$ units of land and z_L unities of the non-spatial composite good (which is taken as the numeraire so that its price is normalized to 1) and earns a wage w_L (that will be determined in the labor market equilibrium). The budget constraints of non-shirking and shirking employed workers are, respectively, given by:

$$R(x) + \tau x + z_L = w_L - e \qquad (4.1)$$

$$R(x) + \tau x + z_L = w_L. \qquad (4.2)$$

The *instantaneous* indirect utilities of an employed non-shirker and a shirker residing at a distance x from the CBD are, respectively, given by:[1]

$$W_L^{NS}(x) = w_L - e - \tau x - R(x) \qquad (4.3)$$

$$W_L^S(x) = w_L - \tau x - R(x). \qquad (4.4)$$

As concerns the unemployed, they commute less often to the CBD since they mainly go there to search for jobs. So, we assume that they incur a commuting cost $s\,\tau$ per unit of distance, with $0 < s < 1$. For example, $s = 1/2$ implies that unemployed only make half as many CBD trips as employed workers. More generally, as in Part 1, s can be interpreted as the search intensity of workers, since it indicates how often workers search for jobs. In this very simple framework, search intensity is only captured through the number of CBD trips and is exogenous.

Each unemployed worker earns a fixed unemployment benefit $w_U > 0$, pays a land rent $R(x)$, consumes $h_U = 1$ units of land, and z_U units of the non-spatial composite good. In this context, because the preferences are given by $\Omega(z_U) = z_U$, the *instantaneous* (indirect) utility of an unemployed worker is equal to:

$$W_U(x) = w_U - s\,\tau x - R(x). \qquad (4.5)$$

As in Part 1, a steady-state equilibrium requires *simultaneously* solving an urban-land-use equilibrium and a labor market equilibrium. It is convenient to first present the former and then the latter.

2.1. Urban-Land-Use Equilibrium

In equilibrium (this will become clear soon), none of the employed workers will shirk so that we only need to analyze the urban-land-use equilibrium with non-shirking workers. Since there are no relocation costs, the urban equilibrium is such that all the employed enjoy the same level of utility $W_L^{NS}(x) \equiv W_L$ while all the unemployed obtain W_U. Thus, we are now able to derive the bid-rents of the (non-shirking) employed workers and the

---

[1] Subscripts NS and S refer to non-shirkers and shirkers, respectively.

unemployed. They are, respectively, given by:

$$\Psi_L(x, W_L) = w_L - e - \tau x - W_L \tag{4.6}$$

$$\Psi_U(x, W_U) = w_U - s \tau x - W_U. \tag{4.7}$$

They are both linear and decreasing in x. We have the following straight-forward result:

Proposition 4.1. *With workers' risk neutrality and fixed housing consumption, the employed reside close to jobs whereas the unemployed live on the periphery of the city.*

It is indeed easily seen that the bid-rent of the employed is steeper than that of the unemployed and thus, the employed will be able to outbid the unemployed to occupy the core of the city. This is because the employed do commute more often to the CBD than the unemployed and thus value the accessibility to the center more. This result is true whatever the preferences chosen, as long as housing consumption is fixed. As a result, since each worker consumes one unit of land, the employed reside between $x = 0$ and $x_b = L$ (x_b is the border between the employed and unemployed workers) whereas the unemployed reside between $x = L$ and $x_f = N$ (x_f is the city fringe) (see Figure 4.1).

Let us now define the urban-land-use equilibrium. We denote the agricultural land rent (the rent outside the city or the opportunity rent) by R_A and, without loss of generality, we normalize it to zero. We have:[2]

Definition 4.1. *An urban-land-use equilibrium with no relocation costs and fixed housing consumption is a 5-tuple* $(W_L^*, W_U^*, x_b^*, x_f^*, R^*(x))$, *such that:*

$$\Psi_L(x_b^*, W_L^*) = \Psi_U(x_b^*, W_U^*) \tag{4.8}$$

$$\Psi_U(x_f^*, W_U^*) = R_A = 0 \tag{4.9}$$

$$\int_0^{x_b^*} \frac{1}{h_L} dx = L \tag{4.10}$$

$$\int_{x_b^*}^{x_f^*} \frac{1}{h_U} dx = N - L \tag{4.11}$$

$$R^*(x) = \max\left\{\Psi_L(x, W_L^*), \Psi_U(x, W_U^*), 0\right\} \; at \; each \; x \in \left(0, x_f^*\right]. \tag{4.12}$$

---

[2] This definition is similar to Definition 1.2 in Chapter 1.

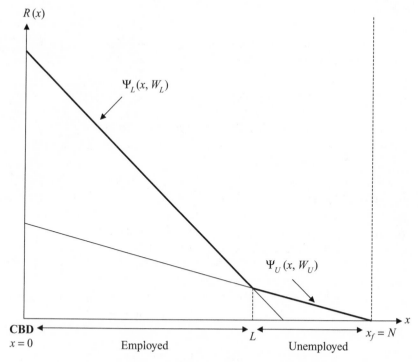

Figure 4.1. Urban equilibrium in the benchmark model.

Equations (4.8) and (4.9) reflect equilibrium conditions in the land market. Equation (4.8) states that in the land market, at the frontier x_b^*, the bid-rent offered by employed workers is equal to the bid-rent offered by the unemployed. Equation (4.9), in turn, says that the bid-rent of the unemployed workers must be equal to the agricultural land at the city fringe. Equations (4.10) and (4.11) give the two population constraints. Finally, equation (4.12) defines the equilibrium land rent as the upper envelope of the equilibrium bid-rent curves of all worker types and the agricultural rent line. Since all N workers must consume 1 unit of housing each, and since there will be no vacant land inside the city in equilibrium, the distance from the CBD to the urban fringe must be given by $x_f^* = N$ and the border by $x_b^* = L$. As a result, the employed reside between 0 and L, whereas the unemployed workers reside between L and N. Furthermore, for this equilibrium to exist (see, e.g., Fujita, 1989), it must be that the equilibrium land rent is everywhere continuous in the city.

By solving (4.8) and (4.9), we easily obtain the equilibrium values of the instantaneous utilities of employed and unemployed workers in the city.

These are given by:

$$W_L^* = w_L - e - \tau x_b^* - s\tau \left(x_f^* - x_b^*\right) \qquad (4.13)$$

$$= w_L - e - \tau L - s\tau (N - L)$$

$$W_U^* = w_U - s\tau x_f^* = w_U - s\tau N. \qquad (4.14)$$

The employment zone (i.e., the residential zone for employed workers) is thus $(0, L]$ and the unemployment zone (i.e., the residential zone for unemployed workers) is thus $[L, N]$.

Observe that in equilibrium all unemployed workers obtain W_U^* and all employed workers obtain W_L^*, whatever their location. This is because mobility is costless and land rent compensates workers for their different locations. By plugging (4.13) and (4.14) into (4.6) and (4.7), we easily obtain the land rent equilibrium $R^*(x)$, which is given by:

$$R^*(x) = \begin{cases} \tau (L - x) + s\tau (N - L) & \text{for } 0 \leq x \leq L \\ s\tau (N - x) & \text{for } L < x \leq N \\ 0 & \text{for } x > N \end{cases} . \qquad (4.15)$$

2.2. Steady-State Equilibrium

We are now able to solve the labor market equilibrium and thus, the steady-state equilibrium.

Definition 4.2. *A steady-state labor market equilibrium consists of a couple* (w_L^*, L^*) *such that firms set an efficiency wage that prevents workers from shirking and determines a labor demand that maximizes their profit.*

Time is continuous and workers and firms live forever. In the labor market, since shirkers add nothing to production, each firm is always motivated to discourage shirking behavior. Each firm is assumed to only have a limited ability to monitor the productivity of its workers. The monitoring capability is taken to be characterized by a *detection rate*, m, which represents the rapidity at which the shirking behavior of any worker can be detected. Equivalently, $1/m$ represents the expected time required to detect shirking behavior. If a worker is caught shirking, he/she is automatically fired. We assume that the changes in employment status are governed by a Poisson process where a is the (endogenous) job acquisition rate and δ the (exogenous) destruction rate. The standard (steady-state) Bellman equations for non-shirkers, shirkers and unemployed are, respectively, given by:[3]

$$r\, I_L^{NS} = w_L - e - \tau\, x_b^* - s\tau\, \left(x_f^* - x_b^*\right) - \delta\,(I_L^{NS} - I_U) \quad (4.16)$$

$$r\, I_L^{S} = w_L - \tau\, x_b^* - s\tau\, \left(x_f^* - x_b^*\right) - (\delta + m)\,(I_L^{S} - I_U) \quad (4.17)$$

$$r\, I_U = w_U - s\tau\, x_f^* + a\,(I_L - I_U), \quad (4.18)$$

where r is the discount rate, I_L^{NS}, I_L^{S} and I_U, represent the discounted expected lifetime utility of a non-shirker, a shirker, and an unemployed worker, respectively, and $W_L^{NS} \equiv W_L$ and W_U are given by (4.13) and (4.14) and $W_L^{S} = W_L + e$. The first equation that determines I_L^{NS} states that a non-shirker today obtains W_L^{NS}, but can lose his/her job with a probability δ and then obtains a negative surplus of $I_U - I_L^{NS}$. For I_L^{S}, we have the same interpretation, except for the fact that a shirker can lose his/her job for two reasons: either the job is destroyed or he/she is caught shirking. The last equation has a similar interpretation.

As can be seen from these equations, there is a trade-off for a worker when deciding whether to shirk or not. There is a short-run gain of shirking because workers do not provide any effort e (the gain is thus $W_L^{S} - W_L^{NS} = e$), but there is a *long-run cost* of shirking because the rate at which workers lose their job is higher ($\delta + m$ instead of δ). Thus, firms must pay enough to prevent shirking, i.e., $I_L^{NS} \geq I_L^{S}$; otherwise workers will provide $e = 0$ and produce nothing. However, there is no need to pay more than the minimum needed to induce effort. Therefore, firms will choose a wage w_L so that $I_L^{NS} = I_L^{S} = I_L$, i.e., the efficiency wage must be set to make workers indifferent between shirking and not shirking.

Using equations (4.16) and (4.17), the condition $I_L^{NS} = I_L^{S} = I_L$ can be written as:

$$I_L - I_U = \frac{e}{m}. \quad (4.19)$$

This highlights the nature of our urban efficiency wage. The surplus of being employed is strictly positive and *does not depend on space*. As in Shapiro and Stiglitz (1984), this a pure incentive effect to deter shirking. This surplus only depends on the monitoring technology, since more monitoring implies less shirking and the effort level provided by workers.

---

[3] See Appendix B at the end of this book for the derivation of the Bellman equations, especially for (4.17) since workers can lose their jobs for two reasons: shirking and technological shocks which involve two Poisson rates m and δ.

Now using (4.13), equation (4.16) can be written as:

$$w_L = e + r I_L + \delta (I_L - I_U) + \tau x_f^* + s\tau \left(x_f^* - x_b^* \right)$$
$$= e + r I_U + (\delta + r)(I_L - I_U) + \tau x_b^* + s\tau \left(x_f^* - x_b^* \right).$$

Furthermore, using (4.18) and (4.19), this can be rewritten as:

$$w_L = w_U + e + \frac{e}{m}(a + \delta + r) + (1 - s)\,\tau\, x_b^*.$$

Finally, in the steady state, flows out of unemployment equal flows into unemployment, i.e.,

$$a\,(N - L) = \delta\, L,$$

so that the efficiency wage is finally given by:

$$w_L^* = w_U + e + \frac{e}{m}\left(\frac{\delta N}{N - L} + r \right) + (1 - s)\,\tau\, x_b^* \qquad (4.20)$$

$$= w_U + e + \frac{e}{m}\left(\frac{\delta N}{N - L} + r \right) + (1 - s)\,\tau\, L.$$

This equation (4.20) is referred to as the Urban No-Shirking Condition (UNSC hereafter), since it is the lowest wage at each level of employment that is necessary to induce workers not to shirk and to stay in the city.

The following comments are in order. First, we have the standard results of the non-spatial efficiency wage literature (Shapiro and Stiglitz, 1984). Indeed, w_L^* increases with L, goes to infinity when L tends to N and has a positive value when $L = 0$. This is because *unemployment acts as a worker discipline device* so that a lower employment level, or an equivalently higher unemployment level, reduces the efficiency wage because the outside option for workers is lower, since it is more difficult to find a job. When there is full employment, $L = N$, then no efficiency wage can be implemented. Indeed, efficiency wages are not compatible with full employment since, in this case, workers will always shirk since, if caught and fired, they will immediately find another job. When there is full unemployment, $U = N$ or $L = 0$, the efficiency wage is strictly positive because firms still have to induce workers to take a job and leave unemployment. Second, we have the following comparative statics effects of the efficiency wage. An increase in the unemployment benefit, w_U, the job destruction rate δ, the discount rate r, or a decrease in the monitoring rate m raises the efficiency wage because firms have to increase their wage to meet the UNSC in order to prevent shirking. To summarize, as in the standard efficiency wage model, firms must *induce workers not to shirk* and there is thus a positive surplus for work as compared to unemployment, which is denoted by ΔSW. It is given by $\Delta SW = \frac{e}{m}\left(\frac{\delta N}{N-L} + r\right)$.

For the spatial elements, τ and s, firms must compensate their employed workers for spatial costs. Indeed, when setting their (efficiency) wage, firms must compensate the spatial cost differential between employed and unemployed. For the employed and the unemployed who both live at L (this is the border distance between employed and unemployed) and thus pay the same land rent, this differential is exactly equal to $(1 - s)\tau L$. Now, since mobility is costless, all employed and unemployed workers obtain, respectively, the same (both instantaneous and intertemporal) utility level whatever their location. Therefore, the spatial cost differential between any employed and unemployed worker is equal to $(1 - s)\tau L$. This is exactly the same compensation effect as the one we found in Chapter 1 (see (1.34)), even though the wage was a result of bargaining between a firm and a worker.

All these elements imply that the efficiency wage has two roles: to prevent shirking (*incentive component*) and ensure that workers are locationally indifferent (*spatial compensation component*). To see this, we can calculate the *spatial costs* of each individual, which consist of transportation plus land rent. In equilibrium, using (4.13) and (4.14), they are given by:

$$SC_L = \tau x_b^* + s\tau \left(x_f^* - x_b^*\right)$$

for employed workers and

$$SC_U = s\tau x_f^*$$

for unemployed workers. Thus, we can determine the spatial cost differential between employed and unemployed workers. It is equal to:

$$\Delta SC \equiv SC_L - SC_U = (1 - s)\,\tau\,x_b^* = (1 - s)\,\tau\,L. \tag{4.21}$$

It is easily seen that ΔSC is precisely the last term of (4.20) and its role is to compensate workers for spatial costs. This implies that the efficiency wage can be written as

$$w_L^* = w_U + e + \underbrace{SW}_{\text{Work Inducement}} + \underbrace{\Delta SC}_{\text{Spatial Compensation}}, \tag{4.22}$$

where $SW = \frac{e}{m}\left(\frac{\delta N}{N-L} + r\right)$ and $\Delta SC = (1 - s)\,\tau\,L$ so that, compared to unemployment, working gives a wage premium of $\Delta SW + \Delta SC$. The first term, $w_U + e$, can be regarded as the *base wage level*, namely the minimum wage level required to induce any individual to leave welfare and expend effort level e in working.

To close the model, let us now determine labor demand L. There are M identical firms in the economy. Each firm $j = 1 \ldots M$ has the same production function $f(el_j)$, which is assumed to be twice differentiable with $f(0) = 0$, $f'(el_j) > 0$ and $f''(el_j) \leq 0$ for all l_j, and satisfy the Inada conditions, i.e., $\lim_{l_j \to 0} f'(el_j) = +\infty$ and $\lim_{l_j \to +\infty} f'(el_j) = 0$. All firms produce the same composite good and sell it at a fixed market price p (this good is taken as the numeraire so that its price p is set to 1). Each firm j chooses l_j which maximizes $f(el_j) - w_L l_j$ (remember that w_L is the efficiency wage that is given by (4.20) and e is the effort level in each firm and thus, the average effort level in the economy)[4] so that $ef'(el_j) = w_L$. At the aggregate level, the total level of employment is given by $L = \sum_{j=1}^{j=M} l_j = M l_j$ so that $f'(el_j)$ is equivalent to $F'(eL)$[5] and, using (4.20), aggregate labor demand is given by:

$$eF'(eL^*) = w_U + e + \frac{e}{m}\left(\frac{\delta N}{N - L^*} + r\right) + (1 - s)\, \tau\, L^*. \qquad (4.23)$$

Definition 4.3. *A steady-state equilibrium* $(R^*(x), x_b^*, x_f^*, w_L^*, L^*)$ *consists of a land rent function, a border between employed and unemployed workers, a city fringe, and wage and employment such that the urban-land-use equilibrium and the labor market equilibrium are solved simultaneously.*

Since labor demand is decreasing in wages and wages are increasing in employment, it is easily shown that the steady-state equilibrium exists and is unique. Figure 4.2 displays this equilibrium: the intersection between the UNSC curve (equation (4.20)) and the labor demand curve gives the equilibrium values of wage $w_L(L)$ and employment L. Observe that at $L = N$, there is full employment and the corresponding wage, w^{pc}, is the wage that would be paid by firms in a perfectly competitive environment. Urban unemployment occurs here because wages are too high $(w_L(L) > w^{pc})$ and downward rigid. *Urban unemployment is thus involuntary.* Indeed, even though unemployed workers are ready to work at a lower wage in order to get a job, firms will never accept this offer because the UNSC will not be respected and all workers will shirk. Therefore, it is the presence of high and sticky wages that creates (involuntary) unemployment. In this context,

---

[4] Since we only consider steady-state equilibria, we can treat firms' decision problems as essentially static, i.e., they maximize instantaneous profit.

[5] Indeed, since $F(eL) = Mf(el_j)$ and $L = M l_j$, we have:

$$eF'(eL) = Mf'(eL/M)(e/M) = ef'(el_j).$$

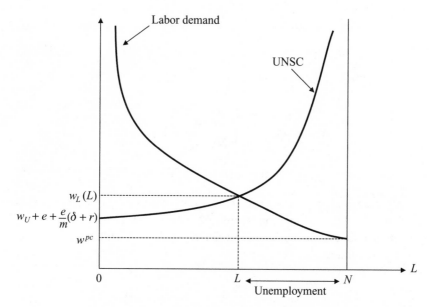

Figure 4.2. Labor equilibrium in the benchmark model.

taking space into account increases the level of unemployment since spatial efficiency wages are higher than in the absence of commuting costs (as, for example, in Shapiro and Stiglitz, 1984).

2.3. Interaction Between Land and Labor Markets

We can now study the interaction between land and labor markets. In fact, in the steady-state equilibrium, the endogenous variables are $R^*(x)$ (land market)[6], determined by (4.15), w_L^* and L^* (labor market), determined by (4.20) and (4.23), respectively, and I_L^* and I_U^* (equations (4.16) and (4.18), respectively).[7]

For the sake of exposition, let us rewrite the five equilibrium equations. We have:

$$R^*(x) = \begin{cases} \tau\ (L^* - x) + s\tau\ (N - L^*) & \text{for } 0 \le x \le L^* \\ s\ \tau\ (N - x) & \text{for } L^* < x \le N \\ 0 & \text{for } x > N \end{cases}$$

---

[6] Because housing consumption is fixed, the city fringe is exogenous and given by $x_f = N$.
[7] Naturally, determining W_L and W_U directly gives the values of I_L and I_U.

$$w_L^* = w_U + e + \frac{e}{m} \left(\frac{\delta\, N}{N - L^*} + r \right) + (1 - s)\, \tau\, L^*$$

$$eF'(eL^*) = w_U + e + \frac{e}{m} \left(\frac{\delta\, N}{N - L^*} + r \right) + (1 - s)\, \tau\, L^*$$

$$W_L^* = w_U + \frac{e}{m} \left(\frac{\delta\, N}{N - L^*} + r \right) - s\, \tau\, N$$

$$W_U^* = w_U - s\, \tau\, N.$$

All these equilibrium equations are a function of only one endogenous variable: L^*. The key equation is thus (4.23) since once L^* is calculated, then all other endogenous variables are determined. By totally differentiating (4.23), we obtain:[8]

$$L^* = L \left(\underset{-}{w_U}, \underset{?}{e}, \underset{-}{\delta}, \underset{+}{N}, \underset{-}{r}, \underset{+}{s}, \underset{-}{\tau} \right).$$

The spatial variables s (the relative fraction of commuting of the unemployed) and τ (the pecuniary commuting cost per unit of distance) have a positive (higher s leads to lower wages and thus higher L^*) and negative (higher τ implies that wages must increase and thus, labor demand will decrease) impact on L^*. In this respect, the impact of the land market on the labor market in this simple model is only through the spatial compensating part of the efficiency wage.

Labor variables also affect the land market. If we differentiate (4.15), we obtain in the employment zone ($0 \leq x \leq L^*$):[9]

$$R^* = R \left(\underset{-}{w_U}, \underset{?}{e}, \underset{-}{\delta}, \underset{+}{N}, \underset{-}{r}, \underset{+}{s}, \underset{?}{\tau} \right),$$

---

[8] The impact of e on L^* is ambiguous because an increase in effort increases wages (thus reduces L^*), but increases productivity (which increases L^*). However, if

$$-\frac{eL\, F''(eL)}{F'(eL)} > 1$$

then the latter effect dominates the former and

$$\frac{\partial L^*}{\partial e} < 0.$$

[9] To be more precise, for τ we have:

$$\frac{\partial R^*}{\partial \tau} = L^* - x + s\left(N - L^* \right) + \tau\, \frac{\partial L^*}{\partial \tau} (1 - s) \gtrless 0.$$

whereas in the unemployment zone ($L^* < x \leq N$), we have:

$$R^* = R \left(\underset{+}{N}, \underset{+}{s}, \underset{+}{\tau} \right).$$

Hence, when, for example, the unemployment benefit w_U increases, labor demand L^* decreases and thus, the employment zone is reduced. This, in turn, increases the instantaneous utility of the employed workers W_L^* (see (4.13)) since the border x_b^* between employed and unemployed workers is smaller and thus, employed workers reduce their bid-rent (the higher is the utility level to achieve, the lower is the bid-rent). The same reasoning applies for the job destruction rate δ since, in a downturn economy, firms hire less people and, because there is less competition in the land market, the equilibrium land rent decreases. As a result, the impact of the labor market on the land market is through labor demand.

3. Endogenous Housing Consumption

In the previous section, one of the key assumptions was that housing consumption was fixed and normalized to 1. This assumption limits the interaction between land and labor markets since the city fringe is exogenous. We now extend the benchmark model to the case of endogenous housing consumption.

3.1. Urban-Land-Use Equilibrium

For the model to be tractable,[10] we assume quasi-linear preferences for all workers. For a worker with employment status $es = L, U$, we have

$$\Omega(h_{es}, z_{es}) = z_{es} + \mho(h_{es}) \tag{4.24}$$

where h_{es} is the *housing* consumption for a worker with employment status $es = L, U$ and $\mho(\cdot)$ is any increasing function of h_{es}, i.e., $\mho'(\cdot) > 0$, with $\mho''(\cdot) \leq 0$. The budget constraints for non-shirking employed and unemployed workers are, respectively, given by:

$$h_L R(x) + \tau x + z_L = w_L - e \tag{4.25}$$

$$h_U R(x) + s\tau x + z_U = w_U, \tag{4.26}$$

---

[10] Indeed, to calculate the efficiency wage, a closed-form solution for the instantaneous utilities and x_b and x_f is needed. For example, with a Cobb-Douglas utility function, this is not possible. It seems that the quasi-linear utility function is the only one allowing us to calculate the efficiency wage.

where, as above, the composite good is taken as the numeraire good with a unit price. Maximizing utility (4.24) subject to (4.25) yields the following *housing (land) demand for non-shirker employed workers* at x:

$$\mho'(h_L^{NS}) = R(x). \tag{4.27}$$

Similarly, maximizing (4.24) subject to (4.26) yields the following *housing (land) demand for unemployed workers* at x:

$$\mho'(h_U) = R(x). \tag{4.28}$$

This implies that

$$h_L^{NS}(x) = h_U(x) = h(x) \tag{4.29}$$

with

$$\frac{\partial h}{\partial R} < 0 \text{ and } h'(x) = \frac{\partial h}{\partial R} R'(x).$$

This result (4.29) is due to the nature of the quasi-linear preferences since housing consumption is independent of income and thus employment status. Not surprisingly, when there is an increase in land price, housing consumption decreases and, if $R'(x) < 0$ (which will be shown below), then workers consume more land farther away from the CBD since land is cheaper there.

Using (4.24) and (4.27), we can now derive the following indirect utility

$$W_L^{NS}(x) = w_L - e - \tau x - h(x) R(x) + \mho(h(x)), \tag{4.30}$$

for each *employed* worker at x and, using (4.24) and (4.28), we have the following indirect utility

$$W_U(x) = w_U - s\tau x - h(x) R(x) + \mho(h(x)), \tag{4.31}$$

for each *unemployed* worker at x.

As in Section 2, because there are no relocation costs, the urban equilibrium is such that all employed enjoy the same level of utility $W_L^{NS}(x) \equiv W_L$, while all unemployed obtain $W_U(x) \equiv W_U$. The bid-rents of the (non-shirking) employed workers and the unemployed are thus equal to:

$$\Psi_L(x, W_L) = \frac{w_L - e - \tau x - W_L + \mho(h(x))}{h(x)} \tag{4.32}$$

$$\Psi_U(x, W_U) = \frac{w_U - s\tau x - W_U + \mho(h(x))}{h(x)}. \tag{4.33}$$

Using the envelope theorem, we easily obtain:

$$\frac{\partial \Psi_L(x, W_L)}{\partial x} = \frac{-\tau}{h(x)} < 0 \text{ and } \frac{\partial^2 \Psi_L(x, W_L)}{\partial x^2} = \frac{\tau\, h'(x)}{[h(x)]^2} > 0$$

$$\frac{\partial \Psi_U(x, W_U)}{\partial x} = \frac{-s\tau}{h(x)} < 0 \text{ and } \frac{\partial^2 \Psi_U(x, W_U)}{\partial x^2} = \frac{s\tau\, h'(x)}{[h(x)]^2} > 0.$$

These are both decreasing and convex in x. Indeed, workers living further away have higher commuting costs (direct effect), but larger lot sizes (indirect effect). The envelope theorem indicates that this indirect effect is negligible when changes in x are small. As a result, we obtain the negative sign since only the direct effect is of importance.

We can now implicitly define the housing consumption of each worker $h(x, W_L)$ and $h(x, W_U)$. Using (4.27) and (4.32) for the employed and (4.28) and (4.33) for the unemployed, we obtain:

$$\mho'(h(x, W_L)) = \frac{w_L - e - \tau x - W_L + \mho(h(x, W_L))}{h(x, W_L)} \tag{4.34}$$

$$\mho'(h(x, W_L)) = \frac{w_U - s\tau x - W_U + \mho(h(x, W_U))}{h(x, W_U)}. \tag{4.35}$$

We have the following straightforward result:

Proposition 4.2. *With quasi-linear preferences such as (4.24) and endogenous housing consumption, employed workers reside close to jobs whereas unemployed workers live on the periphery of the city.*

The proof is given in Appendix A4 at the end of this chapter. When housing consumption is endogenous, no clear urban pattern will be expected to emerge. Indeed, on the one hand, employed workers want to be closer to jobs than the unemployed because of higher commuting costs. On the other hand, because housing is a normal good, they consume more land and therefore prefer to be further away from the CBD since housing is cheaper in that area. However, because we assume quasi-linear preferences, there is *no income effect* and thus, the second effect is nil since at x_b both employed and unemployed workers consume the same amount of land because housing consumption is independent of net income (see (4.27) and (4.28)). As a result, as in the previous section, there is only the commuting cost effect and thus, the employed locate close to jobs. Interestingly, this result is robust if one uses any quasi-linear utility function in which non-linearity is on h.

Because housing consumption is endogenous, we cannot as before equalize x_b to L and x_f to N, but they must be determined. We focus on a closed-city model with absentee landlords (see Appendix A at the end of the book). We have the following definition

Definition 4.4. *An urban-land-use equilibrium is a 5-tuple* $(W_L^*, W_U^*, x_b^*, x_f^*, R^*(x))$ *such that:*

$$\Psi_L(x_b^*, W_L^*) = \Psi_U(x_b^*, W_U^*) \tag{4.36}$$

$$\Psi_U(x_f^*, W_U^*) = R_A \tag{4.37}$$

$$\int_0^{x_b^*} \frac{1}{h_L(x, W_L^*)} dx = L \tag{4.38}$$

$$\int_{x_b^*}^{x_f^*} \frac{1}{h_U(x, W_U^*)} dx = N - L \tag{4.39}$$

$$R^*(x) = \begin{cases} \Psi_L(x, W_L^*) & \text{for } x \leq x_b^* \\ \Psi_U(x, W_U^*) & \text{for } x_b^* < x \leq x_f^* \\ R_A & \text{for } x > x_f^* \end{cases} . \tag{4.40}$$

Obviously, we cannot explicitly determine the values of the endogenous variables.

3.2. Steady-State Equilibrium

As previously, we are now able to solve the labor market equilibrium (the definition is exactly the same as before and given by Definition 4.2). The Bellman equations are still given by (4.16)–(4.18), with the difference that W_L^{NS} and W_U are now defined by (4.50) and (4.51) and that $W_L^S = W_L + e$. Observe that workers are no longer risk neutral since their utility is not equivalent to their income. As above, to determine the efficiency wage, firms choose a wage w_L such that $I_L^{NS} = I_L^S = I_L$. We easily obtain:

$$I_L - I_U = \frac{e}{m}. \tag{4.41}$$

This is exactly as above. The surplus of being employed only depends on the monitoring technology and the effort level provided by workers. We have the following result:

Proposition 4.3. *Assume no relocation costs. If the preferences of the employed and unemployed workers are quasi-linear with respect to* z_{es}, *i.e.,*

$$\Omega(h_{es}, z_{es}) = z_{es} + \mho(h_{es}), \qquad es = L, U$$

where $\mho(\cdot)$ *is any increasing and concave function in* h_{es}, *then the efficiency wage is given by*

$$w_L = w_U + e + \frac{e}{m}\left(\frac{\delta}{u} + r\right) + (1-s)\tau x_b. \tag{4.42}$$

The exact value of x_b *depends on the specific form taken by* $\mho(\cdot)$.

This result is due to the fact that when preferences are quasi-linear, the demand function for good h (housing) does not depend on the individual's wealth (see, e.g., Mas-Colell, Whinston, and Green, 1995), but only on the price of h. As a result, in the same location and thus at the same price $R(x)$, the consumption of housing will be the same for employed and unemployed workers. So, in the same location, which in our case can only be at x_b since employed and unemployed are spatially separated in the city, the only spatial cost difference between employed and unemployed workers is the commuting cost difference, that is $(1 - s)\tau x_b$. Since the efficiency wage has two roles, to prevent shirking (which is not spatially related) and compensate for spatial cost differences, the efficiency wage will always be given by (4.42). Observe that the case of fixed housing consumption normalized to 1 (Section 2) is a special case of this proposition since it assumes that $f(h_k) = f(1) = 1$. In that case, $x_b = L$.

We can close the model exactly as in Section 2 and obtain labor demand in the following way:

$$w_U + e + \frac{e}{m}\left(\frac{\delta N}{N-L} + r\right) + (1-s)\tau x_b = F'(L). \tag{4.43}$$

3.3. Closed-Form Solutions

Because we would like to calculate the exact value of the efficiency wage (and thus of $x_b(L)$) and study the interaction between the two markets (land and labor), we need to take a specific form for the function $f(h_{es})$. Assume that $f(h_{es}) = h_{es}^{1/2}$, which is increasing and concave in h_{es}. It is easily shown that

$$\Psi_L(x, W_L) = \frac{1}{4(W_L - w_L + e + \tau x)} \tag{4.44}$$

$$\Psi_U(x, W_U) = \frac{1}{4(W_U - w_U + s\tau x)} \tag{4.45}$$

and

$$h_L(x, W_L) = 4(W_L - w_L + e + \tau x)^2 \tag{4.46}$$

$$h_U(x, W_U) = 4(W_U - w_U + s\tau x)^2. \tag{4.47}$$

By plugging these values into Definition 4.4 and, without loss of generality, by normalizing R_A to $1/4$, we obtain:

$$x_b^* = \frac{4L^*}{[1 + 4s\tau\,(N - L^*)]\,(1 + 4L^*\tau)} \tag{4.48}$$

$$x_f^* = x_b^* + \frac{4\,(N - L)}{1 + 4s\tau\,(N - L)} \tag{4.49}$$

$$W_L^{NS} = w_L - e + 1 - s\tau\,\left(x_f^* - x_b^*\right) - \tau\,x_b^* \tag{4.50}$$

$$= w_L - e + \frac{1}{1 + 4\tau\,[s\,N + (1 - s)\,L^*]}$$

$$W_U = w_U + 1 - s\tau\,x_f^*$$

$$= w_U + 1 - \frac{4s\tau}{1 + 4s\tau\,(N - L^*)}\left[\frac{L^*}{1 + 4\tau\,[s\,N + (1 - s)\,L^*]} + N - L^*\right] \tag{4.51}$$

$$R(x) = \begin{cases} \dfrac{1}{4}\left(\dfrac{1}{1 + 4s\tau\,(N - L^*) + 4\tau\,L^*} + \tau\,x\right)^{-1} & \text{for } x \le x_b^* \\[2ex] \dfrac{1}{4}\left(1 - \dfrac{4s\tau}{1 + 4s\tau\,(N - L^*)}\left[\dfrac{L^*}{1 + 4s\tau\,(N - L^*) + 4\tau\,L^*}\right.\right. \\[1ex] \quad \left.\left. + N - L^*\right] + s\tau\,x\right)^{-1} & \text{for } x_b^* < x \le x_f^* \\[2ex] \dfrac{1}{4} & \text{for } x > x_f^* \end{cases} \tag{4.52}$$

It can be shown that $x_b^*(L = 0) = 0$ and $\partial x_b^*/\partial L > 0$, and $\partial x_b^*/\partial s < 0$ and

$$\frac{\partial x_b^*}{\partial \tau} \gtrless 0 \Leftrightarrow \tau \lessgtr \frac{1}{4\sqrt{s\,(N - L)\,[L + s\,(N - L)]}}.$$

Hence, if L (the level of employment in this economy) increases, more workers are employed and thus richer and, therefore, the space they occupy increases. It also says that at a given L (in equilibrium, L will itself depend on s and τ), the higher s is (the percentage of unemployed CBD trips), the lower x_b is. Indeed, if unemployed workers commute more often to the CBD, their commuting costs increase and thus their willingness to pay for land decreases (see (4.45)). Since s does not affect the bid-rent of the employed workers, the border x_b decreases. Finally, when τ increases, the impact on x_b is ambiguous. Indeed, the commuting cost τ has a negative effect on both bid-rents (see (4.44) and (4.45)) so that an increase in τ

reduces the willingness to pay for land for both employed and unemployed workers. However, if τ is sufficiently small, then a rise in τ increases x_b, while we have the reverse if τ is sufficiently large. This is because the employed have higher total commuting costs than the unemployed (τx versus $s\tau x$) so if τ is already large, then when τ increases, they will increase their bid-rent less than the unemployed workers and therefore, x_b will decrease. When τ is small, we have the opposite result.

Since $\mho(\cdot)$ has an explicit value, using (4.48)–(4.51), we can determine the efficiency wage. It is given by:

$$w_L^* = w_U + e + \frac{e}{m}\left(\frac{\delta N}{N - L} + r\right) + \Delta SC \qquad (4.53)$$

where

$$\Delta SC = (1 - s)\,\tau x_b^*$$
$$= (1 - s)\left[\frac{1}{1 + 4s\tau\,(N - L)} - \frac{1}{1 + 4s\tau\,(N - L) + 4\tau\,L}\right],$$

is the spatial cost differential between employed and unemployed workers.

Let us interpret ΔSC and the effects of the *spatial* variables, s and τ, on the efficiency wage w_L^*. In fact, the effects of s and τ on w_L^* are exactly those of s and τ on x_b. Since $\Delta SC = (1 - s)\,\tau x_b$ is the spatial compensation that firms must pay to their employed workers, an increase in s (the percentage of unemployed CBD trips relative to employed CBD trips) will always reduce the efficiency wage. Indeed, firms need to compensate employed workers less for their spatial costs since ΔSC decreases with s. However, when the pecuniary commuting cost per unit of distance τ increases, the effect on wages in ambiguous. This is the effect mentioned above where an increase in τ raised x_b only if τ was sufficiently small.

Let us now compare this efficiency wage (4.53) to that obtained where housing consumption was fixed and equal to 1 (see (4.20)). It is easily seen that the only difference between these two wages is the spatial cost differential between employed and unemployed workers, i.e., ΔSC, the spatial component of the wage that firms must set in order to compensate employed workers for their spatial costs (commuting and land rent costs). In fact, since all employed workers obtain the same utility level and since all unemployed workers also obtain the same utility level, we can compare the employed and unemployed workers who live at a distance x_b (i.e., the border between employed and unemployed workers) from the CBD since at x_b, they both pay the same land rent. As a result, in the case of fixed housing (normalized to 1), $x_b = L$ and the only difference between these two workers is the commuting cost differential, which is equal to $\Delta SC = (1 - s)\tau L$. However, in the case of endogenous housing consumption, the spatial difference is also $(1 - s)\tau x_b$, but the value of x_b is now more complicated because it also takes into account the difference in housing consumption between employed and unemployed workers.

3.4. Interaction Between Land and Labor Markets

Compared to the model with fixed housing consumption, the only difference here is that the city fringe x_f is now a function of L and given by (4.49). It is easily shown that $\frac{\partial x_b^*}{\partial L^*} > 0$, but $\frac{\partial x_f^*}{\partial L^*} < 0$ for a reasonable value of the employment rate (i.e., $L^*/N \geq 0.5$). So when employment increases, the employment zone $[0, x_b^*]$ is augmented, but city size x_f^* decreases because the unemployment zone $[x_b^*, x_f^*]$ is reduced; this latter effect being stronger than the former.

4. Open Cities and Resident Landlords

There are other aspects of cities that we would now like to study. They include open cities and non-absent landlords (Fujita, 1989; Appendix A). Indeed, in urban economics, the traditional distinction is between closed and open cities. In closed cities, as we have seen above, the utility of all agents (here, employed and unemployed workers) is endogenous while their population levels are assumed to be exogenous. In open cities where there is free mobility between cities, the utility obtained by city residents becomes exogenous (it is just their outside option), but the number of people living in the city is endogenous. This is what we now want to study. We will further investigate this issue in Chapter 6 when we will analyze rural-urban migration in the efficiency wage framework. Another important issue in urban economics is whether landlords are absentees. We will relax the assumption of absentee landlords and study the full closed city model (see Pines and Sadka, 1986; Fujita, 1989, Appendix A), where urban land is rented from absentee landlords at a price equaling the agricultural rent.

4.1. Open Cities

Let us extend the benchmark model of urban efficiency wages (Section 2) to the case of open cities. The bid-rents of employed and unemployed workers are still given by (4.6) and (4.7) and Proposition 4.1 is still valid so that employed workers reside close to jobs whereas unemployed workers live on the periphery of the city. We must solve (4.8)−(4.12), given that the unknowns are now N and L while W_L and W_U are now exogenous. By solving these equations, we easily obtain $x_f^* = N$ and $x_b^* = L$ as well as:

$$N^* = \frac{w_U - W_U}{s\,\tau} \tag{4.54}$$

$$L^* = \frac{w_L - e - w_U + W_U - W_L}{(1-s)\tau} \tag{4.55}$$

$$R^*(x) = \begin{cases} w_L - e - \tau\,x - W_L & \text{for } 0 \leq x \leq L \\ w_U - s\,\tau\,x - W_U & \text{for } L < x \leq N \\ 0 & \text{for } x > N \end{cases} \tag{4.56}$$

Let us now calculate the efficiency wage. The expected utilities of non-shirking, shirking, and unemployed workers, (4.16)−(4.18), are now modified and equal to:

$$r\,I_L^{NS} = w_L - e - \tau\,L - R(L) - \delta\,(I_L^{NS} - I_U) \tag{4.57}$$

$$r\,I_L^{S} = w_L - \tau\,L - R(L) - (\delta + m)\,(I_L^{S} - I_U) \tag{4.58}$$

$$r\,I_U = w_U - s\tau\,L - R(L) + a(I_L - I_U). \tag{4.59}$$

Observe that the instantaneous utilities of non-shirking, shirking, and unemployed workers (which are exogenous here) are given by (4.3), (4.4) and (4.5), respectively, and are all evaluated at $x = L$. Indeed, since in equilibrium all employed workers obtained the same (instantaneous) utility W_L between $x = 0$ and $x = L$ and all unemployed workers also obtained the same (instantaneous) utility W_U between $x = L$ and $x = N$, it is of no importance which location x we choose. But since the only common location for employed and unemployed workers is $x = L$ (where they pay the same price for land), we have chosen to evaluate the utility in exactly this location. Now, because the optimal efficiency wage contract is such that $I_L^{NS} = I_L^{S} = I_L$, as in the benchmark case, we easily obtain: $I_L - I_U = e/m$. Then, by solving the equations exactly as in the benchmark case, we easily obtain (using (4.54) for the second line):

$$w_L^* = w_U + e + \frac{e}{m}\left(\frac{\delta\,N}{N-L} + r\right) + (1-s)\,\tau\,L \tag{4.60}$$

$$= w_U + e + \frac{e}{m}\left[\frac{\delta\,(w_U - W_U)}{w_U - W_U - s\,\tau\,L} + r\right] + (1-s)\,\tau\,L,$$

which is exactly the efficiency wage (4.20). This is quite natural because there is no reason for the wage to be affected by the type of city we consider (open or closed). Employers just set a wage that deters shirking and induces workers to remain in the city. There is, however, one crucial difference between (4.20) and (4.60) in that N and L are determined by (4.54) and (4.55) in (4.60) while they are parameters in (4.20). For this reason, we can use the value of w_L^* in (4.60) and plug it into (4.55) to obtain:

$$W_L - W_U = \frac{e}{m}\left(\frac{\delta N}{N - L} + r\right). \tag{4.61}$$

Now, plugging back (4.61) into (4.60), we obtain another formulation of the efficiency wage expressed in the (instantaneous) utility difference between employed and unemployed workers. We have:

$$w_L^* = w_U + e + W_L - W_U + (1 - s)\tau L^*. \tag{4.62}$$

The interpretation of this wage is quite intuitive. To deter shirking, the employed must pay the (instantaneous) utility difference between employed and unemployed workers, which is now exogenous. Naturally, here we are not capturing the essence of the efficiency wage model where unemployment "acts as a worker discipline device," that is when L approaches N, w_L tends to infinity, which is why we prefer to use (4.60). We can now close the model exactly as in the benchmark case by adding equation (4.23) which, using (4.54), can be written as

$$eF'(eL^*) = w_U + e + \frac{e}{m}\left[\frac{\delta(w_U - W_U)}{w_U - W_U - s\tau L^*} + r\right] + (1 - s)\tau L^*. \tag{4.63}$$

The equilibrium can be calculated as follows. First, equation (4.23) gives the optimal L^* as a function of parameters only. Then, plugging this value of L^* into (4.60) or (4.62) leads to the efficiency wage w_L^*. Finally plugging w_L^* into (4.56) yields:

$$R^*(x) = \begin{cases} w_U - \tau x - W_U + (1 - s)\tau L^* & \text{for } 0 \leq x \leq L \\ w_U - s\tau x - W_U & \text{for } L < x \leq N \\ 0 & \text{for } x > N \end{cases}. \tag{4.64}$$

If we compare the equilibrium land rent in the closed-city model (equation (4.15)) and the open-city model (equation (4.64)), its value differs substantially in the employment area (i.e., for locations $x \in [0, L]$). Indeed, besides τ, s, L, and x, the land rent depends on w_U and W_U when the city is open and N when it is closed. This is due to the different nature of the two models since, in the latter, utility is endogenous, while in the former it is the size of the population which is endogenous.

As proved by Fujita (1989, Proposition 3.5, pp. 62–63), the closed and open-city models must be consistent with one another. Fujita showed that the open-city model should give the same results as those obtained in the closed-city model using equilibrium utilities W_L^* and W_U^*. Let us now check this. In the closed-city model of Section 2, by plugging the value of w_L^* defined in (4.20) into (4.13), we obtain:

$$W_L^* = w_U + \frac{e}{m}\left(\frac{\delta N}{N-L} + r\right) - s\tau N.$$

Moreover, using (4.14), we have:

$$W_U^* = w_U - s\tau N.$$

Combining these two equations, we obtain:

$$W_L^* - W_U^* = \frac{e}{m}\left(\frac{\delta N}{N-L} + r\right),$$

which is exactly (4.61). The two models (closed and open cities) are thus totally equivalent.

4.2. Landlords are *Not* Absentee

In this section, we return to the benchmark model with a closed city and extend it to the case of resident landlords. We will use the so-called public land ownership model (Fujita, 1989, Ch. 3; Appendix A). To be more precise, the city residents are now assumed to form a government, which rents the land for the city from rural landlords at the agricultural rent R_A. The city government, in turn, subleases the land to city residents at the competitive rent $R(x)$ in each location x. We can define the total differential rent (TDR) from the city as:

$$TDR = \int_0^{x_f} [R(x) - R_A] \, dx$$

$$= \int_0^{x_f} R(x) dx,$$

where R_A has been normalized to zero. The income of each individual is now given by $w_L + TDR/N$ and $w_U + TDR/N$ for employed and unemployed workers, respectively. Observe that since employment and unemployment are not permanent states, but rather transitional, the share of the land obtained by all workers is equal to TDR/N, independently of their employment status. Since TDR/N is taken as given by each individual, the analysis is straightforward and closely follows that of Section 2.

First, it is easily verified that the equilibrium (instantaneous) utilities are given by:

$$W_L^* = w_L + TDR/N - e - \tau L - s\tau \, (N - L) \qquad (4.65)$$

$$W_U^* = w_U + TDR/N - s \tau \, N, \qquad (4.66)$$

while equilibrium land rent is equal to:

$$R^*(x) = \begin{cases} \tau \, (L - x) - TDR/N + s\tau \, (N - L) & \text{for } 0 \leq x \leq L \\ s \tau \, (N - x) - TDR/N & \text{for } L < x \leq N \, . \\ 0 & \text{for } x > N \end{cases}$$
$$(4.67)$$

Second, the efficiency wage is still given by (4.20) and TDR/N is not affected by this wage. This is mainly because employed shirkers and non-shirkers as well as unemployed workers all have the same land revenue TDR/N. Moreover, labor demand L^* is still determined by (4.23). Finally, the main innovation of this model is the fact that equilibrium land rent is affected by resident landlords. We have:

$$TDR^* = \int_0^N R^*(x) dx$$

$$= \int_0^{L^*} \left[\tau \, (L - x) - \frac{TDR}{N} + s\tau \, (N - L) \right] dx$$

$$+ \int_{L^*}^N \left[s \tau \, (N - x) - \frac{TDR}{N} \right] dx.$$

This is equivalent to

$$TDR = \frac{(1-s)\tau}{4} L^{*2} + \frac{s\tau}{4} N^2. \tag{4.68}$$

Plugging (4.68) into (4.65), (4.66), (4.67), and using (4.20), we finally obtain:

$$W_L^* = w_U + \frac{e}{m} \left(\frac{\delta N}{N - L^*} + r \right) + \frac{(1-s)\tau}{4N} L^{*2} - \frac{3}{4} s\tau N \tag{4.69}$$

$$W_U^* = w_U + \frac{(1-s)\tau}{4N} L^{*2} - \frac{3}{4} s\tau N \tag{4.70}$$

$$R^*(x) = \begin{cases} \tau \left(\frac{3}{4} s N - x \right) - (1-s) \left(\frac{L^*}{4N} - 1 \right) \tau L & \text{for } 0 \leq x \leq L \\ s\tau \left(\frac{3}{4} N - x \right) - \frac{(1-s)\tau}{4N} L^{*2} & \text{for } L < x \leq N, \\ 0 & \text{for } x > N \end{cases} \tag{4.71}$$

where L^* is defined by (4.23). Comparing (4.69) and (4.70), we see that:

$$W_L^* - W_U^* = \frac{e}{m} \left(\frac{\delta N}{N - L^*} + r \right),$$

which is exactly (4.61). This is not surprising since all models (closed city, open city, absentee landlords, public land ownership models) must be consistent with one another (see once more Fujita, 1989, Proposition 3.5, pp. 62–63). To conclude, when landlords are not absentee, but reside in the city, the efficiency wage as well as the employment level are not affected and are still given by (4.20) and (4.23). However, the instantaneous utilities are now equal to (4.69) and (4.70) (which also implies that the intertemporal utilities change accordingly) and the equilibrium land rent is now given by (4.71).

5. City Structure

In Section 3, we have endogenized housing consumption, but because of quasi-linear preferences, we have precluded the possibility of differential housing consumption between employed and unemployed workers. Since this becomes very complicated, we return to the assumption of risk-neutral workers (utility equals income) and a closed-city model, but assume different (exogenous) housing consumption between employed and unemployed workers.

5.1. Urban-Land-Use Equilibria

We now assume that employed workers consume $h_L = h > 0$ units of land, whereas the unemployed consume $h_U = \mu h > 0$, with $0 < \mu < 1$. This is a reasonable assumption since, being richer, employed workers in general consume more land than the unemployed. Since all workers are risk neutral, the indirect utility of the (non-shirking) employed and unemployed is now, respectively, given by:

$$W_L^{NS}(x) = z_L = w_L - e - h R(x) - \tau x \qquad (4.72)$$

$$W_U(x) = z_U = w_U - \mu h R(x) - s\tau x. \qquad (4.73)$$

We can compute the bid-rents of all agents. They are given by:

$$\Psi_L(x, W_L) = \frac{w_L - e - \tau x - W_L^{NS}}{h} \qquad (4.74)$$

$$\Psi_U(x, W_U) = \frac{w_U - s\tau x - W_U}{\mu h}. \qquad (4.75)$$

We easily obtain the following result:

Proposition 4.4. *With risk-neutral agents and different housing consumption for the employed and the unemployed, we have:*

(*i*) *If $\mu > s$, then employed workers live close to jobs while unemployed workers reside on the periphery of the city. This is referred to as Equilibrium 1.*

(*ii*) *If $\mu < s$, then unemployed workers live close to jobs while employed workers reside on the periphery of the city. This is referred to as Equilibrium 2.*

The intuition of this result is straightforward. To determine the equilibrium location pattern, there is a trade-off for employed workers between their willingness to reside close to jobs (because they have higher commuting costs than unemployed workers), but also far away from jobs (because they consume more land than unemployed workers and land is cheaper further away from the CBD). As a result, if $\mu > s$, then the second effect (housing consumption differential) dominates the first (commuting cost differential) and the employed occupy the core of the city. If $\mu < s$, we have the reverse location pattern. Figure 4.3 describes the

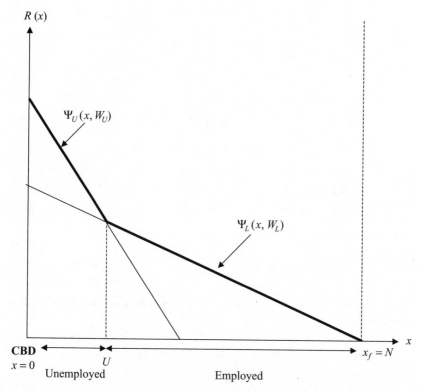

Figure 4.3. Urban equilibrium 2.

urban-land-use pattern of Equilibrium 2, while Figure 4.1 displays that of Equilibrium 1.[11]

We can now give a formal definition of each urban equilibrium. Once more, we normalize the agricultural land rent R_A to zero. Given that $\mu > s$, the definition of Equilibrium 1 is exactly the same as that of Definition 4.1 in Section 2, with $h_L = h$ and $h_U = \mu h$. It is easily seen that, by solving these equations, we obtain:[12]

$$W_L^{1*} = w_L - e - \tau x_b^* - \frac{s\tau \left(x_f^* - x_b^*\right)}{\mu} \qquad (4.76)$$

$$= w_L^1 - e - (1-s)\tau h L^1 - s\tau hN$$

---

[11] These equilibria (and Figures 4.1. and 4.3) are equivalent to the equilibria 1 and 2 (and Figures 1.1 and 1.2) in Chapter 1.

[12] Superscripts 1 and 2 refer to Equilibrium 1 and Equilibrium 2, respectively.

$$W_U^{1*} = w_U - s\tau\, x_f^* \tag{4.77}$$

$$= w_U - s\tau\, h\left[L^1 + \mu\left(N - L^1\right)\right]$$

$$x_b^{1*} = h\, L^1 \tag{4.78}$$

$$x_f^{1*} = h\, L^1 + \mu\, h\left(N - L^1\right) \tag{4.79}$$

$$= h\left(1 - \mu\right)L^1 + \mu\, hN$$

$$R^{1*}(x) = \begin{cases} \left[-x + (1-s)\,hL^1 + shN\right]\tau/h & \text{for } 0 \le x \le x_b^1 \\ \left[-x + hL^1 + \theta\, h\left(N - L^1\right)\right]s\tau/\theta\, h & \text{for } x_b^1 < x \le x_f^1 \\ 0 & \text{for } x > x_f^1 \end{cases} \tag{4.80}$$

For Equilibrium 2, we have:

Definition 4.5. *Assume that $\mu < s$. Then, urban-land-use Equilibrium 2 is a 5-tuple* $(W_L^{2*},\, W_U^{2*},\, x_b^{2*},\, x_f^{2*},\, R^{2*}(x))$ *such that:*

$$\Psi_L(x_b^{2*},\, W_L^{2*}) = \Psi_U(x_b^{2*},\, W_U^{2*}) \tag{4.81}$$

$$\Psi_L(x_f^{2*},\, W_L^{2*}) = 0 \tag{4.82}$$

$$\int_0^{x_b^{2*}} \frac{1}{\mu\, h}\, dx = N - L^2 \tag{4.83}$$

$$\int_{x_b^{2*}}^{x_f^{2*}} \frac{1}{h}\, dx = L^2 \tag{4.84}$$

$$R^{2*}(x) = \max\left\{\Psi_U(x,\, W_U^{2*}),\, \Psi_L(x,\, W_L^{2*}),\, 0\right\} \quad \text{at each } x \in \left(0,\, x_f\right). \tag{4.85}$$

Solving (4.81)–(4.85) gives:

$$W_L^{2*} = w_L^2 - e - \tau\, x_f^{2*} \tag{4.86}$$

$$= w_L^2 - e - \tau\left[hL^2 + \mu\, h\left(N - L^2\right)\right]$$

$$W_U^{2*} = w_U - s\tau\, x_b^{2*} - \mu\,\tau\left(x_f^{2*} - x_b^{2*}\right) \tag{4.87}$$

$$= w_U - s\tau\,\mu\, h\left(N - L^2\right) - \tau\,\theta\, hL^2$$

$$x_b^{2*} = \mu\, h\left(N - L^2\right) \tag{4.88}$$

$$x_f^{2*} = \mu\, h\left(N - L^2\right) + hL^2 \tag{4.89}$$

$$R^{1*}(x) = \begin{cases} \left[-x + \theta\, h\, L^2/s + \theta\, h\left(N - L^2\right)\right] s\tau\,/\left(\theta\, h\right) & \text{for } 0 \le x \le L^1 \\ \left[-x + hL^2 + \theta\, h\left(N - L^2\right)\right] \tau/h & \text{for } L^1 < x \le N\cdot \\ 0 & \text{for } x > N \end{cases} \tag{4.90}$$

5.2. Steady-State Equilibrium 1: Employed Workers Live Close to Jobs

Let us determine labor market Equilibrium 1. We can write the steady-state Bellman equations for non-shirkers, shirkers, and unemployed workers, respectively. Using (4.76) and (4.77), we obtain:

$$r\, I_L^{NS} = w_L - e - \tau\, x_b^* - \frac{s\tau\left(x_f^* - x_b^*\right)}{\mu} - \delta\left(I_L^{NS} - I_U\right) \tag{4.91}$$

$$r\, I_L^{S} = w_L - \tau\, x_b^* - \frac{s\tau\left(x_f^* - x_b^*\right)}{\mu} - (\delta + m)\left(I_L^{S} - I_U\right) \tag{4.92}$$

$$r\, I_U = w_U - s\tau\, x_f^* + a(I_L - I_U). \tag{4.93}$$

Let us now calculate the efficiency wage by having $I_L^{NS} = I_L^{S} = I_L$. We obtain:

$$w_L^1 = w_U + e + \frac{e}{m}\left(\frac{\delta N}{N - L} + r\right) + \Delta SC^1, \tag{4.94}$$

where

$$\begin{aligned} \Delta SC^1 &= (1 - s)\,\tau\, x_b^1 + s\tau\,(1 - \mu)\, h\left(N - L^1\right) \\ &= \tau\, h\left[(1 - s)\, L^1 + s\,(1 - \mu)\left(N - L^1\right)\right] \end{aligned}$$

is the spatial cost differential between employed and unemployed workers.

In the models described above, where *identical housing consumption for employed and unemployed workers* was assumed, the spatial cost differential was equal to $\Delta SC = (1 - s)\,\tau\, x_b^1$ (see (4.20) or (4.42)). Here, spatial compensation is larger because housing consumption is higher for employed than for unemployed workers. This is because firms must not only compensate for commuting costs (which are larger for employed workers), but also for housing consumption (which is also higher for employed workers).

In fact, the difference in commuting costs is given by $(1 - s) \tau x_b^1$ while the difference in housing consumption is equal to $s \tau h \left(N - L^1\right) (1 - \mu)$.

5.3. Steady-State Equilibrium 2: Unemployed Workers Live Close to Jobs

Using exactly the same steps as in the previous section, we can calculate the efficiency wage for Equilibrium 2. We obtain:

$$w_L^2 = w_U + e + \frac{e}{m} \left(\frac{\delta N}{N - L^2} + r \right) + \Delta SC^2, \qquad (4.95)$$

where

$$\Delta SC^2 = (1 - s) \tau x_b^2 + \tau h (1 - \theta) L^2$$
$$= \tau h \left[(1 - s) \mu \left(N - L^2 \right) + (1 - \mu) L^2 \right]$$

is the spatial cost differential between employed and unemployed workers.

5.4. Comparison Between the Two Equilibria

We would now like to compare the two equilibria in terms of urban and labor aspects as well as welfare. Let us thus define welfare as the sum of all utilities (workers, firms, and landlords) in each city. Since wages and land rents are pure transfers, total welfare (which amounts to adding the utilities of all workers, firms, and landlords) in Equilibrium 1 is given by:

$$\mathcal{W}^1 = w_U \left(N - L^1 \right) + F \left(L^1 \right) - e L^1 - \int_0^{x_b^1} \tau x \, dx - \int_{x_b^k}^{x_f^1} s \tau x \, dx,$$

while, in Equilibrium 2, it is equal to:

$$\mathcal{W}^2 = w_U \left(N - L^2 \right) + F \left(L^2 \right) - e L^2 - \int_0^{x_b^2} s \tau x \, dx - \int_{x_b^k}^{x_f^2} \tau x \, dx.$$

To compare welfare across cities, let us proceed to a simple numerical resolution of the model. We use the following Cobb-Douglas function for the production function of equilibrium $k = 1, 2$: $f \left(l^k \right) = \left(l^k \right)^{0.5}$, which implies that

$$F \left(L^k \right) = M f \left(l^k \right) = M^{0.5} \left(L^k \right)^{0.5}$$

and thus,

$$F' \left(L^k \right) = f' \left(l^k \right) = 0.5 \, M^{0.5} L^{-0.5}.$$

The values of the parameters, in yearly terms, are:* $w_U = 80$, $e = 20$, $h = 20$, $\tau = 1$, and $r = 0.05$. The job-destruction rate is $\delta = 0.2$ and the monitoring rate is $m = 1.8$, which means that jobs last on average five years for a non-shirker and six months for a shirker. The number of firms $M = 70,000$ and the total population N are normalized to 1.

First, we fix s and let μ vary. We take $s = 0.2$, which means that the travel frequencies for the unemployed are assumed to be one-fifth of those for employed workers. Table 4.1a describes the results. We have the unemployment rate that is only due to space, $u_s^k = u^k - u_{ns}^k$, where u^k is the unemployment rate, i.e., $\left(N - L^k\right)/N$, and u_{ns}^k is the non-spatial unemployment rate, i.e., the unemployment rate in Shapiro and Stiglitz (1984). Similarly, the wage that is only due to space is $w_s^k = w_L^k - w_{ns}^k$, where w_L^k is the wage defined in this paper and w_{ns}^k is non-spatial wage, i.e., the wage in Shapiro and Stiglitz (1984). Moreover, TLR_L^k, TLR_L^k and $\Sigma\Pi^h$ signify, respectively, total land rent paid by employed workers, total land rent paid by unemployed workers, and the sum of all profits in the city in equilibrium $k = 1, 2$. In this table, we have chosen to vary a key parameter s/μ, the differential ratio of commuting costs and housing consumption between employed and unemployed workers. This parameter s/μ varies from a very low value 0.01 (where city 1 is the prevailing equilibrium) to a very large value 4 (where city 2 is the prevailing equilibrium). The cut-off point is equal to $s/\mu = 1$. The sign '$-$' indicates the 'limit to the left,' whereas the sign '$+$' indicates the 'limit to the right.'[13]

Our comments are as follows. First, it can be seen that switching from a city where the employed live close to jobs (city 1) to a city where the unemployed live close to jobs (city 2) alters some of the variables, but not all. In particular, total welfare is roughly the same. This is not surprising because in this model it is not harmful for the unemployed to be far away from jobs.[14] In particular, the rate at which they leave unemployment is $a^k = \delta L^k/(N - L) = \delta(1 - u^k)/u^k$. Since, for both $s/\mu = 1-$ and $s/\mu = 1+$, $u^k = 0.094$, we have $a^1 = a^2 = 1.927$, which implies that the average duration of unemployment $1/a^k$ is six months. Second, the impact of the spatial variables on labor market outcomes is *not* negligible. If we take the two extreme cases, $s/\mu = 0.2$ (μ close to 1 so that employed and unemployed workers consume the same amount of land; city 1) and

---

* We use different parameter values as compared to that of the urban search models in Part 1. This is due to the different nature of the labor market in the two models.

[13] We did a similar simulation exercise in Table 1.3 of Chapter 1, but the parameter we varied had a very different meaning.

[14] In the search benchmark model of Chapter 1, this was not the case since distance to jobs had a negative effect on the search effort of unemployed workers.

Table 4.1a. *Short-run equilibria when $s = 0.2$ and μ varies*

s/μ (with $s = 0.2$)	City	u^k	u^k_{ns}	u^k_s	$\dfrac{u^k_s}{u^k}$	$\dfrac{w^k_s}{w^k_L}$	$\dfrac{\Delta SC^k}{w^k_L}$	$\dfrac{\Delta WI^k}{w^k_L}$	TLR^k_L	TLR^k_U	x^k_b	x^k_f	$\sum \Pi^k$	W^k
0.2001 ($\mu = 0.9999$)	1	9.32	6.17	3.15	33.77	1.69	10.44	31.97	8.561	0.0174	18.137	20	125.98	66477
0.3 ($\mu = 0.6666$)	1	9.35	6.17	3.18	34.02	1.71	10.53	31.89	8.556	0.0117	18.130	19.38	125.95	66467
0.4 ($\mu = 0.5$)	1	9.37	6.17	3.20	34.15	1.72	10.57	31.86	8.553	0.0088	18.126	19.06	125.94	66461
0.6 ($\mu = 0.3333$)	1	9.39	6.17	3.22	34.28	1.73	10.61	31.82	8.551	0.0059	18.122	18.75	125.92	66456
0.9 ($\mu = 0.22222$)	1	9.40	6.17	3.23	34.36	1.74	10.64	31.80	8.549	0.0039	18.120	18.54	125.92	66452
1− ($\mu = 0.20001$)	1	9.40	6.17	3.23	34.38	1.74	10.65	31.79	8.548	0.0035	18.119	18.50	125.91	66451
1+ ($\mu = 0.19999$)	2	9.40	6.17	3.23	34.38	1.74	10.65	31.79	8.208	0.3440	0.376	18.50	125.91	66446
1.2 ($\mu = 0.16666$)	2	9.57	6.17	3.40	35.50	1.83	11.02	31.47	8.178	0.2914	0.319	18.41	125.80	66387
1.4 ($\mu = 0.143$)	2	9.69	6.17	3.52	36.29	1.89	11.28	31.25	8.157	0.2529	0.277	18.34	125.72	66345
1.6 ($\mu = 0.125$)	2	9.78	6.17	3.61	36.88	1.94	11.48	31.08	8.140	0.2229	0.244	18.29	125.66	66313
1.8 ($\mu = 0.1111$)	2	9.85	6.17	3.68	37.34	1.98	11.63	30.95	8.128	0.1994	0.219	18.25	125.61	66288
4 ($\mu = 0.05$)	2	10.16	6.17	3.99	39.29	2.15	12.29	30.39	8.071	0.0923	0.102	18.07	125.39	66174
200 ($\mu = 0.001$)	2	10.42	6.17	4.25	40.80	2.29	12.81	29.96	8.024	0.0019	0.0021	17.92	125.20	66081

$s/\mu = 200$ (μ close to 0 so that unemployed workers consume a negligible amount of land; city 2), the total unemployment rate increases from 9.32% to 10.42%, but this rise is only due to the spatial part of unemployment, which increases by 35%. This is because city size decreases by 11.6% (from 20 to 17.92), which affects wages and ultimately, totally land prices, which decrease by 6.66% (from 8.5784 to 8.043).

Let us now fix $\mu = 0.2$, which means that housing consumption for unemployed workers is assumed to be 1/5 of that for employed workers, and let s vary. Table 4.1b displays the results of the numerical simulations. The results are similar to those obtained in Table 4.1a, with the difference that the unemployment rate is now higher in city 1 than in city 2, because μ is relatively small. If comparing the two extreme cases, $s/\mu = 0.2$ (s close to 0 so that the unemployed do not very often commute to the CBD; city 1) and $s/\mu = 5$ (s close to 1 so that employed and unemployed workers have the same number of commuting trips; city 2), the decrease in unemployment is once more only due to space. However, in this case, there is nearly no city-size effect but a very strong wage effect. Indeed, since the efficiency wage must compensate for the difference in spatial costs between employed and unemployed workers, a variation in s obviously has large effects. In fact, from s close to 0 to s close to 1, the spatial compensation of wages decreases from 12.39% to 10.45%. This is the main effect which explains the decrease in spatial unemployment from 10.22% to 9.32%.

6. Long-Run Equilibrium with Free Entry

We now study the long-run properties of the urban efficiency wage model in the benchmark model. Firms freely enter the labor market up to a point where profits are equal to zero. If c denotes the fixed entry cost, then, for each equilibrium $k = 1, 2$, the zero-profit condition can be written as:

$$f(l^k) - w_L^k l^k - c = 0.$$

As a result, for each equilibrium $k = 1, 2$, the long-run equilibrium is characterized by four unknowns, l^k, w^k, u^k, M^k, and the four following equations:

$$w_L^k = f'(l^k) \tag{4.96}$$

$$f(l^k) - w_L^k l^k - c = 0 \tag{4.97}$$

$$w_L^k = w_U + e + \frac{e}{m}\left(\frac{\delta}{u^k} + r\right) + \Delta SC^k \tag{4.98}$$

$$1 - u^k = M^k l^k. \tag{4.99}$$

Table 4.1b. Short-run equilibria when $\mu = 0.2$ and s varies

s/μ (with $\mu = 0.2$)	City	u^k	u^k_{ns}	u^k_s	$\frac{u^k_s}{u^k}$	$\frac{w^k_s}{w^k_L}$	$\frac{\Delta SC^k}{w^k_L}$	$\frac{\Delta WI^k}{w^k_L}$	TLR^k_L	TLR^k_U	x^k_b	x^k_f	$\sum\Pi^k$	W^k
0.2001 ($s = 0.04$)	1	10.22	6.17	4.05	39.60	2.18	12.39	30.30	8.135	0.0008	17.957	18.37	125.35	66157
0.3 ($s = 0.06$)	1	10.11	6.17	3.94	38.97	2.12	12.18	30.48	8.189	0.0012	17.978	18.38	125.42	66195
0.4 ($s = 0.08$)	1	10.01	6.17	3.84	38.34	2.07	11.97	30.67	8.243	0.0016	18.000	18.40	125.49	66233
0.6 ($s = 0.12$)	1	9.80	6.17	3.63	37.05	1.95	11.53	31.03	8.348	0.0023	18.040	18.43	125.64	66307
0.9 ($s = 0.18$)	1	9.50	6.17	3.33	35.06	1.79	10.87	31.60	8.500	0.0033	18.100	18.48	125.85	66416
$1 -$ ($s = 0.19999$)	1	9.40	6.17	3.23	34.38	1.74	10.65	31.79	8.548	0.0035	18.119	18.50	125.91	66451
$1 +$ ($s = 0.20001$)	2	9.40	6.17	3.23	34.38	1.74	10.65	31.79	8.208	0.3443	0.376	18.50	125.91	66446
1.2 ($s = 0.24$)	2	9.40	6.17	3.23	34.35	1.74	10.64	31.80	8.209	0.3449	0.376	18.50	125.92	66448
1.4 ($s = 0.28$)	2	9.39	6.17	3.22	34.32	1.73	10.63	31.81	8.209	0.3454	0.376	18.50	125.92	66449
1.6 ($s = 0.32$)	2	9.39	6.17	3.22	34.29	1.73	10.62	31.82	8.210	0.3460	0.376	18.50	125.92	66451
1.8 ($s = 0.36$)	2	9.39	6.17	3.22	34.26	1.73	10.61	31.83	8.211	0.3465	0.375	18.50	125.93	66452
2.5 ($s = 0.8$)	2	9.37	6.17	3.20	34.15	1.72	10.57	31.86	8.214	0.3485	0.375	18.50	125.94	66458
4 ($s = 0.8$)	2	9.34	6.17	3.17	33.92	1.70	10.49	31.92	8.21957	0.3526	0.374	18.51	125.96	66470
4.99 ($s = 0.998$)	2	9.32	6.17	3.15	33.77	1.69	10.45	31.97	8.223	0.3553	0.373	18.51	125.97	66477

Each equilibrium is solved in the following way. First, (4.96) gives labor demand as a function of wage, $l^k(w_L^k) = f'^{-1}(w_L^k)$. Then, we plug this value into (4.97) and obtain the wage $w_L^k(c)$. As already noted by Albrecht and Vroman (1996, 1999), the nice properties of the long-run equilibrium of the shirking model is that, because of the zero-profit condition, wages are solely determined by the parameters of the production function and the value of the entry costs, c. So, for example, if τ, the commuting cost, increases because the free-entry condition must hold, aggregate labor demand shifts in tandem with the urban non-shirking curve in such a way as to keep the equilibrium efficiency wage constant. Then, by plugging $w_L^k(c)$ into (4.98), we obtain $u^k(c, w_U, e, m, \delta, s, \tau)$ and finally using (4.99), we get $M^k(c, b, e, m, \delta, s, \tau)$. It is easily shown that

$$\frac{\partial M^k}{\partial \tau} < 0, \ \frac{\partial M^k}{\partial s} > 0 \ \text{and} \ \frac{\partial M^k}{\partial \mu} > 0 \qquad (4.100)$$

that is, higher commuting costs and/or lower CBD trips for the unemployed imply less entry since they increase unemployment.

For example, if we take $f\left(l^k\right) = \left(l^k\right)^{0.5}$, then (4.96) gives

$$l^k(w_L^k) = \frac{1}{4\left(w_L^k\right)^2}$$

and, using the zero-profit condition (4.97), we obtain:

$$w_L^k = \frac{1}{4c}.$$

This makes the comparative statics calculations very simple. In particular, in the long-run, the wage with and without space is exactly the same and equal to $1/4c$. In other words, in the short run, space affects both wages and unemployment, whereas in the long run, it does not affect wages, but affects unemployment and the number of firms. In fact, it has a stronger effect than in the short run.

Let us once more perform numerical simulations. We use exactly the same parameters as in the previous example. However, M is now endogenous and the fixed-entry cost is $c = 0.0018$. Because the efficiency wage is exactly the same in the short and the long run, we do not reproduce the wage effects in the tables. Moreover, we differentiate between the number of firms when there is no space M_{ns}^k (i.e., in the Shapiro and Stiglitz model) and when space is introduced, $M^k - M_{ns}^k$.

As above, we first fix $s = 0.2$ and let μ vary. Table 4.2a displays the results.

First, the free-entry case shows that the short-run results are quite robust since there is no real change when switching from city 1 $(s/\mu = 1-)$ to city 2 $(s/\mu = 1+)$ and the values of unemployment rates, welfare, etc. are roughly the same. The only difference as compared to the short-run case is really the number of firms that enter the market. Naturally, when s/μ varies, M_{ns}^k is not affected, but $M^k - M_{ns}^k$ increases by 42.6%. Indeed, when μ decreases from 1 to 0, entry cost c and wage w are not affected, but unemployment is and thus entry is reduced (see (4.100)). If we now fix $\mu = 0.2$ and let s vary (Table 4.2b), we obtain the opposite results since, for a given μ, $\frac{\partial M^k}{\partial s} > 0$.

7. Endogenous Unemployment Benefit

To close the benchmark model, let us endogeneize the unemployment benefit w_U. Indeed, so far, it has been assumed that all welfare payments were exogenously financed by taxpayers who resided elsewhere (for example absentee landlords). To add realism to this scenario, we now introduce endogenous taxation. For the sake of simplicity, we consider the case in which all city welfare payments are financed by employee taxes on local firms. In particular, for any given employment level, L, the employee welfare tax, Δ, must satisfy the condition that

$$\Delta(L) = \frac{w_U(N-L)}{L}. \tag{4.101}$$

Indeed, the total benefit of taxation for the government is ΔL, which finances the total cost of welfare payments equal to $w_U(N-L)$. It is easily seen that

$$\Delta'(L) < 0, \quad \lim_{L \to 0} \Delta(L) = +\infty, \quad \lim_{L \to N} \Delta(L) = 0. \tag{4.102}$$

Indeed, more employment means less individual tax and if nobody works, the tax must be infinite to finance the unemployment benefit of everybody. Finally, if all workers are employed ($L = N$), there is no unemployment benefit and $\Delta = 0$.

In this new setting, it follows that the profit function of each firm j is now given by:

$$\Pi_j = f(el_j) - [w_j + \Delta(L)] l_j.$$

Table 4.2a. *Long-run equilibria when* $s = 0.2$ *and* μ *varies*

s/μ (with $s = 0.2$)	City	u^k	u^k_{ns}	u^k_s	$\dfrac{u^k_s}{u^k}$	M^k	M^k_{ns}	$\dfrac{M^k - M^k_{ns}}{M^k}$	TLR^k_L	TLR^k_U	x^k_b	x^k_f	W^k
0.2001 ($\mu = 0.99999$)	1	9.33	5.80	3.53	37.85	69964	72687	3.89	8.560	0.017	18.135	20	66439
0.3 ($\mu = 0.66666$)	1	9.37	5.80	3.58	38.15	69928	72687	3.95	8.553	0.012	18.125	19.375	66391
0.4 ($\mu = 0.5$)	1	9.40	5.80	3.60	38.31	69910	72687	3.97	8.550	0.009	18.121	19.060	66366
0.6 ($\mu = 0.33333$)	1	9.42	5.80	3.62	38.46	69892	72687	4.00	8.546	0.006	18.116	18.744	66341
0.9 ($\mu = 0.22222$)	1	9.44	5.80	3.64	38.57	69879	72687	4.02	8.544	0.004	18.113	18.532	66325
$1 - (\mu = 0.20001$)	1	9.44	5.80	3.64	38.59	69877	72687	4.02	8.543	0.004	18.112	18.490	66321
$1 + (\mu = 0.19999$)	2	9.44	5.80	3.64	38.59	69877	72687	4.02	8.201	0.345	0.378	18.490	66316
1.2 ($\mu = 0.16666$)	2	9.65	5.80	3.86	39.95	69711	72687	4.27	8.162	0.294	0.322	18.391	66081
1.4 ($\mu = 0.143$)	2	9.81	5.80	4.01	40.91	69590	72687	4.45	8.134	0.256	0.281	18.318	65911
1.6 ($\mu = 0.125$)	2	9.93	5.80	4.14	41.64	69496	72687	4.59	8.112	0.226	0.248	18.262	65778
1.8 ($\mu = 0.1111$)	2	10.03	5.80	4.23	42.19	69423	72687	4.70	8.095	0.203	0.223	18.217	65674
4 ($\mu = 0.05$)	2	10.46	5.80	4.67	44.60	69087	72687	5.21	8.017	0.095	0.105	18.012	65201
200 ($\mu = 0.8$)	2	10.83	5.80	5.03	46.48	68803	72687	5.65	7.951	0.002	0.002	17.836	64801

Table 4.2b. *Long-run equilibria when* $\mu = 0.2$ *and s varies*

s/μ (with $\mu = 0.2$)	City	u^k	u_{ns}^k	u_s^k	$\frac{u_s^k}{u^k}$	M^k	M_{ns}^k	$\frac{M^k - M_{ns}^k}{M^k}$	TLR_L^k	TLR_U^k	x_b^k	x_f^k	W^k
0.2001 ($s = 0.04$)	1	10.54	5.80	4.74	44.79	69030	72687	5.30	8.079	0.00089	17.893	18.31	65122
0.3 ($s = 0.06$)	1	10.39	5.80	4.59	44.21	69143	72687	5.13	8.142	0.00130	17.922	18.34	65282
0.4 ($s = 0.08$)	1	10.25	5.80	4.45	43.42	69254	72687	4.96	8.203	0.00168	17.951	18.36	65439
0.6 ($s = 0.12$)	1	9.97	5.80	4.17	41.84	69470	72687	4.63	8.321	0.00238	18.007	18.41	65744
0.9 ($s = 0.18$)	1	9.57	5.80	3.77	39.41	69778	72687	4.17	8.490	0.00330	18.087	18.47	66181
1 − ($s = 0.199999$)	1	9.44	5.80	3.64	38.59	69877	72687	4.02	8.543	0.00356	18.112	18.49	66321
1 + ($s = 0.20001$)	2	9.44	5.80	3.64	38.59	69877	72687	4.02	8.201	0.34550	0.378	18.49	66316
1.2 ($s = 0.24$)	2	9.43	5.80	3.64	38.55	69881	72687	4.02	8.206	0.34217	0.377	18.49	66322
1.4 ($s = 0.28$)	2	9.43	5.80	3.63	38.51	69886	72687	4.01	8.203	0.34655	0.377	18.49	66328
1.6 ($s = 0.32$)	2	9.42	5.80	3.63	38.47	69890	72687	4.00	8.204	0.34706	0.377	18.49	66335
1.8 ($s = 0.36$)	2	9.42	5.80	3.62	38.44	69895	72687	4.00	8.205	0.34758	0.377	18.49	66341
2.5 ($s = 0.5$)	2	9.40	5.80	3.60	38.31	69910	72687	3.97	8.209	0.34938	0.376	18.50	66363
4 ($s = 0.8$)	2	9.35	5.80	3.56	38.03	69942	72687	3.92	8.217	0.35318	0.374	18.50	66409
200 ($s = 0.998$)	2	9.33	5.80	3.53	37.85	69964	72687	3.89	8.222	0.35566	0.373	18.51	66439

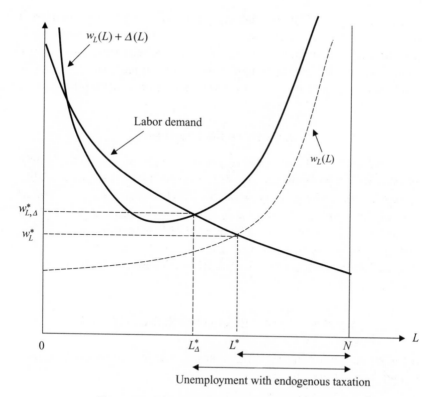

Figure 4.4. Labor equilibrium with tax and subsidy.

Given this modification, the labor market equilibrium condition is now equal to:

$$eF'(eL_\Delta^*) = w_L(L_\Delta^*) + \Delta(L_\Delta^*)$$
$$= w_U + e + \frac{e}{m}\left(\frac{\delta N}{N - L_\Delta^*} + r\right) + (1 - s)\tau L_\Delta^* + \Delta(L_\Delta^*),$$

$$(4.103)$$

where L_Δ^* is the new equilibrium value of employment. This new equilibrium situation is described in Figure 4.4. Notice in particular from (4.102) that when $L \to 0$, the right-hand side of (4.103) approaches infinity at the origin. For simplicity, we do not assume the Inada conditions on the production function and hence, in the endogenous taxation case, there will generally be *multiple equilibria*. However, it should be clear from the monotonicity properties of $F'(.)$ that the equilibrium with the highest employment level (such as L_Δ^* in Figure 4.4) must yield the lowest value of marginal cost, $w_L(L_\Delta) + \Delta(L_\Delta)$ and hence, yield the unique *maximum-profit equilibrium* for firms. Moreover, it is easily seen that this maximum-profit equilibrium is the unique *stable* equilibrium since any reasonable adjustment process will move the system from the low-employment to the high-employment equilibrium level because of the monotonicity properties of $F'(.)$.

8. Notes on the Literature

The benchmark model of Section 2 is based on Zenou and Smith (1995), which is the first paper that incorporates an explicit land market into a labor market analysis. The extensions of this benchmark model (endogenous housing consumption in Section 3, open city and resident landlords in Section 4, different city structures in Section 5, long-run equilibrium in Section 6) have been written specifically for this book. The last extension (financed unemployment benefits in Section 7) is based on Smith and Zenou (1997).

APPENDIX A4. PROOF OF PROPOSITION 4.2

Assume that the two bid-rent functions intersect at x_b (this will be shown below). Then, it must be that:

$$\Psi_L(x_b, W_L) = \Psi_U(x_b, W_U)$$

$$\Leftrightarrow \frac{w_L - e - \tau x_b - W_L + \mho(h(x_b))}{h(x_b)} = \frac{w_U - s\tau x - W_U + \mho(h(x_b))}{h(x_b)}$$

$$\Leftrightarrow W_L - W_U + (1 - s)\tau x_b = w_L - e - w_U. \tag{A4.1}$$

This, in particular, implies that:

$$W_L - w_L + e < W_U - w_U. \tag{A4.2}$$

Let us now show that the employee's bid-rent is steeper than the unemployed worker's bid-rent. For this purpose, we must show that:

$$-\frac{\partial \Psi_L(x, W_L)}{\partial x}\Big|_{x=x_b} > -\frac{\partial \Psi_U(x_b, W_L)}{\partial x}\Big|_{x=x_b}$$

$$\Leftrightarrow [W_U - w_U - (W_L - w_L + e) - (1 - s)\tau x_b]\, h'(x_b) + (1 - s)\tau h(x_b) > 0.$$

Using (A4.2), it is easily seen that $W_U - w_U - (W_L - w_L + e) - (1 - s)\tau x_b > 0$ and since $h'(x) > 0$, $\forall x$, this inequality is always true and thus, the employee's bid-rent is steeper than the unemployed worker's bid rent at

$x = x_b$. We must now verify that the two curves indeed intersect at x_b. For this reason, we must show that

$$\Psi_L(0, W_L) > \Psi_U(0, W_L)$$

$$\Leftrightarrow w_L - e - W_L > w_U - W_U$$

$$\Leftrightarrow W_U - w_U > W_L - w_L + e,$$

which is true by (A4.2). Hence, we have shown that:

(*i*) $\Psi_L(0, W_L) > \Psi_U(0, W_L)$;

(*ii*) the employee's bid-rent function $\Psi_L(x, W_L)$ is steeper than the unemployed worker's bid-rent function $\Psi_U(x, W_U)$ at $x = x_b$;

(*iii*) both functions $\Psi_L(x, W_L)$ and $\Psi_U(x, W_U)$ are decreasing and convex with respect to x.

Since these two functions $\Psi_L(x, W_L)$ and $\Psi_U(x, W_U)$ are well-behaved (in particular continuous and smooth) because the utility function is itself well-behaved, then it must be that they intersect at some point. ∎

CHAPTER FIVE

Extensions of Urban Efficiency Wage Models

1. Introduction

In this chapter, we extend the benchmark urban efficiency wage model developed in Section 2 of Chapter 4 in several directions. First, in the next section, we endogenize the effort function, which becomes a negative function of distance to jobs. Indeed, when workers live far away from jobs and experience long commutes, they may be tired when on the job and provide less of a production effort than if they were residing closer to jobs. The main result of this section is to show that profit-maximizing firms determine an optimal recruitment distance beyond which they will hire workers.

Second, in Section 3, we introduce leisure choice in the benchmark model by considering effort and leisure not to be independent activities. Indeed, if one interprets shirking as a leisure activity on the job, the benefits arising from additional leisure activity on the job are obviously related to the extent of leisure activity at home and vice versa. For example, if effort and leisure are substitutes, then low leisure at home may imply that the worker has less time for rest and relaxation and is more pressed for time at home and, as a result, there is an increase in the benefit of taking leisure or conducting home production (relaxation or errands) while at work. We find that, in equilibrium, residing in a location with a long commute affects the trade-off between effort at work and the frequency of unemployment spells by reducing the time available for leisure. This model suggests that either workers' effort at work or wages vary based upon a worker's residential location, depending upon whether firms can discriminate based on residential location.

Third, as in Chapter 2, Section 3 considers the case with high relocation costs. We find that, in some cases, wages will be an increasing function of distance to jobs. Finally, we develop a model where both leisure and relocation costs are present (Section 5). We find that, in some cases, it may be optimal for firms to allow some shirking in equilibrium.

In all of these models, because workers can provide different effort levels depending on their location, the information available to firms about workers' residence will be of importance in the wage-formation process. As a result, in all models, we will consider two different information structures. In the first, firms can perfectly observe the residential location of all workers. In the second, firms cannot observe workers' residence because such information would either be too costly to obtain or workers would have an incentive to not truthfully reveal where they live. Since city size as well as population density are fixed in our model, differences in information structure could be justified either in terms of country differences (in some countries it may be more costly to obtain information about the residential location of all workers than in others) or culture/race differences (for example, in the United States, African Americans may not want to reveal where they live if this implies spatial discrimination or redlining). In other words, workers who live in "stigmatized" areas (like, for example, Harlem in New York City) may not want to give their true address to their employers, while those who live in good neighborhoods may have incentives for this.

2. Effort as a Function of Distance to Jobs

Consider the benchmark model (of Chapter 4) in which each individual can provide two possible effort levels: either the worker shirks, exerting zero effort, $e = 0$, and contributing zero to production, or he/she does not shirk, providing full effort. Now, in contrast to the benchmark model, we endogenize the effort of non-shirking workers in the following way. Effort equals $e(x) > 0, \forall x \in [0, x_f]$ (with $e(0) = e_0 > 0$), so that a worker located at x contributes to $e(x)$ units of production. We assume that $e'(x) < 0$ and $e''(x) \geq 0$ so that the greater the distance to work, the lower the effort level. For remote locations, the marginal difference in effort is quite small. The former assumption aims at capturing the fact that workers with longer commuting trips are more tired and thus are less able to provide higher levels of effort than those who reside closer to jobs. We discuss the empirical validity of this assumption in depth in Chapter 8 of this book.

Apart from making effort dependent on distance, we keep all other aspects of the benchmark model as previously. The worker's behavior can now be seen as a two-stage decision problem. First, depending on his/her residential location, each worker must decide whether to shirk or not. Since effort is costly, it is clear that workers who live closest to jobs will be more inclined to shirk that those residing further away. Thus, contrary to the benchmark model, *the moral hazard problem here is locationally dependent*. Second, once the worker has decided not to shirk (this is the behavior that will emerge in equilibrium), he/she must decide how much effort he/she will provide. This decision is also locationally dependent since we assume that workers who have longer commutes are more tired and provide less effort than those who live closer to jobs.

As stated in the introduction, we consider two different information structures. For the sake of the presentation, let us first consider the imperfect information case and then the other case.

2.1. Firms Do Not Observe the Residential Location of All Workers

As stated above, this model is identical to the benchmark model with the exception that workers' effort e is now a negative function of distance to jobs, i.e., $e(x)$, with $e'(x) < 0$. How does this affect the urban-land-use equilibrium?

As in the benchmark model, the bid-rent functions are given by

$$\Psi_L(x, W_L) = w_L - e(x) - \tau x - W_L \qquad (5.1)$$

$$\Psi_U(x, W_U) = w_U - s \tau x - W_U. \qquad (5.2)$$

Now, the main difference is that for all workers to reach the same utility level, the land rent does not only need to compensate for commuting costs, but also for effort costs. First, to guarantee that the bid-rent curve of the employed workers is always downward sloping, we assume that, $\forall x$,

$$\tau + e'(x) > 0, \qquad (5.3)$$

which means that $\tau x + e(x)$ is increasing in x despite $e'(x) < 0$. To understand this, observe that the commuting cost τx includes more than just money costs. It also includes the negative effects of a longer commute such as non-work-related fatigue. So even though people benefit from not working as hard on the job as x goes up, the other effects of fatigue (along with the money and time outlay on commuting) make the person worse off overall.

By denoting the recruitment area of firms by x_b, which is equal to the border between employed and unemployed workers, we easily obtain the following result:

Proposition 5.1. *Assume that firms do not observe the residential location of workers. Assume also that*

$$\tau > -e'(x_b)/(1-s). \tag{5.4}$$

Then, in equilibrium, employed workers reside close to the CBD whereas unemployed workers live on the outskirts of the city.

The intuition of this result is as follows. An increase in distance x has offsetting effects on employed workers; they pay higher commuting costs, but lower effort is exerted on the job. The net effect is thus less than the pure commuting cost effect, and the question is whether this net effect is stronger than the shrunken commuting cost effect for unemployed workers, which is smaller than that of employed workers because $s < 1$. In this context, when the commuting cost τ is sufficiently high, employed workers reside close to jobs by outbidding the unemployed.

Using the same definition for urban land use as in the benchmark model (Definition 4.1), we easily obtain the following equilibrium values:

$$x_b^* = L \tag{5.5}$$

$$x_f^* = N \tag{5.6}$$

$$W_U^* = w_U - s \tau N \tag{5.7}$$

$$W_L^* = w_L - e(L) - \tau L - s\tau (N - L) \tag{5.8}$$

$$R^*(x) = \begin{cases} \tau [(1-s)L + s N] + e(L) - [e(x) + \tau x] & \text{for } 0 \le x \le L \\ s \tau (N - x) & \text{for } L < x \le N \\ 0 & \text{for } x > N \end{cases} \tag{5.9}$$

The Bellman equations are the same as in the benchmark model except for the fact that

$$W_L^S(x) = W_L^{NS} + e(x) \tag{5.10}$$
$$= w_L + e(x) - e(L) - \tau L - s\tau (N - L),$$

i.e., the instantaneous utility of the employed shirking workers is now decreasing with distance x.

The efficiency wage must be set to make workers indifferent between shirking and not shirking. However, in contrast to the benchmark model, *the utility of shirkers is not constant over locations whereas it is constant for non-shirkers.* It is in fact easily seen that the utility of shirkers increases as x, the distance to the CBD, decreases (see (5.10)). The intuition is straightforward. Since the land rent compensates for both commuting costs and effort levels, then shirkers, who do not provide any effort, have a higher utility when residing closer to the CBD (since their commuting costs are lower). Formally, we have:

$$\frac{\partial W_L^S}{\partial x} = -\tau - R'(x) = -\tau + e'(x) + \tau = e'(x) < 0.$$

In particular, this implies that the highest utility a shirker can reach is at $x = 0$ (the CBD) and the lowest is at $x = x_b$. As a result, the efficiency wage must be set to make workers indifferent between shirking and not shirking in location $x = 0$ since, if the worker at $x = 0$ does not shirk, then all workers located further away will not shirk. In other words, the condition that determines the efficiency wage is given by

$$I_L^{NS} = I_L^S(0) = I_L.$$

Solving this equation, we first obtain the following incentive condition:

$$I_L - I_U = \frac{e(0)}{m} > 0$$

which guarantees that the surplus of being employed is positive. From this equation, we can easily calculate the efficiency wage, which is equal to:

$$w_L^* = w_U + e(L) + \frac{e_0}{m}\left(\frac{\delta N}{N - L} + r\right) + (1 - s)\tau L, \qquad (5.11)$$

where $e(0) \equiv e_0$.

As in the benchmark model of Chapter 4, the urban efficiency wage has two roles: to prevent shirking (incentive component) and ensure that workers are locationally indifferent (spatial compensation component). The key relation here is the interaction between the effort function $e(\cdot)$ and the location of workers. Hence, there is a fundamental *asymmetry* between workers and firms. Because firms cannot observe workers' residential location, all workers obtain the same efficiency wage whatever their location. However, they do *not* contribute to the same level of production because effort decreases with distance to jobs. In other words, even though the wage cost is location independent, production is not. This implies that the per-worker profit decreases with the distance to jobs. The next natural step of our analysis is therefore to calculate the per-worker profit for each firm and determine the employment level in the city.

There are M identical firms ($j = 1, \ldots, M$) in the economy. We assume that all jobs are obtained through an employment agency which coordinates workers in such a way that each firm employs only one worker in each location.[1] Since all firms and workers are (ex-ante) identical and since the density of workers in each location is M, we focus on a symmetric equilibrium in which each firm sets the same $x_b = L$. This is quite reasonable since, ex-ante (before location), all workers are equally productive (location is not a characteristic of a worker) and, ex-post (once located), they are all indifferent between work in any of the M firms since all firms are located at 0 and offer the same wage, w_L. In this context, since all firms are identical, the employment level in each firm j is equal to: $l_j = l = L/M = x_b$.

We can calculate the total production (or effort) level provided in each firm. This is given by:

$$e^{to} = \int_0^L e(x)dx. \tag{5.12}$$

It is interesting to observe that the average production (or effort) in each firm is given by $e^{av} = \frac{1}{L}\int_0^L e(x)dx$, with

$$\frac{\partial e^{av}}{\partial L} = -\frac{1}{L}\left[e^{av} - e(L)\right] < 0. \tag{5.13}$$

In words, a larger recruitment area decreases the average effort level in each firm since new hired workers produce less effort because they live further away. The aggregate profit function can be written as: $F(e^{to}) - w_L L$, and therefore, equilibrium labor demand is given by:

$$\frac{w_L}{e(L^*)} = F'(e^{to}). \tag{5.14}$$

Indeed, when deciding on the optimal L, each firm takes into account the fact that a higher L increases its workforce, but reduces its average effort

---

[1] In the first period, the timing is as follows. All N workers apply for a job in the employment agency and only L of them obtain a job and locate somewhere in the city (since they are indifferent between all locations between 0 and x_b). Then, the employment agency allocates workers to firms in such a way that each firm recruits one worker in each location. This is true at any moment in time (in particular in the steady state) since, in each period, some workers with different locations lose their job and new workers obtain a job and reside somewhere in the city between 0 and x_b. Then, once more, the employment agency allocates these new workers to firms in such a way that each firm (among those that have lost workers) employs only one worker in each location.

level and thus, average production (see 5.13). It is easily verified that labor demand L is downward sloping in the plane (L, w_L). It can then be shown that there exists a unique labor market equilibrium, which is given by:

$$w_U + e(L^*) + \frac{e_0}{m} \left(\frac{\delta N}{N - L^*} + r \right) + (1 - s)\tau L^* = e(L^*)F'(e^{to}).$$

$$(5.15)$$

Observe that L^* affects both the quality of the workers and the efficiency wage. Indeed, when L^* increases, the average effort level in each firm decreases, but the equilibrium efficiency wage w_L^* increases. The latter result is true only if the workers' effort is not too sensitive to the size of the recruitment area. Let us now investigate the properties of the equilibrium. We have:

Proposition 5.2. *Assume that firms do not observe the residential location of all workers. Assume also that $\tau > -e'(L^*)/(1 - s)$. Then, the equilibrium recruitment area $x_b^* = L^*$ is increasing in the monitoring rate m, in the percentage of CBD trips of the unemployed s and in the size of the active population N, but it is decreasing in the unemployment benefit w_U, the unit commuting cost τ, the effort level e_0 provided in location $x = 0$, the discount rate r, and the job destruction rate δ. For the equilibrium wage w_L^*, we have exactly the opposite effects.*

The following comments are in order. First, a rise in the unemployment benefit shifts the Urban Non-Shirking Condition (UNSC) upward since, in each recruitment area level x_b (or the equivalent employment level), the efficiency wage must increase to deter shirking. This is the standard outside option effect generated by the unemployment benefit. Because wages are higher, it is more costly for firms to hire new workers since they are less productive (they live further away from jobs) and cost more. As a result, firms reduce their recruitment area. In other words, when w_U increases, firms employ workers who live closer to jobs (because they are more productive), but pay them more. Second, we have the opposite result concerning the monitoring technology m. Indeed, if firms monitor their workers more, the efficiency wage is lower so that firms extend their recruitment area. Third, increasing the unit commuting cost τ borne by workers or decreasing the number of CBD trips s reduces the recruitment area x_b. The intuition is exactly the same as for w_U, but here the efficiency wage must increase not to deter shirking, but to spatially compensate employed workers (this is the compensation effect mentioned above). Fourth, when the maximum effort provided in the city, e_0, increases, the efficiency wage increases because all workers provide more effort (a rise in the intercept e_0 shifts upward the non-shirking effort curve $e(x)$). As a result, firms hire less workers and thus reduce x_b. Finally, when the rate at which a technological shock arises increases so that jobs are destroyed more often (δ increases), firms must increase wages to deter shirking and thus, reduce their recruitment area.

2.2. Firms Perfectly Observe the Residential Location of All Workers

Assume now that firms perfectly observe workers' residential location. In that case, they can pay workers according to their location (assuming that there are no anti-discrimination laws that prevent this type of policy). This means, in particular, that the wage is now a function of distance to job, i.e., $w_L(x)$. Thus, bid-rents are now given by:

$$\Psi_L(x, W_L) = w_L(x) - e(x) - \tau x - W_L \qquad (5.16)$$

$$\Psi_U(x, W_U) = w_U - s\tau x - W_U. \qquad (5.17)$$

Observe that

$$\frac{\partial \Psi_L(x, W_L)}{\partial x} = w'_L(x) - e'(x) - \tau.$$

Naturally, at this stage, we do not know the sign of $w'_L(x)$ so we cannot sign this derivative. This is because the land rent does not only compensate for commuting costs, but also for wage differences between different residential locations. If $w'_L(x) < 0$, then the land rent will always be lower further away from the CBD because remote locations imply both longer commutes and lower wages. If, on the contrary, $w'_L(x) > 0$, land rents can increase with distance to jobs if wages are sufficiently high far from the CBD. However, we show below that the latter is never possible.

Let us calculate the efficiency wage. The Bellman equations are given by:

$$r\, I_L^{NS}(x) = w_L - e(x) - \tau x - R(x) - \delta\,(I_L^{NS} - I_U) \qquad (5.18)$$

$$r\, I_L^{S}(x) = w_L - \tau x - R(x) - (\delta + m)\,(I_L^{S} - I_U) \qquad (5.19)$$

$$r\, I_U(x) = w_U - s\tau x - R(x) + a(I_L - I_U). \qquad (5.20)$$

The efficiency wage is such that, *in each location,* we have

$$I_L^{NS}(x) = I_L^S(x) = I_L(x)$$

which is equivalent to

$$I_L(x) - I_U = \frac{e(x)}{m} > 0, \forall x \in [0, N], \tag{5.21}$$

with $\partial (I_L - I_U)/\partial x < 0$. This is an interesting and new result since it shows that the surplus from being employed is a function of distance to jobs. Indeed, since firms observe where workers reside and since they know that effort is inversely related to distance to jobs, they will pay workers less who reside in remote locations compared to those locating closer to jobs. So, the gain from being employed is lower, but still positive for remote workers.

Using this relationship and solving for the efficiency wage in the usual way, we easily obtain the following efficiency wage at each x:

$$w_L(x) = w_U + e(x) + \frac{e(x)}{m}\left(\frac{\delta N}{N - L} + r\right) + (1 - s)\tau x \tag{5.22}$$

with

$$w_L'(x) = e'(x)\left[1 + \frac{1}{m}\left(\frac{\delta N}{N - L} + r\right)\right] + (1 - s)\tau \gtreqless 0.$$

The intuition runs as follows. Firms must decide which wage to pay to each worker, given that they reside in different locations. There are two opposite forces. On the one hand, remote workers providing less effort should be paid less (see (5.21)). This is a pure incentive effect. On the other hand, remote workers should be compensated more to agree to stay in the city. This is a pure spatial compensation effect and it is given by $(1 - s)\tau x$. So the net effect is ambiguous. If (5.22) is plugged into (5.16), one obtains

$$\Psi_L(x, W_L) = w_U + \frac{e(x)}{m}\left(\frac{\delta N}{N - L} + r\right) - s\tau x - W_L$$

with

$$\frac{\partial \Psi_L}{\partial x} = \frac{e'(x)}{m}\left(\frac{\delta N}{N - L} + r\right) - s\tau < 0.$$

So, whatever the sign of $w_L'(x)$, land rents decrease with distance to jobs. When $w_L'(x) < 0$, employed workers who live further away from jobs pay lower land rents to compensate for their low wages and high commuting costs. When $w'_L(x) > 0$, the wage effect is not strong enough to outweigh the commuting cost effect, so that the land rent is still decreasing. We have:

Proposition 5.3. *Assume that firms perfectly observe the residential location of all workers. Then, in equilibrium, employed workers reside close to the CBD whereas unemployed workers live on the outskirts of the city.*

By solving the urban-land-use equilibrium, it is easily seen that x_b^*, x_f^*, W_U^* and $R^*(x)$ are still given by (5.5), (5.6), (5.7), and (5.9), respectively, while W_L^* is now equal to:

$$W_L^* = w_U + \frac{e(L^*)}{m}\left(\frac{\delta N}{N - L^*} + r\right) - s\,\tau\,N. \qquad (5.23)$$

We can finally determine the equilibrium, L^*. Since all firms are totally identical, let us focus on a symmetric (steady-state) equilibrium in which each firm employs the same number of workers and pays the same total wage cost as any other firm. As above, we assume that all jobs are obtained through an employment agency that coordinates workers in such a way that each firm employs only one worker in each location. Aggregate profit is thus given by $F(e^{to}) - w_L^{to}$, where

$$w_L^{to} = \int_0^L w_L(x)dx$$

$$= w_U L + \left[1 + \frac{1}{m}\left(\frac{\delta N}{N - L} + r\right)\right]e^{to} + (1 - s)\tau\,\frac{L^2}{2},$$

and e^{to} is defined by (5.12). The equilibrium employment level L^* is thus determined by:

$$w_U + e(L^*) + \frac{e(L^*)}{m}\left(\frac{\delta N}{N - L} + r\right) + (1 - s)\,\tau\,L^* = e(L^*)F'(e^{to}). \qquad (5.24)$$

Compared to (5.15), the only difference in determining L^* is in the value of the effort function $e(.)$ in front of $\frac{\delta N}{N-L} + r$. So, the results of Proposition 5.2 are basically the same.

3. Effort and Leisure

We would now like to introduce leisure into the model by assuming that leisure and effort are not independent activities. For employed workers, the instantaneous utility function is assumed to be separable and given by:

$$\Omega(z_L, \zeta, e) = z_L + \Gamma(\zeta, e),$$

where z_L is the quantity of a (non-spatial) composite good (taken as the numeraire) consumed by the employed and ζ denotes leisure. $\Gamma(.)$ is assumed to be increasing in leisure ζ and decreasing in effort e, while being concave in both arguments. This choice of the utility function aims at capturing the fact that effort and leisure are not independent activities. Indeed, if one interprets $-e$ as the leisure activity on the job (shirking), then the benefits arising from additional *leisure activity on the job* are obviously related to the extent of *leisure activity at home* and vice versa.

We are now able to write the budget constraint of an employed worker. Each worker purchases z_L units of the composite good and incurs τx in monetary commuting costs when he/she lives at distance x from the CBD. Letting $R(x)$ denote rent per unit of land, the budget constraint of an employed worker residing at distance x can be written as follows:

$$w_L F = z_L + R(x) + \tau x, \tag{5.25}$$

where w_L is the per-hour wage and F denotes the amount of working hours. F is assumed to be the same and constant across workers, an assumption that agrees with most jobs in the vast majority of developed countries.

Each worker provides a fixed amount of labor time F so that the time available for leisure ζ solely depends on commuting time. Thus, denoting by ιx the commuting time from distance x (where $\iota > 0$ is the time commuting cost per unit of distance), the time constraint of an employed worker at distance x can be written as:

$$1 - F = \zeta + \iota x, \tag{5.26}$$

in which the total amount of time is normalized to 1 without loss of generality.

By plugging (5.25) and (5.26) into the utility function, we obtain the following indirect utility for employed workers:

$$W_L(x, e) = z_L + \Gamma(\zeta, e) = w_L F - R(x) - \tau x + \Gamma(1 - F - \iota x, e). \tag{5.27}$$

Let us now focus on unemployed workers. Their budget constraint is given by:

$$w_U = z_U + R(x) + s\tau x. \tag{5.28}$$

To keep the analysis manageable and to be consistent with the utility of employed workers, we assume the unemployed workers' utility function to be: $z_U + \Gamma_U$.[2] In this formulation, Γ_U is a constant utility benefit arising for everyone who is unemployed. Basically, Γ_U is introduced to recognize the inherent disutility of being at work and commuting to work since it ensures that when people have exactly the same z_{es}, those working can receive less utility.

By using (5.28), we obtain the following indirect utility function for unemployed workers:

$$W_U(x) = z_U + \Gamma_U = w_U - R(x) - s\tau x + \Gamma_U. \qquad (5.29)$$

As above, we consider two cases depending on whether firms observe the residential location of all workers or not.

3.1. Firms Do Not Observe the Residential Location of All Workers

The bid-rent functions of workers are given by:

$$\Psi_L(x, W_L) = w_L F - \tau x + \Gamma(1 - F - \iota x, e) - W_L \qquad (5.30)$$

$$\Psi_U(x, W_U) = w_U - s\tau x + \Gamma_U - W_U \qquad (5.31)$$

with

$$\frac{\partial \Psi_L}{\partial x} = -\tau - \iota \Gamma_\zeta < 0$$

$$\frac{\partial \Psi_U}{\partial x} = -s\tau < 0,$$

where $\Gamma_\zeta \equiv \frac{\partial \Gamma(.)}{\partial \zeta}$. For employed workers, land rent compensates both for commuting costs and leisure costs. Indeed, workers living further away have longer commutes which, in turn, implies that they have less time for leisure. For unemployed workers, as usual, it only compensates for the commuting costs. It is straightforward to see that in that case, employed workers reside close to jobs, while unemployed workers live at the periphery of the city. Indeed, employed workers have higher commuting costs than unemployed workers and they suffer from distant locations because of the resulting

---

[2] This formulation assumes that there is no search behavior from the unemployed workers. They just obtain a job randomly. This is consistent with the standard assumptions of exogenous reemployment probability in the efficiency wage model.

loss of leisure. The equilibrium values of the land-use equilibrium are thus given by

$$W_U^* = w_U - s\tau N + \Gamma_U \tag{5.32}$$

$$W_L^* = w_L F + \Gamma^e(L) - \tau L - s\tau(N - L) \tag{5.33}$$

$$R^*(x) = \begin{cases} \tau(L - x) + \Gamma^e(x) - \Gamma^e(L) + s\tau(N - x) & \text{for} \quad 0 \le x \le L \\ s\tau(N - x) & \text{for} \quad L < x \le N \\ 0 & \text{for} \quad x > N \end{cases}$$
$$\tag{5.34}$$

where

$$\Gamma^e(x) \equiv \Gamma(1 - F - \iota x, e).$$

Observe that, since $\Gamma(.)$ is decreasing in x, the highest utility value is at $x = 0$ while the lowest is at $x = L$. Thus, $\Gamma^e(x) > \Gamma^e(L)$.

Let us now calculate the efficiency wage. The Bellman equations of all workers are equal to:

$$r I_L^{NS} = w_L F + \Gamma^e(L) - \tau L - s\tau(N - L) - \delta(I_L^{NS} - I_U) \tag{5.35}$$

$$r I_L^S = w_L F + \Gamma^0(L) - \tau L - s\tau(N - L) - (\delta + m)(I_L^S - I_U) \tag{5.36}$$

$$r I_U = w_U - s\tau N + \Gamma_U + a(I_L - I_U) \tag{5.37}$$

where

$$\Gamma^0(x) \equiv \Gamma(1 - F - \iota x, 0).$$

Indeed, someone who decides to shirk provides no effort, and thus his/her instantaneous utility at x is given by $\Gamma^0(x)$, while a non-shirker enjoys $\Gamma^0(x)$. Solving $I_L^{NS} = I_L^S = I_L$ leads to

$$I_L - I_U = \frac{\Gamma^0(L) - \Gamma^e(L)}{m} > 0.$$

This is the incentive condition to prevent shirking since it gives the surplus obtained from employment. Indeed, workers are more induced to work the larger is the utility difference between shirking and non-shirking behavior. This condition is calculated in location L since it is where employed and unemployed workers pay the same land rent.

Proposition 5.4.

(i) *If effort and leisure are substitutes, i.e.,*

$$\frac{\partial^2 \Gamma(L)}{\partial \zeta \partial e} < 0 \qquad (5.38)$$

then

$$\frac{\partial (I_L - I_U)}{\partial L} < 0.$$

(ii) *If effort and leisure are complements, i.e.,*

$$\frac{\partial^2 \Gamma(L)}{\partial \zeta \partial e} > 0 \qquad (5.39)$$

then

$$\frac{\partial (I_L - I_U)}{\partial L} > 0.$$

This is an interesting and new result since, for the first time, the surplus of being employed (based on an incentive condition) depends on L, the number of employed workers (which here is equal to the location of the last employed worker in the city). Indeed, when L increases, workers located at L are worse off since they are farther away from the CBD and thus, must spend more time commuting. This, in turn, implies that they have less leisure and therefore, less utility. Now, when L increases, in order to increase the surplus and thus the incentive not to shirk, it must be that

$$\frac{\partial \Gamma^0(L)}{\partial \zeta} < \frac{\partial \Gamma^e(L)}{\partial \zeta},$$

that is, in a given location L, the marginal increase in utility following a rise in leisure is lower for shirkers than for non-shirkers. In other words, effort and leisure must be complements. Otherwise, if they are substitutes, we have the reverse effect, i.e., $\partial (I_L - I_U)/\partial L < 0$.

Let us be more precise about these assumptions. Low leisure at home may imply that the worker has less time for rest and relaxation and is more pressed for time at home (less time for relaxation or errands) and, as a result, the benefit from taking leisure or conducting home production (relaxation or errands) while at work rises. This story is consistent with increasing disutility from e as leisure falls or $\partial^2 \Gamma(L)/\partial \zeta \partial e > 0$, and the level of e will fall as there is an increase in commutes. On the other hand, if someone's leisure time at home ζ is reduced, social life may suffer substantially which, in turn, reduces the benefits derived from leisure and leads to less planned activities at home. This decline in quality of social life is likely to reduce overall demand for personal time and activities. As a result, the benefit from doing home production at work falls because in the case of errands, the worker has less overall demand for those activities and in the case of relaxation, a substantial amount of time at home is already available for relaxation. Thus, the worker provides a higher effort e at work. In the extreme case, the worker has less leisure time at home so his/her wife divorces him/her. Once the divorce goes through, the worker has less household errands to run and most of his/her time at home is spent watching TV and relaxing, which is consistent with $\partial^2 \Gamma(L)/\partial \zeta \partial e < 0$.

We can now calculate the efficiency wage and obtain:

$$w_L F = w_U + \Gamma_U - \Gamma^e(L) + \left[\frac{\Gamma^0(L) - \Gamma^e(L)}{m} \right] \left(\frac{\delta N}{N - L} + r \right)$$

$$+ (1 - s)\tau L. \tag{5.40}$$

This efficiency wage is a generalization of that obtained in the previous section (see (5.11)) and in the benchmark case (see (4.20)). We find the same effects of w_U, δ, m, e, s and τ on the efficiency wage w_L. However, the impact of L on w_L is not as straightforward as before. In particular, a sufficient condition for $\partial w_L/\partial L > 0$, which is the essence for the efficiency wage to act as a worker discipline device, is clearly (5.39), i.e., effort and leisure are complements. Indeed, if (5.39) holds, then when there is less unemployment, the surplus of being employed increases (pure incentive effect) and spatial compensation increases. If (5.38) prevails, i.e., effort and leisure are substitutes, then it must be that the spatial costs (commuting costs) are sufficiently large for $\partial w_L/\partial L > 0$.

There is also a new effect, the impact of time cost ι on the efficiency wage. We have:

$$\frac{\partial w_L}{\partial \iota} = L \frac{\partial \Gamma^e(L)}{\partial \zeta} + \frac{L}{m} \left(\frac{\delta N}{N - L} + r \right) \left[\frac{\partial \Gamma^e(L)}{\partial \zeta} - \frac{\partial \Gamma^0(L)}{\partial \zeta} \right].$$

If (5.39) holds, an increase in transportation time increases the efficiency wage. Indeed, when transport time increases (it takes more time to travel the same distance), leisure is reduced. But if it is relatively more reduced for shirkers (effort and leisure are complements), then firms raise the efficiency wage to meet the UNSC. If it is not the case, the net effect is ambiguous.

The labor equilibrium L^* is then calculated in a standard way (wages equal workers' marginal productivity) and is given by:

$$w_U + \Gamma_U - \Gamma^e(L^*) + \left[\frac{\Gamma^0(L^*) - \Gamma^e(L^*)}{m}\right]\left(\frac{\delta N}{N - L^*} + r\right)$$
$$+ (1 - s)\tau L^* = F'(L^*).$$

3.2. Firms Perfectly Observe the Residential Location of All Workers

In that case, firms can pay workers according to their location. The bid-rent functions of all workers are given by:

$$\Psi_L(x, W_L) = w_L(x)F - \tau x + \Gamma^e(x) - W_L$$
$$\Psi_U(x, W_U) = w_U - s\tau x + \Gamma_U - W_U$$

with

$$\frac{\partial \Psi_L}{\partial x} = w'_L(x)F - \tau - \iota\frac{\partial \Gamma^e(x)}{\partial \zeta}.$$

Here, land rent compensates for (pecuniary) commuting costs, wage and leisure differences between residential locations. If $w'_L(x) < 0$, then the land rent will always be lower further away from the CBD because remote locations imply longer commutes, lower wages and less leisure (more time spent commuting). If, on the contrary, $w'_L(x) > 0$, then land rents can increase or decrease with the distance to jobs.

Let us calculate the efficiency wage. The Bellman equations are:

$$r\, I_L^{NS}(x) = w_L F - R(x) - \tau x + \Gamma^e(x) - \delta\,(I_L^{NS} - I_U)$$
$$r\, I_L^{S}(x) = w_L F - R(x) - \tau x + \Gamma^0(x) - (\delta + m)\,(I_L^{S} - I_U)$$
$$r\, I_U(x) = w_U - R(x) - s\tau x + \Gamma_U + a(I_L - I_U).$$

Since firms observe workers' residential location, the efficiency wage is such that, in each location, we have

$$I_L^{NS}(x) = I_L^{S}(x) = I_L(x)$$

which is equivalent to

$$I_L(x) - I_U = \frac{\Gamma^0(x) - \Gamma^e(x)}{m} > 0, \forall x \in [0, N].$$

It is then easily seen that Proposition 5.4 still holds. Using this relationship, $I_L(x) - I_U$, we easily obtain the efficiency wage at each x:

$$w_L(x)F = w_U + \Gamma_U - \Gamma^e(x) + \left[\frac{\Gamma^0(x) - \Gamma^e(x)}{m}\right]\left(\frac{\delta N}{N-L} + r\right)$$
$$+ (1-s)\,\tau x. \tag{5.41}$$

We have:

$$w'_L(x)F = \iota\frac{\partial\Gamma^e(x)}{\partial\zeta} - \frac{\iota}{m}\left(\frac{\delta N}{N-L} + r\right)\left[\frac{\partial\Gamma^0(x)}{\partial\zeta} - \frac{\partial\Gamma^e(x)}{\partial\zeta}\right] + (1-s)\,\tau. \tag{5.42}$$

Now the relationship between wages and distance to jobs is endogenous and determined by (5.42). Thus, as above, if (5.39) holds, then $w'_L(x) > 0$. If, on the contrary, (5.38) prevails, the sign of $w_L(x)$ is ambiguous.

Let us now determine the urban-land-use equilibrium. Using (5.42), we obtain

$$\frac{\partial\Psi_L}{\partial x} = -\frac{\iota}{m}\left(\frac{\delta N}{N-L} + r\right)\left[\frac{\partial\Gamma^0(x)}{\partial\zeta} - \frac{\partial\Gamma^e(x)}{\partial\zeta}\right] - s\tau.$$

The sign is ambiguous because of the three different effects (pecuniary commuting, wage and leisure) mentioned above. If (5.39) holds, i.e., effort and leisure are complements, then $w'_L(x) > 0$ and the bid-rent can be downward or upward sloping. Indeed, workers living further away have less leisure and incur more expenses in commuting, but have higher wages. On the other hand, if $w'_L(x) < 0$, then bid-rents are decreasing. Let us focus on this case. Compared to unemployed workers, the bid-rent of employed workers is steeper and thus, they reside closer to jobs. We can calculate the equilibrium values, which are given by:

$$W^*_L = w_U + \Gamma_U + \left(\frac{\Gamma^0(L)-\Gamma^e(L)}{m}\right)\left(\frac{\delta N}{N-L} + r\right) - s\tau N$$

$$W^*_U = w_U - s\tau N + \Gamma_U.$$

The equilibrium land rent is therefore equal to:

$$R^*(x) = \begin{cases} \left(\frac{\delta N}{N-L} + r\right)\frac{1}{m}\left[\Gamma^0(x) - \Gamma^0(L)\right. \\ \left. - (\Gamma^e(x) - \Gamma^e(L))\right] + s\tau(N-x) & \text{for } 0 \le x \le L \\ s\tau(N-x) & \text{for } L < x \le N \\ 0 & \text{for } x > N \end{cases}.$$

4. High Relocation Costs

The models developed so far had no relocation costs. As in Chapter 2, Section 5, we relax this assumption by considering very high relocation costs so that workers do not change their residence, when a change in their employment status occurs. As a result, *a worker's residential location remains fixed as he/she enters and leaves unemployment.* We also assume perfect capital markets with a zero interest rate. When there is a zero interest rate, workers have no intrinsic preference for the present and thus, they only care about the fraction of time they spend employed and unemployed.

As a result, as in Chapter 2, we consider the average expected utility of a worker rather than the lifetime expected utilities of employed and unemployed workers. At any moment in time, the disposable income (since workers are risk neutral utilities equal to income) of a worker is thus equal to that worker's average income over the job cycle. As before, we assume that changes in employment status (employment versus unemployment) are governed by a continuous-time Poisson (Markov) process. Therefore, the unemployment rate of non-shirkers is given by:

$$u \equiv u^{NS} = \frac{\delta}{a + \delta}, \qquad (5.43)$$

while that of shirkers is equal to:

$$u^S = \frac{\delta + m}{a + \delta + m}, \qquad (5.44)$$

with $u^S > u^{NS}$, $\forall a, \delta, m > 0$.

Since workers have a zero discount rate, they only care about average income over time. For a non shirker located at a distance x from the CBD, it is equal to:

$$E W_L^{NS}(x) = \left(1 - u^{NS}\right) [w_L - e - \tau x - R(x)] + u^{NS} [w_U - s\tau x - R(x)], \qquad (5.45)$$

whereas for a shirker residing at a distance x from the CBD, it is given by:

$$E W_L^S(x) = \left(1 - u^S\right) [w_L - \tau x - R(x)] + u^S [w_U - s\tau x - R(x)]. \qquad (5.46)$$

Once more, because information about residential location is of no importance in wage setting, we will now consider two different information structures.

4.1. Firms Do Not Observe the Residential Location of All Workers

Let us calculate the efficiency wage. Since firms know that wages are increasing with the distance from the CBD, x, they will set the highest possible wage to prevent shirking, i.e.,

$$w_L = w_U + e + \frac{e}{m}\frac{\delta}{u} + (1 - s)\,\tau\,N. \qquad (5.47)$$

Wages are not location-dependent and land rents will therefore only compensate for commuting costs. Let us solve the urban-land-use equilibrium. Plugging (5.47) into (5.45), and denoting the (expected) utility reached by all workers in the city by I, we obtain the following bid-rent:

$$\Psi(x, I) = w_U + \frac{e}{m}\frac{\delta\,(1 - u)}{u} + (1 - u)\,(1 - s)\,\tau\,N$$
$$- [1 - (1 - s)\,u]\,\tau\,x - I. \qquad (5.48)$$

Utility I is determined by the fact that the bid-rent at the city fringe is equal to zero. We obtain:

$$I = w_U + \frac{e}{m}\frac{\delta\,(1 - u)}{u} - s\,\tau\,N. \qquad (5.49)$$

Furthermore, plugging (5.49) into (5.48), we obtain the following equilibrium land rent for $x \in [0, N]$:

$$R(x) = [1 - (1 - s)\,u]\,\tau\,(N - x). \qquad (5.50)$$

We can now determine the labor market equilibrium. Each firm adjusts employment until the marginal product of an additional worker equals the efficiency wage (5.47), so that

$$w_U + e + \frac{e}{m}\frac{\delta}{u} + (1 - s)\,\tau\,N = F'((1 - u)N). \qquad (5.51)$$

4.2. Firms Perfectly Observe the Residential Location of All Workers

To determine the efficiency wage, firms solve $E\,V^{NS}(x) = E\,V^{S}(x)$ at each x. Using (5.45) and (5.46), we easily obtain:[3]

$$w_L(x) = w_U + e + \frac{e}{m}\,(\delta + a) + (1 - s)\,\tau\,x. \qquad (5.52)$$

---

[3] See Appendix A5 at the end of this chapter for a more rigorous demonstration of the derivation of the efficiency wage (5.52).

Since, at the efficiency wage, no worker shirks, we can use the value of a in (5.43) and plug it into (5.52) to obtain:

$$w_L(x) = w_U + e + \frac{e}{m}\frac{\delta}{u^{NS}} + (1-s)\tau x. \qquad (5.53)$$

This efficiency wage has the standard effects of both non-spatial and spatial models (see Chapter 4). This implies, as in Chapter 4, that the efficiency wage has two roles: to prevent shirking and compensate workers for commuting costs.

Now, the main difference here is that the mobility costs are very high so that workers always remain in the same location. So when a worker makes his/her decision of whether to shirk, he/she trades off longer spells of unemployment, but lower effort and lower commuting costs (if he/she decides to shirk) with longer spells of employment, but higher effort and higher commuting costs (if he/she decides not to shirk). As a result, in each location x, the setting of the efficiency wage needs to include these two elements (incentive and spatial compensation). For the spatial compensation element (which varies with x), it must be that, at each x, the compensation is equal to $\tau x(1 - u^{NS} + su^{NS}) - \tau x(1 - u^S + su^S)$, i.e., the average commuting cost when non-shirking minus the average commuting cost when shirking which, using (5.43) and (5.44), is exactly equal to $(1-s)\tau x$.

It is interesting to compare this efficiency wage with that obtained in the case of no relocation costs (Chapter 4) and the case of high relocation costs (like here), but the same commuting costs for employed and unemployed workers, i.e., $s = 1$. In both these models, the equilibrium is such that firms do not observe the residential location of all workers. Recall that in the former, the efficiency wage is equal to:

$$w_L = w_U + e + \frac{e}{m}\frac{\delta}{u^{NS}} + (1-s)\tau\left(1 - u^{NS}\right)N, \qquad (5.54)$$

whereas, in the latter, it is given by:

$$w_L = w_U + e + \frac{e}{m}\frac{\delta}{u^{NS}}. \qquad (5.55)$$

The main difference between (5.53) and (5.54) is that, in the benchmark model of Chapter 4, workers are perfectly mobile and thus, change locations as soon as they change employment status. This implies that employed and unemployed workers have different lifetime utilities. As a result, because of perfect mobility, all employed workers are indifferent to residing between 0 and $(1 - u)N$ (the employment zone) and firms set an efficiency wage at $(1 - u)N$ since, in this location, employed and unemployed workers pay exactly the same land rent, but do not have the same commuting costs, the difference being precisely $(1 - s)\, \tau\, (1 - u)\, N$. This is the spatial compensation role of the efficiency wage highlighted before. The main difference between (5.53) and (5.55) is that, because employed and unemployed workers bear exactly the same commuting costs, the efficiency wage no longer needs to compensate for spatial costs and its role is only to prevent shirking. This is why they obtain exactly the same wage as in Shapiro and Stiglitz (1984).

Let us now solve the urban-land-use equilibrium. We are able to calculate the bid rent of all workers in the city. By plugging (5.53) into (5.45), we obtain the following expected utility of a (non-shirking) worker located at x:

$$E\,W(x) = w_U + \frac{e}{m}\,\frac{\delta\left(1 - u^{NS}\right)}{u^{NS}} - s\tau x - R(x).$$

If we denote that I is the (expected) utility obtained by all workers in the city, then the bid rent is equal to $\Psi(x, I) = w_U + \frac{e}{m}\frac{\delta(1-u^{NS})}{u^{NS}} - s\tau x - I$. This equation highlights the role of land rent, which is to compensate workers for commuting costs and wages. Indeed, workers living further away obtain higher (efficiency) wages, but pay higher commuting costs whereas those living closer to the CBD have the opposite trade-off. In equilibrium, we finally obtain:

$$I = w_U + \frac{e}{m}\frac{\delta\left(1 - u^{NS}\right)}{u^{NS}} - s\tau N \tag{5.56}$$

$$R(x) = s\tau\,(N - x). \tag{5.57}$$

We can now determine the labor market equilibrium. For this purpose, we further assume that when a job is vacant, a firm is always willing to hire a worker whatever his/her location. This means that once a firm has a vacant job, it is always more profitable to hire the first worker that "knocks on its door" rather than waiting for the next worker. This is true for all workers, even for the one located at N, i.e., the worker who obtains the highest wage and lives furthest away from firms.[4] A consequence of this assumption is that each position within a firm will be totally randomly filled by a worker residing between 0 and N.

---

[4] Formally, it suffices to assume that the cost of waiting is sufficiently high as compared to the profit that a firm makes on a worker located at N.

Since all firms are totally identical, let us focus on a symmetric (steady-state) equilibrium in which each firm employs the same number of workers and pays the same total wage cost as any other firm. This means that each firm j hires $l_j = l = L/M$ workers and pays a total wage cost of $\int_0^N 1_{jx} w_L(x) dx = \frac{L}{M} w_L(\frac{N}{2})$, where $1_{jx} = 1$ if a worker is hired by firm j at x, and zero otherwise.[5]

As a result, each firm adjusts employment until the marginal product of an additional worker equals the average efficiency wage so that we have

$$w_L(N/2) = f'(l).$$

This determines labor demand in each firm. Using (5.53), the aggregate equivalent is thus given by:

$$w_U + e + \frac{e}{m} \frac{\delta N}{N - L} + (1 - s) \frac{\tau N}{2} = F'(L). \qquad (5.58)$$

4.3. Comparison Between the Two Equilibria

Let us determine total welfare in each equilibrium. In the perfect information equilibrium, by taking the sum of all (expected) utilities (workers, absentee landlords, and firms), it is easily verified that total welfare in equilibrium $k = pi, ii$ is given by:[6]

$$\mathcal{W}^k = \left(w_U - s\tau \frac{N}{2} \right) (N - L^k) - L^k e + F\left(L^k \right) - \tau \frac{N}{2} L^k$$

where L^{pi} and $L^{ii} < L^{pi}$ are, respectively, given by (5.58) and (5.51).

Proposition 5.5.

(i) *The unemployment rate in the perfect information equilibrium is lower than in the imperfect information equilibrium, i.e., $0 < u^{pi*} < u^{ii*} < 1$.*

(ii) *Wages are such that $w_L^{pi*}(N/2) < w_L^{ii*}$ and $w^{pi*}(x) \gtreqless w^{ii*} \Leftrightarrow x \gtreqless x_d$, where*

$$x_d \equiv N - \frac{e\delta}{m(1 - s)\tau} \left(\frac{1}{u^{pi*}} - \frac{1}{u^{ii*}} \right) > \frac{N}{2}.$$

---

[5] An easy interpretation is that firms only hire workers from an employment agency, which coordinates firms so that they hire workers in a symmetric way.

[6] Superscripts pi and ii refer to the perfect and imperfect information cases.

Furthermore, when N is small enough, $E w_L^{pi*}(x) > E w_L^{ii*}(x), \forall x \in [0, N]$ whereas, when N is large enough, $E w_L^{pi*}(x) \gtreqqless E w_L^{pi*}(x) \Leftrightarrow x \gtreqqless x_{Ed}$, where

$$x_{Ed} = \left(\frac{1 - u^{ii*}}{1 - u^{pi*}} \right) N - \frac{e\delta}{m(1-s)\tau} \left[\frac{1}{u^{pi*}} - \frac{(1 - u^{ii*})}{(1 - u^{pi*}) u^{ii*}} \right].$$

(*iii*) *The equilibrium land rent in the imperfect information equilibrium is always higher than in the perfect information equilibrium, i.e., $R^{ii*}(x) > R^{pi*}(x), \forall x \in [0, N[$ while the expected commuting cost is always higher in the perfect information equilibrium, i.e., $E\tau^{pi*}(x) > E\tau^{ii*}(x), \forall x \in [0, N]$.*

(*iv*) *Workers' expected utility in the perfect information equilibrium is higher than in the imperfect information equilibrium, i.e., $I^{pi*} > I^{ii*} > 0$.*

(*v*) *In terms of total welfare, we have:*

$$W^{pi*} \gtreqqless W^{ii*} \Leftrightarrow \frac{F(L^{pi*}) - F(L^{ii*})}{L^{pi*} - L^{ii*}} \gtreqqless w_U + e + (1-s)\tau \frac{N}{2}.$$

The first result (*i*) is straightforward. Indeed, since firms *on average* pay higher wage costs in the imperfect information equilibrium, they hire less workers and thus, the unemployment rate is lower in the perfect information equilibrium. Even though $w_L^{pi*}(N/2) < w^{ii*}$, this does not mean that wages or expected wages are always higher in the imperfect information equilibrium. Figures 5.1a and 5.1b illustrate (*ii*). Indeed, since $u^{pi*} < u^{ii*}$, then due to the nature of efficiency wages (for which the equilibrium unemployment acts as a worker discipline device), wages should be higher in the perfect information case. However, because firms do not observe residential location, they set the same high wage for all their workers, which implies that wages should be higher in the imperfect information case. So the result is ambiguous. As concerns wages in the case of residential location close to jobs, w_L^{ii} is higher than w_L^{pi} because the first effect dominates the second; the reverse is true for remote locations. For expected wages, more weight is put on the first effect since the unemployment rate measures the time spent in unemployment over workers' lifetime. When N is sufficiently small, the second effect is sufficiently reduced so that $E w_L^{pi}(x) > E w_L^{ii}(x)$, $\forall x$. When N is larger, there is a threshold distance x_{Ed} above which $E w_L^{pi}(x) > E w_L^{ii}(x)$.

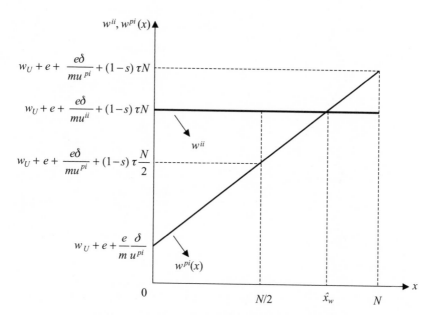

Figure 5.1a. Comparison of wages between equilibria.

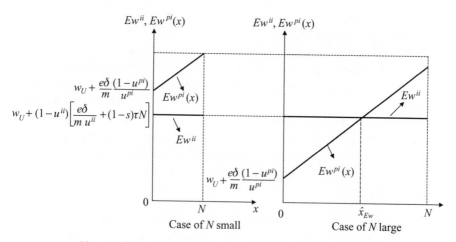

Figure 5.1b. Comparison of expected wages between equilibria.

Figure 5.2 helps us understand result (*iii*). In the two panels, we have drawn the expected values of land rents and commuting costs for each equilibrium. First, whatever the residential location, workers on average bear higher commuting costs (basically because they are less often unemployed

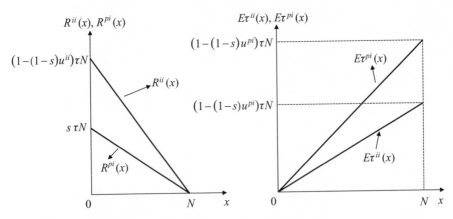

Figure 5.2. Comparison of (expected) land rents expected commuting costs between equilibria.

and commuting is more costly when employed) in the perfect information equilibrium. Second, even if expected wages tend be higher in the perfect information equilibrium, because of higher commuting costs, their capacity to bid for land is reduced and thus, the housing prices are higher everywhere in the city with imperfect information.

The next result is interesting since it shows that the expected utility of workers is always higher in the perfect information equilibrium, even though their wage is in general lower and their expected commuting costs higher. It is really the sharp reduction in land rents that makes them better off.

Finally, not surprisingly, this proposition shows that, in terms of welfare, neither of the equilibria Pareto dominates the other. Indeed, workers are better off, but absentee landlords are worse off in the perfect information equilibrium and, for firms, it is ambiguous since they hire more people and thus have higher production, but, on average pay higher wages.

Let us now examine the properties of these two equilibria.

Proposition 5.6.

(i) *The comparative-statics effects of the unemployment rates and the expected utilities are the same in the two equilibria and are as follows. An increase in the unemployment benefit w_U, effort e, the job-destruction rate, δ, or a decrease in the monitoring rate, m, the relative number of CBD trips for the unemployed, s, increases the unemployment rate, but has an ambiguous effect on expected utility in both equilibria, while an increase in the commuting cost τ increases unemployment, but reduces expected utility in both equilibria.*

(*ii*) *The comparative statics effects of the land rent are different. Indeed, in the perfect-information equilibrium, an increase in s or τ increases R(x). In the imperfect information equilibrium, because R(x) is affected by the unemployment rate, an increase in w_U, e, δ or a decrease in m, s, reduces the land rent while τ has an ambiguous effect.*

The following comments are in order. First, consider the common effects in both equilibria of the *non-spatial exogenous variables*, w_U, e, δ and m on the *non-spatial endogenous variables*, unemployment rate and expected utility. When w_U, e or δ increases or m decreases, the efficiency wage is augmented in order to prevent shirking and thus, the unemployment rate increases. However, the effect on expected utility is ambiguous because there are two opposite forces at work. On the one hand, there is a direct positive effect since wages increase. But, on the other hand, there is an indirect negative effect since it raises unemployment, which implies that workers will experience more unemployment spells. It is clearly ambiguous since, over their lifetime, workers are richer when employed, but spend more time unemployed.

Second, consider the effects of the *spatial exogenous variables*, τ and s on all endogenous variables, i.e., unemployment rate, land rent, and expected utility. In both equilibria, when the commuting cost τ increases (the relative number of CBD trips for the unemployed s decreases), firms raise (reduce) the efficiency wage to deter shirking. As a result, the unemployment rate increases (decreases). Concerning land rent, the effects are different between equilibria. In the perfect-information equilibrium, land rent only depends on s and τ and the relationship is positive because an increase in either s or τ increases the competition for land since access to the CBD becomes more costly. Thus, in the perfect-information equilibrium, when τ increases, wages are higher, but there is an increase in both land rent and unemployment. Since these two negative effects dominate the positive effect on wages, the expected utility decreases. For s, the effect on expected utility is ambiguous because a rise in s decreases wages and increases land rents, but reduces unemployment.

Concerning the imperfect-information equilibrium, the effects of τ and s are more subtle. Indeed, an inspection of (5.50) shows that land rent is both a direct and indirect (via the unemployment rate) function of τ and s. So, when τ increases, there is a direct effect, which leads to more competition and thus a higher land rent in each location, but there is also an indirect effect since it also implies higher wages and higher unemployment, which reduces the capacity to bid for land. The net effect is thus ambiguous.

However, the effect of τ on expected utility is negative because the negative unemployment effect dominates the ambiguous land rent effect. For s, the two effects on $R(x)$ go in the same direction. Indeed, an increase in s leads to more competition and thus, higher land rent, but also a lower wage and lower unemployment and thus a higher capacity to bid for land rents. However, the effect of s on expected utility is ambiguous. Indeed, a rise in s has a negative effect via the increase in land rent, but has a positive effect via the decrease in unemployment.

Finally, consider the effects of the *non-spatial exogenous variables*, w_U, e, δ and m on the *spatial endogenous variable*, land rent $R(x)$. They have no impact in the perfect information equilibrium whereas they strongly affect $R(x)$ in the imperfect information equilibrium via the unemployment rate. Indeed, in the latter, when w_U, e or δ increases or m decreases, the unemployment rate increases. Since workers anticipate that they will experience longer unemployment spells, their capacity to bid for land is lower. Thus, there is less competition in the land market and, as a result, the land rent in each location decreases.

4.4. Free-Entry and Long-Run Equilibrium

Let us study the long-run properties of the two equilibria so that the total number of firms M is not fixed but determined by a free-entry condition, i.e., firms freely enter the labor market up to a point where profits are equal to zero. If c denotes the fixed entry cost then, for each equilibrium $k = pi, ii$, the zero-profit condition can be written as:

$$f(l^k) - w_L^k l^k - c = 0. \tag{5.59}$$

Observe that for the perfect-information equilibrium, the free-entry condition is set for $w_L^{pi} = w_L(N/2)$. Hence, as in Chapter 4, for each equilibrium $k = pi, ii$, the long-run equilibrium is characterized by four unknowns, l^k, w_L^k, u^k, M^k and the following four equations:

$$w_L^k = f'(l^k) \tag{5.60}$$

$$f(l^k) - w_L^k l^k - c = 0 \tag{5.61}$$

$$w_L^k = w_U + e + \frac{e}{m} \frac{\delta}{u^k} + \mathbf{B}^k (1 - s) \tau N \tag{5.62}$$

$$\left(1 - u^k\right) N = M^k l^k, \tag{5.63}$$

where $\mathbf{B}^{pi} = 1/2$, $\mathbf{B}^{ii} = 1$ and $w_L^{pi} = w_L(N/2)$. Here is the way in which each equilibrium is solved. First, (5.60) gives the labor demand of each firm as a function of wage, $l^k(w_L^k) = f'^{-1}(w_L^k)$. Then, by plugging this value into (5.61), we obtain the wage $w_L^k(c)$. Observe that in the perfect information case, it is only the wage at $x = N/2$, that is $w_L^{pi}(N/2)$, which is a function of c; all wages for other locations x are still given by (5.53). Next, by plugging $w_L^k(c)$ into (5.62), we obtain $u^k(c, w_U, e, m, \delta, s, \tau, N)$ and finally, using (5.63), we get $M^k(c, w_U, e, m, \delta, s, \tau, N)$.

Proposition 5.7. *In the long run, we have:*

$$w_L^{pi}(N/2) = w_L^{ii} \equiv w_L(c)$$

$$u^{ii} > u^{pi}, M^{ii} < M^{pi}$$

First, the reason why the long-run wage is constant and only depends on c in the imperfect-information equilibrium is that, in the long run, M adjusts via entry and exit to give zero profits. So, for example, if τ, the commuting cost increases, because the free-entry condition must hold, aggregate labor demand shifts in tandem with the urban non-shirking curve in such a way as to keep the equilibrium efficiency wage constant. For the perfect information equilibrium, we still have a wage distribution because of workers' heterogeneity in terms of location, but the wage at $x = N/2$, i.e., $w_L^{pi}(N/2)$, which is used for the profit function and thus the free-entry condition, is constant. So, if τ increases, the whole wage distribution shifts in such a way as to keep the wage cost per firm equal to $l^{pi}w_L^{pi}(N/2) = l^{pi}w_L(c)$, and aggregate labor demand shifts in tandem with the urban non-shirking curve in such a way as to keep the equilibrium efficiency wage $w_L^{pi}(N/2)$ constant. Second, because wage costs are, on average, higher in the imperfect information equilibrium, unemployment is higher, which leads to less entry so that the total number of firms is lower than in the perfect information equilibrium. Finally, all other results obtained in the short-run case are still valid, but the mechanisms are different because of the free-entry condition, which implies that, in the long run, firms adjust via entry and exit.

5. Effort, Leisure, and Relocation Costs

We would like to reconsider the model of Section 3 by introducing high-relocation costs like in Section 4. This will, in particular, allow us to derive rather than assume the fact that $e'(x) < 0$, i.e., the greater the distance to work, the lower the effort level.

Consider once more two structures of information. Using (5.27) and (5.29), the expected utility of a worker located at x is given by:

$$I = (1 - u)W_L(x, e) + uW_U(x) \tag{5.64}$$
$$= (1 - u)\left[w_L F - R(x) - \tau x + \Gamma^e(x)\right] - R(x) - \tau x + u\left[w_U + \Gamma_U\right].$$

Moreover, since we would consider cases where workers may shirk in equilibrium, we now assume that shirkers provide an effort $\underline{e} > 0$, instead of zero as in the previous cases, while for non-shirkers, the effort is $\overline{e} > \underline{e} > 0$. The contribution to production is equal to $\overline{e}$ and $\underline{e}$ units, respectively.

5.1. Firms Do Not Observe the Residential Location of All Workers

Let us focus on an equilibrium in which some workers may shirk in equilibrium. Using (5.64), and given that all workers obtain the same wage, this implies that the expected indirect utilities of non-shirking and shirking workers are, respectively, equal to:

$$I^{NS}(x, \overline{e}) = (1 - u^{NS})\left[wF + \Gamma^{\overline{e}}(x)\right] - R(x) - \tau x + u^{NS}\Gamma_U$$
$$I^{S}(x, \underline{e}) = (1 - u^{S})\left[wF + \Gamma^{\underline{e}}(x)\right] - R(x) - \tau x + u^{S}\Gamma_U$$

where

$$\Gamma^{\overline{e}}(x) \equiv \Gamma(1 - F - \iota x, \overline{e}) \quad \text{and} \quad \Gamma^{\underline{e}}(x) \equiv \Gamma(1 - F - \iota x, \underline{e}).$$

These are simply the weighted averages of the utility levels of employed and unemployed workers where the share of time spent unemployed is used to form the weights. In equilibrium, all workers (shirkers and non-shirkers) must obtain the same utility level I, which is location independent. Since workers stay in the same location all their life, bid-rents are given by:

$$\Psi^{NS}(x, I) = (1 - u^{NS})\left[wF + \Gamma^{\overline{e}}(x)\right] - \tau x + u^{NS}\Gamma_U - I \tag{5.65}$$

$$\Psi^{S}(x, I) = (1 - u^{S})\left[wF + \Gamma^{\underline{e}}(x)\right] - \tau x + u^{S}\Gamma_U - I. \tag{5.66}$$

Inspecting these two equations shows that, as usual, the bid-rent functions are decreasing in x, with $\partial\Psi^{NS}(x, I)/\partial x < 0$ and $\partial\Psi^{S}(x, I)/\partial x < 0$. In the present model, this reflects the combined influence of the time cost of commuting and the monetary cost. Let us denote the border between non-shirkers and shirkers by x_s. We have the following result.

Proposition 5.8.

(i) *If effort and leisure are complements, i.e., (5.39) holds, then workers who reside close to jobs will choose not to shirk whereas workers located further away will shirk.*

(ii) *If effort and leisure are substitutes, i.e., (5.38) holds, then the location pattern of shirkers and non-shirkers is indeterminate. However, if we assume something stronger than (5.38), that is:*

$$(a + m + \delta) \frac{\partial \Gamma^{\overline{e}}}{\partial \zeta} \Big|_{x=x_s} < (a + \delta) \frac{\partial \Gamma^{\underline{e}}}{\partial \zeta} \Big|_{x=x_s}, \qquad (5.67)$$

then workers who reside close to jobs will choose to shirk whereas workers located further away will not shirk.

As can be seen from this proposition, the crucial assumption is whether $\partial^2 \Gamma (\zeta, e) / \partial \zeta \partial e$ is positive or negative. Neither sign can be ruled out using reasonable restrictions on preferences.[7] If $\partial^2 \Gamma (\zeta, e) / \partial \zeta \partial e > 0$, then disutility from e increases as leisure falls. If this assumption holds, workers residing close to jobs will provide more effort than those residing further away from jobs because they have less commuting time and thus more leisure time at home. This provides a rationale of the assumption $e'(x) < 0$ made in Section 2.

On the other hand, if $\partial^2 \Gamma(\zeta, e)/\partial \zeta \partial e < 0$ is assumed, the location pattern is less obvious. Indeed, workers residing close to jobs have less commuting time and thus, more leisure time at home and, because $\partial^2 \Gamma(\zeta, e)/\partial \zeta \partial e < 0$, provide less effort. So they are more likely to be shirkers and spend a greater fraction of their time unemployed. On the other hand, unemployment offers consumer savings in terms of no commutes during the spell of unemployment, and the benefits of these savings are further away from the CBD. Accordingly, the overall unemployment cost of shirking is lower near the edge of the urban area, which implies less effort in those locations. The net sign is thus ambiguous. If, however, (5.67) holds, which means that the unemployment spells are not too long (because, for example, the monitoring rate m is quite low), shirkers will live close to jobs.

Let us now determine x_s, the boundary between shirking and non-shirking workers where a consumer is indifferent between high and low levels of effort at work. To obtain the value of x_s, we must solve:

---

[7] See Section 3 for more intuition on these assumptions.

$\Psi^{NS}(x_s, I) = \Psi^S(x_s, I)$, which is equivalent to:

$$(1 - u^S)\Gamma^{\underline{e}}(x_s) - (1 - u^{NS})\Gamma^{\overline{e}}(x_s) = (u^S - u^{NS})(wF - \Gamma_U), \quad (5.68)$$

showing a clear trade-off between shirking (higher utility when employed since there is less effort, but a larger number of unemployment spells during the individual's lifetime) and non-shirking. We have the following result.

Proposition 5.9.

(i) *If (5.39) holds, then higher wages imply less shirking in the city, i.e.,* $\partial x_S / \partial w_L > 0$.

(ii) *If (5.67) holds, then higher wages reduce shirking in the city, i.e.,* $\partial x_s / \partial w_L < 0$.

This proposition states that wages affect x_s, i.e., the border between shirkers and non-shirkers. Indeed, if (5.39) holds, i.e., effort and leisure are substitutes, then less workers shirk when wages are higher (the fraction of shirkers $N - x_s$ decreases) since there are more incentives not to shirk (the average wage difference $wF(u^S - u^{NS})$ between shirkers and non-shirkers increases). If effort and leisure are complements and the difference in employment rates between shirkers and non-shirkers is not too large (5.67), then shirkers outbid non-shirkers for central locations and higher wages reduce the fraction of shirkers.

There are thus two urban-land-use equilibria. If (5.39) holds, the first emerges in which non-shirkers reside close to jobs while shirkers reside further away from jobs. If (5.67) holds, then the other equilibrium prevails in which shirkers live close to the CBD, while non-shirkers reside on the outskirts of the city.

Let us now determine the labor market equilibrium for each type of equilibrium. There are M firms in the economy. The profit function of a typical firm can be written as:

$$\Pi = F\left(\phi\left[L^{NS}\overline{e} + L^S\underline{e}\right]\right) - w_L\phi L,$$

where ϕ is the fraction of workers hired by each firm and the total number of non-shirkers in the economy is given by

$$L^{NS} = x_s(1 - u^{NS}), \quad (5.69)$$

the total number of non-shirkers is

$$L^S = (N - x_s)(1 - u^S), \quad (5.70)$$

and the total number of employed workers is $L = L^S + L^{NS}$. Since firms do not observe the residential location, all workers, whatever their location, obtain the same wage. We focus on a symmetric equilibrium where each firm employs the same fraction ϕ of workers (shirkers and non-shirkers). Thus, even if firms know that all workers residing beyond x_s will shirk, they have to pay them the same wage as those who live between 0 and x_s (non-shirkers). Let us now solve the firm's program. By taking $\bar{e}$, $\underline{e}$, u^S and u^{NS} as given, each firm chooses w_L and ϕ that maximize its profit. When choosing w_L, firms will face the following trade-off. Since they affect x_s, higher wages imply that the fraction of shirkers hired will be lower and there will be a decrease in total output, but labor costs are also higher since the wage paid to workers is the same. When choosing ϕ, firms face the following trade-off. Higher ϕ means that more workers are hired; thus higher output, but also higher labor costs.

It can be shown that the optimal wage is given by:

$$w \frac{\partial x_s}{\partial w} = \frac{L\left[(N - x_s)(1 - u^S)\bar{e} + x_s(1 - u^{NS})\underline{e}\right]}{(\bar{e} - \underline{e})\left[(1 - x_s)(1 - u^S)^2 + x_s(1 - u^{NS})^2\right]}. \quad (5.71)$$

In equilibrium, it must be the case that labor supply equals labor demand for non-shirkers and shirkers, respectively. These conditions can be written as:

$$\phi M L^{NS} = (1 - u^{NS})x_s$$

$$\phi M L^S = (N - x_s)(1 - u^S).$$

Using (5.69) and (5.70), this implies that

$$M = \frac{1}{\phi}.$$

5.2. Firms Perfectly Observe the Residential Location of All Workers

The expected utility of each worker is still given by (5.64). Now, as will be shown in the labor market analysis, there will be no shirking in equilibrium, which implies that the unemployment rate of the economy is given by

$$u^{NS} = \frac{\delta}{\theta + \delta}. \quad (5.72)$$

Furthermore, the bid-rent of a (non-shirker) worker is equal to

$$\Psi(x, I) = (1 - u^{NS})\left[w_L(x)F + \Gamma^{\bar{e}}(x)\right] - \tau x + u^{NS}\Gamma_U - I. \quad (5.73)$$

Inspecting this equation shows that

$$\frac{\partial \Psi(x, I)}{\partial x} = (1 - u^{NS}) \left[w'(x)F - \frac{\partial \Gamma^{\bar{e}}}{\partial \zeta} \iota \right] - \tau, \qquad (5.74)$$

which can be positive or negative depending on the sign of $w'(x)$. Since all workers provide the same effort level and are identical in all respects, they just locate anywhere in the city and enjoy the same utility level I, the land rent adjusting for commuting cost differences between different locations. To close the urban equilibrium, we have to check that $\Psi(N, I) = 0$, which is equivalent to:

$$I = (1 - u^{NS}) \left[w(N)F + \Gamma^{\bar{e}}(N) \right] - \tau + u^{NS} \Gamma_U. \qquad (5.75)$$

Let us now solve the labor market equilibrium. In each location in the city ($0 \leq x < N$), each firm must set an NSC (that equates shirking and non-shirking utilities) to prevent shirking. At each x, we obtain:

$$w_L(x) = \frac{(1 - u^S)\Gamma^{\underline{e}}(x) - (1 - u^{NS})\Gamma^{\bar{e}}(x)}{F(u^S - u^{NS})} + \frac{\Gamma_U}{F}. \qquad (5.76)$$

This is the standard Shapiro-Stiglitz style non-shirking condition evaluated in equilibrium for every residential location x. It should be clear here that when firms observe the residential location of workers, it is optimal for them not to allow shirking in equilibrium. In the previous model, this was not possible since each firm had to give the same wage to all its workers and thus, it was somehow optimal to let some workers shirk.

Proposition 5.10.

(*i*) *Assume (5.39). Then, $w'_L(x) > 0$.*
(*ii*) *Assume (5.67). Then, $w'_L(x) < 0$.*

This result is quite intuitive. If leisure and effort are substitutes (i.e., (5.39) holds), then wages have to compensate workers who live further away since they commute more and thus, have less time for leisure at home. If this is not the case and (5.67) holds (which is rather that leisure and effort are complements), then firms have to compensate workers who live closer to jobs for the time they spend employed because they attribute a lower value to leisure.

Using (5.74), Proposition 5.10 implies that when (5.39) holds, $w'_L(x) > 0$ and thus, the sign of $\partial \Psi(x, I)/\partial x$ is ambiguous since there are two opposite effects. On the one hand, workers residing far away have higher wages while on the other, they have higher monetary commuting costs and also higher time costs and thus, lower leisure. The compensation through land rent is therefore not straightforward. The following condition guarantees that land rents decrease from the center to the periphery:

$$0 < \frac{\partial \Gamma^{\bar{e}}}{\partial \zeta} - \frac{\partial \Gamma^{\underline{e}}}{\partial \zeta} < \frac{\tau \, m}{\iota \, a}. \tag{5.77}$$

This condition encompasses (5.61).

Let us determine the labor market equilibrium in each urban-land-use pattern. Let us define the labor demand ϕ of each firm. Firms solve the following program:

$$\max_{\phi} \left[\Pi = F(\phi L \bar{e}) - \phi L \int_0^N w_L(x) dx \right].$$

The first-order condition yields

$$\bar{e} F'(\phi L \bar{e}) = \int_0^N w_L(x) dx. \tag{5.78}$$

Equilibrium condition (labor demand equals labor supply) yields:

$$L = 1 - u^{NS} = \frac{a}{a + \delta}. \tag{5.79}$$

We focus on a symmetric labor market equilibrium in which each firm employs the same number of workers $\phi L = L / M$ so that, once more,

$$M = \frac{1}{\phi}. \tag{5.80}$$

6. Notes on the Literature

In this chapter, we have developed different extensions of the benchmark urban efficiency wage model (Chapter 4) to see how the results change with different assumptions. The models developed in Sections 2 and 4 are based on Zenou (2002) and (2006), respectively. Sections 3 and 5 are both based on Ross and Zenou (2003, 2008). We have seen that the structure of information on workers' residential location is of crucial importance in the efficiency wage setting. We have only discussed two extreme cases where firms can or cannot observe where workers live. An intermediate case may arise if commute time is only partially observed. For example, firms may observe residential location, which provides a noisy signal of a worker's commute, but it is too costly for firms to determine the true commutes of workers. In that case, firms will pay efficiency wages to reduce shirking, but they will not know the exact premium required to eliminate shirking by the worker residing in a given location. Presumably, firms will increase wages until the benefit of reducing the likelihood of shirking for a worker or workers equals the cost of the wage increase. Some workers are likely to shirk in equilibrium because their commute is substantially longer than the firm's estimate of their commute. Therefore, in the intermediate case, the employment and wage conditions may not hold in equilibrium.

APPENDIX A5. BELLMAN EQUATIONS AND EFFICIENCY WAGES WHEN $r \to 0$

Let us calculate the efficiency wage (5.52) using the Bellman equations. When $r > 0$, the standard (steady-state) Bellman equations for non-shirkers, shirkers and unemployed are, respectively, given by:

$$r\, I_L^{NS} = W_L^{NS} - \delta\,(I_L^{NS} - I_U) \tag{A5.1}$$

$$r\, I_L^{S} = W_L^{S} - (\delta + \theta)\,(I_L^{S} - I_U) \tag{A5.2}$$

$$r\, I_U = W_U + a(I_L^{NS} - I_U), \tag{A5.3}$$

where r is the discount rate, I_1^{NS}, I_1^{S} and I_0 represent, respectively, the expected lifetime utility of a non-shirker, a shirker, and an unemployed worker, and $W_L^{NS} = w_L - e - \tau x - R(x)$, $W_L^{S} = w_L - \tau x - R(x)$ and $W_U = w_U - s\tau x - R(x)$.

First, observe that when $r \to 0$, workers are infinitely patient and the value functions of I_1^{NS}, I_1^{S} and I_0 become infinite since there is no more discounting. However, when $r \to 0$, $r\, I_1^{NS}$ and $r\, I_0$ have finite values and, in fact, $r\, I_1^{NS} = r\, I_0$. Indeed, combining (A5.1) and (A5.3), we obtain:

$$r\, I_L^{NS} = \frac{(r + a)(w_L - e) + \delta\, w_U - (r + \delta\, s + a)\tau x}{r + \delta + a} - R(x) \tag{A5.4}$$

$$r\, I_U = \frac{a(w_L - e) + (r + \delta)\, w_U - (r\, s + \delta\, s + a)\tau x}{r + \delta + a} - R(x) \tag{A5.5}$$

so that

$$\lim_{r \to 0} r\, I_L^{NS} = \lim_{r \to 0} r\, I_U = \frac{a(w_L - e) + \delta\, w_U - (\delta\, s + a)\tau x}{\delta + a} - R(x), \tag{A5.6}$$

which obviously has a finite value. This is logical since when $r \to 0$, what is of importance is not the current employment status, but the fraction of time spent in each state.

The efficiency wage is set as follows. Firms set a wage such that the lifetime discounted expected utility of non-shirking is equal to that of shirking, i.e., $r I_L^{NS} = r I_L^S = r I_U$. Let us first derive $r I_L^S$. Combining (A5.2) and (A5.3), we have:

$$r I_L^S = \frac{(r+a)w_L + (\delta+\theta)\, w_U - (r+\delta s + a + \theta s)\tau x}{r + \delta + a + \theta} - R(x)$$

$$(A5.7)$$

with

$$\lim_{r \to 0} r I_L^S = \frac{a w_L + (\delta+\theta)\, w_U - (\delta s + a + \theta s)\tau x}{\delta + a + \theta} - R(x). \qquad (A5.8)$$

In our context, $r I_L^{NS}$ and $r I_L^S$ are well-defined functions since when $r \to 0$, they have finite values. Combining (A5.6) and (A5.8), we obtain the following efficiency wage:

$$w_L(x) = w_U + e + \frac{e}{\theta}\,(\delta+a) + (1-s)\,\tau x,$$

which is (5.52). ∎

CHAPTER SIX

Non-Monocentric Cities and Efficiency Wages

1. Introduction

As in Chapter 3, we will now relax the assumption of a unique job center (monocentric city) and investigate the consequences of multicentric cities on workers' labor market outcomes when firms set efficiency wages.

In Section 2, we extend the Harris-Todaro model with efficiency wages to incorporate a land market. Hence, we analyze the rural-urban migration equilibrium and study its consequences on the labor market. In particular, we find that when the government decreases the unemployment benefit, there is an increase in urban and rural employment while there is a decrease in urban unemployment. We obtain this result because compared to the standard non-spatial model, there is an additional repulsion force due to land-rent escalation following a decrease in the unemployment benefit. Indeed, we find that a reduction in the unemployment benefit reduces the land rent in the unemployment zone, but has an ambiguous effect for employed workers.

Then, we study migration between cities of different sizes in Section 3. We show that there exists a fundamental trade-off between high wages and high land rents in large cities and low wages and low spatial costs in small cities.

In Section 4, we then study migration of workers within a city when workers decide to work somewhere in the area between the Central Business District (CBD) and the Suburban Business District (SBD). We analyze the case when the SBD is exogenous and when it is endogenously formed. We also consider the case of high relocation costs. Efficiency wages and unemployment rates will differ since jobs in the CBD and the SBD are of different natures.

Finally, in Section 5, in a model à la Ogawa-Fujita, we analyze the endogenous formation of the CBD with efficiency wages using firms' externalities in production as the main force of agglomeration. The CBD is endogenously formed of firms that need to bid away workers in order to occupy the center of the city. This implies that labor demand is negatively affected by the commuting cost of workers. Indeed, when a firm wants to hire an additional worker, there is a new additional cost, which is due to the fact that competition in the land market becomes fiercer because access to the center becomes more valuable for this additional worker.

2. Rural-Urban Migration: The Harris-Todaro Model with a Land Market

As in Section 2 in Chapter 3, we analyze a model in which rural workers can migrate to urban areas, so that two job centers (urban and rural) will prevail in equilibrium. Once more, we use a framework similar to that of the Harris-Todaro model (Todaro, 1969; Harris and Todaro, 1970), but focus on efficiency wages instead of search frictions.[1] Using the developments of Chapters 4 and 5, we will analyze a rural-urban migration model à la Harris-Todaro with a land market and efficiency wages.

There are two regions, an urban area (the city, denoted by superscript C) and a rural area (denoted by superscript R). It is assumed that, in cities, jobs are more complex than in rural areas, so that shirking behavior is more likely to arise there.[2] Furthermore, rural wages are assumed to be very flexible so that there is no unemployment in rural areas. Hence, the unemployment level in cities is still given by (3.1), i.e.,

$$U^C = N - L^C - L^R. \tag{6.1}$$

In urban areas, firms set efficiency wages to prevent shirking and consequently, urban unemployment will emerge in equilibrium.

Both regions produce the same good, but use different techniques. In region $g = C, R$, y^g units of output are produced and L^g workers are employed. This is a short-run model where capital is fixed and the production function in region $g = C, R$ is given by

$$y^g = F^g(L^g), F'^g(L^g) > 0, \text{ and } F''^g(L^g) \leq 0. \tag{6.2}$$

---

[1] See Appendix C for a detailed description of the Harris-Todaro model, especially the efficiency wage case.

[2] To justify the possible shirking behavior in cities, it can be assumed that firms are larger in cities than in rural areas. This issue is investigated in more detail in Section 3 below.

We also assume that the Inada conditions hold, that is,

$$\lim_{L^g \to 0} F^{g\prime}(L^g) = +\infty, \quad \lim_{L^g \to +\infty} F^{g\prime}(L^g) = 0. \quad (6.3)$$

The price of the good is taken as a numeraire and, without loss of generality, is normalized to 1.[3] As stated above, in rural areas we assume that jobs are mainly menial and wages are flexible and equal to the marginal product, so that there is no rural unemployment. Thus, we have:

$$w_L^R = F'^R(L^R). \quad (6.4)$$

In cities, jobs are more complex and thus more difficult to monitor. Let us first solve the equilibrium in the land and labor markets in cities and then link rural and urban areas through a migration equilibrium condition.

2.1. The Urban-Land-Use Equilibrium

In region C, all workers are uniformly distributed along a linear, closed, and monocentric city. Their density in each location is taken to be 1. All land is owned by absentee landlords and all firms are exogenously located in the CBD and consume no space. Workers decide on their optimal place of residence between the CBD and the city fringe. There are *no relocation costs*, either in terms of time or money.

The urban-land-use equilibrium is exactly as in Section 2 of Chapter 3 which means that, in cities, employed workers reside close to jobs while unemployed workers live on the outskirts of the city (see Figure 6.1). Rural employed workers reside outside the city.

As a result, the equilibrium instantaneous utilities of employed and unemployed workers and the equilibrium land rent are given by:

$$W_L^C = w_L^C - e - \tau L^C - s\tau \left(N - L^R - L^C\right) \quad (6.5)$$

$$W_U^* = w_U^C - s\tau \left(N - L^R\right) \quad (6.6)$$

$$R^C(x) = \begin{cases} \tau (L^C - x) + s\tau (N - L^R - L^C) & \text{for } 0 \le x \le L^C \\ s\tau (N - L^R - x) & \text{for } L^C < x \le N^C \\ 0 & \text{for } x > N^C \end{cases} \quad (6.7)$$

---

[3] Which means that the city and the rural area produce an export good that is sold on world markets at a fixed price, normalized to 1.

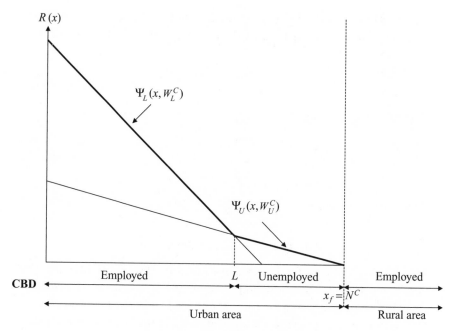

Figure 6.1. Rural-urban equilibrium.

2.2. The Labor Equilibrium in Cities

Using the discounted lifetime expected utilities of non-shirking, shirking, and unemployed workers in the benchmark model of Chapter 4 (determined by (4.16), (4.17), (4.18)), and the fact that $N_C = N - L^R$ and

$$a^C = \frac{\delta L^C}{N - L^C - L^R},$$ (6.8)

we easily obtain the following urban efficiency wage:

$$w_L^C = w_U^C + e + \frac{e}{m}\left[\frac{\delta\left(N - L^R\right)}{N - L^C - L^R} + r\right] + (1 - s)\,\tau\,L^C.$$ (6.9)

This wage is similar to that given in the benchmark model (see (4.20)) with one difference: it depends on rural employment L^R. In particular, the higher rural employment L^R is, the higher the urban efficiency wage w_L^C is. Indeed, a higher L^R implies that fewer rural workers move to the city, so the urban job acquisition rate a^C increases and thus, urban firms raise their wages w_L^C. Urban firms determine their employment level by maximizing their profit. We thus have:

$$w_L^C = F'^C(L^C). \qquad (6.10)$$

By combining (6.9) and (6.10), we obtain:

$$w_U^C + e + \frac{e}{m}\left[\frac{\delta\,(N - L^R)}{N - L^C - L^R} + r\right] + (1 - s)\,\tau\,L^C = F'^C(L^C), \qquad (6.11)$$

which determines L^C as a function of L^R only.

2.3. The Rural-Urban Migration

As in Section 2 of Chapter 3, we assume that a rural worker cannot search from home, but must first be unemployed in the city (to gather information about jobs) and then search for a job. As a result, as described in Figure 6.1, a rural worker who migrates to the city will reside in the unemployment area anywhere between $x = L^C$ and $x = N^C = N - L^R$. Thus, the equilibrium migration condition can be written as (observing that the rural land rent has been normalized to zero):

$$I_U = \int_0^{+\infty} w_L^R\, e^{-rt}dt = \frac{w_L^R}{r},$$

that is, rural workers will migrate to the city up to the point where their expected lifetime utility is equal to the expected utility they will obtain in cities. Using the values of the discounted lifetime expected utilities, $N^C = N - L^R$, and (6.4), we can write this condition as:

$$w_U^C - s\tau\,(N - L^R) + \frac{e}{m}\frac{\delta\,L^C}{N - L^C - L^R} = \frac{F'^R(L^R)}{r}. \qquad (6.12)$$

Observe that we can now check that, in equilibrium, urban workers will never want to migrate to rural areas. Since the utility from staying in rural areas is equal to w_L^R/r and, in equilibrium, is given by (6.12), it suffices to show that $r\, I_L > r\, I_U$. It is easily verified that

$$I_L - I_U = \frac{e}{m} > 0.$$

2.4. The Equilibrium

We have the following definition.

Definition 6.1. *A Harris-Todaro equilibrium with efficiency wages and a land market is a 6-tuple $(w_L^{C*}, L^{C*}, w_L^{R*}, U^{C*}, L^{R*}, R^{C*}(x))$ such that (6.9), (6.10), (6.4), (6.1), (6.12), and (6.7) are satisfied.*

We have the following result (which is proved in Zenou, 2005).

Proposition 6.1. *There exists a unique Harris-Todaro equilibrium with efficiency wages and a land market with $0 < L^{C*} < N$ and $0 < L^{R*} < N$.*

2.5. Interaction Between Land and Labor Markets

Let us first study the comparative statics of our equilibrium. The equilibrium is basically determined by two equations (6.12) and (6.11). If we first totally differentiate (6.12), the equilibrium migration condition, we obtain

$$ L^R = L^R \left(\underset{-}{w_U^C}, \underset{-}{e}, \underset{+}{m}, \underset{-}{\delta}, \underset{+}{N}, \underset{-}{r}, \underset{-}{L^C}, \underset{+}{s}, \underset{+}{\tau} \right). \tag{6.13} $$

First, the impact of the non-spatial variables (w_U^C, e, δ, r, m, N) is as in the non-spatial case (see Appendix C) and is due to the fact that they either have a positive or a negative effect on the intertemporal utility of being unemployed in the city, I_U. Indeed, when the effect is positive (negative) I_U, then more (less) workers leave the rural area, which reduces (increases) L^R. Second, when L^C increases, the urban job acquisition rate a^C increases and more rural workers migrate to the city, thus reducing L^R. Finally, the two spatial variables, s and τ, have a positive effect on the number of people who stay in rural areas, L^R, but the effect goes through the land market. Indeed, when s or τ increases, the capacity to bid for land is augmented (see (6.7)). Competition in the land market becomes fiercer and, as a result, the land rents paid by all workers increase. Thus, unemployed workers are worse off as their expected utility I_U decreases. This discourages rural workers from migrating to the city which, in turn, increases L^R.

If we now totally differentiate the labor demand equation (6.11), we get:

$$ L^C = L^C \left(\underset{-}{w_U^C}, \underset{-}{e}, \underset{+}{m}, \underset{-}{\delta}, \underset{+}{N}, \underset{-}{r}, \underset{-}{L^R}, \underset{+}{s}, \underset{-}{\tau} \right). \tag{6.14} $$

First, the impact of the non-spatial variables (w_U^C, e, δ, r, m, N) is as in the non-spatial case (see Appendix C) and is due to the fact that they either have a positive or a negative effect on the Urban Non-Shirking Condition (UNSC), which is given by (6.9). Indeed, when they have a positive (negative) effect on the UNSC, firms must pay a higher (lower) efficiency wage to prevent shirking. This, in turn, reduces (increases) employment L^C since, because of higher (lower) wage costs, maximizing-profit firms have to reduce (increase) the number of employed. Second, for L^R, the effect is through the job-acquisition rate a^C. Indeed, a higher rural employment L^R increases a^C, which obliges firms to increase their urban efficiency wages which, in turn, reduces urban labor demand L^C because firms maximize their profit. Finally, concerning spatial variables s and τ, they also affect the UNSC; however, not the incentive part, but the spatial compensation part. Indeed, when τ increases or s decreases, firms have to raise the spatial compensation of their employed workers to induce them to stay in the city. This increases the efficiency wage which, in turn, reduces labor demand L^C.

Let us now more specifically focus on the impact of a change in the unemployment benefit w_U^C (a government policy variable) on workers' labor market outcomes. We have the following result:

Proposition 6.2. *In a Harris-Todaro model with urban efficiency wages and a land market, decreasing unemployment benefits lead to*

(i) *an increase in urban employment L^C, i.e., $\partial L^{C*}/\partial w_U^C < 0$;*

(ii) *an increase in rural employment L^R, i.e., $\partial L^{R*}/\partial w_U^C < 0$;*

(iii) *a decrease in urban unemployment (both in level and rate) U^C and u^C, i.e., $\partial U^{C*}/\partial w_U^C > 0$ and $\partial u^{C*}/\partial w_U^C > 0$.*

If making a comparison with the non-spatial case (Appendix C), we obtain exactly the same results. Indeed, when the government decreases the unemployment benefit, this has a direct negative effect on urban efficiency wages and thus, more urban jobs are created. This acts as an attraction force to the city. But there are now three (instead of two) repulsion forces. As in the non-spatial case, the first two repulsion forces are as follows. More job creation indirectly implies that rural wages increase and urban wages become lower. However, there is an additional repulsion force due to *land-rent escalation* in cities, since the initial job creation that triggers migration increases land rents because of a fiercer competition in the land market.

Thus, the results are qualitatively the same, but quantitatively different because of this new force triggered by land rent.

2.6. The Specificity of a Harris-Todaro Equilibrium with a Land Market

Because a land market has been explicitly introduced in this model, it would be interesting to see the effects of a decrease in w_U^C on the equilibrium land rent $R^{C*}(x)$, which is given by (6.7). We have:

Proposition 6.3. *Decreasing the unemployment benefit*

(i) *reduces the equilibrium land rent in the unemployment zone, which is between $x = L^{C*}$ and $x = N$,*

(ii) *but has an ambiguous effect on the equilibrium land rent in the employment zone, which is between $x = 0$ and $x = L^{C*}$, since*

$$\frac{\partial R^C(x)}{\partial w_U^C} = (1 - s)\,\tau\,\frac{\partial L^{C*}}{\partial w_U^C} - s\tau\,\frac{\partial L^{R*}}{\partial w_U^C} \gtrless 0.$$

This proposition is quite intuitive. If the unemployment benefit w_U^C decreases, then less rural workers migrate to the city (L^R increases) and thus, the land rent decreases in the unemployment zone (remember that rural migrants first reside in the unemployment zone) since there is less competition in the land market. This is no longer true in the employment zone because land rent is also affected by L^C. Indeed, when w_U^C decreases, both L^{R*} and L^{C*} are increased (Proposition 6.2) so, one the one hand, there is less competition in the land market because of a higher L^R, but on the other, there is more competition because of a higher L^C. The net effect is thus ambiguous.

3. Migration between Cities of Different Sizes

We would like to develop a model similar to that of Section 2, but focusing on urban-urban migration rather than rural-urban migration. Following Zenou and Smith (1995), we model the migration decision of workers between cities of different sizes. As in the benchmark model of efficiency wages (Chapter 4), each firm is always motivated to discourage shirking behavior because shirkers add nothing to production. Moreover, each firm is assumed to only have a limited ability to monitor the productivity of its workers and the monitoring capability is taken to be characterized by a *detection rate*, m, which represents the speed at which the shirking behavior of any worker can be detected. Since the behavior of single individuals is less conspicuous in large firms, this detection rate now depends on the size of the firm and it is assumed that the larger is the size of the firm, the more difficult it is to detect shirking behavior. Empirical support for this dependency on firm size is given in Brown and Medoff (1989), Rebitzer and Robinson (1991), Zenger (1994), and Oi and Idson (1999). Hence, detection is here taken to be a system variable which varies with average firm size, but which is beyond the control of individual firms. Since there are M identical firms in the economy, the average firm size is L/M (where L is the level of employment in the economy) and thus, our assumption implies that $m(L/M)$, with $m'(L/M) < 0$ and

$$\lim_{L \to 0} m(L/M) = +\infty. \qquad (6.15)$$

This is a boundary condition which says that, as total employment L approaches zero, the detection rate increases without any bound so that the detection of shirkers occurs almost immediately. We can now solve this model of a monocentric city as in the benchmark model of Chapter 4 since the prevailing detection rates are exogenous to the firm and the only way of preventing shirking is to offer the efficiency wage level consistent with the current level of total employment L.

Let us now open the city and allow for the possibility of *between-city* migration. We will consider a closed two-city system with free labor mobility between cities as described by Figure 6.2. This is a bounded one-dimensional continuum with a uniform density of residential land parcels, and with CBDs at each end representing the two cities, designated respectively as city 1 (the big city) and city 2 (the small city). Each city $k = 1, 2$ has a CBD$_i$ that contains the same fixed number of firms M.[4] All firms are assumed to be identical within a CBD and all firms are assumed to be immobile. Each firm is assumed to produce the same good at the same market price (normalized to 1), but firms in the big city (i.e., city 1) have a higher productive capacity than those in the small city (i.e., city 2). This is a well-established empirical fact (see, e.g., Ciccone and Hall, 1996; Glaeser and Maré, 2001) and different reasons have been advanced. Larger cities have a more extensive infrastructure and greater access to other production factors than labor. Moreover, cities have information externalities that increase the

---

[4] This assumption is not necessary to obtain our results.

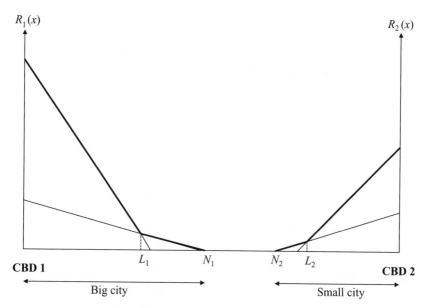

$R_1(x)$ $R_2(x)$

CBD 1 L_1 N_1 N_2 L_2 CBD 2

Big city Small city

Figure 6.2. Two-city equilibrium.

productivity of firms and the presence of greater demand in cities or inputs is cheaper when producers are close to other suppliers. Finally, there are human capital externalities for workers in cities (Duranton, 2006). All these theories predict that the marginal product of labor is higher in larger cities. For example, using data on gross state output in the U.S., Ciccone and Hall (1996) found that a doubling of employment density increases average labor productivity by around 6% and more than half of the variance of output per worker across states can be explained by differences in the density of economic activities.[5] Hence, if the production function for a firm j in city $k = 1, 2$ is denoted by $f_i(el_j)$, then it is assumed that $f'^1(el_j) > f'^2(el_j)$ for all $l_j \geq 0$.[6] Observe that we here assume that e, the effort level of workers, is the same in the two cities. This means that if two identical workers put in

---

[5] There in fact is an important branch of the literature that deals with agglomeration and local labor markets (wage premium in cities, better labor market matching, etc.; see the survey by Duranton and Puga, 2004). We discussed the literature on "better labor market matching in cities" in the "Notes on Literature" at the end of Chapter 3. In section 5, we propose a model that has some of these features. However, apart from this model, the issue of agglomeration and local labor markets has been excluded from the scope of this book.

[6] As usual, we assume the Inada conditions on the production function.

the same effort e, their labor productivity will be higher if they work in city 1 than in city 2.

Turning next to the workers, there is assumed to exist a fixed total population size N in this two-city system, with

$$N = N^1 + N^2 \tag{6.16}$$

where N^k is the number of workers in city k. Workers are freely mobile both within and between cities.

3.1. Urban-Land-Use Equilibrium in Each City

As in the benchmark model (Chapter 4), we can calculate the urban-land-use equilibrium in each city $k = 1, 2$, where the employed reside close to jobs (CBD^k) and the unemployed reside on the periphery of the city. We easily obtain for $k = 1, 2$:

$$W_L^{k*} = w_L^k - e - \tau L^k - s\tau \left(N^k - L^k \right) \tag{6.17}$$

$$W_U^{k*} = w_U - s\tau N^k \tag{6.18}$$

$$R^{k*}(x) = \begin{cases} (1-s)\tau L^k + s\tau N^k - \tau x & \text{for} \quad 0 \le x \le L^k \\ s\tau \left(N^k - x \right) & \text{for} \quad L^k < x \le N^k. \\ 0 & \text{for} \quad x > N^k \end{cases} \tag{6.19}$$

The main difference between the benchmark model and the present one is that there are now another three endogenous variables N^1 and N^2 (which will be determined by the equilibrium migration condition and $N = N^1 + N^2$), and $m^k \equiv m(L^k/M)$. Each endogenous variable is now indexed by $k = 1, 2$ since it is assumed that all exogenous variables (such as τ, s, e, w_U, δ) are the same between the two cities.

3.2. Steady-State Equilibrium

Let us determine the labor market equilibrium. Once more, as in the benchmark model, we can calculate the efficiency wage. For each city $k = 1, 2$, we obtain:

$$w_L^{k*} = w_U + e + \frac{e}{m(L^k/M)} \left(\frac{\delta N^k}{N^k - L_k} + r \right) + (1-s)\tau L^k. \tag{6.20}$$

It is important to notice that we still have the same properties of the efficiency wage with respect to L_k, that is,

$$\frac{\partial w_L^{k*}}{\partial L^k} > 0 \text{ and } \lim_{L \to N_k} w_L^{k*} = +\infty.$$

This is a crucial property of the efficiency wage, since it implies that higher unemployment is associated with lower efficiency wages ("unemployment acts as a worker discipline device") and that full employment is not compatible with efficiency wages. In particular, this implies that larger cities have higher wages because firms are, on average, larger and effort monitoring and detection of shirking is more difficult. The positive relationship between wages and city size is a well-established fact; see in particular Glaeser and Maré (2001).

Aggregate labor demand L^{k*} in city k is the result of firms' profit maximization and, using (6.20), is given by:

$$e F'(e L^{k*}) = w_U + e + \frac{e}{m(L^{k*}/M)} \left(\frac{\delta N^k}{N^k - L^{k*}} + r \right) + (1 - s) \tau L^{k*}.$$

$$(6.21)$$

It is easy to verify that the Inada conditions on the production function of each firm and (6.15) guarantee that there exists a unique labor market equilibrium in each city $k = 1, 2$ and thus, a unique urban-land-use equilibrium $k = 1, 2$.

We would now like to determine the equilibrium for the two-city system. As in the previous section, we assume that workers cannot search from home, but must first be unemployed in the city where they want to migrate (to gather information about jobs) and then search for a job. To write the equilibrium migration condition, we need to determine the (steady-state) expected lifetime utility of an unemployed worker in city k. The corresponding Bellman equation is equal to:

$$r I_U^k = w_U - s\tau N^{k*} + a^k (I_L^k - I_U^k)$$

$$= w_U - s\tau N^{k*} + \frac{\delta L^{k*}}{\left(N^{k*} - L^{k*} \right)} \frac{e}{m(L^{k*}/M)},$$

since $a^k = \delta L^{k*}/(N^{k*} - L^{k*})$ and $I_L^k - I_U^k = e/m(L^{k*}/M)$. In fact, since the *spatial costs* (costs of transportation plus costs of land rent) of the unemployed workers are: $SC_U^k = s \tau N^{k*}$ (see (6.18)) and the *wage surplus* that must be paid to deter shirking is: $SW^k = \delta \, e \frac{L^{k*}}{(N^{k*} - L^{k*}) m(L^{k*}/M)}$, we have:

$$r \, I_U^k = w_U + SW^k - SC_U^k.$$

This expected utility consists of two components. The first one, w_U, is a *base utility* level that can be earned in any of the two cities. The second one, $SW^k - SC_U^k$, is of primary interest for our purpose and represents the difference between SW^k, the *utility gain* from the wage surplus in city k and SC_U^k, and the *utility loss* from the spatial costs in city k. It is this fundamental trade-off that is at the heart of all migration decisions in the present model. Indeed, the equilibrium migration condition between the two cities can be written as $r \, I_U^1 = r \, I_U^2$, which is equivalent to:

$$SW^1 - SW^2 = SC_U^1 - SC_U^2$$

$$\Leftrightarrow \delta \, e \left[\frac{L^{1*}}{(N^{1*} - L^{1*}) \, m(L^{1*}/M)} - \frac{L^{2*}}{(N - N^{1*} - L^{2*}) \, m(L^{2*}/M)} \right]$$

$$= s\tau \left(2N^{1*} - N \right), \tag{6.22}$$

where we use (6.16) for the second equation. It is clear from (6.22) that when deciding to migrate, workers trade off between a higher wage surplus in big cities and lower spatial costs in smaller cities. Compared to small cities, big cities are indeed characterized by higher wages. Indeed, in big cities, firms are, on average, larger and thus monitoring is more difficult so that wages are higher. However, land rents and commuting costs are also higher since individuals are richer and, on average, commute more.

Definition 6.2. *A steady-state equilibrium ($R^{k*}(x)$, w_L^{k*}, L^{k*}, N^{1*}, N^{2*}) for the two-city system described in Figure 6.2 consists of a land rent function (6.19) for each city, a wage (6.20) for each city, an employment level (6.21) for each city, a migration equilibrium condition (6.22), and a population condition (6.16).*

It is easily shown that there exists a unique steady-state equilibrium (Zenou and Smith, 1995). For this purpose, there needs to be a unique solution to (6.22). For example, by introducing a positive migration cost, one can always find a value of the migration cost for the modified equation (6.22) (which takes into account this migration cost). We also have:

Proposition 6.4. *The expected migration utility function in city k, i.e., I_U^k, is always strictly decreasing in L^k.*

The proof of this result is given in Lemma 3.1 in Zenou and Smith (1995). This means that whenever the employment level increases in one city, the expected utility of the unemployed in that city decreases because wages are lower and the chance of finding a job is also lower. This result also establishes the stability of the system equilibrium since any continuous migration process in which migrants move toward higher expected utility must always converge to the unique system equilibrium.

3.3. Interaction Between Land and Labor Markets

The equilibrium conditions for this two-city system are basically given by (6.21), the equilibrium employment level in each city $k = 1, 2$, the equilibrium migration condition (6.22), and the population condition (6.16). Indeed, equation (6.21) gives L^{1*} and L^{2*}. However, since N^{1*} and N^{2*} are now endogenous variables, we cannot, as in the benchmark model, directly calculate the unemployment level in each city, $N^{k*} - L^{k*}$. Conditions (6.22) and (6.16) give N^{1*} and N^{2*}, and the model is solved. The intuition of the equilibrium is as follows. In each city, the size of each firm affects the detection of shirking which, in turn, determines the efficiency wage. Given this wage, firms determine their employment level by maximizing their profit. So employment in each city is basically determined for efficiency wage and monitoring reasons. The wage and employment levels also affect competition in the land market and thus, land rent in each residential location. The complication here is that workers are freely mobile between the two cities, which affects wage determination and the employment level. Indeed, when wages increase in a city, workers are more likely to move there, but unemployment will also increase (since a new migrant must first be unemployed), which implies lower wages (because of the disciplinary nature of the efficiency wage). The net effect is not straightforward. What we have shown is that there is a trade off between space cost differential and wage surplus when deciding to move (see (6.22)). Indeed, larger cities, where workers are assumed to be more productive, offer higher wages, but have higher unemployment rates while housing and commuting costs are also higher. In equilibrium, individuals are indifferent between the two cities because space cost differentials are totally compensated by wage surplus and the discounted lifetime expected utility is the same in each city.

As in the previous section, we would like to analyze the effect of an exogenous variable on equilibrium employment and unemployment levels in each city, for example the effect of a labor market variable such as w_U, the unemployment benefit, or δ, the job destruction rate, on equilibrium land rent $R^{k*}(x)$ in city k.

By totally differentiating (6.21), as in the benchmark model, for each city we obtain that:

$$L^{k*} = L^k \left(\underset{-}{w_U}, \underset{?}{e}, \underset{-}{\delta}, \underset{+}{N^{k*}}, \underset{-}{r}, \underset{+}{s}, \underset{-}{\tau} \right). \qquad (6.23)$$

The intuition of this comparative statics exercise is the same as in the benchmark model. The interesting relationship is between the two endogenous variables N^{k*} and L^{k*}. Indeed, when N^{k*} increases, i.e., there is more people in the city, then there is more unemployment, and hence, for shirking reasons, wages are lower, which means that firms can hire more workers, so that L^{k*} increases. Let us now differentiate (6.22) to analyze the relationship among N^{1*} and L^{1*} and L^{2*}. It is easily verified that:

$$\frac{\partial N^{1*}}{\partial L^{1*}} > 0 \text{ and } \frac{\partial N^{1*}}{\partial L^{2*}} < 0. \qquad (6.24)$$

Indeed, there are two positive effects on N^{1*} when L^{1*} increases: a direct positive effect, which is mechanical since more employment implies more migration to the city because it becomes more attractive (a higher chance of obtaining a job), and an indirect positive effect since higher employment implies that the average size of firms is larger. The detection of shirking being more difficult, wages will be higher so that more people will migrate to the city and N^{1*} increases. For exactly the same reasons (but with the opposite argument), we can explain the negative relationship between N^{1*} and L^{2*}. We can now analyze the effect of the unemployment benefit w_U on N^{1*}. It is easily verified that it is ambiguous because there are two opposite effects. When w_U increases, both L^{1*} and L^{2*} decrease (see (6.23)), since firms have to increase their efficiency wage in both cities to meet the UNSC and thus, reduce their labor demand. Now, because of (6.24), the decrease of L^{1*} will increase efficiency wages in city 1 (monitoring is easier since firm size is lower) and thus increase N^{1*}, but the decrease in L^{2*} will also increase efficiency wages in city 1 and thus, decrease N^{1*}. We have the same kind of ambiguous effect if we analyze the impact of δ on N^{1*}.

We are now able to determine the impact of w_U or δ on equilibrium land rent $R^{k*}(x)$, which is given by (6.19). An increase in w_U or δ has a negative effect on L^{k*} (see (6.23)), but has an ambiguous effect on N^{1*} so that the net effect on land rent is ambiguous. Once more, the intuition is as follows. If, for example, w_U increases, then both cities will have higher wages because of better outside options and thus, higher unemployment. This will increase the land rent in each city in the short run, but as it also affects migration, the net final effect on land rent is ambiguous since N^{1*} will tend to decrease due to the decrease in L^{1*} and tend to increase due to the decrease in L^{2*}.

An interesting extension would be to consider different exogenous variables in the two cities. A natural variable for this is the job destruction rate. It can be assumed that big cities are less affected by shocks because jobs are more diversified and less sensitive to negative shocks as compared to small cities. Start with $\delta^1 = \delta^2 = \delta$. Then, assume that there is a negative shock that only affects a small city (i.e., city 2) so that $\delta^1 = \delta$ and $\delta^2 > \delta$. Let us compare the two steady-states, before ($\delta^1 = \delta^2 = \delta$) and after ($\delta^2 > \delta = \delta^1$) the shock. After the shock, the equilibrium migration condition $r\,I_U^1 = r\,I_U^2$ is different and is given by:

$$
e\left[\frac{\delta\,L^{1*}}{(N^{1*} - L^{1*})\,m(L^{1*}/M)} - \frac{\delta^2\,L^{2*}}{(N - N^{1*} - L^{2*})\,m(L^{2*}/M)} \right]
$$
$$
= s\tau\left(2N^{1*} - N\right). \tag{6.25}
$$

When the shock occurs, L^{1*} is not affected in the short run, but L^{2*} decreases (see (6.23)) since the job creation rate needs to increase for the steady-state condition on flows to be satisfied and thus, there is also an increase in wages. The effect on N^{1*}, given by (6.25), is as follows. Because of (6.24), the decrease in L^{2*} increases N^{1*}. However, there is a direct effect of δ^2 on N^{1*}. Indeed, an increase in δ^2 raises the efficiency wage in the small city, reducing the wage difference between the two cities and thus, more people migrate to the small city, reducing N^{1*}. The net effect on N^{1*} is once more ambiguous, but for a different reason than before.

Consider now two cities located in different countries with different unemployment benefits. Let us start with the same level of unemployment benefit for the two countries, say zero, and then increase the one in city 1, i.e., $w_U^1 > w_U^2 = 0$. The equilibrium migration condition can now be written as:

$$
w_U^1 + \delta\,e\left[\frac{L^{1*}}{(N^{1*} - L^{1*})\,m(L^{1*}/M)} - \frac{L^{2*}}{(N - N^{1*} - L^{2*})\,m(L^{2*}/M)} \right]
$$
$$
= s\tau\left(2N^{1*} - N\right). \tag{6.26}
$$

In that case, when the unemployment benefit in the big city increases, the employment level L^{1*} decreases because of higher efficiency wages in city 1, while L^{2*} is unchanged. The decrease of L^{1*} decreases N^{1*} because it is easier to monitor workers and wages are lower and thus, more people want to migrate to the small city. There is no ambiguous effect here since L^{2*} is not affected and, as in the case of δ, there is no direct effect of w_U on N^{1*}. Furthermore, N^{2*} will increase mechanically since $N^{1*} + N^{2*} = N$. As a result, because of (6.24), L^{1*} will finally decrease and L^{2*} increase. Looking at (6.19), it can be seen that the land rent for all workers will decrease in the big city and increase in the small city, because of the increase in unemployment benefits in the big city.

4. Migration within Cities: Dual Labor Markets in a Duocentric City

We would like to study the mobility of workers within a non-monocentric city. The case of two job centers, the CBD and the SBD, will be considered.

4.1. The Model with a Fixed SBD

Consider a city with two centers, the CBD and the SBD. It is assumed that in the CBD, jobs are complex and detection of shirking is not instantaneous so that an efficiency wage policy prevails. This is referred to as sector 1 (or the primary sector to use the terminology of the dual labor market literature).[7] In contrast, jobs are assumed to be menial in the SBD so that production tasks are easily monitored and shirking is instantaneously detected so that efficiency wages are not needed. This is referred to as sector 2 (or the secondary sector).[8] It is also assumed that the SBD is fixed and located at $x = N$. This assumption will be relaxed below. So basically the CBD is as before (in the benchmark model), even though the efficiency wage will have a different value (see below) because of competition with the SBD. It is also assumed that all non-work activities (such as shopping, interacting with people, etc.) take place in the CBD. Hence, the SBD is only a workplace whereas the CBD is both a workplace and a place for non-work activities.

4.2. Urban-Land-Use Equilibrium

There is a continuum of ex-ante identical workers whose mass is N and a continuum of M identical firms (M_1 firms in the CBD and M_2 firms in the

---

[7] For an overview of this literature, see Saint-Paul (1996).
[8] Subscript 2 refers to sector 2 (SBD) while subscript 1 refers to sector 1 (CBD).

SBD,[9] with $M_1 > M_2$ and $M = M_1 + M_2$). Among the N workers, L_1 are employed in the CBD, L_2 are employed in the SBD and U are unemployed. Therefore,

$$N = L_1 + L_2 + U. \tag{6.27}$$

The density of workers in each location is taken to be 1 (since housing consumption is normalized to 1). The city is *linear, closed,* and *duocentric.* The CBD is located in $x = 0$ while the SBD is located at the other end of the city ($x = N$). All land is owned by absentee landlords and M_1 firms are exogenously located in the CBD while M_2 firms are exogenously located in the SBD. Firms consume no space. Workers are assumed to be infinitely lived, *risk neutral* and to determine their optimal place of residence between the CBD and the SBD. There are *no relocation costs,* either in terms of time or money.

Let us now determine the *instantaneous* indirect utilities of an employed non-shirker and shirker working in the CBD and residing at a distance x from the CBD. They are, respectively, given by:

$$W_L^{NS}(x) = w_L - e_1 - \tau x - R(x) \tag{6.28}$$

$$W_L^S(x) = w_L - \tau x - R(x). \tag{6.29}$$

As in the benchmark model, we assume work trips to be separated from shopping trips, so that non-workers commute to the CBD only for non-work activities and it is assumed that they commute less than the employed, i.e., $0 < s < 1.$[10] Thus, for an unemployed worker, we have:

$$W_U(x) = w_U - s \tau x - R(x). \tag{6.30}$$

For workers employed in the SBD, their instantaneous utility is equal to:

$$W_{L2}(x) = \overline{w}_2 - e_2 - s \tau x - \tau (N - x) - R(x). \tag{6.31}$$

where $\overline{w}_2$ is the wage in the SBD. It should now be clear why we assume work trips to be separated from shopping trips. Indeed, SBD workers located in x need to commute to the CBD for non-work activities and the costs amount to $s \tau x$ (if, for example, $s = 1/2$, then they will go there every other day),

---

[9] Observe that, in this book, *superscript* $k = 1, 2$ denotes the type of city or equilibrium that prevails while *subscript* $j = 1, 2$ denotes the type of sector or employment center that prevails (with $j = 1$ for the CBD and $j = 2$ for the SBD).

[10] Here, s is the fraction of trips for non-work activities and not, as before, for search activities.

but they also need to go to the SBD to work, and the costs are equal to $\tau(N-x)$ since the SBD is located at $x = N$.

In equilibrium, as in the benchmark model, none of the employed workers in the CBD will shirk. Since there are no relocation costs, the urban equilibrium is such that, whatever their location x, all employed workers working in the CBD and in the SBD enjoy the same level of utility $W_L^{NS}(x) \equiv W_{L1}$ and $W_{L2}(x) \equiv W_{L2}$, respectively, while all the unemployed obtain W_U. The bid-rents of the CBD-employed, SBD-employed, and unemployed workers are, respectively, given by:

$$\Psi_{L1}(x, W_{L1}) = w_L - e_1 - \tau x - W_{L1} \qquad (6.32)$$

$$\Psi_{L2}(x, W_{L2}) = \overline{w}_2 - e_2 + (1-s)\tau x - \tau N - W_{L2} \qquad (6.33)$$

$$\Psi_U(x, W_U) = w_U - s\tau x - W_U. \qquad (6.34)$$

Observe that the CBD-employed workers' and unemployed workers' bid-rents are linearly *decreasing* with x while the CBD-employed workers' bid-rent is linearly *increasing* with x. Observe also that the bid-rent of the CBD-employed workers is steeper than that of unemployed workers, so that the employed workers will outbid the unemployed workers to occupy the core of the city. As a result, since each worker consumes one unit of land, the CBD-employed workers reside between $x = 0$ and $x = L_1$, the unemployed between $x = L_1$ and $x = L_1 + U$ and the SBD-employed workers live on the periphery of the city between $x = L_1 + U$ and $x = N$. This city is described by Figure 6.3.

Let us now define the urban-land-use equilibrium. We denote the agricultural land rent (the rent outside the city or opportunity rent) by R_A and, without loss of generality, normalize it to zero. We have:

Definition 6.3. *An urban-land-use equilibrium with no relocation costs and fixed-housing consumption in a duocentric city is a 4-tuple* (W_{L1}^*, W_{L2}^*, W_U^*, $R^*(x)$) *such that:*

$$\Psi_{L1}(L_1, W_{L1}^*) = \Psi_U(L_1, W_U^*) \qquad (6.35)$$

$$\Psi_U(L_1 + U, W_U^*) = 0 \qquad (6.36)$$

$$\Psi_{L2}(L_1 + U, W_{L2}^*) = 0 \qquad (6.37)$$

$$R^*(x) = \max\left\{\Psi_{L1}(x, W_{L1}^*), \Psi_{L2}(x, W_{L2}^*), \Psi_U(x, W_U^*), 0\right\} \quad at\ each$$
$$x \in \left(0, x_f^*\right]. \qquad (6.38)$$

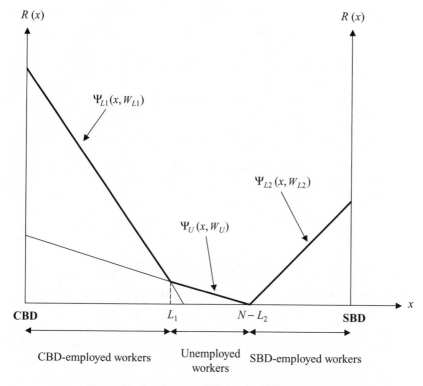

Figure 6.3. Land-use equilibrium in a duocentric city.

By solving (6.35), (6.36), (6.37) and using (6.27), we easily obtain the equilibrium values of the instantaneous utilities of all workers in the city. They are given by:

$$W_{L1}^* = w_L - e_1 - \tau L_1 - s\,\tau\,(N - L_1 - L_2) \qquad (6.39)$$

$$W_{L2}^* = \overline{w}_2 - e_2 + (1 - s)\,\tau\,(N - L_2) - \tau N \qquad (6.40)$$

$$W_U^* = w_U - s\,\tau\,(N - L_2). \qquad (6.41)$$

By plugging (6.39) into (6.32), (6.40) into (6.33), and (6.41) into (6.34), we easily obtain the land rent equilibrium $R^*(x)$. It is given by:

$$R^*(x) = \begin{cases} \tau\,(L_1 - x) + s\,\tau\,(N - L_1 - L_2) & \text{for} \quad 0 \le x \le L_1 \\ s\,\tau\,(N - L_2 - x) & \text{for} \quad L_1 < x \le N - L_2 \\ (1 - s)\,\tau\,[x - (N - L_2)] & \text{for} \quad N - L_2 < x \le N \\ 0 & \text{for} \quad x > N \end{cases}$$

$$(6.42)$$

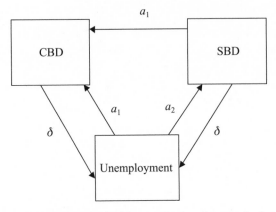

Figure 6.4. Flows in the labor market in a duocentric city.

4.3. Labor Market Equilibrium

Let us now determine the labor market equilibrium first in the CBD, then in the SBD and then the general one in the economy.

Here we use the benchmark framework, that is the detection rate is exogenous and denoted by m. The main difference compared to the benchmark model is that CBD workers now have two outside options if they lose their job. They can be unemployed (as before), but they can eventually find a job in the secondary sector. In this sector, it is assumed that jobs are relatively simple and thus no shirking behavior is possible. Moreover, a minimum wage prevails in sector 2, which is imposed by the government, i.e., $w_2 = \overline{w}_2$. This minimum wage is assumed to be higher than the unemployment benefit, i.e., $\overline{w}_2 > w_U$.

Let us determine the labor market equilibrium. The flows in the labor market are described in Figure 6.4.

It is assumed that the CBD job-acquisition rate is a_1, independently of the employment status of workers. In other words, SBD-employed workers and unemployed workers have exactly the same chance of finding a CBD job in the primary sector. Hence, a_1 represents the (endogenous) *primary-sector job-acquisition rate* for all individuals and it is the common exit rate from both the pool of unemployed and sector 2 into sector 1. Observe that here we have on-the-job search behavior since SBD-employed workers can directly find a CBD job (at rate a_1). Furthermore, the rate at which unemployed workers obtain a CBD job is not equal to that of obtaining an SBD job. Indeed, we have $a_1 \neq a_2$ and thus, a_2 represents the (endogenous) *secondary-sector job acquisition rate* for nonworkers. Otherwise, as in the benchmark model, workers lose their job at the exogenous rate δ.

The state of the economy σ_t evolves following a *three-state* Markov process with states: employed in the CBD, employed in the SBD, and unemployed. We gather the Markov transitions into a matrix P, where its elements $p_{ij} = \Pr\{\sigma_{t+1} = i \mid \sigma_t = j\}$, where $i, j \in \{U, CBD, SBD\}$, that is, rows correspond to t while columns correspond to $t + 1$ (the rows sum up to one). The Markov transition matrix P is given by:

$$
\begin{array}{c}
\\
U \\
CBD \\
SBD
\end{array}
\begin{array}{ccc}
U & CBD & SBD
\end{array}
\left(
\begin{array}{ccc}
1 - (a_1 + a_2) & a_1 & a_2 \\
\delta & 1 - \delta & 0 \\
\delta & a_1 & 1 - (a_1 + \delta)
\end{array}
\right) = P. \qquad (6.43)
$$

We discuss how we compute transitions. For instance, to jump from U to U under a small interval of time it has to be that the unemployed worker found neither a CBD nor an SBD job. Therefore, $\Pr\{\sigma_{t+1} = U \mid \sigma_t = U\} = 1 - (a_1 + a_2)$. Moreover, to jump from SBD to CBD, it must be that the SBD-employed worker did find a CBD job, which occurs at rate a_1. Hence, $\Pr\{\sigma_{t+1} = CBD \mid \sigma_t = SBD\} = a_1$. And so on.

We need to calculate the steady-states values of each state, i.e., the level of employment in the CBD, the SBD, and the level of unemployment. We denote these values by L_1^*, L_2^*, and U^*, respectively. In Appendix A6, at the end of this chapter, we show that they are equal to:

$$
U^* = \frac{\delta N}{a_1 + a_2 + \delta} \qquad (6.44)
$$

$$
L_1^* = \frac{a_1 N}{\delta + a_1} \qquad (6.45)
$$

$$
L_2^* = \frac{a_2 \delta N}{(a_1 + \delta)(a_1 + a_2 + \delta)}. \qquad (6.46)
$$

Let us now determine the efficiency wage in the CBD. The steady-state Bellman equations for the CBD non-shirker, the CBD shirker, the unemployed, and the SBD-employed workers are, respectively, given by:

$$
r I_{L1}^{NS} = w_L - e_1 - \tau L_1 - s\tau (N - L_1 - L_2) - \delta (I_{L1}^{NS} - I_U) \qquad (6.47)
$$

$$
r I_{L1}^{S} = w_L - \tau L_1 - s\tau (N - L_1 - L_2) - (\delta + m)(I_{L1}^{S} - I_U) \qquad (6.48)
$$

$$
r I_U = w_U - s\tau (N - L_2) + a_1 (I_{L1} - I_U) + a_2 (I_{L2} - I_U) \qquad (6.49)
$$

$$
r I_{L2} = \overline{w}_2 - e_2 + (1 - s)\tau (N - L_2) - \tau N - \delta (I_{L2} - I_U)
$$
$$
+ a_1 (I_{L1} - I_{L2}), \qquad (6.50)
$$

where r is the discount rate, I_{L1}^{NS}, I_{L1}^{S}, I_U, and I_{L2} represent the expected lifetime utility of a non-shirking CBD worker, a shirking CBD worker, an unemployed worker, and an SBD worker, respectively. The main differences as compared to the benchmark model are: (i) the lifetime expected utilities of CBD workers, I_{L1}^{NS} and I_{L1}^{S}, are now a function of L_2, (ii) the lifetime expected utility of unemployed workers, I_U, is different since unemployed workers can find a job both in the CBD and in the SBD, and (iii) the lifetime expected utility of an SBD-employed worker, $I_{L,2}$, did not exist before. Because of shirking behavior, firms will choose a wage w_L so that $I_{L1}^{NS} = I_{L1}^{S} = I_{L1}$, i.e., the efficiency wage must be set to make workers indifferent between shirking and not shirking.

Using (6.47) and (6.48), the condition $I_{L1}^{NS} = I_{L1}^{S} = I_{L1}$ can be written as:

$$I_{L1} - I_U = \frac{e_1}{m}. \tag{6.51}$$

This is the same incentive condition as in the benchmark model, which says that the surplus of being employed in the primary sector is strictly positive and a positive function of effort e_1 and a negative function of the detection rate, m. Furthermore, subtracting (6.50) from (6.49), we obtain:

$$I_{L2} - I_U = \frac{\overline{w}_2 - e_2 - w_U - \tau L_2}{r + a_1 + a_2 + \delta}. \tag{6.52}$$

This is the positive surplus of working in the SBD compared to unemployment. It depends on the difference between the net wage in sector 2 and the unemployment benefit, but also on the difference in spatial costs, as captured by $-\tau L_2$, since unemployed workers pay higher land rents than workers in the SBD because of competition with CBD workers. We can now calculate the lifetime expected utility of unemployed workers, which using (6.51) and (6.52) in (6.49), is equal to:

$$r\, I_U = w_U - s\,\tau\,(N - L_2) + a_1\,\frac{e_1}{m} + a_2\left(\frac{\overline{w}_2 - e_2 - w_U - \tau L_2}{r + a_1 + a_2 + \delta}\right). \tag{6.53}$$

Now, using (6.51) and (6.53), (6.47) can be written as:

$$w_L = e_1 + r I_U + (r + \delta)\,(I_{L1} - I_U) + \tau\,L_1 + s\,\tau\,(N - L_1 - L_2)$$

$$= w_U + e_1 + \frac{e_1}{m}\,(r + a_1 + \delta) + a_2\left(\frac{\overline{w}_2 - e_2 - w_U - \tau L_2}{r + a_1 + a_2 + \delta}\right)$$

$$+ (1 - s)\,\tau\,L_1.$$

Rearranging this equation, we easily obtain:

$$w_L = \Upsilon(a_1, a_2) \, w_U + [1 - \Upsilon(a_1, a_2)] \, (\overline{w}_2 - e_2 - \tau L_2)$$
$$+ e_1 + SW_1 + \Delta SC_1 \tag{6.54}$$

where the weighting factor $0 < \Upsilon(a_1, a_2) < 1$ is defined as:

$$\Upsilon(a_1, a_2) = \frac{r + a_1 + \delta}{r + a_1 + a_2 + \delta},$$

and $SW_1 \equiv \frac{e_1}{m}(r + a_1 + \delta)$ is the wage surplus that must be paid to deter shirking and $\Delta SC_1 \equiv SC_{L,1} - SC_U = (1 - s)\tau L_1$ is the spatial-cost differential between CBD-employed workers and unemployed workers.

This efficiency wage is quite similar to that of the benchmark model. The main difference is that the base wage was previously equal to $w_U + e$ whereas it is now equal to a convex combination of w_U and the net wage in the secondary sector (i.e., $\overline{w}_2 - e_2 - \tau L_2$) plus e_1. The other elements of the efficiency wage are exactly the same as those in the benchmark model and consist of work inducement SW_1 and spatial compensation ΔSC_1. Naturally, having $\Upsilon(a_1, a_2) \, w_U + [1 - \Upsilon(a_1, a_2)] \, (\overline{w}_2 - e_2 - \tau L_2)$ instead of w_U reflects the fact that when setting the efficiency wage, firms must take into account the opportunities that workers have outside the CBD labor market. In particular, when deciding whether to shirk, workers take into account the fact that if they are detected and fired, they will be unemployed with a possibility of finding a job not only in the CBD, but also in the SBD in the future. This is why this wage is higher than in the benchmark case since $\Upsilon(a_1, a_2) \, w_U + [1 - \Upsilon(a_1, a_2)] \, (\overline{w}_2 - e_2 - \tau L_2) > w_U$ (it is assumed that $\overline{w}_2 - e_2 - \tau L_2 > w_U$). In some sense, $\Upsilon(a_1, a_2) \, w_U + [1 - \Upsilon(a_1, a_2)] \, (\overline{w}_2 - e_2 - \tau L_2)$ represents the *composite opportunity wage* for individuals outside the primary sector. It can also be interpreted as an *expected discounted wage* for individuals moving between unemployment and SBD jobs. Naturally, when $a_2 = 0$ (no secondary sector), we have returned to the benchmark case since $\Upsilon(a_1, a_2) = 1$. Hence, the efficiency wage in the benchmark case is a special case of (6.54) when $a_2 = 0$ (or, equivalently, $L_2 = 0$).

By using the steady-state flows (6.44), (6.45) and (6.46), we obtain

$$a_1(L_1) = \delta \frac{L_1}{N - L_1} \tag{6.55}$$

$$a_2(L_1, L_2) = \delta \frac{N L_2}{(N - L_1 - L_2)(N - L_1)} \tag{6.56}$$

with $a_1'(L_1) \geq 0$, $\partial a_2(L_1, L_2)/\partial L_1 \geq 0$ and $\partial a_2(L_1, L_2)/\partial L_2 \geq 0$. As a result, the efficiency wage can be expressed in terms of L_1 and L_2 and we obtain:

$$w_L^* = \Upsilon(L_1, L_2) \, w_U + [1 - \Upsilon(L_1, L_2)] \, (\overline{w}_2 - e_2 - \tau L_2) + e_1 \quad (6.57)$$

$$+ \frac{e_1}{m} \left(r + \frac{\delta N}{N - L_1} \right) + (1 - s) \tau L_1$$

where

$$\Upsilon(L_1, L_2) = \frac{[r(N - L_1) + \delta N](N - L_1 - L_2)}{\delta N L_2 + [r(N - L_1) + \delta N](N - L_1 - L_2)}.$$

We need to see if the properties of the efficiency wage ("equilibrium unemployment acts as a worker discipline device") still hold here. We have the following result:

Proposition 6.5. *The two-sector efficiency wage w_L^* is increasing in L_1 over the relevant range* $0 < L_1 < N - L_2$ *and*

$$\lim_{L_1 \to N} w_L^* = +\infty.$$

Furthermore, if the minimum wage is sufficiently large, the two-sector efficiency wage w_L^* is increasing in L_2.

Indeed, higher employment in the CBD leads to higher efficiency wages because workers easily find a CBD job and are thus more incline to shirk. Moreover, the efficiency wages are not compatible with full employment, otherwise there will not be any worker discipline device. Finally, when the level of employment in the SBD increases, CBD firms have to increase their efficiency wages since the prospects for CBD workers are better and they will therefore be more likely to shirk.

In terms of comparative statics of the efficiency wage, we obtain nearly the same results as in the benchmark case. However, there is one important exception and it is the effect of the commuting cost τ on w_L^*. In the benchmark model, an increase in τ always leads to an increase in w_L^* because firms had to compensate more workers for a higher space-cost differential. This is no longer true here. In fact, the sign is now ambiguous since

$$\frac{\partial w_L^*}{\partial \tau} = (1 - s) L_1 - [1 - \Upsilon(L_1, L_2)] L_2 \gtrless 0.$$

Indeed, τ does not only decrease the space-cost differential between CBD-employed and unemployed, but also increases the commuting costs of SBD workers. In particular, if $[1 - \Upsilon(L_1, L_2)] L_2 > (1 - s) L_1$, the increased space costs for individuals outside the primary sector are sufficiently high to make a decrease in efficiency wage levels possible. This dual effect is also present in the time-discounting parameter, r. In the benchmark case, an increase in r always increased w_L^* (since workers value short-run benefits more and thus, are more likely to shirk). While this effect is also present in the two-sector case, it can be countered by the fact that workers fired for shirking always enter unemployment before gaining work in the secondary sector. Hence, if the net wage in sector 2, $\overline{w}_2 - e_2 - \tau L_2$, is sufficiently high relative to w_U, then for a range of increases in r, this short-run loss of income reduces the prospects of individuals leaving the primary sector sufficiently to allow a decrease in efficiency wages.

Let us now determine labor demand L_1 in the primary sector. First, observe that since there is a minimum wage in the economy equal to $\overline{w}_2$, CBD firms cannot pay a wage below $\overline{w}_2$. Thus, the relevant *effective* wage in the CBD is: $w_L^* \equiv w_{L1}(L_1, L_2) = \max\{\overline{w}_2, w_L^*\}$, i.e.,

$$w_{L1}(L_1, L_2)$$
$$= \max\left\{ \begin{array}{c} \overline{w}_2, \Upsilon(L_1, L_2)\, w_U + [1 - \Upsilon(L_1, L_2)](\overline{w}_2 - e_2 - \tau L_2) + e_1 \\ + \frac{e_1}{m}\left(r + \frac{\delta N}{N - L_1}\right) + (1 - s)\tau L_1 \end{array} \right\}.$$

$$(6.58)$$

There are M_1 identical firms in the primary sector. We normalize the price of a product in this sector by 1. By maximizing its profit, each firm determines its labor demand and aggregate labor demand is thus given by: $e_1 F'(e L_1^*) = w_L^*$, which using (6.58) yields:

$$e_1 F'(e L_1^*) = w_{L1}(L_1, L_2). \tag{6.59}$$

Figure 6.5 describes the equilibrium in the labor market for this duocentric city. It shows that for very low levels of employment, L_1, the CBD firms will pay the minimum wage because it is above the UNSC curve $w_{L1}(L_1, L_2)$. Then, when the two-sector efficiency wage is above the minimum wage, it will prevail. Moreover, the dashed curve displays the efficiency wage for the one-sector model (the benchmark case). Indeed, the one-sector efficiency wage $w_{L1}(L_1)$ is always below that set in the two-sector case because workers have more employment opportunities in the latter than in the former.

The production technology in the SBD for the M_2 identical firms in sector 2 can be represented by a production function, $F_2(L_2)$, which is assumed to be twice differentiable with $F_2(0) = 0$, $F_2'(L_2) > 0$, $F_2''(L_2) \le 0$, and to satisfy the Inada conditions, i.e., $\lim_{L_2 \to 0} F'(L_2) = +\infty$ and $\lim_{L_2 \to +\infty} F'(L_2) = 0$. Similarly, it is assumed that all output can be sold

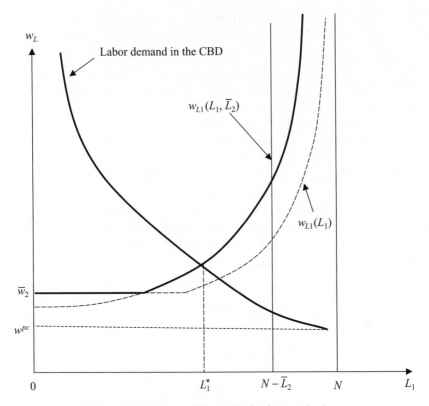

Figure 6.5. Labor equilibrium in the duocentric city.

at a fixed market price, p_2. As stated above, production tasks are relatively simple and easily monitored in sector 2 and hence, it is assumed that the effort expenditure in sector 2, e_2, required for production is much smaller than that of sector 1, i.e., $e_2 < e_2$, and that shirking behavior can be ignored in sector 2. The profit function of the representative firm in sector 2 can thus be written as: $\Pi_2 = p_2 F_2(L_2) - \overline{w}_2 L_2$. Hence, at the minimum wage, $\overline{w}_2$, the firm needs to attract enough workers to maximize its profit. Solving the following program,

$$\max_{L_2} \Pi_2 = p_2 F_2(L_2) - \overline{w}_2 L_2,$$

the equilibrium employment level in sector 2 is obtained:

$$F_2'(\overline{L}_2) = \frac{\overline{w}_2}{p_2}. \tag{6.60}$$

Since $\overline{w}_2$ and p_2 are exogenous variables, so is the employment level in the secondary sector which is why it is denoted by $\overline{L}_2$.

4.4. Steady-State Equilibrium

We have the following definition:

Definition 6.4. *A steady-state equilibrium in the duocentric city ($R^*(x)$, w_L^*, L_1^*) consists of a land rent function (6.42), a wage for CBD workers (6.58) and the employment level in the CBD (6.59), such that the urban-land-use equilibrium and the labor market equilibrium are solved for simultaneously.*

Because of the Inada conditions on the production function, it is easily verified that there exists a unique steady-state equilibrium in the duocentric city (see Smith and Zenou, 1997, for a formal proof).

4.5. Interaction Between Land and Labor Markets

We would like to study how one market affects the other. Observe that, in the CBD employment area, $0 \leq x \leq L_1$, the equilibrium land rent $R^*(x)$ (see (6.42)) depends on the equilibrium employment level in the primary sector L_1^*, determined by (6.59), and other exogenous variables. In the other two areas (the SBD employment area and the unemployment area), the equilibrium land rent is totally determined by $\overline{L}_2$ and thus, the minimum wage $\overline{w}_2$, which are both exogenous.

First, it is interesting to examine whether the SBD-employed workers pay a higher land rent than unemployed workers. We have:

$$R_2^*(N) \gtreqless R_U^*(L_1) \Leftrightarrow s \lesseqgtr \frac{L_2}{L_2 + U},$$

which means that if we compare the highest land rent that these workers pay (at $x = N$ for the SBD-employed workers and at $x = L_1$ for the unemployed workers; see Figure 6.3), then it is indeterminate. In Figure 6.3, we have represented a case where $R_2^*(N) > R_U^*(L_1)$, but this is not always true.

Second, let us analyze the effects of two key exogenous variables, w_U and $\overline{w}_2$ (labor variables) and τ (spatial variable) on the endogenous variables $R^*(x)$ and L_1^*. By totally differentiating (6.59) and focussing on the employment level for which $\max\{\overline{w}_2, w_L^*\} = w_L^*$, we have

$$\frac{\partial L_1^*}{\partial w_U} < 0, \quad \frac{\partial L_1^*}{\partial \overline{w}_2} < 0 \text{ and } \frac{\partial L_1^*}{\partial \tau} \gtreqless 0 \Leftrightarrow (1 - s)\, L_1 \lesseqgtr [1 - \Upsilon(L_1, L_2)]\, L_2.$$

All intuition from these results goes through efficiency wage setting. Indeed, when w_U or $\overline{w}_2$ increases, then CBD firms have to increase their wage to meet the UNSC because workers have better outside options. As a result, since wages are higher, firms recruit less. We have already discussed the ambiguous effect of τ on the efficiency wage, which translates into an ambiguous effect of τ on the employment level in the primary sector.

Let us now analyze the impact of these variables on the land rent paid by individuals working in the CBD (i.e., the employment zone). When L_1 increases, at each $x \in [0, L_1]$, the equilibrium land rent $R^*(x)$ also increases (there is more competition in the land market because more workers are living between 0 and L_1). As a result, for $x \in [0, L_1]$, we have:

$$\frac{\partial R^*(x)}{\partial w_U} = \frac{\partial R^*(x)}{\partial L_1^*} \frac{\partial L_1^*}{\partial w_U} < 0 \,, \quad \frac{\partial R^*(x)}{\partial \overline{w}_2} = \frac{\partial R^*(x)}{\partial L_1^*} \frac{\partial L_1^*}{\partial \overline{w}_2} < 0.$$

Indeed, when the unemployment benefit and/or the minimum wage in the economy increases, workers have better prospects as unemployed and/or as working in the secondary sector. Hence, CBD firms need to increase their wage to deter shirking. This reduces employment in the primary sector and thus, competition in the land market. As a result, land prices decrease in each location between $x = 0$ and $x = L_1$. Observe that land prices outside $[0, L_1]$ are not at all affected by a change in w_U, but will be affected in the following way if there is a variation in the minimum wage:

$$\frac{\partial R^*(x)}{\partial \overline{w}_2} = \frac{\partial R^*(x)}{\partial L_2} \frac{\partial L_2}{\partial \overline{w}_2} > 0 \quad \text{for} \quad L_1 < x \leq N - L_2$$

$$\frac{\partial R^*(x)}{\partial \overline{w}_2} = \frac{\partial R^*(x)}{\partial L_2} \frac{\partial L_2}{\partial \overline{w}_2} < 0 \quad \text{for} \quad N - L_2 < x \leq N.$$

Indeed, for the unemployed workers residing in $L_1 < x \leq N - L_2$, an increase in $\overline{w}_2$ reduces L_2 which, in turn, decreases competition in the land market and thus, the land price in this area. In contrast, for the SBD-employed workers residing in $N - L_2 < x \leq N$, an increase in $\overline{w}_2$ reduces L_2, which now increases competition in the land market and thus, the land price in this area.

Finally, if we analyze the impact of the commuting cost τ on the equilibrium land rent for $x \in [0, L_1]$, we obtain:

$$\frac{\partial R^*(x)}{\partial \tau} = (1 - s) L_1 + s (N - L_2) - x + (1 - s) \tau \frac{\partial L_1^*}{\partial \tau} \gtreqless 0.$$

There are indeed two effects of an increase in τ on land rent. First, there is a *direct positive effect* since access to the CBD is more costly and thus, competition in the land market becomes fiercer, which increases the land price in each location x. Second, there is an *ambiguous indirect effect* via the wage. Indeed, when τ increases, the wage decreases (increases) if the negative indirect effect on the SBD workers mentioned above outweights (is lower than) the positive direct effect on the CBD workers. In that case, labor demand in the CBD increases (decreases) and the land rent increases (decreases). As a result, if $[1 - \Upsilon(L_1, L_2)] L_2 > (1 - s) L_1$, the total effect of the commuting cost τ on equilibrium land rent $R^*(x)$ for $x \in [0, L_1]$ is always positive. Otherwise, it is ambiguous. Observe that an increase in τ always has a positive effect on the equilibrium land rent $x \in [L_1, N]$.

4.6. First Extension: The Case of High Relocation Costs

As in Chapter 5, we would like to extend this model to the case of high mobility costs. We assume that a worker's residential location remains fixed as he/she enters and leaves unemployment. Moreover, we also assume perfect capital markets with a zero interest rate. As in the previous section, we assume that changes in employment status (employment versus unemployment) are governed by a three-state Markov process. Therefore, the unemployment, CBD and CBD employment rates of non-shirkers are, respectively, given by:

$$u^{NS} = \frac{U^{NS}}{N} = \frac{\delta}{a_1 + a_2 + \delta} \tag{6.61}$$

$$l_1^{NS} = \frac{L_1^{NS}}{N} = \frac{a_1}{a_1 + \delta} \tag{6.62}$$

$$l_2^{NS} = \frac{L_2^{NS}}{N} = \frac{a_2 \delta}{(a_1 + \delta)(a_1 + a_2 + \delta)}. \tag{6.63}$$

In the case of shirkers, it is somewhat more complicated. In particular, the Markov transition matrix P is now given by:

$$
\begin{array}{c}
\begin{array}{c} \\ U \\ CBD \\ SBD \end{array}
\begin{array}{ccc}
\;\;\;U & \quad CBD & \quad SBD
\end{array}
\\
\begin{array}{c} U \\ CBD \\ SBD \end{array}
\left(
\begin{array}{ccc}
1 - (a_1 + a_2) & a_1 & a_2 \\
\delta + m & 1 - (\delta + m) & 0 \\
\delta & a_1 & 1 - (a_1 + \delta)
\end{array}
\right) = P.
\end{array}
\tag{6.64}
$$

So the only change as compared to the non-shirking case is that CBD workers can lose their jobs not only because of the exogenous job destruction rate

δ, but also because of their shirking behavior, which is detected at the rate m. In Appendix A6, we show that, in steady-state, we have:

$$u^S = \frac{U^S}{N} = \frac{(\delta + m)(a_1 + \delta)}{(a_1 + \delta + m)(a_1 + a_2 + \delta)} \tag{6.65}$$

$$l_1^S = \frac{L_1^S}{N} = \frac{a_1}{a_1 + \delta + m} \tag{6.66}$$

$$l_2^S = \frac{L_2^S}{N} = \frac{a_2(\delta + m)}{(a_1 + \delta + m)(a_1 + a_2 + \delta)}. \tag{6.67}$$

It is easily verified that:

$$l_1^{NS} - l_1^S = \frac{a_1 m}{(\delta + a_1)(a_1 + \delta + m)} > 0 \tag{6.68}$$

$$u^S - u^{NS} = \frac{a_1 m}{(a_1 + \delta + m)(a_1 + a_2 + \delta)} > 0 \tag{6.69}$$

$$\frac{u^S - u^{NS}}{l_1^{NS} - l_1^S} = \frac{a_1 + \delta}{a_1 + a_2 + \delta} < 1 \tag{6.70}$$

$$l_2^S - l_2^{NS} = \frac{a_1 a_2 m}{(a_1 + \delta + m)(a_1 + a_2 + \delta)(a_1 + \delta)} > 0. \tag{6.71}$$

Indeed, if an individual shirks, the time he/she will spend unemployed and employed will be higher and lower, respectively, than if he/she does not work. Interestingly, $u^S - u^{NS} < l_1^{NS} - l_1^S$, which means that shirkers are losing more in terms of employment than in terms of unemployment. Finally, shirking behavior also affects secondary employment since it implies that shirkers will spend more time in the secondary sector than non-shirkers, because they are more likely to lose their primary sector job.

Since workers have a zero-discount rate, they only care about average net income over time. For a non-shirker located at a distance x from the CBD, it is equal to:

$$E\,W^{NS}(x) = \left(1 - u^{NS} - l_1^{NS}\right)\left[\overline{w}_2 - e_2 + (1 - s)\tau x - \tau N - R(x)\right]$$
$$+ u^{NS}\left[w_U - s\tau x - R(x)\right] + l_1^{NS}\left[w_L - e_1 - \tau x - R(x)\right] \tag{6.72}$$

whereas for a shirker residing at a distance x from the CBD, it is given by:

$$E W^S(x) = \left(1 - u^S - l_1^S\right) \left[\overline{w}_2 - e_2 + (1 - s)\,\tau\,x - \tau N - R(x)\right]$$
$$+ u^S \left[w_U - s\tau x - R(x)\right] + l_1^S \left[w_L - \tau x - R(x)\right]. \quad (6.73)$$

Let us calculate the efficiency wage. It will be determined by $E W_L^{NS}(x) = E W_L^{NS}(x)$, which is equivalent to:

$$w_L^*(x) = \widetilde{\Upsilon}\, w_U + \left(1 - \widetilde{\Upsilon}\right) (\overline{w}_2 - e_2 - \tau N) + e_1 \frac{l_1^{NS}}{l_1^{NS} - l_1^S} + \left(2 - s - \widetilde{\Upsilon}\right) \tau x$$
$$(6.74)$$

where

$$\widetilde{\Upsilon} = \frac{u^S - u^{NS}}{l_1^{NS} - l_1^S}.$$

Using (6.70), we have that $0 < \widetilde{\Upsilon} < 1$.

We assume that firms *do not observe* the residential location of all workers. So we need to know how this efficiency wage varies with location, x. It is easily verified that $\partial w_L/\partial x \geq 0$ since $2 > s + \widetilde{\Upsilon}$ and $s < 1$ and $\widetilde{\Upsilon} < 1$. Indeed, when someone shirks, he/she will spend more time unemployed and working in the SBD (see (6.68), (6.69), and (6.71)) and thus, will commute less to the CBD than those who are not shirking. As a result, workers residing further away from the CBD need to be paid more because they are more likely to shirk than those living closer to the CBD. Since firms know that efficiency wages are increasing with x, i.e., the distance to the CBD, and since they do not know where people live, they will set the highest possible wage to prevent shirking, i.e., at $x = N$. Thus, the efficiency wage in the CBD will be equal for all workers and given by:

$$w_{L1}^* \equiv w_L^*(N) = \widetilde{\Upsilon}\, w_U + \left(1 - \widetilde{\Upsilon}\right) (\overline{w}_2 - e_2) + e_1 \frac{l_1^{NS}}{l_1^{NS} - l_1^S} + (1 - s)\,\tau N.$$
$$(6.75)$$

This efficiency wage is, in fact, very close to that without relocation costs, given in (6.57). Indeed, it consists of three parts: The base wage, $\widetilde{\Upsilon}\, w_U + (1 - \widetilde{\Upsilon})(\overline{w}_2 - e_2)$, the wage surplus for incentive reasons, $e_1 l_1^{NS}/(l_1^{NS} - l_1^S)$, and the spatial cost differential, $(1 - s)\,\tau N$.

Efficiency wages are not location-dependent and land rents will only compensate for commuting costs. Let us solve the urban-land-use equilibrium. By plugging (6.75) into (6.72) or (6.73), we obtain the following expected utility of a (non-shirking) worker located at a distance x from the CBD:

$$E\,W(x) = w_U \left(\frac{l_1^{NS} u^S - u^{NS} l_1^S}{l_1^{NS} - l_1^S} \right) + (\overline{w}_2 - e_2) \left[1 - \left(\frac{l_1^{NS} u^S - u^{NS} l_1^S}{l_1^{NS} - l_1^S} \right) \right]$$

$$+ e_1 \left(\frac{l_1^S l_1^{NS}}{l_1^{NS} - l_1^S} \right) + \tau N \left[(2 - s) l_1^{NS} + u^{NS} - 1 \right] - R(x)$$

$$- \tau x \left[u^{NS} + (2 - s) l_1^{NS} - (1 - s) \right]. \tag{6.76}$$

If we denote that I is the (expected) utility reached by all workers in the city in equilibrium, the bid-rent is equal to

$$\Psi(x, I) = w_U \left(\frac{l_1^{NS} u^S - u^{NS} l_1^S}{l_1^{NS} - l_1^S} \right) + (\overline{w}_2 - e_2) \left[1 - \left(\frac{l_1^{NS} u^S - u^{NS} l_1^S}{l_1^{NS} - l_1^S} \right) \right]$$

$$+ e_1 \left(\frac{l_1^S l_1^{NS}}{l_1^{NS} - l_1^S} \right) + \tau N \left[(2 - s) l_1^{NS} + u^{NS} - 1 \right] - I$$

$$- \tau x \left[u^{NS} + (2 - s) l_1^{NS} - (1 - s) \right]. \tag{6.77}$$

We have the following result (proved by Zenou, 2008g):

Proposition 6.6. *In the duocentric city with high relocation costs, the land rent is decreasing with x, i.e., the distance to the CBD, if $l_1^{NS} + s(u^{NS} + l_2^{NS}) > l_2^{NS}$. A sufficient condition for this to be true is $a_1 > \delta$, that is, the job acquisition rate in the primary sector is greater than the job-destruction rate in the economy.*

Indeed, there are two opposite forces that determine the marginal willingness to pay for land. Distant workers (from the CBD) have higher transportation costs for commuting to the CBD, but lower costs for commuting to the SBD. Because all workers obtain the same utility I in equilibrium, the land rent needs to compensate for both effects. If $a_1 > \delta$ or, more generally, if individuals spend more time unemployed and working in the primary sector than working in the secondary sector, the first effect will dominate the second and the land rent will be decreasing with the distance to the CBD. From now on, we assume that the land rent is always decreasing with x.

As in a standard land-use model, the equilibrium utility I is determined by the fact that the bid-rent at the city fringe is equal to zero (the agricultural land rent). We obtain:

$$I^* = w_U \left(\frac{l_1^{NS} u^S - u^{NS} l_1^S}{l_1^{NS} - l_1^S} \right) + (\overline{w}_2 - e_2) \left[1 - \left(\frac{l_1^{NS} u^S - u^{NS} l_1^S}{l_1^{NS} - l_1^S} \right) \right]$$

$$+ e_1 \left(\frac{l_1^S l_1^{NS}}{l_1^{NS} - l_1^S} \right) - s \tau N. \tag{6.78}$$

Furthermore, plugging (6.78) into (6.77), we obtain the following equilibrium land rent for $x \in [0, N]$:

$$R^*(x) = \tau N \left[(2 - s) l_1^{NS} - (1 - s) + u^{NS} \right]$$

$$- \tau x \left[u^{NS} + (2 - s) l_1^{NS} - (1 - s) \right]. \tag{6.79}$$

We can now determine the steady-state labor market equilibrium. In the primary (CBD) and secondary (SBD) sectors, each firm adjusts employment until the marginal product of an additional worker equals the efficiency wage and the minimum wage, respectively. By focussing on the part of employment for which the efficiency wage is above the minimum wage, we obtain in the CBD:

$$\widetilde{\Upsilon} w_U + \left(1 - \widetilde{\Upsilon} \right) (\overline{w}_2 - e_2) + e_1 \frac{l_1^{NS}}{l_1^{NS} - l_1^S} + (1 - s) \tau N = e_1 F'(e L_1^*)$$

while in the SBD, we have:

$$F_2'(\overline{L}_2) = \frac{\overline{w}_2}{p_2}.$$

Since employment at each center (CBD and SBD) must equal labor demand, the equilibrium unemployment and CBD employment rates satisfy:

$$\left(1 - l_1^* - u^* \right) N = \overline{L}_2$$

$$l_1^* N = L_1^*.$$

The labor market equilibrium condition can thus be written as:

$$\widetilde{\Upsilon} w_U + \left(1 - \widetilde{\Upsilon} \right) (\overline{w}_2 - e_2) + e_1 \frac{l_1^*}{l_1^* - l_1^S} + (1 - s) \tau N = e_1 F'(e l_1^* N)$$

where $l_1^* \equiv l_1^{NS}$ and $\widetilde{\Upsilon} = (u^S - u^{NS})/(l_1^* - l_1^S)$. $\tag{6.80}$

We have the following definition:

Definition 6.5. *A steady-state equilibrium in the duocentric city with high relocation costs* $(R^*(x), w_{L1}^*, l_1^*, u^*, l_2^*, I^*)$ *consists of a land rent function*

(6.79), a wage for CBD workers (6.75), an employment rate in the CBD (6.80), an unemployment rate (6.61), an employment rate in the SBD (6.63), and an (expected) utility level (6.78) such that the urban-land-use equilibrium and the labor market equilibrium are solved for simultaneously.

The equilibrium is calculated as follows. First, since l_2^{NS} is exogenous, one obtains between a_1 and a_2 using (6.63). Then, by solving equation (6.80), one obtains a relationship between l_1^* and a_1 (since u^S, u^{NS}, l_1^S are functions of a_1, a_2 and, because of (6.63), a_2 is a function of a_1) and using equation (6.62), another relationship between l_1^* and a_1 is obtained. By combining these last two equations, a unique solution is found for l_1^*. Using the fact that $1 - l_1^* - l_2 = u^*$, the value of u^* is obtained. Plugging these values into (6.79), (6.75), (6.78), $R^*(x)$, $w_{L,1}^*$ and I^* are obtained, respectively.

4.7. Second Extension: Endogenous Formation of the SBD

So far, the secondary employment center (SBD) has been exogenously fixed. We would now like to study the case of an endogenous formation of an SBD. Let us start with an urban configuration as in the benchmark model where employed workers reside close to jobs and unemployed workers live on the periphery of the city (Figure 4.1). We would like to determine under which condition(s) a single large firm (i.e., the secondary sector) will set up on the periphery of the city.

In choosing a specific location, x, the firm takes into account both location land rent, $R(x)$, and the accessibility of x to the CBD, where the latter effect is represented by a CBD interaction cost, κ, per unit of distance. The latter reflects the occasional need for utilizing city services in the CBD and/or interacting with CBD firms.[11] Hence, the profit function of a SBD firm that decides to locate in a location x is equal to:

$$\Pi(x) = p_2 F(L_2) - \overline{w}_2 L_2 - R(x) - \kappa\, x. \tag{6.81}$$

Denote by x_{SBD} the location of the SBD firm. Then, since ex-ante, workers in the secondary sector do not know where the SBD will be located, their bid-rent function will not be given by (6.33), but by:

$$\Psi_{L2}(x, W_{L,2}) = \overline{w}_2 - e_2 - s\,\tau\,x - \tau\,|x_{SBD} - x| - W_{L2}. \tag{6.82}$$

Hence, the slope of the bid-rent function of SBD workers in all locations x is given by $\Psi_{L2}'(x, W_{L2})$, which is seen to be $(1 - s)\tau$ for all $x < x_{SBD}$, and

---

[11] See the next section for a more elaborate model of interactions between firms.

$-(1 + s)\tau$ for all $x > x_{SBD}$. In other words, it is increasing on the left-hand side of x_{SBD} and decreasing on the right-hand side of x_{SBD} with a steeper slope on the right-hand side. Indeed, we have:

$$\Psi_{L2}^-(x,\, W_{L2}) = \overline{w}_2 - e_2 - s\,\tau\,x - \tau\,(x_{SBD} - x) - W_{L2} \qquad (6.83)$$

$$\Psi_{L2}^+(x,\, W_{L2}) = \overline{w}_2 - e_2 - s\,\tau\,x - \tau\,(x - x_{SBD}) - W_{L2}, \qquad (6.84)$$

where $\Psi_{L2}^-(x,\, W_{L2})$ and $\Psi_{L2}^+(x,\, W_{L2})$ are, respectively, the bid-rent of workers located on the left-hand side and the right-hand side of x_{SBD}. The SBD firm determines $x = x_{SBD}^*$ by maximizing its profit or, equivalently, by minimizing $R(x) + \kappa\,x$. We have a first result (proved by Smith and Zenou, 1997):

Proposition 6.7. *There are three different possible cases:*

(*i*) *If* $x_{SBD} > N - (1 - s)L_2/2$, *the only equilibrium involves an isolated suburb (Figure 6.6a);*

(*ii*) $N - L_2/2 \leq x_{SBD} \leq N - (1 - s)L_2/2$, *the only equilibrium involves an edge city (Figure 6.6b).*

(*iii*) $L_1 + L_2/2 \leq x_{SBD} < N - L_2/2$, *the only equilibrium involves a subcenter (Figure 6.6c).*

In case (*i*), the SBD consists of an isolated suburb since there is a non-empty interval between the smallest distance to the CBD from the SBD (i.e., $x = N - (1 - s)L_2/2$) and the unemployed located the furthest away from the CBD (i.e., at $x = N - L_2$) so that there is no land competition between SBD workers and other workers in the city (see Figure 6.6a). In case (*ii*), this interval is now equal to zero and the two distances mentioned above are equal so that we have an edge city (see Figure 6.6b). In the last case (case (*iii*)), the SBD is located within the unemployment area and thus, forms a subcenter (see Figure 6.6b).

Observe that we do not consider the case for which $x_{SBD} < L_1 + L_2/2$ since, in that case, the land rent will be much higher since SBD workers will compete for land with employed CBD workers. Hence, for each relevant location x_{SBD}, the only possible equilibrium land rent, $R(x_{SBD})$, is seen from Figures 6.6a, 6.6b and 6.6c to be given by:

$$R(x_{SBD}) = \begin{cases} \tau\left(\frac{1+s}{2}\right)L_2 + s\tau\left(N - \frac{L_2}{2} - x_{SBD}\right) & \text{if} \quad L_1 + \frac{L_2}{2} \leq x_{SBD} < N - \frac{L_2}{2} \\ \tau(1 + s)\,(N - x_{SBD}) & \text{if} \quad N - \frac{L_2}{2} \leq x_{SBD} < N - (\frac{L_2}{2})L_2 \\ \tau\,(1 - s)\left(\frac{1+s}{2}\right)L_2 & \text{if} \quad x_{SBD} > N - (\frac{1-s}{2})L_2 \end{cases}$$

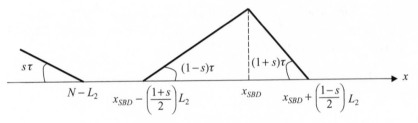

Figure 6.6a. The case of a suburb.

We have the following result:

Proposition 6.8. *If $0 < \varepsilon < s\tau$, the only equilibrium location of the SBD is given by:*

$$x^*_{SBD} = N - \left(\frac{1-s}{2}\right) L_2. \tag{6.85}$$

and the SBD forms an edge city.

Indeed, as described by the profit function (6.81), there are two opposite forces that drive the SBD's location: land rent $R(x)$ (which acts as a repulsion force against the CBD) and interaction costs $\kappa\, x$ (which act as an attraction force to the CBD). So, when the interactions are not too high, the SBD firm decides on the unique location that minimizes $R(x) + \kappa\, x$. This location is given by (6.85). The urban-land-use equilibrium is thus described by Figure 6.7.

The main difference as compared to the case when the SBD was exogeneously located at $x^*_{SBD} = N$ is that now x^*_{SBD} is given by (6.85). As a result, SBD workers now live on both sides of the location of the SBD whereas before, they were always living on its left-hand side (compare Figures 6.3 and 6.7). Therefore, the labor market analysis is exactly as before and thus, the efficiency wage for CBD workers is still given by (6.58), the CBD employment level by (6.59), and the SBD employment level by (6.60). The only difference is the value of the equilibrium land rent $R^*(x)$, which is no longer given by (6.42). Let us define the new urban land-use equilibrium:

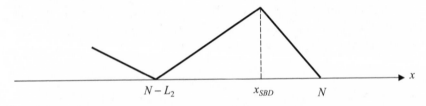

Figure 6.6b. The case of an edge city.

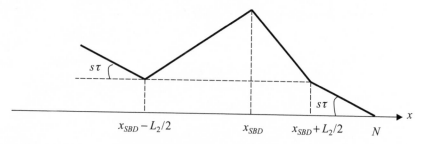

Figure 6.6c. The case of a subcenter.

Definition 6.6. *An urban-land-use equilibrium with no relocation costs and fixed housing consumption in a duocentric city with endogenous SBD is a 4-tuple* $(W_{L1}^*, W_{L2}^*, W_U^*, R^*(x))$ *such that:*

$$\Psi_{L1}(L_1, W_{L1}^*) = \Psi_U(L_1, W_U^*)$$

$$\Psi_U(N - L_2, W_U^*) = \Psi_{L2}^-(N - L_2, W_{L2}^*) = \Psi_{L2}^+(N, W_{L2}^*) = 0$$

$$R^*(x) = \max\left\{\Psi_{L,1}(x, W_{L1}^*), \Psi_{L,2}^-(x, W_{L2}^*), \Psi_{L2}^+(x, W_{L2}^*), \Psi_U(x, W_U^*), 0\right\}$$

at each $x \in \left(0, x_f^*\right].$

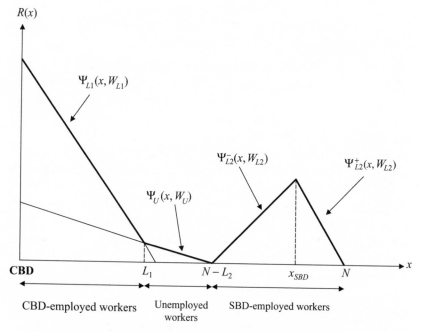

Figure 6.7. Land-use equilibrium in a duocentric city with endogenous SBD.

Solving these equations using (6.85), we easily obtain:

$$W_{L1}^* = w_L - e_1 - \tau\, L_1 - s\,\tau\,(N - L_1 - L_2)$$

$$W_{L2}^* = \overline{w}_2 - e_2 - s\,\tau\,N - \left(\frac{1-s}{2}\right)\tau\, L_2$$

$$W_U^* = w_U - s\,\tau\,(N - L_2)$$

$$R^*(x) = \begin{cases} \tau\,(L_1 - x) \\ \quad + s\,\tau\,(N - L_1 - L_2) & \text{for} \quad 0 \le x \le L_1 \\ s\,\tau\,(N - L_2 - x) & \text{for} \quad L_1 < x \le N - L_2 \\ (1 - s)\,\tau\,(x + L_2 - N) & \text{for} \quad N - L_2 < x \le N - \left(\frac{1-s}{2}\right) L_2 \\ (1 + s)\,\tau\,(N - x) & \text{for} \quad N - \left(\frac{1-s}{2}\right) L_2 < x \le N \\ 0 & \text{for} \quad x > N \end{cases}$$

If we compare these equilibrium values with those obtained in the case of a fixed SBD (see equations (6.39)–(6.42)), we obtain the same values for W_{L1}^* and W_U^*, but naturally, a different one for W_{L2}^* since SBD workers are now located on both sides of the SBD. This is also the reason why the equilibrium land rent $R^*(x)$ has different values between $N - L_2$ and N.

5. Endogenous Formation of Monocentric Cities with Unemployment

So far, firms' location has been assumed to be fixed and the employment center was thus prespecified. There is, in fact, a literature dealing with the endogenous location of firms and the formation of cities by explaining why cities exist, why cities are formed in certain places and why economic activities agglomerate in a small number of places. In their very complete survey of this literature, Fujita and Thisse (2002) give three main reasons for agglomeration economies: externalities under perfect competition (see, e.g., Beckmann, 1976, Borukhov and Hochman, 1977; Fujita and Ogawa, 1980; Papageorgiou and Smith, 1983), increasing returns under monopolistic competition (see, e.g., Abdel-Rahman and Fujita, 1990; Krugman, 1991; Fujita and Krugman, 1995; Fujita and Mori, 1997) and spatial competition under strategic interaction (Hotelling types of models like, for example, D'Aspremont, Gabszewicz, and Thisse, 1979). In this section, we will develop a model of endogenous formation (externalities under perfect competition) of a monocentric city where both employed and unemployed workers compete for land and the labor market is determined by an efficiency wage model.

5.1. The Model

The city is closed, linear, and symmetric. The middle of the city is normalized to 0 and the length of the city is denoted by x_f on its right and by $-x_f$ (symmetry) on its left. There is no vacant land and no cross-commuting (workers cannot cross each other when they go to work) in the city. All land is owned by absentee landlords. There are two types of workers, employed and unemployed workers. All workers (employed and unemployed) consume the same amount of land which, for simplicity, is normalized to 1.

We further assume that the density of workers $\psi(x)$ in each location x of the city within a *residential area* is equal to 1 (a residential area is an area when only households locate). Even though workers and non-workers consume the same amount of land, they differ by their revenue and commuting costs. Let us denote by x_c, $w_L(x_c)$ and w_U, the location of firms (or, equivalently, workers' workplace which will be endogenously determined in equilibrium), the wage at x_c and the unemployment benefit.

For simplicity, we assume that the shopping center is always located exactly at $x = 0$, the middle of the city. This assumption is made to capture the idea of the standard CBD developed in Chapters 4 and 5 where workers go to shop and work. Observe that the shopping center is where consumers buy goods, but not where production takes place, goods being produced by firms in the workplace. The latter will be endogenously determined in equilibrium, but since we focus on a monocentric city, it will be in the city center.

Concerning commuting costs, we have the same assumptions as in previous chapters so that the total commuting cost of an employed worker residing in x and working in x_c is equal to: $s\tau x + (1 - s)\tau |x - x_c|$ while the total commuting cost of an unemployed worker residing in x is equal to: $s\tau x$.

We are now able to write the budget constraint of an employed worker residing in x and working in x_c. This is given by:

$$R(x) + s\tau x + (1 - s)\tau |x - x_c| + z_L = w_L(x_c).$$

The unemployed located in x has the following budget constraint:

$$R(x) + s\tau x + z_U = w_U.$$

We assume the same preferences for all workers as in the benchmark model in Chapter 4. Therefore, each employed and unemployed worker has the following bid-rent function:

$$\Psi_L(x, W_L) = w_L(x_c) - s\tau x - (1 - s)\tau |x - x_c| - W_L \qquad (6.86)$$

$$\Psi_U(x, W_U) = w_U - s\tau x - W_U. \qquad (6.87)$$

There exists a continuum of identical firms, which allows us to treat their distribution in the city in terms of density. Firms' density in each point x of the city is denoted by $\lambda(x)$ and the total mass of firms is equal to M. Each firm uses a fixed quantity of land $\overline{H}$ and a variable quantity of labor l to produce y. The production function in each firm is thus given by: $y = f(\overline{H}, el)$, with $f(\overline{H}, 0) = f(0) = 0, \partial f(.)/\partial l > 0, \frac{\partial^2 f(.)}{\partial l^2} \leq 0$, and the Inada conditions hold, i.e., $f'(0) = +\infty$ and $f'(+\infty) = 0$.

Observe that l is labor demand per firm so that the total employment level in the economy is $L = l M$. Labor demand in each firm, l, is determined by profit maximization. Since all firms are identical, we have $l = L/M$ and the aggregate production function is given by: $F(\overline{H}, L) = Mf(\overline{H}, eL/M)$. Moreover, since $eF'(\overline{H}, eL) = ef'(\overline{H}, eL/M)$, labor demand can be determined by the profit maximization of one (representative) firm.

We shall now model agglomeration forces which is the main original part of this section (compared to the benchmark model). In our framework, the main force of agglomeration is due to the fact that production needs transactions between firms (information exchanges, face to face communication, etc.). There are different ways of modeling these transactions. Since we want to focus on the endogenous formation of a monocentric city, we have chosen the following due to Ogawa and Fujita (1982). The total transaction cost between a firm located at x and all other firms in the city is equal to:[12]

$$\kappa \Theta(x) = \kappa \int_{-x_f}^{x_f} \lambda(\xi) |x - \xi| d\xi$$

$$= \kappa \left[\int_{-x_f}^{x} \lambda(\xi)(x - \xi) d\xi + \int_{x}^{x_f} \lambda(\xi)(\xi - x) d\xi \right]$$

where κ denotes the transaction cost per unit of distance, $\lambda(x)$, the density of firms at x, and $\Theta(x)$, the total distance for the transaction for a firm located at x.

---

[12] In the previous section, interaction between firms was mainly a black box and was such that: $\kappa \Theta(x) = \kappa x$.

This assumption is very important for the urban equilibrium configuration since it affects both workers' and firms' bid-rents. For example, with this type of function, we cannot obtain a duocentric city (see Fujita, 1990, for an extensive discussion of this issue). In fact, as will be seen below, it is essentially the second derivative of $\Theta(x)$ that plays a fundamental role. We further assume that, within a *business area*,[13] the density of firms $\lambda(x)$ is constant and equal to $1/\overline{H}$. Therefore, we have:

$$\Theta'(x) = \int_{-x_f}^{x_f} \lambda(\xi)d\xi - \int_{x}^{x_f} \lambda(\xi)d\xi = 2x\lambda(x) = \frac{2x}{\overline{H}} \qquad (6.88)$$

$$\Theta''(x) = \frac{2}{\overline{H}}, \qquad (6.89)$$

where $\Theta(x)$ is a convex function ($\Theta''(x) > 0$) inside an area where firms are concentrated (business area), i.e., $\lambda(x) > 0$, and is linear ($\Theta''(x) = 0$) in residential areas, i.e., $\lambda(x) = 0$. We are now able to write the profit function of each firm located at x as follows:

$$\Pi(x) = y - R(x)\overline{H} - w_L(x)l - \kappa\Theta(x), \qquad (6.90)$$

where the price of the product is normalized to 1 and $w_L(x)$ is the wage profile that will be defined below. The objective of each firm is to choose a location x that maximizes its profit (6.90). Its bid rent, which is the maximum land rent a firm is ready to pay in location x to achieve profit level Π_F, given the distribution of firms $\lambda(x)$, is therefore given by:

$$\Phi(x, \Pi_F) = \frac{1}{\overline{H}}[y - w_L(x)l - \kappa\Theta(x) - \Pi_F], \qquad (6.91)$$

where Π_F is the equilibrium profit level common to all firms.

Finally, let us spell out our last assumption by using the following definition: two firms located in x_c and x_c' are connected if $|x_c - x_c'| = 0$. There are no commuting costs for workers within connected firms. This assumption is made for simplicity but does not affect the main result. It can be relaxed in two ways. First, workers can bear positive commuting costs within connected firms (as in Fujita and Ogawa, 1982). Second, all workers can have the same total commuting cost whenever they enter the interval of connected firms, which is equal to a fixed cost times the average size of the interval. However, both cases complicate the analysis (the second one being easier) without altering the main results.

---

[13] A business area is an area only when firms locate.

In equilibrium, we will only focus on a monocentric configuration so that all firms will be connected in the middle of the city. In this context, a natural interpretation of this last assumption is that this connected interval corresponds to a shopping mall so that workers have a positive commuting cost to go there, but then, no commuting cost within the mall. The idea is to open the black box of the (spaceless) CBD developed in the urban literature while keeping the same interpretation of a CBD in which individuals work and shop.

5.2. The Urban-Land-Use Equilibrium

We want to find equilibrium conditions for the endogenous formation of a *linear* and *monocentric* city. Thus, we have assumed that the city is symmetric so that we can only consider its right-hand side, that is the interval $[0, x_f]$. A monocentric city is such that (on the right-hand side of 0):

$$\psi(x) = 0 \quad \text{and} \quad \lambda(x) = 1/\overline{H} \quad \text{for} \quad x \in [0, x_e]$$
$$\psi(x) = 1 \quad \text{and} \quad \lambda(x) = 0 \quad \text{for} \quad x \in [x_e, x_f]$$

where $\psi(x)$ is the density of workers at x. This means that firms locate in the CBD, i.e., in the interval $[-x_e, x_e]$ and workers reside outside.

Because of the assumptions of no commuting costs for workers within connected firms and no cross-commuting for workers, the equilibrium wage profile in a monocentric city is given by:

$$w_L(x_c) = w_L, \tag{6.92}$$

where w_L is the efficiency wage that will be determined later. Equation (6.92) means that *there is no wage gradient in the city* since wages do no depend on distance. Using (6.91), this implies that the bid-rent of firms is equal to:

$$\Phi(x, \Pi_F) = \frac{1}{\overline{H}} \left[f(\overline{H}, l) - w_L l - \kappa \Theta(x) - \Pi_F \right] \tag{6.93}$$

$$= \frac{1}{\overline{H}} \left[f(\overline{H}, l) - w_L l - \kappa \left(\frac{x^2 + x_e^2}{\overline{H}} \right) - \Pi_F \right].$$

Thus, we have

$$\Phi'(x, \Pi_F) = \begin{cases} -2\kappa x / \overline{H}^2 < 0 & \text{for} \quad x \in [0, x_e] \\ 0 & \text{for} \quad x \in]x_e, x_f] \end{cases} \tag{6.94}$$

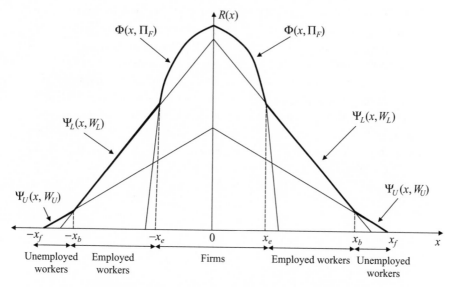

Figure 6.8. Agglomeration economies with unemployment.

and

$$\Phi''(x, \Pi_F) = \begin{cases} -2\kappa/\overline{H}^2 < 0 & \text{for} \quad x \in [0, x_e] \\ 0 & \text{for} \quad x \in \,]x_e, x_f] \end{cases}. \qquad (6.95)$$

We are now able to locate all workers in the city. Using (6.86) and (6.87), employed and unemployed workers have the following bid-rents, respectively:

$$\Psi_L(x, W_L) = w_L - \tau(x - x_e) - W_L \qquad (6.96)$$

$$\Psi_U(x, W_U) = w_U - s\tau(x - x_e) - W_U. \qquad (6.97)$$

Proposition 6.9. *The unemployed reside on the outskirts of the city, whereas employed workers locate in the vicinity of the city center.*

In the present model, Proposition 6.9 is derived because housing consumption is the same for all workers and commuting trips are lower for the unemployed.

Let us denote the border between employed and unemployed by x_b on the right-hand side of 0 (and thus $-x_b$ on the left-hand side of 0). This means that the employed reside between x_e and x_b (on the right-hand side of 0) and the unemployed between x_b and x_f (see Figure 6.8).

The monocentric urban equilibrium configuration is when firms out-bid workers outside the CBD. Consequently, let us write the equilibrium conditions for a monocentric city. As stated above, all firms are located in the CBD between $-x_e$ and x_e (0 being in the middle of this interval), employed workers reside between $-x_b$ and $-x_e$ (on the left-hand side of 0) and between x_b and x_e (on the right-hand side of 0) and unemployed workers reside between $-x_f$ and $-x_e$ (on the left-hand side of 0) and between x_e and x_f (on the right-hand side of 0), as described by Figure 6.8. Since the equilibrium is symmetric, the analysis can only be performed on the right-hand side of the city, i.e., between 0 and x_f. If we denote agricultural land rent (outside the city) by R_A and normalize it to zero, the equilibrium conditions are given by:

Definition 6.7. *An urban-land-use equilibrium with endogenous CBD is a 7-uple* $(W_L^*, W_U^*, \Pi_F^*, x_e^*, x_b^*, x_f^*, R^*(x))$ *such that:*

$$\Phi(x_e^*, \Pi_F^*) = \Psi_L(x_e^*, W_L^*) \tag{6.98}$$

$$\Psi_L(x_b^*, W_L^*) = \Psi_U(x_b^*, W_U^*) \tag{6.99}$$

$$\Psi_U(x_f^*, W_U^*) = R_A = 0 \tag{6.100}$$

$$R^*(x) = max\big\{\Psi_L(x, W_L^*), \Psi_U(x, W_U^*), \Phi(x, \Pi_F^*), 0\big\} \quad \text{for } x \in \big[0, x_f^*\big] \tag{6.101}$$

$$\int_0^{x_e^*} L\lambda(x)dx = \frac{L M}{2} \quad \text{for } x \in \big[0, x_e^*\big] \tag{6.102}$$

$$\int_{x_e^*}^{x_b^*} \psi(x)dx = \frac{L M}{2} \quad \text{for } x \in \big[x_e, x_b^*\big] \tag{6.103}$$

$$\int_{x_b^*}^{x_f^*} \psi(x)dx = \frac{U}{2} \quad \text{for } x \in \big[x_b, x_f^*\big]. \tag{6.104}$$

Let us comment on these equilibrium conditions. The land market condi-tions (6.98)–(6.101) ensure that landlords offer land to the highest bid-rents, that is, in the CBD, firms outbid workers and, outside the CBD, employed workers outbid unemployed workers and the land rent market is continuous everywhere in the city. The last three equations are the standard population constraints. Solving (6.102)–(6.104), we easily obtain:

$$x_e^* = -x_e^* = \frac{\overline{H}M}{2} \tag{6.105}$$

$$x_b^* = -x_b^* = \frac{L + \overline{H}M}{2} \tag{6.106}$$

$$x_f^* = -x_f^* = \frac{N + \overline{H}M}{2}. \tag{6.107}$$

We are now able to determine the equilibrium utility and profit levels. We easily obtain:

$$W_L^* = w_L - \frac{\tau}{2}\left[sN + (1-s)L^*\right] \tag{6.108}$$

$$W_U^* = w_U - s\tau\frac{N}{2} \tag{6.109}$$

$$\Pi_F^* = f(\overline{H}, eL^*/M) - w_L L^*/M - \frac{\tau}{2}\overline{H}\left[sN + (1-s)L^*\right] - \kappa\frac{\overline{H}M^2}{2}, \tag{6.110}$$

where $L^* = l^*M$ is the equilibrium employment level in the economy and $N = L^*M + U$. Observe that the equilibrium profit Π_F^* depends (negatively) on workers' commuting costs τ because of the competition in the land market. Indeed, firms have to bid away employed workers to occupy the core of the city.

Moreover, it is useful to identify the *equilibrium space costs*, i.e., land rent plus travel costs plus transaction costs (the latter are only for firms) for employed workers, unemployed workers, and firms (identified by subscript F). They are, respectively, given by:

$$SC_L^* = \frac{\tau}{2}\left[sN + (1-s)L^*\right] \tag{6.111}$$

$$SC_U^* = s\tau\frac{N}{2} \tag{6.112}$$

$$SC_F^* = \frac{\tau}{2}\overline{H}\left[sN + (1-s)L^*\right] + \kappa\frac{\overline{H}M^2}{2}. \tag{6.113}$$

This yields the following *space-cost differential* between the employed and the unemployed:

$$\Delta SC^* = SC_L^* - SC_U^* = (1-s)\frac{\tau}{2}L^*, \qquad (6.114)$$

which will play a crucial role in the model. In fact, given that the commuting costs are null within the CBD, ΔSC^* corresponds to the commuting costs of the last worker employed by firms. Finally, the equilibrium land rent is given by:

$$R^*(x) = \begin{cases} \tau\left[sN+(1-s)L^*\right]/2 + \kappa\left(\frac{M^2}{4} - \frac{x^2}{\overline{H}^2}\right) & \text{for } x \in \left[-x_e^*, x_e^*\right] \\[2mm] \tau\left[\left(sN+(1-s)L^*+\overline{H}M\right)/2 - |x|\right] & \text{for } x \in \left[-x_b^*, -x_e^*\right] \\ & \text{and } x \in \left[x_e^*, x_b^*\right] \\[2mm] s\tau\left[\left(\overline{N}+\overline{H}M\right)/2 - |x|\right)\right] & \text{for } x \in \left[-x_f^*, -x_b^*\right]. \\ & \text{and } x \in \left[x_b^*, x_f^*\right] \\[2mm] 0 & \text{for } x \in \left[-\infty, -x_f^*\right] \\ & \text{and } x \in \left[x_f^*, +\infty\right] \end{cases} \qquad (6.115)$$

5.3. The Steady-State Equilibrium

As usual, let us solve the labor market equilibrium using the efficiency wage framework. First, observe that $W_L^S = W_L^*$ and $W_L^{NS} = W_L^S - e = w_L - e - \frac{\tau}{2}\left[sN+(1-s)L^*\right]$. Now, to calculate the urban efficiency wage, we have to solve:

$$I_L^{NS} = I_L^S = I_L$$

where

$$r\,I_L^{NS} = w_L - e - \frac{\tau}{2}\left[sN+(1-s)L\right] - \delta\left(I_L^{NS} - I_U\right)$$

$$r\,I_L^S = w_L - \frac{\tau}{2}\left[sN+(1-s)L\right] - (\delta+m)\left(I_L^S - I_U\right)$$

$$r\,I_U = w_U - s\tau\frac{N}{2} + a(I_L - I_U).$$

We easily obtain the following *urban* efficiency wage :

$$w_L = w_U + e + \frac{e}{m}\left(\frac{\delta N}{N - L} + r\right) + (1 - s)\,\tau\frac{L}{2}, \tag{6.116}$$

which is exactly the same efficiency wage as in the benchmark case (L is divided by 2 because we consider the whole city instead of half of it as in the benchmark case).

The labor market equilibrium is now described. Each firm solves the following program:

$$\max_{L} \Pi_F^* \qquad s.t. \quad w \geq w_L^*, \tag{6.117}$$

where Π_F^* is defined by (6.110). The solution to (6.117) is:

$$w_L + (1 - s)\,\tau\overline{H}M/2 = eF'(\overline{H}, eL), \tag{6.118}$$

which defines the labor demand curve. It is important to observe that, in contrast to the case where firms were exogenously located in the CBD (Chapters 4 and 5), the labor demand curve is now negatively affected by τ, the (per unit of distance) commuting cost of workers. Indeed, when a firm wants to hire one additional worker, the gain is $eF'(\overline{H}, eL)$, i.e., the marginal productivity of this worker. However, hiring this worker will impose two costs for the firm: the wage w_L^* as well as the cost resulting from fiercer competition in the land market. Indeed, firms must propose higher bids to push away more employed workers in order to occupy the central part of the city. This leads to an additional cost of $(1 - s)\,\tau\overline{H}M/2$, where $(1 - s)\,\tau$ is the marginal increase in land rent when an additional worker is hired and $\overline{H}M/2$ the location of the firm which is the furthest away, i.e., located at x_e^*. This effect is new and was never present in the models of Chapters 4 and 5, since the location of firms was assumed to be exogenous and the CBD was reduced to a point $x = 0$. This is interesting since it establishes an additional link between land and labor markets. In fact, when a firm hires an additional worker, it anticipates the additional cost in the land market so that the total cost of hiring a new worker is $w_L + (1 - s)\,\tau\overline{H}M/2$, while the gain is $eF'(\overline{H}, eL)$.

We must now check that there exists a unique urban equilibrium as described by Figure 6.8. By plugging the efficiency wage (6.116) into (6.108),

(6.109), and (6.110), we obtain:

$$W_L^* = w_U + e + \frac{e}{m}\left(\frac{\delta N}{N - L} + r\right) - s\tau\frac{N}{2} \tag{6.119}$$

$$W_U^* = w_U - s\tau\frac{N}{2} \tag{6.120}$$

$$\Pi_F^* = f(\overline{H}, eL^*/M) - \left[w_U + e + \frac{e}{m}\left(\frac{\delta N}{N - L} + r\right)\right]\frac{L^*}{M} \tag{6.121}$$

$$- \frac{\tau}{2}\left[(1 - s)\,L^{*2}/M - \overline{H}\left[sN + (1 - s)\,L^*\right]\right] - \kappa\frac{\overline{H}M^2}{2},$$

where $L^* \equiv L^*(\tau, \overline{H}, M, w_U, m, e)$ is defined by (6.118).

We have the following result (due to Zenou, 2000).

Proposition 6.10. *The monocentric city is an equilibrium configuration if the following condition holds:*

$$\tau \leq \frac{\kappa M}{2\overline{H}}. \tag{6.122}$$

The following comments are in order. First, the endogenous formation of a monocentric city is only possible if workers' commuting cost τ is sufficiently low as compared to the firms' transaction cost κ. This is quite intuitive since the transaction cost is the *agglomeration force* to the CBD for firms (via $\kappa\Theta(x)$), and the commuting cost is the *dispersion force* for firms (via the efficiency wage) and the attraction force for workers. Thus, in order to have a monocentric city, it must be that firms bid away workers from the CBD so that the agglomeration forces dominate the dispersion force. Second, the augmentation of $\overline{H}$, the firms' land consumption, has a negative impact on city formation $\overline{H}$, since it has a negative effect on profits and thus firms' bid-rent. Third, the endogenous monocentric city formation is more likely to occur when M, the number of firms, is large since transaction costs increase with M.

Let us be more specific about these effects, which highlight the interaction between the land and the labor markets. First, when τ varies, it modifies the UNSC curve through its effect on the space-cost differential. If, for example, τ decreases, then the UNSC curve shifts downward (or rightward) so that, for any given employment level L, wages are lower as compared to the initial situation. This is because the space-cost differential decreases and thus firms that want to induce workers to remain employed must compensate their workers less in terms of commuting costs. This is what we call the *compensation effect.*

Second, when τ varies, it affects the labor demand curve since the cost of an additional worker is modified because of changes in the intensity of competition in the land market. More precisely, when commuting costs are lower, the attraction to the city center is weaker since it less costly to go there and thus, competition for central location is less intense so that land prices decrease. Therefore, when τ decreases, the labor demand curve shifts upward (or rightward) so that, for any given wage level, employment is higher as compared to the initial case. The explanation is that when a firm hires an additional worker, its marginal cost is lower than before because of weaker competition in the land market. This is referred to as the *spatial effect.*

Third, the net effect of this variation is the following. When τ is reduced, the UNSC curve shifts downward and the labor demand curve shifts upward. Thus, employment unambiguously rises, but wages can either increase or decrease depending on the slopes of these two curves.

6. Notes on the Literature

There is a large literature that introduces an efficiency wage framework in a standard Harris-Todaro model. Stiglitz (1976), Moene (1988), Carter (1998) are prominent examples of this literature. However, none of these models have a land market. The model by Zenou and Smith (1995) is the first that introduces a land market into a Harris-Todaro model with efficiency wages. Sections 2 and 3 are based on this model. Section 2 is also based on Brueckner and Zenou (1999), and Brueckner and Kim (2001). The models developed in Section 4 (sections 4.1 to 4.5) elaborate on Smith and Zenou (1997), and Brueckner and Zenou (2003). The extension with high relocation costs in section 4.6 is due to Zenou (2008g). The extension with endogenous SBD in section 4.7 is due to Smith and Zenou (1997). There are other papers with endogenous formation of subcenters (see, in particular, Fujita and Ogawa, 1980; Ogawa and Fujita, 1982; Henderson and Mitra, 1996; Fujita, Thisse, and Zenou, 1997; for literature surveys, see White, 1999; Fujita and Thisse, 2002), but none of them have unemployment. Finally, there is a large literature on the economics of agglomeration, which is overviewed by Fujita and Thisse (2002). The model developed in Section 5 extends a prominent model of this literature, namely that of Fujita and Ogawa (1980), and Ogawa and Fujita (1982), to incorporate an efficiency wage framework. The model from Section 5 is based on Zenou (2000).

APPENDIX A6. DETERMINATION OF STEADY-STATES VALUES FOR A THREE-STATE MARKOV PROCESS

Proof of (6.44), (6.45), and (6.46)

Let us determine the steady-states values of L_1^*, L_2^*, and U^*, respectively, given by (6.44), (6.45), and (6.46). There are two ways of determining these values.

In the first approach, given a transition matrix P, we must solve the following system:

$$\begin{pmatrix} U & L_1 & L_2 \end{pmatrix} P = \begin{pmatrix} U \\ L_1 \\ L_2 \end{pmatrix}.$$

Now, given that $N = U + L_1 + L_2$ (see (6.27)), this system can be written as:

$$\begin{pmatrix} U & L_1 & N - L_1 - U \end{pmatrix} P = \begin{pmatrix} U \\ L_1 \\ N - L_1 - U \end{pmatrix}. \tag{A6.2}$$

Since the transition matrix P is given by (6.43), this system can be written as:

$$\begin{pmatrix} U & L_1 & N - L_1 - U \end{pmatrix} \begin{pmatrix} 1 - (a_1 + a_2) & a_1 & a_2 \\ \delta & 1 - \delta & 0 \\ \delta & a_1 & 1 - (a_1 + \delta) \end{pmatrix}$$

$$= \begin{pmatrix} U \\ L_1 \\ N - L_1 - U \end{pmatrix}.$$

Solving this system of equations, we easily obtain (observe that the last equation is redundant):

$$U^* = \frac{\delta N}{a_1 + a_2 + \delta}$$

$$L_1^* = \frac{a_1 N}{\delta + a_1}.$$

Then, by using (6.27), we finally obtain:

$$L_2^* = \frac{a_2 \delta N}{(a_1 + \delta)(a_1 + a_2 + \delta)}.$$

These are the values obtained in the text and corresponding to (6.44), (6.45), and (6.46), respectively.

In the second approach, which has more economic intuition, we must write the dynamic equations that describe the different flows in the labor market. From the transition matrix P given by (6.43), we have:

$$\dot{U} = \delta \left(L_{1,t} + L_{2,t} \right) - (a_1 + a_2) U_t$$

$$\dot{L}_1 = a_1 \left(U_t + L_{2,t} \right) - \delta L_{1,t}$$

$$\dot{L}_2 = a_2 U_t - \delta L_{2,t} - a_1 L_{2,t}$$

where $\dot{U} = dU/dt$, $\dot{L}_1 = dL_1/dt$, and $\dot{L}_2 = dL_2/dt$. In steady-state, $\dot{U} = \dot{L}_1 = \dot{L}_2 = 0$ and thus, we obtain

$$\delta \left(L_1 + L_2 \right) = (a_1 + a_2) U$$

$$a_1 \left(U + L_2 \right) = \delta L_1$$

$$a_2 U = \delta L_2 + a_1 L_2.$$

Solving these three equations using (6.27) leads to (6.44), (6.45) and (6.46). ∎

Proof of (6.65), (6.65), and (6.67)
We proceed as in the previous proof, except for the case of shirking.

In the first approach, given that P is determined by (6.64), (A6.2) can now be written as:

$$\begin{pmatrix} U & L_1 & N - L_1 - U \end{pmatrix} \begin{pmatrix} 1 - (a_1 + a_2) & a_1 & a_2 \\ \delta + m & 1 - (\delta + m) & 0 \\ \delta & a_1 & 1 - (a_1 + \delta) \end{pmatrix}$$

$$= \begin{pmatrix} U \\ L_1 \\ N - L_1 - U \end{pmatrix}.$$

Solving this system of equations and using (6.27), we easily obtain (observe that the last equation is redundant):

$$U^{S*} = \frac{(\delta + m)(a_1 + \delta) N}{(a_1 + \delta + m)(a_1 + a_2 + \delta)}$$

$$L_1^{S*} = \frac{a_1 N}{a_1 + \delta + m}$$

$$L_2^{S*} = \frac{a_2 (\delta + m) N}{(a_1 + \delta + m)(a_1 + a_2 + \delta)}.$$

In the second approach, we must write the dynamic equations that describe the different flows in the labor market. From the transition matrix P given by (6.43), we have:

$$\dot{U} = (\delta + m) L_{1,t} + \delta L_{2,t} - (a_1 + a_2) U_t$$

$$\dot{L}_1 = a_1 (U_t + L_{2,t}) - (\delta + m) L_{1,t}$$

$$\dot{L}_2 = a_2 U_t - \delta L_{2,t} - a_1 L_{2,t}$$

where $\dot{U} = dU/dt$, $\dot{L}_1 = dL_1/dt$ and $\dot{L}_2 = dL_2/dt$. In steady-state, $\dot{U} = \dot{L}_1 = \dot{L}_2 = 0$ and thus, we obtain

$$(\delta + m) L_1 + \delta L_2 = (a_1 + a_2) U$$

$$a_1 (U + L_2) = (\delta + m) L_1$$

$$a_2 U = \delta L_2 + a_1 L_2.$$

Solving these three equations using (6.27) leads to (6.65), (6.65), and (6.67). ∎

PART 3

URBAN GHETTOS AND THE LABOR MARKET

Introduction of Part 3

We would now like to use the tools developed in Parts 1 and 2 of this book to understand the relationship between urban ghettos and the labor market outcomes of ethnic minorities. Indeed, most cities in the world are characterized by areas (ghettos) with a high level of poverty and a high concentration of ethnic minorities (see, e.g., Massey and Denton, 1988, 1993; Cutler and Glaeser, 1997; Cutler, Glaeser, and Vigdor, 1999; Anas, 2006). The geographical position of these areas within cities in general coincides with high unemployment and, more precisely, with the absence of jobs in the areas surrounding the ghettos. The labor market is thus a very important channel for the transmission and persistence of poverty across city tracts.

Let us be more precise about the facts. In the United States, it is generally observed that unemployment is unevenly distributed both within and between metropolitan areas. In particular, in most cities, the unemployment rate is nearly twice as high downtown as in the suburbs (see Table 7.1), mainly because of the concentration of blacks in these areas (see Table 7.2), who are mainly unskilled (see Table 7.3). Indeed, because of the massive migration of blacks from the rural south to the urban north after World War I and World War II and because of discrimination in the housing market, blacks had no choice but to live in the central-city ghettos. While there has

301

Table 7.1. *Unemployment rates (%) in 2000*

	Central city	Suburbs
Los Angeles–Long Beach	5.9	4.9
New York	5.7	3.0
Chicago	5.5	3.4
Boston	2.7	2.1
Philadelphia	6.4	3.1
Washington	4.3	2.0
Detroit	6.1	2.5
Houston	5.0	3.2
Atlanta	4.7	2.6
Dallas	3.8	2.5
Ten Largest MSAs	5.4	3.0

Source: Calculated by Gobillon, Selod, and Zenou (2003) from the Census.

Table 7.2. *Percentage of blacks by location in 2000*

	Central city	Suburbs
Los Angeles–Long Beach	11	8
New York	24	12
Chicago	33	8
Boston	11	2
Philadelphia	43	9
Washington	44	22
Detroit	70	6
Houston	24	10
Atlanta	61	25
Dallas	23	9
Ten Largest MSAs	27	11

Source: Calculated by Gobillon, Selod, and Zenou (2003) from the Census.

Table 7.3. *Distribution of jobs and people in 1994 (in %): Pooled sample of MSAs*

	Central city			Suburbs			
	Total central city	Black central city	White central city	Total suburbs	Black suburbs	Integrated suburbs	White suburbs
All Jobs	25.2	7.6	6.2	74.8	3.0	7.0	64.8
Low-skill Jobs*	20.4	10.2	2.7	79.6	2.7	7.5	69.4
People (25 years and older)	27.2	10.1	6.9	72.8	2.5	11.2	59.1
All people							
Black	65.3	57.1	5.3	34.8	10.4	6.6	17.8
White	13.1	2.5	6.3	86.9	1.8	8.7	76.4
H.S. dropouts Black	76.3	67.5	5.0	23.6	7.1	4.2	12.3
H.S. dropouts White	22.2	4.4	10.0	77.9	2.1	10.2	65.6
H.S. dropouts Total	44.8	15.6	7.7	55.2	2.1	12.5	40.6

* No high school (H.S.) diploma; no experience of training; no reading, writing, math.
The black (white) central city is defined as that area within the central area with contiguous census tracts of blacks (whites) representing 50% or more of the population. The black (white) suburbs is defined as that area within the suburbs with contiguous census tracts of blacks (whites) representing 30% (80%) or more of the population. The remaining suburban census tracts are defined as integrated suburban areas.
Source: Stoll, Holzer and Ihlandfeldt (2000).

Table 7.4. *Percentage jobs in central city and average annual growth rates of jobs by workplace, 1980–1990*

	% Job (Central city) 1980	% Job (Central city) 1990	Growth Rate (Central city) 1980–1990	Growth rate (Suburbs) 1980–1990
Los Angeles–Long Beach	51	51	1.9	2.1
New York	91	89	1.1	3.3
Chicago	50	44	−0.2	2.3
Boston	46	41	0.6	2.4
Philadelphia	41	35	−0.0	2.4
Washington	46	38	1.4	4.5
Detroit	38	28	−2.1	2.5
Houston	78	72	1.0	3.9
Atlanta	35	25	0.9	5.6
Dallas	69	60	1.4	5.6
Ten Largest MSAs	57	51	0.8	3.0

Source: Calculated by Gobillon, Selod, and Zenou (2003) from the Census.

been a substantial suburbanization of blacks in some cities, the legacy of that period remains in the form of inner-city ghettos. In the same period, there has been a massive suburbanization of jobs (see Table 7.4). To what extent does this history explain the higher rates of unemployment among blacks than whites?

Since the seminal work of Kain (1968), many economists contend that the spatial fragmentation of cities can entail adverse social and economic outcomes. These adverse effects typically include the poor labor market outcomes of ghetto dwellers (such as high unemployment and low income) and a fair amount of social ills (such as low educational attainment and high local criminality). Even though there is no general theory of ghetto formation, there has been a series of theoretical and empirical contributions, each giving a particular insight into some of the mechanisms at stake.

An interesting line of research revolves around the "spatial mismatch hypothesis," which states that because minorities are physically distant from job opportunities, they are more likely to be unemployed and obtain low net incomes. Table 7.5 documents these findings using Raphael's and Stoll's (2002) measure of spatial mismatch. The authors measure the spatial

Table 7.5. *American MSAs with the worse spatial mismatch for blacks in 2000*

	Blacks			Whites			Total population
	% Pop	SM	% Un	% Pop	SM	% Un	
Atlanta, GA MSA	29	54	8.98	63	40	3.09	4,112,198
Baltimore, MD, PMSA	27	52	11.69	67	37	3.05	2,552,994
Chicago, IL PMSA	19	69	17.27	66	34	4.18	8,272,768
Cleveland-Lorain-Elyria, OH, PMSA	19	62	14.09	77	31	4.17	2,250,871
Detroit, MI, PMSA	23	71	14.89	71	36	4.27	4,441,551
Houston, TX, PMSA	17	57	10.85	61	40	4.46	4,117,646
Los Angeles-Long Beach, CA, PMSA	10	62	15.57	49	37	6.64	9,519,338
Miami, FL, PMSA	20	65	13.44	66	36	6.23	2,253,362
New York, NY, PMSA	25	70	14.63	49	44	5.61	9,314,235
Newark, NJ, PMSA	22	65	13.90	66	34	3.96	2,032,989
Oakland, CA, PMSA	13	55	12.08	55	37	3.95	2,392,557
Philadelphia, PA-NJ, PMSA	20	64	13.93	72	34	4.47	5,100,931
Saint Louis, MO-IL, MSA	18	63	14.21	78	38	4.11	2,603,607
Washington, DC-MD-VA-WV, PMSA	26	56	8.64	60	42	2.63	4,923,153

% Pop: Percentage of (black or white) individuals in the population in the MSA or PMSA.
SM: Measure of the Spatial Mismatch (for black or white) between people and jobs using the Raphael's and Stoll's (2002) dissimilarity index.
% Un: Percentage of (black or white) male unemployed in the MSA or PMSA.
Source: Raphael and Stoll (2002) and Census (2000), calculations from Selod and Zenou (2005).

imbalance between jobs and residential locations using an index of dissimilarity, which ranges from 0 to 100, with higher values indicating a greater geographical mismatch between populations and jobs within a given metropolitan area. For instance, a dissimilarity index of 50 for blacks means that 50% of all blacks residing in the metropolitan area would have to relocate to different neighborhoods within the metropolitan area in order to be spatially distributed in perfect proportion to jobs. Table 7.5 shows that in the largest metropolitan areas in the U.S., access to jobs for blacks is quite elusive (especially in Detroit and New York).

Surprisingly, the numerous empirical works that have tried to test the existence of a causal link between spatial mismatch and the adverse labor market outcomes of minorities (see the surveys by Holzer, 1991; Kain, 1992; Ihlanfeldt and Sjoquist, 1998; Ihlanfeldt, 2006; Zenou, 2008c) are not based on any theory. The typical approach is to look for a relationship between job accessibility and labor market outcomes for blacks, using various levels of aggregation of the data: individual level, neighborhood level, and metropolitan level. Most papers have shown that bad job accessibility deteriorates labor market outcomes, thus confirming the spatial mismatch hypothesis.[1,2] However, following three decades of empirical tests, it is only in the late 1990s that theoretical models of spatial mismatch have begun to emerge. This is why most theoretical models have not yet inspired any specific empirical tests (Zenou, 2006b; Gobillon, Selod, and Zenou, 2007).

How can we proceed in constructing a model consistent with the empirical regularities described in the above tables? Theoretical models of urban labor markets in which unemployment is endogenous must be developed. The aim of this part is precisely to use the urban and the search and efficiency wage models developed in the first two parts of this book to better understand these empirical features and propose different policies aiming at fighting against high unemployment rates among black workers.

Chapters 7 and 8 will provide theories explaining the spatial mismatch hypothesis. In Chapter 7, we use the different urban-search-matching models developed in Part 1 to provide some mechanisms of the spatial mismatch. A first mechanism is that workers' job search efficiency may decrease with the distance to jobs and, in particular, workers residing far away from jobs may have few incentives to search intensively. Moreover, for a given search effort, workers who live far away from jobs have few chances of finding a

---

[1] There are, however, econometric problems since residential location is endogenous because families are not randomly assigned a residential location, but instead choose it. Indeed, self-selection and unobserved heterogeneity (for example unobserved productivity such as motivation or perseverance) rather than distance to jobs may explain why black workers have adverse labor market outcomes. Åslund, Östh, and Zenou (2008) have recently overcome this problem by exploiting a quasi-natural experiment based on a policy in Sweden under which the government assigned refugees to neighborhoods with different degrees of geographic job accessibility. They find that immigrants who in 1990–91 were placed in a location surrounded by few jobs had difficulties of finding work also after several years in 1999. Doubling the number of jobs in the initial location in 1990–91 is associated with 2.9 percentage points higher employment probability in 1999.

[2] Most empirical studies are using U.S. data. Very few are European. Exceptions include Thomas (1998), Fieldhouse (1999), Patacchini and Zenou (2005), for the U.K.; Dujardin, Selod, and Thomas (2007), for Belgium; Gobillon, Magnac, and Selod (2008) for France; and Åslund, Östh, and Zenou (2008) for Sweden.

job because, for instance, they get little information on distant job opportunities. Based on the models exposed in Part 1, these theories state that distance to jobs can be harmful because it implies low search intensities. Indeed, locations near jobs are costly in the short run (both in terms of high rents and low housing consumption), but allow higher search intensities which, in turn, increase the long-run prospects of reemployment. Conversely, locations far from jobs are more desirable in the short run (low rents and high housing consumption), but only allow infrequent trips to jobs and hence, reduce the long-run prospects of reemployment. Therefore, if minority workers are forced to reside far away from jobs, it will then be optimal for them to spend a minimum amount of time searching for jobs and thus, their chance of leaving unemployment will be quite low.

In Chapter 8, we use the theoretical models of Part 2, i.e., the urban efficiency wage theory, to address the issue of the spatial mismatch hypothesis. In particular, we provide two main mechanisms. First, using one of the models of Chapter 5, which assumes that workers' effort negatively depends on distance to jobs, we show that, in equilibrium, it is rational for firms to draw a red line beyond which they will not hire workers. As a result, if housing discrimination against ethnic minorities forces them to live far away from jobs, then even though firms have no prejudices, they are reluctant to hire these workers because they have a relatively lower productivity than whites. Second, using one of the models of Chapter 6, we show that by skewing ethnic workers towards the city center, housing discrimination increases the number of applications for central jobs and decreases the number of applications for suburban jobs. As a result, those workers living in the central part of the city, but working in the suburbs, experience a lower unemployment rate and earn higher wages than ethnic workers living and working in the central part of the city.

The spatial mismatch hypothesis essentially focuses on distance to jobs and claims that it is the main reason for the adverse labor market outcomes of ethnic minorities. However, in cities like New York, Chicago, or Philadelphia, ethnic minorities (especially blacks) reside relatively close to jobs and still experience high rates of unemployment. This means that other aspects than distance to jobs may play a role in explaining these adverse labor market outcomes. Even though the economic literature in that field has not come up with a clear-cut theory, it has stressed a variety of possible mechanisms linking labor market outcomes and residential segregation that are not necessarily linked to distance to jobs. These typically revolve around local externalities in education (Benabou, 1993; Borjas, 1995), labor discrimination (Coate and Loury, 1993; Altonji and Blank, 1999), crime (Glaeser, Sacerdote, and Scheinkman, 1996; Zenou, 2003; Verdier and Zenou, 2004; Raphael and Sills, 2006), housing discrimination (Yinger, 1986; 1997), social distance, social capital, and social networks (Akerlof, 1997; Calvó-Armengol, and Jackson, 2004).

In order to explain the adverse labor market outcomes of black workers living in segregated areas, we will focus on the last aspect in Chapter 9, namely the importance of social networks in the labor market and show how they are linked to urban segregation. Indeed, individuals seeking jobs read newspapers, go to employment agencies, browse on the Web, and mobilize their local networks of friends and relatives. Empirical evidence indeed suggests that about half of all jobs are filled through contacts. Sociologists and labor economists have produced a broad empirical literature on labor market networks. In fact, the pervasiveness of social networks and their relative effectiveness vary with the social group considered. For instance, Holzer (1987, 1988) shows that among 16 to 23-year-old workers who reported job acceptance, 66% use informal search channels (30% direct applications without referral and 36% friends/relatives), while only 11% use state agencies, and 10% newspapers.[3] Networks of personal contacts mediate employment opportunities which flow through word-of-mouth and, in many cases, constitute a valid alternative source of employment information to more formal methods.

Geographical space is linked to social space, however. Topa (2001) argues that the observed spatial distribution of unemployment in Chicago is consistent with a model of local interactions and information spillovers, and may thus be generated by an agent's reliance on informal methods for job search such as networks of personal contacts. Bayer, Ross, and Topa (2008) also document that people who live close to each other, defined as being in the same census block, tend to work together, that is, in the same census block. As a result, residential segregation may be harmful to ethnic minorities (Cutler and Glaeser, 1997) because it deteriorates their social networks and limits their information about jobs (Wilson, 1996; Ihlanfeldt, 1997; O'Reagan and Quigley, 1998; Conley and Topa, 2002).

In Chapter 9, we will see that if ethnic minorities are physically separated from the majority group, they are likely to experience high unemployment rates which, in turn, will affect the quality of their social network. There is a vicious circle of high unemployment rate, segregation, and poor social networks in which ethnic minorities are trapped.

---

[3] See also Corcoran, Datcher, and Duncan (1980) and Granovetter (1995).

CHAPTER SEVEN

The Spatial Mismatch Hypothesis:
A Search-Matching Approach

1. Introduction

In this chapter, we will use the models and results of Part 1 to provide some mechanisms for the spatial mismatch hypothesis. In Section 2, we will adapt the models developed in Chapter 1 to explain the spatial mismatch hypothesis. In this perspective, distance to jobs prevents black workers from obtaining job information, thus isolating them from employment centers. Indeed, little information reaches the area where blacks live, which reduces their search efficiency and thus, their probability of finding a job. We will show that a policy that gives transport subsidies to black workers can increase job creation and the unemployment rate of black workers only if the level of the subsidy is sufficiently high compared to the tax on firms' profits.

Then, in Section 3, we assume that the fixed entry cost of firms is greater in the Central Business District (CBD) than in the Suburban Business District (SBD) and that workers are heterogeneous in their disutility of transportation (or, equivalently, in their search costs). These two fundamental assumptions are sufficient to generate an equilibrium where central city residents (blacks) experience a higher rate of unemployment than suburban residents (whites) and suburban firms create more jobs than central firms (a higher job vacancy rate).

Finally, in the last section, we will show that different transport modes between blacks and whites lead to different search intensities and thus, different probabilities of finding a job. We develop a theoretical model where whites mainly use cars to commute, whereas blacks use public transportation. We show that for both blacks and whites, living in areas where employed workers' average commuting time is higher makes the unemployed search more than in areas with a lower commuting time. Because of access to different transport modes, we also show that white unemployed workers search more intensively than blacks, even if both groups live in areas where employed workers have exactly the same average commuting time. This is due to the fact that using a faster transportation mode allows unemployed whites to accept jobs located further away and thus, to have a higher area of search than blacks.

2. Access to Job Information

In Chapter 1, we developed the benchmark model of urban search-matching. This model was constructed with the European situation in mind, where the unemployment rate is higher in the suburbs (like, e.g., in Paris or London), and was primarily introduced to set out the method of construction of models in urban labor economic theory. This model must obviously be adapted to deal with the U.S. spatial mismatch.

As in the benchmark model, the city is a line whose origin $x = 0$ consists of the CBD, where all firms are located and whose end point is the city fringe denoted by x_f. Workers are uniformly distributed along this line and decide where to locate between $x = 0$ and $x = x_f$. The city is closed so that there is no relation to the outside world, which implies that the population is fixed. All land is owned by absentee landlords. There are no relocation costs, either in terms of time or money.

There are several ways in which this model can be adapted to account for the U.S. spatial mismatch. The easiest way is to flip the city so that the CBD corresponds to a SBD that concentrates all jobs. So, if all jobs are in the suburbs rather than in the CBD, all we require for consistency is to define $x = 0$ to be the workplace location, which is in the suburbs. But, in fact, jobs are more centralized than residences. Indeed, Glaeser and Kahn (2001) have shown that jobs have been suburbanizing faster than residences so that in the large U.S. metropolitan areas, the average job is now only one mile closer to the CBD than the average residence. So, even if we flip the city in the benchmark model of Chapter 1, there seems to be some inconsistency since the unemployment rate in U.S. cities is higher in (central) locations that appear to have better access to jobs. However, since most blacks are unskilled, we need to differentiate between skilled and unskilled jobs. Using both the 1994 Multi-City Study of Urban Inequality (MCSUI) and the 1990 census, Table 7.3 displays the spatial distribution of recently filled low-skill jobs and people by race and education. As pointed out by Stoll, Holzer, and Ihlanfeldt (2000), this table shows that the distribution of low-skill jobs is similar to that of all jobs, except that *there is a greater share of low-skill jobs in general in white suburbs.* This implies that low-skill jobs are much more decentralized than high-skill jobs. If comparing jobs with people, the situation is worse: 79.6% of the lowest skilled jobs in metropolitan areas, but only 23.6% of the least-educated black people (i.e., those with no high school degree) are located in the suburbs. Access to low-skill jobs is thus quite difficult for unskilled black workers. Since unskilled jobs are, on average, further from the CBD than unskilled black workers' housing and since unemployment is a problem for the unskilled, our basic model can be adapted to describe the situation for the *unskilled*, but with $x = 0$ corresponding to a location in the suburbs.

2.1. Search Intensity as a Function of Distance to Jobs

We use both the benchmark model of Chapter 1 and the high-relocation-cost model developed in Chapter 2, Section 5, where $x = 0$ is now the workplace location. The main mechanism proposed here is that inner-city black residents, who are stuck in locations far away from jobs, may face difficulties in gathering information about suburban jobs and therefore, will experience high unemployment rates.

We assume all workers to have very high relocation costs, so that each worker's residential location remains fixed as he/she enters and leaves unemployment. We also assume perfect capital markets with a zero interest rate, i.e., $r \to 0$. As in Chapter 1, workers' search intensity $s(x)$ is assumed to be a negative function of distance to jobs. This relationship was described by equation (1.45), which we rewrite for ease of exposition:

$$s(x) = s_0 - s_a x \qquad (7.1)$$

where $s_0 > 0$ and $s_a > 0$. The key parameter in this formulation is s_a, which measures how quickly job information deteriorates with the distance to jobs. Since the job acquisition rate is defined as: $(s_0 - s_a x)\,\theta q(\theta)$, $s_a\,\theta q(\theta)$ is the marginal decrease in the job acquisition rate for an unemployed worker. Hence, with this formulation, when workers are further away from jobs, they search less intensively. We can now determine $\bar{s}$, aggregate search efficiency in a city, as follows:

$$\bar{s} = s_0 - s_a \bar{x} = s_0 - s_a \frac{N}{2}. \qquad (7.2)$$

Each individual located in x will then spend $u(x)$ of his/her time unemployed,

$$u(x) = \frac{\delta}{\delta + s(x)\,\theta q(\theta)}, \qquad (7.3)$$

where $\theta = V/(\bar{s}u\,N)$ is the labor market tightness in efficiency units. Because $s'(x) < 0$, this means, in particular, that $u'(x) > 0$ so that workers residing further away from jobs spend more time unemployed than those living closer to jobs. The unemployment rate of this economy is then equal to:

$$u = \frac{\delta}{\delta + \bar{s}\,\theta\,q(\theta)}. \tag{7.4}$$

2.1.1. Labor Market Equilibrium. Let us extend the model of Chapter 2, Section 5, to the case of a search intensity defined by (7.1). The wage, which is the result of bargaining between the firm and the worker, is then equal to:

$$w_L^*(x) = \beta(y + c) + (1 - \beta)\{w_U + [1 - s(x)]\,\tau\,x\} \tag{7.5}$$
$$= \beta(y + c) + (1 - \beta)\{w_U + (1 - s_0)\,\tau\,x + s_a\tau\,x^2\}.$$

The wage is increasing and *convex* with distance to jobs x. Firms enter the labor market up to the point where their expected profit is equal to zero. When they enter the labor market, they do not know which wage they will pay, so ex-ante they expect to pay the average wage, $w_L(N/2)$, since workers are uniformly distributed in the city. The free-entry condition is thus $E\,\Pi(N/2) = 0$, which is equivalent to:

$$y - w_U = \left[\frac{\delta}{q(\theta^*)} + \beta\right]\frac{c}{(1 - \beta)} + (1 - s_0)\,\tau\,\frac{N}{2} + s_a\tau\left(\frac{N}{2}\right)^2. \tag{7.6}$$

This is the equilibrium condition that determines job creation θ^*.

2.1.2. Urban-Land-Use and Steady-State Equilibrium. The bid-rent of all workers is given by:

$$\Psi(x, E\,W) = w_U + \beta\,[1 - u(x)]\,\{y - w_U + c - [1 - s(x)]\,\tau x\}$$
$$- s(x)\,\tau x - E\,W. \tag{7.7}$$

Since $u'(x) > 0$, a sufficient condition for the slope of the bid-rent to always be negative is:

$$2s_a\,N < s_0 < 1. \tag{7.8}$$

Here, the land rent does not only compensate workers for commuting costs and wages, as previously, but also for their unemployment rate (or, more exactly, the fraction of their lifetime when they are unemployed) since the further away someone resides, the lower is the search intensity and the longer the time spent unemployed. Using the same definition of urban-land-use equilibrium as in Chapter 2, Section 5, we easily obtain:

$$E\,W^* = w_U + \beta\,[1 - u(N)]\,\{y - w_U + c - [1 - s(N)]\,\tau N\} - s(N)\,\tau N \quad (7.9)$$

$$R^*(x) = \begin{cases} \beta\,[y - w_U + c]\,[u(N) - u(x)] + \tau\,[s(N)\,N - s(x)\,x] & \text{for } x \le N \\ +\tau\beta\,\{[1 - u(N)]\,[1 - s(N)]\,N - [1 - s(x)]\,[1 - u(x)]\,x\} & (7.10) \\ 0 & \text{for } x > N \end{cases}$$

with $s(N) = s_0 - s_a N$ and $u(N) = \delta/\,[\delta + s(N)\,\theta q(\theta)]$.

2.2. Explaining the Spatial Mismatch Hypothesis

Based on the model developed above, we would like to give some theoretical foundation to explain the spatial mismatch between jobs and black workers' residential location.

Assume now that there are two types of workers, black and white, whose mass is given by N_B and N_W, with $N = N_B + N_W$, respectively.[1] Black and white workers have the same productivity y and thus firms have no preference for hiring one type of worker (there is no discrimination). The only difference between black and white workers is due to the job contact rate being different. Indeed, we assume the job contact rate for a type–i worker ($i = B, W$) located at x to be given by $\gamma_i s(x)\,\theta q(\theta)$, where $\gamma_B = \gamma < \gamma_W = 1$. This reflects the fact that blacks and whites have different social networks because blacks tend to be friends with blacks and whites with whites.[2] Since employers are mostly whites and a fraction of them tend to recruit workers via word-of-mouth and friends, then obviously two workers B and W located at the same distance x (and thus having the same $s(x)$) will not have the same chance of having a contact with a firm. This, in particular, implies that when a black worker searches with intensity $s(x)$, his/her returns from search are $\gamma s(x)$ (with $0 < \gamma < 1$) while for whites they are exactly $s(x)$. Hence, there are lower returns to searching for black than for white workers.

Since all workers compete for the same jobs, the matching function is now given by:

$$d(\overline{s}_B\,u_B\,N_B + \overline{s}_W\,u_W\,N_W,\, V),$$

---

[1] Subscripts B and W refer to "black" and "white," respectively.
[2] In Chapter 9, we investigate the impact of social networks on black and white outcomes in more detail.

where $\bar{s}_i$ and u_i are the average search intensity and the unemployment rate of type–i workers, respectively. In this context, the expected utility of a type–i worker is given by:

$$E\,W_i(x) = [1 - u_i(x)]\,W_{iL}(x) + u_i(x)\,W_{iU}(x)$$
$$= [1 - u_i(x)]\,[w_L(x) - \tau\,x] + u_i(x)\,[w_U - s(x)\tau\,x] - R(x),$$

where the time spent unemployed is equal to:

$$u_i(x) = \frac{\delta}{\delta + \gamma_i s(x)\theta q(\theta)}.$$

The wage is still given by (7.5) and only depends on the location of workers. The unemployment rate of a type–i worker is equal to:

$$u_i = \frac{\delta}{\delta + \bar{s}_i\,\theta q(\theta)},$$

where

$$\theta = \frac{V}{\bar{s}_B\,u_B\,N_B + \bar{s}_W\,u_W\,N_W}.$$

As a result, the bid-rent of a type–i worker located at a distance x from the job center is equal to:

$$\Psi_i(x, E\,W_i) = [1 - u_i(x)]\,[w_L(x) - \tau\,x] + u_i(x)\,[w_U - s(x)\tau\,x] - E\,W_i.$$

Assuming (7.8), the bid-rent of a type–i worker is decreasing in x, and it is easily shown that, $\forall x$, we have:

$$\left|\frac{\partial\Psi_W(x, E\,W_W)}{\partial x}\right| > \left|\frac{\partial\Psi_B(x, E\,W_B)}{\partial x}\right|.$$

The intuition is straightforward. Since $\gamma_B = \gamma < \gamma_W = 1$, then, at each x, $u_B(x) > u_W(x)$, i.e., black workers spend more time unemployed over their lifetime than whites. This implies that blacks have lower expected commuting costs than whites, since they are equal to: $[1 - u_i(x)]\,\tau x + u_i(x)s(x)\tau x$ for a type–i worker. As a result, white workers have steeper bid-rents than blacks and thus bid away black workers in order to reside closer to jobs. We now have:

$$\bar{s}_W = s_0 - s_a\frac{N_W}{2}, \qquad \bar{s}_B = s_0 - s_a\frac{(N + N_W)}{2}.$$

Proposition 7.1. *If blacks and whites only differ by their contact rate, then black workers reside further away from jobs, search less intensively, have a lower expected wage, and experience higher spells of unemployment than white workers.*

This is an interesting result that can be explained as follows. Since black workers have a lower contact rate than whites, they are more often unemployed and thus have flatter bid-rents. As a result, they reside further away from jobs. This leads them to search less intensively than whites, i.e., $s_B(x) < s_W(x)$, $\forall x$, which increases their unemployment rate even more because now both γ_i and $s_i(x)$ are lower. By separating black and white workers in the city, space amplifies the effect on unemployment. Since $\forall x$, $u_W(x) \ll u_B(x)$, the expected wage of whites will be much higher than that of blacks, even though they are more compensated for their spatial costs when they work.

To close the model, we need to write the free-entry condition. When a new firm enters the market, it does not know which location and which type of worker it will hire. As a result, the free-entry condition is given by:

$$\frac{N_W}{N} E \Pi_W \left(\frac{N_W}{2} \right) + \left(1 - \frac{N_W}{N} \right) E \Pi_B \left(\frac{N + N_W}{2} \right) = 0. \quad (7.11)$$

Indeed, if a new firm enters the labor market, then with probability N_W/N, it can hire a white worker whose average location is $N_W/2$ while, with probability $1 - N_W/N$, it can hire a black worker, whose average location is $(N + N_W)/2$. Solving this equation, we obtain:

$$y - w_U = \left[(1 + \beta) \frac{\delta}{q(\theta)} + \beta \right] \frac{c}{(1 - \beta)} + (1 - s_0) \tau \frac{N}{2}$$

$$+ s_a \tau \left[\frac{N^2 + N N_W - N_W^2}{4} \right]. \quad (7.12)$$

We can now define the urban-land-use equilibrium as follows:

Definition 7.1. *An urban-land-use equilibrium with black and white workers, high relocation costs, and fixed-housing consumption is a 3-tuple* $(E W_B^*, E W_W^*, R^*(x))$ *such that:*

$$\Psi(N_W, E W_B^*) = \Psi(N_W, E W_W^*) \quad (7.13)$$

$$\Psi(N, E W_B^*) = R_A = 0 \quad (7.14)$$

$$R^*(x) = \max \left\{ \Psi(x, E W_B^*), \Psi(x, E W_W^*), 0 \right\} \quad \text{at each } x \in (0, N]. \quad (7.15)$$

As usual, equations (7.13), (7.14), and (7.15) reflect the equilibrium conditions in the land market. By solving the first two equations, we obtain:

$$E W_B^* = [1 - u_B(N)] \, \beta (y + c - \tau \, N)$$
$$+ [1 - \beta \, (1 - u_B(N))] \, [w_U - s(N)\tau \, N] \qquad (7.16)$$

$$E W_W^* = [u_B(N_W) - u_W(N_W)] \, \beta \, [y - w_U + c$$
$$- (1 - s(N_W)) \, \tau \, N_W] + E W_B^*. \qquad (7.17)$$

Finally, by plugging these values into the bid-rent function, we get:

$$R^*(x) = [1 - u_i(x)] \, [\beta (y + c) + (1 - \beta) \, w_U - \beta \tau \, x]$$
$$- s(x)\tau \, x \, [1 - \beta \, (1 - u_W(x))] + u_i(x) \, w_U - E W_W$$

for $0 \leq x \leq N_W$, and

$$R^*(x) = [1 - u_B(x)] \, [\beta (y + c - \tau \, x)] - [1 - u_B(N)] \, \beta (y + c - \tau \, N)$$
$$+ [1 - \beta \, (1 - u_B(x))] \, [w_U - s(x)\tau \, x]$$
$$- [1 - \beta \, (1 - u_B(N))] \, [w_U - s(N)\tau \, N]$$

for $N_W < x \leq N$.

2.3. Transportation Policy

Let us now consider a simple transportation policy that consists of subsidizing the commuting costs of black workers only, a policy often advocated to fight against the spatial mismatch of black workers (see, e.g., Pugh, 1998). As a result, the commuting cost of white workers is $\tau_W = \tau$, while that of black workers is $\tau_B = (1 - Z^\tau) \tau$, where $0 < Z^\tau < 1$ is the transportation subsidy. The unemployment benefit w_U as well as the transportation subsidy are financed by a tax D^π on firms. This means that when a firm hires a type–i worker ($i = B, W$), its instantaneous profit is equal to: $y - w_{iL}(x) - D^\pi$. The government's budget constraint can be written as:

$$D^\pi (N - u_B N_B - u_W N_W) = w_U (u_B N_B + u_W N_W) + Z^\tau (N_B - u^B N_B).$$

The fiscal policy is such that taxes are kept constant and the budget adjustment is realized through a decrease or an increase in unemployment benefit taxes, w_U. This means that for a constant value of D^π, the unemployment benefit level that balances the budget is given by:[3]

$$w_U = \frac{D^\pi \left(N - u_B N_B - u_W N_W\right) - Z^\tau \left(N_B - u_B N_B\right)}{u_B N_B + u_W N_W}. \tag{7.18}$$

The urban equilibrium is as before with black workers residing far away from jobs and white workers close to jobs. We have the following result (proved by Zenou, 2007b).

Proposition 7.2. *Assume that*

$$Z^\tau > D^\pi \frac{N}{N_B \left(1 - u_B\right)}. \tag{7.19}$$

Then, the higher the transportation subsidy Z^τ, the higher is job creation θ^*, the lower are the unemployment rates of black and white workers, u_B^* and u_W^*, and at each $x \in [0, N]$, the lower are the wages of black and white workers, $w_{BL}^*(x)$ and $w_{WL}^*(x)$.

This proposition states that increasing the transportation subsidy of black workers will not always increase job creation and decrease their unemployment rate. The level of the subsidy must be sufficiently high as compared to the tax on firms' profits. Indeed, when blacks' commuting costs are subsidized, firms can pay a lower wage to these workers because their (long) commutes are less expensive. As a result, more firms enter the labor market and job creation increases. However, there is another effect of the financing of this policy (see (7.18)). Indeed, for given levels of unemployment rates, when subsidies increase, firms are taxed more, which deters entry. Therefore, when the transportation subsidy Z^τ is set at a sufficiently high level compared to the tax rate, then the first effect dominates the second when increasing Z^τ and we obtain Proposition 7.2. An interesting result is that such a policy only targeted at black workers also has an effect on the labor market outcomes of white workers because of the interaction between the land and labor markets.

---

[3] An alternative fiscal policy would be that the unemployment benefits are kept constant, so that taxes are adjusted to balance the budget. In this case, it is well-known that multiple equilibria will emerge (Rocheteau, 1999). Since the focus of this paper is on policy issues and not on multiple equilibria, we focus on the other fiscal policy. Naturally, these two fiscal policies are strictly equivalent, but in one of them (the one we propose here), workers and firms can coordinate on only one equilibrium, whereas this is not possible in the other policy.

2.4. Redlining

One of the interesting and new results of the model with high relocation costs was the positive correlation between wages and distance to jobs (see (7.5)). This can give an explanation for redlining in the labor market. *Geographic redlining* (see, e.g., Ladd, 1998; Lang and Nakamura, 1993) involves differentials in the mortgage loan supply across neighborhoods or space. In other words, mortgage lenders discriminate on basis of the location of the property, so that people living in redlined areas have difficulties in obtaining loans. We would here like to extend this notion of redlining to the labor market where firms may be reluctant to hire workers because of their residential location.[4]

If considering the model with high relocation costs with two stages to matching, a cheap look-at-address-on-resume stage followed by a more costly interview stage, then firms would not interview people who lived far away since they would then find themselves in positions where the firm-worker bargain would lead to a higher wage. They would prefer to interview workers who are residing nearby because they (the firms) would then have more bargaining power.

We will further investigate the issue of redlining in the labor market in Chapter 8.

2.5. Different Search Intensities Between Black and White Workers

Instead of assuming a negative relationship between search intensity and distance to jobs as in (7.1), workers now choose their level of search intensity as in Chapter 1, Section 4. We have shown that this leads to a *nonlinear decreasing* relationship between the residential distance to jobs for unemployed workers and their search intensity s (see Proposition 1.4 and Figure 1.5). This allows us to propose an alternative mechanism for the spatial mismatch hypothesis. Indeed, in Chapter 1, Section 4, using a search-matching model with endogenous housing consumption, we have shown that distance to jobs is harmful because it implies low search intensities. There was a fundamental trade-off between short-run and long-run benefits of various locational choices for the unemployed. Indeed, locations near jobs were costly in the short run (both in terms of high rents and low housing consumption), but make higher search intensities possible which, in turn,

---

[4] To the best of our knowledge, Zenou and Boccard (2000) were the first to propose a formal model of redlining in the labor market.

increase the long-run prospects of reemployment. Conversely, locations far from jobs were more desirable in the short run (low rents and high housing consumption), but only allowed infrequent trips to jobs and hence, reduced the long-run prospects of reemployment. Therefore, for workers residing further away from the workplace, it is optimal to spend the minimal search effort whereas workers residing close to jobs provide a high search effort.

In this context, spatial mismatch can be the result of optimizing behavior by the labor market participants, since the unemployed can choose low amounts of search and long-term unemployment. This implies that the standard U.S.-style mismatch arises because inner-city blacks choose to remain in the inner-city and only search little. They do not relocate to the suburbs because the short run/long run gap is sufficiently large to make locations near the jobs too expensive. The policy implications are thus quite different. In particular, "Moving to Opportunity" programs (such as the so-called Gautreaux program)[5] are just the correct policy device for reducing mismatch, rather than lowering search costs in some other way.

3. Different Entry Costs

To provide another mechanism for the spatial mismatch hypothesis, we will now develop another search urban model based on Coulson, Laing, and Wang (2001). They also use a search framework (similar to that in Chapter 1). However, in contrast to the previous urban search models, they do not explicitly model the intra-urban location of workers, but instead their mobility between two job centers, the CBD and the SBD.

3.1. The Model

The city is *closed* and consists of two zones: a CBD and an SBD, indexed by $j = 1, 2$. Total population in each zone is normalized to 1. There is a continuum of workers who reside in each of the two locations $i = 1, 2$ and who inelastically supply one unit of labor. Thus in terms of notations, the

---

[5] By giving housing assistance (i.e., vouchers and certificates) to low-income families, the MTO programs help them relocate to better and richer neighborhoods. The results of most MTO programs (in particular for Baltimore, Boston, Chicago, Los Angeles, and New York) show a clear improvement in the well-being of participants and better labor market outcomes (see, in particular, Ladd and Ludwig, 2001; Katz, Kling, and Liebman, 2001; Ludwig, Duncan, and Hirschfield, 2001; Rosenbaum and Harris, 2001; Kling, and Katz, 2005). Observe that the MTO programs are not targeted at minority families (such as blacks), but rather at poor families. But this is a good example of an integration policy since the two are correlated.

index $i = 1, 2$ denotes the residential location of workers while $j = 1, 2$ refers to the location of the job or workplace. There is a continuum of firms that provides vacancies in each of the two locations $j = 1, 2$. Once more, it is important to underline that in contrast to the previous approaches, the city consists of two points: the CBD, $j = 1$, and the SBD, $j = 2$, and workers do not reside in between these two centers as, for example, in Chapter 6. There is, in fact, no determination of residential location. Observe, however, that even if workers' location is predetermined, workers are free to search for work in either (or both) locations and commute to work if employment is found outside the zone in which they are domiciled. This model is exactly in the same spirit as the models proposed in Sections 3 and 4 in Chapter 3 where workers' and firms' locations were fixed. The only difference is that here we consider two employment centers while in Chapter 3 there was either a continuum (Section 3) or a finite number (Section 4) of them.

Several assumptions are made. First, ($H1$), firms' entry cost is higher in the CBD than in the SBD, that is $c_1 > c_2$. This captures the fact that jobs have been decentralized in the United States, as documented in Table 7.4, so that it less costly to create a job in the suburbs. Explanations include cheaper land prices in the suburbs, lower taxation, lower labor costs, lower production costs, etc.

Second, ($H2$), workers are heterogeneous in their disutility of commuting, which is captured by parameter ∇. This parameter, which is an inverse measure of disutility of commuting, is uniformly distributed in $[0, 1]$. Moreover, the commuting cost is zero within an area and strictly positive between areas, i.e., $\tau_{ii} = 0$ while for $i = 1, 2, i \neq j$ and $\nabla \in [0, 1]$, we have:

$$\tau_{ij}(\nabla) = \tau_0 - \tau(\nabla) > 0, \qquad (7.20)$$

with $\tau_0 > 0$, $\tau'(.) > 0$, $\tau(0) = 0$ and $\tau(1) = \tau_0$ and where $\tau_{ij}(\nabla)$ is the commuting cost per unit of distance for a worker residing in location $i = 1, 2$ and working in location $j = 1, 2$. This cost function is displayed in Figure 7.1. Equation (7.20) means, in particular, that commuting between the two locations is costly for all but the most able worker, whose commuting cost is normalized to zero. So basically, the higher is ∇, the lower is the disutility of commuting, i.e., $\partial \tau_{ij} / \partial \nabla < 0$. In this section, we will not have an explicit analysis of black and white workers, but it is easy to interpret assumption ($H2$) in terms of race. Indeed, it is well established that most blacks tend to use public transportation while most whites use cars (see the evidence provided in the next section). So it could be assumed that

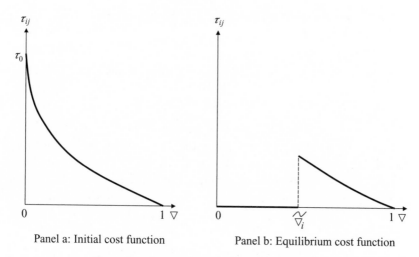

Panel a: Initial cost function   Panel b: Equilibrium cost function

Figure 7.1. Commuting cost function when $i \neq j$.

blacks have a lower ∇ than whites, since there is a lack of good public transportation, especially from the city center to the suburbs, in the United States.

To summarize, what is specific for a location $j = 1, 2$ is the entry cost of firms. This will imply that *wage w_{ij} and productivity y_j will also be location-specific*. However, all other variables will be the same between locations. For example, the job-destruction rate is not location-specific and will thus be denoted by δ.

Independently of where he/she lives, each unemployed worker can look for a job in two locations and each employed worker can work in any of the two locations. L_{ij} and U_{ij} denote the measure of workers residing in i, but working and searching in j. The total labor force residing in i and working and searching in j is: $N_{ij} = U_{ij} + L_{ij}$, which implies that the total labor force in area j is equal to:

$$N_j = N_{1j} + N_{2j}. \tag{7.21}$$

Similarly, we can define the vacancy rate in a location j as:[6]

$$v_j = \frac{V_j}{N_j},$$

---

[6] Contrary to the search models developed in Part 1 and as in Pissarides (2000), the number of vacancies V_j is here defined as a fraction of the total mass of workers N_j and not firms.

and the measure of workers searching for a job in location j as:

$$S_j = U_{1j} + U_{2j}.$$

By normalizing the total population to 1,[7] we finally have:

$$L_i + U_i = L_{i1} + L_{i2} + U_{i1} + U_{i2} = 1, \quad i = 1, 2, \quad (7.22)$$

where $L_i = L_{i1} + L_{i2}$ and $U_i = U_{i1} + U_{i2}$ denote the measure of employed and unemployed workers residing in location i. This means that here, we measure unemployment and employment by *where people live* and not where people search or work. The number of matches per unit of time in location $j = 1, 2$ is thus determined by the following matching function:

$$d_j = d_0\, d\left(S_j, V_j\right), \quad (7.23)$$

where $d_0 > 0$ is a scale parameter of the matching function, $S_j = U_{1j} + U_{2j}$ is the total mass of unemployed workers searching for a job in j and $V_j = v_j N_j$ denotes the total mass of vacancies in location j. As we will see below, workers' search intensity will either be equal to 1 or zero and thus will not appear in the matching function (7.23). As usual, $d(.)$ is assumed to be increasing in both its arguments, be concave and exhibit constant returns to scale (CRS). Thus, the rate at which a firm established in j locates an unemployed worker is given by:

$$\frac{d_j}{V_j} = \frac{d\left(S_j, V_j\right)}{V_j} = d\left(\frac{1}{\theta_j}, 1\right) = q(\theta_j)$$

where

$$\theta_j = \frac{V_j}{S_j} = \frac{V_j}{U_{1j} + U_{2j}}, \quad (7.24)$$

is labor market tightness in area j. Similarly, the rate at which an unemployed worker locates a job offer in area j is equal to:

$$\frac{d_j}{S_j} = \frac{d\left(S_j, V_j\right)}{S_j} = d\left(1, \theta_j\right) = \theta_j\, q(\theta_j).$$

It is crucial to understand the difference between job seekers and unemployed workers. Indeed, for $i \neq j$, we have $S_j = U_{1j} + U_{2j}$ while $U_j = U_{j1} + U_{j2}$. Indeed, job seekers in area j (S_j) include all workers

---

[7] This implies that U_i, the unemployment level in area i, is equal to u_i, the unemployment rate in area i.

who *search* in area j irrespective of their place of residence while unemployed workers in area j (U_j) encompass all individuals who *live* and are unemployed in area j.

We denote by $I_{ijL}(\nabla)$ the discounted lifetime expected utility of an employed worker residing in i, employed in a firm located in j, and having a disutility of commuting equal to ∇. Similarly, $I_{ijU}(\nabla)$ is the discounted lifetime expected utility of an unemployed worker residing in i, searching for a job in j and having a disutility of commuting equal to ∇. In steady-state, the corresponding Bellman equations are, respectively, equal to:

$$r\,I_{ijL}(\nabla) = w_{ij} - \tau_{ij}(\nabla) - \delta\left[I_{ijL}(\nabla) - I_{ijU}(\nabla)\right] \tag{7.25}$$

$$r\,I_{ijU}(\nabla) = w_U - \tau_{ij}(\nabla) + \theta_j\,q(\theta_j)\left[I_{ijL}(\nabla) - I_{ijU}(\nabla)\right]. \tag{7.26}$$

Equation (7.25) states that the flow value of a resident i worker employed in location j equals the present wage minus the commuting costs plus the probability of the worker suffering a capital loss as a result of the breakup of the match. Equation (7.26) has a similar interpretation.

Let e_i and $(1 - e_i)$ denote the effort a resident i worker devotes to search in the CBD ($j = 1$) and the SBD ($j = 2$), respectively. Then, when a resident i worker loses his/her job, he/she must optimally decide where to search. This worker will devote e_i fraction of his/her time to search in area 1 and $1 - e_i$ fraction of his/her time to search in the other area. However,[8] if $I_{i1U}(\nabla) \geq I_{i2U}(\nabla)$, then obviously $e_i = 1$ while if $I_{i1U}(\nabla) < I_{i2U}(\nabla)$, then $e_i = 0$. As a result, although unemployed workers are free to use their unit labor endowment to search for employment in either or both locations, it should be clear that search effort e_i is completely specialized so that e_i is equal to either 0 or 1. Since this decision will clearly depend on the parameter ∇, we have: $e_i(\nabla) = \{0, 1\}$. This implies that, in equilibrium, job seekers will never search simultaneously in two areas. Once they have decided which area gives them the highest expected utility, they put all their effort into this area and stay there for ever. Combining (7.25) and (7.26), we obtain:

$$I_{ijL} - I_{ijU} = \frac{w_{ij} - w_U}{r + \delta + \theta_j\,q(\theta_j)}. \tag{7.27}$$

Observe that although the disutility parameter ∇ appears in both I_{ijL} and I_{ijU}, it is not included in $I_{ijL} - I_{ijU}$ because, once a resident i worker has

---

[8] For simplicity, it is assumed that if $I_{i1U}(\nabla) = I_{i2U}(\nabla)$, then $e_i = 1$, which means that resident i workers only search in location 1.

decided to search and work in a location j, he/she will never change. Using (7.26), this implies that:

$$I_{i1U}(\nabla) \gtrless I_{i2U}(\nabla)$$

$$\Leftrightarrow \tau_{i2}(\nabla) - \tau_{i1}(\nabla) \gtrless \frac{\theta_2 q(\theta_2)(w_{i2} - w_U)}{r + \delta + \theta_2 q(\theta_2)} - \frac{\theta_1 q(\theta_1)(w_{i1} - w_U)}{r + \delta + \theta_1 q(\theta_1)}.$$

$$(7.28)$$

This will determine a value of ∇ such that e_1 will be equal to 1 and 0. It should be clear that workers with a high value of ∇ will be those who will search in the area where they do not live and vice versa.

Let us now write the steady-state Bellman equations for the firms. The discounted lifetime expected profits of a firm located in j with a job filled by a worker residing in i and with an unfilled vacancy are, respectively, given by:

$$r I_{ijF} = y_j - w_{ij} - \delta(I_{ijF} - I_{jV}) \qquad (7.29)$$

$$r I_{jV} = -c_j + q(\theta_j) \left[\left(\frac{U_{1j}}{U_{1j} + U_{2j}} \right) I_{1jF} + \left(\frac{U_{2j}}{U_{1j} + U_{2j}} \right) I_{2jF} - I_V^j \right] \qquad (7.30)$$

where $U_{1j}/(U_{1j} + U_{2j})$ and $U_{2j}/(U_{1j} + U_{2j})$ measure the fraction of workers residing in location 1 (CBD) and 2 (SBD) while searching for a job in j. Equation (7.29) says that the (flow) profit of a firm located in j hiring a resident i worker is the sum of the product of a successful match and the expected capital loss from the break up. In equation (7.30), the bracket term is the expected capital gain from filling a vacancy. Observe that the latter equation reflects the fact that a firm established in j can employ a worker in both locations 1 and 2, which implies that the surplus of a match I_{ijF} may vary with the location of the worker.

3.2. Steady-State Equilibrium

We solve the model in a standard way. Firms enter the labor market up to the point where their expected profits are equal to zero, i.e., $I_{jV} = 0$. Using (7.29) and (7.30), we obtain:

$$I_{ijF} = \frac{y_j - w_{ij}}{r + \delta} \qquad (7.31)$$

$$\frac{c_j(r + \delta)}{q(\theta_j)} = y_j - \left(\frac{U_{1j} w_{1j} + U_{2j} w_{2j}}{U_{1j} + U_{2j}} \right). \qquad (7.32)$$

Wages are determined by a symmetric Nash bargaining between firms and workers, i.e., $\beta = 1/2$. In the bargaining solution, it is assumed that firms do not discriminate among workers according to their residence. In this context, wages are determined by the following sharing of the total surplus:

$$I_{ijF} - I_{jV} = I_{ijL} - I_{ijU} \geq 0, \quad \forall \nabla \in [0, 1].$$

By solving this equation using (7.31) and (7.27), and the fact that $I_{jV} = 0$, we obtain:

$$w_{ij} \equiv w_j = \frac{w_U (r + \delta) + y_j \left[r + \delta + \theta_j q(\theta_j) \right]}{2(r + \delta) + \theta_j q(\theta_j)}, \qquad j = 1, 2. \quad (7.33)$$

Observe that we have $w_{ij} \equiv w_j$ because the agreed bargained wage is independent of each worker's residence i, even though the net income $w_j - \tau_{ij}(\nabla)$ is not. Indeed, if it is optimal for a resident i worker of type ∇ to search for employment in location j, then it remains optimal for him/her to do so in the event that the bargain breaks down, forcing him/her to search for an alternative trading partner.

The steady-state population of job searchers is derived by equating the relevant inflows into and outflows from unemployment. We have $\delta L_{ij} = \theta_j q(\theta_j) U_{ij}$ which, by using the fact that $N_{ij} = U_{ij} + L_{ij}$, can be written as:

$$U_{ij} = \frac{\delta N_{ij}}{\delta + \theta_j q(\theta_j)}, \qquad i = 1, 2, \quad j = 1, 2. \quad (7.34)$$

Now using (7.33) and (7.34) and the fact that $w_{1j} = w_{2j} = w_j$, the job-creation equation (7.32) can be written as:

$$\frac{c_j (r + \delta)}{q(\theta_j)} = y_j - w_{1j}$$

$$\Leftrightarrow \frac{c_j}{q(\theta_j)} = \frac{y_j - w_U}{2(r + \delta) + \theta_j q(\theta_j)}, \qquad j = 1, 2. \quad (7.35)$$

We need to close the model by determining the steady-state distribution of the labor force across the two zones, in particular the workers who are searching outside their residential location. Let us thus rewrite (7.28) using (7.33) and observing that $w_{i1} = w_1$ and $w_{i2} = w_2$. We obtain:

$$\tau_{i2}(\nabla) - \tau_{i1}(\nabla) \gtrless \frac{\theta_2 q(\theta_2)(y_2 - w_U)}{2(r + \delta) + \theta_2 q(\theta_2)} - \frac{\theta_1 q(\theta_1)(y_1 - w_U)}{2(r + \delta) + \theta_1 q(\theta_1)}.$$

$$(7.36)$$

Furthermore, by plugging (7.27) into (7.26), we have:

$$r\,I_{ijU}\,(\nabla) = \frac{w_U\,(r + \delta) + w_{ij}\,\theta_j\,q(\theta_j)}{r + \delta + \theta_j\,q(\theta_j)} - \tau_{ij}\,(\nabla), \qquad (7.37)$$

which implies that $I_{ijU}\,(\nabla)$ is independent of ∇ if $i = j$ (since $\tau_{ii} = 0$) and that $I_{ijU}\,(\nabla)$ is increasing in ∇ if $i \neq j$ (since $\partial\tau_{ij}/\partial\nabla < 0$). Consequently, if commuting occurs in equilibrium, then it is by the workers with the lowest commuting cost, i.e., the highest value of $\nabla \in [0, 1]$. It follows from (7.37) that there exists a unique threshold value $\widetilde{\nabla}_i$, such that every worker residing in location i and having a (high) disutility of commuting $r \in [0, \widetilde{\nabla}_i]$ optimally searches for a job at $j = i$ (i.e., in the same location as their residence), while all workers residing at i and having a disutility $\nabla \in (\widetilde{\nabla}_i, 1]$ optimally search for a job at $j \neq i$ (i.e., in a different location than their residence). Figure 7.1, panel b, displays the equilibrium commuting cost function. Using (7.36), the threshold value $\widetilde{\nabla}_i$ that partitions workers into "stayers" and "movers" is defined by the following equation for $i = 1, 2$:

$$\tau_{i2}\left(\widetilde{\nabla}_i\right) - \tau_{i1}\left(\widetilde{\nabla}_i\right) = \frac{\theta_2\,q\,(\theta_2)\,(y_2 - w_U)}{2\,(r + \delta) + \theta_2\,q(\theta_2)} - \frac{\theta_1\,q\,(\theta_1)\,(y_1 - w_U)}{2\,(r + \delta) + \theta_1\,q(\theta_1)}.$$
$$(7.38)$$

Finally, given the value of ∇, the labor force participating in each location is given by:

$$N_{11} = N_{22} = \widetilde{\nabla}_i \qquad (7.39)$$

and

$$N_{12} = N_{21} = 1 - \widetilde{\nabla}_i. \qquad (7.40)$$

Definition 7.2. *A steady-state search equilibrium is a 14-uple* ($w_1, w_2, \theta_1,$ $\theta_2, U_{11}, U_{12}, U_{21}, U_{22}, \widetilde{\nabla}_1, \widetilde{\nabla}_2, N_{11}, N_{22}, N_{12}, N_{21}$) *such that* (7.33), (7.35), (7.34), (7.38), (7.39), *and* (7.40) *hold.*

It can be shown that there is a unique steady-state search equilibrium (Coulson, Laing, and Wang, 2001).

3.3. Spatial Mismatch

Using this model, we want to characterize a steady-state search equilibrium that has the features of the spatial mismatch. In particular, we are interested in an equilibrium where none of the SBD unemployed workers search for a job in the CBD, i.e., $I_{22U} > I_{21U}\,(\nabla)$, while the opposite is not true, i.e.,

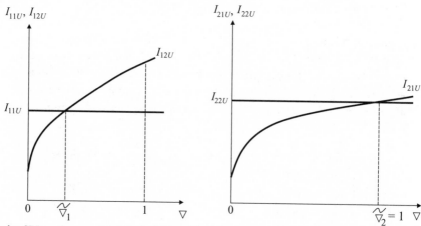

Panel a: CBD workers search both in the CBD and the SBD   Panel b: SBD workers search only in the SBD

Figure 7.2. Equilibrium with asymmetric commuting.

$I_{12U}(\nabla) > I_{11U}$. The latter can be defined as reverse commuting since CBD residents will commute to the SBD. This will create a high unemployment rate in the CBD, a feature consistent with the spatial mismatch hypothesis (see Table 7.1). For this reason, we need to find an *interior* threshold value $\widetilde{\nabla}_1 \in (0, 1)$ and a corner solution $\widetilde{\nabla}_2 = 1$, where these two values are, respectively, defined by:

$$r I_{11U} = \frac{w_U(r+\delta) + w_{11}\theta_1 q(\theta_1)}{r + \delta + \theta_1 q(\theta_1)}$$
$$= \frac{w_U(r+\delta) + w_{12}\theta_2 q(\theta_2)}{r + \delta + \theta_2 q(\theta_2)} - \tau_{12}\left(\widetilde{\nabla}_1\right) = r I_{12U}\left(\widetilde{\nabla}_1\right) \quad (7.41)$$

$$r I_{22U} = \frac{w_U(r+\delta) + w_{22}\theta_2 q(\theta_2)}{r + \delta + \theta_2 q(\theta_2)}$$
$$= \frac{w_U(r+\delta) + w_{21}\theta_1 q(\theta_1)}{r + \delta + \theta_1 q(\theta_1)} - \tau_{21}\left(\widetilde{\nabla}_2\right) = r I_{21U}\left(\widetilde{\nabla}_2\right). \quad (7.42)$$

In particular, we look for the two following conditions to be satisfied:

$$I_{12U}(0) < I_{11U} < I_{12U}(1) \quad (7.43)$$

$$I_{22U} \leq I_{21U}(\nabla) \qquad \forall \nabla \in [0, 1]. \quad (7.44)$$

Figure 7.2 illustrates equations (7.41) and (7.42) for which conditions (7.43) and (7.44) are satisfied.

We have the following result:[9]

Proposition 7.3. *If $\tau_0 > 0$, $c_1 - c_2$ is sufficiently large and $y_1 - y_2$ is sufficiently small so that conditions (7.43) and (7.44) hold, then there exists a unique steady-state search equilibrium in which none of the SBD unemployed workers search for a job in the CBD while CBD unemployed workers search for a job in both centers. In that case, the labor market equilibrium is such that:*

(*i*) *the unemployment rate is higher for central city residents than for suburban residents;*

(*ii*) *the vacancy rate in the CBD is lower than that in the SBD;*

(*iii*) *workers in the suburbs earn a higher wage than those in the CBD.*

As can be seen from this proposition, in equilibrium, the city has the features associated with the spatial mismatch hypothesis. This result strongly depends on assumption (*H*1), i.e., that the entry cost is higher in the CBD than in the SBD. Let us give the intuition of this result.

A higher entry cost for CBD firms implies that these firms will enter less in the labor market (and thus create less jobs) than SBD firms. As a result, the contact rate for workers searching in the CBD $\theta_1 q(\theta_1)$ will be lower than in the SBD while the contact rate for firms in the CBD $q(\theta_1)$ will be higher than in the SBD. In fact, when the difference in entry costs between the CBD and SBD is large enough, which means that the worker contact rate in the CBD is much lower than in the SBD and the firm contact rate is much higher, then it is never profitable for SBD workers to commute to the CBD while the reverse in not true. This is because the threshold value $\widetilde{V}_1$ is affected by these contact rates (see (7.41) and (7.42)).

Also, since the vacancy rate depends inversely on the firm contact rate while the unemployment rate depends inversely on the worker contact rate (see (7.34)), result (*i*) and (*ii*) follow. Concerning the wage, as the entry cost is higher in the CBD, there is a direct negative effect on the wage because of the enhanced bargaining power of firms. In addition, as we have seen, the higher entry cost in the CBD reduces the entry of firms in the CBD and lowers the equilibrium worker contact rate, which also reduces the wage (by weakening each worker's bargaining strength). These two effects work in the same direction, implying an unambiguous lower wage level in the CBD (result (*iii*)).

---

[9] Remember that τ_0 is the constant part of the commuting cost τ_{ij} (∇) defined in (7.20).

Observe also that search frictions are crucial in explaining the results of Proposition 7.3. Indeed, as search frictions vanish, i.e., $d_0 \rightarrow +\infty$, all firms enter the SBD labor market, and no workers are employed in the CBD. This implies that differential entry costs, together with nontrivial search frictions, are sufficient to generate spatial mismatch.

3.4. Policy Implications

What are the policy implications of this model? Since differential entry costs and search frictions are the main culprits in creating spatial mismatch, improvements in the efficiency of the matching function (better information, better market structure organization) and/or in the transportation infrastructure will reduce unemployment. Another policy would be to reduce the differential in the fixed entry cost in order to partially alleviate the spatial mismatch.

Proposition 7.4.

(*i*) *For each job center, a decrease in the entry cost (lower c_j) reduces the unemployment rate and increases the job vacancy rate in both locations;*

(*ii*) *An increase in matching efficacy (higher d_0) reduces both the unemployment rate and the job vacancy rate in both locations;*

(*iii*) *An improvement in the transportation technology (lower τ_0) reduces the unemployment rate for CBD residents but does not affect the vacancy rate in any location.*

Results (*i*) and (*ii*) are not surprising since a reduction in c_j induces firms to create more jobs which, in turn, improves workers' job contact rate $\theta_j q(\theta_j)$ and an increase in d_0 increases the contact rate of both workers and firms. Result (*iii*) is more interesting and can be explained as follows. When τ_0 decreases, the net value of search increases (higher net wages), inducing a greater number of CBD residents to search in the SBD, thus reducing $\widetilde{V}_1$. Since job offers are also given at a faster rate in the SBD than in the CBD, the unemployment rate is reduced in the latter.

Interestingly, policies consisting of subsidizing the entry costs of firms in the CBD have been implemented in the United States and in Europe. Indeed, in the United States, the enterprise zone programs (Papke, 1994; Boarnet and Bogart, 1996; Mauer and Ott, 1999; Bondonio and Engberg, 2000; Bollinger and Ihlanfeldt, 2003; Bondonio and Greenbaum, 2007) consist of designating a specific urban (or rural) area, which is depressed, and targeting it for economic development through government-provided subsidies to labor and capital. In Europe, such policies have also been implemented. In France, for example, any firm that desires to set up in a depressed area ("zone franche") is exempt from tax, but 20% of its workforce must consist of local workers. Typically, such policies act on residential segregation and thus, on redlining, but not on labor discrimination.

4. Different Transport Modes

To more accurately capture the phenomenon of spatial mismatch, we need to take into account the fact that workers can choose between two modes of transportation – mass transit and the car – and that there is a relatively low incidence of car ownership among blacks. This, in fact, will reinforce the spatial mismatch problem for blacks since they are not only far away from jobs, but because of the lack of good public transportation in large U.S. metropolitan areas it is difficult for them to access to these jobs, as confirmed by Table 7.5.

Let us provide some facts about transportation modes. In the United States, blacks essentially take public transports to commute to their workplace, whereas whites are more likely to use their cars. To be more precise, using data drawn from the 1995 Nationwide Personal Transportation Survey, Raphael and Stoll (2001) show that in the Untied States, 5.4% of white households have no automobile while 24% and 12% of black and Latino households, respectively, do not hold a single car.[10] Even more striking, they show that 64% and 46% of black and Latino households, respectively, have one or no car whereas this number was 36% for white households. In Great Britain, using the 1991 census data, Owen and Green (2000) show that people from minority ethnic groups are more than twice as likely as white people to depend on public transportation for commuting journeys (33.2% versus 13.7%), with nearly three-fifths of Black-African workers using public transportation to go to work. Furthermore, 73.6% of the whites use private vehicles while this number is only 56.4% for ethnic minorities (and 39.6% for Black-African workers). Using the Labour Force Survey for England, Patacchini and Zenou (2005) find similar results. They show that the percentage of whites and blacks using coach, bus or British rail train to

---

[10] These differences indicate that black and Latino households are disproportionately represented among households with no automobiles. Indeed, while black and Latino households constituted 11.5% and 7.8% of all households in 1995, respectively, they accounted for 35% and 12% of the households with no vehicles.

travel to work is 15% and 40.2%, respectively, and the percentage of whites and blacks using car or scooters is 79.1% and 57.7%, respectively. On the other hand, the percentage of white and black active job seekers owning or using a motor vehicle is 75.8% and 55.4%, respectively.

We would now like to propose different models that take into account the differential in transport modes between blacks and whites and examine the implications in terms of labor market outcomes.

4.1. A First Simple Model

Consider a continuum of workers and firms. There are two types of workers: black and white $(i = B, W)$. The masses of black and white workers are taken to be N_B and N_W, while the total mass of workers is equal to 1, i.e., $N_B + N_W = 1$. Blacks and whites are totally identical except for the fact that they do not use the same transport mode. We indeed assume that whites mainly use private modes of transportation (cars) whereas blacks mainly use public transportation.[11]

As in the benchmark model of Chapter 1, housing consumption is fixed and normalized to 1 for all workers (employed and unemployed) and the city is linear, monocentric, and closed.

Workers can either be employed or unemployed. The budget constraint of an unemployed worker $i = B, W$ living in the city depends on his/her location, the transport mode, and the information gathered about jobs in the employment center. In our framework, each unemployed individual commutes to the center to gather information about jobs. This is not the only way of obtaining information since (see below) job information can also be obtained by buying newspapers or calling friends. However, each return trip from the residential location to the employment center allows the worker to have some additional information that is not accessible without going to the center (for example, looking at some ads that are locally posted or having interviews with employment agencies that are located at the center). What is crucial for the unemployed is their *job (or information) access* which is measured by both the *physical* distance to jobs and the *time distance* to reach the center (i.e., the trip time). For a worker $i = B, W$, these two "distances" are related:

$$l_i = \frac{x_i}{\varpi_i}, \tag{7.45}$$

---

[11] This choice of transportation will be endogeneized in Section 4.3 below.

where x_i is the physical distance to jobs for a worker i, ϖ_i denotes the average trip speed (which crucially depends on the transport mode) and ι_i is the time for *each return trip* to the employment center. This corresponds to equation (3.14) in Chapter 3. Thus, if τ_i denotes the *pecuniary* cost per unit of physical distance to commute to the employment center and ι^0 a positive constant, then the total cost per return trip to gather information about jobs in the employment center for unemployed workers is given by:

$$\tau_i\, x_i + \iota^0\, \iota_i. \qquad (7.46)$$

In this formulation, there are two types of costs for commuting to the center. The first, $\tau_i\, x_i$, is the total *pecuniary* cost at a distance x_i and the second, $\iota^0\, \iota_i$, is the *time* cost (even though this not explicitly modeled, there is an opportunity cost of traveling because of forgone leisure). We can now express these costs in the same units. If they are expressed in terms of physical distance x_i, they are equal to:

$$\left(\tau_i + \frac{\iota^0}{\varpi_i}\right) x_i$$

whereas, if they are expressed in terms of time distance t_i, they are given by

$$\left(\tau_i \varpi_i + \iota^0\right) \iota_i.$$

Let us focus on time distance rather than physical distance for, in our opinion, job access is crucially determined by the former and not the latter. As a result, we will express all our relations in terms of ι_i and when we write distance to jobs or job access, it means time distance to jobs. We can now determine the *total* cost of gathering information about jobs at a distance ι_i from the employment center. It is given by:

$$\left(\tau_i \varpi_i + \iota^0\right) \iota_i\, s_i, \qquad (7.47)$$

where $0 \leq s_i \leq 1$ is the search-effort rate provided by worker $i = B, W$. Obviously, the higher is s_i, the more often the unemployed worker must travel to the employment center to gather information about jobs. In this formulation, ι_i is a measure of job access (how "well" the unemployed worker is connected to jobs) while s_i is a measure of search intensity (how many hours per day the unemployed worker spends searching for a job).

If the individual *unemployment benefit* is denoted by w_U, the instantaneous budget constraint of an unemployed worker i living at a distance ι_i from the employment center is equal to:

$$w_U = z_i + R(\iota_i \varpi_i) + C(s_i) + \left(\tau_i \varpi_i + \iota^0\right) \iota_i\, s_i, \qquad (7.48)$$

where z_i denotes the composite good consumption (which is taken as the numeraire) for a worker i, $R(\iota_i \varpi_i)$, is the prevailing land rent per unit of land at each distance $x_i = \iota_i \varpi_i$, and $C(s_i)$ denotes all searching costs that are not distance-related. The latter encompasses the costs of buying newspapers, making phone calls, etc. We assume that $C(0) = 0$, $C'(s_i) > 0$ and $C''(s_i) > 0$. In this formulation, the total cost of searching is thus $C(s_i) + (\tau_i \varpi_i + \iota^0) \iota_i s_i$, which encompasses both search costs that are not distance-related and costs that involve commuting to the employment center.

Let us now focus on the employed worker. He/she has the following budget constraint:

$$w_L = z_i + R(\iota_i \varpi_i) + \mathbb{T}_i + \left(\tau_i \varpi_i + \iota^1 w_L \right) \iota_i, \qquad (7.49)$$

where w_L is the wage paid to workers (black or white), ι^1 is a positive constant that is different from ι^0, and $\mathbb{T}_i$ is the fixed cost of transportation irrespective of race. We assume that at the same distance to jobs ι_i, the total cost of search activities for the unemployed is lower than the total commuting cost of the employed, that is, for each $i = B, W$,

$$\left(\tau_i \varpi_i + \iota^0 \right) s_i < \tau_i \varpi_i + \iota^1 w_L. \qquad (7.50)$$

This is a well-documented fact. For instance, Layard, Nickell, and Jackman (1991) show that the time spent in job search activities is quite low compared to the commuting time of the employed. Furthermore, our assumption that whites use cars and blacks public transportation implies that:

$$\mathbb{T}_W > \mathbb{T}_B, \varpi_W > \varpi_B \quad \text{and} \quad \tau_W \varpi_W < \tau_B \varpi_B, \qquad (7.51)$$

i.e., cars used by whites have a higher fixed cost, but are faster and entail a lower variable cost than public transportation for the same time distance, $\iota_B = \iota_W = \iota$.

This is a search model, so let us define the matching function for workers of type $i = B, W$. It is given by:[12]

$$d_i \equiv d(\bar{s}_i u_i N_i, V_i) \qquad (7.52)$$

where, as usual, u_i and V_i denote the unemployment rate and the number of vacancies of type i-workers and $\bar{s}_i$, the average search efficiency for workers of type i in the city. Each individual's search efficiency, s_i, depends on his/her effort e_i, i.e., $s_i \equiv s(e_i)$. We assume decreasing returns to scale to effort, i.e., $s'(e_i) > 0$ and $s''(e_i) \leq 0$. As in Chapter 1, we adopt the standard

---

[12] This matching function assumes that the labor market of blacks and whites are separated. We will relax this assumption below.

assumptions on the matching function. All workers are assumed to be risk neutral and infinitely lived. Therefore, the expected discounted lifetime utility of an employed and an unemployed worker i living at a distance $x_i = \varpi_i \iota_i$ from the employment center is given by:

$$r I_{iL} = w_L - R(\varpi_i \iota_i) - \mathbb{T}_i - (\tau_i \varpi_i + \iota^1) \iota_i - \delta [I_{iL} - I_{iU}(e_i)] \quad (7.53)$$

$$r I_{iU}(e_i) = w_U - R(\varpi_i \iota_i) - C(s(e_i)) - (\tau_i \varpi_i + \iota^0) \iota_i s(e_i)$$

$$+ s(e_i) \frac{d(\bar{s}_i u_i N, V_i)}{\bar{s}_i u_i N} [I_{iL} - I_{iU}(e_i)], \quad (7.54)$$

where $r \in (0, 1)$ is the discount rate and δ the job-destruction rate. By subtracting one equation from the other, we obtain:

$$I_{iL} - I_{iU}(e_i)$$
$$= \frac{w_L - w_U - \mathbb{T}_i + C(s(e_i)) - (\tau_i \varpi_i + \iota^1) \iota_i + (\tau_i \varpi_i + \iota^0) \iota_i s(e_i)}{r + \delta + s(e_i) d(\bar{s}_i u_i N, V_i) / (\bar{s}_i u_i N)}.$$
$$(7.55)$$

4.1.1. *Search Intensity Within Each Race.* Let us now study the search effort decision for each type of worker. In other words, we would like to analyze the search decision within each race (black and white) and examine how s_i is related to job access ι_i. When making the search effort decision, e_i, the unemployed worker of type i takes as given the unemployment rate u in the city where he/she lives, the local number of vacancies V (and thus $\theta = V/(u N)$, the local labor market tightness), the local land rent and the expected discounted lifetime utilities $I_{iL} - I_{iU}(e_i)$. By maximizing (7.54) with respect to e_i, we obtain for $i = B, W$:

$$\frac{\partial I_{iU}(e_i)}{\partial e_i} = -\frac{\partial C}{\partial s} s'(e_i^*) - (\tau_i \varpi_i + \iota^0) \iota_i s'(e_i^*)$$

$$+ s'(e_i^*) \frac{d(\bar{s}_i u_i N, V_i)}{\bar{s}_i u_i N} [I_{iL} - I_{iU}(e_i^*)] = 0, \quad (7.56)$$

where e_i^* is the unique solution to this maximization problem, and $s_i^* = s(e_i^*)$ is the corresponding optimal search efficiency and $I_{iL} - I_{iU}(e_i^*)$ is given by (7.55). Let us give the intuition for (7.56). When choosing e_i^*, there is a fundamental trade-off between short-run and long-run benefits for an unemployed individual i located at a distance ι_i from the job center. On the one hand, increasing search effort e_i to gather more information about jobs is costly in the short run (today) because it decreases instantaneous utility, $-\frac{\partial C}{\partial s} s'(e_i^*) - (\tau_i \varpi_i + \iota^0) \iota_i s'(e_i^*) < 0$, so that the worker consumes less of the composite good (budget constraint). On the other hand, increasing search effort e_i increases the long-run (tomorrow) prospects of employment since it increases the probability of obtaining a job $s'(e_i^*)\frac{d(\bar{s}_i u_i N, V_i)}{\bar{s}_i u_i N} > 0$ and the surplus $I_{iL} - I_{iU}(e_i^*)$ with which it is associated.

Since, within each race, all workers are identical, they all choose the same effort level e_i^* and thus, the average effort level $\bar{e}_i^*$ is equal to individual search effort, i.e. $\bar{e}_i^* = e_i^*$. The average search efficiency of each type of worker is thus given by $\bar{s}_W = s(e_W)$ and $\bar{s}_B = s(e_B)$.

Proposition 7.5. *For both blacks and whites, the worse the access to jobs is (i.e., the longer the time distance), the lower the individual and average search intensities are.*

This result shows that if unemployed workers have poor access to jobs (they are "far away" in terms of time distance), they will search less than those who have better access because *it takes more time (and is thus more costly) to gather information about jobs.* Indeed, when ι_i increases, the instantaneous cost of searching (i.e., gathering information about jobs) increases and the possible surplus of finding a job $I_{iL} - I_{iU}(e_i^*)$ is reduced because of the time spent in search activities being shorter than the commuting time of the employed (see (7.50)). The difference in commuting costs between the employed and the unemployed then increases. As a result, workers residing further away from jobs do not only have a higher cost of gathering information today, but also a higher commuting cost tomorrow if they find a job. This proposition says that if we control for transportation mode (i.e., we fix ϖ_i and τ_i) and thus focus on the search behavior of blacks and whites separately, then remote locations reduce the search intensity for any worker, i.e., $\bar{s}_i'(\iota_i) < 0$, $i = B, W$.

This proposition basically gives a theoretical mechanism for the spatial mismatch. By fixing the transport mode, we are only able to see the impact of job access on search intensity. This result is related to that highlighted in Section 2, where the efficiency of job search decreased with distance to jobs because workers were obtaining less information about distant job opportunities. There is, however, one main difference between the two explanations. First, in Section 2, the instantaneous cost of searching for a job was $C(s_i)$ whereas here it is given by $C(s_i) + (\tau_i \varpi_i + \iota^0)\iota_i s_i$. This implies that here, we in some sense open the black box of the previous model by highlighting the importance of transport mode in acquiring information about jobs. The other mechanism highlighted in Section 2 was that distance to jobs reduced search effort, not because of a higher time cost for obtaining information about jobs, but because of lower land rent, and thus a lower cost of being unemployed. We believe that these three mechanisms explain why distance to jobs reduces search intensity, i.e., lower housing prices, reduced information about jobs, higher costs of gathering information are complementary.

4.1.2. Search Intensity Between Races. We would now like to compare black and white workers with exactly the same access to jobs, i.e., the same time distance $\iota_W = \iota_B = \iota$. In other words, if we take two workers, one black and one white, located at exactly the same time distance ι from the employment center and who only differ by their transportation mode, who will provide the higher search effort? The following proposition provides a clear answer to this question.

Proposition 7.6. *Assume that black workers use public transportation to commute to the job center while whites use private vehicles. If we compare a black and a white unemployed worker who have exactly the same access to jobs (i.e., the same time distance), the white unemployed worker will search more intensively than the black.*

This proposition is in some sense the dual of Proposition 7.5. Indeed, instead of fixing ϖ_i and τ_i and seeing the impact of different degress of job access on search intensities (Proposition 7.5), here we fix job access ι and evaluate the impact of different transport modes on search decisions.

If we are comparing white and nonwhite workers who both live exactly at the same time-distance from the employment center ($\iota_W = \iota_B = \iota$), whites have a lower variable commuting cost of (time) distance because they use a private transport mode, i.e., $\tau_W \varpi_W < \tau_B \varpi_B$ (see (7.51)). As a result, it is less costly for whites to gather information about jobs, and thus they search more intensively than nonwhites. To be more precise, when the variable pecuniary cost is higher, workers have a higher instantaneous cost of gathering information, but also, if they find a job, a higher commuting cost and thus, a lower surplus. Since they have a lower incentive for searching for a job today and tomorrow, their search activity rate is lower.

In this proposition, by fixing job access, we show that transport mode in itself has a significant impact on search intensities. Empirically, Raphael and Stoll (2001) find that raising minority car-ownership rates to the white car-ownership rate would considerably narrow inter-racial employment-rate differentials. Similarly, Raphael, and Rice (2002) show that there is a positive relationship between car ownership and employment outcomes. Using British data, Patacchini and Zenou (2005) show that giving ethnic workers the mean level of white (time) distance to jobs and white car access would close the racial gap in search intensity by 50.31%. Finally, we have the following result.

Corollary 1. *Assume that blacks use public transportation to commute to the center while whites use private vehicles. Assume also that blacks have a worse job access than whites. Then, their search intensity is lower than that of whites.*

This corollary is a straightforward extension of the two previous propositions. It is consistent with empirical studies. In particular, Holzer, Ihlanfeldt, and Sjoquist (1994) found that blacks do not only have longer travel times to work, but also cover less distance while searching. As in our model, this implies that the time cost per mile traveled is thus substantially higher for blacks than for whites. They also find that the higher time cost is partly accounted for by the lower rates of car ownership among blacks.

4.2. A More General Model

Let us now generalize the previous approach by using the model in Chapter 3, Section 3. To be more precise, we would like to develop a model where *blacks and whites are all at equal distance to jobs* and where firms have *no taste for discrimination*. But, if there is a slight difference in wealth between blacks and whites due to historical reasons (slavery, etc.), which implies that blacks choose public transportation while whites choose cars, then we will show that black workers will search less intensively and extensively than whites, experience a higher unemployment rate, and obtain a lower wage even though they are totally identical otherwise.

Thus, we assume that even though blacks and whites are both low-skill workers and have the same level of human capital, they do not compete for the same jobs and thus, their labor markets are separated (or segmented). We also assume that firms perfectly observe the location of all workers.[13] Assuming segmented labor markets between blacks and whites is in accordance with some recent evidence suggesting that blacks are much more likely to be employed in some types of firms that in others (Leonard, 1990; Bound and Holzer, 1993; Holzer, 1998; Holzer and Ihlanfeldt, 1998; Holzer and Reaser, 2000).

---

[13] These two assumptions of segmented labor markets and of perfect information will be relaxed in Section 4.3.

Black and white workers are assumed to be totally identical except for some initial wealth difference that leads them not to use the same transport mode. If $\mathbb{T}$ denotes the per-period fixed cost of using a certain transport mode, then because of initial wealth difference, if $\mathbb{T}$ is high enough for cars, then whites mainly use private modes of transportation (cars), whereas blacks mainly use public transportation. Remember that for a car, $\mathbb{T}$ encompasses the cost of maintaining a car, the insurance fees, etc. So, for example, if $\mathbb{T}$ is very high for cars, then blacks will not be able to afford to buy a car because of credit constraints.

As a result, the total cost of commuting to jobs for employed black and white workers is given by: $\mathbb{T}_B + \iota_B^1 \, w_{BL} \, x/\varpi_B$ and $\mathbb{T}_W + \iota_W^1 \, w_{WL} \, x/\varpi_W$. As before, we assume (7.51), i.e., cars used by whites have higher fixed costs, lower variable costs and are faster. For simplicity, the instantaneous utility of the unemployed workers is: $w_U - R_i - C(s_i)$ and not $w_U - R_i - C(s_i) - (\tau_i \varpi_i + \iota^0) \iota_i \, s(e_i)$ as in the previous section. This means that when they look for a job, the unemployed workers do not need to commute to the job center. Moreover, for employed workers, the instantaneous utility is: $w_{iL} - R_i - \mathbb{T}_i - \iota_i^1 \, w_L \, \iota_i$ instead of $w_{iL} - R_i - \mathbb{T}_i - \iota_i^1 \, w_L \, \iota_i - \iota_i^1 w_{iL} \iota_i$ as in the previous section.

As in Chapter 3, Section 3, workers are located on the circumference of a circle of length 1 so that $0 \leq x \leq 1/2$ denotes the distance between a residential location and a firm. We can write the discounted lifetime expected utilities of unemployed and employed type–i workers as:

$$r\, I_{iU}(s) = w_U - R_i - C(s_i) + s_i\, \theta q(\theta) \left[2\int_0^{\widehat{x}_i} [I_{iL}(x) - I_{iU}(s)]\, dx \right] \quad (7.57)$$

$$r\, I_{iL}(x) = w_{iL}(x) \left(1 - \iota_i^1 \frac{x}{\varpi_i} \right) - R_i - \mathbb{T}_i - \delta\, [I_{iL}(x) - I_{iU}(s)] \quad (7.58)$$

where the wage $w_{iL}(x)$ is a function of x and is given by (3.20) (see Chapter 3, Section 3), s_i is the search intensity and determined by (3.22), and $\widehat{x}_i$, which is given by (3.23), is the maximum geographical distance at which the unemployed worker of type i accepts to take a job (beyond $\widehat{x}_i$, all jobs will be turned down by the type i–unemployed worker). We have the following result.

Proposition 7.7. *We have:*

(*i*) *Whites search more intensively and obtain a higher wage than blacks, i.e., $s_W^* > s_B^*$ and $w_{WL}^* > w_{BL}^*$.*

(*ii*) *Assume for both types of workers that*

$$\widehat{x}_i^* > \frac{\beta \, c \, s_i^* \varpi_i}{y(1-\beta)\iota_i^!} \frac{\partial \theta}{\partial \varpi}, \quad i = B, W, \tag{7.59}$$

then white unemployed have a larger area of search than blacks, i.e., $\widehat{x}_W^* > \widehat{x}_B^*$*, and have a shorter mean time commute, i.e.,* $\overline{\iota}_W^* < \overline{\iota}_B^*$*. Moreover, whites will also experience lower unemployment rates, i.e.,* $u_W^* < u_B^*$*, and a shorter unemployment duration than blacks, and firms will create more jobs for whites, i.e.,* $V_W > V_B$*.*

First, whites who use faster transport modes (higher ϖ) than blacks do search more intensively. Indeed, when whites decide s, they trade off short-run losses against long-run gains. However, because they use a faster transport mode, white unemployed workers anticipate that, for a given s and θ, they can reach jobs located further away so they increase $\widehat{x}$. This, in turn, induces firms to create more jobs and it increases θ, which finally induces white workers to search more because of better opportunities. Since all white workers behave in the same way, their average search intensity is higher than that of blacks. Second, the effect on labor market tightness is now straightforward. Indeed, because of a faster transport mode, for a given s and θ, whites have a higher $\widehat{x}$, which, in turn, induces firms to create more jobs so that θ increases. Third, whites' wages are higher because white workers have better outside options than blacks (because of higher θ and higher $\widehat{x}$).

Finally, the general equilibrium effects of ϖ on $\widehat{x}^*$ are interesting. Indeed, we know from the model in Chapter 3, Section 3 (see equation (3.23)) that, for a given s and a given θ, a faster transport mode increases $\widehat{x}$. This is because a faster transport mode implies a lower opportunity cost of time and thus workers are willing to accept jobs located further way. However, in equilibrium, not only this effect but also the indirect effect of ϖ on search intensity must be taken into account (since when ϖ increases, the effect on s is ambiguous) and on labor market tightness (since when ϖ increases, firms anticipate that workers will accept jobs located further away and thus create more jobs which, in turn, induces workers to be more choosy and thus, to reduce $\widehat{x}$). It turns out that when ϖ increases, only the effects of commuting time and labor market tightness are of importance (indeed, the search intensity effect cancels out because when ϖ increases, workers search more, but it also costs more) and condition (7.59) expresses this result. It says that if the commuting time effect (the left-hand side of (7.59)) dominates the labor market tightness effect (the right-hand side of (7.59)), then a rise in ϖ increases $\widehat{x}^*$. As a result, white unemployed workers will have a smaller area of search than blacks if (7.59) holds. Thus, the average commuting time will be shorter for whites since they use a faster transport mode and have a smaller area of employment if (7.59) holds. Now, if the latter holds, then $\widehat{x}^*_W > \widehat{x}^*_B$ and since whites search more intensively and firms create more jobs, they will experience lower unemployment rates, and a shorter unemployment duration (remember that in a Poisson process unemployment duration is equal to the inverse of the job acquisition rate) than blacks.

Few empirical studies have tried to test these last two results. For the U.K., McCormick (1986) has shown that because of labor discrimination, ethnic minorities (Asian and West Indian workers) are ready to accept jobs in locations that would be unacceptable to whites, either in order to avoid a spell of unemployment or an inferior occupation. This is what we obtain if (7.59) does not hold. Naturally, if discrimination were introduced in our model, then McCormick's result would be stronger. Moreover, most studies have shown that the mean daily commute is shorter for whites than for blacks (see, e.g., Patachini and Zenou, 2005, for the U.K.; Chung, Myers, and Saunders, 2001, and Gottlieb and Lentnek, 2001, for the U.S.). This is what we obtained here because whites use faster transport modes and, if (7.59) holds, because they are on average closer to jobs than blacks. Finally, using the National Longitudinal Survey Youth Cohort (NLSYC) for 1981 and 1982, Holzer, Ihlanfeldt, and Sjoquist (1994) provide results that are very close to that of Proposition 7.7. Here is what they found (Table 7.6).

This data conforms to what we have obtained in Proposition 7.9. First, this table shows lower employment and wages for blacks, as well as durations of unemployment levels that are more than 25 to 30% higher for blacks than for whites. Second, blacks spend significantly more time traveling to work than whites, even though the distance traveled is shorter for blacks. This is certainly due to different transport modes (in their study, 68.5% of white males own a car while this number is 43.8% for blacks; also 4.1% of white males use mass transit while this number is 18.9% for blacks). The time spent per mile traveled is thus considerably higher for blacks–about 46% higher. All these results are quite standard and obtained by most studies. The last outcome concerning the miles traveled searching is less clear since different studies find different results. Here, black job seekers have a smaller area of search than whites. In Proposition 7.9, because of general equilibrium effects, this was not always true and depended on condition (7.59). In fact, using data from the 1994 Los Angeles Survey of Urban Inequality,

Table 7.6. *Search and labor market outcomes for blacks and whites in the U.S.*

	White males	Black males
Miles traveled to work	8.017	6.977
	(11.352)	(9.879)
Miles traveled searching $\hat{x}^*$	19.923	18.558
	(25.328)	(22.718)
Time spent traveling to work $\bar{t}^*$	15.841	18.603
	(15.058)	(17.482)
Time spent per mile traveled	3.351	4.899
	(3.851)	(5.963)
Log (wage), 1981 w_L^*	6.080	5.997
	(0.393)	(0.370)
Log (wage), 1982 w_L^*	6.246	6.112
	(0.447)	(0.421)
Employment, 1981 $1 - u^*$	0.594	0.456
Employment, 1982 $1 - u^*$	0.618	0.452
Log (duration of unemployment)	1.591	1.838
	(0.841)	(0.913)

Values given in this table are means while those given in parentheses are standard deviations.
Source: Holzer, Ihlanfeldt, and Sjoquist (1994).

Stoll (1999) finds that blacks use spatial job search to a greater degree than whites, as measured by the number of areas searched. So there is no real consensus on this issue.

4.3. Firms Do Not Observe Workers' Location, and Labor Markets are Integrated

As in Chapter 3, Section 3, workers' and firms' locations are uniformly distributed on the circumference $\mathbb{C}$ of a circle of length 1. Because the labor market of blacks and whites are now integrated, both types of workers are located in the circle. We restrict attention to initial distribution such that the same proportion of workers (black and white) are unemployed at all locations. This implies that a stationary equilibrium must have a uniform distribution of vacancies at all locations, i.e., $V(j) = V$, for all $j \in \mathbb{C}$. There is a mass of N_i workers of type $i = B, W$, with $N_B + N_W = 1$. Moreover, because the labor market of blacks and whites is integrated, the matching function cannot be written anymore as in (7.52), but as follows:[14]

$$d \equiv d\left(s_B u_B N_B + s_W u_W N_W, V\right). \tag{7.60}$$

Indeed, all unemployed workers (black or white) compete against each other in the same labor market and the number of vacancies V is not race-dependent. In this context, we can define $\theta = V/(s_B u_B N_B + s_W u_W N_W)$ as a measure of labor market tightness in search intensity units so that $s_i\,\theta q(\theta)$ and $q(\theta)$ are the contact rates of workers of type i and firms, respectively.

Because labor markets are integrated, the matching process will be different than that in the previous section. Indeed, for a worker, a match will occur if and only if:

$$\text{Match}_{u_i \to V} = \underbrace{s_i \theta q(\theta)}_{\text{Random contact}} \times \underbrace{2\widehat{x_i}}_{\text{Probability to accept a job offer}} .$$

Similarly, for firms holding a vacancy, a match with a worker of type i will occur if and only if:

$$\text{Match}_{V \to u_i} = \underbrace{q(\theta)\frac{u_i s_i}{s_B u_B N_B + s_W u_W N_W}}_{\text{Random contact}} \times \underbrace{2\widehat{x_i}}_{\text{Probability contact is acceptable}} .$$

As we have seen in Chapter 3, Section 3.2, when firms do not observe workers' locations, they negotiate the wage with workers only on the basis of the observable aspects of workers' characteristics. In particular, firms will infer that the expected distance commuted by each worker is: $\mathbb{E}(x|x \leq \widehat{x_i}) = \widehat{x_i}/2$. Because $\widehat{x_i}/2$ is common knowledge, they know that black workers commute by public transportation and thus $\widehat{x}_B/2 < \widehat{x}_W/2$.

The Bellman equations for workers are the same as in the case of segmented labor markets and defined by (7.57) and (7.58), with the difference that wages are not anymore a function of x. For firms, the Bellman equations are given by:

$$r I_{iF} = y - w_{iL} - \delta\left(I_F - I_V\right) \tag{7.61}$$

$$r I_V = -c + \frac{2q(\theta)}{s_B u_B N_B + s_W u_W N_B}\left[u_W N_W s_W \int_0^{\widehat{x}_W}\left(I_{WF} - I_V\right) dx\right.$$

$$\left. + u_W N_B s_W \int_0^{\widehat{x}_B}\left(I_{BF} - I_V\right) dx\right] \tag{7.62}$$

---

[14] We use s_i instead of $\overline{s}_i$ since, in equilibrium, all workers of type i provide the same search effort $s_i = \overline{s}_i$.

Equation (7.61) is standard but equation (7.62) is not. Indeed, when a firm decides to enter in the labor, it does not know which worker it will employ. With probability $q(\theta) \frac{u_i s_i}{s_B u_B N_B + s_W u_W N_W}$, it will meet a type i-worker who will accept a job offer only if the firm is located at a distance $x \leq \widehat{x}_i$.

Firms enter in the market up to the point where they make zero (expected) profits, i.e., $I_V = 0$. It is easy to show that the free-entry condition is given by:

$$\frac{s_B u_B N_B \widehat{x}_B (y - w_B) + s_W u_W N_W \widehat{x}_W (y - w_W)}{s_B u_B N_B + s_W u_W N_W} = \frac{c(r + \delta)}{2q(\theta)}. \quad (7.63)$$

The wage w_{iL} is determined as in Chapter 3, Section 3.3 and given by (3.28) or (3.30), where $\mathbb{T}$, s, ϖ, ι^1, and $\widehat{x}$ have to be indexed by i. It can also be shown (Gautier and Zenou, 2008) that the optimal search intensity of type i-workers is implicitly determined by:

$$C'(s_i) = \frac{2\theta q(\theta)\beta\widehat{x}_i \left\{ \left[1 - \frac{\iota_i^1 \widehat{x}_i}{2\varpi_i}\right] y - [w_U - C(s_i) - \mathbb{T}_i] \right\}}{(r + \delta)\left[1 - (1 - \beta)\frac{\iota_i^1 \widehat{x}_i}{2\varpi_i}\right] + 2\beta s_i \theta q(\theta)\widehat{x}_i}. \quad (7.64)$$

The maximum distance to jobs $\widehat{x}_i$ can be determined by solving:

$$r I_{iL}(\widehat{x}_i) - I_{iU}(s_i) = 0$$

which, in the case of no information about workers' location, is not equivalent to $I_{iF} - I_V = 0$ because, in the Nash-bargaining process, it is I_{iL} and not $I_{iL}(x)$ which is involved. Finally, the model can be closed by the following steady-state conditions that determine the unemployment rate for each worker of type $i = B$, W:

$$u_i = \frac{\delta}{\delta + 2\widehat{x}_i s_i \theta q(\theta)}. \quad (7.65)$$

Gautier and Zenou (2008) show that, in equilibrium, $w_{WL} > w_{BL}$, $\widehat{x}_W > \widehat{x}_B$, $s_W > s_B$, $u_W < u_B$. So basically this model demonstrates that small initial differences in wealth between blacks and whites, which leads to differences in transport modes, can imply large differences in labor market outcomes between blacks and whites. It is interesting to observe that (7.63) highlights the externalities that workers of different races exert on each other. Apart from the standard search externalities, there are other externalities due to the fact that the labor market is integrated. Indeed, because whites are more (usually) numerous than blacks ($N_W > N_B$), search more intensively ($s_W > s_B$), and have higher $\widehat{x}$ ($\widehat{x}_W > \widehat{x}_B$), then firms are more likely to meet a white than a black worker when entering the labor market.

However, because whites are better paid than blacks ($w_{WL} > w_{BL}$), then firms are less likely to enter the labor market and to create jobs. In other words, the more active are the white unemployed workers in their search activities, the lower is the probability to find a job for a black worker. In some sense, firms would be better off hiring a black worker, but still accept to hire a white worker because it is better than to wait one period since $I_{WF} > I_V$.

4.4. Why Do Whites Use Faster Transport Modes Than Blacks?

We want to explain why $\mathbb{T}_W$, the fixed cost of cars, can be too prohibitive for blacks. Discrimination in the automobile insurance market is a first element that makes $\mathbb{T}_W$ very high. Indeed, it is well-documented that ethnic minorities, especially African Americans, are not treated in the same way as whites in this market and, in particular, tend to pay significantly higher premiums than whites with comparable driving records (see, e.g., Wiegers, 1989; Squires, Velez, and Taeuber, 1991; Harrington and Niehaus, 1998). Similarly, discrimination in the credit market, making loans in the minority community riskier and thus more expensive than for whites, can also explain the relatively low fraction of car owners among black families. Since location and race are highly correlated,[15] insurance and credit companies can engage in racial discrimination in the form of "redlining" that raises prices and restricts the availability of coverage in areas with large minority populations (Squires, Velez, and Taeuber, 1991; Harrington and Niehaus, 1998).

The usual explanation for discrimination in these two markets revolves around either lenders' pure racial discrimination (Becker, 1957), believing that it is riskier to give loans to blacks[16] than to whites, or statistical discrimination (see, e.g., Arrow, 1973 or Phelps, 1972). For the latter, the argument runs as follows. If it is costly to gather information on individual borrowers and if borrowers' race and economic fundamentals are correlated, lenders can rationally use neighborhood racial composition as a low-cost substitute for costly information-gathering (Lang and Nakamura, 1993). Another argument explains redlining as due to neighborhood externalities and information costs (Lang and Nakamura, 1993). The argument goes that

---

[15] The racial homogeneity of neighborhoods is a well-documented phenomenon in U.S. cities. In 1979, for example, the average black lived in a neighborhood that was 63.6% black, even though blacks only constituted 14.9% of the population (Borjas, 1998). The figures were similar (Cutler, Glaeser, and Vigdor, 1999) in the 1990 census.

[16] To explain the argument, we use the credit market, but naturally the same intuition prevails for the automobile insurance market.

in any community, the return on lending depends on the total volume of lending in that particular community and thus lenders concentrate their lendings where other lenders provide loans. This highlights a coordination problem among lenders. As in the statistical discrimination case, loans in the minority community will become riskier.[17]

Smith and Wright (1992) provide an alternative interesting explanation. They want to explain why automobile insurance premiums vary dramatically across localities or cities. Their argument is that high premiums can be attributed to large numbers of uninsured motorists in some localities, while uninsured motorists can be attributed to high premiums. A key assumption is limited liability, or a bankruptcy constraint, since it is the fact that low-income families cannot reimburse their victims (in case of an accident) that makes premiums go up. If we use the same argument and replace low-income families with black families, it can be explained why some localities or areas with a large fraction of black families will have much higher insurance premiums than other areas with fewer blacks.

4.5. Policy Implications

Let us focus on the last model. We have seen that small initial wealth differences between black and whites can lead to large outcome differences. Indeed, if ethnic minorities do not have the initial endowments to invest in efficient transportation modes (like cars), they can search less intensively, have a worse bargaining position, and are more likely to remain unemployed. Any policy that deters people from taking cars will have in our model some positive impact on the labor market outcomes of blacks. For example, increasing taxes on gasoline or imposing a congestion toll as in London or Stockholm will have these effects. This will make the life of whites harder and, because of the externalities mentioned above, will affect positively blacks' outcomes. However, these policies will have rather limited effects. It seems to be much more desirable to invest in fast and efficient public transportation. Most cities in the United States were built around the car, and in many places public transport is now almost non-existent, even in large cities, with only a few cities where public transport is in good condition, like New York City.[18] In light of our model, improving public transport and

---

[17] See the recent literature survey on discrimination in the credit and housing markets by Dymski (2006).

[18] The widespread car usage in the United Stated caused serious problems, such as urban sprawl.

commissioning new rail transit projects will definitively improve the labor market outcomes of black workers. So, basically, in cities, black workers have two main problems due to their residential location. First, they live far away from jobs (spatial mismatch). Second, they use slow transportation mode, which can be extremely problematic in American cities because of the lack of connections. Putting the two together, this implies that black workers are *very* far away from jobs and this can lead to extremly adverse labor market outcomes for them. A public transportation policy will certainly not erase the different outcomes between blacks and whites, but will improve some aspects of the labor market for black workers. Another interesting policy could be based on *microfinance*. A microfinance institution could rent a car to black workers and pay their insurance costs to help them finding a job. Black workers will then pay back when they obtain a job. This policy is based on what has been done in less-developed countries through microfinance (see, in particular, Yunus, 1999). Indeed, often people in less-developed countries don't have enough money when they face a need, so they borrow. The microfinance institution makes small loans to the poor in order to provide for basics and to encourage small-scale private enterprise. These loans must be repaid by saving after the cost is incurred. The same principle could be applied to help black workers obtaining a car and to pay for the insurance costs, especially when they have no job.

5. Notes on the Literature

Despite a large number of empirical studies, it is surprising that very few theoretical attempts have been made to model the spatial mismatch hypothesis. To the best of our knowledge, the first paper to model the spatial mismatch hypothesis is the one by Brueckner and Martin (1998). Since they do not explicitly introduce unemployment in their model, their approach is not considered here. The same applies to Martin (1997) and Arnott (1998). Johnson (2006) proposes a search model to explain the spatial mismatch hypothesis, but the land market is not explicitly introduced.

The models of Section 2 elaborate on Wasmer and Zenou (2002), Smith and Zenou (2003), and Zenou (2007b) while the model of Section 3 is based on Coulson, Laing, and Wang (2001). Sections 4.1 and 4.2 are based on Patacchini and Zenou (2005) and Zenou (2007b), respectively. Finally, the model developed in Section 4.3 elaborates from Gautier and Zenou (2008).

CHAPTER EIGHT

The Spatial Mismatch Hypothesis: An Efficiency-Wage Approach

1. Introduction

We would now like to use some of the urban efficiency wage models developed in Part 2 to provide some microeconomic mechanisms that explain why the spatial mismatch between where blacks (and other ethnic groups) reside and where jobs are located can have adverse labor market outcomes. Since the way the labor market operates is quite different under efficiency wages and search frictions, the mechanisms proposed here are not the same as those exposed in the previous chapter. This will also lead to different policy implications.

We will provide two main mechanisms in this chapter. First, using the model of Section 2 in Chapter 5, which assumes that workers' effort negatively depends on distance to jobs, we will show that, in equilibrium, firms draw a red line beyond which they will not hire workers. This is because, depending on their residential location, workers do not contribute to the same level of production, even though the wage cost is location-independent. As a result, the per-worker profit decreases with distance to jobs and firms stop recruiting workers residing too far away, i.e., when the per-worker profit becomes negative. This model offers an explanation for the spatial mismatch of black workers by focusing on the point of view of firms. If housing discrimination against blacks forces them to live far away from jobs, then even though firms have no prejudices, they are reluctant to hire black workers because they have a relatively lower productivity than whites. This phenomenon is know as *redlining* since firms discriminate workers on basis of their residential address and not on the color of their skin. In the model presented here, it is rational to "redline" workers who live too far away from jobs because of the negative impact on productivity.

Second, using the model of Section 4 in Chapter 6, we introduce two employment centers and high relocation costs so that workers do not change residence as soon as they change employment status. We show that by skewing black workers towards the city center, housing discrimination increases the number of applications for central jobs and decreases it for suburban jobs. As a result, blacks living in the central part of the city, but working in the suburbs, experience a lower unemployment rate and earn higher wages than blacks living and working in the central part of the city.

Finally, further developing the model of Section 4 in Chapter 6 by differentiating between good and bad jobs, we are able to explain how housing discrimination affects the labor market outcomes of black workers. The explanation is similar to that of the previous model, but it focuses on access to jobs before and after discrimination, rather than on unemployment differences between blacks working in the center and in the suburbs.

In all these models, we are able to generate a link between unemployment and a seemingly unrelated phenomenon: racial discrimination in the housing market.

2. The Firms' Perspective

In this section, we adapt the benchmark urban efficiency wage model of Chapter 4 as follows. First, we only focus on low-skill workers (black or white) and low-skill jobs and all workers use the same transport mode (mass transit). Second, $x = 0$ is now the SBD, i.e., the workplace located in the suburbs where all low-skill jobs are located, while $x = x_f$ is now the city center (with no jobs, only people). To be consistent with the basic model, we have normalized the SBD to zero. This means that we take the firms' perspective when calculating distance to jobs, so that x_f, the city center, is now the longest distance from the job center located at $x = 0$. See Figure 8.1 for an illustration of this city. Finally, there is housing discrimination against blacks,[1] which forces them to live downtown (i.e., close to the city center x_f) and causes them to have poorer access to unskilled jobs than whites living in the suburbs.

We focus on the firms' viewpoint to explain the spatial mismatch for black workers. It will be shown that even though firms have no prejudices against black workers, it can be rational for them not to hire black workers if they live too far from jobs (for example, if they live downtown while jobs

---

[1] Housing discrimination against black families is well-documented; see, in particular, Yinger (1986, 1997).

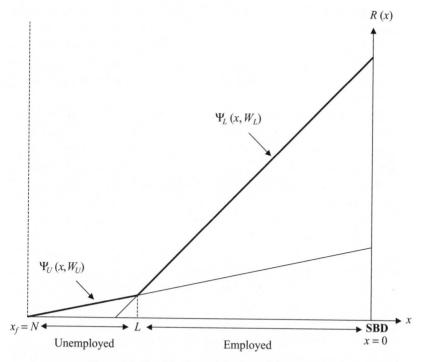

Figure 8.1. Spatial mismatch in the redlining model.

are in the suburbs) because they are less productive than white workers who live closer to jobs.

Based on the model developed in Section 2 of Chapter 5, let us show how we can provide a mechanism for spatial mismatch. Apart of the modifications mentioned above, we use exactly the same benchmark model. There are still only two possible effort levels: either the worker shirks, exerting zero effort, $e = 0$, and contributing zero to production, or he/she does not shirk, providing full effort $e(x) > 0$, $\forall x \in [0, x_f]$, with $e(0) = e_0 > 0$, $e'(x) < 0$, and $e''(x) \geq 0$ so that the greater is the distance to work, the lower is the effort level, and, for a remote location, the marginal difference in effort is quite small.

This assumption $e'(x) < 0$ aims at capturing the fact that workers who have longer commuting trips are more tired and thus are less able to provide higher levels of effort (or productivity) than those who reside closer to jobs. This implies that commuting costs include more than just money and time costs. They also include the negative effects of a longer commute such as non-work-related fatigue. Moreover, this assumption can also capture the fact that workers who reside farther away from jobs have less flexible working hours. For example, in some jobs (e.g., working in a restaurant) there are long breaks during the day (typically between 2 p.m. and 6 p.m.). The worker who lives next door can go back home and relax whereas the others who live far away cannot rest at home. This obviously also affects workers' productivity.

This assumption can be questioned by arguing that one can take a nap on a train. Indeed, driving two hours is tiring, but riding a train is not. This is true if there is a very good public transportation system which, for example, implies that there is a direct train from home to the workplace. Remember that we are dealing with (low-educated) black workers who are forced to live far away from jobs (housing discrimination). It is well-documented that most blacks do not have access to cars and use public transportation.[2] It is also well-documented that in large U.S. Metropolitan Statistical Areas, there is a lack of good public transportation, especially from the city center to the suburbs (see, e.g., Pugh, 1998). For instance, *New York Times* of May 26, 1998, was telling the story of Dorothy Johnson, a Detroit inner-city black female resident who had to commute to an evening job as a cleaning lady in a suburban office. By using public transportation, it took her two hours, whereas had she been able to afford a car, the commute would only have taken 25 minutes. This story illustrates the fact that blacks have a relatively low productivity in suburban jobs because they arrive late at work due to the unreliability of the mass transit system that causes black workers to frequently miss transfers.[*]

The worker's behavior can now be seen as a two-stage decision. First, each worker must decide to shirk or not, depending on his/her residential location. Since effort is costly, it is clear that the worker who lives the closest to jobs will be more inclined to shirk that those residing further away. Thus, as in Section 2 of Chapter 5, *the shirking behavior of workers is here locationally dependent.* Second, once the worker has decided not to shirk (this is the behavior that will emerge in equilibrium), he/she must decide how much effort he/she provides. This decision is also locationally dependent, since we assume that workers who have longer

---

[2] See the beginning of Section 4 in Chapter 7, for evidence on the fact that ethnic minorities (especially blacks) mostly use public transportation to commute to work.

[*] To the best of our knowledge, there is only one paper that tests the relationship between effort and distance to jobs. Indeed, van Ommeren and Gutiérrez-i-Puigarnau (2009), using German data, show that commuting distance induces absenteeism with an elasticity of about 0.07. In other words, on average, absenteeism would be about 16% less if all workers would have a negligible commute.

commutes are more tired and provide less effort than those who live closer to jobs.

Let us first determine the urban-land-use equilibrium and then the labor equilibrium. The entire locational analysis is exactly the same as in Section 2 of Chapter 5, where we have flipped the city so that the CBD corresponds to a SBD where all jobs are concentrated (Figure 8.1). Proposition 5.1 in Chapter 5 still holds and thus, by assuming that $\tau > -e'(L)/(1 - s)$, we can guarantee that the employed reside close to the SBD, whereas the unemployed live close to the city center.[3]

Let us now solve the labor equilibrium. As in the model in Section 2 of Chapter 5, the utility of shirkers is not constant over locations, whereas it is constant for non-shirkers. Because workers are heterogeneous in terms of location, it is clear that workers' residence is of importance in the process of wage formation. We focus on the case where firms do not observe where workers live. Because of housing discrimination, whites live close to jobs while blacks reside further away from jobs.[4] So firms only have this information, but do not know where each worker resides within an area.

It is easily seen that the utility of shirkers increases as x, the distance to the SBD, decreases. This implies, in particular, that the highest utility that a shirker can reach is at the $x = 0$ (the SBD) and the lowest is at L. As a result, because firms cannot discriminate in terms of location or race, the efficiency wage must be set such that workers are indifferent between shirking in location $x = 0$ and not shirking, since if the worker at $x = 0$ does not shirk, all workers located further away will not shirk. In Section 2 of Chapter 5, we have shown that the efficiency wage is given by:

$$w_L(L) = w_U + e(L) + \frac{e_0}{m}\left(\frac{\delta N}{N - L} + r\right) + (1 - s)\tau L. \quad (8.1)$$

This setting thus implies that there is a fundamental *asymmetry* between workers and firms. All workers obtain the same efficiency wage whatever their location. However, they do *not* contribute to the same level of production because their effort decreases with distance to jobs. In other words, even though the wage-cost is location-independent, the contribution to production is not. This implies that the per-worker profit decreases with the distance to jobs, so that firms will determine a red line beyond which they will not hire workers, i.e., when the per-worker profit becomes negative.

---

[3] Remember that τ is the pecuniary commuting cost per unit of distance, L the total level of employment in the economy, but also the border distance between the employed and unemployed, and s the workers' search intensity.

[4] This will be modeled in a more explicit way in the next section.

The interesting implication of this model is that it can explain why firms do not hire remote workers. Indeed, if firms *cannot* discriminate in terms of location (make wages location-dependent), they do anticipate that remote workers will provide a lower effort level. So they stop recruiting workers residing too far away.

To be more precise, all (identical) firms set the same redline $x_s = L$, above which they do not hire workers. The total production (or effort) level provided in each firm is given by: $e^{to} = \int_0^L e(x)dx$. By taking the efficiency wage as given, each firm maximizes its profit to choose the optimal size of the redline (recruitment area L). We obtain: $F'(e^{to}) = w_L/e(L)$. This equation states that the optimal recruitment area $x_s = L$ chosen by each firm is such that the marginal productivity of workers is equal to their cost per efficiency unit of labor. This determines the labor demand for each firm.[5]

This model offers an explanation for the spatial mismatch of black workers by focusing on the point of view of firms. If firms cannot offer different wages for the same job, they can discriminate on the basis of location by setting *higher job rejection rates for those residing far away from jobs*. Since there is housing discrimination against blacks, which forces them to live downtown, they are far away from (low-skill) jobs, which are located at $x = 0$, the SBD. Because firms know that remote workers tend to work less and be less productive than those residing closer to jobs, they prefer not to hire black workers. In other words, even though firms have no prejudices against black workers, it is rational for them not to hire them if they live too far away from jobs (i.e., beyond the recruitment area determined by firms).

The popular press often relates stories about firms that do not want to hire workers living in "bad" neighborhoods, which are in general not well-connected to job centers. In fact, most studies find that employers do use space to screen workers. For example, some of Chicago's inner-city employers revealed in interviews that they take note of the address of job candidates during screening, assuming that residents of public housing projects are unlikely to be good workers (Kirschenman and Neckerman, 1991; Neckerman and Kirschenman, 1991). Tilly, Moss, Kirschenman, and Kennelly (2001) found a similar pattern among some employers in Boston, Atlanta, Detroit, and Los Angeles. Interestingly, in their study of Worcester, Massachusetts, Hanson, and Pratt (1995) found that employers were screening applicants by the distance between the candidate's home

---

[5] This equilibrium exists and is unique because we impose that each firm employs one worker at each location. If this is not the case, then another equilibrium will emerge where firms do not hire workers residing very close to the CBD because of the high efficiency wage required to deter shirking.

and the work site, because they were worried that long work trips would contribute to absenteeism. In some sense, employers were drawing a redline beyond which they were not hiring workers. Moreover, in the United States, African Americans may not want to reveal where they live if it implies spatial discrimination or redlining. In other words, workers who live in "stigmatized" areas may not want to give their true address to employers, while those who live in good neighborhoods may have an incentive to do so.

In his book, based on the Urban Poverty and Family Life Study's survey of a representative sample of Chicago-area employers, Wilson (1996, Ch. 5) indicates that many employers consider inner-city workers to be uneducated, unstable, uncooperative, and dishonest. Some employers pointed out that certain areas of the inner city were to be avoided. For example, one stated: "Before I took this job there were an area of Chicago on the West Side that we'd hired, you know, some groups of employees from . . . and our black management people, who do know the area, they'd say, 'No, stay away from that area. That's a bad area. Anybody who comes from that area . . .' " The president of an inner-city manufacturing firm also expressed a concern about employing residents from certain inner-city neighborhoods: "If somebody gave me their address, uh, Cabrini Green, I might unavoidably have some concerns. That the poor guy probably would be frequently unable to get to work." A welfare mother who lives in a large public housing project put it this way: "Honestly, I believe they look at the address and the – your attitudes, your address, your surround – you know, your environment has a lot to do with your employment status. The people with the best addresses have the best chances, I feel so, I feel so." Another welfare mother of two children from a South Side neighborhood expressed a similar view: "I think that a lot of peoples don't get jobs over here because they live – they live in the projects. I think a lot of people might judge a person because they got a project address. You know, when you put it on an application, they might not even hire you because you live over here."

This first model is consistent with the empirical regularities cited in the introduction of Part 3. Most unskilled jobs are in the suburbs (Table 7.3) and because of housing discrimination most blacks live downtown (Table 7.2). This implies that blacks reside further away from jobs than whites (Table 7.5). As a result, they experience a higher unemployment rate (Tables 7.1 and 7.5) since firms are reluctant to hire them since they have a relatively lower productivity at suburban jobs than whites.

Let us now investigate the policy implications of this model (Figure 4.2 in Chapter 4 describes this labor equilibrium, but for different parameter values). We focus on unemployment benefit and transportation policies. A reduction in the unemployment benefit shifts the UNSC downward since, at each recruitment area level x_s (or the equivalent employment level L), the efficiency wage must decrease to deter shirking. This is the standard outside option effect generated by the unemployment benefit. Since wages are lower, it is less costly for firms to hire new workers, so they increase their recruitment area which is beneficial for black workers. Similarly, decreasing the unit commuting cost τ borne by workers or increasing the number of CBD trips s increases the recruitment area x_s. The intuition is exactly the same as for w_U, but here the efficiency wage must not decrease for incentive reasons, but to spatially compensate employed workers.

As a result, this model strongly advocates a cut in unemployment benefits and subsidies to transportation costs since it increases the recruitment area of firms and reduces unemployment among black workers. In particular, these policies reduce the negative effect of spatial mismatch since firms will be more willing to hire black workers living in remote locations.

3. The Workers' Perspective

In this section, we adapt the basic model in a different way to account for the U.S. spatial mismatch. First, there are N_B black workers and N_W white workers (with $N = N_B + N_W$). Second, there are two job centers, the CBD, located at $x = 0$, and the SBD located at $x = x_f$. We will show that distance to jobs can be harmful to black workers, because they may refuse jobs that involve too long commutes.

Since the model is now quite complicated, following Brueckner and Zenou (2003), it is simplified as follows. First, ($H1$) we assume that employed and unemployed workers have the same commuting cost, i.e., $s = 1$. Second, ($H2$) black workers consume less land than white workers (reflecting lower average black income). If h_i denotes housing consumption for a worker of type i (h_B and h_W stand for the housing consumption of blacks and whites, respectively), then we assume that $h_B < h_W = 1$. Third, as in the previous section, ($H3$) black families are assumed to be discriminated in the housing market, which prevents them from residing in the suburbs. Housing discrimination against blacks is assumed to be so severe that they cannot live in the suburbs, that is between $x = x_{BW}$ and $x = x_f$ (where x_{BW} denotes the border between blacks and whites). They can only reside between $x = 0$ and x_{BW}.

Fourth, ($H4$) we assume relocation costs to be so high that people are not mobile at all and they are stuck in their location. As a result, people stay in the same location when they change their employment status. We also assume perfect capital markets with a zero interest rate, which enable workers to smooth their income over time as they enter and leave unemployment: workers save while employed and reduce their savings when out of work. This is the assumption made in Section 5.5 of Chapter 5. Consequently, there are only four categories of workers defined by their race $i = B$, W and their workplace $j = 1$, 2 (1 if they work in the CBD and 2 in the SBD).

Fifth, ($H5$) blacks and whites do not compete for the same jobs, and thus their labor markets are separated (or segmented). This is the same assumption as that in Chapter 7, Section 4.

A further assumption ($H6$) is such that the SBD job-acquisition rate for workers laid off from the CBD equals zero. Similarly, the CBD job-acquisition rate for workers laid off from the SBD equals zero. These assumptions reflect the underlying idea that laid-off workers cannot simultaneously search for jobs in both employment centers, since most low-skill workers find their jobs through local sources of information within social networks and on-site advertisements (see, e.g., Holzer, 1987, 1988). Assumptions ($H5$) and ($H6$) imply that, for workers of type $i = B$, W, we have:

$$N_{i1} = L_{i1} + U_{i1}, \ N_{i2} = L_{i2} + U_{i2}, \ \text{and} \ N_i = N_{i1} + N_{i2} \qquad (8.2)$$

where L_{ij} and U_{ij} are the employment and unemployment levels of individuals of type $i = B$, W working in job center $j = 1$, 2. Moreover, N_{ij} denotes the number of workers of type $i = B$, W who are "attached" to a job center $j = 1$, 2. Here, "attached to j" means that a worker never looks for a job in the other job center.

We finally assume ($H7$) that black workers are *unskilled* while white workers are *skilled*, but all workers (black or white) use the same public transport mode (mass transit). Shirking may occur in the low-skill job, while high-skill workers do not have the opportunity to shirk. The assumption of different skills and separated labor markets between blacks and whites in particular implies that the labor markets of blacks and whites are different. Following Brueckner and Zenou (2003), we assume that an efficiency wage policy prevails for blacks while there is no shirking problem for whites. Indeed, for unskilled workers (here black workers), shirking can be an issue while for white workers, who are skilled, this should not be the case.[6] As a result, efficiency wages must be paid to black workers in both job centers (i.e., the CBD and the SBD) to prevent low-skill shirking, while high-skill

---

[6] Using the Public Use Microdata sample of the 2000 U.S. Decennial Census, Ross and Zenou (2008) find that efficiency wages tend to be paid to blue-collar workers, who tend to be in occupations that face high levels of supervision because the cost of shirking is high in those occupations.

wages are determined by the usual marginal productivity conditions for whites in both job centers.

To summarize, in this model, blacks are doubly disadvantaged by housing discrimination and by the need to work in jobs where efficiency wages and unemployment are required to maintain work effort.

Let us now intuitively see how the urban-land-use equilibrium works. Since whites have flatter bid-rents (blacks and whites have the same commuting costs, but because they consume more land, whites want to locate in remote locations where the price of land is lower), they reside further away from jobs than blacks. Because of housing discrimination that prevents blacks from residing in the suburbs, the location of workers in the city is as follows. Starting from the CBD, we have blacks working in the CBD (referred to as CBD blacks), then blacks working in the SBD (referred to as SBD blacks), whites working in the CBD (referred to as CBD whites) and finally whites working in the SBD (referred to as SBD whites).

The equilibrium land rent with housing discrimination is described in Figure 8.2 where x_B (x_W) is the border between CBD blacks (whites) and SBD blacks (whites), while x_{BW} is the border between SBD blacks and CBD whites. If there were no housing discrimination against blacks, Figure 4.1 (in Chapter 4) and Figure 8.1 would have to be juxtaposed to obtain Figure 8.3. In this new configuration, starting from the CBD, Figure 8.3 first locates black and then white workers while, starting from the SBD, it first accommodates black and then white workers. The border between CBD whites and SBD whites[7] is at x_1 and the urban configuration is perfectly symmetric around x_1. Now, because of housing discrimination, the urban equilibrium is depicted by Figure 8.2. To understand this pattern, observe that housing discrimination means that whites face no competition for suburban land. Blacks must still outbid whites for land in the central part of the city, however. Therefore, the black bid-rents in this area must be at least as large as the bids offered by CBD whites. This, in turn, implies that the minimum point (which occurs at $x = x_B$) of the black bid-rent curves must lie on the extension of the CBD whites' bid-rents (depicted by the dotted line). Figure 8.2 also shows a dramatic bid-rent discontinuity at $x = x_{BW}$, with SBD black workers offering much more for land in the white area than the white residents themselves. This discrepancy, which would be unsustainable in a competitive market, is a consequence of discrimination by suburban landlords against blacks.

Black workers are skewed towards the CBD and the residences of blacks are thus remote from the SBD. For a black worker, working in the SBD

---

[7] Subscripts 1 and 2 denote the CBD and the SBD, respectively.

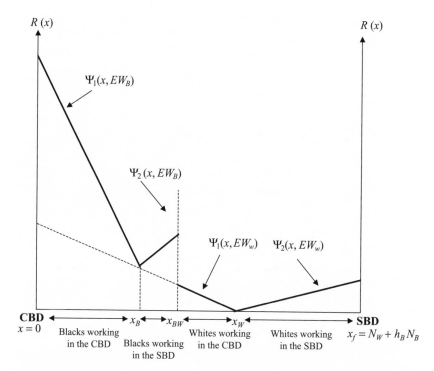

Figure 8.2. Spatial mismatch in a duocentric city with housing discrimination and high relocation costs.

involves high commuting costs, which may deter many black workers from accepting SBD jobs. As a result, the black CBD labor pool is large relative to the black SBD pool, and competition among blacks for central jobs is thus more fierce.

Let us be more precise about the urban-land-use equilibrium. The city is *linear, closed,* and *duocentric.* The CBD is in location $x = 0$ while the SBD is located at the other end of the city (x_f). Since the city's employment areas take up no space, its overall length is then $x_f = N_W + h_B N_B$ and the border between blacks and whites is $x_{BW} = h_B N_B$. Housing discrimination thus implies that blacks cannot reside between $x_{BW} = h_B N_B$ and $x_f = N_W + h_B N_B$. We are now able to write the *instantaneous* indirect utilities of the employed workers of type $i = B, W$ working in the CBD and the SBD. They are, respectively, given by:

$$W_{iL1}^{NS}(x) = w_{i1} - e - \tau x - h_i R(x) \tag{8.3}$$

$$W_{iL2}^{NS}(x) = w_{i2} - e - \tau (N_W + h_B N_B - x) - h_i R(x). \tag{8.4}$$

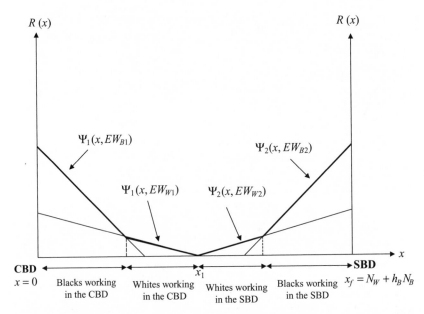

Figure 8.3. Urban equilibrium in a duocentric city with no housing discrimination and high relocation costs.

Here, for example, w_{ij} ($i = B$, W, $j = 1$, 2) denotes the wage of a type–i individual working in job center j. As in Chapter 6, we assume work trips to be separated from shopping trips. We obtain the following *instantaneous* indirect utilities of a type–i worker working in the CBD and the SBD, respectively:

$$W_{iU1}(x) = w_U - \tau x - h_i R(x) \tag{8.5}$$

$$W_{iU2}(x) = w_U - \tau (N_W + h_B N_B - x) - h_i R(x). \tag{8.6}$$

Let us now first determine the labor equilibrium by calculating the efficiency wage for a black person working in $j = 1$, 2. The unemployment rate of non-shirkers is given by:

$$u_{ij} \equiv u_{ij}^{NS} = \frac{\delta}{a_{ij} + \delta}, \tag{8.7}$$

while that of shirkers is equal to:

$$u_{ij}^{S} = \frac{\delta + m}{a_{ij} + \delta + m},$$

with $u_{ij}^{S} > u_{ij}^{NS}$, $\forall a_{ij}$, δ, $m > 0$, where a_{ij} is the job-acquisition rate, δ, the job-destruction rate, and m the firms' monitoring rate. Since, in a

Poisson/Markov process, the unemployment rate also corresponds to the time workers spend unemployed over their lifetime, the expected utility of workers is simply the weighted average of their net incomes, the weights being the unemployment and employment rates. Since firms know that workers have a zero discount rate, to calculate the efficiency wage, they equate the average incomes of a non-shirker and a shirker over time. By observing that $s = 1$ so that firms' information on workers' location is not relevant, we can use the same method as in Section 4 of Chapter 5 to calculate the efficiency wage for a black person working in $j = 1, 2$. We obtain:

$$w_{Bj} = w_U + e + \frac{e}{m} \frac{\delta}{u_{Bj}}, \tag{8.8}$$

where $u_{Bj} = u_{Bj}^{NS}$ since nobody shirks at this efficiency wage. Let us determine the wage of white workers. Each firm in job center $j = 1, 2$ is assumed to produce the same good at the same market price (normalized to 1) and the production function is given by: $F_i(e\, L_{ij})$. Each production function is assumed to be twice differentiable with

$$F_i(e\, L_{ij}) = 0, \quad F_i'(e\, L_{ij}) > 0, \quad F_i''(e\, L_{ij}) \leq 0 \quad \text{for all } e\, L_{ij} \geq 0$$

and to satisfy the Inada conditions, i.e.,

$$\lim_{L_{ij} \to 0} F_i'(e\, L_{ij}) = +\infty, \quad \lim_{L_{ij} \to +\infty} F_i'(e\, L_{ij}) = 0.$$

White workers are paid at their marginal productivity and for $j = 1, 2$ we obtain:

$$w_{Wj} = F_W'(e\, L_{Wj}). \tag{8.9}$$

Thus, we can calculate the equilibrium utility of type$-i$ individuals working in the CBD and SBD. Using $(8.3)-(8.6)$, we obtain:

$$
\begin{aligned}
E\, W_{i1}(x) &= (1 - u_{i1})\, W_{iL1}^{NS}(x) + u_{i1}\, W_{iU1}(x) \tag{8.10} \\
&= (1 - u_{i1})\, (w_{iL1} - e) + u_{i1} w_U - \tau\, x - h_i\, R(x)
\end{aligned}
$$

$$
\begin{aligned}
E\, W_{i2}(x) &= (1 - u_{i2})\, W_{iL2}^{NS}(x) + u_{i2}\, W_{iU2}(x) \\
&= (1 - u_{i2})\, (w_{iL2} - e) + u_{i2} w_U \\
&\quad - \tau\, (N_W + h_B N_B - x) - h_i\, R(x), \tag{8.11}
\end{aligned}
$$

where black wages w_{Bj} and white wages w_{Wj} are given by (8.8) and (8.9), respectively. Observe that wages are not location-dependent and land rents will only compensate for commuting costs.

Let us solve the urban-land-use equilibrium. Since all black and all white workers must obtain the same utility level wherever they work, we denote by $E\,W_i$ the (expected) utility reached by all type−i individuals. Then, by observing that $h_W = 1$ and $h_B = h < 1$, and using (8.8) and (8.9), the bid-rents of workers are equal to:

$$\Psi_1(x, E\,W_B) = \frac{1}{h_B}\left[w_U + \frac{e}{m}\frac{\delta\,(1 - u_{B1})}{u_{B1}} - \tau\,x - E\,W_B\right] \qquad (8.12)$$

$$\Psi_2(x, E\,W_B) = \frac{1}{h_B}\left[w_U + \frac{e}{m}\frac{\delta\,(1 - u_{B2})}{u_{B2}}\right.$$
$$\left. - \tau\,(N_W + h_B\,N_B - x) - E\,W_B\right] \qquad (8.13)$$

$$\Psi_1(x, E\,W_W) = (1 - u_{W1})\left[F_W'(e\,L_{W1}) - e\right] + u_{W1}w_U - \tau\,x - E\,W_W \qquad (8.14)$$

$$\Psi_2(x, E\,W_W) = (1 - u_{W2})\left[F_W'(e\,L_{W2}) - e\right] + u_{W2}w_U$$
$$- \tau\,(N_W + h_B\,N_B - x) - E\,W_W, \qquad (8.15)$$

where $\Psi_i(x, E\,W_j)$ is the bid-rent of a worker of type $i = B, W$ working in job center $j = 1, 2$. As stated above, the role of the land rent here is only to compensate workers for commuting costs. We indeed have:

$$\frac{\partial\Psi_1(x, E\,W_B)}{\partial x} = -\frac{\tau}{h_B} < 0 \qquad \frac{\Psi_2(x, E\,W_B)}{\partial x} = \frac{\tau}{h_B} > 0$$

$$\frac{\partial\Psi_1(x, E\,W_W)}{\partial x} = -\tau < 0 \qquad \frac{\Psi_2(x, E\,W_W)}{\partial x} = \tau > 0.$$

Definition 8.1. *A spatial mismatch land use equilibrium in a duocentric city with housing discrimination (Figure 8.2) is a 5-tuple $(x_B^*, x_W^*, E\,W_B^*, E\,W_W^*, R^*(x))$ such that:*

$$\Psi_1(x_B^*, E\,W_B^*) = \Psi_2(x_B^*, E\,W_B^*) \qquad (8.16)$$

$$\Psi_1(x_W^*, E\,W_W^*) = \Psi_2(x_W^*, E\,W_W^*) \qquad (8.17)$$

$$\Psi_1(x_W^*, E\,W_W^*) = \Psi_2(x_W^*, E\,W_W^*) = 0 \qquad (8.18)$$

$$\Psi_1(x_B^*, E\,W_B^*) = \Psi_1(x_B^*, E\,W_W^*) \qquad (8.19)$$

$$R^*(x) = \max\{\Psi_1(x,\,E\,W_B),\,\Psi_2(x,\,E\,W_B),\,\Psi_1(x,\,E\,W_W),\,\Psi_2(x,\,E\,W_W),\,0\}$$
$$(8.20)$$

at each $x \in (0,\,N_W + h_B\,N_B]$.

Indeed, the equilibrium conditions require that: (i) the black bid-rent curves intersect at x_B^* (equation (8.16)); (ii) the white bid-rent curves intersect at x_W^* (equation (8.17)); (iii) the bid-rent curve of whites equals agricultural land rent (normalized to zero) at x_W^* (equation (8.18)); and (iv) the bid-rent curve of CBD whites intersects with the bid, rent curve of black CBD commuters at x_B^* (equation (8.19)). By solving these equations using (8.12)−(8.15), we obtain:

$$x_B^* = \frac{N_W + h_B\,N_B}{2} + \left[\frac{(1 - u_{B1})}{u_{B1}} - \frac{(1 - u_{B2})}{u_{B2}}\right]\frac{e\delta}{2\tau m} \qquad (8.21)$$

$$x_W^* = \frac{N_W + h_B\,N_B}{2} + (u_{W2} - u_{W1})\left[\frac{F_W'(e\,L_{W1}) - e - w_U}{2\tau}\right] \qquad (8.22)$$

$$E\,W_B^* = w_U\,[1 + h_B(u_{W2} - u_{W1})] \qquad (8.23)$$
$$+ \frac{e\delta}{m}\left[h_B\frac{(1 - u_{B1})}{u_{B1}} + (1 - h_B)\frac{(1 - u_{B2})}{u_{B2}}\right]$$
$$- h_B\left[F_W'(e\,L_{W1}) - e\right]\left(\frac{u_{W2} - u_{W1}}{2}\right) - \frac{(N_W + h_B\,N_B)\tau}{2}$$

$$E\,W_W^* = \left[F_W'(e\,L_{W1}) - e\right]\left(1 - \frac{u_{W1} + u_{W2}}{2}\right) + u_{W2}\,w_U \qquad (8.24)$$
$$- \frac{\tau\,(N_W + h_B\,N_B)}{2}$$

$$R^*(x) = \begin{cases} e\delta\,(1 - h_B)\,[(1 - u_{B1})/u_{B1} & \text{for } x \le x_B \\ \quad - (1 - u_{B2})/u_{B2}]/(h_B\,m) & \\ \quad - w_U(u_{W2} - u_{W1}) & \\ \quad + [F_W'(e\,L_{W1}) - e](u_{W2} - u_{W1})/2 & \\ \quad + \tau[(N_W + h_B\,N_B)/2 - x]/h_B & \\ e\delta[(1 - u_{B2})/u_{B2} - (1 - u_{B1})/u_{B1}]/m & \text{for } x_B \le x \le x_{BW} \\ \quad - w_U\,(u_{W2} - u_{W1}) & \\ \quad + [F_W'(e\,L_{W1}) - e](u_{W2} - u_{W1})/2 & \\ \quad + \tau[x - (N_W + h_B\,N_B)/2]/h_B & \\ (u_{W2} - u_{W1})([F_W'(e\,L_{W1}) - e]/2 - w_U) & \text{for } x_{BW} \le x \le x_W \\ \quad + \tau[(N_W + h_B\,N_B)/2 - x] & \\ [F_W'(e\,L_{W1}) - e](u_{W1} - u_{W2})/2 & \text{for } x_W \le x \le x_f \\ \quad + \tau[x - (N_W + h_B\,N_B)/2] & \end{cases}$$
$$(8.25)$$

Equation (8.21) is easily understood. The border between CBD blacks and SBD blacks is half of the city (i.e., $x_f/2 = (N_W + h_B N_B)/2$) plus or minus the income difference between them. In this model, the income difference between CBD and SBD blacks is just the time spent employed over the life cycle. We have exactly the same intuition for equation (8.22). The two other equations give the equilibrium expected utility levels for blacks and whites. Each equilibrium utility is composed of expected outcome, minus expected commuting costs, which capture competition in the land market. Finally, equation (8.25) determines equilibrium land rent in all locations in the city.

Proposition 8.1. *For the urban equilibrium described in Figure 8.2 to exist, it must be that*

$$m \left[\frac{F'_W(e\, L_{W1}) - e - w_U}{e\delta} \right] > \frac{1}{(u_{W2} - u_{W1})} \left[\frac{(1 - u_{B1})}{u_{B1}} - \frac{(1 - u_{B2})}{u_{B2}} \right].$$

$$(8.26)$$

Indeed, we need to guarantee that $x^*_W > x^*_B$, which using (8.21) and (8.22) is equivalent to (8.26). This condition is assumed to hold because the productivity of white workers is assumed to be sufficiently high so that (8.26) is always satisfied. Observe that for $j = 1, 2$, we have:

$$L_{Bj} = (1 - u_{Bj}) N_{Bj} \quad \text{and} \quad L_{Wj} = (1 - u_{Wj}) N_{Wj}, \qquad (8.27)$$

where N_{ij} is the number of type–i individuals "attached" to job center $j = 1, 2$. As stated above, "attached to j" here means that a worker never looks for a job in the other job center. We can now determine the labor market equilibrium.

Definition 8.2. *A spatial mismatch labor market equilibrium with efficiency wages and high relocation costs is a 8-tuple* $(u^*_{B1}, u^*_{B2}, u^*_{W1}, u^*_{W2}, N^*_{B1}, N^*_{B2}, N^*_{W1}, N^*_{W2})$ *such that:*

$$F'_B \left[e \left(1 - u^*_{B1} \right) N^*_{B1} \right] = w_U + e + \frac{e}{m} \frac{\delta}{u^*_{B1}} \qquad (8.28)$$

$$F'_B \left[e \left(1 - u^*_{B2} \right) N^*_{B2} \right] = w_U + e + \frac{e}{m} \frac{\delta}{u^*_{B2}} \qquad (8.29)$$

$$F'_W \left[e \left(1 - u^*_{W1} \right) N^*_{W1} \right] = w_{W1} \qquad (8.30)$$

$$F'_W \left[e \left(1 - u_{W2} \right) N^*_{W2} \right] = w_{W2} \qquad (8.31)$$

$$N_{B1}^* = \frac{N_W + h_B N_B}{2h_B} + \left[\frac{\left(1 - u_{B1}^*\right)}{u_{B1}^*} - \frac{\left(1 - u_{B2}^*\right)}{u_{B2}^*} \right] \frac{e\delta}{2\tau m h_B} \qquad (8.32)$$

$$N_{B2}^* = N_B - \frac{N_W + h_B N_B}{2h_B} - \left[\frac{\left(1 - u_{B1}^*\right)}{u_{B1}^*} - \frac{\left(1 - u_{B2}^*\right)}{u_{B2}^*} \right] \frac{e\delta}{2\tau m h_B} \qquad (8.33)$$

$$N_{W1}^* = \frac{N_W - h_B N_B}{2} + \left(u_{W2}^* - u_{W1}^*\right) \left[\frac{F'\left[\left(1 - u_{W1}^*\right) N_{W1}^*\right] - e - w_U}{2\tau} \right] \qquad (8.34)$$

$$N_{W2}^* = \frac{N_W + h_B N_B}{2} - \left(u_{W2}^* - u_{W1}^*\right) \left[\frac{F'\left[\left(1 - u_{W1}^*\right) N_{W1}^*\right] - e - w_U}{2\tau} \right]. \qquad (8.35)$$

To calculate the different equilibrium conditions, we have used the fact that $N_{B1} = x_B^*/h_B$ (equation (8.32)), $N_{B2} = N_B - N_{B1}$ (equation (8.33)), $N_{W2} = x_f - x_W^*$ (equation (8.35)), and $N_{W1} = N_W - N_{W2}$ (equation (8.34)).

Labor demand in the CBD and the SBD, respectively, is the result of firms' profit maximization. The labor market equilibrium in each center for each type of labor is depicted in Figure 4.2 in Chapter 4 (for different parameter values). We have the following result (proved by Brueckner and Zenou, 2003):

Proposition 8.2. *Black individuals working in the CBD experience a higher unemployment rate, lower wages, a larger labor pool, and a higher employment level than blacks working in the SBD, i.e. $u_{B1}^* > u_{B2}^*, w_{B1}^* < w_{B2}^*, N_{B1}^* > N_{B2}^*$, and $L_{B1}^* > L_{B2}^*$.*

Since, in equilibrium, it must be that all blacks reach the same utility level wherever they work (in the CBD or the SBD), there must be some compensation for those who commute to the SBD. Indeed, because blacks are discriminated against in the housing market, they are forced to live in the central part of the city. That means those working in the SBD have long commutes that are also costly. So for blacks to obtain the same utility level wherever they work, the SBD workers have to be compensated. Because competition in the land market is quite fierce for blacks, land rent does not totally compensate them and thus, unemployment rates must be lower for SBD black workers as compared to CBD black workers. In other words, *housing discrimination by skewing blacks towards the city center increases the number of job applications of blacks for central jobs and decreases this number for suburban jobs.*

In this context, using for example Figure 4.2 (Chapter 4) to determine the equilibrium in each center $j = C, S$, it is easily seen that the unemployment rate of blacks is higher and their wage lower when they work in the CBD than in the SBD. This is because unemployment acting as a worker discipline device enables employers to pay low wages when unemployment is high. So the main argument of this model is that suburban housing discrimination skews black workers towards the CBD and thus, keeps black residences remote from the suburbs. Since black workers who work in the SBD have more costly commutes, few of them will accept SBD jobs, which makes the black CBD labor pool large relative to the SBD pool. Under an efficiency wage model, this enlargement of the CBD pool leads to a high unemployment rate among CBD workers. These results are consistent with real-world observations where, in U.S. cities, blacks working downtown tend to have higher unemployment rates and lower wages than blacks working in the suburbs (see, for example, Table 3 in Brueckner and Zenou, 2003).

Let us denote by u_B^* the unemployment rate of blacks when they are not discriminated against in the housing market (as in Figure 8.3). Since, in this case, the urban equilibrium is symmetric (Figure 8.3), the labor pool of each center contains half of the black population, $N_B/2$. As a result, u_B^* is determined by the following equation:

$$F'\left[\left(1 - u_B^*\right)\frac{N_B}{2}\right] = w_U + e + \frac{e}{m}\frac{\delta}{u_B^*}.$$

We then have the following result:

Proposition 8.3. *The black unemployment rate without housing discrimination (Figure 8.3) at the two job centers lies between the CBD and SBD black unemployment rates in the discriminating case (Figure 8.2), that is:*

$$u_{B1}^* < u_B^* < u_{B2}^*.$$

The same conclusion applied to (expected) incomes, labor pool $N_B/2$, and employment level $(1 - u_B^*)N_B/2$ at the two centers in the non-discriminating case, each of which lies between the CBD and SBD values in the discriminating equilibrium.

The intuition is straightforward. By keeping black residences in close proximity to the CBD (and remote from the SBD), suburban housing discrimination enlarges the black CBD labor pool relative to the SBD labor pool. This implies a higher unemployment rate in the CBD. The efficiency wages then endogenously adjust, leading to expected income differences as stated in Proposition 8.3.

Furthermore, it easily shown that wherever they work, black workers experience a higher unemployment rate and are paid less than white workers. Indeed, because whites are more skilled and because of housing discrimination of blacks, it is easy to construct an equilibrium where whites are better paid and experience lower rates of unemployment. The intuition is straightforward. Because of housing discrimination, blacks are forced to live in the central part of the city. Since there are more unskilled jobs, in the SBD, most blacks have poor access to unskilled jobs and those who accept to work in the SBD have long and costly commuting costs. As a result, few blacks will accept a job in the SBD and most of them will seek a CBD job. This leads to a high unemployment rate for CBD black workers (which encompasses most blacks) and, because in an efficiency wage framework, unemployment acts as a worker disciplining device, CBD firms can set low wages for black workers without fearing shirking behavior. So, white workers end up with higher wages and lower unemployment rates than black workers, mainly because of housing discrimination.

This model is also consistent with the empirical regularities mentioned in the introduction. The unemployment rate is higher downtown than in the suburbs (Table 7.1) because blacks, who are mainly unskilled (Table 7.3), are forced to live around the city center (Tables 7.2 and 7.3) far away from the suburbs where most unskilled jobs are located (Tables 7.3 and 7.5).

We can determine the extent of housing discrimination in the land market by calculating $\Psi_2(x_{BW}, E\,W_B) - \Psi_1(x_{BW}, E\,W_W)$. Using (8.25) and the fact that $x_{BW} = h_B N_B$, we obtain:

$$\Psi_2(x_{BW}, E\,W_B) - \Psi_1(x_{BW}, E\,W_W)$$
$$= \frac{e\delta}{m}\left[\left(\frac{1 - u_{B2}}{u_{B2}}\right) - \left(\frac{1 - u_{B1}}{u_{B1}}\right)\right] + \tau\,(1 + h_B)\left(\frac{h_B N_B - N_W}{2h_B}\right).$$

As expected, this difference increases in e, the effort level, δ, the job-destruction rate, τ, the commuting cost, h_B, the housing consumption of blacks, N_B, the total number of blacks, and decreases in m, the monitoring rate, and N_W, the total number of whites. More importantly, it also increases in u_{B1}, the unemployment rate in the CBD of black workers, and decreases in u_{B2}, the unemployment rate in the SBD of black workers. Indeed, the higher is u_{B1} or the lower is u_{B2}, the more black workers would like to work in SBD, but are discouraged by long commutes due to housing discrimination.

We finally have the following policy-oriented result:

Proposition 8.4. *For black workers, a decrease in the commuting cost τ leads to a lower unemployment rate in the CBD and a higher unemployment rate in the SBD, with*

$$\frac{\partial u^*_{B1}}{\partial \tau} > 0, \quad \frac{\partial u^*_{B2}}{\partial \tau} < 0.$$

The severity of the distortion caused by housing discrimination depends on the magnitude of the commuting cost parameter τ. A larger value for this parameter effectively increases the remoteness of the SBD from the black residential area (between $x = 0$ and $x = x_{BW} = h_B N_B$). Proposition 8.4 shows that this effect increases the extent to which the black labor force is skewed toward the CBD, thus amplifying the disparities between the two labor markets. Thus, the effects of spatial mismatch are magnified when the friction of space, as captured by τ, is more substantial.

Even though the mechanism is totally different, this model has similar implications in terms of policy as the redlining model of the previous section. Both a policy that reduces unemployment benefits and a policy that subsidizes commuting costs will reduce unemployment for blacks. However, this is not due to the fact that the recruitment area (the red-line) increases. Indeed, in the first policy, wages are reduced so that labor demand increases in both employment centers. In the second policy, SBD black workers are more willing to accept jobs at a longer distance which increases their labor supply. Both policies, although different, reduce the negative consequences of blacks' spatial mismatch on their labor market outcomes.

So how relevant is the mechanism highlighted in this section? Interestingly, Zax and Kain (1996) have in some sense illustrated this by studying a "natural experiment" (the case of a large firm in the service industry that relocated from the center of Detroit to the suburb Dearborn in 1974). They show that, among workers whose commuting time was increased, black workers were over-represented and not all could follow the firm. This had two consequences. First, as in our model, segregation forced some blacks to quit their jobs. Second, there was a drastical decrease in the share of black workers applying for jobs at the firm (53% to 25% in 5 years before and after the relocation), and the share of black workers in hires also fell from 39% to 27%. Fernandez (1994) also analyzes a "natural experiment" by studying the relocation of a Milwaukee food-processing plant from the city's CBD to the suburban ring. He finds similar results. This evidence suggests that black workers may indeed refuse jobs that involve too long commutes.

4. A More General Model

We would now like to extend the previous model to allow for some competition between the two job centers, the CBD and the SBD. For this purpose, we keep assumptions ($H2$), i.e., black workers consume less land than white workers; ($H3$) i.e. black families are discriminated in the housing market; ($H5$) the labor markets of blacks and whites are separated; and ($H7$) i.e. black workers are *unskilled* while white workers are *skilled*, all workers (black or white) use the same public transport mode (mass transit), and blacks are paid efficiency wages while white workers are not.

However, we relax assumption ($H1$) so that employed and unemployed workers now have *different commuting costs*, which implies that $0 < s < 1$, and ($H4$) so that all workers now have *zero relocation costs*. More importantly, we also relax assumption ($H6$) so that workers can search everywhere in the city. This was a crucial assumption in the previous section, which enormously simplified the model since the labor market was exactly as in the benchmark model of Chapter 4. In particular, there was no interaction between the CBD and the SBD and, therefore, the Markov process in the labor market in each center was only characterized by two states: employed in center $j = 1, 2$ or unemployed. By relaxing ($H6$), we will now have to consider a three-state Markov process (employed in the CBD, employed in the SBD and unemployed) so that the efficiency wage will have to reflect the opportunities not only of being unemployed, but also of working in the SBD. We will now use the model developed in Chapter 6, Section 4.

Finally, in contrast to the previous section, it is assumed that, for blacks, each center is specialized. Even if all jobs for blacks are unskilled, it is assumed that information and moral hazard problems only prevail in the CBD so that CBD firms pay efficiency wages to their workers. In contrast, no such problems arise in the SBD and workers are paid a minimum wage imposed by the government. For whites, we assume, for simplicity, that they are never unemployed and that wages are exogenously higher in the CBD than in the SBD (where a minimum wage also prevails). This is just capturing the fact that CBD firms have access to a better infrastructure so that productivity is higher in the CBD than in the SBD. The assumption about whites is not important, since we will once more mainly focus on black workers and their labor market outcomes.

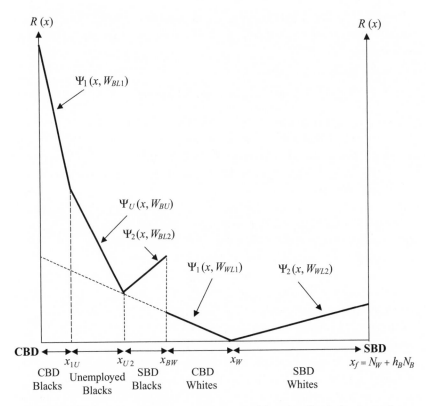

Figure 8.4. Spatial mismatch in a duocentric city with housing discrimination and zero relocation costs.

The urban-land-use equilibrium with housing discrimination is depicted in Figure 8.4, which is similar to Figure 8.2, but includes a new category of workers – black unemployed workers.

An important difference between the two figures is that the utility level of workers of type i is no longer the same in Figure 8.4, mainly because of zero location costs. Indeed, in steady-state, there will now be three groups of black workers with different utilities, CBD, SBD, and unemployed workers, and two groups of white workers, CBD and SBD workers. We denote by W_{iL1}, W_{iL1} and W_{BU} the instantaneous utility reached by all workers of type i working in the CBD, the SBD and being unemployed. The bid-rent functions of employed workers of type $i = B, W$ in the CBD are equal to:

$$\Psi_1(x, W_{iL1}) = \frac{w_{i1} - e - \tau x - W_{iL1}}{h_i}, \qquad (8.36)$$

where $h_B < h_W = 1$. We assume work trips to be separated from shopping trips, so that non-workers commute to the CBD only for non-work activities; it is also assumed that they commute less than the employed, i.e., $0 < s < 1$. Thus, for an unemployed black worker, we have:

$$\Psi_U(x, W_{BU}) = \frac{w_U - s \tau x - W_{BU}}{h_B}. \tag{8.37}$$

For workers of type $i = B, W$ employed in the SBD, their bid rents are equal to:

$$\Psi_2(x, W_{iL2}) = \frac{\overline{w}_2 - s \tau x - \tau (N_W + h_B N_B - x) - W_{iL2}}{h_i}, \tag{8.38}$$

where $\overline{w}_2$ is the exogenous minimum wage in the SBD common for all workers. For simplicity, the effort exerted on simple jobs in the SBD is normalized to zero. Here, SBD workers located in x need to commute to the CBD for non-work activities and the costs amount to $s \tau x$, but they also need to go to the SBD to work, and the costs are equal to $\tau(x_f - x)$ since the SBD is located in $x_f = N_W + h_B N_B$.

Let us now define the urban-land-use equilibrium. We denote agricultural land rent (the rent outside the city or the opportunity rent) by R_A and, without loss of generality, we normalize it to zero. We first have:

$$N_B = L_{B1} + L_{B2} + U_B \quad \text{and} \quad N_W = L_{W1} + L_{W2}, \tag{8.39}$$

where L_{ij} is the employment level for individuals of type $i = B, W$ working in job center $j = 1, 2$. It is interesting to compare (8.39) with (8.2) from the previous model. Indeed, because we relax assumption ($H6$), we do not need N_{i1} and N_{i2} since black and white workers are no longer defined in terms of their "attachment" to a job center, but rather in terms of their employment situation with respect to a job center. Denoting the border between CBD blacks and black unemployed workers by $x_{1U} = h_B L_{B1}$, the border between black unemployed workers and SBD blacks by $x_{U2} = h_B (N_B - L_{B2})$ and the border between CBD white and SBD black workers by $x_W = h_B N_B + L_{W1}$, we have the following definition:

Definition 8.3. *An urban-land-use equilibrium with no relocation costs and housing discrimination in a duocentric city (Figure 8.4) is a 6-tuple* $(W^*_{BL1}, W^*_{BL2}, W^*_{BU}, W^*_{WL1}, W^*_{WL2}, R^*(x))$ *such that:*

$$\Psi_1(x_{1U}, W^*_{BL1}) = \Psi_U(x_{1U}, W^*_{BU}) \tag{8.40}$$

$$\Psi_U(x_{U2}, W^*_{BU}) = \Psi_2(x_{U2}, W^*_{BL2}) \tag{8.41}$$

$$\Psi_1(x_W, W^*_{WL1}) = \Psi_2(x_W, W^*_{WL2}) = 0 \qquad (8.42)$$

$$\Psi_U(x_{U2}, W^*_{BU}) = \Psi_1(x_{U2}, W^*_{WL1}) \qquad (8.43)$$

$$R^*(x) = \max\left\{\Psi_{L,1}(x, W^*_{L,1}), \Psi_{L,2}(x, W^*_{L,2}), \Psi_U(x, W^*_U), 0\right\}$$
$$\text{at each} \quad x \in (0, x^*_f]. \qquad (8.44)$$

As stated above, an important difference between this model and the previous one is that all workers of type i do not need to obtain the same utility level in equilibrium. In fact, there will be different utility levels between individuals working in the CBD and the SBD. By solving these equations, we obtain:

$$W^*_{BU} = w_U - s\,\tau\,h_B\,(N_B - L_{B2}) - \tau h_B\,(L_{W1} + h_B L_{B2}) \qquad (8.45)$$

$$W^*_{BL1} = w_{B1} - e - s\tau\,h_B\,(N_B - L_{B1} - L_{B2})$$
$$- \tau h_B\,(L_{W1} + L_{B1} + h_B L_{B2}) \qquad (8.46)$$

$$W^*_{BL2} = \overline{w}_2 - \tau\,[N_W + h_B L_{W1} + h_B L_{B2}\,(1 + h_B)] - s\,\tau\,h_B\,(N_B + L_{B2})$$
$$\qquad (8.47)$$

$$W^*_{WL1} = w_{W1} - e - \tau\,(h_B N_B + L_{W1}) \qquad (8.48)$$

$$W^*_{WL2} = \overline{w}_2 - s\,\tau\,(h_B N_B + L_{W1}) - \tau\,L_{W2} \qquad (8.49)$$

$$R^*(x) = \begin{cases} s\,\tau\,(N_B - L_{B1} - L_{B2}) \\ \quad + \tau(L_{W1} + L_{B1} + h_B L_{B2} - x/h_B) & \text{for } x \le x_{1U} \\[4pt] s\,\tau(N_B - L_{B2} - x/h_B) \\ \quad + \tau(L_{W1} + h_B L_{B2}) & \text{for } x_{1U} \le x \le x_{U2} \\[4pt] \tau[L_{W1} + (1 + h_B - s)L_{B2}] \\ \quad - (1-s)\tau(N_B - x/h_B) & \text{for } x_{U2} \le x \le x_{BW} \ . \\[4pt] \tau(h_B N_B + L_{W1} - x) & \text{for } x_{BW} \le x \le x_W \\[4pt] \tau(L_{W1} - h_B N_B + x) \\ \quad + s\,\tau(h_B N_B + L_{W1} - x) & \text{for } x_W \le x \le x_f \end{cases}$$
$$\qquad (8.50)$$

Let us now study the labor market. For black workers, we follow exactly the same model as in Section 4 of Chapter 6, where it is assumed that the CBD job-acquisition rate is a_{B1}, independently of the employment status of workers. Moreover, the rate at which the unemployed workers obtain a CBD job is not equal to that for obtaining an SBD job. We indeed have $a_{B1} \ne a_{B2}$ and thus, a_{B2} represents the *secondary-sector job acquisition rate*

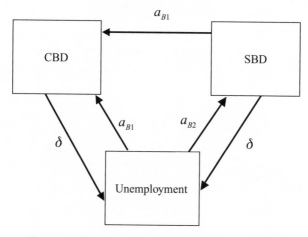

Figure 8.5. Flows in the labor market for black workers.

for nonworkers. Figure 8.5 describes the flows in the labor market for blacks, where δ is the job-destruction rate.

The flows in the labor market for whites, who are never unemployed, are displayed in Figure 8.6. It is assumed that CBD jobs are better paid than SBD jobs, and thus all workers would like to work there. Workers in the CBD lose their jobs at the rate δ and instantaneously, find a lower-paid SBD job. They can then once more find a CBD job at the rate a_{W1}.

As a result, for black workers, the state of the economy evolves following a *three-state* Markov process with states: employed in the CBD, employed in the SBD and unemployed. Using the same procedure as in Section 4 of Chapter 6, we easily obtain:

$$\frac{U_B^*}{N_B} = \frac{\delta}{a_{B1} + a_{B2} + \delta} \tag{8.51}$$

$$\frac{L_{B1}^*}{N_B} = \frac{a_{B1}}{\delta + a_{B1}} \tag{8.52}$$

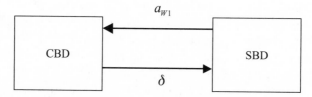

Figure 8.6. Flows in the labor market for white workers.

$$\frac{L^*_{B2}}{N_B} = \frac{a_{B2}\,\delta}{(a_{B1} + \delta)\,(a_{B1} + a_{B2} + \delta)}.$$ (8.53)

For white workers, the state of the economy evolves following a *two-state* Markov process: employed in the CBD and employed in the SBD. We easily obtain:

$$\frac{L^*_{W1}}{N_W} = \frac{a_{W1}}{\delta + a_{W1}}.$$ (8.54)

Let us now determine the efficiency wage in the CBD for black workers. In steady-state, the lifetime expected utilities of black workers I^{NS}_{L1}, I^{S}_{L1}, I_U and I_{L2} are given by:

$$r\,I^{NS}_{BL1} = W^*_{BL1} - \delta\,(I^{NS}_{BL1} - I_{BU})$$ (8.55)

$$r\,I^{S}_{BL1} = W^*_{BL1} + e - (\delta + m)\,(I^{S}_{BL1} - I_{BU})$$ (8.56)

$$r\,I_{BU} = W^*_{BU} + a_{B1}\,(I_{BL1} - I_{BU}) + a_{B2}\,(I_{BL2} - I_{BU})$$ (8.57)

$$r\,I_{BL2} = W^*_{BL2} - \delta\,(I_{BL2} - I_{BU}) + a_{B1}\,(I_{BL1} - I_{BL2}),$$ (8.58)

where r is the discount rate. Because of shirking behavior, firms will choose a wage w_{B1} so that $I^{NS}_{BL1} = I^{S}_{BL2} = I_{BL1}$, i.e., the efficiency wage must be set to make (black) workers indifferent between shirking and not shirking. By proceeding as in Section 4 of Chapter 6, we obtain the following efficiency wage:

$$w^{HD*}_{B1} = \Upsilon(a_{B1}, a_{B2})w_U$$ (8.59)
$$+ [1 - \Upsilon(a_{B1}, a_{B2})]\,[\overline{w}_2 - \tau\,(N_W + h_B L_{B2})]$$
$$+ e + \frac{e_1}{m}\,(r + \delta + a_{B1}) + (1 - s)\,\tau\,h_B L_{B1}$$

where the weighting factor $0 < \Upsilon(a_{B1}, a_{B2}) < 1$ is defined as:

$$\Upsilon(a_{B1}, a_{B2}) = \frac{r + a_{B1} + \delta}{r + a_{B1} + a_{B2} + \delta}.$$ (8.60)

For blacks, the efficiency wage (8.59) in the CBD is a convex combination of the unemployment benefit w_U and the (minimum) wage $\overline{w}_2$ offered in the SBD. This reflects the fact that when setting the efficiency wage, firms must take into account the opportunities that workers have outside the CBD labor market. In particular, when deciding whether to shirk or not, workers take into account that if they are detected and fired, they will be unemployed with a possibility of finding a job in the future, not only in the CBD, but also in the SBD. This is in contrast to the efficiency wage determined in the previous section and given by (8.8). In that wage, only w_U was taken into account because of assumption (A6), which implies that a CBD worker could not search for an SBD job and vice versa. We are now able to define a labor market equilibrium:

Definition 8.4. *A spatial mismatch labor market equilibrium with efficiency wages and zero relocation costs is a 5-tuple* $(w_{B1}^{HD*}, L_{B1}^*, L_{B2}^*, L_{W1}^*, L_{W2}^*)$, *such that (8.59),*

$$F_B' \left(e L_{B1}^*\right) = w_{B1}^* \tag{8.61}$$

$$F_B' \left(L_{B2}^*\right) = \overline{w}_2 \tag{8.62}$$

$$F_W' \left(e L_{W1}^*\right) = w_{W1} \tag{8.63}$$

$$F_W'(L_{W2}^*) = \overline{w}_2 \tag{8.64}$$

are satisfied.

In contrast to the model of the previous section, it is not interesting to compare the difference in employment levels between the CBD and the SBD since different wage structures prevail. However, it can be seen that the unemployment level in this economy is affected by housing discrimination. Indeed, most blacks live close to the CBD where an efficiency wage policy is implemented, leading to a high level of unemployment. In the suburbs, where other types of jobs are available, some blacks prefer to be unemployed rather than to work in the SBD because of the long commutes involved.

To further investigate the impact of housing discrimination on labor market outcomes of black workers, let us consider the case of no housing discrimination. Its urban equilibrium is depicted in Figure 8.7.

In this figure, it is assumed that $s < h_B$ so that black unemployed workers have a flatter bid-rent than CBD white employed workers. Using the bid-rents (8.36)–(8.38), the urban equilibrium displayed in Figure 8.7 leads to the following equilibrium utilities and land rents:

$$W_{BL1}^* = w_{B1} - e - \tau h_B \left(L_{B1} + L_{W1}\right) - s \tau h_B \left(N_B - L_{B1} - L_{B2}\right)$$

$$W_{BL2}^* = \overline{w}_2 - s \tau \left[h_B \left(N_B - L_{B2}\right) + L_{W1}\right] - \tau \left(L_{W2} + h_B L_{B2}\right)$$

$$W_{BU}^* = w_U - s \tau \left[h_B \left(N_B - L_{B2}\right) + L_{W1}\right]$$

$$W_{WL1}^* = w_{W1} - e - \tau \left(h_B L_{B1} + L_{W1}\right) - s \tau \left(N_B - L_{B1} - L_{B2}\right)$$

$$W_{WL2}^* = \overline{w}_2 - s \tau \left(L_{W1} + h_B N_B - h_B L_{B2}\right) - \tau \left(L_{W2} + h_B L_{B2}\right)$$

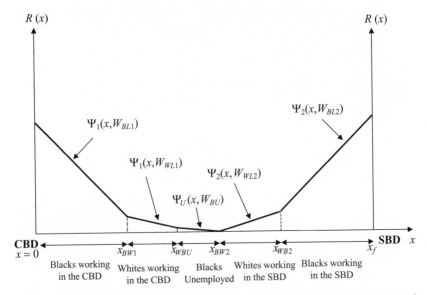

Figure 8.7. Urban equilibrium in a duocentric city with no housing discrimination and zero relocation costs.

$$
R^*(x) = \begin{cases}
\tau(L_{B1} + L_{W1} - x/h_B) & \text{for} \quad x \le x_{BW1} \\
\quad + s\,\tau(N_B - L_{B1} - L_{B2}) & \\
\tau(h_B L_{B1} + L_{W1} - x) & \text{for } x_{BW1} \le x \le x_{WBU} \\
\quad + s\,\tau(N_B - L_{B1} - L_{B2}) & \\
s\,\tau[(N_B - L_{B2}) + (L_{W1} - x)/h_B] & \text{for } x_{WBU} \le x \le x_{BW2} \\
s\,\tau(L_{W1} + h_B N_B - h_B L_{B2} - x) & \text{for } x_{BW2} \le x \le x_{WB2} \\
\quad + \tau[x - h_B(N_B - L_{B2}) - L_{W1}] & \\
s\,\tau[(N_B - L_{B2}) + (L_{W1} - x)/h_B] & \text{for } x_{WB2} \le x \le x_f \\
\quad + \tau[(x - L_{W1})/h_B - (N_B - L_{B2})]
\end{cases}
$$

Let us calculate the efficiency wage. Once more, following the model in Section 4 of Chapter 6, we obtain:

$$
w_{B1}^{ND*} = \Upsilon(a_{B1}, a_{B2})\,w_U + [1 - \Upsilon(a_{B1}, a_{B2})]\,[\overline{w}_2 - \tau\,(L_{W2} + h_B L_{B2})]
$$
$$
+ e + \frac{e}{m}\,(r + \delta + a_{B1}) + (1 - s)\,\tau\,h_B L_{B1} + \tau\,L_{W1}\,(h_B - s),
$$

where $\Upsilon(a_1, a_2)$ is defined by (8.60). If we compare w_{B1}^{HD*}, define (8.59) and w_{B1}^{ND*}, we have:

Proposition 8.5. *The wage difference due to housing discrimination is equal to:*

$$w_{B1}^{ND*} - w_{B1}^{HD*} = \tau L_{W1} \left[1 - \Upsilon(a_{B1}, a_{B2}) + h_B - s \right]$$

$$= \tau L_{W1} \left[\frac{a_{B2}}{r + a_{B1} + a_{B2} + \delta} + h_B - s \right]$$

where $w_{B1}^{ND*} > w_{B1}^{HD*}$.

The main difference with the housing discrimination case is that there are fewer workers who are unemployed because now workers who find a job in the SBD relocate to the area close to the SBD whereas before (Figure 8.4) they could not; they could only relocate to area $[x_{U2}, x_{BW}]$ which is quite far away from the SBD. In other words, workers are here unemployed, not because they refuse a job in the SBD, but because they prefer to wait for a CBD job. In the case with housing discrimination, there were two reasons why black workers were unemployed: waiting for a CBD job *and* refusing to take an SBD job because of long commutes.

We can determine the extent of housing discrimination in the land market by calculating $\Psi_2(x_{BW}, W_{BL2}) - \Psi_1(x_{BW}, W_{WL1})$, which using (8.50) and the fact that $x_{BW} = h_B N_B$, is equal to: $\tau (1 + h_B - s) L_{B2}$. Not surprisingly, this difference increases with τ, the commuting cost, h_B, the housing consumption of blacks and decreases with s, the part of the commuting costs dedicated to non-work activities. More importantly, it also increases with the employment level of black workers in the SBD, since the larger the number of black workers commuting to the SBD, the higher is the cost (in terms of land price) of housing discrimination.

5. Notes on the Literature

As explained in previous chapters, there are few theoretical models on the spatial mismatch hypothesis and even fewer that incorporate both the labor (especially the efficiency wage model) and the land market in their analysis, a crucial feature for understanding the spatial mismatch hypothesis. Section 2 is based on Zenou (2002) while Section 3 elaborates on Brueckner and Zenou (2003). The model developed in Section 4 has been written specifically for this book.

CHAPTER NINE

Peer Effects, Social Networks, and Labor Market Outcomes in Cities

1. Introduction

In the two previous chapters, distance to jobs was put forward as the main reason for explaining the high unemployment rates and the low wages of black workers and other ethnic minorities (the so-called spatial-mismatch hypothesis). This is obviously not the only determinant since both in cities where black workers reside *close* to jobs (such as New York, Chicago, or Philadelphia) and in cities where they live *far away* from jobs (such as Los Angeles, Atlanta, or Houston), black workers do experience adverse labor market outcomes. In the present chapter, we would like to focus on another important aspect, namely the role of *social networks* in finding a job.

A social network is a social structure made of *nodes* (which are individuals or firms) that are *tied* by one or more specific types of interdependency, such as values, friends, kinship, etc. As a result, any social network analysis studies social relationships in terms of *nodes* and *ties*. Nodes are the individual actors within the networks, and ties are the relationships between the actors. These concepts are often displayed in a social network diagram, where nodes are the points and ties are the lines. In the present chapter, we mainly focus on ties between friends who can exchange information about jobs. The study of social networks in labor markets highlights the nature of labor market transactions as very different from trading in goods, and postulates that access to information is heavily influenced by social structure. Individuals use connections with others, such as friends and social and professional acquaintances, to maintain information networks.[1]

---

[1] Sociologists have been studying the importance of social networks in the labor market for a long time. See, in particular, Granovetter (1995).

It should be clear that social networks are also localized, which means that residential segregation and distance to jobs can isolate black workers and reduce their social contacts with whites, thus limiting their information about jobs (Holzer, 1987, 1988; Wilson, 1996; Ihlanfeldt, 1997; O'Reagan and Quigley, 1998; Kleit, 2001; Topa, 2001; Conley and Topa, 2002; Bayer, Ross, and Topa, 2008). Urban segregation, distance to jobs, and social networks are therefore linked together. The aim of this chapter is to study these three aspects together to get a better understanding of urban ghettos and their consequences on the labor-market outcomes of ethnic minorities.

There is a growing literature on peer effects and social interactions (see, e.g., Akerlof, 1997; Glaeser, Sacerdote, and Scheinkman, 1996; and the literature survey by Durlauf, 2004) and social networks (Jackson and Wolinsky, 1996; Bala and Goyal, 2000; Ballester, Calvó-Armengol, and Zenou, 2006; Bramoullé and Kranton, 2007; Calvó-Armengol, Patacchini, and Zenou (2008); the literature surveys by Jackson, 2005, 2006, 2007, and recent books by Vega-Redondo, 2007; Goyal, 2007; Jackson, 2008). The former literature studies how the behavior of individual agents is affected by that of their peers.[2] Peer effects are conceived as an average intra-group externality that identically affects all members of a given group. As a result, the group boundaries for such homogeneous effects are often arbitrary and set at quite an aggregate level. For instance, peer effects in crime are often defined at the neighborhood level, peer effects in school at the classroom or school level, etc. In contrast, the latter literature builds on the smallest unit of analysis for the cross influence of individuals, the dyad. The collection of dyadic bilateral relationships constitutes a *social network*. What is of importance is not only the influence of direct friends or peers on an individual's behavior but also that of friends of friends, etc. In this context, the *geometry* of the social network is crucial for understanding individuals' outcomes.

These two literatures are very relevant in education, crime, labor markets, fertility, participation in welfare programs, etc. In particular, there is a rich literature on the role of social networks in the labor market (see the literature surveys by Granovetter, 2005; Ioannides and Loury, 2004; Calvó-Armengol

---

[2] In fact, social interactions refer to particular forms of externalities in which the actions of a reference group affect an individual's preferences. The reference group depends on the context and is typically an individual's family, neighbors, friends, or peers. As Scheinkman (2008) put it, "social interactions are sometimes called *non-market interactions* to emphasize the fact that these interactions are not regulated by the price mechanism."

and Ioannides, 2008), but until recently, the network literatures in both sociology (Fernandez and Su, 2004) and economics have tended to ignore space, especially from a theoretical point of view.[3,4]

In the present chapter, we focus on the relationship between non-market interactions (or peer effects and social networks) and urban economics through the labor market. In particular, we will study how residential location determines social interactions which, in turn, affect labor market outcomes. This will help us explain why ethnic minorities end up with very adverse labor market outcomes. In all models presented in this chapter, the role of the social network is to help unemployed workers obtain a job. There are, however, some models in which social networks help firms screen workers in the hiring process,[5] which is not what we are doing here.

To be more precise, we present three different models of labor social networks in cities. We start with an urban model where the social network is not explicitly modeled, but captured by externalities (Section 2), so that we are basically dealing with peer effects. Then, we propose a framework where individuals belong to mutually exclusive two-person groups, referred to as *dyads* (Section 3). The land market is explicitly modeled, but the social network is reduced to dyads. Finally, in the last part of the chapter (Section 4), the social network is explicitly modeled using a graph of relationships (as in Goyal, 2007 or Jackson, 2008), but the land market is not explicitly introduced. In all these models, we determine the impact on labor market outcomes of ethnic minorities.

---

[3] In his review article, Glaeser (2000) emphasizes the natural connections between non-market interactions and urban economics. First, the demand for cities is largely driven by non-market interactions (information and idea flows, crime, prejudice, etc.). Second, interactions tend to be determined by spatial proximity.

[4] Using using the 1998 Egyptian Labor Market Survey, Wahba and Zenou (2005) find that the probability to find a job through social networks, relative to other search methods, increases with population density and thus with urban density.

[5] For example, Montgomery (1991b) emphasizes the role of networks and their advantages for the employer relative to other channels as providing a screening device against low-ability workers. Indeed, it is widely documented that individuals tend to interact with individuals similar to themselves (a property often called assortative matching or inbreeding bias). Therefore, currently employed, high-ability workers (whose type has already been revealed to the employer) are more likely to refer workers of the same type. For this reason, employers often delegate the screening function of finding a suitable employee to the network of their current workforce. Finneran and Kelly (2003) use a similar idea to show that below a critical density of referrals, workers have no chance of being hired.

2. Social Networks as Externalities

2.1. The Model

Let us develop an urban search model similar to that presented in Chapter 1. Consider a continuum of equally productive workers (blacks and whites) uniformly distributed along a linear and closed city. Blacks and whites have low skills. All land is owned by absentee landlords and all firms are exogenously located in the Central Business District (CBD).

In contrast to the two previous chapters, we would now like to consider two types of black workers: status-seeker and conformist blacks. The former group mainly prefers interactions with whites (they want to increase their *status*) while the latter has strong preferences for mainly interacting with blacks (they want to *conform* to the norm of their group). Indeed, it has been observed that in the United States, African Americans tend to "choose" to adopt what is termed *oppositional identities*, that is, some actively reject the dominant ethnic (e.g., white) behavioral norms while others totally assimilate them (see, in particular, Ainsworth-Darnell and Downey, 1998). Studies in the U.S. (but also in the U.K.) have, for example, found that African American students in poor areas may be ambivalent about learning standard English and performing well at school because this may be regarded as "acting white" and adopting mainstream identities (Fordham and Ogbu, 1986; Wilson, 1987; Delpit, 1995; Akerlof, 1997; Ogbu, 2003; Austen-Smith and Fryer, 2005; Fryer and Torelli, 2005; Selod and Zenou, 2006; Battu, McDonald, and Zenou, 2007). In some instances, oppositional identities produce significant economic and social conflicts.

Thus, there are three groups of workers: two types of blacks denoted by BS (status-seeker blacks) and BC (conformist blacks), respectively, and one type of whites, denoted by W. For whites, it is assumed that they prefer to mainly interact with other whites. While there are some models in which the choice of oppositional identities is endogenous,[6] here we consider it to be exogenous and directly model it in the agents' preferences (see below).

The fact that whites mainly prefer to interact with whites, while this behavior is divided for blacks, is well-documented in economics, but also in sociology and psychology where adolescents feel more comfortable around

---

[6] See, in particular, Akerlof and Kranton (2000); Austen-Smith and Fryer (2005); Battu, McDonald, and Zenou (2007); Patacchini and Zenou (2006b); and De Martí and Zenou (2008).

others of their own race (Clark and Ayers, 1988; Hallinan and Tuma, 1979). Cutler, Glaeser, Vigdor (1999) also find similar attitudes among blacks. They use the following question from the General Social Survey in the United States in 1982: "If you could find the housing that you would want and like, would you rather live in a neighborhood that is all black, mostly black, half black, half white, or mostly white?" On average, 67% of blacks choose either the third or fourth option, meaning that a large fraction of blacks would like to interact with whites (either because they like whites or because they anticipate the positive effects on education and labor market outcomes), but also 33% of them would like to mostly interact with blacks. Using data from the National Longitudinal Survey of Adolescent Health (AddHealth) in the United States, which contains detailed information on a nationally representative sample of 90,118 pupils in roughly 130 private and public schools, entering grades 7–12 in the 1994–1995 school year, Patacchini and Zenou (2006b) study the choice of best friends among these adolescents. Figure 9.1 displays the empirical distribution of teenagers by the share of same-race friends for blacks and whites, respectively. It shows that 65% of the white pupils have more than 80% of same-race friends (see the lower panel of Figure 9.1). It also shows that blacks are more heterogenous in their choice of friends than whites, since there are mainly three modes in the distribution of friends: for 32% of the black teenagers 80% of their friends are blacks, for 25% there are 70% of their friends who are whites and for 10% there are 60% of their friends who are blacks (and thus 40% are whites).

The sizes of these population groups are, respectively, denoted by N_{BS}, N_{BC}, and N_W, with $N_{BS} + N_{BC} + N_W = 1$, so that the end of the city is at a distance 1 from the CBD. We assume that $N_W > N_B$, which is the case in most cities ($N_B = N_{BS} + N_{BC}$). In the labor market, we assume that firms only resort to two types of recruitment methods: word of mouth or posting "want ads" in local newspapers. We also assume that even though blacks and whites are both low-skill workers and thus have the same level of human capital, they do not compete for the same jobs and thus, their labor markets are separated (or segmented).[7]

2.1.1. Racial Preferences and Utilities. We assume that groups always form spatially homogenous communities. In other words, we only focus on equilibria where all members of a given community live together and do not mix with members of other communities. Let us now express the utility

---

[7] For some evidence on this issue, see Chapter 7.

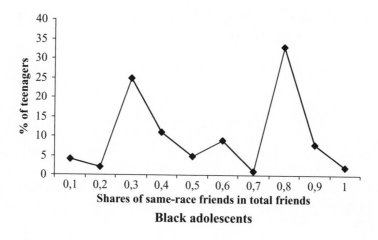

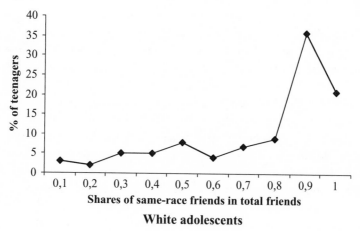

Figure 9.1. Percentage of same race-friends for adolescents. *Source:* AddHealth in the 1994–1995 school year (Calculation by Patacchini and Zenou, 2006b).

functions of workers. For this purpose, let us consider an individual located at x in the city. If this individual is white, we denote by x_B the location of the closest black worker from a white worker. If this individual is a conformist or a status-seeking black, we denote by x_W the location of the closest white from this black worker. Since communities are assumed to be homogenous, observe that, by definition, the location of the closest black (white) individual is the location of the closest border between communities. This is because two close neighbors share the same closest neighborhood border. The respective utility functions for a white, a status-seeking black, and a conformist black worker of employment status $es = L, U$ residing in location x are then assumed to be given by:

$$\Omega_{Wes}(x) = w_{es} - \tau x - R(x) + \bowtie_W |x - x_B| \tag{9.1}$$

$$\Omega_{BSes}(x) = w_{es} - \tau x - R(x) + \bowtie_{BS} |x - x_W| \tag{9.2}$$

$$\Omega_{BCes}(x) = w_{es} - \tau x - R(x) + \bowtie_{BC} |x - x_W|, \tag{9.3}$$

where w_{es} is the exogenous income of a worker of employment status $es = L, U$,[8] τ is the commuting cost per unit of distance, $R(x)$ is the land rent at a distance x from the BD and $\bowtie_W$, $\bowtie_{BS}$, and $\bowtie_{BC}$ measure the racial preferences for whites, status-seeker blacks, and conformist blacks, respectively.

The following comments are in order. First, irrespective of race, all workers are paid the same (minimum) wage, w_L. This is because all workers have the same education level and are equally productive. Second, unemployed and employed workers bear the same commuting cost per unit of distance. This assumption can be justified by considering that when unemployed, workers still have to go to the CBD in order to shop. Third, in our formulation, the racial externality incurred by a worker of one community is expressed through the distance to the other community. Therefore, *racial preferences are here captured by the fact that individuals may want to live far from or close to the other community so as to avoid contact or interact with members of the other group.* We assume that all whites want to live far away from blacks and that some blacks (labeled "conformist blacks") want to live far away from whites. In our framework, this requires $\bowtie_W > 0$ and $\bowtie_{BC} > 0$. We also assume that there is another group of blacks (labeled "status-seeker blacks") who would like to live close to whites, implying $\bowtie_{BS} < 0$. It is then easily seen that for status-seeker blacks, utility increases with proximity to the boundary between communities, reflecting the benefit of living close to the other community.

2.1.2. Job Search, Social Networks, and Arrival Rates.

In the following, we use subscript $i = B, W$ for blacks and whites and among blacks, we use subscript $r = C, S$ to distinguish conformists from status seekers. Consequently, we shall use the double subscript ir with $ir = W, BC, BS$ to refer to each of our three groups. Let us start by presenting the stocks in the labor

---

[8] In this section, we assume that both wages and unemployment benefits are exogenous with $w_L > w_U > 0$.

market. There are M jobs (or firms since each firm only hires one worker) in the economy.[9] This implies that:

$$M = L + V \tag{9.4}$$

$$1 = L + U, \tag{9.5}$$

where L, U, and V are, respectively, the total number of employed workers, unemployed workers, and vacancies in the economy (since each firm only hires one worker, L is also the total number of filled jobs).

As stated above, there are only two types of jobs in the economy: one for blacks and one for whites. In other words, some firms will only hire white workers (type W–firms), while others will only hire black workers (type B–firms). Consequently, the matching function is race-specific and equal to:

$$d_i \equiv d(\bar{s}_i U_i, V_i) \qquad i = B, W, \tag{9.6}$$

where U_i and V_i are, respectively, the total number of unemployed workers and vacancies of type $i = B$, W in the economy, and $U_B = U_{BC} + U_{BS}$. Each unemployed worker of type W, BC, BS provides a search intensity s_{ir} (which will be determined below). Accordingly,

$$\bar{s}_W = s_W \text{ and } \bar{s}_B = \frac{s_{BC} U_{BC} + s_{BS} U_{BS}}{U_{BC} + U_{BS}} \tag{9.7}$$

is a group-specific index of aggregate information about economic opportunities. As a result, the rate at which the vacancies of firms of type $i = B$, W are filled is given by:

$$\frac{d(\bar{s}_i U_i, V_i)}{V_i} = d\left(\frac{1}{\theta_i}, 1\right) \equiv q(\theta_i),$$

where $\theta_i = V_i / (\bar{s}_i U_i)$ is a measure of labor market i's tightness, in units of information intensity or search efficiency. Similarly, the group-specific job arrival rate for workers of type $ir = W$, BC, BS is given by:

$$s_{ir} \frac{d(\bar{s}_i U_i, V_i)}{\bar{s}_i U_i} = s_{ir} d(1, \theta_i) \equiv s_{ir} \theta_i q(\theta_i).$$

For workers of type $ir = W$, BS, BC, finding a job depends on the interplay of two factors: the rate at which they gather information (which is group-specific and given by s_{ir}) and the search externalities (which are race-specific and captured by θ_i).

---

[9] The number of jobs is fixed to M and hence, in contrast to the benchmark model of urban search (Chapter 1), there will not be a free-entry condition.

As in the models of Chapter 1, s_{ir} *establishes a link between labor and land markets* since it is a function of workers' location and thus of city structure. It is equal to:

$$s_{ir} = s_0 + s_g\, g_{ir} - s_x\, \overline{x}_{ir} \qquad ir = W,\ BS,\ BC, \qquad (9.8)$$

where $s_0 > 0$ is the common information about jobs available to anyone (independently of race or space), g_{ir} denotes the (endogenous) local social network of a worker of type ir and $\overline{x}_{ir}$ is the (endogenous) average distance to the employment center for workers of type ir. Observe that s_g and s_x are positive parameters that measure the respective impacts of social networks and distance to jobs on s_{ir}.

As stated above, s_{ir} is the rate at which workers gather information about jobs. Formula (9.8) differs from (1.45) since it assumes that besides the common knowledge factor. There are two ways of learning about jobs: either employed workers hear about a job and transmit this information to all their residential unemployed neighbors or the unemployed directly read about job opportunities in the newspapers published in their area of residence.

Let us now present in detail the two channels through which information about jobs can be gathered. *The first channel operates via peer effects (referred to as social networks here) which are built on local connections.* The local connections that individuals from a given group ir can use to find a job are measured by g_{ir}, which we assume to be a positive function of that group's employment rate $1 - u_{ir}$. In other words, when the unemployment rate is high among a particular group, individuals in that group have few connections that can refer them to jobs and their social network is poor.

As far as whites are concerned, individuals only use (local) connections with other whites, so that their social network is simply defined by:

$$g_W = 1 - u_W. \qquad (9.9)$$

Since we have two groups for blacks (conformists and status seekers), there are two cases depending on their respective residential location in the city. If blacks from group $r = C, S$ reside far away from whites, they only benefit from their own connections to jobs, which implies that:

$$g_{Br} = 1 - u_{Br}. \qquad (9.10)$$

If, on the contrary, blacks from group r reside in the same neighborhood as whites (or, more accurately in our model, in an adjacent neighborhood) they benefit from their own connections to jobs and also from part of the social network of whites (because of the local interactions between the two neighboring groups). Observe that even if black and white labor markets are segmented, employed whites can still transmit information about job opportunities to unemployed blacks since, being employed, they have access to a wider range of information than the unemployed. Thus, the social network of blacks from group ir depends on their own employment rate, but also on that of their white neighbors, so that we have:

$$g_{Br} = g_0(1 - u_W) + (1 - g_0)(1 - u_{Br}),\qquad(9.11)$$

with $0 < g_0 < 1$. This local externality causes the employment rate in the black neighborhood to be positively affected by the employment rate in the adjacent white area.

The second way workers can learn about jobs involves local formal sources of information. This part is different from (1.45) where search intensity was *continuously* decreasing with distance to jobs x. Here, what we have in mind is the amount of information conveyed by ads in local newspapers at a neighborhood level. Obviously, this type of information is available to all workers residing in the same neighborhood since they can all buy the same local newspaper. Since employers tend to post more ads in newspapers that cover areas adjacent to their firms, we assume that the quantity of information available in each neighborhood decreases with the *neighborhood*'s distance to the CBD. This is why, in (9.8), we have considered that the job acquisition rate of type-i workers negatively depends on $\overline{x}_{ir}$, the workers' average distance to the CBD – which should be considered as a measure of the district's distance to firms. As we have seen in Chapter 7, several empirical studies on job search confirm that distance to jobs deteriorates the information on job opportunities and that job accessibility is crucial for getting a job. In this model, as far as firms are concerned, they only use local recruitment methods (such as local newspapers or relying on word-of-mouth communication), which further emphasizes the adverse effect of physical distance to jobs.

2.1.3. Unemployment and Labor Discrimination. As usual, we can determine the steady-state unemployment rates u_{ik} for workers of type $ir = W, BS, BC$. They are given by:

$$u_W = \frac{\delta}{s_W \theta_W q(\theta_W) + \delta}\qquad(9.12)$$

$$u_{BS} = \frac{\delta}{s_{BS} \theta_B q(\theta_B) + \delta}\qquad(9.13)$$

$$u_{BC} = \frac{\delta}{s_{BC} \theta_B q(\theta_B) + \delta}.\qquad(9.14)$$

As in Chapters 2 and 5, we assume perfect capital markets with a zero interest rate and very high relocation costs. Therefore, the expected utility of a worker of type $ir = W, BS, BC$ residing in x is given by:

$$E\,W_{ir} = (1 - u_{ir})\Omega_{iL}(x) + u_i\Omega_{iU}(x),$$

where $\Omega_{ies}(x)$ are given by (9.1)–(9.3).

As in Becker (1957), firms have a taste for discrimination. In our framework, firms specialize in one of the two jobs available in the economy and, by doing so, decide to hire either black or white workers, but not both. Without loss of generality, we assume that each firm can only hire one worker. There exists a continuum of employers (or firms) whose mass is normalized to $M > 0$ and whose taste for discrimination M is uniformly distributed on $[0, M]$ (i.e., there is one firm at each point in the interval $[0, M]$). When working in a firm, each worker, black or white, has the same productivity $y > 0$ and receives the same wage, w_L. Employers are more or less prejudiced against blacks (depending on the value of their taste for discrimination M). In this framework, parameter M corresponds to the psychological cost of hiring and working with a black person and will enter in the profit function as a cost associated with the hiring of a black worker. It measures the intensity of the employer's racial preferences. In this context, the subjective cost of hiring a black worker takes into account both wage and psychological costs and is given by $w_L + M$.

In this context, the instantaneous profit function for a firm of type M hiring a black worker is given by:

$$\Pi_B(M) = y - w_L - M$$

whereas for a firm hiring a white worker, it is equal to:

$$\Pi_W = y - w_L,$$

where $y > w_L$ is the worker's productivity.

Since blacks and whites are totally identical and are paid the same wage, one may wonder why some firms with prejudices would ever hire a black worker. Naturally, if our model were static and there were no turnover, then a black worker would never be hired. As we will see, some firms will hire black workers because the duration of their vacancy is shorter and thus, the expected profit is higher than for whites. Let us explain this trade-off in detail.

For this purpose, we need to determine the expected profit for discriminating and non-discriminating firms. There is also a Poisson process on the firm's side where $q(\theta_i)$ is the (group-specific) job-contact rate and δ is the exogenous job-separation rate. In the steady state, flows into and out of vacancies are equal. Therefore, the vacancy rate for discriminating firms is equal to:

$$v_W = \frac{\delta}{q(\theta_W) + \delta} \tag{9.15}$$

whereas for non-discriminating firms, we have:

$$v_B = \frac{\delta}{q(\theta_B) + \delta}. \tag{9.16}$$

With zero interest rate and assuming that the cost of holding a vacant job is c, we have:

$$E\Pi_W = (1 - v_W)(y - w_L) - v_W c$$

$$E\Pi_B(M) = (1 - v_B)(y - w_L - M) - v_B c,$$

where $E\Pi_W$ and $E\Pi_B$, respectively, stand for the steady-state expected profit of a discriminating firm (which only hires white workers) and the expected profit of a non-discriminating firm (which only hires black workers) and $c > 0$ is the cost of maintaining a vacancy.

Since $E\Pi_W$ is constant with M and $E\Pi_B(M)$ is decreasing with M, then there must exist a threshold value $\widetilde{M}$ such that all firms with prejudice $M \in [0, \widetilde{M}]$ only hire black workers, whereas all firms with prejudice $M \in [\widetilde{M}, \overline{M}]$ only hire white workers. This threshold $\widetilde{M}$ is such that

$$E\Pi_W = E\Pi_B(\widetilde{M})$$

which, using the above equations, yields:

$$\widetilde{M} = \left(\frac{v_W - v_B}{1 - v_B} \right)(y - w_L + c). \tag{9.17}$$

It can easily be seen from (9.17) that $\widetilde{M} > 0$, whenever $v_W > v_B$, which is equivalent to $\theta_W > \theta_B$, i.e., when the labor market of whites is tighter than that of blacks. Now, it is quite clear why some firms will hire black workers. Indeed, since all workers obtain the same wage, it must to be that the expected duration of a vacancy is shorter for blacks than for whites for any prejudiced firm to be willing to hire a black worker, i.e., $q(\theta_W) < q(\theta_B)$. Here, firms specialize in one of the two jobs by calculating their expected profit. If their $M \leq \widetilde{M}$, then they will specialize in jobs available to black workers while if $M > \widetilde{M}$, they will only hire white workers. Specialization here is irreversible so that no whites will apply to a 'black' firm. For example, if blacks work as plumbers and whites as electricians, then a white electrician will never apply for a job as a plumber. Therefore, when deciding in which job to specialize, firms trade off their prejudice cost M against the cost of a vacancy, given that a vacant job for a black worker, on average, lasts for a shorter period than for a white worker. Naturally, only firms with a sufficiently low M will hire black workers.

2.2. The Different Equilibria

In equilibrium, all workers of the same type ir reach the same (expected) utility level I_{ir}. Therefore, we can determine the bid-rent of each type of worker. In equilibrium, absentee landlords allocate land to the highest bids. Since we assume that groups always form spatially homogenous communities and since bid-rents are all linear in x, it is easy to verify that six different equilibrium land-use configurations can arise depending on the relative ranking of whites (W), status-seeker blacks (BS) and conformist blacks (BC) in the city. However, under a reasonable assumption (for details, see Selod and Zenou, 2006), only two equilibria can be sustained: Equilibrium 1 in which, moving outward from the CBD, we have the location of the following groups: W, BS, BC (see Figure 9.2) and Equilibrium 2 in which, starting from the BD, we have: BC, BS, W (see Figure 9.3). We will refer to Equilibrium 1 as the *spatial-mismatch equilibrium* since, in that equilibrium, blacks reside far away from jobs, while Equilibrium 2 corresponds to a situation in which blacks reside close to jobs which we will call the *spatial-match equilibrium*. We have the following result, for which proof is given in Selod and Zenou (2006):

Proposition 9.1. *Assume that*

$$\bowtie_{BC} < |\bowtie_{BS}| < \bowtie_W. \tag{9.18}$$

Then, we have multiple equilibria in which either the spatial-mismatch equilibrium (Equilibrium 1) or the spatial-match equilibrium (Equilibrium 2) occurs.

Assuming $\bowtie_{BC} < |\bowtie_{BS}| < \bowtie_W$ means that whites are more eager to isolate themselves from blacks than status-seeker blacks are to have contacts with whites ($\bowtie_W > |\bowtie_{BS}|$), while status-seeker blacks are more eager to have contacts with whites than conformist blacks are to isolate themselves from whites ($|\bowtie_{BS}| > \bowtie_{BC}$). The reasons why only Equilibrium 1 and Equilibrium 2 can be sustained under assumption (9.18) are quite easy to understand. The assumption that $\bowtie_{BC} < |\bowtie_{BS}|$ is used to rule out the

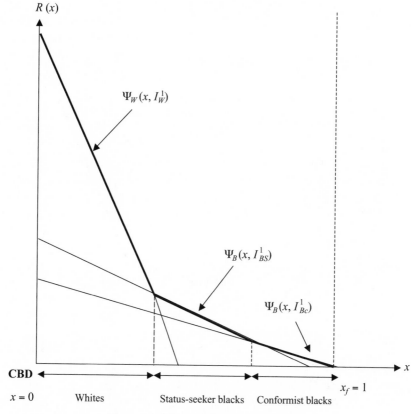

Figure 9.2. The spatial-match equilibrium.

two urban configurations in which whites locate in between status-seeker blacks and conformist blacks, so that status-seeker blacks and conformist blacks must locate on the same side as whites. Moreover, the two other urban configurations where conformist blacks locate in between whites and status-seeker blacks can never be sustained, since the two black groups will always prefer to switch locations (since $\bowtie_{BC} > 0$ and $\bowtie_{BS} < 0$). It follows, using $\bowtie_W > |\bowtie_{BS}|$, that status-seeker blacks must always locate in between whites and conformist blacks, so that only Equilibrium 1 and Equilibrium 2 can exist.

The reason why we have multiple equilibria is because *the driving force behind the location of communities is racial preferences*, since commuting costs do not discriminate among blacks and whites (the commuting cost per unit of distance is the same for both races). Therefore, multiple equilibria emerge since what is of importance is only the desire of workers to live or not

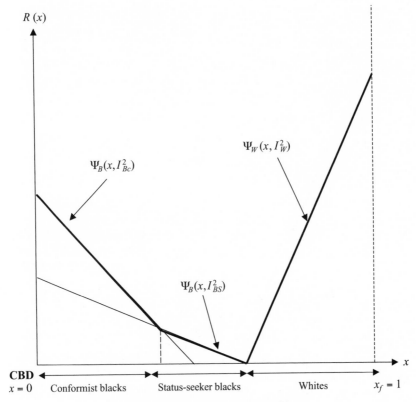

Figure 9.3. The spatial-mismatch equilibrium.

to live with other individuals of their communities. In this context, which equilibrium will prevail only depends on the coordination of workers.

If we focus on the spatial-mismatch equilibrium, we have the following result:

Proposition 9.2. *In the spatial-mismatch equilibrium (Figure 9.2) with discrimination, i.e., when* $0 < \widetilde{M}^{1*}/M < N_B$,

(*i*) *communities that live closer to jobs have lower unemployment rates:*

$$u_W^{1*} < u_{BS}^{1*} < u_{BC}^{1*}.$$

In particular, whites live close to jobs, have the lowest unemployment rate and experience the shortest unemployment spells.

(*ii*) *blacks who value interacting with other blacks most (conformist blacks) live further away from jobs, have a higher unemployment rate and experience longer unemployment spells than status-seeker blacks.*

In this equilibrium, it is clear that whites and conformist blacks are the most and less favored group, respectively. Indeed, whites have very good access to jobs (because they are closest to jobs), are not discriminated against, and benefit from a good social network. In contrast, conformist blacks have very bad access to jobs, have a poor social network (in particular because they reside far away from whites), and are discriminated against. Therefore, in this equilibrium, the place where conformist blacks live can be viewed as a ghetto: unemployment is rampant and peer pressure (to conform to the ghetto's norm and accept adverse racial preferences) has negative effects on those sensitive to it. These results are partly based on the fact that information about jobs can only be acquired locally, either through social networks (employed friends), or via formal sources of information (local newspapers). In this respect, conformist blacks are totally isolated from jobs, both physically and through their local contacts and have very little information on job opportunities in the CBD. The situation is different for status-seeker blacks who do not live in the ghetto, but seek contact with whites. They are less isolated from jobs, both physically and because they have contacts with whites.

If we now focus on the spatial-match equilibrium, we obtain:

Proposition 9.3. *In the spatial-match equilibrium (Figure 9.2) with discrimination, i.e., $0 < \widetilde{M}^{2*}/M < N_B$, unemployment rates cannot be ranked. However:*

(*i*) *If $\bowtie_W N_W - \bowtie_{BS} N_{BS} - \bowtie_{BC} N_{BC} > \tau(1 + N_{BS})$, then whites living far away from jobs on average pay higher land rents than blacks residing in the vicinity of the CBD.*

(*ii*) *Even though status-seeker blacks are further away from jobs than conformist blacks, they can have a lower unemployment rate than conformist blacks because they reside close to whites and therefore benefit from their social network.*

(*iii*) *Even though whites are the furthest away from jobs, they can experience the lowest unemployment rate when they are sufficiently favored by employers (because of racial discrimination against blacks).*

First, condition (*i*) guarantees that the average land rent paid by whites is strictly greater than the land rent paid by blacks close to the CBD. This condition is obviously satisfied whenever there is a sufficiently large number of whites, which is the case for most U.S. cities. It is easily seen that, in this equilibrium, whites are ready to pay a very high land rent in order to separate themselves from blacks. This may be one of the explanations for high land prices in American residential suburbs. Second, one of the main results in this proposition is to show that access to jobs is more crucial for blacks than for whites (which is in accordance with the spatial-mismatch literature). Indeed, in an equilibrium in which whites are the furthest away from jobs, whites can still have the lowest unemployment rate in the city (if discrimination is sufficiently high). Because of their advantage in terms of labor-market discrimination, whites can easily find a job even if they reside far away from jobs. In other words, for *high levels of labor discrimination, whites may benefit from a much better social network than blacks, even if they are physically isolated from jobs.* In contrast, *the social networks of blacks are strongly connected to their physical distance to jobs.* However, if there are strong social network spillovers across adjacent neighborhoods, then, *for status-seeker blacks, proximity to the white community may be even more crucial than proximity to jobs.*

2.3. Comparison Between the Two Equilibria

Since this model leads to multiple equilibria, it is quite natural to compare the utilities of agents between the different urban configurations. This involves comparing gains and losses associated with variations in permanent income, transportation costs, and land consumption. Even though analytical comparisons do not enable us to systematically rank these two equilibria, it is quite easily shown that, under a plausible condition on parameters, all workers are better off in Equilibrium 2 than in Equilibrium 1. We indeed have:

Proposition 9.4. *If*

$$\tau N_W - \bowtie_{BC} N_{BC} - \bowtie_{BS} N_{BS} > w_L - w_U \qquad (9.19)$$

then all workers are better off in the spatial-match equilibrium than in the spatial-mismatch equilibrium.

Proposition 9.4 states that if blacks are sufficiently keen on interacting with whites, i.e., if status seekers are very eager to have contacts with whites ($\bowtie_{BS}$ sufficiently negative) and conformists are not too conformist ($\bowtie_{BC}$ small enough), then workers are better off in the spatial-match equilibrium (Equilibrium 2) than in the spatial-mismatch equilibrium (Equilibrium 1).

The intuition runs as follows. Racial preferences (as well as transport costs) are completely capitalized in land rents. Comparing the two equilibria, condition (9.19) guarantees that reductions in land rents more than compensate possible losses in permanent income or that increases in land rents do not completely offset possible gains in permanent income. Conformist blacks are better off in the spatial-match equilibrium (Equilibrium 2) because they are much less unemployed than in the spatial-mismatch equilibrium (Equilibrium 1) and because, even if they reside closer to jobs, the increase in land rent is quite limited. Whites are better off even though their unemployment rate is higher since, residing far away from jobs, they now face lower land rents. The same intuition applies to status-seeker blacks.

Observe that in Proposition 9.4, we only compare the utilities of workers. If comparing the total surplus which includes the utility of absentee landlords and the profit of firms, then the two equilibria cannot be ranked analytically. However, in the numerical simulations proposed below (and in many others that we do not display), the total surplus is greater in the spatial-match equilibrium than in the spatial-mismatch equilibrium.

2.4. Policy Implications

We would now like to consider two different policies that can improve the situation of blacks as well as increase social welfare in the economy. We thus add one more stage in the timing of the model. In stage 0, the government announces its policy (affirmative action or employment subsidy) and then we solve the three next stages as before.

2.4.1. Affirmative Action.[10] Let us start by considering an affirmative action policy that is designed to give a preferential treatment to minority groups, for example by imposing minimum hiring quotas to firms. In particular, we would like to assess the efficiency of such a policy and determine whether different quotas should be imposed depending on the structure of the city.

In the present model, an affirmative action policy consists in imposing a quota to all firms that do not choose to hire blacks voluntarily, i.e., the discriminating firms. Since each firm only employs one worker at a time, imposing a quota means that a discriminating firm has to fill a vacancy with a black worker ϕ_B percent of the time and with a white worker $1 - \phi_B$ percent of the time. To put it short, a "white firm" must turn into a "black firm" ϕ_B percent of the time. In the context of our model, this means that when a firm chooses to specialise in 'white' jobs (say jobs that involve

---

[10] For overviews on the different viewpoints on the pros and cons of affirmative action policies, see, in particular, Holzer and Newmark (2000, 2006), Leonard (1990).

customers that are mostly whites or manufacturing jobs), it anticipates that it has to hire ϕ_B percent of its time a black worker (who may be unpopular with white consumers or specialized in service jobs).

Implementing an affirmative action policy has the following effects (as shown by Selod and Zenou, 2006). First, in both city structures, quotas significantly reduce the unemployment rates of blacks, while only raising slightly that of whites. Consequently, the equilibrium utility of whites decreases while those of blacks increase. Second, it also reduces (respectively increases) the labor market tightness, the vacancy rate, and the vacancy duration on the white labor market (respectively on the black labor market). Finally, in terms of quotas, there are stark differences between the different city structures of implementing an affirmative action policy. Indeed, the optimal quota has to be quite high in the urban configuration in which blacks are far away from jobs (the spatial-mismatch equilibrium or Equilibrium 1) and quite low in the urban configuration in which they are close to jobs (the spatial-match equilibrium or Equilibrium 2). This result is due to the fact that blacks are more discriminated against when they live far away from jobs. Therefore, when an affirmative action policy is implemented in order to eliminate discrimination or to maximize the total welfare, it is thus natural that the quota has to be higher in the spatial-mismatch equilibrium so as to compensate for this discrepancy between the two equilibria. This suggests that *affirmative action policies have different impacts depending on city structure and are more justified in cities where blacks reside far away from jobs*.

2.4.2. Employment Subsidies. We now consider another policy in which the (local) government gives a subsidy to all firms that accept to hire a black worker. This policy is financed with a lump-sum tax on all profits.

The effects of such a policy are as follows. First, as with the previous policy, the unemployment rates of blacks decrease with the subsidy while the unemployment rate of whites increases. Also, even if the total cost of discrimination monotonically increases with the subsidy, the total welfare first increases and then decreases with the subsidy. The mechanism at stake is however quite different from the previous policy since firms that are subsidized now *freely chose* whether it is more profitable for them to hire a black worker or not. Second, as the subsidy increases, the labor market tightness of whites decreases while taht of blacks increases. Indeed, since the number of firms which hire black workers increases, the number of firms which hire white workers decreases, and thus it becomes easier for blacks and more difficult for whites to find a job. Finally, it can be shown that the optimal subsidy (and thus the optimal taxation) is higher in a city where blacks are far away from jobs than in a city where blacks are closer to jobs. Indeed, the main problem for isolated blacks in Equilibrium 1 is that their job-acquisition rate is very low. So even when there are many unemployed black workers as in Equilibrium 1 (which should imply that the vacancy-filling rate of black firms should be quite high), firms are in fact *seldom contacted by black workers* (which explains why the duration of a black vacancy is higher in the spatial-mismatch equilibrium than in the spatial-match equilibrium). As a result, in order to reduce discrimination or in order to maximize total welfare, *a more intense employment-subsidy policy is required in the city where blacks are further away from jobs.*

3. Social Networks as Dyads

In the previous model, especially in the Spatial-Mismatch Equilibrium, conformist blacks have very poor access to jobs, a weak social network, and are discriminated against. Since information about jobs can only be acquired locally, either through social networks (employed friends), or via formal sources of information (local newspapers), the cost of not interacting with whites and living far away from jobs is very high for conformist blacks. We would now like to present a different model where the social network is more explicit so that not only direct friends (strong ties), but also friends of friends (weak ties) are of importance for the labor market outcomes of black and white workers.

3.1. The Model

Consider a continuum of (black and white) workers uniformly distributed along a linear and closed city. The total mass of individuals is normalized to 1 and there are N_B black workers and N_W white workers, with $N_B + N_W = 1$. All land is owned by absentee landlords and all firms are exogenously located in the CBD. As usual, the density of residential land parcels is taken to be unity, so that there are exactly x units of housing within a distance x from the CBD. We assume that blacks and whites only differ by their productivity levels so that they do not earn the same wage. The black-white wage gap is well-documented (Neal, 2006) so that it is assumed that $w_{BL} < w_{WL}$, where w_{iL} is the wage of a worker of type $i = B, W$.

3.1.1. *Dyads.* Individuals belong to mutually exclusive two-person groups referred to as *dyads*. We say that two individuals belonging to the same dyad hold a *strong tie* to each other. We assume that dyad members do not change over time. A strong tie is created once and forever and can never be broken. Thus, we can think of strong ties as links between members of the same family, or between very close friends. However, each dyad partner can meet other individuals outside the dyad partnership, referred to as *weak ties* or random encounters. By definition, weak ties are transitory and only last for one period.

3.1.2. Social Interactions. Time is continuous and individuals live forever. We assume repeated random pairwise meetings over time. Matching can take place between dyad partners or not. At time t, each individual has a probability Ξ_t of meeting a weak-tie member and thus $1 - \Xi_t$ is the probability of meeting the strong-tie member at time t. We assume these probabilities to be constant and exogenous, not to vary over time and thus, they can be written as Ξ and $1 - \Xi$.

It is assumed that strong *and* weak ties (i.e., dyads) are made between two friends of the *same race*. For example, drawing on a survey of residents of the Detroit area, Sigelman, Bledsoe, Welch, and Combs (1996) "examine how blacks and whites interact with each other. They show that much contact between blacks and whites consists of brief, superficial encounters while shopping, attending sport events, and the like. Nearly half of the city's black residents do not have a single white friend, and almost the same proportion of whites in the Detroit suburbs has neither a friend nor a social acquaintance who is black.[11]

It should be clear that the relationships with strong ties are in general not costly while relationships with weak ties, which are random encounters, involve some costs. Here, we mainly focus on spatial costs and assume that weak ties only meet in the CBD, which involves (both pecuniary and time) costs of commuting to the CBD.[12] For example, individuals go to a bar, go bowling, or go shopping and may then meet other people. In our dynamic model, people meet different weak ties in each period. Henning and Lieberg (1996) investigate the structure of networks and the content of ties in selected neighborhoods in Linköping, Sweden. Strong ties were those of importance to the respondent and were characterized by regular contact. Weak ties consisted of nodding acquaintances and conversational contacts.

---

[11] Similar results are obtained by Fong and Isajiw (2000) for the case of Canada.

[12] Using a different model, Helsey and Strange (2007) model social interactions in a similar way since all social interactions occur in a single location (the "center") and are defined as the number of visits to the center.

Henning and Lieberg found that the neighborhood where people live was relatively unimportant in weak ties relationships for both white-collar and blue-collar residents – three-quarters of these contacts took place outside the local area.

To capture these ideas, we assume that Ξ is a decreasing function of x, the distance to the CBD, i.e., $\Xi(x)$ with $\Xi'(x) < 0$. As expressed by Glaeser (2000), "social influences decay rapidly with distance." Indeed, interacting with strong ties (family members or best friends) has no real cost: either they live in the same location or one just needs to make a phone call to have a contact with a strong tie. So basically, strong ties provide information at no cost, especially no spatial costs. This is well-documented empirically. For example, Topa (2001) and Bayer, Ross, and Topa (2008) found evidence of significant social interactions operating at the block level.[13] In the present model, these are interactions between strong ties since they are repeated over time.

3.1.3. Information Transmission. Each job offer is taken to arrive only to employed workers, who can then direct it to one of their contacts (through either strong or weak ties). This is a convenient modelling assumption which stresses the importance of on-the-job information. The gist of the analysis would be preserved if this assumption is relaxed. To be more precise, employed workers hear of job vacancies at the exogenous rate a while they lose their job at the exogenous rate δ. All jobs are identical and workers within the same ethnic group $i = B, W$ are also identical so that all employed workers of type i obtain the same wage w_{iL}. So, employed workers of type i, who hear about a job, pass this information on to their current matched partner, who is, by assumption, of the same type. This transmission of information can also take place through a random acquaintance (i.e., a weak tie). In that case, a type–i worker can only transmit job information to a worker of the same race i.

As a result, the rate at which a black or a white worker within a dyad hears of a job from either a weak or a strong tie is the same and equal to: $[1 - \Xi(x) + \Xi(x) l_i] a$ since his/her best friend will always give him/her job information if he/she is aware of it (this occurs at rate $[1 - \Xi(x)] a$) and for weak ties, it only depends on how many of them are employed in the economy (this occurs at rate $\Xi(x) l_i a$, where $l_i = L_i / N_i$ is the employment rate of type–i workers in the economy).

---

[13] See also Kan (2007) who shows social capital to be very local.

This information transmission protocol defines a Markov process. The state variable is the relative size of each type of dyad. Transitions depend on labor market turnover and the nature of social interactions as captured by $\Xi(x)$. We can define the average rate of meeting a weak tie for a type–i worker as $\overline{\Xi}_i$. Because of the Markov/Poisson process, the probability of a two-state change is zero (small order) during a small interval of time t and $t + dt$. This means, in particular, that both members of a dyad cannot change their status at the same time. For example, two unemployed workers cannot find a job at the same time, i.e., during t and $t + dt$, the probability assigned to a transition from a d_{iU}–dyad to a d_{iL}–dyad is zero. Similarly, two employed workers (d_{iL}–dyad) cannot both become unemployed, i.e., switch to a d_{iU}–dyad during t and $t + dt$. This applies to all other dyads mentioned above.

3.1.4. Aggregate State. Individuals of race $i = B, W$ can be in either of two different states: employed or unemployed. Dyads, which consist of paired individuals, can thus be in three different states,[14] which are the following:

(i) both members are employed – we denote the number of such dyads by d_{iL};

(ii) one member is employed and the other is unemployed (d_{iLU});

(iii) both members are unemployed (d_{iU}).

Here, d_{iU} is the number of dyads with two unemployed workers while d_{iLU} and d_{iL} constitute the number of dyads with one unemployed and one employed worker, and two employed workers, respectively. By denoting the total employment and unemployment levels for workers of type i at time t by $L_i(t)$ and $U_i(t)$, we have:

$$\begin{cases} L_i(t) = 2d_{iL}(t) + d_{iLU}(t) \\ U_i(t) = 2d_{iU}(t) + d_{iLU}(t) \end{cases}. \tag{9.20}$$

Furthermore

$$L_i(t) + U_i(t) = N_i \tag{9.21}$$

or, alternatively,

$$d_{iL}(t) + d_{iLU}(t) + d_{iU}(t) = \frac{N_i}{2}. \tag{9.22}$$

---

[14] The inner ordering of dyad members is of no importance.

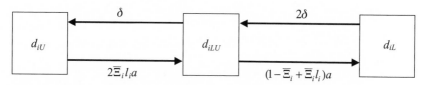

Figure 9.4. Flows in a labor market characterized by dyads for workers of race $i = B, W$.

3.1.5. Flows of Dyads Between States. It is readily checked that the net flow of dyads from each state between t and $t + dt$ is given by:

$$
\begin{cases}
\dot{d}_{iL}(t) = \left[1 - \overline{\Xi}_i + \overline{\Xi}_i \, l_i(t)\right] a \, d_{iLU}(t) - 2\delta d_{iL}(t) \\[2mm]
\dot{d}_{iLU}(t) = 2\overline{\Xi}_i \, l_i(t) a \, d_{iU}(t) \\[1mm]
\quad - \left\{\delta + \left[1 - \overline{\Xi}_i + \overline{\Xi}_i \, l_i(t)\right] a\right\} d_{iLU}(t) + 2\delta d_{iL}(t) \\[2mm]
\dot{d}_{iU}(t) = -2\overline{\Xi}_i \, l_i(t) a \, d_{iU}(t) + \delta \, d_{iLU}(t)
\end{cases}
\quad (9.23)
$$

These dynamic equations reflect the flows across dyads. This is graphically illustrated in Figure 9.4.

For instance, in the first equation, the variation of dyads composed of two employed workers ($\dot{d}_{iL}(t)$) is equal to the number of d_{iLU}–dyads in which the unemployed worker has found a job (through either his/her strong tie with probability $(1 - \Xi(x))a$ or his/her weak tie with probability $\overline{\Xi}_i l_i(t)a$) minus the number of d_{iL}–dyads in which one of the two employed has lost his/her job. All the other equations have a similar interpretation.

Observe that the assumption stated above that both members of a dyad cannot lose their status at the same time is reflected in the flows described by (9.23). What is crucial in our analysis is that members of the same dyad (strong ties) always remain together throughout their life. So, for example, if a d_{iL}–dyad becomes a d_{iU}–dyad, the members of this dyad are exactly the same; they have just changed their employment status.

3.2. Steady-State Equilibrium Analysis

3.2.1. Labor Market Equilibrium. By solving (9.23) in steady-state, we obtain for $i = B, W$:

$$
d_{iL}^* = \frac{(1 - \overline{\Xi}_i + \overline{\Xi}_i \, l_i^*)a}{2\delta} d_{iLU}^* \tag{9.24}
$$

$$
d_{iLU}^* = \frac{2\overline{\Xi}_i \, l_i^* a}{\delta} d_{iU}^* \tag{9.25}
$$

where

$$d_{iU}^* = \frac{N_i}{2} - d_{iL}^* - d_{iLU}^* \tag{9.26}$$

$$L_i^* = 2d_{iL}^* + d_{iLU}^* \tag{9.27}$$

$$U_i^* = N_i - L_i^*. \tag{9.28}$$

Since the labor markets of blacks and whites are totally separated, they can be studied separately. In a steady-state $(d_{iL}^*, d_{iLU}^*, d_{iU}^*)$, each of the net flows in (9.23) is equal to zero. The following result is demonstrated by Zenou (2008e):

Proposition 9.5.

   (*i*) *There always exists a steady-state equilibrium $\mathcal{U}_i$ where all individuals are unemployed and only d_{iU}–dyads exist, that is $d_{iL}^* = d_{iLU}^* = L_i^* = 0, d_{iU}^* = N_i/2$ and $U_i^* = N_i$.*

  (*ii*) *If*

$$\delta < a[\overline{\Xi}_i + \sqrt{\overline{\Xi}_i(4 - 3\overline{\Xi}_i)}]/2 \tag{9.29}$$

there exists a steady-state equilibrium $\mathcal{I}_i$ where $0 < L_i^* < N_i$ is defined by:

$$\frac{L_i^*}{N_i} = \frac{\delta^2}{2d_{iU}^* a^2 \overline{\Xi}_i^2} - \frac{\delta}{a\,\overline{\Xi}_i} - \frac{\left(1 - \overline{\Xi}_i\right)}{\overline{\Xi}_i} > 0, \tag{9.30}$$

$0 < U_i^* < N_i$, and $0 < d_{iU}^* < N_i/2$ is the unique solution of the following equation:

$$-\frac{a\left(1 - \overline{\Xi}_i\right)}{\delta} d_{iU}^{*2} - \frac{d_{iU}^*}{2\overline{\Xi}_i} + \left[\frac{\delta}{2a\overline{\Xi}_i}\right]^2 = 0. \tag{9.31}$$

The other dyads are given by:

$$d_{iLU}^* = \frac{2a\overline{\Xi}_i L_i^*}{\delta N_i} d_{iU}^* \tag{9.32}$$

$$d_{iL}^* = \frac{a^2\overline{\Xi}_i\left[N_i - \overline{\Xi}_i\left(N_i - L_i^*\right)\right] L_i^*}{\delta^2 N_i^2} d_{iU}^*. \tag{9.33}$$

First, observe that if condition (9.29) holds, then an interior equilibrium always exists. Observe also that Proposition 9.5 characterizes the equilibrium values of dyads for both black and white workers. It can be seen that the only difference between them is $\overline{\Xi}_i$, the average contact rate with weak ties, which depends on their average location in the city. We now turn to this issue by studying the urban-land-use equilibrium. Since the steady-state equilibrium U_i is obviously uninteresting, from now on, we only focus on the labor market equilibrium I_i and thus, assume that condition (9.29) holds.

3.2.2. Urban Land-Use Equilibrium. The *instantaneous* indirect utilities of an employed and unemployed worker of type $i = B, W$ at distance x are given by:

$$W_{iL}(x) = w_{iL} - \tau x - R(x) \tag{9.34}$$

$$W_{iU}(x) = w_U - s\tau x - R(x). \tag{9.35}$$

We are now able to calculate the expected utility of each worker. As in the previous section, we assume perfect capital markets with a zero interest rate and high relocation costs, so that the disposable income of a worker is equal to his/her average net income over the job cycle. Therefore, the expected utility of a worker residing in x is given by:

$$E\,W_i(x) = l_i^*(x)\,W_{iL}(x) + \left[1 - l_i^*(x)\right] W_{iU}(x).$$

In steady-state, each employed worker spends $l_i^*(x) = [2d_{iL}^*(x) + d_{iLU}^*(x)]/N_i$ of his/her time employed and $1 - l_i^*(x)$ of his/her time unemployed. If replacing $\overline{\Xi}_i$ by $\Xi_i(x)$, then the values of $d_{iL}^*(x)$ and $d_{iLU}^*(x)$ are given by (9.24), (9.25), where $d_{iU}^*(x)$ is defined by (9.31). Indeed, we are now calculating the fraction of time each worker spends in each dyad which depends on his/her residential location x. It can be shown that:

$$l_i^*(x) = \frac{1}{a\,\Xi(x)N_i} \left[\frac{\delta^2}{2\Xi(x)ad_U^*} - \delta \right] - \frac{[1 - \Xi(x)]}{\Xi(x)N_i} \tag{9.36}$$

where d_U^* is the solution to

$$-\frac{[1 - \Xi(x)]\,a}{\delta}d_U^{*2} - \frac{d_U^*}{2\Xi(x)} + \left[\frac{\delta}{a\Xi(x)}\right]^2 = 0.$$

Condition (9.29) guarantees that there is a unique solution to this equation in d_U^*. It can be shown that

$$\frac{\partial l_i^*(x)}{\partial x} < 0. \tag{9.37}$$

Indeed, for workers living far away from jobs, it is more costly to travel to the CBD and thus, they are less likely to meet weak ties who can provide information about jobs. For example, if someone is unemployed and belongs to a d_{iU}–dyad, the only individuals who can provide information about jobs are weak ties. But if a person lives far away from the CBD, he/she will go less often to the CBD and thus, will have little information about jobs. As a result, workers who live far away from jobs will spend less time employed than those living closer to jobs.

The result (9.37) is not always true and, in fact, depends on the value of a (the job-contact rate) relative to the value of δ (the job-destruction rate). A sufficient condition for (9.37) to hold is $\delta/a < \sqrt{\Xi(x)/6}, \forall x \in [0, 1], \forall i = B, W$. Indeed, individuals belong to mutually exclusive groups, the dyads, and weak tie interactions spread information across dyads. Parameter $\Xi(x)$ measures the proportion of social interaction that occurs outside the dyad, i.e., the inter-dyad interactions. When $\Xi(x)$ is high, social cohesion between employed and unemployed workers is high and thus, they are in close contact with each other. In this context, increasing $\Xi(x)$ induces more transitions from unemployment to employment and, l_i^*, the unemployment rate of type i–workers increases. However, even though l_i^* increases, the effect of $\Xi(x)$ on d_{iL}^* and d_{iLU}^* is ambiguous.

Now, using (9.34) and (9.35), the expected utility $E\,W_i(x)$ can be written as:

$$E\,W_i(x) = l_i^*(x)\left[w_{iL}\left(1 - \iota\,x\right) - w_U - (1 - s)\,\tau x\right] + w_U - s\tau x - R(x),$$

where $l_i^*(x)$ is given by (9.36). We can now calculate the bid rent of workers $\Psi_L(x, E\,W_i)$. We obtain:

$$\Psi_L(x, E\,W_i) = l_i^*(x)\left[w_{iL}\left(1 - \iota\,x\right) - w_U - (1 - s)\,\tau x\right]$$
$$+ w_U - s\tau x - E\,W_i$$

with

$$\frac{\partial\Psi_L(x, E\,W_i)}{\partial x} < 0.$$

In this model, bid-rents compensate workers for different commuting costs and for the fact that the time spent employed and unemployed over lifetime is location dependent. Those who live close to jobs pay higher land rents because they have both low time and pecuniary commuting costs and spend less time unemployed during their lifetime. Since white workers have higher wages, they value access to the center more than black workers because of a higher opportunity cost of time. As a result, they bid away black workers to occupy the center of the city.

We can now solve the urban equilibrium so that the bid-rent at the city fringe is equal to the agricultural land and blacks' and whites' bid-rents intersect at $x = N_W$ to obtain $E W_B^*$, $E W_W^*$ and $R^*(x)$.

In this context, because blacks live further away from jobs, they have less contacts with weak ties and thus, have difficulties leaving a d_{BU}–dyad. As a result, they will experience higher unemployment rates than whites. Indeed, their source of information about jobs mainly comes from their strong ties. So when they are in a d_{BU}–dyad, their chances of leaving unemployment are very low, especially if they live very far away from jobs. They are stuck in an unemployment state and we here obtain some duration dependence only due to network effects. Indeed, the probability of finding a job depends on: (i) with whom one is linked and (ii) the location in the city since it affects the interactions with weak ties. So, if, on average, people live far away from jobs and thus spend more time in a d_{iU} dyad, then their unemployment duration will be much higher than for those who live closer to jobs.

3.3. Choosing Social Interactions

It is easy to extend the model so that Ξ is chosen by individuals. We assume that there is some cost of interacting with weak ties and κ denotes the marginal cost of these interactions. The expected utility of type–i workers is now given by:

$$E W_i(\Xi_i, x) = \frac{L_i(\Xi_i)}{N_i} (w_L - \tau x) + \left[1 - \frac{L_i(\Xi_i)}{N_i}\right] (w_U - s\tau x)$$
$$- R(x) - \kappa\, \Xi_i,$$

where $\frac{L_i(\Xi)}{N_i}$ is defined by (9.30). Each individual i optimally chooses Ξ_i that maximizes $E W_i(\Xi, x)$. The first-order condition yields:

$$\frac{\partial E W_i(\Xi, x)}{\partial \Xi_i} = \frac{\partial L_i(\Xi_i)}{\partial \Xi_i} [w_L - w_U - (1 - s)\tau x] - \kappa = 0.$$

We have the following result:

Proposition 9.6. *There exists a unique interior Ξ_i^* that maximizes $E W_i(\Xi, x)$ and* (*i*) *workers living further away from jobs will interact less with weak ties than those residing closer to jobs, i.e.,*

$$\frac{\partial \Xi_i^*}{\partial x} < 0;$$

(*ii*) *higher wages or lower unemployment benefits will increase the interactions with weak ties, i.e.,*

$$\frac{\partial \Xi_i^*}{\partial w_L} > 0 \qquad \frac{\partial \Xi_i^*}{\partial w_U} < 0;$$

(*iii*) *higher commuting costs will decrease the interactions with weak ties, i.e.,*

$$\frac{\partial \Xi_i^*}{\partial \tau} < 0.$$

Workers want to interact with weak ties because it increases their probability of being employed (or, equivalently, the time they spend employed during their lifetime), i.e., $\frac{\partial L_i(\Xi_i)}{\partial \Xi_i} > 0$. However, because it is always more expensive to commute to the business district when employed than when unemployed (i.e., $\tau > s\tau$), the marginal gain of interacting with weak ties is higher for workers residing closer to jobs than for those locating further away. As a result, workers residing closer to jobs will interact more with weak ties than those residing further away from jobs. Concerning wage w_L and unemployment benefit w_U, a higher w_L or w_U increases the value of employment and, since L_i and Ξ_i are positively related, workers will interact more with weak ties. The same intuition applies for commuting costs τ.

If, for example, black workers are forced to live further away from jobs because of housing discrimination,[15] they will experience higher unemployment. This is because they choose not to have access to weak ties so that their main source of information about jobs will be provided by their strong ties. But if the latter are themselves unemployed, the chance of escaping unemployment will be very low.

4. Social Networks as Explicit Graphs

Let us now deepen our analysis of social networks by modeling weak ties in a more explicit way. The whole structure of the network will now be of importance in explaining workers' labor market outcomes. Since it becomes

---

[15] It may also well be that blacks prefer to mainly interact with other blacks and may end up residing far away from jobs as in Section 2 of this chapter.

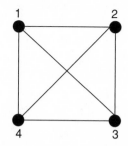

Figure 9.5. The complete network.

quite complicated, we will not model the land market. Let us start with some definitions.

4.1. Some Basic Definitions from Graph Theory[16]

A *network* is a set of individuals, called *nodes* or *vertices*, $N = \{1, \ldots, n\}$, and a set of *links* or *edges* between them. In other words, $N = \{1, \ldots, n\}$ is a set of individuals connected in some pairwise-dependent relationship. These links are represented by a graph $\mathbf{g}$, where $g_{ij} = 1$ if i has a link with j (denoted by ij) and $g_{ij} = 0$ otherwise (*unweighted* graphs/networks). Links are taken to be reciprocal, so that $g_{ij} = g_{ji}$ (*undirected* graphs/networks). By convention, $g_{ii} = 0$.

The direct contacts of the set of i's are: $N_i(\mathbf{g}) = \{j \neq i \mid g_{ij} = 1\}$, which is of size $n_i(\mathbf{g})$. A network $\mathbf{g}$ can be defined by an $n-$square matrix $\mathbf{A}$, called the *adjacency* matrix. This matrix keeps track of all *direct connections* in network $\mathbf{g}$.

Let us illustrate these concepts for $n = 4$ with three prominent networks: the complete, the star-shaped, and the circle network. The *complete network* is such that each agent is in a direct relationship with all other agents so that each node i has $n - 1$ direct contacts. Formally, the complete graph is the set of all subsets of N of size 2. In the case of 4 individuals, $N = \{1, 2, 3, 4\}$ and $\mathbf{g} = \{12, 13, 14, 23, 24, 34\}$. This network is illustrated in Figure 9.5.

The corresponding adjacency matrix is given by:

$$\mathbf{A} = \begin{bmatrix} 0 & 1 & 1 & 1 \\ 1 & 0 & 1 & 1 \\ 1 & 1 & 0 & 1 \\ 1 & 1 & 1 & 0 \end{bmatrix}.$$

---

[16] For a much more extensive overview of the way networks can be viewed as graphs, see Wasserman and Faust (1994) or Jackson (2008).

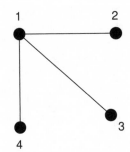

Figure 9.6. The star-shaped network.

The *star-shaped network* is when one central individual is in direct contact with all other peripheral individuals who, in turn, are only connected to this central individual in the star. Agents hold very asymmetric positions, as one agent has $n-1$ direct links while all other agents only have 1 direct link. For four individuals, $N = \{1, 2, 3, 4\}$, $\mathbf{g} = \{12, 13, 14\}$, so that individual 1 holds a central position whereas individuals 2, 3, and 4 are peripherals. The following figure displays this network.

The corresponding adjacency matrix is equal to:

$$\mathbf{A} = \begin{bmatrix} 0 & 1 & 1 & 1 \\ 1 & 0 & 0 & 0 \\ 1 & 0 & 0 & 0 \\ 1 & 0 & 0 & 0 \end{bmatrix}.$$

Finally, the *circle* is such that each individual has two direct contacts. In the case of four individuals, $N = \{1, 2, 3, 4\}$ and $\mathbf{g} = \{12, 14, 23, 34\}$. Figure 9.7 displays the circle network.

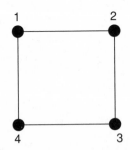

Figure 9.7. The circle network.

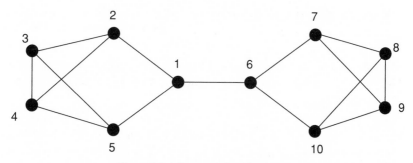

Figure 9.8. The network with a bridge.

The corresponding adjacency matrix is equal to:

$$\mathbf{A} = \begin{bmatrix} 0 & 1 & 0 & 1 \\ 1 & 0 & 1 & 0 \\ 0 & 1 & 0 & 1 \\ 1 & 0 & 1 & 0 \end{bmatrix}.$$

So far, we have mainly described the direct links between individuals. However, one of the key features of networks/graphs is that not only *direct*, but also *indirect* links are of importance.

Definition 9.1. *A path of length k from i to j in network* $\mathbf{g}$ *is a sequence* $\langle i_0, i_1, \ldots, i_k \rangle$ *of players such that* $i_0 = i$, $i_k = j$, $i_p \neq i_{p+1}$, *and* $g_{i_p i_{p+1}} = 1$, *for all* $0 \leq p \leq k - 1$, *that is, players* i_p *and* i_{p+1} *are directly linked in* $\mathbf{g}$. *If such a path exists, then individuals i and j are path-connected.*

In other words, a *path* between two individuals i and j is an ordered set of agents $(i, i_1, \ldots, i_k, j)$ of N, where an agent can appear several times, such that $i \neq j$. We say that a path belongs to network $\mathbf{g}$ if $g_{i i_1} g_{i_1 i_2} \cdots g_{i_k j} \neq 0$. A path is *simple* if all individuals in the path are different. Figure 9.8 represents a network/graph with $N = \{1, 2, 3, 4, 5, 6, 7, 8, 9, 10\}$ and

$$\mathbf{g} = \{12, 15, 16, 23, 24, 34, 35, 45, 46, 67, 610, 78, 79, 89, 810, 910\}.$$

In this network, $\{1, 2, 3, 4\}$ is a *simple path* of length 3 in $\mathbf{g}$ from 1 to 4 (the path is $12 \to 23 \to 34$) while $\{1, 2, 1, 2, 3, 4\}$ is a *path* of length 4 in $\mathbf{g}$ that is *not simple* from 1 to 4 (the path is $12 \to 21 \to 12 \to 23 \to 34$).

Some networks are *regular* (or *symmetric*). This is when all individuals have the same number of direct contacts, and thus hold symmetric positions in the network. For example, the complete network and the circle are regular networks.

We would like finally to give some properties of the adjacency matrix $\mathbf{A}$. Let $\mathbf{A}^k$ be the kth power of the adjacency matrix $\mathbf{A}$ with coefficients $g_{ij}^{[k]}$, where k is some non-zero integer. This matrix keeps track of the indirect connections in the network. Indeed, $g_{ij}^{[k]} \geq 0$ measures the number of paths of length $k \geq 1$ in g from i to j. In particular, $\mathbf{A}^0 = \mathbf{I}$, that is, $g_{ii}^{[0]} = 1$ and $g_{ij}^{[0]} = 0$ for all $i \neq j$.

Proposition 9.7. *Let g be a graph with adjacency matrix $\mathbf{G}$. The number of different paths of length k from i to j, where k is a positive integer, equals the (i, j)th entry of $\mathbf{G}^k$.*

The proof of this proposition uses simple mathematical induction and can be found in any graph theory book. Let us illustrate this proposition using the circle network described in Figure 9.6 for three agents only, where agent 1 is the star. The adjacency matrix is given by

$$\mathbf{A} = \begin{bmatrix} 0 & 1 & 1 \\ 1 & 0 & 0 \\ 1 & 0 & 0 \end{bmatrix}.$$

Its is a straightforward algebra exercise to compute the powers of this matrix, which are:

$$\mathbf{A}^{2k} = \begin{bmatrix} 2^k & 0 & 0 \\ 0 & 2^{k-1} & 2^{k-1} \\ 0 & 2^{k-1} & 2^{k-1} \end{bmatrix} \quad \text{and} \quad \mathbf{A}^{2k+1} = \begin{bmatrix} 0 & 2^k & 2^k \\ 2^k & 0 & 0 \\ 2^k & 0 & 0 \end{bmatrix}, k \geq 1.$$

For instance, we deduce from $\mathbf{A}^3$ that there are exactly two paths of length 3 between agents 1 and 2, namely, $12 \to 21 \to 12$ and $13 \to 31 \to 12$. Obviously, there is no path of this length (and, in general, of odd length) from any agent to himself. Indeed,

$$\mathbf{A}^3 = \begin{bmatrix} 0 & 2 & 2 \\ 2 & 0 & 0 \\ 2 & 0 & 0 \end{bmatrix}.$$

Using Proposition 9.7, any path of length k from i to j in network $\mathbf{g}$ can easily be determined. It suffice to calculate $\mathbf{G}^k$.

4.2. The Setup

Let us now describe a labor market model that explicitly incorporates a network as a graph g. It must be noted that there is no explicit land market in this model since the focus is on social space and not on urban space.

We will show that social space will segment workers into different groups, and thus black workers can end up experiencing a high unemployment rate because their social network is of "bad" quality, i.e., mainly composed of unemployed workers. Since social space in some sense reflects urban space, social segregation can lead to urban segregation, which in turn reinforces social segregation.

The model can be described as follows. There are n agents. Time evolves in discrete periods indexed by t. The vector σ_t describes the employment status of workers at time t. If individual i is employed at the end of period t, then $\sigma_{it} = 1$ and if i is unemployed, then $\sigma_{it} = 0$.

A period t begins with some agents being employed and others not, as described by status σ_{t-1} from the last period. Next, information about job openings is obtained. In particular, any given individual hears about a job opening with a probability a between 0 and 1. This job arrival process is independent across individuals. If the individual is unemployed, then he/she will take the job. However, if the individual is already employed, then he/she will pass the information along to a direct unemployed friend. A graph $\mathbf{g}$ thus summarizes the links of all agents, where $g_{ij} = 1$ indicates that i and j know each other, and share their knowledge about job information, while $g_{ij} = 0$ indicates that they do not know each other. It is assumed that $g_{ij} = g_{ji}$, meaning that the acquaintance relationship is reciprocal.

Observe that if an employed worker hears about a job, but all his/her friends (i.e., direct links) are already employed, then the job is lost. Here we focus on a model where wages are exogenous and identical for all workers.[17] So there is no room in this model for an employed worker to exploit a job offer to increase his/her current wage.

Finally, the last thing that happens in a period is that some agents lose their jobs. This happens randomly according to an exogenous breakup rate, δ, between 0 and 1. In contrast to most models developed in this book, time is here discrete.

We are able to write the probability $\mathbb{P}_{ij}$ of the joint event that individual i learns about a job and this job ends up in individual j's hands. It is equal to:

$$\mathbb{P}_{ij}(\sigma) = \begin{cases} a & \text{if} & \sigma_i = 0 \text{ and } i = j \\ a/\sum_{k:\sigma_k=0} g_{ik} & \text{if} & \sigma_i = 1, \sigma_j = 0, \text{ and } g_{ij} = 1, \\ 0 & & \text{otherwise} \end{cases} \quad (9.38)$$

where vector σ describes the employment status of all individuals at the beginning of the period. In (9.38), a is the probability of obtaining information about a job without using friends and relatives. Three cases

---

[17] Calvó-Armengol and Jackson (2007) propose a similar framework with endogenous wages.

Figure 9.9. Employment correlations in a star-shaped network.

may then arise. If individuals i and j are unemployed ($\sigma_i = \sigma_j = 0$), the probability that j will obtain a job is just a since individual i will never transmit any information to j. If individual i is already employed and his/her friend j is not ($\sigma_i = 1$, $\sigma_j = 0$), then individual i transmits this job information to all his/her direct unemployed neighbors, whose total number is $\sum_{k:\sigma_k=0} g_{ik}$. It is assumed that all unemployed neighbors are treated on an equal footing, meaning that the employed worker who has the job information does not favor any of his/her direct neighbors. As a result, the probability of an unemployed worker j being selected among the $\sum_{k:\sigma_k=0} g_{ik}$ unemployed direct neighbors of an employed worker j is given by: $a/\sum_{k:\sigma_k=0} g_{ik}$. Finally, if individual j is employed, then he/she does not need any job information, at least not in the current period.

4.3. Correlations in Employment Status Between Path-Connected Workers

The first important result is to show that, in steady-state, there is a positive correlation in employment status between two path-connected workers (see Definition 9.1). As we will see, this result is not at all easy to obtain since, in the short run, the correlation is negative. Indeed, in a static model, if an employed worker is directly linked to two unemployed workers, then if he/she is aware of a job, he/she will share this job information with his/her two unemployed friends (see (9.38)). These two individuals, who are path-connected (path of length two), are thus in competition and one (randomly chosen) will obtain the job and be employed while the other will remain unemployed. So their employment status will be negatively correlated (see Calvó-Armengol, 2004 and Calvó-Armengol and Zenou, 2005). Let us now show that this negative correlation result does *not* hold in a dynamic labor-market model. To get the main intuition, we will focus on the case with three workers with a star-shaped network (Figure 9.9), i.e., $n = 3$ and $g_{12} = g_{23} = 1$.

4.3.1. *The Employment Stochastic Dynamics.* Let us first present an example that makes it clear why a full analysis of the dynamics of employment is subtle.

Consider the network described in Figure 9.9 with three individuals and suppose employment from the end of the last period to be $\sigma_{t-1} = (0, 1, 0)$. In the figure, a black node represents an employed worker (individual 2), while unemployed workers (1 and 3) are represented by white nodes. Conditional on this state, σ_{t-1}, employment states σ_{1t} and σ_{3t} are negatively correlated. As stated above, this is due to the fact that individuals 1 and 3 are "competitors" for any job news that is first heard by individual 2.

Despite this negative (conditional) correlation in the shorter run, individual 1 can benefit from individual 3's presence in the longer run. Indeed, individual 3's presence helps improve individual 2's employment status. Moreover, when individual 3 is employed, individual 1 is more likely to hear about any job that individual 2 hears about. These aspects of the problem counter the local (conditional) negative correlation and help induce a positive correlation between the employment status of individuals 1 and 3.

In what follows, we describe how this long-run positive correlation is obtained. Once more, consider the network described in Figure 9.9, but without imposing any employment status on workers. In that case, there are eight possible employment states: 000, 100, 010, 001, 110, 101, 011, 111, where, for example, 000 means that all individuals 1, 2, and 3 are unemployed. As a result, the state of the economy σ_t evolves following a Markov process $\mathcal{M}(a, \delta)$ where a is the job-arrival rate that takes place in the first half of each period, while δ is the job-destruction rate that takes place in the second half of each period. We gather the Markov transitions into a matrix $\mathbb{P}_{ij} = \Pr\{\sigma_{t+1} = i \mid \sigma_t = j\}$, where $i, j \in \{000, 100, 010, 001, 110, 101, 011, 111\}$, that is, rows correspond to $t + 1$ while columns correspond to t (the columns sum up to one as in all Markov matrices).

4.3.2. The Subdivided Dynamics. As highlighted above, an important issue in this case is the short-run negative correlation versus the long-run (possibly) strictly positive correlation. To sort out the short- and longer-run effects, we divide a and δ both by some larger and larger factor, so that we are looking at arbitrarily short time periods. We call this the "sub-division" of periods. More precisely, instead of analyzing the Markov process $\mathcal{M}(a, \delta)$, we analyze the associated Markov process $\mathcal{M}(a/T, \delta/T)$, which we name the *T–period subdivision* of $\mathcal{M}(a, \delta)$, with steady state distribution μ^T. We show that there exists some T' such that, for all $T \geq T'$, the employment statuses of any path-connected agents are positively correlated under μ^T.

4.3.3. The Approximated Subdivided Dynamics. Consider $\mathcal{M}(a/T, \delta/T)$. For this Markov process, in every period, every shock (be it a job arrival a/T

or a job breakdown δ/T) is very unlikely when T is high enough. Having two shocks or more in every such period is thus much less unlikely. Instead of analyzing $\mathcal{M}(a/T, \delta/T)$, we analyze an approximated Markov process $\mathcal{M}^*(a/T, \delta/T)$ where we only keep track of one-shock transitions, and disregard transitions involving two shocks or more. We denote the corresponding steady-state distribution by μ^{*T}. The higher is T, the closer are the transitions of the approximated Markov process $\mathcal{M}^*(a/T, \delta/T)$ to those of the true Markov process $\mathcal{M}(a/T, \delta/T)$ and thus, the closer is μ^{*T} to μ^T.

To simplify matters, we set $a = \delta$ and write $\varepsilon = a/T = \delta/T$. We write the transitions for $\mathcal{M}^*(\varepsilon)$ and compute the corresponding steady state μ^*. The states can take eight different values 000, 100, 010, 001, 110, 101, 011, 111. Exploiting symmetries, we analyze the coarsened Markov process with six states 000, 100, 010, 110, 101, 111. If we denote the corresponding steady-state distribution by ν^*, we have $\mu^*_{100} = \mu^*_{001} = \nu^*_{100}/2$ and $\mu^*_{110} = \mu^*_{011} = \nu^*_{110}/2$.

We order states as described below

$$
P^* = \begin{array}{c} \\ 000 \\ 100 \\ 101 \\ 010 \\ 110 \\ 111 \end{array}
\begin{array}{cccccc}
000 & 100 & 101 & 010 & 110 & 111 \\
\left[\begin{array}{cccccc}
1 - 3\varepsilon & \varepsilon & 0 & \varepsilon & 0 & 0 \\
2\varepsilon & 1 - 4\varepsilon & 2\varepsilon & 0 & \varepsilon & 0 \\
0 & \varepsilon & 1 - 5\varepsilon & 0 & 0 & \varepsilon \\
\varepsilon & 0 & 0 & 1 - 5\varepsilon & \varepsilon & 0 \\
0 & 2\varepsilon & 0 & 4\varepsilon & 1 - 4\varepsilon & 2\varepsilon \\
0 & 0 & 3\varepsilon & 0 & 2\varepsilon & 1 - 3\varepsilon
\end{array}\right]
\end{array}.
$$

Note that transitions are non-zero only for adjacent states, that is, states that only differ for the state of one single agent. Indeed, other transitions require at least two states, and we set them to zero in the approximated Markov process.

We discuss how we compute transitions. For instance, to jump from 101 to 111, there are three different possibilities because, given the communication possibilities in the network, it suffices that any agent gets a job offer. Therefore, $\Pr\{\sigma_{t+1} = 111 \mid \sigma_t = 101\} = 3\varepsilon$.

Let us now compute $\Pr\{\sigma_{t+1} = 100 \mid \sigma_t = 101\}$. We need either of the employed agents to be hit by a negative breakdown job. Indeed, recall that in the coarsened Markov process, state 100 corresponds to both 100 and 001. The transition probability is thus 2ε. Finally, let us compute $\Pr\{\sigma_{t+1} = 111 \mid \sigma_t = 110\}$. The coarsened state 110 can either be 110 or 011, each with equal probability $1/2$. For each such state profile, two shocks make it possible to jump to 111: either the unemployed individual hears about the job directly, or the central employed agent does and communicates it. So, the transition occurs with probability $(1/2)\,2\varepsilon + (1/2)\,2\varepsilon = 2\varepsilon$. And so on.

The steady-state equations for the approximated dynamics are therefore given by:

$$3v_{000} = v_{100} + v_{010}$$
$$2v_{100} = v_{000} + v_{101} + \frac{1}{2}v_{110}$$
$$5v_{101} = v_{100} + v_{111}$$
$$5v_{010} = v_{000} + v_{110}$$
$$2v_{110} = 2v_{010} + v_{111} + \frac{1}{2}v_{100}$$
$$3v_{111} = 3v_{101} + 2v_{110}.$$

After some algebra, we obtain:

$$v^* = \left(v_{000}^*, v_{100}^*, v_{101}^*, v_{010}^*, v_{110}^*, v_{111}^*\right) = \frac{1}{774}\,(61,\,124,\,70,\,59,\,234,\,226),$$

from which we easily deduce μ^* for the non-coarsened approximated process.

4.3.4. *Intra-Group Correlations.* How should these intragroup correlation patterns be qualified? In particular, how should correlations between individual spoke and hub, correlations between either individual spoke or hub and the two other agents, be qualified?

The state of the economy is a binary random vector. The long-run behavior is described by a steady-state distribution over the possible outcomes for this random vector. This is a joint distribution, characterized by $2^n - 1$ variables. It allows for a richer set of internal correlations than a joint distribution characterized by a collection of individual Bernoulli (n variables) together with pairwise correlations across the different individual outcomes ($n(n-1)/2$ variables). Indeed,

$$2^n - 1 > \frac{n(n+1)}{2}\ \text{for}\ n \geq 3.$$

Hence, a joint distribution can display richer intragroup correlation patterns than simple pairwise comparisons. Calvó-Armengol and Jackson (2004) introduce the concept of stochastic association, which qualifies the presence of such richer correlation patterns. Stochastic association is self-domination, where domination is a stochastic ordering over joint distributions that extends first-order stochastic domination.

By definition (actually, this is a Lemma in Calvó-Armengol and Jackson, 2004, which derives from the definition for domination that extends first-order stochastic domination from random variables to random vectors), we say that μ is strongly stochastically associated if and only if $\mu\,(\mathbb{L}\cap\mathbb{L}') > \mu\,(\mathbb{L})\,\mu\,(\mathbb{L}')$ for all increasing sets $\mathbb{L}$, $\mathbb{L}'$. The set of increasing sets is

$$\mathcal{E} = \{\mathbb{L} \subset \{0, 1\}^n \mid s \in \mathbb{L}, s' \geq s \Rightarrow s' \in \mathbb{L}\}$$

that is, the set of subsets of states such that if one state is in the event then all states with at least as high employment status (person by person) are also in the event. Note that here we do not use coarsened state space, but true state space with eight different states, as we need to discriminate agents by their labels.

We check that μ^*, the steady-state distribution for the approximated subdivided Markov process, is strongly stochatistically associated. First, let $\mathbb{L} = \{100, 101, 110, 111\}$ and $\mathbb{L}' = \{011, 111\}$. $\mathbb{L}$ is the set of states for which agent 1 is employed, while $\mathbb{L}'$ is the set of states for which agents 2 and 3 are employed. Then, $\mu^*\,(\mathbb{L}) = v^*_{100}/2 + v^*_{101} + v^*_{110}/2 + v^*_{111}$ is the marginal employment probability for agent 1, while $\mu^*\,(\mathbb{L}') = v^*_{110}/2 + v^*_{111}$ is the marginal employment probability for agents 2 and 3 together. Then, $\mu^*\,(\mathbb{L}\cap\mathbb{L}') = v^*_{111}$. The inequality can be checked immediately.

Second, let $\mathbb{L} = \{010, 011, 110, 111\}$ and $\mathbb{L}' = \{101, 111\}$. $\mathbb{L}$ is the set of states for which agent 2 is employed, while $\mathbb{L}'$ is the set of states for which agents 1 and 3 are employed. Then, $\mu^*\,(\mathbb{L}) = v^*_{010} + v^*_{110} + v^*_{111}$ is the marginal employment probability for agent 2, while $\mu^*\,(\mathbb{L}') = v^*_{101} + v^*_{111}$ is the marginal employment probability for agents 1 and 3 together. Then, $\mu^*\,(\mathbb{L}\cap\mathbb{L}') = v^*_{111}$. The inequality can be checked immediately. We can also check for standard pairwise correlations, etc.

4.3.5. The Final Result. We have shown that strong stochastic association holds for the Markov process that approximates the T–period subdivision of the true Markov process. The approximation is more accurate the higher is T. Therefore, with a sufficiently high T–period subdivision, we can immediately conclude that the true (subdivided) Markov process is weakly stochastically associated, as strict inequalities turn into weak inequalities "at the limit."

As a matter of fact, we can show a much stronger result, namely that the true (subdivided) Markov process is also strongly stochastically associated. Proving that inequalities remain strict at the limit is a far from trivial endeavour, the details of which we skip here.

To conclude, we reproduce the following general result for n individuals and any social network structure from Calvó-Armengol and Jackson (2004):

Proposition 9.8. *Under sufficiently fine subdivisions of periods, the unique steady-state, long-run distribution on employment is such that the employment statuses of any path-connected agents are positively correlated.*

The proposition shows that despite the short-run conditional negative correlation between the employment of competitors for jobs and information, any interconnected workers' employment is positively correlated in the longer run. This implies that there is a clustering of workers by employment status, and employed workers tend to be connected with employed workers, and vice versa.

4.3.6. Why Does the Network Matter? Suppose that there is no network in the population, and the three agents are isolated. The Markov transition then changes, as there are no communication possibilities. The new matrix is:

$$
\begin{bmatrix}
1 - 3\varepsilon & \varepsilon & 0 & \varepsilon & 0 & 0 \\
2\varepsilon & 1 - 3\varepsilon & 2\varepsilon & 0 & \varepsilon & 0 \\
0 & \varepsilon & 1 - 3\varepsilon & 0 & 0 & \varepsilon \\
\varepsilon & 0 & 0 & 1 - 3\varepsilon & \varepsilon & 0 \\
0 & \varepsilon & 0 & 2\varepsilon & 1 - 3\varepsilon & 2\varepsilon \\
0 & 0 & \varepsilon & 0 & \varepsilon & 1 - 3\varepsilon
\end{bmatrix}.
$$

The new steady-state distribution is such that $\mu^*_{ijk} = 1/8$. Indeed, the Markov transitions for the isolated agent are:

$$
\begin{bmatrix}
1 - \varepsilon & \varepsilon \\
\varepsilon & 1 - \varepsilon
\end{bmatrix},
$$

with steady-state $(1/2, 1/2)$. With no communication, states are independent. It can also be checked that positive correlation holds even when communication is imperfect.

To illustrate the fact that not only the network is of importance, but also its structure, let us consider a network with four workers $n = 4$. We assume that the job-acquisition rate a and the job-destruction rate δ are such that $a = 0.100$ and $\delta = 0.015$. If we interpret the time period as a week, then a worker loses a job on average once every 67 weeks and directly hears about a job on average once every ten weeks. Using numerical simulations, Table 9.1 depicts the value of unemployment probabilities of

Table 9.1. *Correlations in employment statuses and network structure*

g	$\Pr(\sigma_1 = 0)$	$Cor(\sigma_1, \sigma_2)$	$Cor(\sigma_1, \sigma_3)$
(network)	0.132	–	–
(network)	0.083	0.041	–
(network)	0.063	0.025	0.019
(network)	0.050	0.025	0.025

worker 1, i.e., $\Pr(\sigma_1 = 0)$, and the correlations between workers 1 and 2, $Cor(\sigma_1, \sigma_2)$, and between workers 1 and 3, in the long-run steady-state. These results are calculated using numerical simulations repeated for a sufficiently long period of time. First, when there is no social network so that no information is exchanged between workers, the unemployment rate of each agent is just equal to its steady-state value, that is $u = \delta/(\delta + a) = 0.132$. Thus, the probability of being unemployed for each worker is 13.2%, given that they cannot rely on other workers to get information about jobs and the only chance they can have of obtaining a job is by direct methods. Imagine now that only one link is added in this network so that workers 1 and 2 are directly linked to each other, $g_{12} = g_{21} = 1$. Steady-state unemployment decreases substantially for workers 1 and 2, from 13.2% to 8.3%. When more links are added, the unemployment rate for each worker decreases even more from 13.2% when there are no links to 5% when the social network is complete. Another important feature of Table 9.1 is the positive correlation between employment statuses of different workers. Indeed, it can be seen that correlation in employment statuses between direct and indirect friends is always positive in the long run, even if this correlation is smaller for indirect than direct neighbors. The latter is due to the fact that direct connections provide job information while indirect connections only help by indirectly providing information that keeps friends, and friends of friends, etc., employed. For example, in the third network in Table 9.1, workers 1 and 3 are not directly connected, but are *path-connected* (length 2)

Table 9.2. *Duration dependence and network structure*

g	1 period	2 periods	10 periods
	0.099	0.099	0.099
	0.176	0.175	0.170
	0.305	0.300	0.278

and their correlation is 1.9%, while workers 1 and 2, who are directly connected (length 1) have a correlation of 2.5%. To summarize, Table 9.1 illustrates the fact that the structure of the network is crucial for understanding the labor market outcomes of workers. Switching from a circle to a complete network does not only have a strong effect on the unemployment rate of workers but also on their correlation in employment statuses.

4.3.7. Duration Dependence and Persistence in Unemployment. Another important result is the fact that social networks can help us understand *duration dependence* among certain groups of workers. This is illustrated in Table 9.2 where it is once more assumed that $a = 0.100$ and $\delta = 0.015$. Let us calculate the individual probability of being employed at the end of a period, given that this person has been unemployed for at least each of the last T periods preceding this period. Columns 1, 2, 3 correspond, respectively, to $T = 1, 2, 10$. When there is no social network of relationships, workers do not experience any duration dependence since the probability of being employed is independent of the time spent unemployed. This probability is just the probability of hearing about a job and not losing this job during the period, i.e., $a(1 - \delta) = 0.099$. Once a social network is introduced, workers start to exchange job information and duration dependence prevails. It can, in particular, be seen that the probability of being employed after spending some time unemployed decreases with the number of links. For example, when the network is complete, the probability of finding a job for a worker who has been unemployed for 10 periods (27.8%) is much higher that for a worker who has been unemployed for only 1 period (17.6%) located in a network where only workers 1 and 2 have a link. This shows that not only direct links, but also indirect links are of importance. Indeed, take workers 1 and 2. In the first network, each of them has one direct link while, in the complete network, they have three links each. This is not sufficient to explain the difference probabilities. The main difference is that there are no path-connected friends that can eventually provide information about jobs in the first network while, in the complete network, everybody helps each other.

We can now state a more general result due to Calvó-Armengol and Jackson (2004).

Proposition 9.9. *Under sufficiently fine subdivisions of periods and starting under the steady-state distribution, the conditional probability that an individual will become employed in a given period is decreasing with the length of his/her observed (individual) unemployment spells.*

This is a very powerful result which indicates that past unemployment histories are of importance in calculating individual probabilities of finding a job. If the unemployed worker's network is of poor quality because he/she either has few friends or few contacts with employed workers, then his/her chance of hearing about a job will be low, especially in a world where the majority of jobs are advertised through informal methods.

4.3.8. Urban Segregation and Social Networks. In this model, there is no explicit land market. It is indeed difficult to reconcile the network perspective with a *finite* number of agents and a monocentric city model with a *continuum* of workers. However, the social analysis can easily be transposed into an urban space. Indeed, as in spatial econometrics (Anselin, 1988), the adjacency matrix **A** (see Section 4.1) could be defined in the *geographical space* instead of the *social space*. In that case, if the nodes are areas (neighborhoods, regions, etc.), then links between nodes can be represented by a graph **g**, where $g_{ij} = 1$ if area i is contiguous to (or at a certain road distance from) area j and $g_{ij} = 0$ otherwise.[18] Another way to spatially define the adjacency matrix **A** is to represent links by proximity in terms of time distance so that $g_{ij} = 1$ if area i is at an average road journey time less than a certain threshold (in minutes) from area j and $g_{ij} = 0$ otherwise. This is the strategy adopted by Patacchini and Zenou (2008) to test the model

---

[18] See, for example, Patacchini and Zenou (2007) who use such an approach.

of section 4. In other words, they approximate the *social proximity* by the *geographical proximity*, drawing a link between the social and geographical spaces. Focussing on ethnic minorities in the U.K., their conjecture is that the density of people belonging to the same ethnicity and living in the same area constitutes a good approximation for the number of direct friends one has, i.e., *strong ties*. In the same spirit, the density of individuals living in neighboring areas is a measure of friends of friends, i.e., *weak ties*. From the adjacency matrix **A**, now defined in terms of time distance thresholds, they can easily calculate the indirect connections between any path-connected areas (or people) of any length (see Definition 9.1 and Proposition 9.7). Consistently with the theoretical model of section 4, they find that the higher the percentage of a given ethnic group living nearby, the higher the employment rate of this ethnic group. This effect decays very rapidly with distance, losing significance beyond approximately 90 minutes travel time.

There is clearly a strong correlation between the social and the geographical space. In the introduction to this part, we have seen that social networks are localized and many contacts take place within the neighborhood where people live. In cities, especially American cities, ethnic minorities are usually spatially isolated. This residential segregation reduces their social contacts with whites. As a result, if the main source of job information for black workers is from the other black workers living in the same neighborhood, then it is very likely that the quality of their social network will be poor. In other words, being isolated in the physical space (segregation) can lead to an isolation in the social space (low-quality social networks). Using the model developed above, it is easy to understand why black workers will experience high unemployment rates and long spells of unemployment in segregated neighborhoods.

5. Discussion

The different models presented in this chapter have in common that social networks are of importance in explaining the high unemployment rates experienced by ethnic minorities in cities. This explanation is complementary to that provided in Chapters 7 and 8 where distance to jobs was seen as the main reason for these.

In Section 2 of Chapter 9, black workers who do not desire to interact with whites pay a high price in the labor market, especially if they end up in an equilibrium where they live far away from jobs. However, even if they reside close to jobs, they will still experience high unemployment rates because of their poor-quality social networks since they have no interaction with whites. In Section 3 of Chapter 9, building on Granovetter (1973)'s idea that weak ties are superior to strong ties when providing support in getting a job, we develop a model where black workers who live far away from jobs tend to have less connections to weak ties. This is because black workers who live in distant neighborhoods are limited in getting information about possible jobs. Because of the lack of good public transportation in the U.S., it is costly (both in terms of time and money) to commute to business centers to meet other types of people (especially whites) who can provide other sources of information about jobs. If distant workers mainly rely on their strong ties (mainly blacks) and if the latter are unemployed, there is little chance of escaping unemployment and finding a job.

The last section of Chapter 9 instead proposes a model where the notion of weak ties is much more elaborate since it corresponds to all workers who are path-connected. These indirect links prove to be crucial in explaining the high unemployment rates of minority workers. In particular, even if it is not true in the short run, the employment statuses of weak ties are positively correlated in the long run. This implies that, not only direct friends, but also indirect friends (i.e., friends of friends, friends of friends of friends, etc.) are decisive in evaluating the quality of a social network. Weak ties (as defined by friends of friends) will indirectly help individuals because, by providing job information to their strong ties, they help them become employed. duration dependence might then be less severe for workers who are well-connected in a good-quality network.

An important result of this last model is to show that there is clustering since, in the long run (i.e., steady-state), employed workers tend to be friends with employed workers. As a result, if some black workers are unemployed due to some initial condition (say history), then in steady-state they will still be unemployed because both their strong and weak ties will also be unemployed. In the other two models, it is segregation and distance to jobs that make black workers only interact with strong ties who are themselves likely to be unemployed.

To conclude, we believe that weak ties generate "bridging" social capital. Bridging social capital refers to ties across networks that may make the resources existing in one network accessible to a member of another (Burt, 1992). These social relationships make it possible for members to "get ahead." They are needed to extend beyond family to connect to a broader range of resources and opportunities that exist in networks to which they are otherwise not connected. If black workers do not have access to weak ties (especially whites), in particular because they are segregated and separated from business centers, their main source of information about jobs will be provided by their strong ties. But if the latter are themselves unemployed, the chances of escaping unemployment will be very low.

6. Notes on the Literature

As stated in the introduction, there is a large empirical literature showing the importance of social networks in finding a job. There are, however, very few theoretical models that have tried to model urban space and social space together, in particular social networks in the labor market. The models presented in Chapter 3, Section 4, based on Brueckner, Thisse, and Zenou (2002), were a first attempt in this direction. These models show that low-skill workers are distant from firms in both *skill* and *urban* spaces. Since skill space is highly correlated with social space, this provided a rationale for the existence of *socio-economic ghettos*, occupied by workers who are "socially" and physically distant from their employers. In this framework, *socio-economic ghettos emerge as workers with poor skill matches are also those who incur the highest commuting costs.* However, in these models, there were no social networks (or social interactions) so that workers just found a job randomly.[19] There are some job-search models where workers find jobs through social contacts (Calvó-Armengol and Zenou, 2005; Diamond, 1981; Mortensen and Vishwanath, 1994), but there is no urban space. Section 2, based on Selod and Zenou (2006), was a first attempt at combining urban space and social networks. However, the modeling of social networks was quite shallow since it was captured by the employment rate of workers of the same race. The model of Section 3, which has been specifically written for this book and can be found as a working paper in Zenou (2008e), tried to go further by introducing the notion of weak and strong ties in helping an individual find a job.[20] However, the structure of the network was quite limited since we only considered dyads. In Section 4, which elaborates

---

[19] There are some papers that combine social interactions and urban spatial structure (Helsley and Strange, 2007; Brueckner and Lagey, 2008). However, in all these papers, the social network is not explicitly modeled. Social interactions are captured by externalities and only average effects are considered.

[20] Granovetter (1973, 1983) was the first to introduce the idea of weak and strong ties in the labor market. The way of modeling strong and weak ties as in Section 3 is due to Montgomery (1992, 1994). Calvó-Armengol, Verdier, and Zenou (2007) has proposed a similar model focussing on the interaction between the labor and the crime market.

on Calvó-Armengol and Jackson (2004), the network was totally explicit, but the land market was not modeled. It must be emphasized that it is very difficult to have an explicit network analysis with a *finite* number of individuals and a monocentric city with a *continuum* of individuals together in the same model.

General Conclusion

The aim of this book has been twofold. First, we have provided different models of urban labor economics (Parts 1 and 2) to acclimatize the reader to these new tools. Different models incorporating search-matching frictions or efficiency wages into an urban framework have been proposed and the reader is expected to master these new tools after the first two parts. Second, we have provided different mechanisms for explaining the consequences of segregation on ethnic minorities' labor market outcomes (Part 3). Distance to jobs and poor social networks have been put forward as the main reasons for the adverse labor market outcomes experienced by ethnic minorities.

This book has been written because the link between urban economics and labor economics has been almost totally ignored, as least from a theoretical perspective. We believe that many issues in urban economics can be analyzed in a new and deeper way when the labor market is introduced. Similarly, introducing a land market in a labor market analysis allows us to address standard issues in a different way. One prominent example is the analysis of urban ghettos, which is difficult to understand if the land (or more generally space) and the labor market are not incorporated together. Indeed, space is often a constraining factor for people in the labor market, especially for racial minorities. The spatial-mismatch hypothesis (developed in Chapters 7 and 8) is a good example of this since it posits that spatial arrangements diminish minorities' access to job opportunities, resulting in greater joblessness for minorities compared to non-minorities. Space works as a barrier for minorities. In particular, we have seen that discrimination in the housing market introduces a key frictional factor that prevents minorities from improving access to job opportunities by relocating residences closer to suburban jobs.

Social networks (developed in Chapter 9), which are a crucial feature of the labor markets, also tend to be affected by space. Indeed, social networks tend to be localized so that workers who are *physically close* to jobs can be *socially far away* from them. For example, Kasinitz and Rosenberg (1996) find that poor, black residents of the Red Hook section of Brooklyn are cut off from good jobs on the waterfront, even though these jobs are spatially very close by. Since people only tend to be hired to these jobs through connections with union members who already work there, and because few African Americans are currently employed on the waterfront, African Americans have difficulties in obtaining these jobs; they are "missing the connection" as argued by the authors.

We have highlighted distance to jobs (spatial-mismatch hypothesis) and social networks as the main explanation for the adverse labor market outcomes of ethnic minorities. Naturally, there are other explanations that can be added to these and for which space plays an important role. Identity formation, cultural transmission, role models, and peer effects do also affect the labor market outcomes of ethnic minorities.[1]

It has indeed been stipulated that black students in predominantly white schools who study hard are often subject to peer ridicule. They are accused of "acting white" by other blacks (Fordham and Ogbu, 1986; Austen-Smith and Fryer, 2005; Fryer and Torelli, 2005). This so-called "ghetto chic" in the form of peer pressure to shun academic pursuits undoubtedly has a dragging effect on the average black student's Scholastic Assessment Test (SAT) and other test scores. The late John Ogbu, professor of anthropology at Berkeley, believed that broad cultural attributes among blacks – such as parental style, commitment to learning, and work ethic – bear a heavy responsibility for the black-white educational gap. In his last book, Ogbu (2003) wrote that even black students in the affluent homes of doctors and lawyers often consider rappers in ghettos as their role models. Students talk about what it takes to be a good student, Ogbu wrote, but few put forth the effort required to get good grades. This type of behavior is typical, Ogbu said, of racial minorities adapting to oppression and lack of opportunities. Ogbu, much as Bill Cosby has done recently, also placed the blame on black parents. He believed that many black parents are not offering sufficient guidance, do not spend enough time helping with homework, and do not pay adequate attention to their children's educational progress.

Even for adults, the same phenomenon has been observed in terms of work ethics. The existence of a low work ethic has been pointed out by several scholars as an important element in the set of values defining the prevalent

---

[1] In Chapter 9, we have mentioned the importance of oppositional identity and its impact on blacks' labor market outcomes.

culture in inner-city neighborhoods. This is consistent with more general evidence from sociology and anthropology,[2] suggesting the existence of a persistent "ghetto culture," which is transmitted from one generation to the next. As argued by Wilson (1987, 1996), it is the social, rather than the physical distance, that often separates poor blacks from good jobs. This is particularly true for the African American community, which has experienced high levels of segregation for at least a century (Massey and Denton, 1993; Cutler, Glaeser, and Vigdor, 1999).

"Inner-city social isolation also generates behavior not conducive to good work histories. The patterns of behavior that are associated with a life of casual work (tardiness and absenteeism) are quite different from those that accompany a life of regular or steady work (e.g., the habit of waking up early in the morning to a ringing alarm clock). In neighborhoods in which most families do not have a steadily employed breadwinner, the norms and behavior patterns associated with steady work compete with those associated with casual or infrequent work." (Wilson, 1996)

In the words of a counsellor about a training program aimed at exposing black workers to more conventional working values:

"To adopt a regular pattern, you have to break with this environment. Your friends laugh at you for going to work, that's hell, they think you are trying to be better than them! You have to have strong character to resist this pressure. If all your friends and families went to work, they would help you adopt a regular schedule." (cited in Bonney, 1975)

The importance of family and social environment in the transmission of personality traits has been widely documented (see, e.g., Boyd and Richerson, 1985, and Cavalli-Sforza and Feldman, 1981).[3] To the extent that some of those traits are important in determining individual performance in the workplace, it is also important to understand the mechanism of transmission. Evidence from sociological literature suggests that children's families and the communities where they live are important elements in shaping their attitudes towards work. If employers are reluctant, as they declare to be, to hire members from the black group because of the prevalent values in their communities, then the incentives of parents to transmit different habits may be affected and policies promoting integration may have a positive effect on blacks (Saez-Marti and Zenou, 2005).

---

[2] See, in particular, Hannerz (1969), Lewis (1969), Wilson (1987), and Katz (1993).

[3] Bisin and Verdier (2000, 2001) were the first to analyze the role of cultural transmission in economics. For empirical applications focussing on identity issues, see Bisin, Topa, and Verdier (2004), and Bisin, Patacchini, Verdier, and Zenou (2006, 2008).

The interactions between urban economics and labor economics are multi-dimensional. In particular, the issues of urban ghettos, ethnic minorities, and their labor market outcomes are extremely complex and no simple recipe can be found to solve these urban/labor problems. This book has provided some answers and we hope that it will encourage more people to work on these issues.

APPENDIX A

Basic Urban Economics

In this Appendix, we give the basic ingredients of the standard urban economic model. Modern urban economics is based on the concept of bid-rent curves, first introduced by von Thünen (1826) in the context of agricultural land use. Alonso (1964) is the first author who successfully generalizes von Thünen's concept of bid-rent curves to an urban context. For a deeper understanding of these types of models, the reader is strongly advised to read Fujita (1989). It is important to observe that, throughout this book, we follow the Alonso's approach in the sense that individuals consume land directly and thus we use the terms "land" and "housing" interchangeably. Mills (1967) and Muth (1969) proposed a more realistic model where land is an intermediate input in the production of housing, which is the final consumption good. We refer to Brueckner (1987) for a unified treatment of these two approaches.

1. The Basic Model with Identical Agents

We assume that the city is *linear* and *monocentric*. This means that the city is described by a line in which all jobs and all firms (which are assumed to be identical) are located in the Central Business District (CBD), which is, for simplicity, normalized to zero and all workers/consumers endogenously decide their residential location between 0 and the city fringe x_f. Landlords allocate the land to the highest bids in the city. All workers/consumers are employed and are identical in all respects. There are exactly N identical workers. There are neither mobility costs within the city nor migration costs between the city and and the area outside the city. However, individuals do incur commuting costs to go to work.

1.1. The Individual Location Choice

The question we must solve is the following: What is the optimal residential choice of each individual? In fact, each individual is a worker and thus works every day in the CBD. He/she obtains a monthly wage of w_L and incurs a monthly pecuniary commuting cost at a distance x from the CBD equal to τx, where τ is the commuting cost per unit of distance.

Each individual is also a consumer. He/she consumes housing (or land) and a non-spatial composite good (it is a mixture of all goods that are not related to location). More precisely, he/she optimally determines the lot size of the house h_L and the optimal consumption of the non-spatial composite good, z_L.

To solve this question, we must determine the preferences of this worker/consumer. For simplicity, we use preferences that are well-behaved; i.e., preferences are continuous and increasing at all $h_L > 0$ and $z_L > 0$ and all indifference curves are strictly convex and smooth and do not cut axes. The utility function (that represents these preferences) is given by:

$$\Gamma(z_L, h_L) \tag{A.1}$$

with

$$\frac{\partial \Gamma(z_L, h_L)}{\partial h_L} > 0 \qquad \frac{\partial \Gamma(z_L, h_L)}{\partial z_L} > 0,$$

and the function $\Gamma(z_L, h_L)$ is strictly quasi-concave.

We can also write the budget constraint. Each worker has a net monthly wage of $w_L - \tau x$ and spends money on the composite good z_L plus housing $h_L R(x)$, where $R(x)$ is the land price at a distance x from the CBD. The budget constraint is thus given by:

$$w_L - \tau x = h_L R(x) + z_L. \tag{A.2}$$

Each individual chooses h_L and z_L which maximize $\Gamma(z_L, h_L)$ under the budget constraint (A.2). We need to calculate the bid-rent of each individual; that is, how much he/she is ready to pay for land in each location x in order to reach a utility level $\Gamma(z_L, h_L)$. There are three different approaches that are all equivalent (Fujita, 1989, Ch. 2).

1.1.1. *The Indirect Marshallian Approach.*
In this approach, each individual solves the following program:

$$\max_{h_L, z_L} \Gamma(z_L, h_L) \text{ s.t. } w_L - \tau x = h_L R(x) + z_L. \tag{A.3}$$

This is equivalent to:

$$\max_{h_L} \Gamma(w_L - \tau x - h_L R(x), h_L), \tag{A.4}$$

where $z_L = w_L - \tau x - h_L R(x)$. First- and second-order conditions of (A.4) give a unique Marshallian demand for housing (lot size) $h_L^M(R(x), w_L)$, which is implicitly defined as:

$$-\frac{\partial \Gamma}{\partial z_L} R(x) + \frac{\partial \Gamma}{\partial h_L} = 0. \tag{A.5}$$

By using the budget constraint, we obtain the Marshallian demand for the composite good:

$$z_L^M(R(x), w_L) = w_L - \tau x - h_L^M(x, w_L) R(x). \tag{A.6}$$

The indirect utility function can be written as:

$$W(w_L, \tau, x, R) = \Gamma(w_L - \tau x - h_L^M(R(x), w_L) R(x), h_L^M(R(x), w_L))$$
$$\equiv W_L, \tag{A.7}$$

where W_L is the equilibrium utility level in the city. Finally, we can solve equation (A.7) to obtain the so-called bid-rent (see below for an exact definition) for specific preferences:

$$\Psi_L(x, W_L). \tag{A.8}$$

Let us explain the Marshallian approach using Figure A.1. The aim of each individual is to solve (A.3), that is to find the highest utility level compatible with the budget constraint (A.2). Thus, by fixing the budget constraint as in Figure A.1, we vary the utility functions W_Ls and the solution to (A.3) is given by (z_L^*, h_L^*), which is precisely the highest utility level compatible with the budget constraint; in Figure A.1, it corresponds to $W_{L,2}$.

We would like to know where this representative individual chose his/her residential location in the city. For that, he/she solves the following program:

$$\max_{x} \Gamma(w_L - \tau x - h_L R(x), h_L).$$

It is easily checked that this leads to:

$$\tau + h_L R'(x) = 0, \tag{A.9}$$

which is the so-called Alonso-Muth condition. It says that, by optimally choosing his/her location, each individual faces the following trade-off. If the individual decides to reside closer to the city center (here 0), then he/she pays a higher marginal land rent ($R'(x) < 0$), but incurs a lower

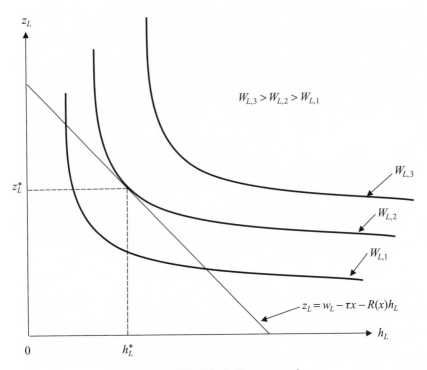

Figure A.1. The Marshallian approach.

marginal commuting cost ($\tau > 0$). In contrast, if he/she locates closer to the periphery of the city, then the marginal land rent is lower, but the marginal commuting cost is greater. Naturally, in equilibrium, all (identical) individuals are indifferent between all locations since they reach the same utility level W_L (there is no mobility costs).

1.1.2. *The Direct Approach.* Defining the concept of bid-rent in a more direct way is referred to as the *direct* approach to calculating the bid-rent.

Definition A.1. *The bid-rent $\Psi_L(x, W_L)$ is the maximum rent per unit of land that an individual can pay for residing at a distance x from the CBD, while enjoying a fixed utility level W_L.*

Using the budget constraint (A.2), this bid-rent can be written as:

$$\Psi_L(x, W_L) = \max_{z_L, h_L}\left\{\frac{w_L - \tau x - z_L}{h_L} \mid \Gamma(z_L, h_L) = W_L\right\}, \quad (A.10)$$

where, for an individual residing at x, $w_L - \tau x - z_L$ is the money available for land rent and where $(w_L - \tau x - z_L)/h_L$ represents the land rent per unit of land. Solving the equation $\Gamma(z_L, h_L) = W_L$, we obtain a composite good consumption, which is a function of h_L and W_L; that is, $Z_L(h_L, W_L)$ and thus we can write (A.10) as:

$$\Psi_L(x, W_L) = \max_{h_L} \left\{ \frac{w_L - \tau x - Z_L(h_L, W_L)}{h_L} \right\}. \tag{A.11}$$

Solving (A.11) leads to the optimal lot size, which is a function of x and W_L, that is $h_L^d(x, W_L)$, which is implicitly defined by:

$$\frac{\partial Z_L(h_L^d(x, W_L), W_L)}{\partial h_L} h_L + w_L - \tau x - Z_L(h_L^d(x, W_L), W_L) = 0. \tag{A.12}$$

Plugging $h_L^d(x, W_L)$ back into (A.11), we obtain:

$$\Psi_L(x, W_L) = \frac{w_L - \tau x - Z_L(h_L^d(x, W_L), W_L)}{h_L^d(x, W_L)}. \tag{A.13}$$

We can illustrate the direct approach using Figure A.2. To solve program (A.10), the utility level must be fixed to W_L and then the highest bid-rent $\Psi_L(x, W_L)$ compatible with W_L must be found. Since in the (h_L, z_L)-plane, $\Psi_L(x, W_L) = R(x)$ is the slope of the budget constraint, i.e., $z_L = w_L - \tau x - R(x) h_L$, graphically solving program (A.10) means finding the optimal slope of the budget constraint that is compatible with W_L. In Figure A.2, it is $\Psi_{L,2}(x, W_L)$.

Once more, we can calculate the optimal location for each individual. By differentiating (A.13) with respect to x, we obtain:

$$\begin{aligned}
\frac{\partial \Psi_L(x, W_L)}{\partial x} &= \frac{1}{h_L^2} \left\{ \left[-\tau - \frac{\partial Z_L(h_L, W_L)}{\partial h_L} \frac{\partial h_L}{\partial x} \right] h_L \right. \\
&\quad - [w_L - \tau x - Z_L(h_L, W_L)] \frac{\partial h_L}{\partial x} \Bigg\} \\
&= \frac{1}{h_L^2} \left\{ -\tau h_L - \frac{\partial h_L}{\partial x} \left[\frac{\partial Z_L(h_L, W_L)}{\partial h_L} h_L \right. \right. \\
&\quad + [w_L - \tau x - Z_L(h_L, W_L)] \Bigg] \Bigg\},
\end{aligned}$$

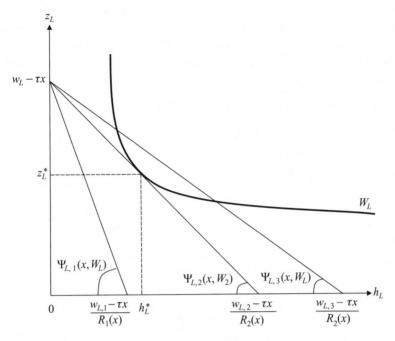

Figure A.2. The direct approach.

where $h_L \equiv h_L^d(x, W_L)$. Now observing from (A.12) that $\frac{\partial Z_L(h_L, W_L)}{\partial h_L} h_L - [w_L - \tau x - Z_L(h_L, W_L)] = 0$, we obtain (this is known as the Envelope Theorem):

$$\frac{\partial \Psi_L(x, W_L)}{\partial x} = -\frac{\tau}{h_L^d(x, W_L)}.$$

In equilibrium, $\Psi_L(x, W_L) = R(x)$ and thus this equation is exactly equivalent to (A.9).

1.1.3. The Indirect Hicksian Approach. The last approach consists of using Hicksian compensated demand for land. In that case, the consumer minimizes his/her expenses in order to reach a certain level of utility (this is referred to as the expenditure-minimization problem), that is:

$$\mathbf{E}(x, W_L) \equiv \min_{z_L, h_L} \{z_L + h_L R(x) + \tau x \mid \Gamma(z_L, h_L) = W_L\}, \qquad (A.14)$$

where $\mathbf{E}(x, W_L)$ is the expenditure function. Once more solving $\Gamma(z_L, h_L) = W_L$, we obtain $Z_L(h_L, W_L)$. Thus, this program can be written as:

$$\mathbf{E}(x, W_L) \equiv \min_{h_L} \{Z_L(h_L, W_L) + h_L R(x) + \tau x\},$$

which implicitly defines $h_L^H(R(x), W_L)$, the (compensated) Hicksian demand for land, as follows:

$$\frac{\partial Z_L(h_L^H(R(x), W_L), W_L)}{\partial h_L} + R(x) = 0. \tag{A.15}$$

Plugging $h_L^H(R(x), W_L)$ back into the expenditure function, we easily obtain:

$$\mathbf{E}(x, W_L) \equiv Z_L(h_L^H(R(x), W_L), W_L) + h_L^H(R(x), W_L) R(x) + \tau x. \tag{A.16}$$

From the budget constraint (A.2), we have

$$\mathbf{E}(x, W_L) = w_L,$$

which using (A.16) is equivalent to:

$$Z_L(h_L^H(R(x), W_L), W_L) + h_L^H(R(x), W_L) R(x) = w_L - \tau x. \tag{A.17}$$

Inverting this equation and observing that $\Psi_L(x, W_L) = R(x)$, we obtain the bid-rent function.

Now, by differentiating equation (A.17), we obtain:

$$\begin{aligned}
\frac{\partial \Psi_L(x, W_L)}{\partial x} &= \frac{1}{h_L^2} \left\{ \left[-\tau - \frac{\partial Z_L(h_L, W_L)}{\partial h_L} \frac{\partial h_L}{\partial x} \right] h_L \right. \\
&\quad \left. - [w_L - \tau x - Z_L(h_L, W_L)] \frac{\partial h_L}{\partial x} \right\} \\
&= \frac{1}{h_L^2} \left\{ -\tau h_L - \frac{\partial h_L}{\partial x} \left[\frac{\partial Z_L(h_L, W_L)}{\partial h_L} h_L \right. \right. \\
&\quad \left. \left. + w_L - \tau x - Z_L(h_L, W_L) \right] \right\},
\end{aligned}$$

where $h_L \equiv h_L^H(R(x), W_L)$. Using the budget constraint (A.2), we have

$$w_L - \tau x - Z_L(h_L, W_L) = h_L \Psi_L(x, W_L)$$

and thus

$$\begin{aligned}
&\frac{\partial Z_L(h_L, W_L)}{\partial h_L} h_L + [w_L - \tau x - Z_L(h_L, W_L)] \\
&= \left[\frac{\partial Z_L(h_L, W_L)}{\partial h_L} + \Psi_L(x, W_L) \right] h_L.
\end{aligned}$$

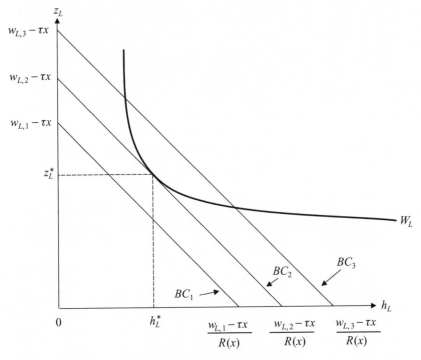

Figure A.3. The Hicksian approach.

Observing that in equilibrium $\Psi_L(x, W_L) = R(x)$ and using (A.16), it is easily seen that (Envelope Theorem):

$$\frac{\partial Z_L(h_L, W_L)}{\partial h_L} h_L + w_L - \tau x - Z_L(h_L, W_L) = 0$$

and thus

$$\frac{\partial \Psi_L(x, W_L)}{\partial x} = -\frac{\tau}{h_L^H(x, W_L)} < 0.$$

We can explain the Hicksian approach using Figure A.3. It is easily seen that this approach is the dual of the Marshallian approach, since we are fixing the utility function at some level, here W_L, and we vary the budget constraint. Indeed, to solve program (A.14), the *lowest* budget constraint compatible with utility W_L must be found and in Figure A.3 it is BC_2.

Finally, if we compare the different approaches, it is easily verified that:

$$h_L^*(x, W_L) \equiv h_L^M(R(x), w_L) = h_L^d(x, W_L) = h_L^H(R(x), W_L), \quad \text{(A.18)}$$

when $h_L^M(R(x), w_L)$ and $h_L^H(R(x), W_L)$ are evaluated at $R(x) = \Psi_L(x, W_L)$. Therefore, the three approaches are totally equivalent. By differentiating equation (A.18), it is easily shown that:

$$\frac{\partial h_L^*(x, W_L)}{\partial x} < 0, \quad \frac{\partial h_L^*(x, W_L)}{\partial W_L} > 0, \quad \frac{\partial h_L^*(x, W_L)}{\partial w_L} < 0.$$

Indeed, people living further away from the CBD will consume more land because it is cheaper there (remember that $\frac{\partial \Psi_L(x, W_L)}{\partial x} < 0$). When utility W_L increases, bid-rent decreases and thus, individuals increase their housing consumption because land is cheaper. The same reasoning applies to w_L since when it increases, they are able to pay more for land, and thus reduce their housing consumption.

Moreover, in all these approaches, it is easily shown that:

$$\frac{\partial \Psi_L(x, W_L)}{\partial w_L} > 0, \quad \frac{\partial \Psi_L(x, W_L)}{\partial W_L} < 0, \quad \frac{\partial \Psi_L(x, W_L)}{\partial \tau} < 0.$$

Indeed, the bid-rent increases (decreases) with the wage w_L (the commuting cost τ) because when individuals are richer (poorer), they are able to offer more (less) for land in each location x. On the other hand, the bid-rent decreases with utility W_L because the higher the utility level to be reached, the lower the bid-rent individuals can afford.

1.2. The Urban-Land-Use Equilibrium

We must now to determine the equilibrium of this city. We will have different cases depending on whether the city is closed or open and whether the landlords are absent or not.

1.2.1. The Closed City With Absentee Landlords.
We must now determine the equilibrium of this city. The fact that the city is closed means that the utility level W_L is endogenous while the size of the population N is given. Moreover, landlords do not reside in the city, and thus the revenue for land does not appear in the income of any resident. We have the following definition:

Definition A.2. *A closed-city urban equilibrium where landlords are absentee and individuals are all employed is a vector* $(W_L, x_f, R(x))$, *such that:*

$$\Psi_L(x_f, W_L) = R_A \tag{A.19}$$

$$\int_0^{x_f} \frac{1}{h_L^*(x, W_L)} dx = N \tag{A.20}$$

$$R^*(x) = \begin{cases} \max\{\Psi_L(x_f, W_L), R_A\} & \text{for } x \le x_f \\ 0 & \text{for } x > x_f \end{cases}, \tag{A.21}$$

where x_f *is the city fringe and* R_A *agricultural land rent outside the city and* $h_L^*(x, W_L)$ *is defined by (A.18).*

Equation (A.21) means that the land is offered to the highest bids in the city. In equation (A.19), the bid-rent at the city fringe is equal to agricultural rent (normalized to zero for simplicity). Equation (A.20) is the population constraint condition. By solving the last two equations, we obtain the equilibrium values of the two unknowns W_L^* and x_f^* as functions of the exogenous variables w_L, τ.

Naturally, these conditions are written for a linear city. To better understand them, let us explain the case of a circular city. Let there be $n(x)dx$ individuals residing in a circular ring whose inner radius is x and outer radius is $x + dx$. Their total *demand for land* in that ring is thus $h_L^*(x, W_L)n(x)dx$. On the other hand, total supply of land in that ring is $2\pi x dx$. Then, in equilibrium, the supply of land must equal demand, that is:

$$h_L^*(x, W_L)n(x)dx = 2\pi x dx$$

which can be written as

$$n(x)dx = \frac{2\pi x}{h_L^*(x, W_L)}.$$

As a result, the equilibrium condition for space is given by:

$$N = \int_0^{x_f} n(x)dx = \int_0^{x_f} \frac{2\pi x}{h_L^*(x, W_L)} dx,$$

which is exactly the population constraint (A.20) for the case of a circular city since $2\pi x$ is the circumference of a circle of radius x. Indeed, at a distance x from the CBD, there is 1 piece of land available in a linear city and $2\pi x$ in a circular city. The second equilibrium condition (A.19) is independent of the type of city (linear or circular) and is mainly the result of perfect competition in the land market.

1.2.2. *The Open City With Absentee Landlords.* We can easily extend this model to the case of an open city. In that case, where mobility is free between cities, the utility obtained by city residents W_L becomes exogenous (it is just their outside option), but the number of people N living in the city is endogenous. The definition of equilibrium is exactly as in definition A.2, but one must solve (A.19), (A.20), and (A.21) in terms of N, x_f and $R(x)$. It can be shown (see Fujita, 1989, Proposition 3.5, pp. 62–63) that the closed-city and open-city models are identical if one uses the value of equilibrium utility W_L^* of the closed-city model in the open-city case.

1.2.3. *The Case of Resident Landlords.* In both closed and open cities, landlords can reside in the city. This is referred to as the *public-land-ownership* model. To be more precise, the city residents are now assumed to form a government which rents the land for the city from rural landlords at agricultural rent R_A. The city government, in turn, subleases the land to city residents at the competitive rent $R(x)$ in each location x. We can define the total differential rent (TDR) from the city as:

$$TDR = \int_0^{x_f} [R(x) - R_A]\, dx \qquad (A.22)$$

$$= \int_0^{x_f} R(x)dx - R_A\, x_f.$$

This will lead us to study the case where urban land is rented from absentee landlords at a price equaling the agricultural rent (see, for example, Pines and Sadka, 1986, for the full closed-city model, i.e., a closed-city model with public land ownership).

The analysis of this case in both closed and open cities is quite straightforward. The only difference is that the income of each individual is now given by $w_L + TDR/N$ (instead of w_L). Since TDR/N is taken as given by each individual, the analysis is straightforward and closely follows that of the benchmark case. Once more, Fujita (1989, Proposition 3.5, pp. 62–63) has shown that the absentee landlord and public-land-ownership models are identical if they are evaluated with the same values.

1.3.   Example A.1. Cobb-Douglas Utility Function with Endogenous Housing Consumption

1.3.1. *The Individual Location Choice.* We will now illustrate all results of the previous section using a Cobb-Douglas utility function. Let us first focus on the individual problem. We assume that all individuals have the following preferences:

$$\Gamma(z_L, h_L) = z_L^\alpha h_L^\omega,$$

with $\alpha + \omega \le 1$. We will first determine the bid-rent using the Marshallian *indirect* approach. From the budget constraint (A.2), we have: $z_L = w_L - \tau x - h_L R(x)$ and thus, the Cobb-Douglas utility function can be written as:

$$\Gamma(h_L) = [w_L - \tau x - h_L R(x)]^\alpha h_L^\omega. \tag{A.23}$$

Solving (A.4) leads to the following Marshallian demand for housing:

$$h_L^M(R(x), w_L) = \left(\frac{\omega}{\alpha + \omega}\right) \frac{(w_L - \tau x)}{R(x)}, \tag{A.24}$$

and, using the budget constraint, we obtain:

$$z_L^M(R(x), w_L) = \left(\frac{\alpha}{\alpha + \omega}\right)(w_L - \tau x). \tag{A.25}$$

We can compute the indirect utility function by plugging (A.24) into (A.23):

$$\Gamma(z_L^M(R(x), w_L), h_L^M(R(x), w_L)) = \frac{\alpha^\alpha \omega^\omega}{(\alpha + \omega)^{\alpha + \omega}} \frac{(w_L - \tau x)^{\alpha + \omega}}{R(x)^\omega} \equiv W_L.$$

By inverting this function, we obtain the following bid-rent:

$$\Psi_L(x, W_L) = \frac{\omega \alpha^{\alpha/\omega}}{(\alpha + \omega)^{(\alpha + \omega)/\omega}} (w_L - \tau x)^{(\alpha + \omega)/\omega} W_L^{-1/\omega}. \tag{A.26}$$

Let us now determine the bid-rent by the *direct* approach. Using the definition given by (A.10), we have:

$$\Psi_L(x, W_L) = \max_{z_L, h_L} \left\{ \frac{w_L - \tau x - z_L}{h_L} \mid z_L^\alpha h_L^\omega = W_L \right\}. \tag{A.27}$$

Solving $z_L^\alpha h_L^\omega = W_L$, we obtain: $Z_L(h_L, W_L) = W_L^{1/\alpha} h_L^{-\omega/\alpha}$ and thus, (A.27) can be written as:

$$\Psi_L(x, W_L) = \max_{h_L} \left\{ \frac{w_L - \tau x - W_L^{1/\alpha} h_L^{-\omega/\alpha}}{h_L} \right\}. \tag{A.28}$$

Solving this program leads to:

$$h_L^d(x, W_L) = \left(\frac{\alpha + \omega}{\alpha}\right)^{\alpha/\omega} \frac{W_L^{1/\omega}}{(w_L - \tau x)^{\alpha/\omega}}. \tag{A.29}$$

Thus, we have:

$$z_L^d(x, W_L) = W_L^{1/\alpha} h_L^{-\omega/\alpha} \tag{A.30}$$

$$= \left(\frac{\alpha}{\alpha + \omega}\right)(w_L - \tau x).$$

Now, by plugging the value of h_L^d from (A.29) into (A.28), we obtain exactly (A.26), demonstrating that the direct and indirect approaches are totally identical.

Finally, let us calculate the bid-rent under the Hicksian *indirect* approach. Observing that $Z_L(h_L, W_L) = W_L^{1/\alpha} h_L^{-\omega/\alpha}$, the program (A.16) can be written as:

$$\mathbf{E}(x, W_L) \equiv \min_{h_L}\left\{W_L^{1/\alpha} h_L^{-\omega/\alpha} + h_L R(x) + \tau x\right\}.$$

The first-order condition gives:

$$h_L^H(R(x), W_L) = \left(\frac{\alpha}{\omega}\right)^{-\alpha/(\alpha+\omega)} W_L^{1/(\alpha+\omega)} R(x)^{-\alpha/(\alpha+\omega)}. \tag{A.31}$$

Plugging $h_L^H(R(x), W_L)$ back into the expenditure function, we easily obtain:

$$\mathbf{E}(x, W_L) \equiv \left(\frac{\alpha + \omega}{\omega}\right) h_L^H(R(x), W_L) R(x) + \tau x$$

$$= \frac{(\alpha + \omega)}{\omega^{\omega/(\alpha+\omega)}\alpha^{\alpha/(\alpha+\omega)}} W_L^{1/(\alpha+\omega)} R(x)^{\omega/(\alpha+\omega)} + \tau x.$$

By the budget constraint, we know that $\mathbf{E}(x, W_L) = w_L$ and thus, we can obtain the bid-rent function by solving the following equation:

$$\mathbf{E}(x, W_L) = \frac{(\alpha + \omega)}{\omega^{\omega/(\alpha+\omega)}\alpha^{\alpha/(\alpha+\omega)}} W_L^{1/(\alpha+\omega)} R(x)^{\omega/(\alpha+\omega)} + \tau x = w_L.$$

This gives:

$$\Psi_L(x, W_L) = \frac{\omega \alpha^{\alpha/\omega}}{(\alpha + \omega)^{(\alpha+\omega)/\omega}}(w_L - \tau x)^{(\alpha+\omega)/\omega} W_L^{-1/\omega},$$

which is identical to (A.26).

In all these approaches, by differentiating (A.26), we have:

$$\frac{\partial \Psi_L(x, W_L)}{\partial x} = -\tau \left(\frac{\alpha}{\alpha + \omega}\right)^{\alpha/\omega} (w_L - \tau x)^{\alpha/\omega} \, W_L^{-1/\omega} < 0$$

$$\frac{\partial^2 \Psi_L(x, W_L)}{\partial x^2} = \tau^2 \frac{\alpha^{(\alpha+\omega)/\omega}}{\omega \, (\alpha + \omega)^{\alpha/\omega}} W_L^{(\alpha-\omega)/\omega} (w_L - \tau x) \, W_L^{-1/\omega} > 0.$$

The intuition is as follows. To guarantee that all individuals have the same utility level W_L, the bid-rent decreases with distance to the city center (CBD) because it compensates individuals for their increasing commuting costs. This decrease is a marginally increasing (convex function) because the further individuals reside from the CBD, the higher is the compensation for ensuring the same utility.

Finally, let us verify (A.18) to check that the three different approaches yield the same result.

First, for the Marshallian direct approach, let us plug the value of the bid-rent function $\Psi_L(x, W_L) = R(x)$ given by (A.26) into (A.24). We obtain:

$$\begin{aligned}
h_L^M\left(R(x), w_L\right) &= \left(\frac{\omega}{\alpha + \omega}\right) \frac{(w_L - \tau x)}{R(x)} \\
&= \left(\frac{\alpha + \omega}{\alpha}\right)^{\alpha/\omega} \frac{W_L^{1/\omega}}{(w_L - \tau x)^{\alpha/\omega}},
\end{aligned}$$

which is exactly the value of $h_L^d(x, W_L)$ given in (A.29). Second, for the Hicksian indirect approach, we plug the value of the bid-rent function $\Psi_L(x, W_L) = R(x)$ given by (A.26) into (A.31). We obtain:

$$\begin{aligned}
h_L^H(R(x), W_L) &= \left(\frac{\alpha}{\omega}\right)^{-\alpha/(\alpha+\omega)} W_L^{1/(\alpha+\omega)} R(x)^{-\alpha/(\alpha+\omega)} \\
&= \left(\frac{\alpha + \omega}{\alpha}\right)^{\alpha/\omega} \frac{W_L^{1/\omega}}{(w_L - \tau x)^{\alpha/\omega}},
\end{aligned} \tag{A.32}$$

which is exactly the value of h_L^d given in (A.29). As a result, we have shown that

$$\begin{aligned}
h_L^*(x, W_L) &\equiv h_L^M\left(R(x), w_L\right) = h_L^d(x, W_L) = h_L^H(R(x), W_L) \\
&= \left(\frac{\alpha + \omega}{\alpha}\right)^{\alpha/\omega} \frac{W_L^{1/\omega}}{(w_L - \tau x)^{\alpha/\omega}},
\end{aligned}$$

where $R(x) = \Psi_L(x, W_L)$.

We are now able to determine the Alonso-Muth condition (A.9). Differentiating the utility function (A.23) with respect to x, we have:

$$\frac{\partial \Gamma(h_L)}{\partial x} = -\alpha \left[\tau + h_L\, R'(x)\right] \left[w_L - \tau\, x - h_L\, R(x)\right]^{\alpha-1} h_L^\omega = 0.$$

Since $w_L - \tau\, x - h_L\, R(x) \neq 0$, $h_L \neq 0$ and $\alpha \neq 0$, this implies that $t + q\, R'(x) = 0$ or equivalently

$$R'(x) = -\frac{\tau}{h_L^*(x,\, W_L)},$$

which is the Alonso-Muth condition.

1.3.2. The Urban-Land-Use Equilibrium. Using (A.26) and (A.32), equilibrium conditions (A.19) and (A.20) can be written as:

$$\omega\, \alpha^{\alpha/\omega} \left(w_L - \tau\, x_f^*\right)^{(\alpha+\omega)/\omega} = (\alpha + \omega)^{(\alpha+\omega)/\omega}\, W_L^{1/\omega}\, R_A \qquad \text{(A.33)}$$

$$w_L^{(\alpha+\omega)/\omega} - \left(w_L - \tau\, x_f^*\right)^{(\alpha+\omega)/\omega} = \omega^{-1}\alpha^{-\alpha/\omega}\, (\alpha + \omega)^{(\alpha+\omega)/\omega}\, \tau\, N\, W_L^{1/\omega}. \qquad \text{(A.34)}$$

Furthermore, from equation (A.33), we obtain:

$$\left(w_L - \tau\, x_f^*\right)^{(\alpha+\omega)/\omega} = \omega^{-1}\alpha^{-\alpha/\omega}\, (\alpha + \omega)^{(\alpha+\omega)/\omega}\, W_L^{1/\omega}\, R_A. \qquad \text{(A.35)}$$

By plugging this value into (A.34), we get:

$$w_L^{(\alpha+\omega)/\omega} = \omega^{-1}\alpha^{-\alpha/\omega}\, (\alpha + \omega)^{(\alpha+\omega)/\omega}\, W_L^{1/\omega}\, (\tau\, N + R_A). \qquad \text{(A.36)}$$

First, let us solve the case of *closed city with absentee landlords*. From (A.36), we obtain:

$$W_L^* = \frac{\omega^\omega \alpha^\alpha}{(\alpha + \omega)^{(\alpha+\omega)}}\, \frac{w_L^{(\alpha+\omega)}}{(\tau\, N + R_A)^\omega}. \qquad \text{(A.37)}$$

Now plugging this value of W_L^* into (A.35), we have:

$$x_f^* = \frac{w_L}{\tau} \left[1 - \left(\frac{R_A}{\tau\, N + R_A}\right)^{\omega/(\alpha+\omega)}\right], \qquad \text{(A.38)}$$

which is always strictly positive since $1 > \left(\frac{R_A}{\tau\, N + R_A}\right)^{\omega/(\alpha+\omega)}$. We can now calculate the equilibrium land rent (A.21) by plugging the value of W_L^* in

(A.37) into (A.26). We obtain:

$$R^*(x) = \begin{cases} (w_L - \tau x)^{(\alpha+\omega)/\omega} \, w_L^{-(\alpha+\omega)/\omega} \, (\tau \, N + R_A) & \text{for} \quad x \le x_f^* \\ R_A & \text{for} \quad x > x_f^*, \end{cases}$$

(A.39)

where x_f^* is defined by (A.38).

Second, let us solve the case of *open city with absentee landlords*. The great advantage over the closed-city case is that the two equations (A.33) and (A.34) can be solved independently for x_f^* and N^*. Indeed, from (A.36), we obtain:

$$N^* = \frac{\omega \, \alpha^{\alpha/\omega} \, (\alpha + \omega)^{-(\alpha+\omega)/\omega} \, W_L^{-1/\omega} w_L^{(\alpha+\omega)/\omega} - R_A}{\tau},$$

(A.40)

while from (A.35), we have:

$$x_f^* = \frac{w_L - \omega^{-\omega/(\alpha+\omega)} \alpha^{-\alpha/(\alpha+\omega)} \, (\alpha + \omega) \, W_L^{1/(\alpha+\omega)} R_A^{\omega/(\alpha+\omega)}}{\tau}.$$

(A.41)

For x_f^* and N^* to be strictly positive, it must be assumed that R_A is not too high, i.e.

$$R_A < \frac{\omega \, \alpha^{\alpha/\omega}}{(\alpha + \omega)^{(\alpha+\omega)/\omega}} \, W_L^{-1/\omega} \min \left\{ w_L^{(\alpha+\omega)/\omega}, w_L \right\}.$$

Moreover, we can determine the equilibrium land rent (A.21) by directly using the value of the bid-rent in (A.26) (since it is expressed in terms of exogenous values only). We obtain:

$$R^*(x) = \begin{cases} \omega \, \alpha^{\alpha/\omega} \, (\alpha + \omega)^{-(\alpha+\omega)/\omega} \, (w_L - \tau x)^{(\alpha+\omega)/\omega} \, W_L^{-1/\omega} & \text{for } x \le x_f^* \\ R_A & \text{for } x > x_f^*, \end{cases}$$

(A.42)

where x_f^* is defined by (A.41).

Third, we can analyze the case of a *closed city with resident landlords*. Using (A.38) and (A.39), the total differential rent, TDR^*, (A.22) is equal to:

$$\begin{aligned} TDR^* &= \int_0^{x_f} R^*(x)dx - R_A x_f^* \\ &= \int_0^{x_f} \left[\left(w_L + \frac{TDR}{N} - \tau x \right)^{(\alpha+\omega)/\omega} \left(w_L + \frac{TDR}{N} \right)^{-(\alpha+\omega)/\omega} (\tau \, N + R_A) \right] dx, \\ &\quad - R_A \left(\frac{w_L}{\tau} + \frac{TDR}{\tau N} \right) \left[1 - \left(\frac{R_A}{\tau \, N + R_A} \right)^{\omega/(\alpha+\omega)} \right] \end{aligned}$$

which is equivalent to:

$$(\alpha + 2\omega)\, TDR$$

$$= \left(w_L + \frac{TDR}{N}\right)\left[\omega N - \frac{(\alpha + \omega)}{\tau} R_A \left[1 + \left(\frac{R_A}{\tau N + R_A}\right)^{\omega/(\alpha+\omega)}\right]\right].$$

By solving this equation, we finally obtain:

$$TDR^* = \frac{\left[\omega - \frac{(\alpha+\omega)}{\tau N} R_A \left[1 + \left(\frac{R_A}{\tau N + R_A}\right)^{\omega/(\alpha+\omega)}\right]\right]}{(\alpha + \omega)\left[1 + \frac{R_A}{\tau N}\left[1 + \left(\frac{R_A}{\tau N + R_A}\right)^{\omega/(\alpha+\omega)}\right]\right]}\, w_L N. \qquad (A.43)$$

We can now solve the whole model since it suffices to replace w_L by $w_L + TDR^*/N$ in (A.37), (A.38) and (A.39) to obtain W_L^*, x_f^* and $R^*(x)$.

Fourth and last, we can analyze the case of an *open city with resident landlords*. Using (A.41) and (A.42), the total differential rent, TDR^*, (A.22) is equal to:

$$TDR^* = \int_0^{x_f} R^*(x)dx - R_A x_f^*$$

$$= \omega \alpha^{\alpha/\omega} (\alpha + \omega)^{-(\alpha+\omega)/\omega} W_L^{-1/\omega} \int_0^{x_f} (w_L + TDR/N - \tau x)^{(\alpha+\omega)/\omega} dx$$

$$- R_A \frac{w_L + TDR/N - \omega^{-\omega/(\alpha+\omega)}\alpha^{-\alpha/(\alpha+\omega)} (\alpha + \omega)\, W_L^{1/(\alpha+\omega)} R_A^{\omega/(\alpha+\omega)}}{\tau},$$

which is equivalent to:

$$TDR^*\left(\frac{\tau N + R_A}{N}\right) = (w_L + TDR/N)^{(\alpha+2\omega)/\omega} \frac{\alpha^{\alpha/\omega}\omega^2}{(\alpha + 2\omega)(\alpha + \omega)^{(\alpha+\omega)/\omega}} W_L^{-1/\omega}$$

$$+ \frac{(\alpha + \omega)}{\alpha^{\alpha/(\alpha+\omega)}} W_L^{1/(\alpha+\omega)} R_A^{(\alpha+2\omega)/(\alpha+\omega)}\omega^{-\omega/(\alpha+\omega)}\left[1 - \frac{\omega^{(\alpha-\omega)/(\alpha+\omega)}}{(\alpha + 2\omega)}\right] - w_L R_A.$$

This can be shown, under some condition that there is a unique solution in TDR^* to this equation. Once more, we can solve the whole model since it suffices to replace w_L by $w_L + TDR^*/N$ in (A.40), (A.41) and (A.42) to obtain N^*, x_f^* and $R^*(x)$.

1.4. Example A.2. Exogenous Housing Consumption

To make the algebra simpler, we make the following assumption. All individuals consume the same amount of land, which is normalized to 1. This means that $h_L = 1$.

This assumption implies that the utility function of each individual (A.1) can be rewritten as:

$$\Gamma(z_L, 1) \tag{A.44}$$

and the budget constraint (A.2) as

$$w_L - \tau x = R(x) + z_L. \tag{A.45}$$

Now solving (A.45) and replacing z_L into (A.44) yields

$$\Gamma(w_L - \tau x - R(x), 1).$$

For simplicity, we use the following indirect utility function:[1]

$$\Gamma(w_L - \tau x - R(x), 1) \equiv W_L = w_L - \tau x - R(x), \tag{A.46}$$

which is quite intuitive since it expresses a net income, i.e., wage minus commuting costs minus housing cost. In this context, the bid-rent (A.10) or (A.11) can be written as:

$$\Psi_L(x, W_L) = w_L - \tau x - W_L. \tag{A.47}$$

It is easily checked that

$$\frac{\partial \Psi_L(x, W_L)}{\partial x} < 0 \qquad \frac{\partial \Psi_L(x, W_L)}{\partial w_L} > 0 \qquad \frac{\partial \Psi_L(x, W_L)}{\partial \tau} < 0$$

$$\frac{\partial \Psi_L(x, W_L)}{\partial W_L} < 0.$$

Let us determine the urban-land-use equilibrium in the *closed-city case with absentee landlords.* Solving (A.19) and (A.20) yields:

$$x_f^* = N \tag{A.48}$$

$$W_L^* = w_L - \tau N - R_A \tag{A.49}$$

with

$$\frac{\partial x_f^*}{\partial N} > 0$$

$$\frac{\partial W_L^*}{\partial w_L} > 0 \qquad \frac{\partial W_L^*}{\partial \tau} < 0 \qquad \frac{\partial W_L^*}{\partial N} < 0 \qquad \frac{\partial W_L^*}{\partial R_A} < 0.$$

When wages increase or commuting costs decrease, workers are richer and their utility level increases. Concerning N, the effect is less obvious. When

---

[1] This is the primary utility function that we are using in this book.

N rises, the city becomes larger (since the city fringe is equal to N) and workers are, on average, further away from jobs. This means that their commuting costs increase, implying a reduction in their utility level. In this very simple model, larger cities imply lower levels of utility as compared to smaller cities since only commuting costs are taken into account. However, it is well known that large cities offer more diversity and more amenities than smaller cities. For example, one can think of the variety of restaurants, the nice theatres, and the fine architecture of monuments that are offered by big cities. If we introduce these elements into the model, then there will obviously be a trade-off between commuting costs and amenities so that big cities do not always imply lower utility levels.

We can now calculate the equilibrium land rent in the city. For this purpose, we plug the value of (A.49) into (A.47) and easily obtain:

$$R^*(x) = \begin{cases} \tau(N - x) + R_A & \text{if} \quad x \leq N \\ R_A & \text{if} \quad x > N \end{cases} . \qquad (A.50)$$

A comparative statics analysis shows that within the city (i.e., $x \leq N$), land rent linearly decreases from the city center ($x = 0$) to the city fringe ($x_f = N$) at the rate τ. The interesting result here is that N is positively correlated with $R(x)$, which means that land prices in big cities are higher than in small cities. In this model, the intuition runs as follows. When N increases, the size of the city increases so that everybody is further away from jobs, so they, incur more commuting costs (even though the commuting per unit of distance τ remains the same). Now, for all workers to obtain the same utility level, the land rent must decrease.

Now study the *open-city case with absentee landlords*, that is utility W_L is now given by N being endogenous. Solving equations (A.19) and (A.20) leads to:

$$x_f^* = N^* = \frac{w_L - W_L - R_A}{\tau} \qquad (A.51)$$

with

$$\frac{\partial x_f^*}{\partial w_L} = \frac{\partial N^*}{\partial w_L} > 0 \qquad \frac{\partial x_f^*}{\partial W_L} = \frac{\partial N^*}{\partial W_L} < 0 \qquad \frac{\partial x_f^*}{\partial \tau} = \frac{\partial N^*}{\partial \tau} < 0.$$

Therefore, when wages increase and/or commuting costs decrease, the city becomes larger because more individuals are attracted to the city. However, when the (exogenous) utility level W_L outside the city increases, more workers are induced to stay outside the city, and thus city size is reduced.

Using (A.47), we can calculate the equilibrium land rent in the open-city case:

$$R^*(x) = \begin{cases} w_L - \tau x - W_L & \text{if} \quad x \leq N \\ R_A & \text{if} \quad x > N \end{cases} \, . \tag{A.52}$$

We have the same type of figure as for the closed-city case (linearly decreasing in x with a slope of τ). However, different parameters affect equilibrium land rent. Higher wages imply higher land rents (the willingness to pay is higher) and higher outside utility implies lower land rents (this is a direct consequence of the definition of the bid-rent function where bid-rents and utility are negatively correlated).

We now study the case of a *closed city with resident landlords.* Using (A.48) and (A.50), the total differential rent, TDR^*, (A.22) is equal to:

$$TDR^* = \int_0^{x_f} R^*(x)dx - R_A x_f^*$$
$$= \int_0^{x_f} [\tau(N - x) + R_A]\,dx - R_A N$$

and thus

$$TDR^* = \frac{\tau N^2}{2}. \tag{A.53}$$

In this equilibrium, we have:

$$W_L^* = w_L + \frac{TDR^*}{N} - \tau N - R_A$$
$$= w_L - \frac{\tau N}{2} - R_A, \tag{A.54}$$

while $x_f^* = N$ and the equilibrium land rent $R^*(x)$ is still given by (A.50).

Finally, in the case of an *open city with resident landlords,* by using (A.51) and (A.52), we have:

$$TDR^* = \int_0^{x_f} R^*(x)dx - R_A x_f^*$$
$$= \int_0^{x_f} [w_L - \tau x - W_L]\,dx - R_A \frac{w_L - W_L - R_A}{\tau}$$

and thus

$$TDR^* = \frac{(w_L - W_L - R_A)^2}{2\tau}. \tag{A.55}$$

In that case, we have the following equilibrium values:

$$x_f^* = N^* = \frac{w_L + TDR^*/N - W_L - R_A}{\tau}$$

$$= (w_L - W_L - R_A)\left(\frac{1}{\tau} + \frac{w_L - W_L - R_A}{2N}\right) \qquad (A.56)$$

$$R^*(x) = \begin{cases} w_L - W_L + \frac{(w_L - W_L - R_A)^2}{2\tau N} - \tau x & \text{if} \quad x \le N \\ R_A & \text{if} \quad x > N \end{cases}. \qquad (A.57)$$

It is easily seen that the four different cases are totally equivalent.

2. The Basic Model with Heterogenous Agents

Relax the assumption that all workers are identical and that there are two types of workers: employed workers who earn w_L and unemployed workers whose wage is w_U, with $w_L > w_U$. Furthermore, the employed commute to the CBD more often than the unemployed so that their total costs are τx at distance x from the CBD, while for the unemployed they are equal to $s\tau s$, with $0 < s < 1$. There are L employed workers and U unemployed workers. We need to determine where they reside in the city. A standard result (Fujita, 1989) is that steeper bid-rents imply locations closer to the CBD. This is because landlords allocate land to the highest bids so that workers with steeper bid-rents will bid away the workers with flatter bid-rents.

Let us verify this rule in our model. Assume land to be a normal good, that is

$$\frac{\partial h_{es}(x, W_{es})}{\partial w_{es}} > 0. \qquad (A.58)$$

where subscript $es = U, L$ denotes the employment status of workers. In other words, when households become richer, they increase their housing consumption. Assume that the bid-rent of each household intersects at some distance x_b. In this context, if land is a normal good, it must be the case that

$$h_U(x_b, W_U) < h_L(x_b, W_L).$$

This is equivalent to:

$$\frac{s\tau}{h_U(x_b, W_U)} \underset{>}{\overset{\leqq}{=}} \frac{\tau}{h_L(x_b, W_L)},$$

and thus, using (A.58), this is equivalent to:

$$-\frac{\partial \Psi_U(x_b, W_U)}{\partial x} \lesseqqgtr -\frac{\partial \Psi_L(x_b, W_L)}{\partial x}.$$

The intuition of this ambiguity is quite simple. For employed households, there exists *an attraction force* to the CBD because of higher pecuniary commuting costs than for the unemployed as well as a *repulsion force* from the CBD because of housing consumption (or lot size) since land is a normal good and land price is cheaper in the periphery. In other words, when deciding to locate, employed and unemployed households trade off commuting costs and housing consumption.

Proposition A.1. *If land is a normal good and employed workers have higher commuting costs than the unemployed, then the location pattern is ambiguous.*

Imagine that the commuting-cost effect dominates the lot-size effect. What matters most for employed workers is reducing their commuting costs. Then they will relocate closer to jobs while the unemployed will reside on the periphery of the city. In this case, we have the following definition for a closed-city model.

Definition A.3. *An urban equilibrium with full employment and two types of workers is a vector* $(W_L^*, W_U^*, x_b^*, x_f^*, R^*(x))$, *such that:*

$$\Psi_L(x_b^*, W_L^*) = \Psi_U(x_b^*, W_U^*) \qquad (A.59)$$

$$\Psi_U(x_f^*, W_U^*) = R_A \qquad (A.60)$$

$$\int_0^{x_b^*} \frac{1}{h_L(x, W_L^*)} dx = L \qquad (A.61)$$

$$\int_{x_b^*}^{x_f^*} \frac{1}{h_U(x, W_U^*)} dx = U \qquad (A.62)$$

$$R^*(x) = \max\left\{\Psi_L(x, W_L^*), \Psi_U(x, W_U^*), 0\right\} \quad \textit{at each } x \in \left(0, x_f^*\right]. \quad (A.63)$$

Equation (A.59) says that, in the land market, at the frontier x_b^*, the bid-rent offered by the employed is equal to the bid-rent offered by the unemployed. Equation (A.60), in turn, says that the bid-rent of the unemployed must be equal to the agricultural land at the city fringe. Equations (A.61) and (A.62) give the two population constraints. Finally, equation (A.63) defines equilibrium land rent as the upper envelope of the equilibrium bid-rent curves of all worker types and the agricultural rent line.

2.1. Example A.3. Quasi-Linear Utility Function with Endogenous Housing Consumption

Let us now assume quasi-linear preferences. For workers with employment status $k = L, U$, we therefore have:

$$\Omega(h_k, z_k) = z_k + g(h_k), \tag{A.64}$$

where h_k is the *housing* consumption for a worker with employment status $k = L, U$ and $g(\cdot)$ is any increasing function with $g''(\cdot) \leq 0$. For simplicity, we take

$$g(h_k) = \sqrt{h_k}.$$

The budget constraints for employed and unemployed workers are, respectively, given by:

$$h_L R(x) + \tau x + z_L = w_L \tag{A.65}$$

$$h_U R(x) + s\tau x + z_U = w_U, \tag{A.66}$$

where, as above, the composite good is taken as the numeraire good with a unit price.

Maximizing utility (A.64) subject to (A.65) for the employed and subject to (A.66) yields the following Marshallian *housing (land) demand* for workers of employment status $k = L, U$:

$$h_k^M = \frac{1}{[2R(x)]^2}, \tag{A.67}$$

which implies that

$$h_L(x) = h_U(x) = h(x) = \frac{1}{[2R(x)]^2}. \tag{A.68}$$

This result (A.68) is due to the nature of the quasi-linear preferences since housing consumption is independent of income and thus, employment status. Using (A.64) and (A.67), we can now derive the following indirect utility

$$W_L = w_L - \tau x + \frac{1}{4R(x)} \qquad (A.69)$$

for each *employed* worker at x,

$$W_U = w_U - s\tau x + \frac{1}{4R(x)} \qquad (A.70)$$

for each *unemployed* worker at x.

Thus, bid-rents of the employed and the unemployed are, respectively, equal to:

$$\Psi_L(x, W_L) = \frac{1}{4(W_L - w_L + \tau x)} \qquad (A.71)$$

$$\Psi_U(x, W_U) = \frac{1}{4(W_U - w_U + s\tau x)}. \qquad (A.72)$$

Plugging (A.71) into (A.67) and (A.72) in (A.67), we obtain the housing consumption of the employed and unemployed. These are, respectively, given by:

$$H_L(x, W_L) = 4(W_L - w_L + \tau x)^2 \qquad (A.73)$$

$$H_U(x, W_U) = 4(W_U - w_U + s\tau x)^2. \qquad (A.74)$$

We have the following straightforward result:

Proposition A.2. *With quasi-linear preferences and endogenous housing consumption, the employed reside close to jobs whereas the unemployed live on the periphery of the city.*

Since we assume quasi-linear preferences, as in the previous section, there is only the commuting cost effect, and thus the employed locate close to jobs. Interestingly, this result is robust if using any quasi-linear utility function where the non-linearity is on h.

Since housing consumption is endogenous, we cannot (as before) equate x_b to L and x_f to N, but they must be determined. We focus on a *closed city with absentee landlords*. We have exactly the same definition as Definition A.3. Solving equations (A.59)–(A.63) and, without loss of generality, normalizing R_A to $1/4$, we obtain:

$$x_b^* = \frac{4L}{[1 + 4s\tau\,(N - L)]\,(1 + 4L\tau)}$$

$$x_f^* = 4\frac{N + 4L\tau\,(N - L)}{[1 + 4s\tau\,(N - L)]\,(1 + 4L\tau)}$$

$$W_L^* = w_L + \frac{1}{1 + 4\tau\,[s\,N + (1 - s)\,L]}$$

$$W_U^* = w_U + 1 - \frac{4s\tau}{1 + 4s\tau\,(N - L)}\left[\frac{L}{1 + 4\tau\,[s\,N + (1 - s)\,L]} + N - L\right]$$

$$R^*(x) = \begin{cases} \frac{1}{4}\left(\frac{1}{1 + 4s\tau(N-L) + 4\tau L} + \tau\,x\right)^{-1} & \text{for } x \leq x_b^* \\[2mm] \frac{1}{4}\left(1 - \frac{4s\tau}{1 + 4s\tau(N-L)}\left[\frac{L}{1 + 4s\tau(N-L) + 4\tau L}\right.\right. \\ \left.\left. + N - L\right] + s\tau\,x\right)^{-1} & \text{for } x_b^* < x \leq x_f^* \\[2mm] \frac{1}{4} & \text{for } x > x_f^* \end{cases}.$$

The same type of computations can be made for an open city with absentee landlords, a closed city with resident landlords, and an open city with resident landlords. We leave this as an exercise. Naturally, all results should be equivalent if properly evaluated.

2.2. Example A.4. Exogenous Housing Consumption

Now assume that all individuals consume the same amount of land, which is normalized to 1, that is $h_L = h_U = 1$. Assume the same preferences as in (A.46), then the bid-rents for the employed and unemployed are, respectively, given by:

$$\Psi_L(x,\,W_L) = w_L - \tau\,x - W_L \tag{A.75}$$

$$\Psi_U(x,\,W_U) = w_U - s\,\tau\,x - W_U. \tag{A.76}$$

Then, solving (A.59)–(A.63) for the *closed-city model with absentee landlords* gives the following equilibrium values:

$$x_b^* = L \tag{A.77}$$

$$x_f^* = N \tag{A.78}$$

$$W_L^* = w_L - \tau\,L - s\tau\,(N - L) - R_A \tag{A.79}$$

$$W_U^* = w_U - s\,\tau\,N - R_A. \tag{A.80}$$

The employment zone (i.e. the residential zone for employed workers) is thus $(0, L]$ and the unemployment zone (i.e. the residential zone for unemployed workers) is thus $[L, N]$. By plugging (A.79) and (A.80) into (A.75) and (A.76), we easily obtain the land rent equilibrium $R(x)$ which is given by:

$$
R^*(x) = \begin{cases} \tau\,(L-x) + s\tau\,(N-L) + R_A & \text{for} \quad 0 \le x \le L \\ s\tau\,(N-x) + R_A & \text{for} \quad L < x \le N \ . \\ R_A & \text{for} \quad x > N \end{cases}
$$

$$(A.81)$$

Let us analyze the *closed city with resident landlords case* (the computations of the equilibrium values of an open city with absentee landlords and with resident landlords are straightforward and are left as an exercise). Using (A.77), (A.78) and (A.81), the total equilibrium land rent TDR^* is given by:

$$
\begin{aligned}
TDR^* &= \int_0^{x_f^*} R^*(x)dx - R_A x_f^* \\
&= \int_0^L [\tau\,(L-x) + s\tau\,(N-L) + R_A]\,dx \\
&\quad + \int_L^N [s\tau\,(N-x) + R_A]\,dx - R_A N
\end{aligned}
$$

which is equivalent to:

$$
\begin{aligned}
TDR^* &= \frac{\tau L^2}{2} + \frac{s\tau}{2}\left(N^2 - L^2\right) \\
&= \frac{\tau}{2}\left[(1-s)\,L^2 + s\,N^2\right].
\end{aligned}
$$

$$(A.82)$$

The equilibrium values of W_U^* and $R^*(x)$ are still given by (A.80) and (A.81), respectively, while W_L^* is now equal to (the revenue of each employed individual is now $w_L + TDR/N$):

$$
W_L^* = w_L - \tau L\left(\frac{2N-L}{2N}\right) - \frac{s\tau}{2N}(N-L)^2 - R_A.
$$

$$(A.83)$$

Poisson Process and Derivation of
Bellman Equations

1. Poisson Process

Let us first define the exponential distribution.

Definition B.1. *A continuous random variable X is said to have an exponential distribution with parameter $\lambda > 0$ if its cumulative distribution function (cdf) is given by:*

$$F(t) = \mathbb{P}\{X < t\} = 1 - e^{-\lambda t}$$

for all $t \geq 0$. This implies that the probability density function (pdf) is equal to:

$$f(t) = \lambda e^{-\lambda t}$$

for all $t \geq 0$. The exponential distribution has mean

$$\mathbb{E}[X] = \int_0^{+\infty} t\, f(t)dt = \frac{1}{\lambda}$$

and variance

$$\mathbb{V}[X] = \mathbb{E}[X^2] - (\mathbb{E}[X])^2 = \frac{1}{\lambda^2}.$$

It is straightforward to show the following proposition:

Proposition B.1. *The exponential distribution with parameter (or rate) $\lambda > 0$ has the following properties:*

(i) Independence:

$$\mathbb{P}\{X > t + t'\} = \mathbb{P}\{X > t\}\,\mathbb{P}\{X > t'\}$$

(*ii*) *Memoryless*

$$\mathbb{P}\left\{X > t + t' \mid X > t\right\} = \mathbb{P}\left\{X > t'\right\} \qquad \forall t, t' \geq 0.$$

Observe that the exponential distribution is the unique distribution possessing the memoryless property. Following Ross (1996), let us now define a *counting* process (and its properties) and then a *Poisson* process.

Definition B.2. *Let* $\{X_n, n \geq 1\}$ *be a sequence of random variables representing the inter-event times. Define* $S_0 = 0$, $S_n = X_1 + \cdots + X_n$. *Then* S_n *is the time of occurrence of the nth event. Define*

$$\mathbb{S}(t) = \max\{n \geq 0 \mid S_n \leq t\}, t \geq 0.$$

Thus $\mathbb{S}(t)$ *represents the total number of events that have occurred up to time* t. *A stochastic process* $\{\mathbb{S}(t), t \geq 0\}$ *is called a counting process.*

Definition B.3. *A counting process* $\{\mathbb{S}(t), t \geq 0\}$ *is said to possess:*

(*a*) *independent increments if the number of events which occur in disjoint intervals are independent, i.e., for* $0 \leq t_1 \leq \cdots \leq t_n$, *the increments* $\mathbb{S}(t_1)$, $\mathbb{S}(t_2) - \mathbb{S}(t_1)$, $\ldots$, $\mathbb{S}(t_n) - \mathbb{S}(t_{n-1})$ *are independent random variables, or*

(*b*) *stationary increments if the distribution of the number of events which occur in any interval of time only depends the length of the time interval, i.e., the distribution of* $X(t + t') - X(t')$ *is independent of* t'.

A Poisson process is frequently used as a model for counting events occurring one at a time. Let us now define formally a Poisson process.

Definition B.4. *The counting process* $\{\mathbb{S}(t), t \geq 0\}$ *is said to be a Poisson process having rate* $\lambda > 0$, *if:*

(*i*) *The process has stationary and independent increments;*

(*ii*) *The number of events in any interval of length t is Poisson distributed with mean* λt. *That is, for all* $t \geq 0$,

$$\mathbb{P}\{\mathbb{S}(t) = n\} = e^{-\lambda t}\frac{(\lambda t)^n}{n!}, \qquad n = 0, 1, \ldots \qquad \text{(B.1)}$$

We have the following alternative definition.[1]

---

[1] A function $f \colon \mathbb{R} \to \mathbb{R}$ is said to be an $o(h)$ function if;

$$\lim_{h \to 0} \frac{f(h)}{h} = 0$$

Definition B.5. *The counting process* $\{\mathbb{S}(t), t \geq 0\}$ *with* $\mathbb{S}(0) = 0$ *is said to be a Poisson process having rate* $\lambda > 0$, *if:*

   (*i*) *The process has stationary and independent increments;*
   (*ii*) $\mathbb{P}\{\mathbb{S}(h) = 1\} \equiv \mathbb{P}\{\mathbb{S}(t+h) - \mathbb{S}(t) = 1\} = \lambda h + o(h);$
   (*iii*) $\mathbb{P}\{\mathbb{S}(h) \geq 2\} \equiv \mathbb{P}\{\mathbb{S}(t+h) - \mathbb{S}(t) \geq 2\} = o(h).$

This definition helps us understand how "randomness in time" can be interpreted. Condition (*i*) implies that what happens under non-overlapping time intervals is independent. Condition (*ii*) states that rate λ is constant over time while condition (*iii*) says that two (or more) events cannot occur at the same time. Ross (1996) shows that these two definitions (i.e., definitions B.4 and B.5) are equivalent.

Example B.1. Consider a person who receives a lot of "junk" mail in his/her mailbox. Assume that the amount of junk mail follows a Poisson process having the rate of 2 per hour.

B.1.1. What is the probability that no "junk" mail arrives between 9 a.m. and 11 a.m.?

This probability is defined by $\mathbb{P}\{\mathbb{S}(11) - \mathbb{S}(9) = 0\}$. Using Definition B.4 and in particular equation (B.1), we obtain (for $\lambda = 2$):

$$\mathbb{P}\{\mathbb{S}(11) - \mathbb{S}(9) = 0\} = e^{-2t}\frac{(2t)^0}{0!} = e^{-2\times2} \cong 0.0183.$$

Observe that, because of time homogeneity, this probability is the same as the probability that no junk mail arrives between 2:00 p.m. and 4:00 p.m. or any other times as long as there are two hours difference.

B.1.2. What is the expected amount of junk mail that arrives during 8 hours?

The expected amount of junk mail that arrives during 8 hours is:

$$\mathbb{E}[\mathbb{S}(8)] = \lambda \times 8 = 16.$$

B.1.3. What is the probability that one piece of junk mail arrives between 1:00 p.m. and 2:00 p.m. *and* two pieces of junk mails arrive between 1:30 p.m. and 2:30 p.m.?

Using time homogeneity and using hours as units of time, start at $t = 0$ (which corresponds to 1:00 p.m.) so that 2:00 p.m. corresponds to $t = 1$ (1 hour corresponds to 1 unit of time). Then 1:30 p.m. corresponds to $t = 0.5$ and 2:30 p.m. to $t = 1.5$. Thus, the probability that one piece of junk mail arrives between 1:00 p.m. and 2:00 p.m. *and* two pieces of junk mail arrives between 1:30 p.m. and 2:30 p.m. can be written as:

$$\mathbb{P}\{\mathbb{S}(1) = 1, \mathbb{S}(1.5) - \mathbb{S}(0.5) = 2\}.$$

Using the fact that increments over (0, 0.5], (0.5, 1], and (1, 1.5] are independent, we can write the following:

$$\mathbb{P}\{\mathbb{S}(1) = 1, \mathbb{S}(1.5) - \mathbb{S}(0.5) = 2\}$$

$$= \sum_{n=0}^{1} \mathbb{P}\{\mathbb{S}(0.5) = n, \mathbb{S}(1) - \mathbb{S}(0.5) = 1 - n, \mathbb{S}(1.5) - \mathbb{S}(1) = 1 + n\}.$$

For this equation, we divide time in three intervals: (0, 0.5], (0.5, 1], and (1, 1.5], that is between 1:00 p.m. and 1:30 p.m., 1:30 p.m. and 2:00 p.m., 2:00 p.m. and 2:30 p.m. Then, in order to have 1 junk mail between $t = 0$ (i.e., 1:00 p.m.) and $t = 1$ (i.e., 2:00 p.m.), it has to be that *either* no junk mail arrives between $t = 0$ and $t = 0.5$ (i.e., 1:30 p.m.) and 1 piece arrives between $t = 0.5$ and $t = 1$ *or* 1 piece of junk mail arrives between $t = 0$ and $t = 0.5$ and 0 arrives between $t = 0.5$ and $t = 1$. Similarly, in order to have 2 pieces of junk mail between $t = 0.5$ and $t = 1.5$ (i.e., 2:30 p.m.), it has to be that *either* no junk mail arrives between $t = 0.5$ and $t = 1$ and 2 arrive between $t = 1$ and $t = 1.5$ *or* 2 pieces of junk mail arrive between $t = 0.5$ and $t = 1$ and 0 arrives between $t = 1$ and $t = 1.5$ *or* 1 piece of junk mail arrives between $t = 0.5$ and $t = 1$ and 1 piece of arrives between $t = 1$ and $t = 1.5$. By combining all these possibilities, it has to be that:

$$\mathbb{P}\{\mathbb{S}(1) = 1, \mathbb{S}(1.5) - \mathbb{S}(0.5) = 2\}$$
$$= \mathbb{P}\{\mathbb{S}(0.5) = 0, \mathbb{S}(1) - \mathbb{S}(0.5) = 1, \mathbb{S}(1.5) - \mathbb{S}(1) = 1\}$$
$$+ \mathbb{P}\{\mathbb{S}(0.5) = 1, \mathbb{S}(1) - \mathbb{S}(0.5) = 0, \mathbb{S}(1.5) - \mathbb{S}(1) = 2\}.$$

In other words, *either* no junk mail arrives between $t = 0$ and $t = 0.5$ and 1 piece of junk mail arrives both between $t = 0.5$ and $t = 1$ and between $t = 1$ and $t = 1.5$, *or* 1 piece of junk mail arrives between $t = 0$ and $t = 0.5$, 0 junk mail between $t = 0.5$ and $t = 1$ and 2 between $t = 1$ and $t = 1.5$.
  We have:

$$\sum_{n=0}^{1} \mathbb{P}\{\mathbb{S}(0.5) = n, \mathbb{S}(1) - \mathbb{S}(0.5) = 1 - n, \mathbb{S}(1.5) - \mathbb{S}(1) = 1 + n\}$$

$$= \sum_{n=0}^{1} \mathbb{P}\{\mathbb{S}(0.5) = n\} \times \mathbb{P}\{\mathbb{S}(1) - \mathbb{S}(0.5) = 1 - n\}$$
$$\times \mathbb{P}\{\mathbb{S}(1.5) - \mathbb{S}(1) = 1 + n\}$$
$$= \sum_{n=0}^{1} e^{-1} \frac{(1)^{n}}{n!} e^{-1} \frac{(1)^{1-n}}{(1-n)!} e^{-1} \frac{(1)^{1+n}}{(1+n)!}$$
$$= e^{-3} \sum_{n=0}^{1} \frac{1}{n!\,(1-n)!\,(1+n)!}$$
$$= e^{-3} \left(1 + \frac{1}{2}\right) = 1.5 e^{-3} \simeq 0.0747. \qquad \blacksquare$$

Consider a Poisson process $\{\mathbb{S}(t), t \geq 0\}$ and denote the time of the first event by T_1. Moreover, for $n > 1$, let T_n denote the elapsed time between the $(n-1)$th and the nth event. The sequence $\{T_n, n = 1, 2, \ldots\}$ is called the sequence of *interarrival* times. We can now determine the distribution of the T_n. We have the following result:

Proposition B.2. $T_n, n = 1, 2$, *are independent identically distributed (i.i.d.) exponential random variables having mean* $1/\lambda$. *This means, in particular, that,*

$$\mathbb{P}\{T_1 > t\} = \mathbb{P}\{\mathbb{S}(t) = 0\} = e^{-\lambda t}$$

and

$$\mathbb{P}\{T_2 > t \mid T_1 = t'\} = e^{-\lambda t}$$

etc. Furthermore, the arrival time of the nth event, also called the waiting time until the nth event and denoted by Σ_n, is given by,

$$\Sigma_n = \sum_{i=1}^{n} T_i, \qquad n \geq 1$$

Σ_n *has a gamma distribution with parameters n and λ. That is, the probability density of Σ_n is:*

$$f_{\Sigma_n}(t) = \lambda e^{-\lambda t} \frac{(\lambda t)^{n-1}}{(n-1)!}$$

2. An Intuitive Way of Deriving the Bellman Equations

First, derive the expected lifetime utility of an unemployed worker I_U. This analysis is valid for both search-matching (Part 1) and efficiency wage (Part 2) models. During a small interval of time dt, the unemployed worker obtains W_U, and during this time, he/she may find a job and enjoy an expected lifetime-utility level of I_E at time $t + dt$. The probability that he/she finds a job is: $adt + o(dt)$ with $\lim_{dt \to 0} o(dt)/dt = 0$. If he/she does not find a job, then he/she enjoys utility I_U at time $t + dt$. Observe that during this small interval of time dt, the probability that the unemployed worker leaves unemployment and then straightaway loses his/her new job is negligible with respect to dt (since it is a term in $(dt)^2$). We have:[2]

$$I_U(t) = W_U(t)dt + \frac{1}{1 + rdt} \left[adt\, I_L(t + dt) + (1 - adt)I_U(t + dt)\right].$$

---

[2] We could have discounted in a different way,

$$I_U(t) = \frac{1}{1 + rdt} \left[W_U(t)dt + adt I_E(t + dt) + (1 - adt)I_U(t + dt)\right]$$

i.e., before starting the period. In this case, it is easily verified that the Bellman equation would have been exactly the same.

This is equivalent to

$$(1 + rdt) I_U(t) = (1 + rdt) W_U(t)dt + adt\, I_L(t + dt)$$
$$+ (1 - adt) I_U(t + dt)$$

$$\Leftrightarrow r I_U(t)dt = W_U(t)dt + r W_U(t)(dt)^2 + adt\,[I_L(t + dt) - I_U(t + dt)]$$
$$+ I_U(t + dt) - I_U(t).$$

Now, by dividing everything by dt, we obtain (observe that $(dt)^2$ is negligible compared to dt)

$$r I_U(t) = W_U(t) + a\,[I_L(t + dt) - I_U(t + dt)] + \frac{I_U(t + dt) - I_U(t)}{dt}.$$

By taking the limit when $dt \to 0$, we get

$$r I_U(t) = W_U(t) + a\,[I_L(t) - I_U(t)] + \dot{I}_U(t)$$

since

$$\dot{I}_U(t) \equiv \frac{dI_U(t)}{dt} = \lim_{dt \to 0} \frac{I_U(t + dt) - I_U(t)}{dt}.$$

In steady-state, $\dot{I}_U(t) = 0$ and $I_U(t) = I_U$ and $I_L(t) = I_L$. The steady-state lifetime expected utility of an unemployed worker is given by:

$$r I_U = W_U + a\,(I_L - I_U).$$

Now determine the expected lifetime utility of a non-shirking employed worker I_L. We have:

$$I_L(t) = W_L^{NS}(t)dt + \frac{1}{1 + rdt}\left[\delta dt\, I_U(t + dt) + (1 - \delta dt) I_L^{NS}(t + dt)\right].$$

By replicating the same analysis as for the unemployed, we easily obtain for employed workers:

$$r I_L = W_L^{NS} - \delta\,(I_E - I_U).$$

Now focus more specifically on efficiency wage models (Part 2). Determining the case of shirking is more complicated since shirking workers can lose their jobs either by an exogenous shock δ or by being caught shirking at rate m. We have

$$I_L^S(t) = W_L^S(t)dt + \frac{1}{1 + rdt}\,[\delta dt\, I_U(t + dt) + mdt\, I_U(t + dt)$$

$$+ (1 - (\delta + m)\,dt)\, I_L^S(t + dt)].$$

By replicating the same analysis, we obtain:

$$r I_L^S = W_L^S - (\delta + m)\left(I_L^S - I_U\right). \tag{B.2}$$

3. A Formal Way of Deriving the Bellman Equations

As previously stated, changes in employment status are assumed to be governed by a Poisson process with two states: employed or unemployed. Consider a Poisson process (as defined by Definition B.4 or Definition B.5). As shown in Proposition B.2, the key feature of these stochastic processes is that the duration time spent in each state is a random variable with exponential distribution. More precisely, if we denote the (random) unemployment and employment duration times by T_a and T_δ, then

$$F(T_a) = \mathbb{P}\{T_a < t\} = 1 - e^{-a\,T_a}$$

$$F(T_\delta) = \mathbb{P}\{T_\delta < t\} = 1 - e^{-\delta\,T_\delta}.$$

This implies that the probability densities are given by:

$$f(T_a) = a\,e^{-a\,T_a} \tag{B.3}$$

$$f(T_\delta) = \delta\,e^{-\delta\,T_\delta}. \tag{B.4}$$

As a result, the average time spent in each state is equal to (see Definition B.1):

$$
\begin{aligned}
\mathbb{E}\,[T_a] &= \int_0^{+\infty} T_a\,f(T_a)dT_a \\
&= \int_0^{+\infty} a\,T_a\,e^{-a\,T_a}dT_a \\
&= \int_0^{+\infty} e^{-a\,T_a}dT_a - \left[T_a\,e^{-a\,T_a}\right]_0^{+\infty} \\
&= -\frac{1}{a}\left[e^{-a\,T_a}\right]_0^{+\infty} - \left[T_a\,e^{-a\,T_a}\right]_0^{+\infty} \\
&= \frac{1}{a}
\end{aligned}
$$

since

$$\lim_{T_a \to +\infty} T_a\,e^{-a\,T_a} = \lim_{T_a \to 0} T_a\,e^{-a\,T_a} = 0.$$

Similarly,

$$\mathbb{E}\left[T_\delta\right] = \int_0^{+\infty} T_\delta \, f(T_\delta) dT_\delta = \frac{1}{\delta}.$$

As above, let us first determine the expected lifetime utility of an unemployed worker, I_U. It is given by:

$$I_U = \mathbb{E}_{T_a}\left[\int_0^{T_a} W_U \, e^{-rt} dt + e^{-rT_a} I_L\right]. \tag{B.5}$$

I_U is thus the discounted value at time $t = 0$. The unemployed worker remains unemployed during a random period of time T_a. During this period, he/she earns w_U discounted at rate r. Then, after this period T_a, he/she becomes employed and obtains an expected utility of I_L discounted at rate r starting at time $t = T_a$.

By developing (B.5), we obtain:

$$I_U = \int_0^{+\infty} \left[\int_0^{T_a} W_U \, e^{-rt} dt\right] f(T_a) dT_a + \int_0^{+\infty} e^{-rT_a} I_E \, f(T_a) dT_a.$$

Since

$$\int_0^{T_a} W_U \, e^{-rt} dt = W_U \left[\frac{1 - e^{-rT_a}}{r}\right],$$

and using (B.3), it can be rewritten as:

$$I_U = a\frac{W_U}{r}\int_0^{+\infty} \left(1 - e^{-rT_a}\right) e^{-a\,T_a} dT_a + aI_L \int_0^{+\infty} e^{-rT_a} e^{-a\,T_a} dT_a$$

$$= a\frac{W_U}{r}\left[\int_0^{+\infty} \left(e^{-a\,T_a} - e^{-(r+a)T_a}\right) dT_a\right] + a\,I_L \int_0^{+\infty} e^{-(r+a)T_a} \, dT_a$$

$$= \frac{W_U}{r + a} + \frac{a}{r + a} I_L.$$

We finally obtain:

$$r\,I_U = W_U + a\,(I_L - I_U). \tag{B.6}$$

Similarly, we can calculate the expected lifetime utility of an employed worker I_L (non-shirking in the efficiency wage model). It is:

$$I_L^{NS} = E_{T_\delta}\left[\int_0^{T_\delta} W_L^{NS} e^{-rt} dt + e^{-rT_\delta} I_U\right]. \tag{B.7}$$

By making exactly the same analysis, one easily obtains:

$$r I_L^{NS} = W_L^{NS} - \delta \left(I_L - I_U \right). \tag{B.8}$$

For the efficiency wage model, we need to consider the case of a shirker. It is more complicated since, when employed, a shirker can lose his/her job because either he/has been caught shirking or the job has been eliminated. Denote by T_m the (random) length of time until the next control of shirking occurs. This implies that T_a is still the (random) unemployment duration time whereas $\min(T_\delta, T_m)$ is now the employment duration time for a shirker. Since we know (see, for example, Kulkarni, 1995, ch. 5) that $\min(T_\delta, T_m)$ is a random variable characterized by an exponential distribution of parameter $\delta + m$, i.e.,

$$F(\min(T_\delta, T_m)) = \mathbb{P}\left[\min(T_\delta, T_m) < t\right] = 1 - e^{-(\delta+m)\min(T_\delta, T_m)}$$

then the expected lifetime utility of a shirker I_L^S is equal to:

$$I_L^S = E\left[\int_0^{\min(T_\delta, T_m)} W_L^S e^{-rt} dt + e^{-r \min(T_\delta, T_m)} I_U\right].$$

By doing exactly the same kind of manipulations as above, we obtain (B.2).

The Harris-Todaro Model

In two seminal papers, Todaro (1969) and Harris and Todaro (1970) have developed a canonical model of rural-urban migration. These papers have been so influential that they are referred to as the Harris-Todaro model in the literature. Even though these papers were written for developing countries, the general mechanism put forward can be applied to developed countries. In this appendix, we expose in a synthetic way the same model with different extensions.

1. A Simple Model with Exogenous Wages

There are two regions: rural and urban. The crucial assumption of the Harris-Todaro model is that workers base their migration decision on their expected incomes. Since the basic model is static, the expected income is just the weighted average of the urban wage and the unemployment benefit, the weights being the probabilities of finding and not finding an urban job. It is assumed that the rural wage is flexible enough to guarantee that there is no rural unemployment; this wage is denoted by w_L^R. The urban wage is exogenous and set at a high-enough level, so that urban unemployment prevails in equilibrium; this wage is denoted by w_L^C and we assume that $w_L^C > w_L^R$ (superscript C is used for cities and superscript R for rural areas). There is a continuum of ex-ante identical workers whose mass is N. Among the N workers, N^C and N^R live in cities and rural areas, respectively, i.e., $N = N^C + N^R$, and

$$N^C = L^C + U^C$$
$$N^R = L^R$$

where L^g and U^g are, respectively, the total employment and unemployment levels in region $g = C, R$. As stated above, there is no unemployment in rural areas. Thus, by combining these two equations, we obtain:

$$U^C = N - L^C - L^R. \tag{C.1}$$

The unemployment rate is then given by:

$$u^C = \frac{U^C}{U^C + L^C} = \frac{N - L^C - L^R}{N - L^R}. \tag{C.2}$$

As a result, the probability of finding an urban job is:

$$a^C \equiv \frac{L^C}{L^C + U^C} = \frac{L^C}{N - L^R}. \tag{C.3}$$

What is crucial here is that the probability of finding a job in cities depends on the number of jobs available in cities, L^C, but also on the number of employed workers in rural areas, L^R. Observe that L^C, the number of urban jobs, is exogenously fixed here. This means that rural workers will decide to migrate if

$$w_L^C \frac{L^C}{N - L^R} > w_L^R.$$

The equilibrium is reached when

$$w_L^C \frac{L^C}{N - L^R} = w_L^R, \tag{C.4}$$

which is equivalent to

$$L^R = N - \frac{w_L^C}{w_L^R} L^C. \tag{C.5}$$

This is the fundamental equation of the Harris-Todaro model. We have the following definition:

Definition C.1. *A Harris-Todaro equilibrium with exogenous wages is a couple (U^C, L^R) such that (C.1) and (C.5) are satisfied.*

In this simple model, it is easy to calculate an equilibrium. Indeed, given that the wages w_L^C, w_L^R, the total population N and the number of urban jobs L^C are exogenous, the number of rural employed workers L^R can be calculated by solving the equilibrium migration condition (C.5). Then, using this value and the exogenous values of L^C and N, the level of urban unemployment U^C can be determined using (C.1).

A key question that has been studied is the effect of increasing urban jobs on urban unemployment. In developing countries, it has been shown that an increase in urban jobs can lead to an increase rather than a decrease in urban unemployment, because of the induced effect of migration. This is referred to as the *Todaro paradox*. We have the following result.

Proposition C.1. *In a Harris-Todaro model with exogenous wages, a Todaro paradox exists if and only if*

$$-\frac{\partial L^R}{\partial L^C} > 1 + \frac{U^C}{L^C}. \qquad (C.6)$$

To understand this result, we must differentiate between a Todaro paradox in unemployment level, i.e., $\frac{\partial U^C}{\partial L^C} > 0$, and a Todaro paradox in unemployment rate, i.e., $\frac{\partial u^C}{\partial L^C} > 0$. By totally differentiating (C.1) and (C.2) and observing that L^R is a function of L^C (because of the migration equilibrium condition), we obtain (C.6). To be more precise, a Todaro paradox in unemployment level exists if and only if:

$$-\frac{\partial L^R}{\partial L^C} > 1, \qquad (C.7)$$

while a Todaro paradox in unemployment rate exists if and only if

$$-\frac{\partial L^R}{\partial L^C} > 1 + \frac{U^C}{L^C}. \qquad (C.8)$$

It is clear that if a Todaro paradox in unemployment rate exists, then a Todaro paradox in unemployment level also exists, but the reverse in *not* true. The intuition of (C.7) is as follows. If this condition holds, then the initial increase in urban jobs (L^C increases) induces rural workers to migrate to cities (since the probability a^C of obtaining an urban job is higher and thus rural workers' expected income is also higher), which implies that the reduction in L^R is higher than the increase in L^C. Since $U^C = N - L^C - L^R$, urban unemployment increases.

In our model, by totally differentiating (C.5), we easily obtain:

$$\frac{\partial L^R}{\partial L^C} = -\frac{w_L^C}{w_L^R} < -1. \qquad (C.9)$$

This means that a *Todaro paradox in unemployment level always exists in this model*. Indeed, if the number of urban jobs is raised by one unit, rural employment falls by w_L^C / w_L^R units. This is because creating one additional job in the urban sector induces w_L^C / w_L^R people to migrate into the urban sector and since $w_L^C > w_L^R$ and $U^C = N - L^C - L^R$, it has to be that urban unemployment U^C increases for N to remain constant. Observe that the higher is the wage gap between urban and rural areas, the higher is this effect. Concerning the unemployment rate, using (C.8), we have:

$$\frac{\partial u^C}{\partial L^C} > 0 \Leftrightarrow \frac{w_L^C}{w_L^R} < 1 + \frac{U^C}{L^C},$$

which is not always true and thus, in this model with exogenous wages, it may well be that increasing urban jobs increases the urban unemployment level, but decreases or does not affect the urban unemployment rate. This is the case if

$$1 < \frac{w_L^C}{w_L^R} \leq 1 + \frac{U^C}{L^C}. \tag{C.10}$$

Example C.1. We illustrate this last result with a numerical example. Let $N = 1100, L^C = 800, w_L^C = 90, w_L^R = 80$, so that $w_L^C / w_L^R = 9/8$. Calculate the Harris-Todaro equilibrium of this economy. Using (C.5) and (C.1), we obtain:

$$L^R = 1100 - \frac{9}{8}800 = 200$$

and

$$U^C = 1100 - 800 - 200 = 100.$$

The unemployment rate is given by

$$u^C = \frac{1100 - 800 - 200}{1100 - 200} = 11.11\%.$$

To summarize, the equilibrium is characterized by:

$$N = 1100, \ w_L^C = 90, \ w_L^R = 80, \ L^C = 800, \ L^R = 200$$
$$U^C = 100 \text{ and } u^C = 11.11\%.$$

Now, the government decides to create 50 urban jobs, i.e., $L_{AP}^C = 850$[1] and thus, $\Delta L^C \equiv L_{AP}^C - L^C = 50$. Now because of (C.9), we have

$$\frac{\partial L^R}{\partial L^C} = -\frac{w_L^C}{w_L^R} = -\frac{9}{8},$$

---

[1] All variables with subscript "AP" denote equilibrium variables after a policy has been implemented. For example, L_{AP}^C is the equilibrium urban employment after the policy of creating 50 urban jobs has been implemented.

so that (in discrete units):

$$\Delta L^R \equiv L^R_{AP} - L^R = -\frac{9}{8}\Delta L^C = -56.25.$$

As a result,

$$L^R_{AP} = -56.25 + L^R = 143.75.$$

This means that the creation of 50 urban jobs has triggered a migration to the city of $\frac{9}{8}\Delta L^C = 56.25$ rural workers, so that rural employment has decreased from $L^R = 200$ to $L^R_{AP} = 143.75$. Because $\Delta L^C = 50 < 56.25 = |\Delta L^R|$, urban unemployment has increased by 6.25 workers since

$$U^C_{AP} = N - L^C_{AP} - L^R_{AP} = 106.25.$$

This is the fundamental idea of Harris and Todaro, and this is why it is referred to as the *Todaro paradox*. Indeed, creating urban jobs may lead to an increase rather than a decrease in urban unemployment because of the induced rural-urban migration that may outweight the initial increase in urban jobs. In this example, there are 50 more urban jobs, but 56.25 more migrants. So the net result is an increase in urban unemployment. Observe that what is crucial in a Harris-Todaro model is that $N^C = N - L^R$ is endogenous (since it is a function of L^R) and determined by (C.5), whereas in a model without migration (autarky) it would be exogenous.

So, an increase of $(\Delta L^C/L^C =)$ 6.25% of urban jobs has increased urban unemployment by $(\Delta U^C/U^C =)$ 6.25%. This means that the unemployment rate has not been affected. Indeed,

$$u^C_{AP} = \frac{U^C_{AP}}{N - L^R_{AP}} = \frac{1100 - 850 - 143.75}{1100 - 143.75} = 11.11\%,$$

so that *there is no Todaro paradox in the unemployment rate*. Indeed, using (C.8), we have:

$$1 < -\frac{\partial L^R}{\partial L^C} = \frac{w^C_L}{w^R_L} = \frac{9}{8} = 1 + \frac{U^C}{L^C},$$

which means that we are in the case when (C.10) holds. To summarize, after the policy of creating 50 urban jobs, the equilibrium is characterized by:

$$N = 1100, \ w^C_{L,AP} = 90, \ w^R_{L,AP} = 80, \ L^C_{AP} = 850, \ L^R_{AP} = 143.75$$
$$u^C_{AP} = 106.25 \text{ and } u^C_{AP} = 11.11\%.$$

2. The Harris-Todaro Model with Minimum Wages

Naturally, the previous analysis, though useful, was quite limited (and mechanical) since, apart of the migration decision, all variables were exogenous. We now describe the Harris-Todaro model in more detail where L^C and w_L^R are endogenously determined, but w_L^C is still exogenous (as in the original formulation). There are still two regions: rural and urban. Both regions produce the same good, but use different techniques. In region $g = C, R$ (C for cities and R for rural areas) y^g units of output are produced and L^g workers are employed. This is a short-run model where capital is fixed and the production function in region $g = C, R$ is given by

$$y^g = F^g(L^g), \quad F'^g(L^g) > 0 \text{ and } F''^g(L^g) \leq 0. \quad (C.11)$$

We also assume that the Inada conditions hold, that is $\lim_{L^g \to 0} F^{g\prime}(L^g) = +\infty$ and $\lim_{L^g \to +\infty} F^{g\prime}(L^g) = 0$. As before, we have:

$$U^C = N - L^C - L^R, \quad (C.12)$$

and, in the rural area, wages are flexible so that there is no rural unemployment. The price of the good is taken as a numeraire and, without loss of generality, normalized to 1. In the urban area, it is assumed that the government imposes a minimum wage w_m^C (which is downward rigid) that is above $w_L^C = F^{C\prime}(L^C)$, i.e., w_m^C is above the wage that would prevail if wages were set at their competitive level. The profit maximization condition in region $g = C, R$ can be written as:

$$w_L^g = F^{g\prime}(L^g). \quad (C.13)$$

As before, the equilibrium migration condition is given by (C.5). However, using the fact that $w_L^C = w_m^C$ and (C.13), this condition can be written as:

$$F^{R\prime}(L^R) = w_m^C \frac{L^C}{N - L^R}. \quad (C.14)$$

Definition C.2. *A Harris-Todaro equilibrium with a minimum wage is a 4-tuple (L^C, w_L^R, U^C, L^R) such that*

$$w_m^C = F^{C\prime}\left(L^C\right) \quad (C.15)$$

$$w_L^R = F^{R\prime}\left(L^R\right), \quad (C.16)$$

(C.12), (C.14) are satisfied.

In this model, an equilibrium is calculated as follows. First, the number of urban employed workers L^C can be calculated by solving (C.15). Second, using this value L^C and given that both w_m^C and N are exogenous, the number of rural employed workers L^R can be determined by solving the equilibrium migration condition (C.14). Then, by plugging this value L^R into (C.16), we obtain w_L^R. Finally, given that N is exogenously given and using the values of L^C and L^R calculated above, U^C is obtained by solving (C.12). It is easily verified that the Inada conditions guarantee that (C.14) has a unique solution in L^R.

We can now totally differentiate (C.14) and we easily obtain

$$\frac{\partial L^R}{\partial L^C} = \frac{w_m^C}{\left(N - L^R\right) F^{R\prime\prime}(L^R) - w_m^C L^C / \left(N - L^R\right)} < 0. \quad \text{(C.17)}$$

Contrary to the previous model, neither a Todaro paradox in unemployment rate nor in unemployment level can be guaranteed in this model. The Todaro paradox is not always true because there are two opposite effects. Indeed, an increase in the number of urban jobs raises the number of rural migrants (attraction force to the city) since it increases their probability of finding a job in cities, but because there are less workers in rural areas (due to migration), the rural wage w_L^R, which is a decreasing function of rural employment L^R, i.e., $w_L^R = F^{R\prime}(L^R)$, increases and this tends to reduce migration (repulsion force to the city). The net effect is thus ambiguous.

Example C.2. We illustrate this result with an example that was calibrate so that the equilibrium is identical to that of Example C.1. Let $N = 1100$, $F^C(L^C) = 5091.2\sqrt{L^C}$, $F^R(L^R) = 2262.7\sqrt{L^R}$, and the government imposes a minimum wage of $w_m^C = 90$. Since $w_m^C = F^{C\prime}(L^C) = 2545.6/\sqrt{L^C}$, this implies that $L^C = 800$. Using the migration equilibrium condition (C.14), we can calculate L^R, which by observing that $F^{R\prime}(L^R) = 1131.4/\sqrt{L^R}$, is equal to $L^R = 200$. We can calculate the rural wage by solving (C.16). We easily obtain

$$w_L^R = F^{R\prime}\left(L^R\right) = \frac{1131.4}{\sqrt{200}} = 80.$$

Finally, U^C is obtained by solving (C.12). We get: $U^C = 100$ and the unemployment rate is $u^C = 11.11\%$. So we study an equilibrium that has exactly the same values (both exogenous and endogenous) as in Example C.1.

Indeed, the equilibrium is characterized by:

$$N = 1100, \ w_m^C = 90, \ w_L^R = 80, \ L^C = 800, \ L^R = 200$$
$$U^C = 100 \text{ and } u^C = 11.11\%.$$

Let us implement exactly the same policy, which consists of creating 50 urban jobs, i.e., $L_{AP}^C = 850$ and thus, $\Delta L^C \equiv L_{AP}^C - L^C = 50$. In this model, because L^C is endogenous, it is easy to verify that to create 50 urban jobs, the government must reduce the minimum wage by nearly 3%, i.e., from $w_m^C = 90$ to $w_{m,AP}^C = 87.313$. Using (C.14), one can calculate L_{AP}^R by solving the following equation:

$$\frac{1131.4}{\sqrt{L_{AP}^R}} = 87.313 \frac{850}{1100 - L_{AP}^R}.$$

We obtain $L_{AP}^R = 191.72$, which implies that $\Delta L^R \equiv L_{AP}^R - L^R = -8.28$. Using (C.16), we obtain

$$w_L^R = \frac{1131.4}{\sqrt{191.72}} = 81.711.$$

Finally, the unemployment level and the unemployment rate are, respectively, given by:

$$U_{AP}^C = 1100 - 850 - 191.72 = 58.28$$

$$u_{AP}^C = \frac{58.28}{58.28 + 850} = 6.42\%.$$

To summarize, here are the new equilibrium values after the government policy:

$$N = 1100, \ w_{m,AP}^C = 87.31, \ w_{L,AP}^R = 81.71, \ L_{AP}^C = 850, \ L_{AP}^R = 191.72$$
$$U_{AP}^C = 58.28 \text{ and } u_{AP}^C = 6.42\%.$$

If we compare these equilibrium values with those before the policy, it is easy to see that the unemployment level as well as the unemployment rate have been divided by two. This is mainly because the reduction in the urban wage has created fifty new urban jobs, but has also increased the rural wage because of migration and the induced higher productivity. As a result, the wage gap has narrowed from $9/8 = 1.125$ to $87.31/81.71 = 1.069$. In this example, *there is no Todaro paradox* (both in unemployment level and rate) and the policy is efficient in reducing unemployment.

3. The Harris-Todaro Model with Efficiency Wages

We now want to go further by endogenizing both urban wages and urban unemployment. We use the standard efficiency wage model, as proposed by Shapiro and Stiglitz (1984) and extensively developed in Part 2 of this book. The model is now dynamic and we assume that if rural workers want to get an urban job, they must first move to the city, be unemployed, and gather information about jobs, and can then eventually obtain an urban job. In the two previous models, which were static, the implicit assumption was that rural workers could directly find an urban job by searching from rural areas. We still have

$$U^C = N - L^C - L^R. \qquad \text{(C.18)}$$

The steady-state Bellman equations for non-shirkers, shirkers, and unemployed workers are, respectively, given by:

$$r \, I_L^{NS} = w_L^C - e - \delta \, (I_L^{NS} - I_U) \qquad \text{(C.19)}$$

$$r \, I_L^{S} = w_L^C - (\delta + m) \, (I_L^{S} - I_U) \qquad \text{(C.20)}$$

$$r \, I_U = w_U + a^C (I_L - I_U), \qquad \text{(C.21)}$$

where w_L^C, w_U are the urban wage and the unemployment benefit, respectively, e is the effort level, r the discount rate, δ, m and a denote the job-destruction, monitoring and job-acquisition rates, respectively. Firms set the efficiency wage such that $I_L^{NS} = I_L^{S} = I_L$ and we obtain that $I_L - I_U = e/m$. By combining these equations (as in Chapter 4), and observing that in steady-state, flows out of unemployment equal flows into unemployment, i.e.,

$$a^C = \frac{\delta \, L^C}{N - L^C - L^R}, \qquad \text{(C.22)}$$

we easily obtain the following urban efficiency wage:

$$w_L^C = w_U^C + e + \frac{e}{m} \left[\frac{\delta \, (N - L^R)}{N - L^C - L^R} + r \right]. \qquad \text{(C.23)}$$

Observe that L^R has a positive effect on w_L^C since more employment in rural areas implies a higher urban job-acquisition rate a^C (indeed a higher L^R leads to a decrease in urban unemployment since there is less competition for urban jobs) and thus, urban firms must increase their wages to meet the Urban Non-Shirking Condition (C.23). In cities, firms decide on their employment level by maximizing their profit. Thus, we have:

$$w_L^C = F'^C(L^C). \tag{C.24}$$

In rural areas, we assume that jobs are mainly menial and wages are flexible and equal to the marginal product, so that there is no rural unemployment. Thus, we have:

$$w_L^R = F'^R(L^R). \tag{C.25}$$

We assume that the Inada conditions on both production functions hold. Concerning rural-urban migration, as stated above, we assume that a rural worker cannot search from home, but must first be unemployed in the city and then search for a job. Thus, the equilibrium migration condition can be written as:

$$I_U = \int_0^{+\infty} w_L^R e^{-rt} dt = \frac{w_L^R}{r}. \tag{C.26}$$

The left-hand side is the intertemporal utility of moving to the city (remember that a migrant must first be unemployed) while the right-hand side corresponds to the intertemporal utility of staying in rural areas. Using (C.19)–(C.22), $I_L^{NS} = I_L^S = I_L$ and (C.25), we can write condition (C.26) as:

$$w_U^C + \frac{e}{m} \frac{\delta L^C}{N - L^C - L^R} = F'^R(L^R), \tag{C.27}$$

where L^C is determined by (C.24).

Definition C.3. *A Harris-Todaro equilibrium with efficiency wages is a 5-tuple* $(w_L^C, L^C, w_L^R, U^C, L^R)$ *such that (C.23), (C.24), (C.25), (C.18), and (C.27) are satisfied.*

In this model, given that w_U^C, e, m, δ, N, r are exogenous, an equilibrium is calculated as follows. First, from (C.23), the urban efficiency wage can be calculated as a function of L^C and L^R, that is $w_L^C(L^C, L^R)$. Second, by plugging this value $w_L^C(L^C, L^R)$ into (C.24), one obtains a relationship between L^C and L^R, that we write $L_w^C(L^R)$ and is given by

$$w_U^C + e + \frac{e}{m} \left[\frac{\delta (N - L^R)}{N - L^C - L^R} + r \right] = F'^C(L^C). \tag{C.28}$$

By totally differentiating (C.28) and using the Inada conditions, we easily obtain:

$$\frac{\partial L_w^C}{\partial L^R} < 0, \quad \lim_{L^R \to 0} L_w^C = L_0^C, \quad \lim_{L_w^C \to 0} L^R = N,$$

where $0 < L_w^C(L^R) < L_0^C < N$ is the unique solution of the following equation

$$w_U^C + e + \frac{e}{m} \left[\frac{\delta N}{N - L_0^C} + r \right] = F'^C(L_0^C).$$

Third, the equilibrium migration condition (C.27) gives another relationship between L^C and L^R, that we denote by $L_h^C(L^R)$ and which has the following properties:

$$\frac{\partial L_h^C}{\partial L^R} < 0, \quad \lim_{L^R \to 0} L_h^C = N, \quad \lim_{L_h^C \to 0} L^R = L_0^R = F'^{-1}\left(r w_U^C\right),$$

where $0 < L_h^C(L^R) < L_0^R < N$. Figure C.1 describes the two curves (C.28) (labor demand equation) and (C.27) (migration equilibrium condition) in the plane (L^R, L^C) and it is easily seen that there exists a unique equilibrium that gives a unique value of L^C and a unique value of L^R that we denote by (L^{R*}, L^{C*}).

Finally, plugging L^{R*} and L^{C*} into (C.23), (C.25), and (C.18) gives the equilibrium values of $w_L^{C*}, w_L^{R*}, U^{C*}$, respectively.

Let us now study the Todaro paradox in this model. Naturally, since L^C is an endogenous variable, it is difficult to study the impact of L^C on U^C or u^C. However, we can study the impact of a reduction of unemployment benefit w_U^C on urban unemployment since w_U^C has a direct impact on L^C. We have the following definition:

Definition C.4. *In a model where wage w_L^C and employment L^C are endogenous, a Todaro paradox prevails if an increase or a decrease in a policy variable leads to an increase in the equilibrium values of both L^C and U^C (or u^C). If, for example, one takes the unemployment benefit w_U^C, then a Todaro paradox prevails if by reducing w_U^C, both L^C and U^C (or u^C) increase, that is $\partial L^C / \partial w_U^C < 0$ and $\partial U^C / \partial w_U^C < 0$ (or $\partial u^C / \partial w_U^C < 0$). Differentiating (C.18) implies that a Todaro paradox exists if and only if*

$$\frac{\partial L^{R*}}{\partial w_U^C} > -\frac{\partial L^{C*}}{\partial w_U^C} > 0. \tag{C.29}$$

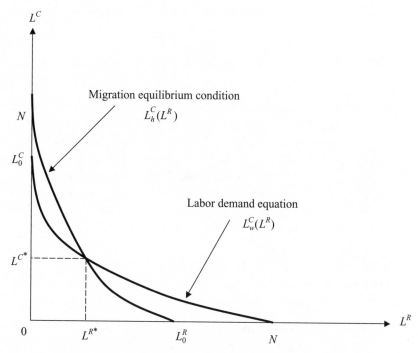

Figure C.1. Harris-Todaro equilibrium with efficiency wages.

Using this definition, let us now study the Todaro paradox in this model. As stated, the equilibrium is determined by two equations (C.27) and (C.28). If we differentiate (C.27), we obtain

$$L^R = L^R \left(\underset{-}{w_U^C}, \underset{-}{e}, \underset{+}{m}, \underset{-}{\delta}, \underset{+}{N}, \underset{-}{r}, \underset{-}{L^C} \right). \tag{C.30}$$

Indeed, a higher unemployment benefit, w_U^C, or effort level, e, or job-destruction rate, δ, or discount rate, r, or a lower monitoring rate, m, or total population, N, makes the city more attractive because of a higher intertemporal utility of being unemployed in the city, I_U (remember that $I_L - I_U = e/m$). Thus, more workers leave the rural area, which reduces L^R. When L^C increases, the urban job-acquisition rate a^C increases and once again, more rural workers migrate to the city, thus reducing L^R.

If we now differentiate (C.28), we get:

$$L^C = L^C \left(\underset{-}{w_U^C}, \underset{-}{e}, \underset{+}{m}, \underset{-}{\delta}, \underset{+}{N}, \underset{-}{r}, \underset{-}{L^R} \right) \tag{C.31}$$

where

$$\frac{\partial L^C}{\partial L^R} = -\frac{\frac{e}{m}\delta L^C}{\frac{e}{m}\delta\left(N - L^R\right) - \left(N - L^C - L^R\right)^2 F''^C(L^C)} < 0. \quad \text{(C.32)}$$

Indeed, a higher w_U^C, or e, or δ, or r, or a lower m, or N, shifts upward the Non-Shirking Condition (C.23), so that firms have to pay a higher efficiency wage to prevent shirking. This, in turn, reduces employment since maximizing-profit firms must reduce the number of employed because of higher wage costs. For L^R, the effect is through the job-acquisition rate, a^C. Indeed, a higher rural employment L^R increases a^C, which obliges firms to increase their urban efficiency wages which, in turn, reduces urban labor demand L^C because firms maximize their profit. We obtain the following result (proved by Zenou, 2005):

Proposition C.2. *In a Harris-Todaro model with urban efficiency wages, a decreasing unemployment benefit leads to*

(*i*) *an increase in urban employment L^C, i.e., $\partial L^{C*}/\partial w_U^C < 0$;*
(*ii*) *an increase in rural employment L^R, i.e., $\partial L^{C*}/\partial w_U^C < 0$;*
(*iii*) *a decrease in urban unemployment (both in level and rate) U^C and u^C, i.e., $\partial U^{C*}/\partial w_U^C > 0$ and $\partial u^{C*}/\partial w_U^C > 0$.*

As a result, there is no Todaro paradox.

There is thus no Todaro paradox in this model. The intuition is as follows. When the government decreases the unemployment benefit, this has a direct negative effect on urban wages and thus, more urban jobs are created. This is the attraction force of the city. But there are two repulsion forces. As before, this implies that rural wages increase, but since there are more jobs in cities and efficiency wages act as a worker's disciplining device, urban firms reduce their wages because it becomes more difficult to find a job. Since the repulsion forces are sufficiently strong, the net effect is that creating urban jobs via a reduction in unemployment benefit reduces urban unemployment because of the discouraging effect of efficiency wages on migration.

These results are quite interesting. Let us see what happens in the autarky case; i.e., the case of no mobility between rural and urban areas. Indeed, now imagine that migration was totally controlled and that workers, especially rural workers, could *not* migrate to cities. In that case, the two regions

(C and R) would be totally independent and we would have

$$U^C = N^C - L^C$$

$$L^R = N^R,$$

so that the unemployment rate would be given by

$$u^C = \frac{U^C}{U^C + L^C} = \frac{N^C - L^C}{N^C}.$$

Here, only L^C and not L^R is endogenous. Thus, the job-acquisition rate and the urban efficiency wage would be given by:

$$a^C = \frac{\delta \, L^C}{N - L^C}$$

$$w_L^C = w_U + e + \frac{e}{m} \left[\frac{\delta \, N^C}{N - L^C} + r \right] \tag{C.33}$$

and labor demand would still be given by (C.24). The urban labor equilibrium would then be defined as:

$$w_U + e + \frac{e}{m} \left[\frac{\delta \, N^C}{N - L^C} + r \right] = F'(L^C). \tag{C.34}$$

Definition C.5. *An efficiency wage equilibrium with no mobility is a triple* $(w_e^{C*}, L^{C*}, w^{R*})$ *such that (C.33) (C.24) and (C.25) are satisfied.*

From this definition and by totally differentiating (C.34), we obtain the following result:

Proposition C.3. *In an efficiency wage equilibrium with no mobility, decreasing the unemployment benefit* w_U *always increases urban employment and decreases urban unemployment (both in level and rate), that is*

$$\frac{\partial L^C}{\partial w_U} < 0, \quad \frac{\partial U^C}{\partial w_U} > 0, \quad \frac{\partial u^C}{\partial w_U} > 0.$$

This result is not surprising since when w_U decreases, firms can reduce their efficiency wages and thus hire more workers. There is no effect on rural workers. However, even when rural-urban migration is authorized, we obtain the same results because the repulsion forces are sufficiently strong to thwart the attraction force of a reduction in the unemployment benefit.

4. The Harris-Todaro Model with Urban Search Externalities

We would like to endogenize both urban wages and urban unemployment using a standard search-matching model as in Mortensen and Pissarides (1999) and Pissarides (2000). This model has been extensively analyzed in Chapter 1 of this book. The starting point is the following matching function

$$d(U^C, V^C),$$

where U^C and V^C are the total number of urban unemployed and urban vacancies, respectively. This matching function captures the frictions implied by search behaviors of both firms and workers. It is assumed that $d(.)$ is increasing in its arguments, concave and homogeneous of degree 1. Thus, the rate at which vacancies are filled is $d(U^C, V^C)/V^C = d(1/\theta^C, 1) \equiv q(\theta^C)$, where

$$\theta^C = \frac{V^C}{U^C} \tag{C.35}$$

is a measure of *labor market tightness* in cities and $q(\theta^C)$ is a Poisson intensity. Similarly, the rate at which an unemployed worker leaves unemployment (job-acquisition rate) is now given by

$$a^C = \frac{d(U^C, V^C)}{U^C} \equiv \theta^C q(\theta^C). \tag{C.36}$$

In steady-state, the Bellman equations for the employed and unemployed are, respectively, given by:

$$r I_L = w_L^C - \delta (I_L - I_U) \tag{C.37}$$

$$r I_U = w_U^C + \theta^C q(\theta^C) (I_L - I_U). \tag{C.38}$$

For firms with filled and vacant jobs, we have the following Bellman equations:

$$r I_F = y^C - w_L^C - \delta(I_F - I_V) \tag{C.39}$$

$$r I_V = -c + q(\theta^C)(I_F - I_V), \tag{C.40}$$

where c is the search cost for the firm and y^C is the product of the match. Because of free entry, $I_V = 0$, and using (C.39)–(C.40), we obtain the following decreasing relation between labor market tightness and wages:

$$\frac{c}{q(\theta^C)} = \frac{y^C - w_L^C}{r + \delta}. \tag{C.41}$$

Wages are negotiated between the firm and the worker. By solving the following Nash-program (where β is the bargaining power of workers):

$$w_L^C = \arg\max_{w_L^C}(I_L - I_U)^\beta (I_F - I_V)^{1-\beta},$$

we obtain the following wage (see Chapter 4):

$$w_L^C = (1 - \beta) w_U^C + \beta \left(y^C + c\,\theta^C \right). \tag{C.42}$$

As previously, the unemployment level in cities in equal to:

$$U^C = N - L^C - L^R. \tag{C.43}$$

In steady-state, flows into and out of unemployment must be equal and we obtain the following relationship in cities:

$$L^C = \frac{\theta^C q(\theta^C)}{\delta + \theta^C q(\theta^C)} \left(N - L^R \right). \tag{C.44}$$

In rural areas, as before, there is no unemployment and the following condition holds:

$$w_L^R = F'^R(L^R). \tag{C.45}$$

Finally, we assume that a rural worker cannot search from home, but must first be unemployed in the city and then search for a job. Thus, the equilibrium migration condition can be written as:

$$I_U = \frac{w_L^R}{r}.$$

Using (C.37) and (C.38), and observing that

$$I_L - I_U = \frac{w_L^C - w_U^C}{r + \delta + \theta^C q(\theta^C)},$$

this can be written as:

$$\frac{(r + \delta)\, w_U^C + \theta^C q(\theta^C) w_L^C}{r + \delta + \theta^C q(\theta^C)} = F'^R(L^R). \tag{C.46}$$

Definition C.6. *A Harris-Todaro equilibrium with urban search external-ities and bargained wages is a 5-tuple $(w_L^C, \theta^C, w_L^R, L^C, U^C, V^C, L^R)$ such that (C.42), (C.41), (C.45), (C.44), (C.43), (C.35) and (C.46) are satisfied.*

Here is the way the equilibrium is calculated. The system is recursive. First, by combining (C.42) and (C.41), we obtain a unique θ^{C*} that is only a function of parameters and given by:

$$(1 - \beta)\left(y^C - w_U^C\right) - \beta c \theta^C = \frac{c(r + \delta)}{q(\theta^C)}. \tag{C.47}$$

Second, by combining (C.42) and (C.46), we obtain:

$$\frac{(r + \delta) w_U^C + \theta^C q(\theta^C)\left[(1 - \beta) w_U^C + \beta\left(y^C + c\theta^C\right)\right]}{r + \delta + \theta^C q(\theta^C)} = F'^R(L^R), \tag{C.48}$$

which, using θ^{C*}, gives a unique L^{R*} as a function of parameters only. Furthermore, by plugging θ^{C*} and L^{R*} into (C.42), we obtain a unique L^{C*}. Figure C.2 illustrates the way in which the equilibrium is calculated.

Finally, by plugging L^{C*} and L^{R*} into (C.45) and (C.43), we obtain, respectively, w_L^{R*} and U^{C*} and by plugging θ^{C*} into (C.47), we obtain w_L^{C*}. Moreover, using the values of θ^{C*} and U^{C*} in (C.35), we obtain the equilibrium number of vacancies in cities, V^{C*}.

Here the migration process is more complex. If the government reduces the unemployment benefit, this will once more have a direct effect by in-creasing urban jobs. Indeed, since the wage is reduced (see (C.42)), more firms enter the market (see (C.41)) and thus, more urban jobs are created. There will still be a repulsion force because of the positive effect on rural wage. But since workers face less search frictions (more firms enter the mar-ket), more rural workers will migrate to the cities which, in turn, increases workers' search frictions. We have the following result (proved by Zenou, 2005 and 2008b):

Proposition C.4. *In a Harris-Todaro model with urban search externalities and bargained wages, a decreasing unemployment benefit w_U^C leads to:*

(*i*) *an increase in both urban job creation θ^C and urban employment L^C,*
(*ii*) *an ambiguous effect on both rural employment L^R and urban unem-ployment (both in level and rate) U^C and u^C.*

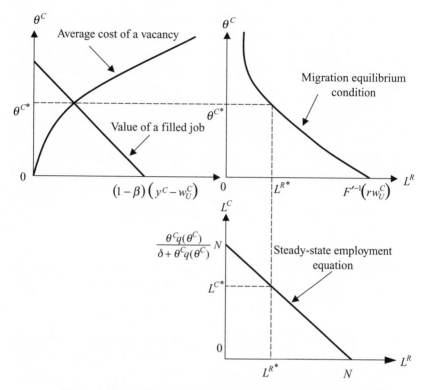

Figure C.2. Harris-Todaro equilibrium with search externalities.

Furthermore, if the following condition holds,

$$w_L^C - w_L^R/r + \frac{\beta c}{\frac{\partial\left[\theta^C q(\theta^C)\right]}{\partial\theta^C}} < -F''^R(L^R)\left(N - L^R\right)\frac{\delta\left[r + \delta + \theta^C q(\theta^C)\right]}{r\left[\delta + \theta^C q(\theta^C)\right]^2}$$

then a Todaro paradox prevails, that is decreasing w_U^C increases both urban employment and unemployment.

A decrease in w_U^C has a direct negative effect on bargained wages. As a result, because it is cheaper and thus more profitable to hire a worker, more firms enter the urban labor market and more jobs are created, consequently θ^C and L^C increase. However, the effect on rural-urban migration and thus on L^R is more subtle. Indeed, when w_U^C decreases, there is a *direct negative effect* on migration since urban wages are lower, and thus less rural workers migrate (thus L^R increases). There is also an *indirect positive effect* on migration since a lower w_U^C increases w_L^C, and thus more firms enter the urban labor market (if the search cost c is not too large) and more jobs are created. This increases rural-urban migration and reduces L^R. The net effect is thus ambiguous. The same ambiguity arises when one studies the effect of w_U^C on urban unemployment. These results mean that there is a possibility for a Todaro paradox; that is, a decrease in the unemployment benefit can increase both urban employment and unemployment. This is true if at least the indirect positive effect on migration is larger than the direct negative effect mentioned previously.

As in the efficiency wage model, let us study the case with no mobility between the two regions. The wage w_L^C and the job creation rate θ^C are still given by (C.42) and (C.47), respectively, but L^C is now equal to:

$$L^C = \frac{\theta^C q(\theta^C)}{\delta + \theta^C q(\theta^C)} N^C. \tag{C.49}$$

Definition C.7. *A search equilibrium with no mobility is a triple* $(w^{C*}, \theta^{C*}, L^{C*}, w^{R*})$ *such that (C.42), (C.47), (C.49), and (C.25) are satisfied.*

By totally differentiating (C.47), (C.49), and (C.43), we have the following result:

Proposition C.5. *In a search equilibrium with no mobility, decreasing the unemployment benefit* w_U *increases both urban job creation* θ^C *and urban employment* L^C *and decreases urban unemployment (both in level and rate), that is:*

$$\frac{\partial \theta^C}{\partial w_U} < 0, \quad \frac{\partial L^C}{\partial w_U} < 0, \quad \frac{\partial U^C}{\partial w_U} > 0, \quad \frac{\partial u^C}{\partial w_U} > 0.$$

Here, in contrast to the efficiency wage model, the results are different from the free-mobility case because of the induced effects on rural-urban migration.

Bibliography

Abdel-Rahman, H.M. and M. Fujita. "Product Variety, Marshallian Externalities, and City Sizes." *Journal of Regional Science* 30(1990):165–183.

Abdel-Rahman, H.M. and P. Wang. "Toward a General-Equilibrium Theory of a Core-Periphery System of Cities." *Regional Science and Urban Economics* 25(2005):529–546.

Agell, J. and P. Lundborg. "Theories of Pay and Unemployment: Survey Evidence from Swedish Manufacturing Firms." *Scandinavian Journal of Economics* 97(1995):295–307.

Ainsworth-Darnell, J.W. and D.B. Downey. "Assessing the Oppositional Culture Explanation for Racial/Ethnic Differences in School Performance." *American Sociological Review* 63(1998):536–553.

Akerlof, G.A. "Social Distance and Social Decisions." *Econometrica* 65(1997):1005–1027.

Akerlof, G.A. and R.E. Kranton. "Economics and Identity." *Quarterly Journal of Economics* 115(2000):715–753.

Akerlof, G.A. and J.L. Yellen. *Efficiency Wage Models of the Labor Market*, Cambridge, MA: Cambridge University Press, 1986.

Albrecht, J.W. and B. Axell. "An Equilibrium Model of Search Unemployment." *Journal of Political Economy* 92(1984):824–840.

Albrecht, J.W., Gautier, P.A., Tan, S. and S.B. Vroman. "Matching with Multiple Applications Revisited." *Economics Letters* 84(2004):311–314.

Albrecht, J.W., Navarro, L. and S.B. Vroman. "The Effects of Labor Market Policies in an Economy with an Informal Sector." *Economic Journal* 2009, forthcoming.

Albrecht, J.W. and S.B. Vroman. "A Note on the Long-Run Properties of the Shirking Model." *Labour Economics* 3(1996):189–195.

Albrecht, J.W. and S.B. Vroman. "Unemployment Compensation Finance and Efficiency Wages." *Journal of Labor Economics* 17(1999):141–167.

Alonso, W. *Location and Land Use*, Cambridge, MA: Harvard University Press, 1964.

Altonji, J.G. and R.M. Blank. "Race and Gender in the Labor Market." *Handbook of Labor Economics, Vol. 3*, North Holland: Elsevier Science, pp. 3143–3259, 1999.

Anas, A. "Ethnic Segregation and Ghettos." In: R. Arnott and D. McMillen (Eds.), *A Companion to Urban Economics*, Boston: Blackwell Publishing, pp. 536–554, 2006.

Anas, A., Arnott, R. and K. Small. "Urban Spatial Structure." *Journal of Economic Literature* 36(1998):1426–1464.

Anselin, L. *Spatial Econometrics: Methods and Models*, Boston: Kluwer Academic Publishers, 1988.

Armstrong, H. and J. Taylor. *Regional Economics*, London: Harvester Wheatsheaf, 1993.

Arnott, R. "Economic Theory and the Spatial Mismatch Hypothesis." *Urban Studies* 35(1998):1171–1185.

Arrow, K.J. "The Theory of Discrimination." In: O. Ashenfelter and A. Rees (Eds.), *Discrimination in Labor Markets*, Princeton: Princeton University Press, pp. 3–33, 1973.

Åslund, O., Östh, J. and Y. Zenou. "How Crucial is Distance to Jobs for Ethnic Minorities? Old Question-Improved Answer." Unpublished manuscript, Stockholm University, 2008.

Austen-Smith, D. and R.D. Jr. Fryer. "An Economic Analysis of 'Acting White,'" *Quarterly Journal of Economics* 120(2005):551–583.

Bala, V. and S. Goyal. "A Non-Cooperative Model of Network Formation." *Econometrica* 68(2000):1181–1229.

Ballester, C., Calvó-Armengol, A. and Y. Zenou. "Who's Who in Networks. Wanted: The Key Player." *Econometrica* 74(2006):1403–1417.

Barber, A. *Recruiting Employees: Individual and Organizational Perspectives*, London: Sage Publications, 1998.

Banerjee, B. "Information Flow, Expectations and Job Search: Rural-to-Urban Migration Process in India." *Journal of Development Economics* 15(1984):239–257.

Bartik, T.J. "The Distributional Effects of Local Labor Demand and Industrial Mix: Estimates Using Individual Panel Data." *Journal of Urban Economics* 40(1996):150–178.

Basu, K. *Analytical Development Economics: The Less-Developed Economy Revisited*, Cambridge, MA: MIT Press, 1997.

Battu, H., McDonald, M. and Y. Zenou. "Oppositional Identities and the Labor Market." *Journal of Population Economics* 20(2007):643–667.

Bayer, P., Ross, S.L. and G. Topa. "Place of Work and Place of Residence: Informal Hiring Networks and Labor Market Outcomes." *Journal of Political Economy* 116(2008): 1150–1196.

Becker, G.S. *The Economics of Discrimination*, Chicago: The University of Chicago Press, 1957.

Beckmann, M. "Spatial Equilibrium in the Dispersed City." In: Y.Y. Papageorgiou (Ed.), *Mathematical Land Use Theory*, Lexington, MA: Lexington Books, pp. 117–125, 1976.

Benabou, R. "Workings of a City: Location, Education, and Production." *Quarterly Journal of Economics* 108(1993):619–52.

Berliant, M., R.R. Reed III and P. Wang. "Knowledge Exchange, Matching, and Agglomeration." *Journal of Urban Economics* 60(2006):69–95.

Bewley, T.T. *Why Wages Don't Fall During a Recession?* Cambridge, MA: Harvard University Press, 1999.

Bhaskar, V. and T. To. "Minimum Wage Laws for Ronald McDonald Monopsonies: A Theory of Monopsonistic Competition." *Economic Journal* 109(1999): 190–203.

Binmore, K., Rubinstein, A. and A. Wolinsky. "The Nash Bargaining Solution in Economic Modelling." *Rand Journal of Economics* 17(1986):176–188.

Bisin, A., Patacchini, E. Verdier, T. and Y. Zenou. "'Bend it Like Beckham': Identity, Socialization, and Assimilation." CEPR Discussion Paper No. 5662, 2006.

Bisin, A., Patacchini, E. Verdier, T. and Y. Zenou. "Are Muslim Immigrants Different in Terms of Cultural Integration?" *Journal of the European Economic Association* 6(2008):445–456.

Bisin, A., Topa, G. and T. Verdier. "Religious Intermarriage and Socialization in the United States." *Journal of Political Economy* 112(2004):615–664.

Bisin, A. and T. Verdier. "Beyond the Melting Pot: Cultural Transmission, Marriage, and the Evolution of Ethnic and Religious Traits." *Quarterly Journal of Economics* 115(2000):955–988.

Bisin, A. and T. Verdier. "The Economics of Cultural Transmission and the Dynamics of Preferences." *Journal of Economic Theory* 97(2001):298–319.

Blanchard, O.J. and P.A. Diamond. "The Beveridge Curve." *Brookings Papers of Economic Activities* 1(1989):1–76.

Blanchard, O.J. and P.A. Diamond. "The Aggregate Matching Function." In: P.A. Diamond (Ed.), *Growth, Productivity, and Unemployment*, Cambridge, MA: M.I.T. Press, pp. 159–206, 1990.

Blanchard, O.J. and P.A. Diamond. "Ranking, Unemployment Duration, and Wages." *Review of Economic Studies* 61(1994):417–434.

Blanchflower, D.G. and A.J. Oswald. *The Wage Curve*, Cambridge, MA: M.I.T. Press, 1994.

Blinder, A. and D. Choi. "A Shred of Evidence on Theories of Wage Stickiness." *Quarterly Journal of Economics* 105(1990):1003–1015.

Boarnet, M.G. and W.T. Bogart. "Enterprise Zones and Employment: Evidence from New Jersey." *Journal of Urban Economics* 40(1996):198–215.

Bollinger, C.R. and K.R. Ihlanfeldt. "The Intraurban Spatial Distribution of Employment: Which Government Interventions Make a Difference." *Journal of Urban Economics* 53(2003):396–412.

Bondonio, D. and J. Engberg. "Enterprise Zones and Local Employment: Evidence from the States' Program." *Regional Science and Urban Economics* 30(2000):519–549.

Bondonio, D. and R.T. Greenbaum. "Do Local Tax Incentives Affect Economic Growth? What Mean Impact Miss in the Analysis of Enterprise Zone Policies?" *Regional Science and Urban Economics* 37(2007):121–136.

Bonney, N. "Work and Ghetto Culture." *British Journal of Sociology* 26(1975):435–447.

Borjas, G.J. "Ethnicity, Neighborhoods, and Human Capital Externalities." *American Economic Review* 85(1995):365–390.

Borjas, G.J. "To Ghetto or not to Ghetto: Ethnicity and Residential Segregation." *Journal of Urban Economics* 44(1998):228–253.

Borukhov, E. and O. Hochman. "Optimum and Market Equilibrium in a Model of a City Without a Predetermined Center." *Environment and Planning A* 9(1977):849–856.

Bound, J. and H.J. Holzer. "Industrial Shifts, Skill Levels, and the Labor Market for White and Black Males." *Review of Economics and Statistics* 75(1993): 387–395.

Boyd, R. and P.J. Richerson. *Culture and the Evolutionary Process*, Chicago: University of Chicago Press, 1985.

Bramoullé, Y. and R.E. Kranton. "Public Goods in Networks." *Journal of Economic Theory* 135(2007):478–494.

Brown, C. and J. Medoff. "The Employer Size Wage Effect." *Journal of Political Economy*, 97(1989):1027–1059.

Brueckner, J.K. "The Structure of Urban Equilibria: A Unified Treatment of the Muth-Mills Model." In: E.S. Mills (Ed.), *Handbook of Regional and Urban Economics*, Amsterdam: Elsevier Science, pp. 821–845, 1987.

Brueckner, J.K. "Urban Sprawl: Diagnosis and Remedies." *International Regional Science Review* 23(2000):160–171.

Brueckner, J.K. and H.-A. Kim. "Land Markets in the Harris-Todaro Model: A New Factor Equilibrating Rural-Urban Migration." *Journal of Regional Science* 41(2001):507–520.

Brueckner, J.K. and A.G. Largey. "Social Interaction and Urban Sprawl." *Journal of Urban Economics* 64(2008):18–34.

Brueckner, J.K. and R.W. Martin. "Spatial Mismatch: An Equilibrium Analysis." *Regional Science and Urban Economics* 27(1997):693–714.

Brueckner, J.K. and H. Selod. "The Political Economy of Urban Transport-System Choice." *Journal of Public Economics* 90(2006):983–1005.

Brueckner, J.K., Thisse, J.-F. and Y. Zenou. "Why is Central Paris Rich and Downtown Detroit Poor? An Amenity-Based Theory." *European Economic Review* 43(1999):91–107.

Brueckner, J.K., Thisse, J.-F. and Yves Zenou. "Local Labor Markets, Job Matching and Urban Location." *International Economic Review* 43(2002):155–171.

Brueckner, J.K. and Y. Zenou. "Harris-Todaro Models with a Land Market." *Regional Science and Urban Economics* 29(1999):317–339.

Brueckner, J.K. and Y. Zenou. "Space and Unemployment: The Labor-Market Effects of Spatial Mismatch." *Journal of Labor Economics* 21(2003):242–266.

Burdett, K. and K.L. Judd. "Equilibrium Price Dispersion." *Econometrica* 51(1983):955–970.

Burdett, K. and D.T. Mortensen. "Wage Differentials, Employer Size, and Unemployment." *International Economic Review* 39(1998):257–273.

Burdett, K., Shi, S. and R. Wright. "Pricing and Matching with Frictions." *Journal of Political Economy* 109(2001):1060–1085.

Burt, R.S. *Structural Holes*, Cambridge, MA: Harvard University Press, 1992.

Butters, G. "Equilibrium Distributions of Sales and Advertising Prices." *Review of Economic Studies* 44(1979):465–491.

Cahuc, P. and A. Zylberberg. *Labor Economics*, Cambridge, MA: MIT Press, 2004.

Calvó-Armengol, A. "Job Contact Networks." *Journal of Economic Theory* 115(2004):191–206.

Calvó-Armengol, A. and Y.M. Ioannides. "Social Networks in Labor Markets." In: L. Blume and S. Durlauf (Eds.), *The New Palgrave, A Dictionary of Economics, Second Edition*, London: MacMillan Press, 2008.

Calvó-Armengol, A. and M.O. Jackson. "The Effects of Social Networks on Employment and Inequality." *American Economic Review* 94(2004):426–454.

Calvó-Armengol, A. and M.O. Jackson. "Social Networks in Labor Markets: Wage and Employment Dynamics and Inequality." *Journal of Economic Theory* 132(2007):27–46.

Calvó-Armengol, A., Patacchini, E. and Y. Zenou. "Peer Effects and Social Networks in Education." *Review of Economics Studies*, forthcoming, 2009.

Calvó-Armengol, A., Verdier, T. and Y. Zenou. "Strong and Weak Ties in Employment and Crime." *Journal of Public Economics* 91(2007):203–233.

Calvó-Armengol, A. and Y. Zenou. "Job Matching, Social Network and Word-of-Mouth Communication." *Journal of Urban Economics* 57(2005):500–522.

Campbell, C. and K. Kamlani. "The Reasons for Wage Rigidity: Evidence from a Survey of Firms." *Quarterly Journal of Economics* 112(1997):759–789.

Cao, M. and S. Shi. "Coordination, Matching, and Wages." *Canadian Journal of Economics* 33(2000):1009–1033.

Cappelli, P. and K. Chauvin. "An Interplant Test of the Efficiency Wage Hypothesis." *Quarterly Journal of Economics* 106(1991):769–787.

Carmichael, L. "Self-Enforcing Contracts, Shirking, and Life Cycle Incentives." *Journal of Economic Perspectives* 3(1989):65–84.

Carter, T.J. "Urban Productivity, Urban Unemployment, and Labor Market Policies." *Regional Science and Urban Economics* 28(1998):329–344.

Cavalli-Sforza, L.L. and M.W. Feldman. *Cultural Transmission and Evolution*. Princeton, NJ: Princeton University Press, 1981.

Cheshire, P. "Inner Areas as Spatial Labour Markets: A Critique of the Inner Area Studies." *Urban Studies* 16(1979):29–43.

Cho, Y. and C. Whitehead. "Residential Mobility of Social Tenants and Households Entering Low-Cost Home Ownership: A Comparison Between London and the Northern Regions." Dataspring Report 10, The Cambridge Centre for Housing and Planning Research, 2005.

Chung, C., Myers, S.L. Jr. and L. Saunders. "Racial Differences in Transportation Access to Employment in Chicago and Los Angeles, 1980 and 1990." *American Economic Review, Papers and Proceedings* 91(2001):174–177.

Ciccone, A. and R. Hall. "Productivity and the Density of Economic Activity." *American Economic Review* 86(1996):54–70.

Clark, M.L. and M. Ayers. "The Role of Reciprocity and Proximity in Junior High School Friendships." *Journal of Youth and Adolescence* 17(1988):403–411.

Coate, S. and G.C. Loury. "Will Affirmative-Action Policies Eliminate Negative Stereotypes?" *American Economic Review* 83(1993):1220–1240.

Conley, T.G. and G. Topa. "Socio-Economic Distance and Spatial Patterns in Unemployment." *Journal of Applied Econometrics* 17(2002):303–327.

Corcoran, M., Datcher, L. and G.J. Duncan. "Most Workers Find Jobs Through Word of Mouth." *Monthly Labor Review* 103(1980):33–35.

Coulson, E., Laing, D. and P. Wang. "Spatial Mismatch in Search Equilibrium." *Journal of Labor Economics*, 19(2001):949–972.

Crampton, G.R. "Urban Labour Markets." In: E.S. Mills and P. Cheshire (Eds.), *Handbook of Regional and Urban Economics Vol. 3*, Amsterdam: Elsevier Science, pp. 1499–1557, 1999.

Cutler, D.M. and E.L. Glaeser. "Are Ghettos Good or Bad?" *Quarterly Journal of Economics* 112(1997):827–872.

Cutler, D.M., Glaeser, E.L. and J. Vigdor. "The Rise and Decline of the American Ghetto." *Journal of Political Economy* 107(1999):455–506.

D'Aspremont, C., Gabszewicz, J.J. and J.-F. Thisse. "On Hotelling's Stability in Competition." *Econometrica* 47(1979):1045–1050.

David, Q. "Does the Opening of a City Affect City Structure, Job Search, and Welfare?" Unpublished manuscript, ECARES, 2008.

Davis, S.J., Haltiwanger, J.C. and S. Schuh. *Job Creation and Destruction*, Cambridge, MA: MIT Press, 1996.

Delpit, L. *Other People's Children: Cultural Conflict in the Classroom*, New York: The Free Press, 1995.

De Martí, J. and Y. Zenou. "Friendship Formation, Oppositional Identity, and Segregation." CEPR Discussion Paper, 2008.

Devine, T.J. and N.M. Kieffer. *Empirical Labor Econonomics. The Search Approach*, Oxford: Oxford University Press, 1991.

Diamond, P.A. "A Model of Price Adjustment." *Journal of Economic Theory* 3(1971):156–168.

Diamond, P.A. "Mobility Costs, Frictional Unemployment, and Efficiency." *Journal of Political Economy* 89(1981):798–812.

Diamond P.A. "Aggregate Demand Management in Search Equilibrium." *Journal of Political Economy* 89(1982):798–812.

Dickens, W.T. and L.F. Katz. "Inter-Industry Wage Differences and Industry Characteristics." In K. Lang and J.S. Leonard (Eds.), *Unemployment and the Structure of Labor Markets*, New York: Basil Blackwell, pp. 48–89, 1987.

Dujardin, C., Selod, H. and I. Thomas. "Residential Segregation and Unemployment: The Case of Brussels." *Urban Studies* 45(2008):89–113.

Duranton, G. "Human Capital Externalities in Cities: Identification and Policy Issues." In: R. Arnott and D. McMillen (Eds.), *A Companion to Urban Economics*, New York: Blackwell, pp. 24–39, 2006.

Duranton, G. and D. Puga. "Micro-Foundations of Urban Agglomeration Economies." In: J.V. Henderson and J.-F. Thisse (Eds.), *Handbook of Regional and Urban Economics Vol. 4*, Amsterdam: Elsevier Science, pp. 2063–2117, 2004.

Durlauf, S.E. "Neighborhood Effects." In: J.V. Henderson and J.-F. Thisse (Eds.), *Handbook of Regional and Urban Economics Vol. 4*, Amsterdam: Elsevier Science, pp. 2173–2242, 2004.

Dymski, G.A. "Discrimination in the Credit and Housing Markets: Findings and Challenges." In: W.M. Rodgers III (Ed.), *Handbook on the Economics of Discrimination*, Northampton, MA: Edward Elgar, pp. 215–259, 2006.

Eberts, R.W. "Urban Labor Markets." Upjohn Institute Staff Working Paper 95-32, 1994.

Eberts, R.W. and J.A. Stone. *Wage and Employment Adjustment in Local Labor Markets*, Kalamazoo, MI: W.E. Upjohn Institute for Employment Research, 1992.

Eckstein, Z. and G.J. Van den Berg. "Empirical Labor Search: A Survey." *Journal of Econometrics* 136(2007):531–564.

Economides, N. "Symmetric Equilibrium, Existence and Optimality in a Differentiated Product Market." *Journal of Economic Theory* 47(1989):178–194.

Fehr, E. and A. Falk. "Wage Rigidity in a Competitive Incomplete Contract Market." *Journal of Political Economy* 107(1999):106–134.

Fehr, E. and L. Goette. "Do Workers Work More if Wages are High? Evidence from a Randomized Field Experiment." *American Economic Review* 97(2007):298–317.

Fehr, E., Kirchsteiger, R. and A. Riedl. "Involuntary Unemployment and Non-Compensating Wage Differentials in an Experimental Labour Market." *Economic Journal* 106(1996):106–121.

Fernandez, R.M. "Race, Space, and Job Accessibility: Evidence From a Plant Relocation." *Economic Geography* 70(1994):390–416.

Fernandez, R.M. and C. Su. "Space in the Study of Labor Markets." *Annual Review of Sociology* 30(2004):545–569.

Fieldhouse, E. "Ethnic Minority Unemployment and Spatial Mismatch: The Case of London." *Urban Studies* 36(1999):1569–1596.

Fields, G.S. "Rural-Urban Migration, Urban Unemployment and Underemployment, and Job-Search Activity in LDCs." *Journal of Development Economics* 2(1975):165–187.

Fields, G.S. "On-the-Job Search in a Labor Market Model. Ex-Ante Choices and Ex-Post Outcomes." *Journal of Development Economics* 30(1989):159–178.

Finneran, L. and M. Kelly. "Social Networks and Inequality." *Journal of Urban Economics* 53(2003):282–299.

Fiorillo, F., Santacroce, S. and S. Staffolani. "Monopsonistic Competition for the 'Best' Workers." *Labour Economics* 7(2000):313–334.

Fisher, M.M. and P. Nijkamp. *Regional Labour Markets. Analytical Contributions and Cross-National Comparisons*, Amsterdam: Elsevier Science, 1987.

Fong, E. and W. Isajiw. "Determinants of Friendship Choices in Multiethnic Society." *Sociology Forum* 15(2000):249–271.

Fordham S. and J.U. Ogbu. "Black Students' School Success: Coping with the Burden of Acting White." *The Urban Review* 18(1986):176–206.

Fryer, R.G. Jr. and P. Torelli. "An Empirical Analysis of 'Acting White.'" NBER Working Paper No. 11334, 2005.

Fujita, M. *Urban Economic Theory*, Cambridge, MS: Cambridge University Press, 1989.

Fujita, M. "Spatial Interactions and Agglomeration in Urban Economics." In: M. Chatterji and R.E. Kunne (Eds.), *New Frontiers in Regional Sciences*, London: Macmillan, pp. 184–221, 1990.

Fujita, M. and P. Krugman. "When is the Economy Monocentric?" *Regional Science and Urban Economics* 25(1995):505–528.

Fujita, M., Krugman, P. and A.J. Venables. *The Spatial Economy. Cities, Regions, and International Trade*, Cambridge, MA: MIT Press, 1999.

Fujita, M. and T. Mori. "Structural Stability and Evolution of Urban Systems." *Regional Science and Urban Economics* 27(1997):399–442.

Fujita, M. and H. Ogawa. "Equilibrium Land Use Patterns in a Nonmonocentric City." *Journal of Regional Science* 20(1980):455–475.

Fujita M. and J. F. Thisse. "Spatial Competition with a Land Market: Hotelling and von Thünen Unified." *Review of Economic Studies* 53(1986):819–841.

Fujita, M. and J.-F. Thisse. *Economics of Agglomeration. Cities, Industrial Location, and Regional Growth*, Cambridge: Cambridge University Press, 2002.

Garreau, J. *Edge City. Life on the New Frontier*, New York: Doubleday, 1991.

Gaumont, D., M. Schindler and R. Wright. "Alternative Theories of Wage Dispersion." *European Economic Review* 50(2006):831–848.

Gautier, P.A. "Unemployment and Search Externalities in a Model with Heterogeneous Jobs and Workers." *Economica* 69(2002):21–40.

Gautier, P.A. and Y. Zenou. "How Transport Mode Affects the Labor-Market Outcomes of Ethnic Minorities?" CEPR Discussion Paper No. 7061, 2008.

Glaeser, E.L. "The Future of Urban Economics: Non-Market Interactions." *Brookings-Wharton Papers on Urban Affairs* 1(2000):101–150.

Glaeser, E.L., Sacerdote, B. and J.A. Scheinkman. "Crime and Social Interactions." *Quarterly Journal of Economics* 111(1996):508–548.

Glaeser, E.L. and M.E. Kahn. "Decentralized Employment and the Transformation of the American City." *Brookings-Wharton Papers on Urban Affairs* 2(2001):1–64.

Glaeser, E.L. and M.E. Kahn. "Sprawl and Urban Growth." In: J.V. Henderson and J.-F. Thisse (Eds.), *Handbook of Regional and Urban Economics Vol. 4*, Amsterdam: Elsevier Science, pp. 2498–2527, 2004.

Glaeser, E.L., M.E. Kahn and J. Rappaport. "Why Do the Poor Live in Cities? The Role of Public Transportation." *Journal of Urban Economics* 63(2008):1–24.

Glaeser, E.L. and D.C. Maré. "Cities and Skills." *Journal of Labor Economics* 19(2001):316–342.

Gobillon, L., Magnac, T. and H. Selod. "The Effect of Location on Finding a Job in the Paris Region," LEA Working Paper 0703, INRA, 2007.

Gobillon, L., Selod, H. and Y. Zenou. "Spatial Mismatch: From the Hypotheses to the Theories." CEPR Discussion Paper No. 3740, 2003.

Gobillon, L., Selod, H. and Zenou, Y. "The Mechanisms of Spatial Mismatch." *Urban Studies* 44(2007):2401–2427.

Goldsmith, A.H., Veum, J.R. and W. Jr. Darity. "Working Hard for the Money? Efficiency Wages and Worker Effort." *Journal of Economic Psychology* 21(2000):351–385.

Gordon, I.R. *Unemployment, the Regions and Labour Markets: Reactions to Recession*, London: Pion, 1987.

Gottlieb, P.D. and B. Lentnek. "Spatial Mismatch is Not Always a Central-City Problem: An Analysis of Commuting Behavior in Cleveland, Ohio, and its Suburbs." *Urban Studies* 38(2001):1161–1186.

Goyal, S. *Connections: An Introduction to the Economics of Networks*, Princeton, NJ: Princeton University Press, 2007.

Granovetter, M.S. "The Strength of Weak Ties." *American Journal of Sociology* 78(1973):1360–1380.

Granovetter, M.S. "The Strength of Weak Ties: A Network Theory Revisited." *Sociological Theory* 1(1983):201–233.

Granovetter, M.S. *Getting a Job: A Study of Contacts and Careers*, Second Edition, Chicago, IL: Chicago University Press, 1995.

Granovetter, M.S. "The Impact of Social Structure on Economic Outcomes." *Journal of Economic Perspectives* 19(2005):33–50.

Hall, R. "An Aspect of the Economic Role of Unemployment." In: G.C. Harcourt (Ed.), *The Microeconomic Foundations of Macroeconomics*, London: McMillan, 1977.

Hall, R. "A Theory of the Natural Unemployment Rate and the Duration of Employment." *Journal of Monetary Economics* 5(1979):153–169.

Hallinan, M. and N. Tuma. "Classroom Effects on Change in Children's Friendships." *Sociology of Education* 51(1979):270–282.

Hamilton, J., Thisse, J.-F. and Y. Zenou. "Wage Competition with Heterogeneous Workers and Firms." *Journal of Labor Economics* 18(2000):453–472.

Hannerz, U. *Soulside: Inquiries into Ghetto Culture and Community*, New York: Columbia University Press, 1969.

Hanson, S. and G. Pratt. *Gender, Work, and Space*, New York: Routledge, 1995.

Harrington, S.E. and G. Niehaus. "Race, Redlining, and Automobile Insurance Prices." *Journal of Business* 71(1998):439–469.

Harris, J.R. and M.P. Todaro. "Migration, Unemployment and Development: A Two-Sector Analysis." *American Economic Review*, 60(1970):126–142.

Hartwick, J.M., Schweizer, U. and P. Varaiya. "Comparative Statics of a Residential Economy with Several Classes." *Journal of Economic Theory* 13(1976):396–413.

Helsey, R.W. and W.C. Strange. "Matching and Agglomeration Economies in a System of Cities." *Regional Science and Urban Economics* 20(1990):189–222.

Helsey, R.W. and W.C. Strange. "Social Interactions and Urban Spatial Structure." *Journal of Economic Geography* 7(2007):119–138.

Henderson, J.V. and A. Mitra. "The New Urban Landscape Developers and Edge Cities." *Regional Science and Urban Economics* 26(1996):613–643.

Henning, C. and M. Lieberg. "Strong Ties or Weak Ties? Neighbourhood Networks in a New Perspective." *Scandinavian Housing and Planning Research* 13(1996):3–26.

Holzer, H.J. "Informal Job Search and Black Youth Unemployment." *American Economic Review* 77(1987):446–452.

Holzer, H.J. "Search Method Used by Unemployed Youth." *Journal of Labor Economics* 6(1988):1–20.

Holzer, H.J. *Unemployment, Vacancies and Local Labor Markets*, Kalamazoo, MI: W.E. Upjohn Institute for Employment Research, 1989.

Holzer, H.J. "The Spatial Mismatch Hypothesis: What Has the Evidence Shown? *Urban Studies* 28(1991):105–122.

Holzer H. J. "Why Do Small Establishments Hire Fewer Blacks than Larger Ones?" *Journal of Human Resources* 33(1998):896–814.

Holzer H.J. and K.R. Ihlanfeldt. "Customer Discrimination and the Employment Outcomes of Minority Workers." *Quarterly Journal of Economics* 113(1998):835–867.

Holzer, H.J., Ihlanfeldt, K.R. and D.L. Sjoquist. "Work, Search and Travel Among White and Black Youth." *Journal of Urban Economics* 35(1994):320–345.

Holzer, H.J. and J. Reaser. "Black Applicants, Black Employees, and Urban Labor Market Policy." *Journal of Urban Economics* 48(2000):365–387.

Holzer, H.J. and D. Newmark. "Assessing Affirmative Action." *Journal of Economic Literature* 38(2000):483–568.

Holzer, H.J. and D. Newmark. "Affirmative Action: What Do We Know?" *Journal of Policy Analysis and Management* 25(2006):463–490.

Hosios, A. "On the Efficiency of Matching and Related Models of Search and Unemployment." *Review of Economic Studies*, 57(1990):279–298.

Hughes, G. and B. McCormick. "Did Migration in the 1980's Narrow the North-South Divide?" *Economica* 61(1994):509–527.

Ihlanfeldt, K. "Information on the Spatial Distribution of Job Opportunities within Metropolitan Areas." *Journal of Urban Economics* 41(1997):218–242.

Ihlanfeldt, K.R. "A Primer on Spatial Mismatch within Urban Labor Markets." In: R. Arnott and D. McMillen (Eds.), *A Companion to Urban Economics*, Boston, MA: Blackwell Publishing, pp. 404–417, 2006.

Ihlanfeldt, K.R. and D.L. Sjoquist. "Job Accessibility and Racial Differences in Youth Employment Rates." *American Economic Review* 80(1990):267–276.

Ihlanfeldt, K.R. and D.L. Sjoquist. "The Spatial Mismatch Hypothesis: A Review of Recent Studies and Their Implications for Welfare Reform." *Housing Policy Debate* 9(1998):849–892.

Ioannides, Y.M. and D.L. Loury. "Job Information Networks, Neighborhood Effects, and Inequality." *Journal of Economic Literature* 42(2004):1056–1093.

Isserman, A., Taylor, C., Gerking, S. and U. Schubert. "Regional Labor Market Analysis." In: P. Nijkamp and E.S. Mills (Eds.), *Handbook of Regional and Urban Economics* Vol. 1, Amsterdam: Elsevier Science, pp. 543–580, 1986.

Jackson, M.O. "The Stability and Efficiency of Economic and Social Networks." In: B. Dutta and M.O. Jackson (Eds.), *Networks and Groups: Models of Strategic Formation*, Heidelberg: Springer Verlag, pp. 99–140, 2003.

Jackson, M.O. "A Survey of Models of Network Formation: Stability and Efficiency." In: G. Demange and M. Wooders (Eds.), *Group Formation in Economics: Networks, Clubs and Coalitions*, Cambridge, MA: Cambridge University Press, pp. 11–57, 2004.

Jackson, M.O. "The Economics of Social Networks." In: R. Blundell, W.K. Newey, and T. Persson (Eds.), *Advances in Economics and Econometrics. Theory and Applications, Ninth World Congress, Vol. I*, Cambridge, MA: Cambridge University Press, pp. 1–56, 2007.

Jackson, M.O. *Social and Economic Networks*, Princeton, NJ: Princeton University Press, 2008.

Jackson, M.O and A. Wolinsky. "A Strategic Model of Social and Economic Networks." *Journal of Economic Theory* 71(1996):44–74.

Jayet, H. "Spatial Search Processes and Spatial Interaction: 1. Sequential Search, Intervening Opportunities, and Spatial Search Equilibrium." *Environment and Planning A* 22(1990a):583–599.

Jayet, H. "Spatial Search Processes and Spatial Interaction: 2. Polarization, Concentration, and Spatial Search Equilibrium." *Environment and Planning A* 22(1990b):719–732.

Jellal, M., Thisse, J.-F. and Y. Zenou. "Demand Uncertainty, Mismatch and Unemployment." *Economics Letters* 88(2005a):33–39.

Jellal, M., Thisse, J.-F. and Y. Zenou. "Demand Uncertainty, Mismatch and Unemployment. Erratum." *Economics Letters* 89(2005b):248–254.

Johnson, R.C. "Landing a Job in Urban Space: The Extent and Effects of Spatial Mismatch." *Regional Science and Urban Economics* 36(2006):331–372.

Julien, B., Kennes, J. and I. King. "Bidding for Labor." *Review of Economic Dynamics* 3(2000):619–649.

Kain, J.F. "Housing Segregation, Negro Employment, and Metropolitan Decentralization." *Quarterly Journal of Economics* 82(1968):175–197.

Kain, J.F. "The Spatial Mismatch Hypothesis: Three Decades Later." *Housing Policy Debate* 3(1992):371–460.

Kan, K. "Residential Mobility and Social Capital." *Journal of Urban Economics* 61(2007):436–457.

Kasinitz, P. and J. Rosenberg. "Missing the Connection: Social Isolation and Employment on the Brooklyn Waterfront." *Social Problems* 43(1996):180–193.

Kats, A. "More on Hotelling's Stability in Competition." *International Journal of Industrial Organization* 13(1995):89–93.

Katz, M.B. *The "Underclass" Debate: Views From History*, Princeton, NJ: Princeton University Press, 1993.

Katz, L.F., Kling, J.R. and J.B. Liebman. "Moving to Opportunity in Boston: Early Results of a Randomized Mobility Experiment." *Quarterly Journal of Economics* 116(2001):607–654.

Kaufman, R. "On Wage Stickiness in Britain's Competitive Sector." *British Journal of Industrial Relations* 22(1982):101–112.

Kim, S. "Labor Specialization and the Extent of the Market." *Journal of Political Economy* 97(1989):692–705.

Kim, S. "Heterogeneity of Labor Markets and City Size in an Open Spatial Economy." *Regional Science and Urban Economics* 21(1991):109–126.

Kirschenman, J. and K.M. Neckerman. "'We'd love to hire them but...': The Meaning of Race for Employers." In: C. Jencks and P.E. Peterson (Eds.), *The Urban Underclass*, Washington, DC: Brookings Institution, pp. 155–174, 1991.

Kleit, R.G. "The Role of Neighborhood Social Networks in Scattered-Site Public Housing Residents' Search for Jobs." *Housing Policy Debate* 12(2001):541–573.

Kling, J.R., Ludwig, J. and L.F. Katz. "Neighborhood Effects on Crime for Female and Male Youth: Evidence from a Randomized Housing Voucher Experiment." *Quarterly Journal of Economics* 120(2005):87–130.

Kruger, A. and Summers, L. "Efficiency Wages and the Inter-Industry Wage Structure." *Econometrica* 56(1988):259–293.

Krugman, P. "Increasing Returns and Economic Geography." *Journal of Political Economy* 99(1991):483–499.

Kulkarni, V.G. *Modeling and Analysis of Stochastic Systems*, London: Chapman & Hall, 1995.

Ladd, H.F. "Evidence on Discrimination in Mortgage Lending." *Journal of Economic Perspectives* 12(1998):41–62.

Ladd, H.F. and J. Ludwig. "Federal Housing Assistance, Residential Relocation, and Educational Opportunities: Evidence from Baltimore." *American Economic Review* 87(1997):272–277.

Lagos, R. "An Alternative Approach to Search Frictions." *Journal of Political Economy* 108(2000):851–873.

Laing, D., Park, C. and P. Wang. "A Modified Harris-Todaro Model of Rural-Urban Migration for China." In: F. Kwan and E. Yu (Eds.), *Critical Issues in China's Growth and Development*, London: Ashgate, pp. 245–264, 2005.

Lang, W.W. and L.I. Nakamura. "A Model of Redlining." *Journal of Urban Economics* 33(1993):223–234.

Layard, R., Nickell, S. and R. Jackman. *Unemployment: Macroeconomic Performance and the Labour Market*, Oxford: Oxford University Press, 1991.

Leonard, J.S. "The Impact of Affirmative Action Regulation and Equal Opportunity Law on Black Employment." *Journal of Economic Perspectives* 4(1990):47–54.

LeRoy, S.F. and J. Sonstelie. "Paradise Lost and Regained: Transportation Innovation, Income, and Residential Location." *Journal of Urban Economics* 13(1983):67–89.

Lewis, O. "Culture of Poverty." In: D.P. Moynihan (Ed.), *On Understanding Poverty: Perspectives from the Social Sciences*, New York: Basic Books, pp. 187–220, 1969.

Lucas, R. and E. Prescott. "Equilibrium Search and Unemployment." *Journal of Economic Theory* 7(1974):188–209.

Ludwig, J., Duncan, G.J. and P. Hirschfield. "Urban Poverty and Juvenile Crime: Evidence from a Randomized Housing-Mobility Experiment." *Quarterly Journal of Economics* 116(2001):655–679.

Madden, J.F. "Urban Wage Gradients: Empirical Evidence." *Journal of Urban Economics* 18(1985):291–301.

Manning, A. "The Real Thin Theory: Monopsony in Modern Labour Markets." *Labour Economics* 10(2003):105–131.

Marimon R. and F. Zilibotti. "Unemployment Versus Mismatch of Talents: Reconsidering Unemployment Benefits." *Economic Journal* 109(1999):266–291.

Marston, S.T. "Two Views of the Geographic Distribution of Unemployment." *Quarterly Journal of Economics* 100(1985):57–79.

Martin, R.W. "Job Decentralization with Suburban Housing Discrimination: An Urban Equilibrium Model of Spatial Mismatch." *Journal of Housing Economics* 6(1997):293–317.

Martin, R.W. "The Adjustment of Black Residents to Metropolitan Employment Shifts: How Persistent is Spatial Mismatch?" *Journal of Urban Economics* 50(2001):52–76.

Mas-Colell, A., Whinston, M.D. and J.R. Green. *Microeconomic Theory*, Oxford: Oxford University Press, 1995.

Massey, D.S. and N.A. Denton. "Suburbanization and Segregation in U.S. Metropolitan Areas." *American Journal of Sociology* 94(1988):592–626.

Massey, D.S. and N.A. Denton. *American Apartheid: Segregation and the Making of the Underclass*, Cambridge, MA: Harvard University Press, 1993.

Mauer, D.C. and S.H. Ott. "On the Optimal Structure of Government Subsidies for Entreprise Zones and Other Locational Development Programs." *Journal of Urban Economics* 45(1999):421–450.

McCormick, B. "Employment Opportunities, Earnings, and the Journey to Work of Minority Workers in Great Britain." *Economic Journal* 96(1986):375–397.

Mieszkowski, P. and E.S. Mills. "The Causes of Metropolitan Suburbanization." *Journal of Economic Perspectives* 7(1993):135–147.

Mills, E.S. *Urban Economics*, Glenview, IL: Scott Foresman, 1972.

Moen, E.R. "Competitive Search Equilibrium." *Journal of Political Economy* 105(1997):385–411.

Moene, K.O. "A Reformulation of the Harris-Todaro Mechanism with Endogenous Wages." *Economic Letters* 27(1988):387–390.

Mohtadi, H. "Migration and Job Search in a Dualistic Economy. A Todaro-Stigler Synthesis." *Economics Letters* 29(1989):373–378.

Montgomery, J.D. "Equilibrium Wage Dispersion and Interindustry Wage Differentials." *Quarterly Journal of Economics* 106(1991a):163–179.

Montgomery, J.D. "Social Networks and Labor-Market Outcomes: Toward and Economic Analysis." *American Economic Review* 81(1991b):1408–1418.

Montgomery, J.D. "Job Search and Network Composition: Implications of the Strength-of-Weak-Ties Hypothesis." *American Sociological Review* 57(1992):586–596.

Montgomery, J.D. "Weak Ties, Employment, and Inequality: An Equilibrium Analysis." *American Journal of Sociology* 99(1994):1212–1236.

Mortensen, D.T. "Job Search and Labor Market Analysis." In: O. Ashenfelter and R. Layard (Eds), *Handbook of Labor Economics Vol. 2*, Amsterdam: North-Holland, pp. 849–920, 1986.

Mortensen, D.T. "Matching: Finding a Partner for Life or Otherwise." *American Journal of Sociology* 94(1988):S215–S240.

Mortensen, D.T. and C.A. Pissarides. "Job Creation and Job Destruction in the Theory of Unemployment." *Review of Economic Studies* 61(1994):397–415.

Mortensen, D.T. and C.A. Pissarides. "New Developments in Models of Search in the Labor Market." In: D. Card and O. Ashenfelter (Eds.), *Handbook of Labor Economics Vol. 3B*, Amsterdam: Elsevier Science, pp. 2567–2627, 1999a.

Mortensen, D.T. and C.A. Pissarides. "Job Reallocation, Employment Fluctuations, and Unemployment." In: J.B. Taylor and M. Woodford (Eds.), *Handbook of Macroeconomics Vol. 1B*, Amsterdam: Elsevier Science, pp. 1171–1228, 1999b.

Mortensen, D.T. and T. Vishwanath. "Personal Contacts and Earnings. It Is Who You Know!" *Labour Economics* 1(1994):187–201.

Murphy, K.M. and R.H. Topel. "Efficiency Wage Reconsidered: Theory and Evidence." In: Y. Weiss and G. Fishelson (Eds.), *Advances in the Theory and Measurement of Unemployment*, St. Martin's Press, New York, pp. 104–240, 1990.

Muth, R.F. *Cities and Housing*, Chicago, IL: University of Chicago Press, 1969.

Nagin, D.S., J.B. Rebitzer, S. Sanders and L.J. Taylor. "Monitoring, Motivation, and Management: The Determinants of Opportunistic Behavior in a Field Experiment." *American Economic Review* 92(2002):850–873.

Neal, D. "Supervision and Wages Across Industries." *Review of Economics and Statistics* 75(1993):409–417.

Neal, D. "Why Has Black-White Skill Convergence Stopped?" In: E. Hanushek and F. Welch (Eds.), *Handbook of the Economics of Education Vol. 1*, Amsterdam: Elsevier Science, pp. 511–576, 2006.

Nechyba, T.J. and R.P. Walsh. "Urban Sprawl." *Journal of Economic Perspectives* 18(2004):177–200.

Neckerman, K.M. and J. Kirschenman. "Hiring Strategies, Racial Bias, and Innercity Workers: An Investigation of Employers' Hiring Decisions." *Social Problems* 38(1991):801–815.

O'Reagan, K. and J. Quigley. "Where Youth Live: Economic Effects of Urban Space on Employment Prospects." *Urban Studies* 35(1998):1187–1205.

Ogawa, H. and M. Fujita. "Multiple Equilibria and Structural Transition of Nonmonocentric Urban Configurations." *Regional Science and Urban Economics* 12(1982):161–196.

Ogbu, J.U. *Black American Students in an Affluent Suburb: A Study of Academic Disengagement*, City, New Jersey: Lawrence Erlbaum, 2003.

Oi, W.Y. and T.L. Idson. "Firm Size and Wages." In: O. Ashenfelter and D. Card (Eds.), *Handbook of Labor Economics Vol. 3*, Amsterdam: Elsevier Science, pp. 2165–2214, 1999.

Ortega, J. "Pareto-Improving Immigration in an Economy with Equilibrium Unemployment." *Economic Journal* 110(2000):92–112.

Osborne, M.J. and A. Rubinstein. *Bargaining and Markets*, San Diego, CA: Academic Press, 1990.

Owen, D. and A.E. Green. "Estimating Commuting Flows for Minority Groups in England and Wales." *Journal of Ethnic and Migration Studies* 26(2000):581–608.

Papageorgiou, Y.Y. and T.R. Smith. "Agglomeration as Local Instability of Spatially Uniform Steady-States." *Econometrica* 51(1983):1109–1119.

Papke, L. "Tax Policy and Urban Development: Evidence from the Indiana Enterprise Zone Program." *Journal of Public Economics* 54(1994):37–49.

Patacchini, E. and Y. Zenou. "Spatial Mismatch, Transport Mode and Search Decisions in England." *Journal of Urban Economics* 58(2005):62–90.

Patacchini, E. and Y. Zenou. "Search Activities, Cost of Living and Local Labor Markets." *Regional Science and Urban Economics* 36(2006a):227–248.

Patacchini, E. and Y. Zenou. "Racial Identity and Education." CEPR Discussion Paper No. 5607, 2006b.

Patacchini, E. and Y. Zenou. "Spatial Dependence in Local Unemployment Rates." *Journal of Economic Geography* 7(2007):169–191.

Patacchini, E. and Y. Zenou. "Ethnic Networks and Employment Outcomes." IZA Discussion Paper No. 3331, 2008.

Peters, M. "Ex Ante Price Offers in Matching Games Non-Steady States." *Econometrica* 59(1991):1425–1454.

Petrongolo, B. and C.A. Pissarides. "Looking into the Black Box: A Survey of the Matching Function." *Journal of Economic Literature* 39(2001):390–431.

Phelps, E. "The Statistical Theory of Racism and Sexism." *American Economic Review* 62(1972):659–661.

Pines, D. and E. Sadka. "Comparative Statics Analysis of a Fully Closed City." *Journal of Urban Economics* 20(1986):1–20.

Pissarides, C.A. "Job Matchings with State Employment Agencies and Random Search." *Economic Journal* 89(1979):818–833.

Pissarides, C.A. *Equilibrium Unemployment Theory*, Second edition, Cambridge, MA: MIT Press, 2000.

Postel-Vinay, F. and J.-M. Robin. "Microeconometric Search-Matching Models and Matched Employer-Employee Data." In: R. Blundell, W.K. Newey, and T. Persson (Eds.), *Advances in Economics and Econometrics. Theory and Applications, Ninth World Congress, Vol. II*, Cambridge, MA: Cambridge University Press, pp. 279–310, 2007.

Pugh, M. "Barriers to Work: The Spatial Divide Between Jobs and Welfare Recipients in Metropolitan Areas." Washington, DC: The Brookings Institution, 1998.

Raphael, S. and M. Sills. "Urban Crime, Race, and the Criminal Justice System in the United States." In: R. Arnott and D. McMillen (Eds.), *A Companion to Urban Economics*, Boston, MA: Blackwell Publishing, pp. 515–535, 2006.

Raphael, S. and M.A. Stoll. "Can Boosting Minority Car-Ownership Rates Narrow Inter-Racial Employment Gaps?" *Brookings-Wharton Papers on Urban Economic Affairs* 2(2001):99–145.

Raphael, S. and M.A. Stoll. "Modest Progress: The Narrowing Spatial Mismatch Between Blacks and Jobs in the 1990s." Washington, DC: The Brookings Institution, 2002.

Ray, D. *Development Economics*, Princeton, NJ: Princeton University Press, 1998.

Rebitzer, J.B. "Is There a Trade-off Between Supervision and Wages? An Empirical Test of Efficiency Wage Theory." *Journal of Economic Behavior and Organization* 28(1995):107–129.

Rebitzer, J.B. and M. Robinson. "Plant Size and Dual Labor Markets." *Review of Economics and Statistics*, 73(1991):710–715.

Rocheteau, G. "Balanced-Budget Rules and Indeterminacy of the Equilibrium Unemployment Rate." *Oxford Economic Papers* 51(1999):399–409.

Rogerson, R., Shimer, R. and R. Wright. "Search Theoretic Models of the Labor Market: A Survey." *Journal of Economic Literature* 43(2005):959–988.

Rosenbaum, E. and L.E. Harris. "Residential Mobility and Opportunities: Early Impacts of the Moving to Opportunity Demonstration Program in Chicago." *Housing Policy Debate* 12(2001):321–346.

Rosenthal, S.S. "A Residence Time Model of Housing Markets." *Journal of Public Economics* 36(1988):87–109.

Ross, S.L. and Y. Zenou. "Shirking, Commuting and Labor Market Outcomes." Unpublished Manuscript, Department of Economics Working Paper No. 2003-41, University of Connecticut, 2003.

Ross, S.L. and Y. Zenou. "Are Shirking and Leisure Substitutable? An Empirical Test of Efficiency Wages Based on Urban Economic Theory." *Regional Science and Urban Economics* 38(2008):498–517.

Ross, S.M. *Stochastic Processes*, Second Edition, New York: Wiley, 1996.

Rouwendal, J. and J. Van Ommeren. "Recruitment in a Monopsonistic Labour Market: Will Travel Costs be Reimbursed?" Unpublished manuscript, Free University in Amsterdam, 2007.

Roy, A.D. "Some Thoughts of the Distribution of Earnings." *Oxford Economic Papers* 3(1951):135–146.

Saez-Marti, M. and Y. Zenou. "Cultural Transmission and Discrimination." IZA Discussion Paper No. 1880, 2005.

Saint-Paul, G. *Dual Labor Markets: A Macroeconomic Perspective*, Cambridge, MA: MIT Press, 1996.

Salop, S. "Monopolistic Competition with Outside Goods." *Bell Journal of Economics* 10(1979):141–156.

Sasaki, K. "Income Class, Modal Choice, and Urban Spatial Structure." *Journal of Urban Economics* 27(1990):322–343.

Satchi, M. and J. Temple. "Labor Markets and Productivity in Developing Countries." *Review of Economic Dynamics* 12(2009): 183–204.

Sattinger, M. "Assignment Models of the Distribution of Earnings." *Journal of Economic Literature* 31(1993):831–880.

Sato, Y. "Labor Heterogeneity in an Urban Labor Market." *Journal of Urban Economics* 50(2001):313–337.

Sato, Y. "City Structure, Search, and Workers' Job Acceptance Behavior." *Journal of Urban Economics* 55(2004a):350–370.

Sato, Y. "Migration, Frictional Unemployment and Welfare Improving Labor Policies." *Journal of Regional Science* 44(2004b):773–793.

Scheinkman, J.A. "Social Interactions (Theory)." In: L. Blume and S. Durlauf (Eds.), *The New Palgrave, A Dictionary of Economics, Second Edition*, London: MacMillan Press, 2008.

Seater, J. "Job Search and Vacancy Contacts." *American Economic Review* 69(1979):411–419.

Selod, H. and Y. Zenou. "Private Versus Public Schools in Post-Apartheid South African Cities. Theory and Policy Implications." *Journal of Development Economics* 71(2003):351–394.

Selod, H. and Y. Zenou. "City Structure, Job Search, and Labour Discrimination. Theory and Policy Implications." CEPR Discussion Paper No. 5009, 2005.

Selod, H. and Y. Zenou. "City-Structure, Job Search, and Labour Discrimination. Theory and Policy Implications." *Economic Journal* 116(2006):1057–1087.

Shapiro, C. and J.E. Stiglitz. "Equilibrium Unemployment as a Worker Discipline Device." *American Economic Review* 74(1984):433–444.

Sigelman, L., Bledsoe, T., Welch, S. and M.W. Combs. "Making Contact? Black-White Social Interaction in an Urban Setting." *American Journal of Sociology* 101(1996):1306–1332.

Simpson, W. *Urban Structure and the Labour Market: Worker Mobility, Commuting, and Underemployment in Cities,* Oxford: Clarendon Press, 1992.

Small, K. *Urban Transportation Economics,* Chur: Harwood Academic Publisher, 1992.

Smith, E. and R. Wright. "Why is Automobile Insurance in Philadelphia so Damn Expensive?" *American Economic Review* 82(1992):756–772.

Smith, T.E. and Y. Zenou. "Dual Labor Markets, Urban Unemployment, and Multicentric Cities." *Journal of Economic Theory,* 76(1997):185–214.

Smith, T.E. and Y. Zenou. "Spatial Mismatch, Search Effort and Urban Spatial Structure." *Journal of Urban Economics,* 54(2003a):129–156.

Smith, T.E. and Y. Zenou. "Spatial Mismatch, Search Effort and Urban Spatial Structure." CEPR Discussion Paper No. 3731, London, 2003.

Smith, T.E. and Y. Zenou. "A Discrete-Time Stochastic Model of Job Matching." *Review of Economic Dynamics* 6(2003c):54–79.

Squires, G.D., Velez, W. and K.E. Taeuber. "Insurance Redlining, Agency Location, and the Process of Urban Disinvestment." *Urban Affairs Quarterly* 26(1991):567–587.

Stevens, M. "A Theoretical Model of On-the-Job Training with Imperfect Competition." *Oxford Economic Papers* 46(1994):537–562.

Stevens, M. "New Microfoundations for the Aggregate Matching Function." *International Economic Review* 48(2007):847–868.

Stigler, G.J. "The Economics of Information." *Journal of Political Economy* 70(1961):94–104.

Stiglitz, J.E. "The Efficiency Wage Hypothesis, Surplus Labour and the Distribution of Income in LDCs." *Oxford Economic Papers* 28(1976):185–207.

Stokey, N.L. "Job Differentiation and Wages." *Quarterly Journal of Economics* 95(1980):431–449.

Stoll, M.A. "Spatial Job Search, Spatial Mismatch, and the Employment and Wages of Racial and Ethnic Groups in Los Angeles." *Journal of Urban Economics,* 46(1999):129–155.

Stoll, M.A., Holzer, H.J. and K.R. Ihlanfeldt. "Within Cities and Suburbs: Racial Residential Concentration and the Spatial Distribution of Employment Opportunities Across Submetropolitan Areas." *Journal of Policy Analysis and Management* 19(2000):207–231.

Strobl, E. and F. Walsh. "Estimating the Shirking Model with Variable Effort." *Labour Economics* 14(2007):623–637.

Tasnadi, A. "A Way of Explaining Unemployment Through a Wage-Setting Game." *Labour Economics* 12(2005):191–203.

Teulings, C.N. and P.A. Gautier. "Search and the City." *Regional Science and Urban Economics,* forthcoming, 2009.

Thisse, J.-F. and Y. Zenou. "How to Finance Education When the Labor Force is Heterogeneous?" In: G. Barba Navaretti, P. Dasgupta, K.-G. Mäler and D. Siniscalco (Eds.), *Creation and Transfer of Knowledge: Institutions and Incentives,* Berlin: Springer Verlag, pp. 209–223, 1998.

Thisse, J.-F. and Y. Zenou. "Skill Mismatch and Unemployment." *Economics Letters* 69(2000):415–420.

Thomas, J.M. "Ethnic Variation in Commuting Propensity and Unemployment Spells: Some UK Evidence." *Journal of Urban Economics* 43(1998):385–400.

Tilly, C., Moss, P., Kirschenman, J. and I. Kennelly. "Space as a Signal: How Employers Perceive Neighborhoods in Four Metropolitan Labor Markets." In: A. O'Connor, C. Tilly and L.D. Bobo (Eds.), *Urban Inequality: Evidence from Four Cities*, New York: Russell Sage Foundation, pp. 304–340, 2001.

Todaro, M.P. "A Model of Labor Migration and Urban Unemployment in Less Developed Countries." *American Economic Review* 59(1969):138–148.

Topa, G. "Social Interactions, Local Spillovers and Unemployment." *Review of Economic Studies* 68(2001):261–295.

Topel, R.H. "Local Labor Markets." *Journal of Political Economy* 94(1986):S111–S143.

Van Ommeren, J.N. and E. Gutiérrez-i-Puigarnau. "Are Workers with a Long Commute Less Productive? An Empirical Analysis of Absenteeism." Unpublished manuscript, Free University, Amsterdam.

Van Ommeren, J.N. and P. Rietveld. "Commuting and Reimbursement of Residential Relocation Costs." *Journal of Transport Economics and Policy* 41(2007):51–73.

Van Ommeren, J.N., Rietveld, P. and P. Nijkamp. "Spatial Moving Behavior of Two-Earner Households." *Journal of Regional Science* 38(1998):23–41.

Van Ommeren, J.N., Rietveld, P. and P. Nijkamp. "Job Moving, Residential Moving, and Commuting: A Search Perspective." *Journal of Urban Economics* 46(1999):230–253.

Van Ommeren, J.N., Van der Vlist, A. and P. Nijkamp. "Transport-Related Fringe Benefits: Implications for Moving and the Journey to Work." *Journal of Regional Science* 46(2006):493–506.

Van Ommeren, J.N. and M. Van Leuvensteijn. "New Evidence of the Effect of Transaction Costs on Residential Mobility." *Journal of Regional Science* 45(2005):681–702.

Vega-Redondo, F. *Complex Social Networks*, Econometric Society Monograph Series, Cambridge: Cambridge University Press, 2007.

Verdier, T. and Y. Zenou. "Racial Beliefs, Location and the Causes of Crime." *International Economic Review* 45(2004):731–760.

Von Thünen, J.H. *Der Isolierte Staat in Beziehung auf Landwirtschaft und Nationalökonomie*, Hamburg: Perthes. English translation: *The Isolated State*, Oxford: Pergammon Press, 1966.

Wahba, J. and Y. Zenou. "Density, Social Networks and Job Search Methods: Theory and Applications to Egypt." *Journal of Development Economics* 78(2005):443–473.

Wasmer, E. and Y. Zenou. "Equilibrium Urban Unemployment." Centre for Economic Performance (CEP) Discussion Paper No. 368, 1997.

Wasmer, E. and Y. Zenou. "Does City Structure Affect Job Search and Welfare?" *Journal of Urban Economics* 51(2002):515–541.

Wasmer, E. and Y. Zenou. "Equilibrium Search Unemployment with Explicit Spatial Frictions." *Labour Economics* 13(2006):143–165.30.

Wasserman, S. and K. Faust. *Social Network Analysis: Methods and Applications*, Cambridge, MA: Cambridge University Press, 1994.

Wauthy, X. and Y. Zenou. "How Does Imperfect Competition in the Labor Market Affect Unemployment Policies?" *Journal of Public Economic Theory* 4(2002):417–436.

Weiss, A. *Efficiency Wage Models of Unemployment, Layoffs, and Wage Dispersion*, Oxford: Clarendon Press, 1991.

Wheeler, C.H. "Search, Sorting, and Urban Agglomeration." *Journal of Labor Economics* 19(2001):879–899.

White, M.J. "Urban Areas with Decentralized Employment: Theory and Empirical Work." In: E.S. Mills and P. Cheshire (Eds.), *Handbook of Regional and Urban Economics Vol. 3*, Amsterdam: Elsevier Science, pp. 1375–1412, 1999.

Wial, H. "Getting a Good Job: Mobility in a Segmented Labor Market." *Industrial Relations* 30(1991):396–416.

Wiegers, W.A. "The Use of Age, Sex, and Marital Status as Rating Variables in Automobile Insurance." *University of Toronto Law Journal*, 39(1989):149–210.

Wilson, W.J. *The Truly Disadvantaged: The Inner City, the Underclass, and Public Policy*, Chicago: University of Chicago Press, 1987.

Wilson, W.J. *When Work Disappears: The World of the New Urban Poor*, New York: Alfred A. Knopf, 1996.

Yashiv, E. "Labor Search and Matching in Macroeconomics." *European Economic Review* 51(2007):1859–1895.

Yinger, J. "Measuring Racial Discrimination with Fair Housing Audits." *American Economic Review* 76(1986):881–893.

Yinger, J. "Cash in Your Face: The Cost of Racial and Ethnic Discrimination in Housing." *Journal of Urban Economics* 42(1997):339–365.

Yunus, M. *Banker to the Poor: Micro-Lending and the Battle Against World Poverty*, New York: Public Affairs, 1999.

Zax, J.S. "Compensation for Commutes in Labor and Housing Markets." *Journal of Urban Economics* 30(1991):192–207.

Zax, J. and J.F. Kain. "Moving to the Suburbs: Do Relocating Companies Leave their Black Employees Behind? *Journal of Labor Economics* 14(1996):472–493.

Zenger, T.R. "Explaining Organizational Diseconomies of Scale in R&D: Agency Problems and the Allocation of Engineering Talent, Ideas, and Effort by Firm Size." *Management Science* 40(1994):708–729.

Zenou, Y. "Unemployment in Cities." In: J.-M. Huriot and J.-F. Thisse (Eds.), *Economics of Cities*, Cambridge, MA: Cambridge University Press, pp. 343–389, 2000.

Zenou, Y. "Urban Unemployment, Agglomeration and Transportation Policies." *Journal of Public Economics* 77(2000):97–133.

Zenou, Y. "How do Firms Redline Workers?" *Journal of Urban Economics* 52(2002):391–408.

Zenou, Y. "The Spatial Aspects of Crime." *Journal of the European Economic Association* 1(2003):459–467.

Zenou, Y. "The Todaro Paradox Revisited." CEPR Discussion Paper No. 5402, 2005.

Zenou, Y. "Efficiency Wages and Unemployment in Cities: The Case of High Relocation Costs." *Regional Science and Urban Economics* 36(2006a):49–71.

Zenou, Y. "Urban Labor Economic Theory." In: R. Arnott and D. McMillen (Eds.), *A Companion to Urban Economics*, Boston, MA: Blackwell Publishing, pp. 418–439, 2006b.

Zenou, Y. "Endogenous Job Destruction and Job Matching in Cities." IZA Discussion Paper No. 2695, 2007a, *Journal of Urban Economics*, forthcoming.

Zenou, Y. "High-Relocation Costs in Search-Matching Models: Theory and Application to Spatial Mismatch." IZA Discussion Paper No. 2739, 2007b, *Labor Economics*, forthcoming.

Zenou, Y. "Why do Black Workers Search Less? A Transport-Mode Based Theory." CEPR Discussion Paper No. 6155, 2007c.

Zenou, Y. "Search in Cities." CEPR Discussion Paper No. 6197, 2008a, *European Economic Review*, forthcoming.

Zenou, Y. "Job Search and Mobility in Developing Countries. Theory and Policy Implications." *Journal of Development Economics* 86(2008b):336–355.

Zenou, Y. "The Spatial Mismatch Hypothesis." In: L. Blume and S. Durlauf (Eds.), *The New Palgrave, A Dictionary of Economics, Second Edition*, London: MacMillan Press, 2008c.

Zenou, Y. "Search, Wage Posting, and Urban Spatial Structure." IZA Discussion Paper No. 3339, 2008d.

Zenou, Y. "Social Interactions and Labor Market Outcomes in Cities." IZA Discussion Paper No. 3283, 2008e.

Zenou, Y. "Search, Migration, and Urban Land Use. Theory and Policy Issues." IZA Discussion Paper, 2008f.

Zenou, Y. "Formal Versus Informal Sector in Cities. The Case of Transportation Policies." Unpublished manuscript, Stockholm University, 2008g.

Zenou, Y. and N. Boccard. "Racial Discrimination and Redlining in Cities." *Journal of Urban Economics* 48(2000):260–285.

Zenou, Y. and T.E. Smith. "Efficiency Wages, Involuntary Unemployment and Urban Spatial Structure." *Regional Science and Urban Economics* 25(1995):821–845.

Author Index

Subject Index